Developing Diversity, Equity, and Inclusion Policies for Promoting Employee Sustainability and Well-Being

Sónia P. Gonçalves
ISCSP, Universidade de Lisboa, Portugal

Paula Cristina Nunes Figueiredo
Universidade Lusófona, Portugal

Eduardo Luis Soares Tomé
ULHT, Universidade Lusófona, Portugal

José Baptista
ISCSP, Universidade de Lisboa, Portugal

A volume in the Advances in Human Resources Management and Organizational Development (AHRMOD) Book Series

Published in the United States of America by
IGI Global
Business Science Reference (an imprint of IGI Global)
701 E. Chocolate Avenue
Hershey PA, USA 17033
Tel: 717-533-8845
Fax: 717-533-8661
E-mail: cust@igi-global.com
Web site: http://www.igi-global.com

Copyright © 2023 by IGI Global. All rights reserved. No part of this publication may be reproduced, stored or distributed in any form or by any means, electronic or mechanical, including photocopying, without written permission from the publisher. Product or company names used in this set are for identification purposes only. Inclusion of the names of the products or companies does not indicate a claim of ownership by IGI Global of the trademark or registered trademark.
    Library of Congress Cataloging-in-Publication Data

Names: Gonçalves, Sónia, 1982- editor.
Title: Developing diversity, equity, and inclusion policies for promoting
   employee sustainability and well-being / Sonia Gonçalves, Paula
   Figueiredo, Eduardo Tome, and Jose Baptista, editor.
Description: Hershey, PA : Business Science Reference, [2022] | Includes
   bibliographical references and index. | Summary: "This book will analyze
   the state of the art of employee sustainability and well-being by
   exploring the implications of diversity, equity and inclusion practices
   on the sustainability and well-being of the employees for a more
   sustainable and healthier workplace"-- Provided by publisher.
Identifiers: LCCN 2022001834 (print) | LCCN 2022001835 (ebook) | ISBN
   9781668441817 (hardcover) | ISBN 9781668441824 (paperback) | ISBN
   9781668441831 (ebook)
Subjects: LCSH: Diversity in the workplace. | Quality of work life. |
   Personnel management.
Classification: LCC HF5549.5.M5 D478 2022 (print) | LCC HF5549.5.M5
   (ebook) | DDC 658.3008--dc23/eng/20220114
LC record available at https://lccn.loc.gov/2022001834
LC ebook record available at https://lccn.loc.gov/2022001835

This book is published in the IGI Global book series Advances in Human Resources Management and Organizational Development (AHRMOD) (ISSN: 2327-3372; eISSN: 2327-3380)

British Cataloguing in Publication Data
A Cataloguing in Publication record for this book is available from the British Library.

All work contributed to this book is new, previously-unpublished material. The views expressed in this book are those of the authors, but not necessarily of the publisher.

For electronic access to this publication, please contact: eresources@igi-global.com.

Advances in Human Resources Management and Organizational Development (AHRMOD) Book Series

Patricia Ordóñez de Pablos
Universidad de Oviedo, Spain

ISSN:2327-3372
EISSN:2327-3380

Mission

A solid foundation is essential to the development and success of any organization and can be accomplished through the effective and careful management of an organization's human capital. Research in human resources management and organizational development is necessary in providing business leaders with the tools and methodologies which will assist in the development and maintenance of their organizational structure.

The **Advances in Human Resources Management and Organizational Development (AHRMOD) Book Series** aims to publish the latest research on all aspects of human resources as well as the latest methodologies, tools, and theories regarding organizational development and sustainability. The **AHRMOD Book Series** intends to provide business professionals, managers, researchers, and students with the necessary resources to effectively develop and implement organizational strategies.

Coverage

- Corporate Governance
- Compliance
- Employee Evaluation
- Workplace Discrimination
- Change Management
- Human Resources Development
- Human Relations Movement
- Diversity in the Workplace
- Disputes Resolution
- Employee Communications

IGI Global is currently accepting manuscripts for publication within this series. To submit a proposal for a volume in this series, please contact our Acquisition Editors at Acquisitions@igi-global.com or visit: http://www.igi-global.com/publish/.

The Advances in Human Resources Management and Organizational Development (AHRMOD) Book Series (ISSN 2327-3372) is published by IGI Global, 701 E. Chocolate Avenue, Hershey, PA 17033-1240, USA, www.igi-global.com. This series is composed of titles available for purchase individually; each title is edited to be contextually exclusive from any other title within the series. For pricing and ordering information please visit http://www.igi-global.com/book-series/advances-human-resources-management-organizational/73670. Postmaster: Send all address changes to above address. Copyright © 2023 IGI Global. All rights, including translation in other languages reserved by the publisher. No part of this series may be reproduced or used in any form or by any means – graphics, electronic, or mechanical, including photocopying, recording, taping, or information and retrieval systems – without written permission from the publisher, except for non commercial, educational use, including classroom teaching purposes. The views expressed in this series are those of the authors, but not necessarily of IGI Global.

Titles in this Series

For a list of additional titles in this series, please visit: www.igi-global.com/book-series

Talent Acquisition and Retention Strategies in Global Startups
Neetima Agarwal (Symbiosis International University, India) Leo Paul Dana (Kingston University, UK) and Sujata Khandai (Amity University, ndia)
Business Science Reference • © 2023 • 305pp • H/C (ISBN: 9781668475140) • US $250.00

Female Entrepreneurship as a Driving Force of Economic Growth and Social Change
Ana Dias Daniel (Universidade de Aveiro, Portugal) and Cristina Fernandes (Universidade da Beira Interior, Porugal)
Business Science Reference • © 2023 • 320pp • H/C (ISBN: 9781668476697) • US $250.00

Strategic Human Resource Management in the Hospitality Industry A Digitalized Economic Paradigm
Kannapat Kankaew (Suan Sunandha Rajabhat University, Thailand)
Business Science Reference • © 2023 • 309pp • H/C (ISBN: 9781668474945) • US $250.00

Corporate Sustainability as a Tool for Improving Economic, Social, and Environmental Performance
Bartolomé Marco-Lajara (University of Alicante, Spain) Javier Martínez-Falcó (University of Alicante, Spain & Stellenbosch University, South Africa) and Luis A. Millán-Tudela (University of Alicante, Spain)
Business Science Reference • © 2023 • 337pp • H/C (ISBN: 9781668474228) • US $250.00

Handbook of Research on Dissecting and Dismantling Occupational Stress in Modern Organizations
Adnan ul Haque (Yorkville University, Canada)
Business Science Reference • © 2023 • 559pp • H/C (ISBN: 9781668465431) • US $315.00

Managing Technology Integration for Human Resources in Industry 5.0
Naman Sharma (Indian Institute of Foreign Trade, India) and Kumar Shalender (Chitkara University, India)
Business Science Reference • © 2023 • 294pp • H/C (ISBN: 9781668467459) • US $215.00

Leadership Perspectives on Effective Intergenerational Communication and Management
Fatma Ince (Mersin University, Turkey)
Business Science Reference • © 2023 • 289pp • H/C (ISBN: 9781668461402) • US $230.00

Examining the Aging Workforce and Its Impact on Economic and Social Development
Bruno de Sousa Lopes (University of Aveiro, Portugal) Maria Céu Lamas (School of Health, Polytechnic of Porto, Portugal) Vanessa Amorim (Porto Accounting and Business School, Polytechnic of Porto, Portugal) and Orlando Lima Rua (Porto Accounting and Business School, Polytechnic of Porto, Portugal)
Business Science Reference • © 2023 • 215pp • H/C (ISBN: 9781668463512) • US $225.00

701 East Chocolate Avenue, Hershey, PA 17033, USA
Tel: 717-533-8845 x100 • Fax: 717-533-8661
E-Mail: cust@igi-global.com • www.igi-global.com

Editorial Advisory Board

Celina Alonso, *UFBA, Brazil*
Manfred Bornemann, *Austrian Research Center Seibersdorf, Austria*
Mary Cartlotto, *CNPq, Brazil*
Dália Costa, *ISCSP, Universidad de Lisboa, Portugal*
Stephen Deepak, *School of Management, Kristu Jayanti College, India*
Ozgun Sarimehmet Duman, *Hacettepe University, Turkey*
João Farinha, *ISLA Santarém, Portugal*
Catarina Gomes, *Universidade Lusófona, Portugal*
Sónia Gondim, *Universidade Federal de Uberlândia, Brazil*
Pedro Goulart, *ISCSP, Universidad de Lisboa, Portugal*
Daniela Lima, *Instituto Politécnico de Setúbal, Portugal*
Sílvia Luís, *Universidade Lusófona, Portugal*
Mariana Marcelino, *ISCSP, Universidad de Lisboa, Portugal*
Ana Marôco, *ISCSP, Universidad de Lisboa, Portugal*
Isabel Marques, *ISCSP, Universidad de Lisboa, Portugal*
Albertina Monteiro, *Instituto Politécnico do Porto, Portugal*
Ana Moreira, *ISPA, Portugal*
Catarina Neves, *ISCSP, Universidad de Lisboa, Portugal*
Francisco Ribeiro, *ISCSP, Universidad de Lisboa, Portugal*
Ana Rocha, *UCAN, Brazil*
Arlinda Rodrigues, *ISCSP, Universidad de Lisboa, Portugal*
José Rouco, *Universidade Lusófona, Portugal*
Darlene Russ-Eft, *Oregon State University, USA*
Khodor Shatila, *IProCares International Research Center, Beirut, Lebanon*
Tuğçe Şimşek, *Gümüşhane University, Turkey*
Maria Soares, *ISEG, Universidad de Lisboa, Portugal*
Fátima Suleman, *ISCTE-IUL, Portugal*
Basak Ucanok Tan, *Istanbul Bilgi University, Turkey*
Maria Velez, *ISCTE-IUL, Portugal*
Ana Veloso, *Universidade do Minho, Portugal*
Joana Vieira dos Santos, *Universidade do Algarve, Portugal*

Table of Contents

Foreword xv

Preface xvi

Acknowledgement xx

Chapter 1
Beyond Economics: Focusing on the Well-Being of Organizations 1
    Susana Dias, Instituto Universitário de Lisboa, Portugal
    Sílvia Luís, Universidade Lusófona de Humanidades e Tecnologias de Lisboa, Portugal

Chapter 2
Worker Nutrition Program: A Health and Wellness Promoting Policy at the Workplace? 22
    Celina Maria Pereira Alonso, Universidade Federal da Bahia, Brazil & ISCSP, Universidade de Lisboa, Portugal
    Maria da Conceição Pereira Fonseca, Universidade Federal da Bahia, Brazil
    Carlos Rodrigo Nascimento de Lira, Universidade Federal da Bahia, Brazil
    Sónia P. Gonçalves, ISCSP, Universidade de Lisboa, Portugal

Chapter 3
The Smart Job Factory: Creating Sustainable Jobs by Defining Work Process Roles Based on a Digital Ecosystem Model 40
    Christian-Andreas Schumann, Westsächsische Hochschule Zwickau, Germany
    Chantal Runte, Westsächsische Hochschule Zwickau, Germany
    Cornelia M. Enger, Westsächsische Hochschule Zwickau, Germany
    Anna-Maria Nitsche, Westsächsische Hochschule Zwickau, Germany

Chapter 4
Job Insecurity and Performance: Contributions for an Integrative Theoretical Framework 61
    Ligia Portovedo, University of Minho, Portugal
    Ana Veloso, University of Minho, Portugal
    Miguel Portela, University of Minho, Portugal

Chapter 5
The Impact of Irregular Schedules on Worker Lives: Theoretical Considerations and Implications for Practice 99
    Isabel S. Silva, CICS.NOVA, University of Minho, Portugal
    Liliana Fernandes, University of Minho, Portugal
    Daniela Costa, University of Minho, Portugal
    Ana Veloso, CICS.NOVA, University of Minho, Portugal

Chapter 6
Work Passion and Workaholism: Antecedents of Psychological Well-Being and Burnout 117
    Joana Vieira dos Santos, Psychology Research Centre, University of Algarve, Portugal
    Gabriela Gonçalves, University of Algarve, Portugal
    Catia Sousa, University of Algarve, Portugal
    Alexandra Gomes, University of Algarve, Portugal

Chapter 7
Workplace Ostracism and Subjective Well-Being: A Reflection on Understanding the Experiences of Syrian Asylum Seekers in Turkey 134
    Basak Ucanok Tan, Istanbul Bilgi University, Turkey
    Fatma Nur Bayır, United Work, Turkey

Chapter 8
Environment of Inclusion and Diversity Management on Perceived Diversity Climate 153
    Stephen Deepak, Kristu Jayanti College, India
    Syed Khalid Perwez, Vellore Institute of Technology, India

Chapter 9
The Effect of Gender Diversity and Locus of Control on Employee Sustainability: The Mediating Effect of Equity and Engagement — A Comparative Study Between Lebanon and Europe 166
    Khodor Shatila, IProCares International Research Center, Lebanon

Chapter 10
Gender Diversity Management in the Labor Market: The Integration of Trans People 183
    José Baptista, ISCSP, Universidade de Lisboa, Portugal
    Dália Costa, ISCSP, Universidade de Lisboa, Portugal
    Sónia P. Gonçalves, ISCSP, Universidade de Lisboa, Portugal

Chapter 11
Work Identity, Meaning, and Meaningfulness of Work in the Immigration Context: Systematic Literature Review 198
    Silvana Curvello de Cerqueira Campos, Universidade Federal da Bahia, Brazil
    Sônia Maria Guedes Gondim, Universidade Federal da Bahia, Brazil
    Juliana Paranhos Moreno Batista, Universidade Federal da Bahia, Brazil

Chapter 12
Flexibility of Work During the Pandemic: The Cases of Portugal and Greece 226
    Özgün Sarımehmet Duman, Hacettepe University, Turkey

Chapter 13
Levers of Control and Employee Groupwork to Develop a Novel Strategy in the Post-COVID-19 Era 244
    Marco Borria, Ca' Foscari University of Venice, Italy
    Maurizio Massaro, Ca' Foscari University of Venice, Italy
    Carlo Bagnoli, Ca' Foscari University of Venice, Italy

Chapter 14
Chess as a Way of Inclusion of Prisoners: A Portuguese Experience 257
    Eduardo Tomé, Universidade Lusófona de Humanidades e Tecnologias, Portugal
    Cátia Godinho, GOVCOPP Research Centre, Universidade de Aveiro, Portugal
    António José F. Lopes, Academia de Xadrez de Gaia, Portugal

Compilation of References 270

About the Contributors 324

Index 331

Detailed Table of Contents

Foreword xv

Preface xvi

Acknowledgement xx

Chapter 1
Beyond Economics: Focusing on the Well-Being of Organizations 1
    Susana Dias, Instituto Universitário de Lisboa, Portugal
    Sílvia Luís, Universidade Lusófona de Humanidades e Tecnologias de Lisboa, Portugal

With the increasing debate about the sustainability of our actions and the importance of a people-centered development approach, the role of employees has become an emerging topic of high relevance. A study was conducted through interviews with stakeholders. The analyses of the six interviews identified four categories of themes, such as: I) Reasons for the extensive use of economic-financial metrics; II) Shift from the extensive use of economic-financial metrics to complementarity with other metrics; III) Position of companies regarding the measurement of well-being; and IV) Feasibility of applying well-being indices to the business environment. The extensive use of economic-financial metrics is related to knowledge, utility, composition, culture, and time. Shifting is possible with training/education, politics, investigation, entrepreneurship, society, and economic theory. The company's position depends on legislation, indicators, marketing, availability, and external pressure. Finally, standardization and composition are associated with the feasibility of applying well-being indices.

Chapter 2
Worker Nutrition Program: A Health and Wellness Promoting Policy at the Workplace? 22
    Celina Maria Pereira Alonso, Universidade Federal da Bahia, Brazil & ISCSP, Universidade de Lisboa, Portugal
    Maria da Conceição Pereira Fonseca, Universidade Federal da Bahia, Brazil
    Carlos Rodrigo Nascimento de Lira, Universidade Federal da Bahia, Brazil
    Sónia P. Gonçalves, ISCSP, Universidade de Lisboa, Portugal

Within the scope of attention that workers' health deserves to be given, the implementation of worker's food policies is essential for the promotion of their health, and are shown to be excellent tools for promoting the health and well-being of these workers. Brazil is a country that has an important trajectory in the implementation and monitoring of food and nutritional security (SAN), given its entire historical context. In this chapter, the authors will carry out a deep reflection on the importance of implementing policies for work nutrition and quality of life and well-being of workers in companies, based on the experience of implementing the PAT from 1976 to the present, highlighting the benefits, and proceeding with a critical assessment based on several published studies.

Chapter 3
The Smart Job Factory: Creating Sustainable Jobs by Defining Work Process Roles Based on a Digital Ecosystem Model.. 40
 Christian-Andreas Schumann, Westsächsische Hochschule Zwickau, Germany
 Chantal Runte, Westsächsische Hochschule Zwickau, Germany
 Cornelia M. Enger, Westsächsische Hochschule Zwickau, Germany
 Anna-Maria Nitsche, Westsächsische Hochschule Zwickau, Germany

The labor market is confronted with social, environmental, and economic developments that affect working conditions and individual labor relations. Lately, the Covid-19 pandemic has demonstrated and reinforced the importance of inclusive growth and sustainable work relationships. In this chapter, the smart job factory, a metamodel that supports the creation of new forms of work by redefining roles in labor, is introduced. The smart job factory is based on social entrepreneurship principles to drive innovative, sustainable, and long-term solutions to social challenges. For practical application, the model can be translated into a software solution that supports employers in the assessment of current working conditions and job roles within their companies and helps to redefine work relationships and to create new jobs. Thus, the smart job factory supports the labor market transition by systematically and proactively shaping new forms of work based on the triple bottom line of sustainable development.

Chapter 4
Job Insecurity and Performance: Contributions for an Integrative Theoretical Framework................. 61
 Ligia Portovedo, University of Minho, Portugal
 Ana Veloso, University of Minho, Portugal
 Miguel Portela, University of Minho, Portugal

Based on published literature between 2000 and 2020 and applying a systematic review, the authors reflect on the theoretical bases that describe the effects of psychological moderating and mediating variables in the relationship between job insecurity and performance. An aggregating theoretical model is proposed, anchored on the conservation of resources theory, social exchange theory, and trust to describe the process in which job insecurity impacts performance, through or in the presence of the variables found.

Chapter 5
The Impact of Irregular Schedules on Worker Lives: Theoretical Considerations and Implications for Practice 99
 Isabel S. Silva, CICS.NOVA, University of Minho, Portugal
 Liliana Fernandes, University of Minho, Portugal
 Daniela Costa, University of Minho, Portugal
 Ana Veloso, CICS.NOVA, University of Minho, Portugal

In the recent decades, work schedules have diversified, leading to the implementation of different schedules like shift work or irregular hours. This chapter primarily focuses on irregular work schedules, and is structured in three parts. The first part is dedicated to the theoretical framework of the subject, particularly dealing with the main effects of irregular work schedules for the workers. Next, a study carried out in the

Portuguese context is presented, where the impacts of irregular work schedules of different types (i.e., depending on their degree of irregularity) on the workers were evaluated, specifically in terms of health, family, and social spheres, as well as satisfaction with work schedule. In general, the results indicate that the greater the irregularity of work schedule, the greater the negative impact on the worker. The third part discusses possible strategies for managing non-standard work schedules by organizations, especially at the level of personnel management.

Chapter 6
Work Passion and Workaholism: Antecedents of Psychological Well-Being and Burnout 117
    Joana Vieira dos Santos, Psychology Research Centre, University of Algarve, Portugal
    Gabriela Gonçalves, University of Algarve, Portugal
    Catia Sousa, University of Algarve, Portugal
    Alexandra Gomes, University of Algarve, Portugal

The passion for work can be a predictor of positive behaviors and attitudes, but can also be negative and harmful to the well-being of employees. The aim of this chapter is to test a model in which workaholism presents itself as the main variable and seeks to analyze antecedents (passion for work) and consequences (burnout and psychological well-being). With a sample of 441 participants from different professional areas, aged between 18 to 63 years ($M = 12.47$, $SD = 1.46$), the results show that harmonious work passion contributes to an explanation of workaholism and an individual's well-being. No statistically significant effects were observed on burnout levels. Organizations should seek to foster work environments that favor the harmonious passion of their employees, thus contributing to an increase in their psychological well-being.

Chapter 7
Workplace Ostracism and Subjective Well-Being: A Reflection on Understanding the Experiences of Syrian Asylum Seekers in Turkey 134
    Basak Ucanok Tan, Istanbul Bilgi University, Turkey
    Fatma Nur Bayır, United Work, Turkey

There is growing recognition that better adaptation and settlement is achieved amongst refugees when they obtain meaningful and humane employment in the host country. However, asylum seekers face significant barriers to not only finding work, but also experience difficulties integrating into the workplace and face discrimination at work. Such discrimination may take the form of ostracism and is likely to lead to decreased identification with the employing organization along with colleagues and supervisors. The current chapter is thus a non-systematic review of the literature on workplace ostracism and calls for immediate discussion on refugee and asylum seekers' work experiences, and how neglect and discriminatory practices may lead to undesirable work outcomes and socio-cultural integration problems.

Chapter 8
Environment of Inclusion and Diversity Management on Perceived Diversity Climate 153
    Stephen Deepak, Kristu Jayanti College, India
    Syed Khalid Perwez, Vellore Institute of Technology, India

Diversity at the workplace refers to the environment where individuals from different social backgrounds work together to pursue organizational goals. It is often difficult for individuals to accept members who belong to a different country, culture, religion, and other backgrounds. To manage this, organizations must encourage a climate that appreciates diversity and fosters inclusivity. Diversity climate in organizations is an indication of the extent that working individuals in organizations appreciate diversity related management policies, practices, and action plans aimed to accommodate everyone equally. Employees experience a sense of inclusion when their feelings of uniqueness and belongingness are addressed by the firm's inclusive initiatives making them contribute to the objectives of the organization. This study conceptually provides a theoretical understanding that inclusion and diversity management positively influences the perceived diversity climate which in turn motivates employees towards higher organizational performance.

Chapter 9
The Effect of Gender Diversity and Locus of Control on Employee Sustainability: The Mediating Effect of Equity and Engagement — A Comparative Study Between Lebanon and Europe 166
Khodor Shatila, IProCares International Research Center, Lebanon

Workplaces in Lebanon have a wide range of diversity, including cultural, linguistic, and religious diversity, which all contribute to a better work environment for everyone. Women in Lebanon have not been able to fully exploit the basic right granted to them because of a variety of financial difficulties, stereotypes, and hidden discrimination. Data had been collected using survey distributed among 300 respondents; only 257 respondents filled the questionnaires maintaining 80% response rate. The data had been analyzed using SPSS to evaluate the mediating effect of equity and engagement on the relationship of gender diversity and locus of control on employee performance. The findings stated that the perception of gender diversity in the workplace is expected to enhance feelings of adequacy, empowerment, and physical and emotional well-being, has empirically supported a positive relationship between perceived gender diversity and employees performance. In the workplace, job equality has a significant impact on the performance of employees.

Chapter 10
Gender Diversity Management in the Labor Market: The Integration of Trans People 183
José Baptista, ISCSP, Universidade de Lisboa, Portugal
Dália Costa, ISCSP, Universidade de Lisboa, Portugal
Sónia P. Gonçalves, ISCSP, Universidade de Lisboa, Portugal

Managing diversity in the labor market means adopting flexible management measures that recognize and respect each workers individuality, taking into account that everyone works differently but allowing for everyone to feel recognised, valued, and safe. Within the very broad issue of diversity in human resources, this chapter means to focus on transgender people, often forgotten when discussing this issue. The main goal of this piece of work is to bring this very timely issue to the discussion lineup - not only for research purposes, but for organizations and society as a whole.

Chapter 11
Work Identity, Meaning, and Meaningfulness of Work in the Immigration Context: Systematic Literature Review 198

    Silvana Curvello de Cerqueira Campos, Universidade Federal da Bahia, Brazil
    Sônia Maria Guedes Gondim, Universidade Federal da Bahia, Brazil
    Juliana Paranhos Moreno Batista, Universidade Federal da Bahia, Brazil

The objective of this chapter is to find evidence of empiric relations among work identity, meaning and meaningfulness of work in the immigration context. The method used was systematic literature review, adopting PRISMA recommendations. The following database has been consulted: Scopus, Web of Science, SciELO, PsycInfo and Lilacs. Empiric articles available between 2010 and 2020 have been used, with work identity, meaning and meaningfulness of work, immigration and immigrant descriptors in Portuguese and English. Data was analyzed with thematic content analysis. Results show twenty-seven articles have been found. The created categories considered each construct separately, being three for work identity, two for meaning of work, and none for meaningfulness of work. The main conclusions were that work identity in a host country depends a lot of the environment characteristics, institutional recognition and social status, and on immigrant personal characteristics. In addition, the type of career favors or hinders redefinition of work identity.

Chapter 12
Flexibility of Work During the Pandemic: The Cases of Portugal and Greece 226

    Özgün Sarımehmet Duman, Hacettepe University, Turkey

Economic recovery programmes implemented in Portugal and Greece during the Eurozone crisis prioritised atypical forms of work to increase the efficiency and productivity of labour. Just after they exited their structural adjustment programmes, there happened the COVID-19 outbreak with further challenges to their economic wellbeing and labour-capital relations. This chapter aims to comparatively analyse the labour market indicators in flexible forms of work before and during the pandemic. It argues that the economic policies implemented during the COVID-19 crisis had initially aimed to contain the adverse effects of the pandemic on societies, by simply limiting the contagion among individuals. With their widespread coverage, COVID-19 measures tended to sustain the already-in-place flexibilisation policies with increasing numbers in part-time and temporary employment relations. In this respect, COVID-19 practices in the labour market simply consolidated the economic recovery policies implemented in the post-crisis years in Portugal and Greece.

Chapter 13
Levers of Control and Employee Groupwork to Develop a Novel Strategy in the Post-COVID-19 Era 244

    Marco Borria, Ca' Foscari University of Venice, Italy
    Maurizio Massaro, Ca' Foscari University of Venice, Italy
    Carlo Bagnoli, Ca' Foscari University of Venice, Italy

Since the onset of the COVID-19 pandemic, businesses are competing in an unknown, ever-changing environment. This turbulence generates new forms of uncertainty and risks that not only affect business performance but also the wellbeing of employees. Groupwork as a management control system can support business risk reduction and increase employee wellbeing. However, while groupwork can help companies develop a novel strategy apt to face unprecedented competitive scenarios, it can also bring new challenges in terms of practical organization and efficiency. Moving from this premise, the chapter will discuss how groupwork can be used as a management control system using the levers of control lens. Opportunities and challenges both for businesses and employee wellbeing will be discussed.

Chapter 14
Chess as a Way of Inclusion of Prisoners: A Portuguese Experience 257
Eduardo Tomé, Universidade Lusófona de Humanidades e Tecnologias, Portugal
Cátia Godinho, GOVCOPP Research Centre, Universidade de Aveiro, Portugal
António José F. Lopes, Academia de Xadrez de Gaia, Portugal

This paper describes a Portuguese ongoing experience of policies aiming at including people in society and ultimately in the labour market, promoting sustainability in wellbeing. Namely, if focuses on the teaching of chess to prisoners in Portuguese jails, and the following participation of these prisoners in championships as the first Hybrid European Championship for Prisoners held in October of 2021. the authors base the study in theories about social inclusion and relate them to chess. Then they explain in detail experiences dealing with the inclusion of chess in society. Furthermore, they explain the Portuguese case. The chapter concludes that chess has been a very interesting tool for the social integration of prisoners in Portugal as well as in other countries. Therefore, the experience is worth being pursued and developed worldwide.

Compilation of References 270

About the Contributors 324

Index 331

Foreword

The book *Developing Diversity, Equity, and Inclusion Policies for Promoting Employee Sustainability and Well-Being* is a significant contribution to the knowledge on people management and workplace issues. Human resource management field is a dynamic and also passion area, with several gold topics that should be in the professional and academic agenda.

This book reinforces and reflect several of these goal issue, by highlighting people-centered development approach and the importance of well-being, namely, related with physical, mental and emotional health. The book also stresses new ways of work based in digital ecosystem model, irregular schedules and job insecurity. Unhealthy workplaces, were workaholism and ostracism can be present, are subject of reflection in this book. Four chapters highlighted issues related with diversity and inclusion based namely with in gender and nationality. Authors have not forgot the pandemic challenges related with flexibility of work and employee groupwork. Finally, the last chapter present an intervention that aims to promote inclusion and well-being.

The research discussed in the book has the potential to increase critical thinking and understanding in universities, workplaces, and throughout society. The objective is to encourage organizations to think and act to promote a more healthy and sustainable workplaces promoting innovation and best practices.

Sincerely,

Pedro Ramos
Associação Portuguesa de Gestão das Pessoas, Portugal

Preface

A quick search in *B-on database* with the keywords "employee wellbeing" and "sustainability" shows that twice as many articles have been published in the last five years compared to the period between 1970 and 2017 (6.100 articles vs 3.015 articles). Thus, employee well-being and sustainability have been increasingly important discussions in today's academic and business world. The reason is because well-being has proved to be an important outcome in the literature of the social sciences, namely, organizational behavior, psychology and industrial, organizational sociology and work, when related to other variables, namely, work performance (e.g., Taris & Schaufeli, 2018). Besides that, workers' attitudes and behaviors, including well-being, may play a central role in explanatory models of the relationship between human resource management practices and organizational performance (Peccei, 2004). Guest (2017) also adds that there is a strong ethical argument to focus on the worker's well-being, derived from changes in work conditions and contexts that can reduce their health and well-being. In this sense, the organization, as an integral part of this context, will have the co-responsibility for contributing to the health and well-being of workers, namely through strategic and sustainable human resource system.

Also, in the actual dynamic context businesses may have difficulty implementing a successful long-term policy due to a lack of knowledge, limited resources, and a short-term focus; however, the effects have shown a potential strategic and growth advantage. Promoting employee sustainability is an important step towards greater competitive advantage, creation of added value to the business, and a greater identity among society and within the organization itself. Therefore the develop of a more Sustainable Human Resource Management - "characterized by the maximization and balancing of economic, environmental, and social organizational goals" (Bush, 2018, p. 2) is an important and urgent goal, because can enable corporate sustainability.

Developing Diversity, Equity, and Inclusion Policies for Promoting Employee Sustainability and Well-Being analyzes the current state of employee sustainability policies, systematizes the factors that promote a more sustainable and healthier workplace, explores the implications of diversity and inclusion practices on the well-being of employees, and collects policy options aimed at finding solutions to enhance well-being. The target audience of the book is composed of academicians, researchers, scholars, practitioners, policymakers, business owners, managers, government officials, instructors, and students.

The book is organized in 14 chapters, that covered several topics (Figure 1) such as, well-being, news forms of work organization, work characteristics, insecurity, work passion, nutrition, workaholism, workplace ostracism, inclusion and diversity, performance and COVID-19.

Here is a brief description of the main ideas of each chapter.

Preface

Figure 1. Chapters keywords

Chapter 1, titled "Beyond Economics: Focusing on the Well-Being of Organizations", written by Susana Dias e Sílvia Luís, highlights, through interviews, namely the people-centered development approach as complementary alternative to the use of economic-financial metrics.

Chapter 2, titled "Worker Nutrition Program: A Health and Wellness Promoting Policy at the Workplace?" written by Celina Maria Pereira Alonso, Maria da Conceição Pereira Fonseca, Carlos Rodrigo Nascimento de Lira e Sónia P. Gonçalves, ia a deep reflection on the importance of implementing policies for work nutrition and quality of life and well-being of workers in companies, based on the experience of implementing a Worker's Food Program in Brazil from 1976 to the present.

In Chapter 3, titled "The Smart Job Factory: Creating Sustainable Jobs by Defining Work Process Roles Based on a Digital Ecosystem Model", written by Christian-Andreas Schumann, Chantal Runte, Cornelia M. Enger, and Anna-Maria Nitsche, the Smart Job Factory, a metamodel that supports the creation of new forms of work by redefining roles in labour, is introduced.

Chapter 4, titled "Job Insecurity and Performance: Contributions for an Integrative Theoretical Framework", written by Lígia Portovedo, Ana Veloso, and Miguel Portela, presents a systematic review focused in the psychological moderating and mediating variables in the relationship between Job Insecurity and Performance and based in this revision an aggregating theoretical model is proposed.

Chapter 5, titled "The Impact of Irregular Schedules on the Worker Lives: Theoretical Considerations and Implications for Practice", written by Isabel S. Silva, Liliana Fernandes, Daniela Costa, and Ana Veloso, focuses on a very actual and relevant issue, the effect of irregular schedules on the workers' health, family, and social spheres through a study carried out in the Portuguese context that show that the greater the irregularity of work schedule, the greater the negative impact on the worker. The authors also discuss the practical implications related with strategies for managing non-standard work schedules by organizations and workers.

Chapter 6, "Work Passion and Workaholism: Antecedents of Psychological Well-Being and Burnout", written by Joana Vieira dos Santos, Gabriela Gonçalves, Cátia Sousa, and Alexandra Gomes, shows that harmonious work passion contributes to an explanation of workaholism and an individual's well-being, highlighting the organizations should seek to foster work environments that favor the harmonious passion of their employees.

Chapter 7, titled "Workplace Ostracism and Subjective Well-Being: A Reflection on Understanding the Experiences of Syrian Asylum Seekers in Turkey", written by Basak Ucanok Tan and Fatma Nur Bayır, is a non-systematic review of the literature on workplace ostracism discrimination and calls for immediate discussion on refugee and asylum seekers' work experiences and how neglect and discriminatory practices may lead to undesirable work outcomes and socio-cultural integration problems

Chapter 8, titled "Environment of Inclusion and Diversity Management on Perceived Diversity Climate", written by Stephen Deepak and Syed Khalid Perwez, provides a theoretical understanding that inclusion and diversity management positively influences the perceived diversity climate which in turn motivates employees towards higher organizational performance.

Chapter 9, titled "The Effect of Gender Diversity and Locus of Control on Employee Sustainability, the Mediating Effect of Equity, and Engagement: A Comparative Study Between Lebanon and Europe", written by Khodor Shatila, presents a study that evaluate the mediating effect of equity and engagement on the relationship of gender diversity and locus of control on employee performance. The findings supported a positive relationship between perceived gender diversity and employee's performance. And also, that job equality has a significant impact on the performance of employees.

Chapter 10, titled "Gender Diversity Management in the Labor Market: The Integration of Trans People", written by José Baptista, Dália Costa, and Sónia P. Gonçalves, means to focus on transgender people and their integration on labor market.

Chapter 11, titled "Work Identity, Meaning, and Meaningfulness of Work in the Immigration Context: Systematic Literature Review", written by Silvana Curvello de Cerqueira Campos, Sônia Maria Guedes Gondim e Juliana Paranhos Moreno Batista, presents a Systematic literature review aiming to find evidence of empiric relations among work identity, meaning and meaningfulness of work in the immigration context. The main conclusions were that work identity in a host country depends from multidimensional factors: environment characteristics, institutional recognition, social status and immigrant personal characteristics.

Chapter 12, titled "Flexibility of Work During the Pandemic: The Cases of Portugal and Greece", written by Özgün Sarımehmet Duman, aims to comparatively analyse the labour market indicators in flexible forms of work before and during the pandemic in Portugal and Greece.

Chapter 13, titled "Levers of Control and Employee Groupwork to Develop a Novel Strategy in the Post-COVID-19 Era", written by Marco Borria and Carlo Bagnoli, discusses how groupwork can be used as a management control system using the levers of control lens.

Finally, Chapter 14, titled "Chess as A way of Inclusion of Prisoners: A Portuguese Experience", written by Eduardo Tomé, Cátia Godinho, and António José F. Lopes, brings to us an ongoing experience focused in the teaching of chess to Prisoners in Portuguese jails and the following participation of prisoners in the first Hybrid European Chess Championship for Prisoners held in October of 2021. The goal of this intervention is to promote social inclusion and well-being.

The book brings together authors from different countries and presents different methodological approaches, aspects that are enriching for the readers. The book focuses on workers well-being aiming at clarifying several emergent topics that are relevant for sustainability of human resource management. The book's goal was to bring together chapters that consider all three main areas that are connected and are interdependent: Workers, Organizations and Social context. A healthy and sustainable workplace is constructed through a synergic dynamic of these three key actors.

Preface

    We deeply thank all the authors of the chapters and hope readers will have a great time reading this book.

Sónia P. Gonçalves
ISCSP, Universidade de Lisboa, Portugal

Paula Cristina Nunes Figueiredo
Universidade Lusófona, Portugal

Eduardo Luis Soares Tomé
ULHT, Universidade Lusófona, Portugal

José Baptista
ISCSP, Universidade de Lisboa, Portugal

REFERENCES

Bush, J. T. (2018). Win-win-lose? Sustainable HRM and the promotion of unsustainable employee outcomes. *Human Resource Management Review*, *30*(3), 1–10. doi:10.1016/j.hrmr.2018.11.004

Guest, D. (2017). Human resource management and employee well-being: Towards a new analytic framework. *Human Resource Management Journal*, *27*(1), 22–38. doi:10.1111/1748-8583.12139

Peccei, R. (2004). *Human resource management and the search for the happy workplace. Erasmus Research Institute of Management* , Erasmus University.

Taris, T. W., & Schaufeli, W. B. (2018). Individual Well-Being and Performance at Work. In C. Cooper (Ed.), *Current issues in work and organizational psychology* (pp. 15–34). Routledge. doi:10.4324/9780429468339-11

Acknowledgement

Organizing a book is a challenge project, but when we see the final product it is very rewarding. None of this would have been possible without the authors that entrust their work to our book. It is important to highlight the role of reviewers, that are an important key for the project, they give their time, ideas and feedback with little recognition.

Thanks to all!

Chapter 1
Beyond Economics:
Focusing on the Well-Being of Organizations

Susana Dias
Instituto Universitário de Lisboa, Portugal

Sílvia Luís
Universidade Lusófona de Humanidades e Tecnologias de Lisboa, Portugal

ABSTRACT

With the increasing debate about the sustainability of our actions and the importance of a people-centered development approach, the role of employees has become an emerging topic of high relevance. A study was conducted through interviews with stakeholders. The analyses of the six interviews identified four categories of themes, such as: I) Reasons for the extensive use of economic-financial metrics; II) Shift from the extensive use of economic-financial metrics to complementarity with other metrics; III) Position of companies regarding the measurement of well-being; and IV) Feasibility of applying well-being indices to the business environment. The extensive use of economic-financial metrics is related to knowledge, utility, composition, culture, and time. Shifting is possible with training/education, politics, investigation, entrepreneurship, society, and economic theory. The company's position depends on legislation, indicators, marketing, availability, and external pressure. Finally, standardization and composition are associated with the feasibility of applying well-being indices.

INTRODUCTION

Humanity should be concerned with the sustainable development of the planet, progress indicators measured only in monetary or social terms are limited and unsustainable. It is necessary to change the global knowledge of what progress is, shifting the discussion from growth to sustainable development and human well-being (Giannetti et al., 2015).

DOI: 10.4018/978-1-6684-4181-7.ch001

Climate changes, regulatory pressures, and societal demands for greater environmental and social responsibility are reasons that are motivating organizations worldwide to shift the focus to sustainability, and this means different ways of doing business than traditional (Cohen et al., 2012). The results of Adebanjo et al. (2016) also showed that external pressures can influence the adoption of sustainable practices. However, the challenging times that we are living, caused by uncertainties, continuous technological advancement, increasing speed of innovation, and overall socioeconomic, legal and political forces, add difficulty to this task of going beyond economics (Randev & Jha, 2019).

Nevertheless, in the last decades, there has been an increased interest in the sustainability of organizations, evidenced by stakeholders, customers, and general public. The application of sustainability principles at the employee level can constitute a differentiating practice and make the brand stand out from its competitors, being viewed as a responsible employer in the labor market (Hronová & Špaček, 2021).

The concepts and definitions of sustainability and well-being are complex, interdependent, and interdisciplinary (Qasim, 2017), which demonstrates the importance of looking at the sustainability and well-being of employees in an interconnected way.

Human well-being has been a main concern for humankind since Greek philosophers in BC times until today. But in the twentieth century, with the first industrial revolution, the importance of human well-being was displaced. There is no doubt this period was of great importance, with deep change and transformation and significant impact on societies, economies, and people. But history shows that a focus on human well-being in the workforce cannot be a marginal subject and there is a lot to improve. During this millennium, concern for well-being has gained increasing attention in the workplace and many areas and disciplines, particularly to understand more about it in these different areas and learn how to improve and consolidate it in synchrony with organizational well-being (Ochoa et al., 2018).

The following work aims to analyze the state of the art in employee sustainability and well-being; and to explore policy options aimed at finding solutions to enhance employee sustainability and well-being. Most studies on employee well-being focus on micro-level variables. The approach that will be developed in this chapter assumes that employee well-being is a complex and multidimensional concept that can only be grasped when macro, meso, and micro-level variables of economic, social, and environmental nature are considered. For instance, the air quality of the area where the organization is located, organizational policies towards employee engagement in decision making, and perceived fairness of one's income interact to influence the employee's well-being at work.

EMPLOYEE SUSTAINABILITY

With the current challenges that our society lives and increased interest in sustainability, the idea of extending the focus from a purely economic one to include ecological and social responsibility gained traction (Kainzbauer & Rungruang, 2019). The called "triple bottom line", a term coined by John Elkington in 1994 as a challenge for business leaders to rethink capitalism (Elkington, 2018), introduced a broader perspective on how firms create value and how they can simultaneously deliver positive results for the people, planet, and profit. This perspective was accompanied by a shift in focus from short-term profitability to longer-term success based on various indicators (Kainzbauer & Rungruang, 2019).

In the human resource management (HRM) literature, this shift in perspective led to the emergence of a new research focus on sustainable human resource management, or S-HRM, a term that was introduced around the turn of the millennium. Despite a growing number of recent publications on S-HRM, research in this field remains in the emerging phase (Kainzbauer & Rungruang, 2019). The rise of the Sustainable Development (SD) concept and its recognized importance contributed to the increasing interest in practices encompassing the S-HRM, recognized by many researchers as a new paradigm in the area of HRM (Mazur & Walczyna, 2020).

At the base of S-HRM, one can see the process of change driven by the organization, where attention is equally distributed to the three pillars of sustainability – economic, social, and environmental – and incorporated into the organizational strategy. The concept of incorporating human resources into sustainability and vice-versa, as it is a reciprocal process, has evolved over the years and has changed the scope of the literature on the S-HRM as well as its' understanding and definitions (Mazur & Walczyna, 2020). Thus, S-HRM can be defined as "the adoption of HRM strategies and practices that enable the achievement of financial, social, and ecological goals, with an impact inside and outside of the organization and over a long-term time horizon while controlling for unintended side effects and negative feedback" (Ehnert et al., 2016, p. 90).

The emerging field of S-HRM incorporates a macro perspective, namely on how HRM contributes to sustainable outcomes and promotions of organizational sustainability, as well as the meso and micro perspectives on how to make HRM itself more sustainable, by studying the sustainability of its' practices (Kainzbauer & Rungruang, 2019).

Regarding the meso and micro perspectives, Gollan (2000) developed one of the pioneering studies presenting the sustainability aspect of HRM. In this study, it is indicated that for true corporate sustainability, an organization must recognize, value, and promote the capability of its people, or it is highly likely that the organization will lose its talents. The human resources policies and practices need to be integrated for sustained business performance and positive employee outcomes of equity, development, and well-being so that human resource sustainability can be achieved (Gollan, 2000).

The study by Kainzbauer and Rungruang (2019) has showed that the majority of the top-cited S-HRM documents focused on the relationship between HRM and environmental management, as well as the relationship between HRM and Corporate Social Responsibility (CSR). This focus corresponds to the macro perspectives of S-HRM which focus the potential of HRM in promoting sustainability. Another interesting fact is that very few among the top-cited documents in this study's database explore several aspects of sustainability simultaneously (environmental, social, and economic). Also, only one paper in top 20 list focused on the sustainability of HRM processes, demonstrating the need of more research on the sustainability of HRM processes and practices, the meso and micro perspectives focusing on HR systems, and employee well-being.

The sustainable management of employees, who are fundamental organizational assets, uses human resources tools and helps to embed the sustainability strategy into organizations (Cohen et al., 2012). The goal of human resource management is to provide motivated, qualified, and loyal employees, with sustainable human resource management being the next logical step, after incorporating sustainability into a company's processes (Hronová & Špaček, 2021).

Consulting the KPMG Sustainability reporting survey, it was possible to see that sustainability reporting rates in Portugal are lower than the global average (less than 77%) and have decreased by 8% between 2017 and 2020. In 2020, 72% of the largest companies in Portugal reported their sustainable activities (KPMG, 2020).

In terms of the presence of Portuguese companies in the Dow Jones Sustainability Index, one of the world's reference indices in the area of sustainability, created in 1999, in the results from November 12,

2021 to March 21, 2022, only 2 Portuguese companies were part of this group, namely EDP and Galp (S&P Global, 2021).

Non-financial reporting on the sustainability of HR can help to offset the imbalance concerning the lack of publicly available information about the company's activities and procedures, with sustainability and S-HRM reporting can also be pragmatically perceived as a tool used to enhance the positive image and reputation of a company (Hronová & Špaček, 2021).

EMPLOYEE WELL-BEING

WHO defines health and well-being in its constitution as "a state of complete physical, mental and social well-being and not merely the absence of disease or infirmity" (WHO, 1946, p. 2). As part of its "better life" initiative, the OECD has developed a range of objective indicators of well-being but has also focused on subjective well-being, defined as "good mental states, including all the various evaluations, positive and negative, that people make of their lives, and the affective reaction of people to their experiences" (OECD, 2013, p. 10).

Employee well-being has expanded beyond physical well-being to focus on building a culture of holistic well-being, that includes concerns about physical, emotional, financial, social, career, community, and purpose (Meister, 2021).

Organizational concerns about employees' well-being are growing exponentially due to the global term VUCA (volatile, uncertain, complex, ambiguous) environment (Ochoa et al., 2018), and, more recently, the term BANI (brittle, anxious, nonlinear, incomprehensible) environment (Bustos, 2021). In these environments, organizational success is no longer simply based on short-term revenue maximization, capital investments, or sales, but increasingly depends on people's well-being, human capital, and the development of human talent to ensure sustained and sustainable growth and performance (Ochoa et al., 2018).

Given the breadth of well-being factors and the disparity in theoretical models and definitions of what employees' well-being is, the selection of instruments for measuring it is a challenge (Jarden et al., 2018).

Organizations are entities with great importance and relevance in various aspects of society, including aspects that are fundamental to its safety and well-being. As a result, companies have become more powerful actors and often assume a political role, directly or indirectly. This has important implications for how we understand and manage the responsibilities of business to society (Rasche et al., 2017), given its significant impact on people's economic and social conditions, as well as on environmental outcomes (Shinwell & Shamir, 2018).

Given its importance, well-being should play a central role in businesses and companies. Businesses have a strong impact on people's well-being not only in current terms and within the national borders of a country, but also on future well-being and across different territories (Durand & Boarini, 2016).

Investing in well-being ensures business resilience, with healthier employees performing better, and entailing fewer organizational costs and risks (Kowalski & Loretto, 2017). In contrast, poor employee well-being is strongly related to increased absenteeism, problems related to stress and turnover, and recruitment costs (Chartered Institute of Personnel and Development, 2019).

Although there is a growing number of analyses of the impact of companies on well-being and value creation beyond financial wealth, there is no common agreement on how to measure these impacts, making analysis and drawing conclusions particularly difficult (OECD, n.d.-a).

Beyond Economics:

The phenomenon of well-being is markedly multidimensional, and its measurement encourage reflection and debate. However, reflecting on such complex information can be a challenge (OECD, n.d.-b). In this vein, recent occupational studies have been evidencing the multidimensional nature of well-being. It has been found to depend on individual conditions, such as financial situation, employment type, socioeconomic status, social networks, marital status, and demographic factors, and on organizational conditions, such as organizational culture and safety and health at work (e.g., Berrill et al., 2020; Puciato et al., 2022.; Kamau et al., 2022).

The construction of multidimensional measures of well-being is also supported by new data that shows that quality of life is related to the social and physical environment, personal activities, safety, political voice, in addition to health, education, material wealth, and income (Barrington-Leigh & Escande, 2018). In sum, only a multidimensional definition will be able to grasp the full meaning of well-being (Stiglitz et al., 2009).

In The 2019 Edelman Trust Barometer global report, whose data were collected between October and November 2018, 76% of the more than 33.000 respondents worldwide indicate that they want companies to lead the transition to a new model of sustainable development instead of waiting for the government to impose it (Edelman, 2019). The same pattern was observed in 2020, with 74% wanting the same shift, out of more than 34.000 respondents (Edelman, 2020).

Regarding Portugal, the National Statistics Institute (INE) has been producing the *Índice de Bem-Estar* (IBE) since 2013, with the first release occurring that year and covering the period from 2004 to 2011. The IBE makes it possible to assess well-being and social progress based on 74 indicators, grouped into ten domains of analysis, which represent two main aspects: material living conditions of families and quality of life (INE, 2017). The IBE essentially seeks to portray the evolution of the standard of quality of life, so in the concept adopted by INE, well-being is not equivalent to subjective well-being, even though the latter influences the former. It is also not a happiness index nor does have the objective of assessing the degree of people's happiness (INE, n.d.).

One of the major goals of IBE is to stimulate dialogue among the various actors that promote economic and social progress, so that this index can be a useful tool for a wide range of opinion leaders, public and private decision-makers, the media, and the general public (INE, n.d.).

Initially, the IBE was based on key dimensions identified in the OECD well-being framework (Figure 1), since these indicators have been chosen based on several statistical criteria and in consultation with OECD member countries. The OECD framework covers dimensions of well-being that are relevant to all human beings, and some countries and cultures may include additional aspects which are relevant to their context and history (OCDE, n.d.).

Also, the Better Life Index (BLI) draws on the OECD Well-being Framework, being one of the several projects in the OECD's Better Life Initiative, that contribute to well-being in OECD countries (OCDE, n.d.). The study carried out by Shinwell and Shamir (2018) uses the OECD well-being approach to better understand how business practices might affect the well-being of employees, consumers, and communities, defending that the OECD well-being framework offers a conceptual framework against which the various impacts of business activities can be assessed. In Figure 2 the authors demonstrate how business activities might affect the different well-being dimensions and which circles of impact are most pertinent.

In their findings on the different measurement methods and practices, after reviewing thirty-five business frameworks and initiatives that measured the impacts of business on people's well-being and sustainability, the authors identified a number of common characteristics and challenges:

Figure 1. OECD Well-Being Framework

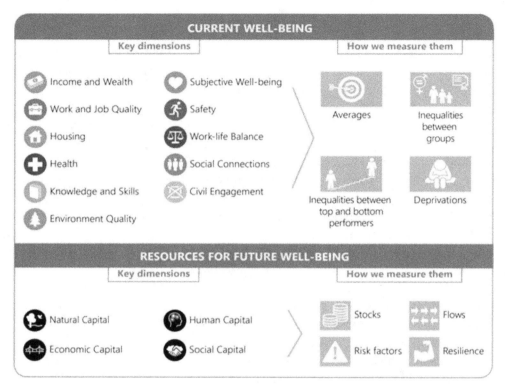

1. Measurement frameworks are not detailed and transparent enough about metrics and methodologies;
2. Company reporting is highly compartmentalized, and results that the variation in the structure and content of annual reports is significant among different companies and from year to year;
3. High quality and up-to-date data on business impacts feature in several reporting frameworks targeted to investors, however, they tend to charge fees compared to boards that target other stakeholders, as their aim is to widen exposure to as many stakeholders as possible;
4. Industry-specific metrics, which on the one hand increases the accuracy of the data but on the other makes comparability a challenge;
5. The development of an enterprise-wide SDG measurement metric is still a distant goal (Shinwell & Shamir, 2018, p. 33).

The authors further conclude that the landscape of the business impact measurement field is fragmented and insufficient, with the proliferation of measurement frameworks are a burden on businesses and stakeholders, and does not make business impact data comprehensible, comparable and actionable. It would be important the adoption of a common framework for assessing how business operations affect people's well-being and sustainability (Shinwell & Shamir, 2018).

Therefore, one of the goals of this chapter is to explore barriers to the development and use of such measures.

Beyond Economics:

Figure 2. Illustration of How Business Activities Might Affect Various Well-Being Dimensions

Dimension	Potential Business impact	Affected circles
Jobs and Earnings	Businesses are the main provider of jobs and directly affect **employees'** employment and pay conditions. These effects may extend through the supply chain, and businesses may in some cases have the means to ensure that their **suppliers** pay adequate (or living) wages to their workers, that safety standards are applied and that school-age children are not employed. Wages paid by business may also impact on earnings inequalities throughout **society**, and in some countries publicly held corporations are now required to disclose information on the compensation of their CEO and management, which allows computing measures of within-company earnings inequality (e.g. between managers and workers) and of how firms reward shareholders relative to employees.	Employees, either directly or through supply-chains; Suppliers; Society at large
Income and Wealth	Businesses affect people's income and wealth in other ways than wages. They may provide employer-sponsored pension plans, savings benefits, loans under preferential terms or financial protection in the event of non-work-related personal injury. **Shareholders and investors** are also affected through company value, profits and dividends.	Employees; Shareholders and investors
Work-Life Balance	Businesses affects **employees'** work-life balance through working hours, overtime, commuting, as well as through their ability to work part-time, flexitime, or telework. Offering flexible working arrangements also allows more people, including women and disabled persons, to get into the labour market. Families are particularly affected, as workers' ability to combine work, family commitments and personal life is important for the well-being of all household members. It is also important for **society as a whole**, as it ensures that people have time to socialise and participate in the life of their community. Some business products and services that reduce the time spent on domestic work can affect **consumers**, allowing more time for leisure activities, and extend to **society at large** through spill-over effects.	Employees and their families; Consumers; Society at large
Health	Businesses affect **employees'** health by creating secure and healthy work environments, providing healthcare coverage to workers and their families, and through supplementary health-promotion programmes. They may also affect workers in their **supply chain** through health and safety directives to suppliers. In many industries, such as food and beverages, infrastructure, communication and electronics, businesses affect **consumers'** health either positively (by providing products with nutritional value and product safety) or negatively. **Society at large** might also be affected through spill-overs, such as better health service infrastructure and CSR activities promoting public health and health awareness.	Employees and their families, directly or through supply-chains; Consumers; Society at large, future generations
Education and Skills	Businesses affect the skills of their **employees**, by providing on-the-job training, opportunities to learn new things on the jobs and to use the skills they already have. In some cases, businesses might also contribute to building up the skills of workers, **their offspring and communities** in countries where they operate through educational CSR activities, scholarships, training opportunities to students and philanthropy.	Employees and their families, directly or through supply-chains; Society at large, future generations
Political Voice and Governance	Corporate governance, ethical business practices, opportunities for **workers** to organise and express their voice are ways in which business affect people's experiences in this dimension. **Investors and shareholders** are affected by businesses competitive behaviour, transparency and integrity. **Employees** are affected through business initiatives to increase workforce diversity, avoid discrimination, allow freedom of association, comply with human rights and provide opportunities to workers to voice their concerns on how the business is run. Businesses also affect **consumers** through fair marketing and product labelling, and **society at large** through philanthropy and volunteering activities.	Employees; Investors and shareholders; Consumers; Society at large
Environment	People's lives are affected by the healthiness of their physical environment, which business impacts through pollutants, hazardous substances and noise. These impacts may be limited to **workers** but also extend to **society as a whole**. Energy use, water and waste management, use of natural resources are the main channels through which businesses influence environmental quality. Through their products and services, businesses can raise **consumer** awareness and screen suppliers based on environmental criteria.	Society at large, future generations; Employees; Consumers
Social Connections	Businesses contribute to the social connections of their **workers** by encouraging meaningful relationships in the work-place. They may also affect **consumers**, through products that support social networks, and **society at large** by investing in local communities, organising volunteering activities and community support programmes.	Employees; Consumers; Society at large, future generations
Housing	While only few business provide housing to their employees, financial institutions and construction firms influence **people's** ability to get access to good and affordable housing.	Consumers
Personal Security	Business operations may affect people's personal security through the provision of security-enhancing goods and services offered to **consumers**.	Consumers
Subjective Well-being	As people spend most of their adult lives at work, business can impact people's subjective well-being, through employees' job satisfaction as well as **consumers'** satisfaction.	Employees; Consumers

EMPLOYEE SUSTAINABILITY AND WELL-BEING

Deloitte's 2021 Global Human Capital Trends Report shared that in the past two years, 44% of millennials and 49% of Generation Z said that their personal ethics influence their choices about the type of work they are prepared to do and the organizations for which they are willing to work (Volini et al., 2021), and this fact translates into overall employee engagement (Meister, 2021). A recent Gartner survey revealed that the proportion of workers who were considered highly engaged increased from 40% to 60% when an organization acted on today's social issues (Gartner, 2020).

A good example of the efforts being made is the launch of the OECD Centre on Well-being, Inclusion, Sustainability and Equal Opportunity (WISE) in November 2020:

WISE's mission includes strengthening the measurement of well-being, inequalities, inclusion, and sustainability, as well as better understanding the impact that policies and business actions have on people's lives today, and on the sustainability of well-being over time. WISE strives to deliver timely responses to today's challenges while keeping long-term objectives in mind as we enter the "decade of action" for the SDGs (OECD, 2020, p. 1).

The development of these themes by relevant international organizations is important, for the means available to develop the themes, for the greater possibility of bringing these themes to more people, as well as for the possibility of encouraging more people to develop these emerging themes.

In today's interconnected and ever-changing world, the paradigm shift from the entrenched approaches of the industrial past to a human-centered methodology makes it possible to meet the needs of people and organizations around the world. Current challenges include issues of human development, responsible leadership, financial accountability, and social responsibility, which can only be understood and resolved through inputs from different disciplines including management, psychology, economics, and others. The emergence of increasingly complex and disruptive problems requires solutions that build resilience through the incorporation of effective multidisciplinary models in building productive organizations, transparent markets, sustainable economies, and inclusive societies (Ochoa et al., 2018).

Hence, for the purpose of this study, interviews were carried out to explore the possible complementarity relationship of different metrics, to investigate the position of companies regarding the measurement of well-being, and the feasibility of applying well-being indices to the organizational context.

METHODOLOGY

The goal of the semi-structured interview was to acquire information on the reasons for the current extensive use of economic-financial metrics, understand how to promote the transition from extensive use of economic-financial metrics to complementarity with other metrics, to determine the position of companies regarding the measurement of well-being, and the feasibility of applying well-being indices to the business environment.

Six interviews were conducted with stakeholders of different backgrounds, that were mapped due to their professional activity being linked to the theme (see Table 1 in Appendix 1). Four of them were academics working in the economics, psychology, and sustainability areas, one was a statistician working in the well-being area, and the other one was the general secretary of a business association working towards sustainability. The study aimed to explore and develop the topic, so the interviewees selected were mostly academics because of their broader potential to provide insight into current developments in the topic.

The interview guides were sent to the interviewees in advance, for a better understanding of the topics that would be addressed during the interview. The interviews were held via zoom session, and to be able to carry out a full analysis of the data, an audio and video record needed to transcribe the interview verbatim. The technique of analysis by categories was used, which works through operations of dismembering the text into units, in categories according to analogical regroupings. Three steps were performed: 1) pre-analysis; 2) the exploration of the material; and 3) the treatment of results and interpretation (Bardin, 1977). Data were analyzed through a conceptual content analysis, a research tool that helps identify the presence or quantify the number of times a word/phrase or text appears in each interview fragment. After identifying the research question and having the interviews for analysis, the text was coded into manageable content categories, being a process of selective reduction, and where the content categories represent an idea, attitude, or behavior relevant to the research question. By reducing the text into categories, the authors were able to focus and code specific words or patterns that inform the research question (Columbia University, n.d.). Due to the lack of available information on the application of well-being indices in the business context, the interviews were exploratory, and the categories emerged from these, that is, they were not previously built based on a literature review.

For each category of themes identified, tables were built with the summary of the analysis performed, containing excerpts from the interviews carried out. The tables intend to demonstrate the knowledge, lack of knowledge, or uncertainty of the participants regarding each of the discussed categories, as well as the identification of a favorable (☺), unfavorable (☹), or neutral position (☻) of the interviewed regarding the topic. The number of mentions gave an idea of the frequency the same content is referred to.

It is possible to see the summary of the research methodology represented in Figure 3.

RESULTS

Four categories were identified in the content analysis: I) Reasons for the extensive use of economic-financial metrics; II) Shift from the extensive use of economic-financial metrics to complementarity with other metrics; III) Attitudes of companies regarding the measurement of well-being; and IV) feasibility of applying well-being indices to the business environment.

Five reasons were found for the extensive use of economic-financial metrics identified in the Portuguese context: knowledge, utility, composition, culture, and time. The fact that they are widely known and widespread metrics, which provide useful information and allow a simple and clear assessment, are the reasons why most sustain their use. We live in a market economy, dominated by financial markets, where these indicators are useful and have been used over time, allowing the collection of data over time are also reasons that encourage their use (Table 1).

In the second category, "Shift from the extensive use of economic-financial metrics to complementarity with other metrics", six ways to promote the transition to an approach using complementary metrics, such as well-being indices, were identified: training/education, politics, research, entrepreneurship, citizens and society themselves, and economic theory (Table 2). Only training/education was mentioned by more than one expert, although the experts' opinions diverged.

Figure 3. Summary of Research Methodology

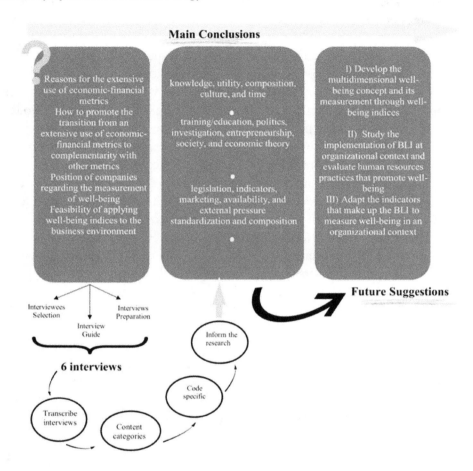

Table 1. Reasons for the Extensive Use of Economic-Financial Metrics

Institution	Functions and Study Areas
Institute of Statistics	Statistics Technician Role in the production of the Portuguese Well-being Index (IBE)
Business Association	General secretary
University	Professor
University	Professor Research interests: Environmental and Natural Resource Economics Sustainability in Higher Education Institutions
University	Professor Researcher in Positive Psychology, Public Happiness and Well-being, Peace and Corporate Virtues
University	Professor Research interests: educational economics, family economics and social demography

Table 2. Shift from Extensive Use of Economic-Financial Metrics to Complementarity with Other Metrics

Category	Knowledge / Mention	Nº of citations	Example	Position	Nº of citations	Example
1) Reasons for the Extensive Use of Economic-Financial Metrics	Yes	1	We were always praising everything that had to do with the economic dimension in such a way that we ended up reducing everything or almost everything to the economic dimension.	☺	1	We believed that there is only what is measured, economics is a science that has many measuring instruments.
				☺	1	The economy and its indicators] were always those most visible in the media and considered most relevant
1) Knowledge	Yes	2	Because they're the ones that people know, basically there's a lot of inertia in these kinds of things.	☺	1	These are all indicators that are well known to everyone, both the public and the policymakers themselves.
2) Utility				☺	2	They are true indicators that have their utility for measuring the things they measure and therefore they hold true because people continue to believe that the things that are measured here are important.
3) Composition				☺	1	It's because they are objective indicators, which allow us to assess clearly. (...) it immediately eliminates some subjectivity, and also makes the activity of the country and the companies more transparent
4) Culture	Yes	1	This economy is also dominated by financial markets, which place a high value on company results, hence all this pressure for objectives and quantified financial indicators.			
5) Time				☺	1	One of the reasons why we use all economic data is because they are calculated in terms of long series from Banco de Portugal since the 1940s and from INE.

The third category describes the current positioning of Portuguese companies in measuring the well-being of their employees. Five subcategories emerged: legislation, indicators, marketing, availability, and external pressure. Legislative developments have promoted analyses using other non-economic indicators. The development of different indicators, with different uses and application objectives, also contribute to promoting their use, however, well-being still does not seem to be part of the interest of companies. Exploring this question of "well-being semantics" is pointed out as one of the reasons. Well-being does not seem to be attractive because it is often confused with subjective well-being and happiness, and it is not thought of as a multidimensional concept. However, it was pointed out that the lack of availability can be overcome by the external pressure that companies tend to suffer (Table 3).

The last category that emerged was "Feasibility of applying well-being indices to the business environment". This category described the opinion of the experts regarding the application of different well-being indices to the business world. More specifically interviewees were asked about the application of the Portuguese Well-being Index (IBE) or Better Life Index (BLI) to the business environment. None of the interviewees mentioned it was unfeasible, and their attitudes were favorable. Two reasons operationalized the feasibility of applying well-being indices: standardization of information and composition of the indices. These results demonstrate that it would be possible to apply indices such as the IBE or the BLI to the business context, obtaining consistency of information and comparability (Table 4).

Table 3. Position of Organizations Regarding the Measurement of Well-Being

Category	Knowledge / Mention	N° of citations	Example	Position	N° of citations	Example
II) Moving from the extensive use of economic-financial metrics to complementarity metrics	Yes	2	I think that in recent years there have been some changes, even in economics as an economic science. (...) especially in the younger generations, there is more and more concern	🙂	1	There are signs, but I repeat, these processes will take a long time because the economy is the center of our life, it was always thought, its GDP as it has always been considered essential to assess the development
				😐	1	An improvement in their well-being, and it's those kinds of indicators that I really feel are missing and that even in the news, in the media, there is a very large preponderance of hardcore economic information
				☹	2	This isn't like in Physics, where you do an experiment and show that it was a lie after all and changes everything
1) Training/ education	Yes	3	Schools in the areas of training in economics or management (...) are introducing new themes, spaces for reflection on new economic models	🙂	2	There are already at the university, at least in Portugal, at least in a discipline that I know of, where these issues are already alerted to students, they take them to their personal and professional lives, and they go with this awareness and attention to this theme
				☹	2	It's really difficult because there are also colleagues who think this is a waste of time
				😐	1	It's interesting that it has been students, in some countries like the USA and UK, who have created movements to change university curricula. (...) students ask for the curriculum to be more connected to reality
2) Politics	Yes	1	One of the areas where you need to enter is the political area			
3) Research	Yes	2	A very important place for researchers (...) the more it's possible to investigate, explore, with scientific knowledge, new models	🙂	1	When funders start saying "they only get funding now if they show they contribute to SDG A, B, or C", people start thinking about SDGs A, B, or C
4) Entrepreneurship	Yes	1	Make visible all the projects that are being born, in multiple places; therefore, entrepreneurship and visibility			
5) Society	Yes	1	Economic theory is important, but society, citizens, and politics, it's here that they also have an important role in changing this focus on some indicators			
6) Economic theory	Yes	1	The change in terms of the economic theory involves recognizing that human beings have other goals in addition to financial goals			

Table 4. Feasibility of Applying Well-Being Indices to the Business Environment

Category	Knowledge / Mention	N° of citations	Example	Position	N° of citations	Example
III) Position of companies regarding the measurement of well-being	Yes	2	The opening to integrate these 3 factors - environmental, social, and corporate governance is increasing	🙂	1	The companies themselves no longer only have a strict analysis in terms of results and financial values, they are also concerned with other types of indicators, naturally that the domain still remains the economic and financial indicators
				😐	1	It's certain that if companies do everything well in the most objective and quantifiable things they are contributing to well-being. (...) But it's easier to measure upstream than to measure downstream, to measure well-being, which is a super difficult thing to measure.
1) Legislation	Yes	1	There are major developments in terms of legislation, but not just legislation, in obliging companies to disclose their impacts (whether negative or positive) and in telling the story of what happens beyond the financial dimension	🙂	1	There has to be more regulation, and within the regulation, incentives, on the one hand positive (...) and on the other hand negative
2) Indicators	Yes	1	The GRI (Global Reporting Initiative), which is one of the most followed reporting standards	🙂	1	What is at stake is measuring the impacts of companies, which will then translate into public health, it will translate into well-being, it will translate into quality of life
				😐	1	Measuring greenhouse gas emissions, impacts on the biosphere (...) this is still more or less objective. Now getting into the issue of well-being, of course, there are companies that have more subjective reporting dimensions (...) but companies are obviously not there
3) Marketing				😐	1	The question is also a question of terminology, of semantics. Companies, well-being... Companies like tangible things, that's why they like accounting, numbers, the economic-financial part, it's measured well, it's comparable with the past and with others, it's comparable in space and in time
4) Availability				🙂	1	There are also increasing opportunities for financing sustainability
	No	1	I also notice and I am told "we have difficulty measuring our own effectiveness, let alone now gather in the management practices of organizations and people, having time, space, opportunity and scope, to be concerned with the SDGs" (...) It's often a language of companies that do not have a vision, and that do not see themselves as part of the collective, do not see themselves as elements of interdependence	☹	2	Let alone ask them to measure happiness or well-being.
5) External pressure	Yes	2	Portuguese companies are feeling the pressure from 4 types of stakeholders: investors, regulators, customers, and employees	🙂	1	Due to pressure from the end customer, but also the corporate customer, our companies are increasingly forced to make this transition

Beyond Economics:

Summary of the Results

Exploratory interviews with experts in the different fields of knowledge that cover the well-being area suggest that change towards more comprehensive metrics of well-being will be viable but challenging. These metrics are at risk of being perceived as "subjective" and, therefore "untrue". In addition, the competitor indicators are tough. The current economic indicators that are used to tap well-being, such as the GDP, are well known, objective, and have been widely used for many decades. The change will take time and societal efforts. External pressure from society, such as customers and employees, accompanied by the development, standardization, and availability of comprehensive well-being indicators to organizations would help change the current paradigm.

DISCUSSION

When discussing the extensive use of economic-financial metrics, one of the main reasons identified by experts was the knowledge, as these metrics are of general and widespread knowledge. Economic tools have become almost mandatory to produce information that is common to all countries, companies, organizations, or others. In the past, these organisms only had economic tools as a means of comparison. Another reason is the utility of these metrics since they are indicators that provide useful information and whose importance is recognized. The information obtained through economic-financial metrics has many applications, and its utility has been developed and adjusted to the needs over time. Its composition is pointed out as another reason, given that they are objective indicators, which allow a clear assessment of what is intended to be evaluated. Obtaining information on the composition of these metrics is something that can be done and there are different indicators for different objectives. On the other hand, the culture in which we operate is identified as another reason, consistent with the fact that we live in a market economy, dominated by financial markets, that encourages the extensive use of economic-financial metrics. Finally, the fact that financial metrics have existed for several years, allowing the accumulation of data and information over time. Economic measures have been widely used for a long time and in a generalized way, which has allowed the development and adaptation of these measures to the different needs. The importance of these measures is recognized, but economic measures are not enough to reflect on the sustainability and well-being of employees, because despite the economic factor having an impact on the lives of employees, it does not reflect on everything else.

Regarding the complementarity of financial metrics with other metrics, such as well-being indices, and according to the opinion of the experts, this shift can take place through the investment in education and training of students and people overall. It is important to include themes like the importance of a holistic view and not only financial metrics view in schools, universities, and training sites. The investment in education and training should include those currently in leadership roles. This change can also be fostered through politics, being one of the areas where it is necessary to enter and act. Politics is very important, given the high impact it has on society and people's lives. If policies has a people-centered focus and not just a financial information base, the measures and decisions taken will certainly be different. The information that is measured and analyzed is very important, as it may influence political measures, which consequently have a great impact on people's lives. Through research, investment in the exploration of new models, and scientific knowledge, it is also expected to develop the complementarity of financial metrics with other metrics. Research is important because it allows the identification of problems, the diagnosis of causes, and the collection of evidence for theories, which allows the identification of potential solutions, the decision of the action to be taken, as well as the monitoring and evaluation of the action and the results. All this with the aim of contributing to the advancement of knowledge in a field of study.

Entrepreneurship was also pointed out as a possible promoter of this transition, through the visibility that entrepreneurship can provide from the application of these new models. Entrepreneurship promotes innovation through the right practices of research and development, as well as entrepreneurship can promote social changes as entrepreneurs are the pioneer of bringing new technologies and systems that ultimately bring changes to society (Mohamed, 2020).

Society will also play an important role throw the citizen being essential for changes to occur. Citizens can act "as agents of change" in their everyday life, individual choices, or actions on a local level (Kuleta-Hulboj, 2016), but also in sustainable citizenship, where those citizens not only engage in sustainable household practices but respect the importance of raising awareness, discussing, and debating sustainability policies for the common good and maintaining the Earth's ecosystems (Horne et al., 2016). This can be extrapolated to the role of the employee, who must play an active role in achieving sustainability and well-being.

Finally, and not so consensual, the renewal of economic theory can also promote the complementarity of economic-financial metrics with other metrics. This means that economic theory could be adjusted to people's current living conditions, and their current interests and reflect a more holistic view of what people's lives are like.

On the topic referring to the position of companies regarding the measurement of well-being, it is worth highlighting the increasing openness of companies to integrate the three factors – environmental, social, and corporate governance. Legislative developments have led companies to carry out analyses that are not strictly limited to financial factors and are also concerned with other types of indicators. The fact that there are more and more indicators and their recognition, is favorable, however, the requirements of some indicators (such as those with subjective measures) can constitute an obstacle to their implementation. Increasingly, there is a movement to support the inclusion of subjective measures in this type of indicator, such as environmental organizational citizenship behaviors, and studies show that these measures are valid and an asset in promoting sustainability (Luís & Silva, 2022). Yet, the existence of different indicators with different objectives turns out to be a facilitator for the use of different metrics, an attraction. However, the marketing of well-being indices seems to have a problem, given that it is often confused with subjective well-being and/or happiness, and this is not what multidimensional well-being is mainly concerned with. Note that the terms happiness and well-being are often used to describe the same situations, but there are differences between them. "Happiness" is an emotion that everyone generally experiences, but being an emotion, it is a transitory state. On the contrary, "well-being" is a more stable state of contentment, resulting from a series of variables that go far beyond the emotion of happiness (Theobald & Cooper, 2012). Generally, well-being is defined as the presence of the best standard of quality of life in the broadest sense of the term, and the concept of well-being encompasses not only the material conditions of life but also other factors that explain the level of quality of life (INE, n.d.). Choosing a more holistic approach taking into account individual, organizational, and contextual aspects will make possible to present with more accuracy the factors that influence employees' well-being (Kowalski & Loretto, 2017).

Regarding the availability of companies, they do not seem to be very motivated to measure well-being. Nevertheless, the external pressure that companies suffer from stakeholders can stimulate the transition to measuring aspects beyond merely economics. Organizations feel pressured to react and evolve to meet the expectations of their employees and be attractive to attract new talent, given the increasing importance that these issues have in employees' choices.

At the business level, companies are increasingly concerned about carrying out analyses using different types of metrics, however, the well-being indices, for reasons of semantics, still do not seem to be an attractive index. To counteract this, it would be important to invest in marketing and dissemination of information about what are well-being indices, and how they are constituted and constructed, allowing to deconstruct the idea that well-being indices focus on happiness and subjective well-being, bridging the existing semantic problem with these indices.

On the topic of the feasibility of applying well-being indices to the business environment, the responses obtained were favorable, with the main reasons identified being the standardization of the indicators used at the business level, and the composition of the aforementioned indicators, IBE and BLI, likely to be adjusted to the business context. Today, with the wide dispersion of well-being indicators, organizations collecting data on the well-being of their employees are free to choose which data to measure and explore, and the choice can be made in terms of how easy it is to obtain the data, or in terms of which data is most beneficial to expose. Standardization of the information produced by companies will allow the comparison of companies and healthy competition, promoting innovation and development. It was mentioned in two interviews that this information is included in the Global Reporting Initiative (GRI), one of the most important organizations that promote the use of sustainability reports to foster more sustainable organizations. Based on this statement, the indicators that make up the BLI and the GRI were reviewed. However, after comparing all the indicators, few similarities were found in the indicators of both indices. Although the GRI Standards are an important reporting tool, very broad and diverse in their composition, in terms of well-being, this tool has little information that can be used to improve the well-being of its employees. This fact demonstrates the level of misinformation about multidimensional well-being, which consequently affects its integration at the business level or any other level.

This study illustrates the perspectives of a limited number of experts, mainly because the number of people currently focusing their work on it is still small, and only from one country. Nevertheless, it provides a starting point for building on the fundamental issue of applying multidimensional well-being indexes in the organizations as a means to diagnose, compare, and promote employee well-being and, therefore, fully adopt S-HRM practices. Developing the idea of Shinwell and Shamir (2018), who used the OECD framework to try to better understand how business practices can affect workers' well-being, would be an avenue for further research.

CONCLUSION

This work illustrated the state of the art in sustainability and employee well-being and explored policy options based on experts' opinions aimed at finding solutions to improve employee sustainability and well-being. The study presented above also aimed to explore the topic of using metrics beyond merely economic ones, trying to understand the existing knowledge, as well as the company's position in the measurement of well-being. The results of the study remind us of the need to raise awareness of the multidimensional well-being concept and study indicators that allow organizations to access information about the employees' well-being. A future agenda would be to: I) develop the multidimensional well-being concept and its measurement through well-being indices; II) study the implementation of BLI at the organizational level and evaluate human resources practices that promote well-being; and III) adapt the indicators of BLI to measure well-being to the organizational context. It is necessary to establish a common agreement on the constitution of a well-being index and how to measure its impacts on the business level in a way that facilitates analyzing, comparing, and drawing conclusions. This information will then be used to work on the relationship between the companies and well-being.

Experts sustain that it is viable to invest in the implementation of well-being indices in an organizational context by first introducing the theme of well-being in politics, that latter being translated into dedicated policies, training, and education. At the same time, is fundamental to promote research and the development of the subject at the academic level, to support projects that work with well-being, and to promote a societal discussion of this subject. We hope this chapter contributes to fostering this discussion.

REFERENCES

Adebanjo, D., Teh, P.-L., & Ahmed, P. (2016). The impact of external pressure and sustainable management practices on manufacturing performance and environmental outcomes. *International Journal of Operations & Production Management, 36*(9), 995–1013. doi:10.1108/IJOPM-11-2014-0543

Bardin, L. (1977). Análise de Conteúdo. In L. Edições 70 (Ed.), *Revista Educação, 22*(37). http://books.google.com/books?id=AFpxPgAACAAJ%5Cnhttp://cliente.argo.com.br/~mgos/analise_de_conteudo_moraes.html#_ftn1

Barrington-Leigh, C., & Escande, A. (2018). Measuring Progress and Well-Being: A Comparative Review of Indicators. *Social Indicators Research, 135*(3), 893–925. doi:10.100711205-016-1505-0

Berrill, J., Cassells, D., O'Hagan-Luff, M., & Stel, A. van. (2020). *The Relationship Between Financial Distress and Well-Being : Exploring the role of self-employment.* Sage. doi:10.1177/0266242620965384

Bustos, A. (2021). *El futuro del trabajo y cómo prepararnos para afrontarlo* (Issue March). Research Gate. https://www.researchgate.net/profile/Alfonso-Bustos/publication/350043257_El_futuro_del_trabajo_y_como_prepararnos_para_afrontarlo/links/604d1e7e92851c2b23c90685/El-futuro-del-trabajo-y-como-prepararnos-para-afrontarlo.pdf

Chartered Institute of Personnel and Development. (2019). *Health and Wellbeing Survey Report.* CIPD. https://www.cipd.co.uk/Images/health-and-well-being-at-work-2019.v1_tcm18-55881.pdf

Cohen, E., Taylor, S., & Muller-Camen, M. (2012). *Effective Practice Guidelines Series HRM's Role in Corporate Social and Environmental Sustainability.* HRM. https://www.shrm.org/hr-today/trends-and-forecasting/special-reports-and-expert-views/Documents/Corporate-Social-Environmental-Sustainability.pdf

Columbia University. (n.d.). *Content Analysis.* Columbia University. https://www.publichealth.columbia.edu/research/population-health-methods/content-analysis

Durand, M., & Boarini, R. (2016). Well-Being as a Business Concept. *Humanistic Management Journal, 1*(1), 127–137. doi:10.100741463-016-0007-1

Edelman. (2019). 2019 Edelman Trust Barometer Global Report. In *Edelman Trust Barometer*. https://cms.edelman.com/sites/default/files/2017-03/2009-Trust-Barometer-Global-Deck.pdf

Edelman. (2020). *Edelman Trust Barometer 2020*. Edelman.

Ehnert, I., Parsa, S., Roper, I., Wagner, M., & Muller-Camen, M. (2016). Reporting on sustainability and HRM : A comparative study of sustainability reporting practices by the world's largest companies. *International Journal of Human Resource Management*, *27*(1), 88–108. doi:10.1080/09585192.2015.1024157

Elkington, J. (2018). 25 Years Ago I Coined the Phrase "Triple Bottom Line." Here's Why It's Time to Rethink It. *Harvard Business Review*. https://hbr.org/2018/06/25-years-ago-i-coined-the-phrase-triple-bottom-line-heres-why-im-giving-up-on-it

Gartner. (2020). *Gartner Identifies Three Dimensions That Define The New Employer-Employee Relationship*. https://www.gartner.com/en/newsroom/press-releases/2020-10-13-gartner-identifies-three-dimensions-that-define-the-new-employer-employee-relationship

Giannetti, B. F., Agostinho, F., Almeida, C. M. V. B., & Huisingh, D. (2015). A review of limitations of GDP and alternative indices to monitor human wellbeing and to manage eco-system functionality. *Journal of Cleaner Production*, *87*(1), 11–25. doi:10.1016/j.jclepro.2014.10.051

Gollan, P. J. (2000). *Human Resources, Capabilities And Sustainability*. London School of Economics. https://www.agrh.fr/assets/actes/2000gollan038.pdf

Horne, R., Fien, J., Beza, B. B., & Nelson, A. (2016). *Sustainability Citizenship in Cities*. Routledge.

Hronová, Š., & Špaček, M. (2021). Sustainable HRM practices in corporate reporting. *Economies*, *9*(2), 75. doi:10.3390/economies9020075

INE. (2017). *ÍNDICE DE BEM ESTAR 2004-2016*. INE. https://www.ine.pt/xportal/xmain?xpid=INE&xpgid=ine_publicacoes&PUBLICACOESpub_boui=313010615&PUBLICACOESmodo=2

INE. (n.d.). *O que é o Índice de Bem-estar?* INE. https://www.ine.pt/xportal/xmain?xpid=INE&xpgid=ine_indbemestar&xlang=pt

Jarden, R. J., Sandham, M., Siegert, R. J., & Koziol-Mclain, J. (2018). Quality appraisal of workers' wellbeing measures: A systematic review protocol. *Systematic Reviews*, *7*(1), 1–5. doi:10.118613643-018-0905-4 PMID:30572952

Kainzbauer, A., & Rungruang, P. (2019). Science mapping the knowledge base on sustainable human resource management, 1982-2019. *Sustainability (Switzerland)*, *11*(14), 3938. doi:10.3390u11143938

Kamau, J. W., Schader, C., Biber-Freudenberger, L., Stellmacher, T., Amudavi, D. M., Landert, J., Blockeel, J., Whitney, C., & Borgemeister, C. (2022). A holistic sustainability assessment of organic (certified and non - certified) and non - organic smallholder farms. *Environment, Development and Sustainability*, *24*(5), 6984–7021. doi:10.100710668-021-01736-y

Kowalski, T. H. P., & Loretto, W. (2017). Well-being and HRM in the changing workplace. *International Journal of Human Resource Management, 28*(16), 2229–2255. doi:10.1080/09585192.2017.1345205

KPMG. (2020). *The time has come: The KPMG Survey of Sustainability Reporting 2020*. KPMG. https://home.kpmg/xx/en/home/insights/2020/11/the-time-has-come-survey-of-sustainability-reporting.html

Kuleta-Hulboj, M. (2016). The global citizen as an agent of change: Ideals of the global citizen in the narratives of polish NGO employees. *The Journal for Critical Education Policy Studies, 14*(3), 220–250.

Luís, S., & Silva, I. (2022). Humanizing sustainability in organizations: a place for workers' perceptions and behaviors in sustainability indexes? *Sustainability: Science. Practice and Policy, 18*(1), 371–383. doi:10.1080/15487733.2022.2068751

Mazur, B., & Walczyna, A. (2020). *Bridging Sustainable Human Resource Management and Corporate Sustainability*. Sustainability., doi:10.3390u12218987

Meister, J. (2021). *The Future Of Work Is Employee Well-Being*. https://www.forbes.com/sites/jeannemeister/2021/08/04/the-future-of-work-is-worker-well-being/?sh=4d7124984aed

Mohamed, N. (2020). Takeaways On The Importance of Entrepreneurship. *Duke Sanford*. https://dcid.sanford.duke.edu/importance-of-entrepreneurship/.

OCDE. (n.d.). *What's the Better Life Index?* OCDE. https://www.oecdbetterlifeindex.org/about/better-life-initiative/

Ochoa, P., Lepeley, M.-T., & Essens, P. (2018). *Wellbeing for Sustainability in the Global Workplace*. Routledge. doi:10.4324/9780429470523

OECD. (2013). *OECD Guidelines on Measuring Subjective Well-being*. https://www.oecd-ilibrary.org/economics/oecd-guidelines-on-measuring-subjective-well-being_9789264191655-en

OECD. (2020). *Putting people's well-being at the top of the agenda*. OECD. https://www.oecd.org/wise/Peoples-well-being-at-the-top-of-the-agenda-WISE-mission.pdf

OECD. (n.d.-a). *Measuring Business Impacts on People's Well-being and Sustainability*. OECD. https://www.oecd.org/investment/measuring-business-impacts-on-peoples-well-being.htm

OECD. (n.d.-b). *What's the Better Life Index?* OECD. https://www.oecdbetterlifeindex.org/about/better-life-initiative/

Puciato, D., Rozpara, M., Bugdol, M., & Gorgoń, B. M. (2022). Socio - economic correlates of quality of life in single and married urban individuals : A Polish case study. *Health and Quality of Life Outcomes, 20*(1), 1–16. doi:10.118612955-022-01966-2 PMID:35366910

Qasim, M. (2017). Sustainability and Wellbeing: A Scientometric and Bibliometric Review of the Literature. *Journal of Economic Surveys, 31*(4), 1035–1061. doi:10.1111/joes.12183

Randev, K. K., & Jha, J. K. (2019). *Sustainable Human Resource Management : A Literature-based Introduction*. Sage. doi:10.1177/2631454119873495

Beyond Economics:

Rasche, A., Morsing, M., & Moon, J. (2017). The Changing Role of Business in Global Society: CSR and Beyond. In Cambridge University Press (Ed.), *Corporate Social Responsibility Strategy, Communication, Governance.*

Shinwell, M., & Shamir, E. (2018). *Measuring the impact of businesses on people's well-being and sustainability: Taking stock of existing frameworks and initiatives.* OECD.

S&P Global. (2021). *Dow Jones Sustainability Indices components.* S&P Global. https://www.spglobal.com/esg/csa/csa-resources/dow-jones-sustainability-indices-components-bh19

Stiglitz, J. E., Sen, A., & Fitoussi, J.-P. (2009). *Report by the Commission on the Measurement of Economic Performance and Social Progress.* Europa. https://ec.europa.eu/environment/beyond_gdp/reports_en.html

Theobald, T., & Cooper, C. (2012). The relationship between happiness and wellbeing. In *Doing the Right Thing.* Palgrave Macmillan. doi:10.1057/9780230359017_3

Volini, E., Schwartz, J., Eaton, K., Mallon, D., Van Durme, Y., Hauptmann, M., Scoble-Williams, N., & Poynton, S. (2021). The worker-employer relationship disrupted. In *Deloitte Insights.* https://www2.deloitte.com/us/en/insights/focus/human-capital-trends/2021/the-evolving-employer-employee-relationship.html/#endnote-7

WHO. (1946). *Constitution of the World Health Organization.*

ADDITIONAL READING

Council of the European Union. (2019). *The Economy of Wellbeing - Draft Council Conclusions.* EU. https://www.consilium.europa.eu/en/press/press-releases/2019/10/24/economy-of-wellbeing-the-council-adopts-conclusions/

Durand, M., & Scott, S. (2016). *Measuring multidimensional well-being and sustainable development*, 33–36. doi:10.1787/9789264264687-6-en

Guest, D. E. (2017). Human resource management and employee well-being: Towards a new analytic framework. *Human Resource Management Journal*, *27*(1), 22–38. doi:10.1111/1748-8583.12139

OECD. (2018). *Compendium of Selected Papers on Measuring the Impacts of Business on Well-Being and Sustainability.* OECD. https://www.oecd.org/statistics/Measuring-impacts-of-business-on-well-being.pdf

OECD. (2020). How's Life? 2020: Measuring Well-being. OECD Publishing, Paris. OECD.

KEY TERMS AND DEFINITIONS

BANI world: A concept used to explain new world dynamics. In this case, a brittle, anxious, non-linear, incomprehensible world, the successor to the VUCA world.

Better Life Index: An interactive tool developed by OECD, one project of the OECD's Better Life Initiative, that aims to involve citizens in well-being debate.

Multidimensional approach: With the increasing complexity of emerging topics, it is important to use multidimensional indices instead of traditional metrics with single measures.

People-centered approach: The belief that people's best interests should be at the center of decisions.

Sustainable citizenship: The role that citizens can play to help improve social justice, safeguard nature or any action that contributes to sustainable development and that make the world a better place to live.

Triple bottom line: A term created with the aim of rethinking the traditional way of doing business, putting environmental and social issues on the same level as economic ones.

VUCA world: Big developments, instability and changes were characteristics of the world that led to the creation of the VUCA concept, defined as a world volatile, uncertain, complex and ambiguous.

APPENDIX 1

Table 5. Interviewees' Information

Category	Knowledge / Mention	N° of citations	Example	Position	N° of citations	Example
IV) Feasibility of applying well-being indices to the business environment	Yes	3	*I think it's a possible path*	☺	2	There is a set of subjective evaluation indicators in the IBE that could be transported to the corporate level
1) Standardization				☺	2	Trying to understand if some of the indicators are similar at the national and business level would create a greater correspondence. Not meaning that in the end they were directly comparable, but at least some consistency was maintained
2) Composition				☺	2	Among all the indicators from BLI, I think you can find parallels
				☹	1	I think that if it's not based on something that companies already have information about, such as the GRI, it won't do any good because no one will use it

Chapter 2
Worker Nutrition Program:
A Health and Wellness Promoting Policy at the Workplace?

Celina Maria Pereira Alonso
https://orcid.org/0000-0002-1350-3809
Universidade Federal da Bahia, Brazil & ISCSP, Universidade de Lisboa, Portugal

Maria da Conceição Pereira Fonseca
Universidade Federal da Bahia, Brazil

Carlos Rodrigo Nascimento de Lira
https://orcid.org/0000-0001-7266-1367
Universidade Federal da Bahia, Brazil

Sónia P. Gonçalves
ISCSP, Universidade de Lisboa, Portugal

ABSTRACT

Within the scope of attention that workers' health deserves to be given, the implementation of worker's food policies is essential for the promotion of their health, and are shown to be excellent tools for promoting the health and well-being of these workers. Brazil is a country that has an important trajectory in the implementation and monitoring of food and nutritional security (SAN), given its entire historical context. In this chapter, the authors will carry out a deep reflection on the importance of implementing policies for work nutrition and quality of life and well-being of workers in companies, based on the experience of implementing the PAT from 1976 to the present, highlighting the benefits, and proceeding with a critical assessment based on several published studies.

DOI: 10.4018/978-1-6684-4181-7.ch002

INTRODUCTION

The human resources management paradigm has found more and more ground on workers as key elements of the organizational performance process (e.g, Wright & Nishii, 2007). This line of thought indicates towards the literature on healthy workplaces, which has been broadly expanding, and also to the importance for organizations to constitute themselves as generators of resources to workers, through the promotion and implementation of practices and programs that promote health and wellness of workers (Affonso, 2005), thus contributing to their life quality and subsequent performance (Shain & Kramer, 2004).

Thereby, Thiry-Cherques (1991) considers that workers' life quality influences their productivity, which hence directly affects their life quality, that is, they are intertwined. In the face of this, paying attention to life quality on the workplace aids the workers on the development of their activities in a more coherent way, which repercussion on productivity, final product quality and mainly in their health because, as Silva (2005) states, if there aren't safe conditions of life and work, consequently, there will be no health. Caldas JR (1995) also reinforces the development of a company is linked to the health of its workers.

Life quality (LQ) is conceptualized as the "perception of the individual of his life insertion on the context of the culture and value systems in which he lives and also of his objectives, expectations, standards and concerns" (WHOQOL GROUP, 1994, p. 15). It has become a noted feature on society's agenda, highlighting organizations and human resources management, which has taken an active role on the matter.

Therefore, one important component of LQ is the assessment of life at the workplace. Providing LQ on the workplace potentiates the areas of workers' health, wellness, safety management, career plan, competence development, among others (Ruževičius, 2014). In this regard, the forms/conditions on the workplaces pervades the workers' experiences in one of the dimensions of their lives.

On this perspective, the construct Life Quality at the Workplace (LQW) was born on the 20th century from studies on the relation man/work. The definition of LQW, such as LQ, is also broad and multidisciplinary. Therefore, is treated in a differentiated way by numerous authors, defending the company has social responsibility to address the needs of their workers, based on the humanization principle, and defining practices which establish the individual's relation with his work. This author suggests eight categories to evaluate LQW: 1) proper and just salary; 2) safe and healthy work conditions; 3) opportunities to use/develop human capabilities; 4) growth opportunity assurance; 5) social integration on the workplace organization; 6) constitution on the workplace organization; 7) total work and life span; 8) social relevance of professional life.

The LQW is described as the favorable workplace that supports and promotes satisfaction, providing the staff with rewards, work safety, career growth opportunities etc. Given the interdisciplinary character of this construct, the evaluation process is very distinct and, sometimes, complex. However, it is possible to find consensus points, considering a bio-psycho-social view, where the individual is formed by the biological, psychological and social (Limongi-França, 1996). Hence, it is also important sustaining a healthy, complete and balanced nutrition, physical activity and preventive behavior regarding relationships and stress control (Nahas, 2001).

Nutrition is, undoubtedly, one of the factors which contribute to this assurance, and the offer of meals with an appropriate nutritional value and hygienic-sanitary quality is fundamental to the collaboration of QVT (Silva, 2005) since, given proper food offer, there is more chance to reduce the risk of professional accidents/illnesses (Amil et al., 2021; Barros et al., 2016). The concern regarding hygienic-sanitary aspects on all stages of the meals' production process, as well as available spaces to nutrition and permanence of workers on the resting period, contributes to workers' nutrition and workplace wellness. Hence, the trilogy health, healthy nutrition and wellness are determinant factors (Pegado, 1995).

A recent study by Amil et al. (2021) objectified relevance assessment and orientation of global dietary quality on the context of a health promotion program at the workplace and its effects on the cardio-metabolic health rates. It concluded that improving general dietary quality through interventions on the workplace lifestyle may have direct effects on cardio-metabolic risk, particularly in women, as well as indirect effects on both men and women given the effects on abdominal adiposity.

There is evidence that nutrition on the workplace contributes to a better ingestion of healthy food, calories and micro-nutrients (Lassen et al., 2004). After extensive research on workers' nutrition, scientists from the National Institute of Health and Wellness (Finland) have demonstrated that having lunch at the workplace contributes positively to workers' nutrition quality. It derives from the fact that a significant portion of the nutrition offered is rich in nutrients and it may present low energetic value, by providing food such as: vegetables, whole grains, fish and low-fat dairy. Studies also stress that eating regularly at restaurants on the workplace has improved Finnish employees' diet, substantially increasing the ingestion of vegetables (Lassen et al., 2004; Raulio et al., 2009, 2010). Aspects related to the workplace, such as low social support, physically demanding jobs, high mental tensions and long work journeys are also involved on dietary outcomes, such as the frequent use of packed meals, snack consumption substituting meals, among others (Raulio et al., 2010; Tamrakar et al., 2020).

Health promoting programs must be increasingly integrated to the Human Resources Management (HRM) practices, capacitating and motivating workers, as well as preparing them emotionally and physically to understand and interact about these health-related issues. Inside these organizations, rethinking work and employment is an issue which defies managers to create mechanisms which can improve the workers' relation with work and with life, promoting the adaptation of people, minimizing the inevitable effects of transition situations, and building a support environment (Silva, 2005). The implementation of Worker's Nutritional Policies is essential to the promotion of their health and reveals itself an excellent tool for the promotion of health and wellness of this public.

Therefore, studies have shown the efficacy of educational programs on nutrition and LQ on the workplace, improving the workers' dietary habits (Lassen et al., 2004; Mazzon, 1992, 1996, 2001, 2006; Raulio et al., 2010). Globally, there are several Worker Nutrition Programs[1] (WNP), however, WNP in Brazil (PAT) was pointed by Barros et al. (2016) as one of the largest in the world.

Brazil is a country with an important trajectory regarding the implementation and monitoring of Food and Nutritional Safety (FNS), its Worker's Nutrition Program (PAT) was implemented in 1976, and despite some limitations, in general, it has helped a lot on the improvement of the condition of workers' health.

In this chapter, we will focus on this program promoting a detailed description and a critical perspective on the program itself, and on the challenges for HRM on interface with governmental policies.

OVERVIEW ON THE WORKERS' NUTRITION AND ON NUTRITION PROGRAMS AROUND THE WORLD

A healthy nutrition to workers has a positive socioeconomical impact on companies, on workers and on the countries' economies (Barros et al., 2016). For this reason, many nations have invested on incentives to Workers' Nutrition since the 1950s, after the 2nd World War (Bezerra, 2015). Research by Barros et al.

(2016) has pointed out that about 40 countries offer their workers nutrition systems, in order to improve nutritional and health conditions, aiming better development and productivity rates (Table 1).

England was the pioneer country on the incentive to worker's nutrition in 1946, and only 16 years later France rapidly stood out among the other countries, by instituting the worker's nutrition program, using the Ticket system and offering tax deduction (Barros et al., 2016; Bezerra, 2015). Italy and Brazil have taken the initiative only 14 years after France did, while Portugal has instituted it in 1979, three years after Brazil and Italy (Table 1). Hungary also stands out as one of the nations that offers broader coverage, reaching 80% of its workers (Bezerra, 2015).

Table 1. Tax characteristics of worker nutrition programs by country and year of creation listed in the study by Barros et al. (2016)

Countries/year of creation	Employer		Employee		Proportion paid per voucher	Maximum exemption limit per voucher per meal	There is a tax benefit if the payment is cash?
	Tax deductible	Contribution Exemption for Social Security	Income Tax Exemption	Contribution Exemption for Social Security	Employee employer		
United Kingdom England - 1946	No	No	No	No	-	-	No
France 1962	Yes	Yes	Yes	Yes	From 50 to 60% employer; From 50 to 40% employed	€0.72	No
Belgium 1965	Yes	Yes	Yes	Yes	€5.91/€1.09 (2015) €6.91/€1.09 (2016)	€7.00 (2015) €8.00 (2016)	No
Brazil 1976	Yes	Yes	Yes	Yes	80% employer/20% employed	-	No
Italy 1976	Yes	Yes	Yes	Yes	Defined between the employer and the employee	€5.29 paper voucher €7.00 Electronic Voucher	No
Portugal 1979	Yes	Yes	Yes	Yes	100% employer	€6.83 Voucher €4.27 Received as Money	Yes
México 1982	Yes	Yes	Yes	Yes	80% employer/20% employed	MxS 71.10 (€3.37)	No
Japan 1987	No	Yes	Yes	Yes	50% employer/50% employed	¥159.10 (€1.23)	No
Czech Republic 1992	Yes	Yes	Yes	Yes	55% employer/45% employed	€3.80	No
Turquia 1995	Yes	Yes	Yes	Yes	100% employer	TL = 2.33 (€0.78) in cash TL = 14.00 (€4.27) in voucher	No
India 1997	No	Yes	Yes	Yes	100% employer	€50.00 (€0.85)	No
Morocco 2003	Yes	Yes	Yes	Yes	100% employer	DH 20 (€1.83)	No

Around the world, worker nutrition programs in general have some similar characteristics regarding their implementation and fiscal benefits, as the possibility to have meals on the company's cafeteria or receiving vouchers/tickets/electronic currency to eat on restaurants close to the workplace. Only Portugal allows subsidy payment in cash, and in this case, there is no assurance the value will be used exclusively on nutrition, different from the company practice of providing meals on the institutional environment, therefore preventing this benefit to be used on other expenses, such as products that are injurious to health, like tobacco and alcoholic beverages (Barros et al., 2016).

The Inter-union Statistics and Socio-economic Studies Department (DIEESE, 2013)[2] and Bezerra (2015) explains that worker nutrition programs which have managed to develop satisfactorily were generally combined with some kind of governmental fiscal benefit and/or exemption of pension benefits, even if it implies that, in the absence of these incentives, the number of contemplated workers becomes quite reduced and the program, of very low importance.

WORKER NUTRITION PROGRAM - BRAZILIAN PAT

PAT's Conception, Objectives and Initial Developments

The Brazilian Worker Nutrition Program, known as *Programa de Alimentação do Trabalhador* or PAT, created in April, 1976 (Lei n° 6.321, de 14 de abril de 1976 da Presidência da República do Brasil, 1976) is recognized as the main exclusive public policy of workers. It was conceived as a component of the II National Food and Nutrition Program (II Programa Nacional de Alimentação e Nutrição - II PRONAN), presenting as prerogative the character of a nutrition supplementation program for low-income workers (up to 5 minimum-wages (MW)) (Decreto n° 77.116, de 6 de fevereiro de 1976. da Presidência da República do Brasil, 1976). It is also included in the National Policy for Health and Safety at Work and on the National Policy of Health Promotion *(Política Nacional de Alimentação e Nutrição*, 2002; *Política Nacional de Saúde e Segurança no Trabalho*, 2004).

It is a shared management program among the Ministries of Work, Health and Finance, sharing costs among the beneficiated worker and company (respectively 20% and 80% of the costs) and the government (tax exemptions). Therefore, it characterizes a benefit program for the worker, with incentives to the company and tax waiver for the government (Decreto n° 349, de 21 de novembro da Presidência da República do Brasil, 1991) (Figure 1).

The objectives of PAT entail the relation health/work, since it aims the improvement of the worker's nutritional state and, consequently, increase in productivity reduction of work accidents and absenteeism, and the promotion of better LQ to the workers (Bezerra, 2020; Decreto n° 78.676, de 08 de novembro da Presidência da República do Brasil, 1976; Lei n° 6.321, de 14 de abril de 1976 da Presidencia da República do Brasil, 1976; Strasburg & Redin, 2014; Vanin et al., 2006).

Generally speaking, the PAT has constituted itself in two dimensions: tax and nutrition. It is important to stress that PAT provides nutrition without linking this concession to the employees' salaries. Therefore, it causes both beneficiary companies and workers to be exempt from pension and labor charges taxes. Furthermore, the government establishes that only companies who declare to adopt the Real Profit tax modality are allowed to subscribe to PAT (Bezerra, 2015). In this respect, the Union's Comptroller General (CGU)[3] indicates that, based on projections by the Worker Nutrition Program Division of the Labor Inspection Secretary of the Labor Ministry (extraofficial projection), the program exempts companies of about R$1 billion annually on tax incentives, in addition to exempting the tax collection of R$20 billion on social taxation. This way, the great tax incentive for beneficiary companies to adhere to PAT is not the tax exemption, but the social taxation exemption (CGU, 2017). Also, the program does not address micro and small companies, because of their option for SIMPLES taxation modality or Assumed Profit modality (Bezerra, 2015).

Figure 1. PAT dimensions, benefits to the agents involved and management formats

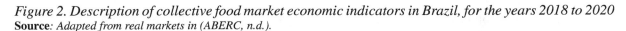

The creation of PAT had a strong influence of the Brazilian socioeconomic sector, providing a new space on the scope of HRM, given the training process, professional formation and worker's nutrition, considering the rising market originated on tax exemptions and also on the growth of large urban centers. Therefore, the involvement of the private sector on the creation and strengthening of the program is evident, through different modalities of services provision (figure 2). Perhaps this relation between "public and private" sectors and the financial primacy evidenced by PAT, on the beginning of PRONAN, have contributed for it to become a permanent program in Brazil (Araújo, 2002; Souza, 2013).

Figure 2. Description of collective food market economic indicators in Brazil, for the years 2018 to 2020
Source: *Adapted from real markets in (ABERC, n.d.).*

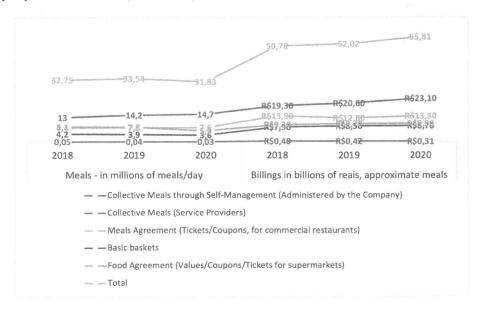

This way, in order to execute PAT, the involvement and organization of some kinds of companies happen: 1) beneficiary company and 2) collective nutrition entities, which might be sub-divided in companies that supply collective nutrition and facilitating companies for the acquisition of meals and foodstuffs (figure 3).

Figure 3. Types of companies involved with the Nutrition Program in Brazil.

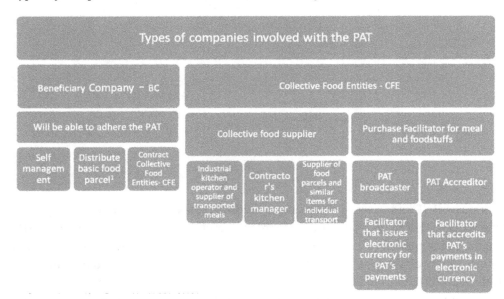

PAT Over the Years: Main Changes and Critical Analysis

Considering the economic aspect, PAT has had great importance to the collective nutrition sector, since it was propelled by the tax incentives (income tax deductions) and social taxation exemptions from nutrition expenses established by the program. In addition, this sector is in constant growth, since even during the pandemic/2020, the sector has managed to increase half a million meals/day, considering the period of 2019 to 2020, also presenting there an increase of approximately R$23 billion in 2020, offering 250 thousand jobs (ABERC, n.d.).

Regarding changes on fiscal aspects, the reduction of tax incentives stands out, from 5% to 4%, as well as regulations to build and unbuild bureaucracy around the accession process of the Beneficiary Company (BC) and the registration of Supply Companies for Meal/Nutrition to Workers (SCM/NW). On the program's social dimension, in 1997, the PAT Three-way Commission was created, identified as an important element for social control. Currently, the commission is made of representatives from the Labor, Finance, Health, Social Security, Social Development and Hunger Confrontation Ministries; workers and employers have other attributions, that is, monitoring, overseeing, and assessing PAT's execution (Portaria Interministerial 66, de 25 de agosto do Gabinete do Ministro, 2006.

In respect of the workers' productivity assessment, productivity increase and workplace accidents' reduction, results indicate that, between 2004 and 2014 there has been a productivity gain of 18%, at 1.7% average a year, and each percentual point of increase on PAT's diffusion is associated with a 0.78UDS/

worked-hour raise. It is also estimated that each percentage point of PAT penetration on the formal work force is associated with a 0.77 pp[4] reduction on work accidents/100 workers (Barros et al., 2016).

On the nutritional dimension few changes are observed, despite great alterations on nutritional standards, and on nutritional and health conditions of Brazilian workers. Initially, the program advocates a minimum 1400 calories on larger meals (Table 2), adequate to the 67% calory-deficient and energetic-protein malnutrition scenery of the population (IBGE, 1977). This way, recommendations assessed the nutritional need of the low-income population (Veloso, 2005).

Regarding macro and micronutrients, a minimum lipidic margin was adjusted (15-30%), increasing the maximum carbohydrate margin (55-75%), establishing a maximum margin for the caloric protein percentage (NDpCAL) (<10%), total and saturated fat (<10%), sodium levels (£ 2400mg) and introducing fibers (>25g), fruits, green vegetables, aside from nutritional education (Table 3) (Inter-ministry Ordinance 66, August 25, Ministry Office, 2006).

Table 2. General dietary guidelines in caloric terms for main and smaller meals from 1976 to 2021

Regulations	Until 1999	Inter-ministerial Ordinance No. 05, November 30, 1999	Interministerial Ordinance No. 66/2006
Main Meals (Lunch, Dinner and Supper)			
Total Energy Value (Valor Energético Total - VET)	Minimum 1,400 calories	1,400 calories (a reduction to 1,200 calories is allowed for workers in light activity, or an increase to 1,600 calories for intense activity)	Contain from 600 to 800 calories - can have an increased by 20% (400 calories) in relation to the VET of 2000 calories
NDpCal	6% of NDpCal	6% of NDpCal	Minimum 6% and maximum 10%.
Presence of Fruits/vegetables	-	Offer at least a portion of fruits and a portion of vegetables at meals	
Smaller Meals (Breakfast and Snack)			
Total Energy Value (Valor Energético Total - VET)	Minimum 300 calories	300 calories	They must contain 300 to 400 calories, providing an increase of 20% (400 calories) compared to the VET of 2000 calories per day.
NDpCal	6%	-	
Presence of Fruits	-	Offer at least a portion of fruits per meal	
Other changes (Food and Nutrition)			- Promote nutritional education, including making available, in a place visible to the public, a suggestion of a healthy menu to workers. - The VET calculation will be changed, in compliance with work requirements, for the benefit of the worker's health, provided that it is based on nutritional diagnostic studies. - The beneficiary companies must provide workers with diseases related to food and nutrition, properly diagnosed, with adequate meals and conditions for the treatment of their pathologies, and a periodic nutritional assessment of these workers must be carried out.

Changes in nutritional orientation and recommendation were late and insufficient. In 1999 alone, 23 years later, there has been alteration on the initial caloric recommendation and on the incentive for implantation of Food and Nutrition Education (FNE) action, even during the ongoing transitional nutrition process. The second shift on nutritional recommendation occurred in 2006, seven years later, reducing up to 600 calories on main meals and increasing up to 500 calories on small meals (Table 2).

Table 3. Daily values of macro and micronutrients and Total Energy Value (VET) to be adopted by beneficiary companies in the execution of food planning related to the PAT

NUTRIENTS	DAILY RECOMMENDATIONS	RECOMMENDATION MAIN MEAL	RECOMMENDATION MEAL MINORS
Total Energy Value - VET (Kcal)	2000 calories	600-800 (with a 20% increase, i.e. 400 calories)	300-400 (with a 20% increase, i.e. 400 calories)
Carbohydrates (%)	55 - 75	60	60
Proteins (%)	over 15	15	15
Total fat (%)	15-30	25	25
Saturated fat (%)	< 10	0-10	0-10
Fibers (g)	> 25 g (in small meals and 7-10 g in main meals)	7-10	4-5
Sodium (mg)	≤ 2400mg	720-960	360-480
Protein Percentage - Calorie (N4PCal)	Minimum 6% and maximum 10%		

Source: Based on Inter-ministry Ordinance n°66/2006 (Portaria Interministerial 66, de 25 de agosto do Gabinete do Ministro, 2006).

Despite enforcing the suggested alterations, these changes are not considered to have a contributing impact to an alteration on the workers' nutritional epidemic profile. Through an integrative review with the objective of verifying adherence of companies to the program before and after the Inter-ministry Ordinance n°66/2006, Bezerra (2020) has analyzed 12 studies and concluded that companies enlisted on PAT did not follow the designed nutritional directives before or after its reformulation in 2006. This fact may have contributed to the observed consequences on excessive weight among workers.

Beyond criticism related to tardiness on nutritional directive changes, late approaches were equally identified regarding different food and nutrition dimensions: social, economic and cultural, considering the importance of these dimensions to the resolution of unfolding nutritional transition in course and to the promotion of the workers' health (Araújo, 2002; Bandoni et al., 2006; Bezerra, 2020; Guilherme et al., 2019; Veloso, 2005). Since only in 1999 the PAT, through normative regulation, has broadened the nutritional dimension to other contexts, such as nutritional evaluation, healthy nutrition incentive, EAN and SAN, and also de setting of nutritional directives restricted to the indication of macro and micro-nutrients (Portaria Interministerial n° 05, de 30 de novembro do Ministério do Trabalho e Previdência/ Gabinete do Ministro, 1999).

Despite the use of directives through Ordinance n°66/2006, incorporating the logics of promoting health based on EAN demands, studies show that most responsible parties or administrative managers and technicians involved on the execution of the EB program have assimilated very little of the mandatory actions required by EAN or ignore them completely (Bandoni et al., 2006; Guilherme et al., 2019). However, Guilherme et al. (2019) have verified the fulfilment of EAN's actions in 57% of beneficiary companies that participated the study, even lacking the knowledge of their mandatory character.

It stands out that EAN's actions are fundamental to improve workers' LQ, given the relation between healthy nutrition and LQ, given that it provides workers with guidance towards better nutritional choices and consequently promoting health. Besides, collective nutrition spaces, such as company restaurants, are to be seen as places that provide actions towards health promotion, through nutrition and also by the possibility of mobilizing groups of workers, who generally share similar problems, enabling the articulation of actions (Bezerra, 2020; Santos et al., 2007; Veloso, 2005).

Another aspect that must be approached on the nutritional dimension is the issue of Food and Nutrition Insecurity (FNI) that has always been present in Brazil, both in the form of malnutrition, as in the beginning of PAT, and also in the excessive weight condition, which has been portrayed in the country during the last decades (Batista Filho & Rissin, 2003; Kac & Velásquez-Meléndez, 2003). This concern with FNI in Brazil has increased, given the devastating consequences of the COVID-19 pandemic, which has highlighted economic crisis, social inequalities and an unemployment increase spiral (Food and Agriculture Organization of the Unided Nations (FAO), n.d.; Rede PENSAN, 2021).

On the 2nd Nacional Inquiry on Nutrition Insecurity, this time in the context of COVID-19 pandemic, organized by the Brazilian Network of Research on Food and Nutrition Security and Sovereignty (Rede PENSSAN)[5], it was disclosed that Brazil has over 33 million Brazilians in famine situation, reding to the same level as 30 years ago, when PAT was operating for only 16 years. It means half the population (58.7%) is in nutrition insecurity, that is, does not have guaranteed food every day, nor in quantity, nor in quality. In this context, it is the role of food and nutrition programs committed to SAN, among them the PAT, to fight against such situation (Rede PENSAN, 2021).

The PAT has been evaluated on the aspect of its scope. Thus, Mazzon (1992, 1996, 2001, 2006), DIEESE (2013) and more recently Barros et al. (2016) have concluded the 40-year evaluation of the program, showing that until 2016 about 79 billion meals have been served, corresponding to over 40 million tons of agricultural commodities. The registered annual growth of workers is 8.7%, the companies', 14.5%. This way, about 83% of the target public is reached (workers who receive up to 5 MW), estimated to represent 38% of the formal workforce (in 2014, about 37.5%), reaching about 20 million beneficiated workers, in over 223 thousand BC during its existence around the country. This effort has demanded the participation of about 670 thousand people to work directly on nutrition services, therefore favoring the creation of jobs and contributing to national economy (Barros et al., 2016).

In respect of the nutrition dimension, recommendations of PAT remain inadequate to the population's new profile regarding nutrition and employment. In addition, menus presenting a caloric content higher than recommended by the programs were registered, and also the absence of the directives' adaptation to specific nutrition planning of each BC, considering workers' specific characteristics, such as epidemic profile and workstation, as well as EAN actions directed to healthy nutrition and LQ. An unfamiliarity regarding the mandatory character of EAN's actions by the managers is also noted, and probably of other elements of Ordinance n°66/2006 (Bandoni et al., 2006; Bezerra, 2020; Canella et al., 2011; de Paula & Dias, 2017; Santos et al., 2007; Veloso et al., 2007).

In addition, it is observed that, despite PAT's long years of existence, the program is still unknown by many, both in civil society and among company managers (technical and administrative managers) who demonstrate to ignore the program's existence or important details such as essential objectives and other elements important to its execution (Bandoni et al., 2006; Guilherme et al., 2019; Santos et al., 2007). In this context, it is possible to observe an exposure of workers to inadequate nutrition on the workplace.

Despite forementioned limitations, the program proposes benefits that reach all the different agents involved. In general, positive effects of a proper and healthy nutrition on the workers' life will impact productivity. Furthermore, it offers the government a tax collection increase, given the activity expansion on the nutrition sector. Finally, society benefits with the improvement on the population's health and consequent decrease in demand for public health assistance and reduced health related expenses (DIEESE, 2013).

Figure 4. PAT's benefits to the agents involved

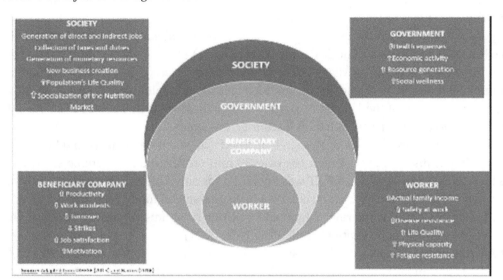

PAT Today: Critical Analysis and Suggestions

For an analysis of the program considering the current context, reports from audit on the program promoted by the Transparency Ministry and the Union's Comptroller General (CGU) were used, as well as the new labor legislation, disposed on Law n°13.467, July/2017 and Decree n°10.854, November/2021, which regulate the new Labor Law.

CGU's report was based on the program's audit from 2017, considering its goals and respective control mechanisms, pointing out the PAT did not achieve its goals regarding the nutrition dimension. It also indicates control frailties on the processes which have severely influenced PAT's evaluation process, including the public policy's effectiveness verification and managers' (re)orientation of decision-making processes. The CGU has verified the absence of national scope studies which lead to conclusions over the program's capability of achieving the objectives defined by law, considering overall that the current national scenery is totally different from the one previous to the program's creation. This way, it is important to promote broader discussions for reassessing the goals and social control systems of the PAT (CGU, 2017).

Another consideration refers to the latest alterations on the labor legislation that significantly modify 1943's Consolidation of Labor Laws (CLT)[6] causing meaningful impact to the workforce and the PAT. Such alterations regard mainly the new text of Article 457, which establishes the non-incorporation of the meal allowance to the employment contract, therefore not constituting a calculation-base figure to any labor or social security taxation. This way, the exemption of social taxation, considered the main attractive of PAT, no longer required adherence to the program, for it was assured by CLT (CGU, 2017).

Thereat, the management team of PAT, along with the Labor Ministry, has reassessed Article 457 through a conjoint articulation with the Civil House and PAT's partners (IRS, Federal Nutrition Council, Brazilian Association of Brazilian Companies Beneficial to the Workers) with the intention of assessing the inclusion of a temporary order to alter incise 2° of Article 457, on a new restriction regarding PAT. Until this study was concluded, there was no further development on the estimated temporary order (CGU, 2017).

During the COVID-19 pandemic, in 2020, another relevant situation also became part of the political scenery regarding PAT. A Project of Law establishing the possibility the worker opts for the PAT benefit in cash during the pandemic. Such proposal was in transit on the assigned government agencies when this manuscript was written, and no definition of its conclusion was available (Projeto de Lei PL 2704/2020, 2020).

On November 10, 2021, Decree n°10.854 was published, regulation several aspects of the new Labor Law in Brazil, also regulation PAT and relevant aspects of the Workers' Health, considering them indispensable to the worker's LQ. It focuses on work-inherent risk reduction, prevention of work accidents and occupational illnesses, and workers' health and safety promotion. Regarding PAT, Article 173 stands out, reinforcing responsibility to the beneficiary companies to dispose of programs destined to promote and monitor health and improve workers' food and nutrition security. Also, Article 180 determines the Labor, Social Security and Economy Ministries should elaborate periodical assessment studies of PAT, analyzing costs, effectiveness, reach and acceptance of the payment instruments (Decreto n° 10.854, de 10 de novembro da Presidência da República do Brasil, 2021).

From the conjoint assessment on the 2017 CGU report and on the 2021 Decree n°10.854, some questions must be raised about the better analysis on the execution and assumptions regarding PAT. It is indispensable to stand out that CGU presents three statements in the 2017 audit related to PAT:

1. Distortions on the allocation of low-income workers' benefit are presented;
2. It does not assure the reach of the stablished objectives as to its formulation, nor it reflects the socioeconomic changes occurred since its creation;
3. Frailty on the instituted administrative controls for the program's management.

In respect of the first statement, the CGU has identified that the PAT is presenting greater attractiveness to companies with higher income level workers. Hence, it has recommended the evaluation of the program to subsidize decisions that assure bigger reach to low-income workers. It is believed that, given the CGU report, it should be at least partially contemplated or at least evaluated on this Decree's elaboration, since it did not directly observe the CGU's recommendations regarding the low-income workers' reach, especially when it comes to the Article 171.

Regarding the second statement, considering the program's established objectives and the fact that it does not reflect on socioeconomic changes occurred since its creation, it was intensely discussed on this study (CGU, 2017). However, considering such aspect related to Decree n°10.854 substantial changes are not made on this aspect, only the BC's higher responsibility is stressed. This aspect has been criticized, given that, with Article 173, the government is exempt from important responsibility related to PAT's main goal (Decree n°10.854, November 10, Presidential Office, 2021). However, the Decree has advanced on determining the program's need of assessment, as previously mentioned.

Regarding the administrative control's frailties (statement 3), which are potentially damaging to the program's management and assessment, CGU (2017) has observed the absence of regulation to establish specific control procedures or activities to be performed by the agency in charge of tax exemptions. For this reason, it recommends the necessary information to be required to the IRS itself, enabling the program's assessment on this respect. As the use of information from the PAT online system to evaluate the achievement of the program's objectives, the definite periodicity to the reports' emissions, to the evaluation and presentation of conclusions to the CTPAT. On this aspect, the Decree n°10.854/2021 has only advanced through its Article 180, which indicates the program's systematic evaluation, as forementioned.

Therefore, as perspective for PAT in Brazil, considering the dimensions approached in this study and trying to overcome some of the program's limitations, we have listed a few suggestions of improvement:

1. To acquire the largest possible number of workers with income lower than 5 minimum salaries, which might be done by extending the fiscal benefit to the companies that participate on the National SIMPLES taxation modality, thus reaching micro and small companies;
2. Facilitate studies to include informal workers on the program;
3. Considering the international scenery, reducing the cost paid by the worker on the program;
4. Contribute to fight nutritional disorders (malnutrition, overweight and obesity), in a way of favoring better health conditions, life quality and reduction of health expenses. Therefore, nutritional orientation must be more articulated with reality and with epidemic studies about workers in Brazil;
5. The government needs to regulate efforts to execute sensibilization campaigns about good nutrition and the importance of the company's enrollment on the program;
6. Larger program inspection by the government, both on the tax and nutrition dimensions;
7. Promoting larger articulation, through the Labor, Economy and Social Security Ministries, with Universities and/or Research Centers, in order to develop an evaluation program for the PAT in all its dimensions, on a national and systematic character, by implanting multicentric studies, organized by Higher Education institutions.

4. FINAL CONSIDERATIONS

Public policies are tools used by the State to guarantee the effectiveness of human rights, and since food and nutrition are basic elements to promote and protect health, and also to improve life quality and citizenship. The Universal Declaration of Human Rights and specifically the Human Right to Proper Nutrition defend these rights to all people, including workers (Bezerra, 2015).

This way, Workers' Nutrition is a public policy which started in several countries to guarantee a worker's basic right, and also to increase the workers' productivity and life quality. The Worker's Nutrition Program in Brazil (PAT) is noted as one of the largest worker nutrition programs in the world by the volume of its reach; however, it presents difficulties in control, given its magnitude.

Thus, as all public policies, the evaluation stage is a crucial systematic method of investigation about a program's determined configuration or policy, which evaluates its implementation, effectiveness, and possibility of broadening potentialities. The assessment enables the examination of the results obtained, difficulties met, and alternatives presented to the confrontation and resolution of problems (Bezerra, 2015).

The Brazilian experience has shown that, more than the promulgation of regulations, an effective regular evaluation process is essential to the Program's success, and also, it needs to be accordingly to science and to the needs of society. According to CGU (2017), the main limitations to PAT's control reside on the absence of information, result of the undeveloped nationwide impact assessment over the past 46 years.

Although several critics directed at PAT cannot deny the importance of the program, its need to be sustained and broadened to a larger portion of the economic active population, especially the poorest (workers with income lower than 5MW/informal) and, overall, contributing to the nutritional health of workers. On the other hand, the program needs a broad redefinition of its strategy which must include other important aspects to the subjects' integral health and not only the guarantee of meals.

However, rethinking aspects related to energetic quality and adequation to the needs of every worker is a primary factor, especially considering the context of excessive weight and prevalence of chronic untransmissible illnesses, not to mention the renewed concern of hunger and malnutrition in the country, partially as result of the socioeconomic crisis originated from the COVID-19 pandemic (Rede PENS-SAN, 2021).

On this matter, nutritionists are technically responsible for the adequation of collective nutrition to the directives of the Program, taking into consideration the collectives' specificity and the elements of healthy nutrition and life quality, among others. For that, it must favor the development of constant action of EAN, which must be organized around specific studies of their collectivity. Bezerra (2015) emphasized that continued education actions to the food and nutrition of workers must be valued through formation actions, aiming the promotion of healthy nutritional practices and choices, respecting regional cultural nutrition.

The HRM area has an extremely important role, as responsible, by regulation, for the formation and wellness programs. Therefore, it matters to refine the sensibility of the area so healthy nutrition is included on the annual formation plans, as well as the implementation of programs that might find support on the data about nutrition or on the availability of healthy meals along the day.

Despite the fact that the program has not fulfilled its objective entirely, its importance resides on the impact it might have on the targeted public. Therefore, it is essential to value its existence and permanence, with the reformulation of its objectives, which must be broadened to a more holistic view of nutrition and life quality for workers. For that, social control and surveillance of the program are important, with active participation of the workers on this process and also its decentralization (Bezerra, 2015).

Generally speaking, as presented along this chapter, PAT's proposal is highly relevant to all society, since with it comes benefits to the government, for example, through the reduction of public expenses on illnesses, also to companies through productivity increase, larger motivation at work and, overall, to workers in terms of an improved health condition, more work safety, better life quality, among others.

REFERENCES

ABERC. (n.d.). *Mercado Real*. [Real Market]. ABERC. https://www.aberc.com.br/mercado-real/

Affonso, C. (2005). Nutrição, Prevenção e Qualidade de Vida. In A. Gonçalves, G. Gutierrez, & R. Vilarta (Orgs.), Gestão da Qualidade de Vida na Empresa (p. 141–146). IPES Editorial.

Amil, S., Lemieux, I., Poirier, P., Lamarche, B., Després, J.-P., & Alméras, N. (2021). Targeting Diet Quality at the Workplace: Influence on Cardiometabolic Risk. *Nutrients*, *13*(2283), 2283. doi:10.3390/nu13072283 PMID:34209458

Araújo, M. da P. N. (2002). *Avaliação do Programa de Alimentação do Trabalhador: um estudo da evolução normativa e do acesso de trabalhadores e empresas baianas* [Dissertação de Mestrado em Nutrição, Repositório Institucional da Universidade Federal da Bahia]. https://repositorio.ufba.br/handle/ri/11163

Bandoni, D. H., Brasil, B. G., & Jaime, P. C. (2006). Programa de Alimentação do Trabalhador: representações sociais de gestores locais Workers' Food Program: local managers' social representations. *Revista de Saude Publica*, *40*(5), 837–842. doi:10.1590/S0034-89102006000600013 PMID:17301905

Barros, F., Zilveti, F., Isabella, G., Carvalho, H., Marques, J., Guilhoto, J., & Mazzon, J. (2016). *40 anos do Programa de Alimentação do Trabalhador: conquistas e desafios da política nutricional com foco em desenvolvimento econômico e social.* (J. Mazzon (org.)). Blucher.

Batista Filho, M., & Rissin, A. (2003). A transição nutricional no Brasil: Tendências regionais e temporais. *Cadernos de Saude Publica*, *19*(suppl.1), 181–191. https://doaj.org/article/1988797ea06e4cfb8f4fac9687292f2a. doi:10.1590/S0102-311X2003000700019

Bezerra, I. W. L. (2015). *Avaliação da Efetividade do Programa de Alimentação do Trabalhador*. Universidade Federal do Rio Grande do Norte.

Bezerra, J. M., Matos, M. F., Oliveira, E. de S., & Costa, A. M. M. (2020). valiação da adesão do programa de alimentação do trabalhador: Uma revisão integrativa. *Research. Social Development*, *9*(5), 9–25.

Caldas, L. M. R. Jr. (1995). *O combustível da empresa moderna*. Inovação Empresarial.

Canella, D. S., Bandoni, D. H., & Jaime, P. C. (2011). Densidade energética de refeições oferecidas em empresas inscritas no programa de alimentação do Trabalhador no município de São Paulo. *Revista de Nutrição*, *24*(5), 715–724. doi:10.1590/S1415-52732011000500005

CGU. (2017). *RELATÓRIO N° 201702245*. CGU. https://eaud.cgu.gov.br/relatorios/download/11004.pdf

da Silva, T. (2005). Pensando a Gestão Estratégica, Saúde e a Qualidade de Vida. In A. Gonçalves, G. L. Gutierrez, & R. Vilarta (Orgs.), Gestão da Qualidade de Vida na Empresa (p. 147–152). IPES Editorial.

de Paula, C. L. C., & Dias, J. C. R. (2017). Avaliação do consumo alimentar e perfil nutricional de colaboradores atendidos por uma Unidade de Alimentação e Nutrição (UAN). *Revista Ciências Nutricionais Online*, *1*(1), 11–20. https://unifafibe.com.br/revistasonline/arquivos/cienciasnutricionaisonline/sumario/46/27032017152056.pdf

Decreto nº 10.854, de 10 de novembro da Presidência da República do Brasil, Pub. L. No. Diário Oficial da União-Seção 1-11/11/202; Edição 212 Seção 1;Página 3 (2021). https://www.in.gov.br/en/web/dou/-/decreto-n-10.854-de-10-de-novembro-de-2021-359085615

Decreto nº 349, de 21 de novembro da Presidência da República do Brasil, Pub. L. No. Diário Oficial da União-Seção 1-22/11/1991, Página 26443 (1991).

Decreto nº 77.116, de 6 de fevereiro de 1976. da Presidência da República do Brasil, Pub. L. No. Diário Oficial da União-Seção 1-6/2/1976, Página 1745 (1976). https://www2.camara.leg.br/legin/fed/decret/1970-1979/decreto-77116-6-fevereiro-1976-425734-publicacaooriginal-1-pe.html

Decreto nº 78.676, de 08 de novembro da Presidência da República do Brasil, Pub. L. No. Diário Oficial da União-Seção 1-9/11/1976, Página 14807 (1976). https://www2.camara.leg.br/legin/fed/decret/1970-1979/decreto-78676-8-novembro-1976-427964-publicacaooriginal-1-pe.html

Departamento Intersidical de Estatística e Estudos Socioeconômicos (DIEESE). (2013). *Relatório Final sobre o Programa de Alimentação do Trabalhador*. PAT.

Food and Agrivulture Organization of the Unided Nations (FAO). (n.d.). *Insegurança Alimentar e Covid-19 no Brasil*. [Food Insecurity and Covid-19 in Brazil].

Guilherme, R. C., Canuto, R., Clark, S. G. F., de Vasconcelos, F. N., Padilha, V. M., & Tavares, F. C. de L. P., Pessoa, R. F. de M., & de Lira, P. I. C. (2019). Worker's nutrition: An evaluation in industries in North-Eastern Brazil. *Ciencia & Saude Coletiva*, 25(10), 4013–4020. doi:10.1590/1413-812320202510.29512018

IBGE. (1977). *Estudo Nacional da Despesa Familiar (ENDEF): Tabelas de Composição dos Alimentos*. IBGE.

Kac, G., & Velásquez-Meléndez, G. (2003). A transição nutricional e a epidemiologia da obesidade na América Latina The nutritional transition and the epidemiology of obesity in Latin America. *Cadernos de Saude Publica*, 19(suppl 1), S4–S5. doi:10.1590/S0102-311X2003000700001 PMID:12886430

Lassen, A. AV, T., Trolle, E., Elsig, M., & Ovesen, L. (2004). Successful strategies to increase the consumption of fruits and vegetables: results from the Danish "6 a day" Work-site Canteen Model Study. In Public health nutrition, 7(2), 263–270. doi:10.1079/PHN2003532

Lei nº 6.321, de 14 de abril de 1976 da Presidencia da República do Brasil, Pub. L. No. Diário Oficial da União-Seção 1-19/4/1976, Página 4895 (1976). https://www.planalto.gov.br/ccivil_03/leis/l6321.htm

Limongi-França, A. C. (1996). *Indicadores empresariais de qualidade de vida no trablaho: Esforço empresarial e satisfação dos empregados no ambiente de manufaturas com cetificação ISO 9000*. FEA/USP.

Mazzon, J. A. (1992). PAT – Programa de Alimentação do Trabalhador. Uma avaliação histórica e impactos socioeconômicos (2o ed). São Paulo: Abrh; Assert; Aberc; Abracesta.

Mazzon, J. A. (1996). PAT - Programa de Alimentação do Trabalhador - 20 Anos de desenvolvimento: uma avaliação histórica e impactos socioeconômicos (1o ed). Abrh; Assert; Aberc; Abracesta.

Mazzon, J. A. (2001). Programa de Alimentação do Trabalhador - 25 anos de contribuições ao desenvolvimento do Brasil (1o ed). FIA - USP.

Mazzon, J. A. (2006). PAT - Programa de Alimentação do Trabalhador: 30 anos de contribuições ao desenvolvimento do Brasil (1o ed). FIA-USP.

Nahas, M. V. (2001). *Atividade física, saúde e qualidade de vida: conceitos e sugestões para um estilo de vida ativo* (2ª). Midiograf.

Pegado, P. (1995). *Saúde e Produtividade. Revista Proteção, 44*. VII.

Política Nacional de Saúde e Segurança no Trabalho, (2004). http://www.prevideenciasocial.gov.br/arquivos/office/3_081014-105206-701.pdf

Portaria Interministerial 66, de 25 de agosto do Gabinete do Ministro, Pub. L. No. Diário Oficial da União-Seção 1-nº 165; 28/08/2006 Pag. 153/154 (2006). https://www.gov.br/trabalho-e-previdencia/pt-br/servicos/empregador/programa-de-alimentacao-do-trabalhador-pat/arquivos-legislacao/portarias-interministeriais/pat_portaria_interministerial_66_2006.pdf

Portaria Interministerial nº 05, de 30 de novembro do Ministério do Trabalho e Previdência/Gabinete do Ministro, Pub. L. No. Diário Oficial da União 03/12/1999 (1999). https://www.gov.br/trabalho-e-previdencia/pt-br/servicos/empregador/programa-de-alimentacao-do-trabalhador-pat/arquivos-legislacao/portarias-interministeriais/pat_portaria_interministerial_05_1999_atualizada.pdf

Raulio, S., Roos, E., Ovaskainen, M.-L., & Prättälä, R. (2009). Food use and nutrient intake at worksite canteen or in packed lunches at work among Finnish employees. *Journal of Foodservice*, *20*(6), 330–341. https://doi.org/10.1111/j.1748-0159.2009.00157.x

Raulio, S., Roos, E., & Prättälä, R. (2010). School and workplace meals promote healthy food habits. In *Public health nutrition*, *13*(6A), 987–992. doi:10.1017/S1368980010001199

Rede, P. E. N. S. A. N. (2021). VIGISAN: Inquérito Nacional sobre Insegurança Alimentar no Contexto da Pandemia da Covid-19 no Brasil. In Rede PENSSAN. Rede Pensan.

Ruževičius, J. (2014). Quality of life and of working life: conceptions and research. *17th Toulon-Verona International Conference, May*, 317–334. https://citeseerx.ist.psu.edu/viewdoc/download?doi=10.1.1.829.6991&rep=rep1&type=pdf

Santos, L. M. P., & Araújo, M. da P. N., Martins, M. C., Veloso, I. S., Assunção, M. P., & Santos, S. M. C. dos. (2007). Avaliação de políticas públicas de segurança alimentar e combate à fome no período 1995-2002: 2 - the Workers' Nutriti. *Cadernos de Saúde Pública*, *23*(8), 1931–1945. doi:10.1590/S0102-311X2007000800020

Shain, M., & Kramer, D. M. (2004). Health promotion in the workplace: Framing the concept; reviewing the evidence. *Occupational and Environmental Medicine*, *61*(7), 643–648. https://doi.org/10.1136/oem.2004.013193

Souza, J. (2013). *A gênese do Programa de Incentivo Fiscal à Alimentação do Trabalhador (PIFAT/PAT)*. [Tese de Doutoramento em Saúde Pública, Repositório Institucional da Universidade Federal da Bahia]. https://repositorio.ufba.br/handle/ri/11477

Strasburg, V. J., & Redin, C. (2014). O Contexto Da Alimentação Institucional Na Saúde Do Trabalhador Brasileiro. *Revista Eletrônica em Gestão, Educação e Tecnologia Ambiental*, *18*(0), 127–136. doi:10.5902/2236117013028

Tamrakar, D., Shrestha, A., Karmacharya, B. M., Rai, A., Malik, V., Mattei, J., & Spiegelman, D. (2020). Drivers of healthy eating in a workplace in Nepal: A qualitative study. *BMJ Open*, *10*(2). https://doi.org/10.1136/bmjopen-2019-031404

Thiry-Cherques, H. R. (1991). A guerra sem fim: sobre a produtividade administrativa. *Revista de Administração de Empresas*, *31*(3), 37–46. doi:10.1590/S0034-75901991000300004

Vanin, M., Southier, N., Novello, D., & Francishetti, V. A. (2006). ADEQUAÇÃO NUTRICIONAL DO ALMOÇO DE UMA UNIDADE DE ALIMENTAÇÃO E NUTRIÇÃO DE GUARAPUAVA - PR Lunch nutritional adequacy in a Meal and Nutrition Unit in Guarapuava - PR Resumo. *Revista Sallus-Guarapuava-PR*, *1*(1), 31–38.

Veloso, I. S. (2005). *Programa de Alimentação do Trabalhador e os efeitos sobre a saúde* [Tese de Doutoramento em Saúde Pública, Repositório Institucional da Universidade Federal da Bahia]. https://repositorio.ufba.br/handle/ri/27084

Veloso, I. S., Santana, V. S., & Oliveira, N. F. (2007). Programas de alimentação para o trabalhador e seu impacto sobre ganho de peso e sobrepeso The Brazilian Workers' Food Program and its impact on weight gain and overweight. *Revista de Saude Publica*, *41*(5), 769–776. https://doi.org/10.1590/S0034-89102007000500011

Walton, R. E. (1973). Quality of Working Life: What Is It. *Sloan Management Review*, *15*(1), 11–21. https://search.ebscohost.com/login.aspx?direct=true&db=bth&AN=4009978&site=eds-live

WHOQOL GROUP. (1994). Development of the WHOQOL: Rationale and Current Status. *International Journal of Mental Health*, *23*(3), 24–56. https://doi.org/10.1080/00207411.1994.11449286

Wright, P. M., & Nishii, L. H. (2007). Strategic HRM and organizational behavior: Integrating multiple levels of analysis. *CAHRS Working Paper Series*, 468. http://digitialcommons.ilr.cornell.edu/cahrswp/468

ENDNOTES

1. [N.T.] In Portuguese, Programas de Alimentação do Trabalhador (PAT).
2. [NT] Departamento Intersidical de Estatística e Estudos Socioeconômicos (DIEESE) on the original.
3. [NT] The *Controladoria Geral da União* (CGU) is responsible for assisting the Brazilian Presidential Office regarding the defense of public property and the assurance of management transparency.
4. pp: Percentage Point
5. [NT] In Portuguese, Rede Brasileira de Pesquisa em Soberania e Segurança Alimentar e Nutricional, Rede PENSSAN.
6. [NT] In Portuguese, Consolidação das Leis do Trabalho (CLT).

Chapter 3
The Smart Job Factory:
Creating Sustainable Jobs by Defining Work Process Roles Based on a Digital Ecosystem Model

Christian-Andreas Schumann
Westsächsische Hochschule Zwickau, Germany

Chantal Runte
https://orcid.org/0000-0002-9064-1973
Westsächsische Hochschule Zwickau, Germany

Cornelia M. Enger
Westsächsische Hochschule Zwickau, Germany

Anna-Maria Nitsche
Westsächsische Hochschule Zwickau, Germany

ABSTRACT

The labor market is confronted with social, environmental, and economic developments that affect working conditions and individual labor relations. Lately, the Covid-19 pandemic has demonstrated and reinforced the importance of inclusive growth and sustainable work relationships. In this chapter, the smart job factory, a metamodel that supports the creation of new forms of work by redefining roles in labor, is introduced. The smart job factory is based on social entrepreneurship principles to drive innovative, sustainable, and long-term solutions to social challenges. For practical application, the model can be translated into a software solution that supports employers in the assessment of current working conditions and job roles within their companies and helps to redefine work relationships and to create new jobs. Thus, the smart job factory supports the labor market transition by systematically and proactively shaping new forms of work based on the triple bottom line of sustainable development.

DOI: 10.4018/978-1-6684-4181-7.ch003

INTRODUCTION

The massive dislocations and changes in employment in the wake of the Covid-19 pandemic have, in a new dimension, highlighted that the development and well-being of the population as a whole, as well as of individuals, is strongly dependent on purposeful and meaningful activity in social groups. At the same time, the current events have demonstrated a deficit of skilled workers and professionals, for example in the health and logistics sectors and companies with a focus on well-being and services to the public. Unemployment or change of employment, change of work content and processes, modification forms of work and tasks, etc. have a significant adverse impact on the psychosocial work environment, social security, performance, mental health, and well-being of employees (European Commission, 2010; OECD, 2017; Pohlan, 2019). Ultimately, personality development, as well as the social well-being of the population, depends on the design of sustainable work relationships.

Changes in the goals and tasks for employees´ work activities triggered by the dynamics of science and technology, globalization, digitalization, and climate change, as well as changes in the external circumstances, are leading to permanent changes in employment relationships (Dolphin, 2015; Leichenko & Silva, 2014). These changes are difficult to manage in a highly complex system of hybrid forms of work, thus causing difficulties for employees to secure a decent job and for employers to find and retain a suitable workforce. This leads to an imbalance in the job market and employee-employer relationships. Consequently, conventional approaches to job design, which solely depend on traditional corporate and social responsibility considerations, have become insufficient for the development of new forms of work. Approaches toward the transition to sustainable work need to be economically, ecologically and socially balanced to systematically and proactively shape new professional activities in new forms of work. A concept that addresses the establishment and transition of businesses towards sustainability, including sustainable forms of work, is Social Entrepreneurship (SE) (Javed, Yasir & Majid, 2019). The balancing of social and economic motives as a guiding principle of social enterprises (Chell, 2007) is a widely discussed concept on which this chapter builds to propose a novel model that supports sustainable business development.

A systematic and proactive design of new occupational activities in new forms of work is required to enable an economically, ecologically and socially sustainable change in the external living conditions of the society as a whole, as well as a balanced development of new forms of work. In this chapter, the Smart Job Factory (SJF) is being introduced, a holistic methodology for the role-based generation of sustainable jobs in the form of a metamodel. The basis for the concept development of the SJF was the role conception in the use case diagrams of the Unified Modelling Language (UML) (see Object Management Group, n.d.). Accordingly, in a use case, an actor creates a system with specific activities that can be connected with other actors. Actors can be real people, computer systems or external events. Thus, they do not represent the physical person or system, but rather the roles of these objects. Transferring this method to the example of labor reorganization by filling tasks, responsibilities and behavioral expectations, the role conception can be completed with an actor that best fits the requirements of the organization. That does not imply that tasks fulfilled by humans are substituted by machines, but that roles are better designed to fit individuals, contributing to their satisfaction in pursuing their work. Hence, the purpose of the SJF is to enable the transition to sustainable new forms of work by evaluating and further developing the sustainability of new forms of work concerning employee wellness and motivation, social impact, and welfare by orienting along the principles of SE. This chapter is aiming to explore the current issues in the sustainability of work relations, identify the potential for the design and application of the SJF as well provide an outlook for prospective opportunities for the application and development of the SJF.

BACKGROUND

Sustainable work has recently been a highly debated topic (Mohrman & Worley, 2010; van Dam et al., 2017; Rhee et al., 2021) with ethics, quality of work, and job satisfaction fuelling the discussion around predictors of sustainability and feasibility in businesses (Sheel et al., 2012; Sadri & Jayashree, 2013; Sadri & Goveas, 2013). Generally, the sustainability paradigm seeks to guide economic and social actions toward the support of the triple bottom line of sustainable development (people, planet, profit) (Docherty et al., 2009; United Nations, 1972). Sustainable development was introduced to policy debates with the Brundtland report in 1987, where the United Nations defined Sustainable Development as "development which meets the needs of the present without compromising the ability of future generations to meet their own needs" (United Nations, 1987, p. 16). Projecting this onto work, it means that companies should strive to establish work relations that maintain and strengthen their workforce opposed to their exploitation to make sure these (human) resources remain available and willing to work in the future (Docherty et al., 2009; Hedge, 2008; Mohrman & Worley, 2010; van Dam et al., 2017). Consequently, sustainable work can be defined as the degree to which employees are capable and keen to remain in their employment situation in the present and future (Van Vuuren, 2012; Van der Klink et al. 2010 as referred to by Peters et al., 2015).

Van Dam et al. (2017) suggests three indicators of sustainable work. Firstly, workers employability: the capability of worker´s to appropriately perform their work in present and future employment relationships in the internal and external labor market (Berntson, Sverke, & Marklund, 2006; Fugate et al., 2004; Van Dam, 2004). Second, work engagement: an optimistic, engaged attitude and mood at work that represents one´s mental resilience in the job (Bakker & Demerouti, 2007). Lastly, affective commitment: the emotional attachment workers have cultivated toward the company (van Dam et al., 2017). These three indicators are widely considered crucial for employers to retain efficient and valuable employees (Fugate, Kinicki, & Ashforth, 2004; Semeijn et al., 2015; van Dam et al., 2017), and can be regulated by executive interventions (van Dam et al., 2017). Nangoy et al. (2020) suggested a three-level approach in interventions for enhancing employees work well-being. On the primary level, the occupational conditions are adapted concerning the individual staff member's well-being, in particular job redesign, work culture and environment changes, and work-life balance policies. On the secondary level, the individual consciousness, resilience and capabilities are comprised. These factors can be mediated by managing stress factors at work in the form of better recruitment and selection practices, and career development programmes that entail coping strategies and activities that focus on health-oriented routines. Finally, the individual support of employees facing issues in private or professional concerns through counselling or assistance services are the intervention on the third level. According to Nangoy et al. (2020) the interventions on all levels ought to be recognized by the top management and fundamentally embedded in the strategic decision-making processes of an organization to become effective. Martínez-Garcia et al. (2018) summarized several individual organizational factors that have an impact on the job quality and need to be considered when planning and executing interventions: the size of the company, the industry, the strategy, type of labor practices, diffusion of innovation and technology as well as external factors such as labor unions and labor market policy and laws.

The Smart Job Factory

To keep up with global competition and technological transformation, companies are constantly under pressure to innovate to maintain their long-term competitive advantage (Tsai, 2011; Dobni, 2008). For this reason, it is crucial for employers to encourage an innovative spirit in their workers who are the main source of the creation, implementation, and application of new ideas and solutions in a company (Janssen, 2000; Tierney and Farmer, 2002; Tang et al., 2021). In line with the raising awareness and attention to sustainable development, companies are beginning to approach the topic of innovation more strongly from the perspective of the contribution to social solutions (Gebauer et al., 2013). In this context, the terminology of Social Entrepreneurship (SE) is often utilized. In academic research there are many definitions of SE (Zahra et al., 2014), but as it represents a fairly young research stream, none of them is supported by the majority (García-Morales et al., 2020; Austin et al., 2006; Bornstein, 2007; Zahra et al., 2014; McSweeney, 2020). Most definitions comprise a focus on the social mission: "creating social value by providing solutions to social problems' (Dacin et al. 2011, p. 2). Furthermore, the entrepreneurial approach to solving social problems can either be understood as an introduction or diffusion of innovations to a business model and market income, or the application of management methods and tools is part of many interpretations (Gebauer et al., 2013; Zahra et al., 2014). In this chapter, SE comprises small and medium-sized enterprises (SMEs) that not only are orientated towards financial performance but also social problems and pursue social or environmentally oriented goals.

The SE approach focuses on innovation and solving social problems. However, a comprehensive approach that considers essential factors to create a positive social contribution such as internal and external interactions and feedbacks and questions of organizational governance in the larger social, cultural and economic system are often neglected (Gebauer et al., 2013; Roundy, 2017). For this reason, the authors included stakeholder theory and the context of digital ecosystems to develop a comprehensive approach with the SJF. Stakeholder theory (e.g. Freeman, 1984) considers not only the organization under study, but also its unilateral, bilateral, or even multilateral relationships (Parmar et al., 2010). Through this approach, relationships can be effectively managed and shaped, values can be distributed to the various stakeholders and diverse needs considered in a moral and sustainable way (Attanasio, Battistella, & Preghenella, 2021). Business transformation enabled by digitalization can have wide-ranging implications, often in the forms of disruptions that require strategic responses (Vial, 2019) and product or marketing innovation (Stone et al., 2017). In an academic context, digitalization is commonly referred to as the advancement or facilitation of processes by leveraging digital technologies and their dispersion among the society in terms of for instance labor, domestic and free-time activities (Lehn, 2020). Specifically, in the context of the labor market, empirical studies have not yet reached a point of widely accepted consensus on the implications of digitalization, making it difficult to frame the impact (Piroșcă et al., 2021). So far, the empirical literature in the field of digitalization and the labor market is more deeply explored in terms of labor distribution, training and remuneration. Complementary, in the theoretical conceptualization, certain advances have been achieved by authors like Schlogl and Sumner (2018), Acemoglu and Restrepo (2018), and Leduc and Liu (2021). Still, a broad appraisal of the implications and anticipation of negative social impact is still missing. Therefore, it becomes crucial to develop a comprehensive understanding of the relevant digital processes and to develop a systematic multi-dimensional stakeholder approach that integrates several levels of intervention (Brunetti et al., 2020). To do so, viewing organizations and their environments as digital ecosystems can benefit the development of a systematic strategy. Li et al. (2012, p. 119) suggested that digital ecosystems are "open, loosely coupled, domain clustered, demand-driven, self-organizing agent environment, where each agent of each species is proactive and responsive regarding its benefit/profit but is also responsible to its system." More recently, Valdez-De-Leon, (2019,

p. 44) defined digital ecosystems as "loose networks of interacting organizations that are digitally connected and enabled by modularity, and that affect and are affected by each other's offerings". For the purpose of this chapter the following definition is suggested: digital ecosystems are interacting, digitally connected organizations that are embedded in a self-organizing, demand-driven system which is shaped by the dynamics between the stakeholders, available resources as well as relevant policy. Accordingly, organizations face individual system conditions that affect their knowledge accumulation, innovative capacity, and the range of potential intervention measures when encountering new and transformative developments. These need to be recognized and managed to seize the opportunities the developments provide in terms of sustainability, the creation of decent work, and advanced competitive advantages (Brunetti et al., 2020).

BARRIERS TO SUSTAINABILITY IN TODAY'S WORK RELATIONS

With the aggravation of complexity in the labor market at the beginning of the fourth industrial revolution, caused by digital transformation and globalization, job characteristics, i.e. the requirements for certain skills and competencies, or the organization of production processes are constantly undergoing rapid change (Amelia, 2018; Colombo et al., 2019). Digitalization increases the potential for further flexibilization in the world of work in several respects, whether it is the division of labor or flexibilization of place and time. It will have an impact on future labor markets and thus influence productivity, innovative capacity and the (inter)national division of labor. It entails sectoral structural change as well as occupational and qualification-related effects, i.e. new or changed competencies, qualification requirements and job profiles. As one of the consequences, the competition to recruit and retain the top talents becomes more and more fierce (Sung et al., 2020). Despite this, recruiting and career development processes in organizations often lack efficiency, leading to the loss of talents. A study by the German software provider Softgarden from 2019 states that almost 60% of the 6,000 respondents had already withdrawn a job application, even though they were interested in the advertised position due to a cumbersome application process (Softgarden, 2019). If companies take too long to decide, applicants interpret this as disinterest and lack of respect, the study says. At the same time, longer processes become costlier for the employer, demonstrating the need to create effective short processes. The challenges of inefficient recruiting and career development processes need to be overcome to make it easier for qualified people to find appropriate employment without delay after completing their training or certification in times of "war for talent". Provided that employers behave socially and pay attention to sufficient further training and sustainably designed work in the company, labor retention needs to be improved on the one hand to anticipate job losses and on the other hand to expand fruitful employment relationships.

Conventionally, companies recruit staff based on job descriptions that comprise the responsibilities and qualifications that individuals need to match with a certain set of competencies, skills and knowledge (Tang et al., 2021). This approach, however, neglects the compatibility between the employee's characteristics and values as well as their adaptability to the organizational culture, mission and managerial strategy which are essential in long-term-oriented, successful employer-employee relationships and organizational development (Tang et al., 2021). For this reason, the fit between employees and their work environment (person-organization fit) has received an increasing amount of attention in research in recent years (see Edwards and Billsberry, 2010; Kristof-Brown et al., 2005; Tang et al., 2021). Organizations now need to dynamically and actively adapt their workforce to external and internal changes which highlight the need for a person-organization fit as opposed to a rigid recruiting and career development strategy (Tang et al., 2021). At the same time, retaining staff and motivating them to utilize their full potential in their work requires employers to make their employees satisfied and pleased with their jobs (Gratton, 2011; Schotanus-Dijkstra et al., 2016). The more organizations understand and focus on the significance of person-organization fit and employee motivation and encouragement, the higher the likelihood of a scale-up that drives social transformation.

Social changes or transformations require transitions in society and (between) cultures, in institutional structures, organizational contexts as well as individual life situations. To be able to recognize the transition from "before and after", it needs the "new" or also the "other". In this respect, they are by no means simple, transitory services from one state to the other. Rather, they are transitioning into a risky mode of increasing dynamics, diversification, complexity, fragility and contingency. Such a mode requires reflexive modernity, specifically a detachment from classical status-passage thinking into a "thinking in transitions" - a consideration of transitions and their process character. In the development of the labor force, this means that in addition to the former transfer of standardized highly specialized skills, nowadays the development of flexible skills and competencies of employees is necessary to keep up with a high-paced transformative society and economy (Suleimankadieva et al., 2021). Societal learning cultures, as well as institutional and individual learning environments, are needed to deal with transitions in a way that promotes learning. In the European Union, about 50% of the study programs and qualification measures are currently being converted to a direct reference to digitalization and sustainability (European Commission, 2020). The other half is being fundamentally modernized, in which all subjects are enriched with elements of digitalization and sustainability. The European education system seems to be on the path to training labor that respects the availability of employment opportunities in the future.

The implementation of the redesign of work towards sustainable development cannot unilaterally happen by an organization but requires the consideration of a wide set of stakeholder interactions that are relevant to the person filling a position, the organization and also the society. The challenges now lie in identifying and developing partly newly defined identities and cultures at the various levels - whether at the micro-level, meso-level or macro-level - in the sense of a broadly applicable concept, and in stimulating their establishment and stabilization. The primary design framework refers to the individual characteristics and content-related visions of persons (personal), the interaction with the various stakeholders (relational), and the social contexts in which institutions or companies operate (contextual) (Cortelazzo et al., 2019). Policies on educating employees that support the maintenance of employability, work engagement and affective commitment are still too inadequate. As these factors are intrinsically connected to the intellectual, innovative and professional capital development of the labor force they should be of interest to an organization from a self-preservation standpoint.

The hitherto rather superior focus of the technocratic side of digital transformation is no longer sufficient, as behavioral-analytical, but also structural perspectives need to be considered as well. This does not rule out the possibility that some rather ambivalent relationships between the desire for and the reality of digital transformation projects at the individual, organizational and societal levels will remain a challenge in the future. However, it also demonstrates that new approaches, concepts, and tools are needed to translate, shape and adopt digital transformation in businesses in the future of work for better social value.

THE SMART JOB FACTORY AS A MODEL FOR CREATING SUSTAINABLE FORMS OF WORK

General Model Approach for the Smart Job Factory

The changing world of work with its framework conditions offers multi-layered design possibilities that basically cannot be seen in isolation from their conditional contexts. To address this complexity, the authors suggest a new metamodel (see Figure 1) that supports work redesign towards sustainable work through the lens of newly formed roles in organizations. These newly formed roles are based on three relations levels and three different determinants with their connected attributes. The individual, institutional/corporate and socio-political relations levels are considered influencing factors. For example, (social) policy measures result from legal, economic, social and institutional conditional contexts, between controversial constraints on adaptation and entrenched protection of the status quo. Context-related questions open up about given educational, labor and social standards and the need for appropriate adjustments to state and company social policy frameworks and regulations.

The determinants of the metamodel need to be used subsequently. The first determinant is a requirement profile for sustainable work which comprises the transformation of current labor and employment relations and their consequences and challenges for sustainable work and workplaces. New forms of work are triggered by a wide variety of social, economic, and technological changes such as digitalization, occupational safety, ecology, economy, career development prospects, social and ethical norms, health, fair pay, and equality. The consequences of these changes can be localized to a varying degree at the relations levels. The aspects are specifically considered in the metamodel utilizing parameters or suitable factors for identifying and evaluating a requirements model, which functions as a universal orientation in the first step.

As more sustainable forms of businesses and jobs already exist, a reference when redesigning work can provide valuable insights. SE in this context has proven to provide a combination of sustainability and innovation orientation with which organizations and policy-makers can comply. SE supports the development of sustainable jobs, thus significantly advancing the positive transformation of society whenever occupational profiles, work tasks and forms are changed or redesigned. For this reason, the second determinant of the SJF is a semantic SE reference model. From the duality of SE in the creation of economic and social value, managers of organizations may learn how social innovations can better be integrated into business practices while a wider awareness of the necessity of addressing societal objectives and stakeholder needs can support the cooperative norms on national or even global scales (Phillips et al., 2015, García-Morales et al., 2020, Estrin et al., 2013). The previously introduced classification of SE serves the purpose of a reference for best practices within the framework of the SJF to provide a new perspective on the corporate problem and need orientation as well as align companies towards a more innovative and sustainable path. Consequently, the SJF model intends to contribute to the shared responsibility for value creation and greater interlinking of economic and social value creation in the sense of blended value understanding (see Emerson 2003; Elkington 1997; Nicholls, 2010; Bornstein, 2007). To do so, parameters like the motivation of social entrepreneurs, the kinds of business ideas and models they create and the nature of jobs and working environments they establish, are integrated as references for the creation of new jobs and the design of sustainable work. The insights into SE can be gained from the analysis of entrepreneurship databases like GEM (see GEM Global Entrepreneurship Monitor, n.d.), PSED (see Curtin & Davidson, 2018) or send-ev (see Scharpe & Wunsch, 2019).

The Smart Job Factory

The third determinant of the SJF comprises organization-specific parameters that are essential for the design of the roles, specifically factors that determine the work task and work environment as well as organizational values that majorly affect the behavioral expectations of the organization towards its labor force.

Figure 1. Scheme of the Smart Job Factory metamodel

	Requirements Profile	Social Entrepreneurship Reference Model	Organisation Specificities
Socio-Political	Equality; Ecology; Digitalisation; Fair Pay	Success Factors of SE; Motivation Factors; Business Models & Ideas	Corporate strategy; Legal environment; Digital Ecosystem; Size
Institutional	Career Development Prospects; Economy; Health	Characteristics of Work Environment; Innovative spirit	Degree & Potential of Automation; Location; Industry/Sector
Individual	Occupational Safety; Social & Ethical Norms	Characteristics of Jobs; Application Strategies	Types of labour practices; Partners & Competitors

Within the metamodel, the parameters are evaluated and matching factors in the requirement profile and the gained insights on the SE reference model in the context of digital ecosystems are identified and connected with the organization-specific parameters. Thus, the characteristics, functions, and behavioral expectations for sustainable work are implemented in the design of digital ecosystems and consequently get implemented into a role. The role description goes beyond a pure function and job description since, in addition to functions, tasks and characteristics, responsibilities and expectations of behavior are also defined within the role. Once these attributes have been identified and documented, they are expanded and modified to reflect future expectations. Individuals who then assume the role are motivated and guided to behave socially, ecologically, and economically by aligning the target system with social and corporate sustainability and innovation. For the matching process in an organizational context, applicants or employees need to be carefully assessed by Human Resource Management (HRM) to identify, besides the relevant "hard facts" (experience, education, competencies etc.), "soft facts" like motivation, potential and social behavior as well as identification with the organizations' mission, the responsibilities and career expectations. Policy-makers on the other hand can test the implications and interdependencies of policy interventions in constructed examples by changing single attributes of the model or deriving factors that are essential when designing a new policy that seeks to support and encourage the spread of ideas for sustainable work and innovation promotion. The systematic view that the digital ecosystem perspective provides, with the interconnected complex stakeholder networks and feedback thereby examines the inside and outside of the organizational environment in sync to directing policy, practice, and research. As a next step, the development of the SJF model requires the exploration of the connections within networks, determinants, and parameters in an empirical setting. To do so, the development of a software solution may be a promising test setting for the development of the SJF for practice.

Modelling and Software Solution of the Smart Job Factory

For practical application, the SJF metamodel can be realized in form of a software solution with different access and applicability levels. The advantage of the metamodel is that a simplification and visualization of real facts (specifically use cases, actors and work systems) enables a better understanding of complex interrelationships. In this form, it offers immediate starting points to focus on model-relevant and result-relevant aspects, expand options, minimize a fading out of relevant information, promote the basis for a common understanding of complex interrelationships and improve the making of well-founded decisions. The SJF software tool can be set up to provide an interface to a knowledge base that offers various formats for knowledge acquisition, processing, storage, and distribution to facilitate easy access and use for policymakers and managers of the SJF tools. In this context, the use of artificial intelligence can open up new opportunities for mastering the adaption effort, especially regarding including and calculating essential labor-related factors such as workload and role clarity (the precise delimitation of the role to other roles) to guarantee the feasibility of a role. When the SJF tool is introduced and applied for the first time, it is likely to be dependent on using a high proportion of standard values and thus, only containing an approximate solution, which can then be further improved by determining and entering company-specific values. Over time, when more use cases are developed, the SJF tool is going to become more precise and valuable.

The design of roles in practice can first be based on Unified Modelling Language (UML) in form of a use case diagram. According to UML, a use case specifies some behavior that a subject can perform in collaboration with one or more actors" (Object Management Group, n.d., p. 638). The scheme of the SJF metamodel is the system, including the sub-systems requirement profile, SE reference model and organizational specificities. At the same time, specific use-cases are shown in Figure 1, e.g., Equality or Digitalisation for the requirement profiles sub-system, or Motivation Factors or Innovation Spirit for the SE Reference Model sub-system, in addition to verbs, for example, "creating Equality" instead of "Equality". Actors may represent roles played by human users (e.g., a candidate applying), external stakeholders (e.g., policymakers), or IT systems (e.g. AI systems). The behaviors of the actors, namely the set of potential execution in reaction to developments within the organization, then need to be modelled to be able to identify the perfect fit between potential actor and defined role.

The Application of the Smart Job Factory

It can be assumed that the successful application of the SJF depends on several factors and their interdependencies, that need to be studied carefully in the further development of the SJF:

- **Factor 1:** The regulatory framework of policy actors should create incentives for managers to recognise the benefits of SE and be motivated to follow this path permanently. The balancing of social and entrepreneurial interests within the framework of the social market economy implies that this concept can be anchored in everyday business practice as well as in social culture through targeted regulatory measures.

- **Factor 2:** As the preservation of the enterprise and the employment relationships associated with it is crucial, the goal of any entrepreneurship is ought to be sustainability instead of short-term profit-seeking. Business owners should recognise their labor force as human capital and the most important resource for the successful long-term development of the enterprise. Therefore, organizations should be oriented towards sustainability.
- **Factor 3:** It is advisable that the parameters of the SE reference model and their use in describing the roles for generating sustainable employment are reviewed regularly and, if necessary, adapted to changes in science and technology or changes in the relationship between human labor, automation, and digitalisation up to the application of AI. This is not just about securing employment, but rather about better working conditions and making work easier.
- **Factor 4:** Roles for business and work processes, in which work tasks are to be described and sustainably optimised for humans, are subject to permanent changes. Their adaptation, which is necessary at intervals, has consequences for the employees, which consist of successively further qualifying the workers, not only through on-the-job training but also through politically supported periods for additional qualification measures. This qualification offensive is a mandatory prerequisite for the generation of sustainable work and therefore should be part of the understanding of SE.
- **Factor 5:** Preconditions should be created and considered for policy advice. Entrepreneurial training, as well as qualifications and information of employees, could be designed in such a way that they are prepared in a manner that is suitable for the target groups.
- **Factor 6:** The adaptation of the model application, especially the parameters for the role model to sector-specific and nationally specific conditions and regulations, may require additional effort. Organizations need to strive to adapt to these specificities and to describe the roles for their work processes from which sustainable work is to be generated.

The SJF model has the potential to be applied in an individual organisation context as well as in the development of policy interventions. For the latter, the SJF model will provide an actual overview of the most recent developments of digital transformation and connected recruiting and career development processes while providing suggestions for policy interventions that support sustainable development. Accordingly, the model can serve several target groups and additionally has a wide range of beneficiaries. Starting from a social science perspective, the focus is on people, their interaction or society as a whole and its development in the form of analysis and collection of empirical facts. The aim is to describe the functions and characteristics of roles in the work process that result from new developments in the social, economic and societal environment employing the model. The basis for this is the analysis of existing use cases in occupation and work, for the definition of roles and their changes. Based on the actions of the actors, which are described by attributes (key figures), a direct connection between use cases, actors and work systems may be possible to observe.

Stakeholders of the Smart Job Factory Application

Organizations and their actions are majorly affected by their external and internal environment, which Freeman (1984, p. 46) described as stakeholders: "(…) any group or individuals who can affect or is affected by the achievement of the organization's objectives". Thus, for a valuable contribution to social change and sustainable development, business outcomes need to be oriented towards a specific set of stakeholders (Phillips et al., 2015) and interventions should be planned to integrate the interests of the relevant stakeholders. In the case of the application of the SJF, special features of all levels (individual, organizational and socio-political) and the different stakeholders are embedded, starting from the individual, the individual employee, the individual social entrepreneur, over the individual corporations and organizations, to the surrounding, regionally, and locally perceived community and its representatives, the relevant sectors, the actors in the field of SE education (in training and further education), as well as research and science (see Figure 2). In addition to national policy actors, the consideration of international operating actors such as supranational policymakers also represent the universality and upscaling of the application potential.

Figure 2. Stakeholders of the Smart Job Factory

- **Stakeholder Group One - Individual Employee:** The individual employee will benefit from SJF through the application by their organization. The redefined roles and new forms of work and sustainable work relationships will have a significant impact on the psychosocial work environment, social security, performance, mental health and well-being of employees, and consequently on the personality development and the social well-being of the individual and the workforce as a whole.
- **Stakeholder Group Two - Individual Social Entrepreneur:** On the micro-level, the SJF model addresses the consequences of a changed awareness of role-related responsibilities and behavioral expectations regarding attention, reflection, and training. Especially (aspiring) social entrepreneurs need the support of self-efficacy and the definition of outcome expectations in their activity. For this, the first two steps of the model, the requirement profile and SE reference model will be of specific interest to this target group as well as the concrete measures (practice-supporting action guidelines/recommendations for action) that serve as a basis for exchange and discussion and their need for action. Moreover, best practices for the development of social entrepreneurial projects will be derived in the second phase of the SJF model.
- **Stakeholder Group Three - Individual Organizations:** Individual organizations and corporations will benefit from the application of the SJF itself in the redefinition of their job roles, more

efficient deployment of the workforce, improved working conditions and higher satisfaction levels among staff through more sustainable forms of work. For innovation promoters acting at the company level, the metamodel offers an orientation framework for social innovations and thus the expansion of social innovations and fundamentally of an innovation promotion. Corresponding direct starting points and measures are also offered by the presentation and discussion of the detailed specifics of the metamodel and developed, practical approaches to solutions.

- **Stakeholder Group Four - Surrounding Community:** For sustainable development in a digital ecosystem, the surrounding community and its representatives, the regionally and locally perceived social context is essential. There is a need to debate and stimulate social change and sustainable development, specifically the role of social enterprises in society. Whether the educational sector, the business community or individual consumers, the aim is to raise awareness for the way social entrepreneurs act and do business and to orient them so that they feel connected to a social added value and thus to social enterprises. From a long-term perspective, the surrounding community can reinforce this replication process by sharing experiences. This comprehensive involvement of stakeholders of all kinds needs to be promoted in the application of the SJF model and software solution by the executing organization and also in the case of the application by policy-makers.
- **Stakeholder Group Five - National Policy Actors:** In the socio-political context, social and employment policy actors such as social partners, social insurance institutions and social economy organizations, but also responsible ministries, employment agencies, trade unions or new forms of participation-oriented trade union work, employers' associations and labor organizations. They support the legitimization of social enterprises and the development of a changed awareness on the issue of the 'new self-employment' as well as social security for social entrepreneurs.
- **Stakeholder Group Six – Sector:** The industry reference supports and promotes new perspectives in industry and society on the roles and thus the position in the company, in the organization. This closes the connection to the already mentioned stakeholder group of innovation promoters acting at the company level.
- **Stakeholder Group Seven - Supranational Policy Actors:** Policymakers and social and employment policy actors for example EU level are potential users of the SJF tool. The derived policy measures from the SJF are intended to shape the regulatory framework for new, sustainable forms of work, in particular, to avoid socioeconomic inequalities and generate wealth through long-term stable employment relationships that are capable of development inside and outside of Europe.
- **Stakeholder Group Eight - Social Entrepreneurship Educators:** Actors in the field of SE education (training and further education) constitute a special future-oriented target group. Through an increased promotion of SE in education and training, especially concerning role-related responsibilities and behavioral expectations. The promotion of competencies is characterized by corresponding requirement profiles and role-specific ways of thinking and acting.
- **Stakeholder Group Nine - Researchers and Scientists:** The field of science and research offers another space respectively target group, nationally and internationally. In particular, the measurement of social impact, the importance of hybrid organizations and venture philanthropy will be significantly advanced. Due to the metamodeling approach, the potential recommendations that can get derived can be applied to different industries and the services sectors and thus provide a comprehensive approach towards the advancement of new forms of work.

Looking at the previously described applications that the SJF can provide, the breadth of potential beneficiaries becomes clear. However, these are likely to depend on the holistic nature and severity of SJF-based interventions. For individuals, the greatest potential lies in opportunities for social well-being and personal growth. At the business and community level, strengthening efficiency, innovation capacity, and sustainability is a promising prospect that can be supported by the SJF. In addition, national policy actors and entire sectors can be provided with a tool to monitor and measure labor market development and social security improvement. The same could be transferred to the supranational level, but addressing national or regional adjustment needs will play a crucial role in the potential for effectiveness. Finally, for researchers and academics, the new model means that it will draw attention to the issue of SE and sustainability in the labor market and provide several starting points for further research on the topic and the model itself.

FUTURE RESEARCH DIRECTIONS

As the first presentation of a new model, this chapter opens numerous future research avenues. The multi-layeredness and the associated interdisciplinarity of the SJF model have advantages concerning the perspective orientation and thus the added value of the model, but at the same time, it also poses the challenge of consistent compatibility and understanding of the different levels and dimensions. When applied, the quality of the output of the SJF depends on the careful selection of data that is fed into the system. An adaptive design with feedback implementation is needed for the establishment of the legitimacy of the model. As a logical next step, the SJF needs to be prototyped and tested from the semantic model introduced in the chapter to the technical level to facilitate the estimation of the social system change capabilities of the SJF model, and to identify application potentials and barriers. With the results, maturity studies can build up on the findings that for example could include a social study that identifies the relevant factors for the requirement profile as well as a SE study to identify the best practices in SE as a reference.

What needs to be considered is that the SJF only recognizes the demand side in the role so far. For the successful practical application, a representative and comprehensive profile of a potential candidate who might fill a role need to be developed by HRM. A pre-structured and normed profile with predetermined techniques for information retrieval may benefit such profile development (e.g. selection test or interviews) but still needs to be developed and adapted from a testing process. The baseline in the development of such a profile should aim for the most efficient and sound design of the recruitment process to save costs for the organization and to provide candidates with a fair and effective experience without unnecessary obstacles.

Other fields of potential and exploration of sustainable work could be the more profound inclusion of the issue of a declining workforce and demographic change. The related themes that have already been discussed in research and may benefit the further development of the SJF are reduced-load work (e.g. Kossek & Ollier-Malaterre, 2020), occupational health (e.g. Moreira et al., 2017), and ageing workforce (e.g. van Dam et al., 2017). Overall, the exploration of hybrid forms of ventures in the sense of blended value and its impact on sustainable development needs further research. Reporting or accounting standards for the measurement of social impact and blended value may also provide a valuable component for the fine-tuning of the SJF and create a wider generalizability.

CONCLUSION

Business development and employment relationships have been subject to increasing dynamization for years, which becomes apparent in digital ecosystems. This includes the major challenges of current social development such as demographic change, globalization, digitalization, and green transition. Apart from these predictable, ongoing developments, the Covid-19 pandemic has demonstrated how changes of a disruptive nature can massively affect and change the social dimension of the contemporary labor market. Due to these manifold demands on new forms of work, each occupation and sector needs to be analyzed, designed, and applied regarding its conformity with the sustainable development of the labor market in the context of overall societal development. In the case of the pandemic, this for example showed in the rise of the significance of telework opportunities and online platforms. If the labor market is redesigned and shaped according to this concept, future jobs will also meet the requirements of the tangential social and welfare systems. With the SJF this trend can potentially be actively encountered in a flexibly through the transition to sustainable, smart, and social new forms of work. The SJF design is not directed toward maximizing short-term economic profit but to optimize long-term sustainable development through SE. The importance of SE, for social innovation and in the sense of new social practices and organizational models, needs to be emphasized.

Sustainable roles are used to develop forms of work and activity profiles that meet future societal requirements, new jobs are created, and existing jobs are transformed. The SJF seeks to ensure stable forms of work and employment relationships that promote personal development and lifelong learning as well as to suggest additions to an appropriate regulatory framework. This has a direct impact on the social security and welfare of the individuals concerned. The general mental health and well-being of the people and their environment are improved. A prerequisite for this is the integration of a change mentality in labor interventions into the strategic decision-making processes and therefore the corporate culture of an organization.

In the medium and long term, the application results of the SJF should also be evaluated in terms of welfare. The goal of social policy is to ensure that everyone has sufficient resources to live independently and with a certain standard of living. In this case, independent also means independence from state measures to increase social and material well-being, and this is also in the sense of the social state or welfare state, to prevent emergencies if necessary. Strengthening sustainable forms of work and employment thus also makes a lasting contribution to strengthening welfare in the economic sense. Future-oriented competencies, from change competence to learning competence, to questions of future-oriented activity and investment priorities, and also the perception of future challenges (trend sensitivity) clarify the multi-layered requirements with a focus on the creation of sustainable jobs. Requirements that also want to clarify a discrepancy with the established as well as optimized processes and name counter-arguments in case of resistance, whether in companies or society.

In the end, the SJF offers the potential to advance the labor market through a transition toward more human-centered and oriented toward sustainable development and innovation.

REFERENCES

Acemoglu, D., & Restrepo, P. (2018). The Race between Man and Machine: Implications of Technology for Growth, Factor Shares, and Employment. *The American Economic Review*, *108*(6), 1488–1542. doi:10.1257/aer.20160696

Amelia, A. (2018). *Employer branding: When HR is the new marketing*. Penerbit Buku Kompas.

Attanasio, G., Battistella, C., & Preghenella, N. (2021). *Sustainable Value and Stakeholders: a Conceptual Framework from Multiple Case Studies*. Paper presented at the International Forum on Knowledge Asset Dynamics (IFKAD), Rome, Italy.

Austin, J., Stevenson, H., & Wei-Skillern, J. (2006). Social and commercial entrepreneurship: Same, different, or both? *Entrepreneurship Theory and Practice*, *30*(1), 1–22. doi:10.1111/j.1540-6520.2006.00107.x

Bakker, A. B., & Demerouti, E. (2007). The job demands-resources model: State of the art. *Journal of Managerial Psychology*, *22*(3), 309–328. doi:10.1108/02683940710733115

Berntson, E., Sverke, M., & Marklund, S. (2006). Predicting perceived employability: Human capital or labor market opportunities? *Economic and Industrial Democracy*, *27*(2), 223–244. doi:10.1177/0143831X06063098

Bornstein, D. (2007). *How to change the world: Social entrepreneurs and the power of new ideas*. Penguin Books.

Brunetti, F., Matt, D. T., Bonfanti, A., De Longhi, A., Pedrini, G., & Orzes, G. (2020). Digital transformation challenges: Strategies emerging from a multi-stakeholder approach. *The TQM Journal*, *32*(4), 697–724. doi:10.1108/TQM-12-2019-0309

Chell, E. (2007). Social enterprise and entrepreneurship: Towards a convergent theory of the entrepreneurial process. *International Small Business Journal*, *25*(1), 5–26. doi:10.1177/0266242607071779

Colombo, E., Mercorio, F., & Mezzanzanica, M. (2019). AI meets labor market: Exploring the link between automation and skills. *Information Economics and Policy*, *47*, 27–37. doi:10.1016/j.infoecopol.2019.05.003

Cortelazzo, L., Bruni, E., & Zamperie, R. (2019). The Role of Leadership in a Digitalized World: A Review. *Front Psychology, 10*(1938), 1–21.

Curtin, R. T., Davidson, R., & Paul, D. (2018). Panel Study of Entrepreneurial Dynamics, PSED II, United States, 2005-2011: Version 1 [Data set]. Inter-University Consortium for Political and Social Research. doi:10.3886/ICPSR37202.V1

Dacin, P. A., Dacin, M. T., & Matear, M. (2010). Social entrepreneurship: Why we don't need a new theory and how we move forward from here. *The Academy of Management Perspectives*, *24*(3), 37–57.

Dobni, C. B. (2008). The DNA of innovation. *The Journal of Business Strategy*, *29*(2), 43–50. doi:10.1108/02756660810858143

Docherty, P., Kira, M., & Shani, A. B. (2009). What the world needs now is sustainable work systems. In P. Docherty, M. Kira, & A. B. Shani (Eds.), *Creating sustainable work systems: Developing social sustainability* (pp. 1–32). Routledge.

Dolphin, T. (Ed.). (2015). *Technology, Globalisation and the future of work in Europe: Essays on employment in a digitised economy.* Institute for Public Policy Research. https://www.ippr.org/publications/technology-globalisation-and-the-future-of-work-in-europe

Edwards, J. R., & Billsberry, J. (2010). Testing a multidimensional theory of person-environment fit. *Journal of Managerial Issues*, 22, 476–493. https://www.jstor.org/stable/25822526

Elkington, J. (1997). *Cannibals with Forks: The Triple Bottom Line of 21st Century Business.* Capstone Publishing.

Emerson, J. (2003). The blended value proposition: Integrating social and financial returns. *California Management Review*, 45(4), 35–51. doi:10.2307/41166187

Estrin, S., Mickiewicz, T., & Stephan, U. (2013). Entrepreneurship, Social Capital, and Institutions: Social and Commercial Entrepreneurship across Nations. *Entrepreneurship Theory and Practice*, 37(3), 479–504. doi:10.1111/etap.12019

European Commission. (2010). *Psychosocial risks and health effects of restructuring.* EC. https://www.google.com/url?sa=t&rct=j&q=&esrc=s&source=web&cd=&cad=rja&uact=8&ved=2ahUKEwiE7KatwOr0AhV7Q_EDHT34DqwQFnoECAgQAQ&url=https%3A%2F%2Fec.europa.eu%2Fsocial%2FBlobServlet%3FdocId%3D6245%26langId%3Den&usg=AOvVaw22OtHLcxEg4sZ2xJsmrYCw

European Commission. (2020). *Commission staff working document-Digital Education action Plan 2021-2027 Resetting education and training for the digital age* (SWD No. 2020, 209 final). EC. https://ec.europa.eu/education/sites/default/files/document-library-docs/deap-swd-sept2020_en.pdf

Freeman, R. E. (1984). *Strategic management: A stakeholder approach.* Pitman.

Fugate, M., Kinicki, A. J., & Ashforth, B. E. (2004). Employability: A psycho-social construct, its dimensions, and applications. *Journal of Vocational Behavior*, 65(1), 14–38. doi:10.1016/j.jvb.2003.10.005

García-Morales, V. J., Martín-Rojas, R., & Garde-Sánchez, R. (2020). How to Encourage Social Entrepreneurship Action? Using Web 2.0 Technologies in Higher Education Institutions. *Journal of Business Ethics*, 161(2), 329–350. doi:10.100710551-019-04216-6

Gebauer, J., Schirmer, H., Fels, M., Lange, F., & Meyer, N. (Eds.). (2013). Unternehmerisch und verantwortlich wirken? Forschung an der Schnittstelle von Corporate Social Responsibility und Social Entrepreneurship. IÖW, Institut für ökologische Wirtschaftsforschung.

Global Entrepreneurship Monitor. (n.d.). *Entrepreneurial behaviour and attitudes. GEM* Global Entrepreneurship Monitor. https://www.gemconsortium.org/data/sets

Gratton, L. (2011). *The shift: The future of work is already here.* HarperCollins Publisher.

Hedge, J. W. (2008). Strategic human resource management and the older worker. *Journal of Workplace Behavioral Health*, 23(1-2), 109–123. doi:10.1080/15555240802189513

Janssen, O. (2000). Job demands, perceptions of effort-reward fairness and innovative work behaviour. *Journal of Occupational and Organizational Psychology, 73*(3), 287–302. doi:10.1348/096317900167038

Javed, A., Yasir, M., & Majid, A. (2019). Is Social Entrepreneurship a Panacea for Sustainable Enterprise Development? *Pakistan Journal of Commerce and Social Sciences, 13*(1), 29.

Kossek, E. E., & Ollier-Malaterre, A. (2020). Desperately seeking sustainable careers: Redesigning professional jobs for the collaborative crafting of reduced-load work. *Journal of Vocational Behavior, 117*, 103315. doi:10.1016/j.jvb.2019.06.003

Kristof-Brown, A. L., Zimmerman, R. D., & Johnson, E. C. (2005). Consequences of individuals' fit at work: A meta-analysis of person-job, person-organization, person-group, and person-supervisor fit. *Personnel Psychology, 58*(2), 281–342. doi:10.1111/j.1744-6570.2005.00672.x

Leduc, S., & Liu, Z. (2021). *Robots or Workers? A Macro Analysis of Automation and Labor Markets*. Federal Reserve Bank of San Francisco.

Leichenko, R., & Silva, J. A. (2014). Climate change and poverty: Vulnerability, impacts, and alleviation strategies. *Wiley Interdisciplinary Reviews: Climate Change, 5*(4), 539–556. doi:10.1002/wcc.287

Li, W., Badr, Y., & Biennier, F. (2012). Digital ecosystems: challenges and prospects. *Proceedings of the international conference on management of Emergent Digital EcoSystems,* ACM. https://dl.acm.org/doi/pdf/10.1145/2457276.2457297

Martínez-Garcia, E., Sorribes, J., & Celma, D. (2018). Sustainable Development through CSR in Human Resource Management Practices: The Effects of the Economic Crisis on Job Quality: Sustainable development: economic crisis and job quality. *Corporate Social Responsibility and Environmental Management, 25*(4), 441–456. doi:10.1002/csr.1471

McSweeney, M. J. (2020). Returning the 'social' to social entrepreneurship: Future possibilities of critically exploring sport for development and peace and social entrepreneurship. *International Review for the Sociology of Sport, 55*(1), 3–21. doi:10.1177/1012690218784295

Mohrman, S. A., & Worley, C. G. (2010). The organizational sustainability journey. *Organizational Dynamics, 39*(4), 289–294. doi:10.1016/j.orgdyn.2010.07.008

Moreira, S., Vasconcelos, L., & Santos, C. S. (2017). Sustainability of green jobs in Portugal: A methodological approach using occupational health indicators. *Journal of Occupational Health, 59*(5), 374–384. doi:10.1539/joh.17-0045-RA PMID:28794392

Nangoy, R., Mursitama, T. N., Setiadi, N. J., & Pradipto, Y. D. (2020). Creating sustainable performance in the fourth industrial revolution era: The effect of employee's work well-being on job performance. *Management Science Letters*, 1037–1042. doi:10.5267/j.msl.2019.11.006

Nicholls, A. (2010). The Legitimacy of Social Entrepreneurship: Reflexive Isomorphism in a Pre-Paradigmatic Field. *Entrepreneurship Theory and Practice, 4*(34), 611–633. doi:10.1111/j.1540-6520.2010.00397.x

Object Management Group. (n.d.). Unified Modeling Language, v2.5.1. *Unified Modeling Language*, 796.

OECD. (2017). *OECD Guidelines on Measuring the Quality of the Working Environment*. OECD. doi:10.1787/9789264278240-

Parmar, B. L., Freeman, R. E., Harrison, J. S., Wicks, A. C., Purnell, L., & De Colle, S. (2010). Stakeholder theory: The state of the art. *The Academy of Management Annals*, *4*(1), 403–445. doi:10.5465/19416520.2010.495581

Peters, V., Engels, J. A., de Rijk, A. E., & Nijhuis, F. J. N. (2015). Sustainable employability in shiftwork: Related to types of work schedule rather than age. *International Archives of Occupational and Environmental Health*, *88*(7), 881–893. doi:10.100700420-014-1015-9 PMID:25578669

Phillips, W., Lee, H., Ghobadian, A., O'Regan, N., & James, P. (2015). Social Innovation and Social Entrepreneurship. *Group & Organization Management*, *40*(3), 428–461. doi:10.1177/1059601114560063

Piroşcă, G. I., Şerban-Oprescu, G. L., Badea, L., Stanef-Puică, M.-R., & Valdebenito, C. R. (2021). Digitalization and Labor Market—A Perspective within the Framework of Pandemic Crisis. *Journal of Theoretical and Applied Electronic Commerce Research*, *16*(7), 2843–2857. doi:10.3390/jtaer16070156

Pohlan, L. (2019). Unemployment and social exclusion. *Journal of Economic Behavior & Organization*, *164*, 273–299. doi:10.1016/j.jebo.2019.06.006

Rhee, C. S., Woo, S., Yu, S.-J., & Rhee, H. (2021). Corporate Social Responsibility and Sustainable Employability: Empirical Evidence from Korea. *Sustainability*, *13*(14), 8114. doi:10.3390u13148114

Roundy, P. T. (2017). Social entrepreneurship and entrepreneurial ecosystems: Complementary or disjoint phenomena? *International Journal of Social Economics*, *44*(9), 1252–1267. doi:10.1108/IJSE-02-2016-0045

Sadri, S., & Jayashree, S. (2013). *Human Resources Management in Modern India (concepts and cases)*. Himalaya Publishing Co.

Scharpe, K., & Wunsch, M. (n.d.). *Social Entrepreneuship Netzwerk Deutschland e.V. (SEND)*. 92.

Schlogl, L., & Sumner, A. (2018). The Rise of the Robot Reserve Army: Automation and the Future of Economic Development, Work, and Wages in Developing Countries. SSRN *Electronic Journal*. doi:10.2139/ssrn.3208816

Schotanus-Dijkstra, M., Pieterse, M. E., Drossaert, C., Westerhof, G. J., de Graaf, R., ten Have, M., Walburg, J. A., & Bohlmeijer, E. T. (2016). What factors are associated with flourishing? Results from a large representative national sample. *Journal of Happiness Studies*, *17*(4), 1351–1370. doi:10.100710902-015-9647-3

Semeijn, J. H., Van Dam, K., Van Vuuren, T., & Van der Heijden, B. I. J. M. (2015). Sustainable labor participation and sustainable careers. In A. VosDe, A., Van der Heijden, B. (Eds.), The handbook of research on sustainable careers. Cheltenham: Edward Elgar Publishing.

Sheel, S., Sindhwani, D. B. K., Goel, S., & Pathak, S. (2012). *Quality of work life, employee performance and career growth opportunities: a literature review*, *2*, 10.

Softgarden. (2019, January 1). *Bewerbungsreport 2019: Wie nehmen Kandidaten aktuell Recruitingprozesse wahr?* Softgarden. https://softgarden.com/de/studie/bewerbungsreport-wie-nehmen-kandidaten-aktuell-recruitingprozesse-wahr/

Stone, M., Aravopolou, E., Gerardi, G., Todeva, E., Weinzerl, L., Laughlin, P., & Scott, R. (2017). How platforms are transforming customer information management. *The Bottom Line (New York, N.Y.)*, *30*(3), 216–235. doi:10.1108/BL-08-2017-0024

Suleimankadieva, A., Petrov, M., & Kuznetsov, A. (2021). Digital educational ecosystem as a tool for the intellectual capital development. *SHS Web of Conferences*, *116*, 00060. 10.1051hsconf/202111600060

Sung, S. H., Seong, J. Y., & Kim, Y. G. (2020). Seeking sustainable development in teams: Towards improving team commitment through person-group fit. *Sustainability*, *12*(15), 6033. doi:10.3390u12156033

Tang, Y., Shao, Y.-F., Chen, Y.-J., & Ma, Y. (2021). How to Keep Sustainable Development Between Enterprises and Employees? Evaluating the Impact of Person–Organization Fit and Person–Job Fit on Innovative Behavior. *Frontiers in Psychology*, *12*, 653534. doi:10.3389/fpsyg.2021.653534 PMID:33995213

Tierney, P., & Farmer, S. M. (2002). Creative self-efficacy: Its potential antecedents and relationship to creative performance. *Academy of Management Journal*, *45*(6), 1137–1148. doi:10.2307/3069429

Tsai, C. H. (2011). Innovative behaviors between employment modes in knowledge intensive organizations. *International Journal of Humanities and Social Science*, *1*, 153–162.

Unified Modeling Language, v2.5.1. (n.d.). *Unified Modeling Language*, 796. UML.

United Nations. (1972). *Stockholm 1972: Declaration of the United Nations Conference on the Human Environment*. UN. https://www.unep.org/Documents.Multilingual/

Valdez-De-Leon, O. (2019). How to Develop a Digital Ecosystem – a Practical Framework. *Technology Innovation Management Review*, *9*(8), 43–54. doi:10.22215/timreview/1260

Van Dam, K. (2004). Antecedents and consequences of employability orientation. European Journal of Work and Organizational Psychology, 13, 29–51.

Van Dam, K., van Vuuren, T., & Kemps, S. (2017). Sustainable employment: The importance of intrinsically valuable work and an age-supportive climate. *International Journal of Human Resource Management*, *28*(17), 2449–2472. https://doi.org/10.1080/09585192.2015.1137607

Van der Klink, J. J. L. (2010). *Duurzaam inzetbaar: werk als waarde. Rapport in opdracht van ZonMw ten behoeve van het programma Participatie en Gezondheid*. Rijksuniversiteit Groningen.

Van Vuuren, T. (2012). Vitality management: One does not need to be ill to get better! *Gedrag en Organisatie*, *25*, 400–418.

Vial, G. (2019). Understanding digital transformation: A review and a research agenda. *The Journal of Strategic Information Systems*, *28*(2), 118–144.

vom Lehn, D. (2020). Digitalization as "an Agent of Social Change" in a Supermarket Chain: Applying Blumer's Theory of Industrialization in Contemporary Society. *Symbolic Interaction*, *43*(4), 637–656. doi:10.1002ymb.502

Zahra, S. A., Newey, L. R., & Li, Y. (2014). On the Frontiers: The Implications of Social Entrepreneurship for International Entrepreneurship. *Entrepreneurship Theory and Practice*, *38*(1), 137–158. https://doi.org/10.1111/etap.12061

ADDITIONAL READING

Briken, K., Chillas, S., Krzywdzinski, M., & Marks, A. (2017). Labor Process Theory and the New Digital Workplace. In K. Briken, S. Chillas, M. Krzywdzinski, & A. Marks (Eds.), *The New Digital Workplace* (pp. 1–17). Palgrave Macmillan. doi:10.1057/978-1-137-61014-0_1

Eberhard, B., Podio, M., Alonso, A. P., Radovica, E., Avotina, L., Peiseniece, L., Sendon, M. C., Lozano, A. G., & Solé-Pla, J. (2017). Smart Work: The Transformation of the Labor Market to the Fourth Industrial Revolution. *International Journal Business and Economic Sciences Applied Research.*, *10*(3), 47–66.

Gawrycka, M., & Szymczak, A. (2021). A Panel Analysis of the Impact of Green Transformation and Globalization on the Labor Share in the National Income. *Energies*, *14*(21), 1–14. doi:10.3390/en14216967

Grassl, W. (2012). Business Models of Social Enterprises: A Design Approach to Hybridity. *ACRN Journal of Entrepreneurship Perspectives.*, *1*(1), 37–60.

Jaiswal, A. (2018). Effect of Work Environment Characteristics on Job Involvement in an Organization: An Empirical Review. *Research Review International Journal of Multidisciplinary.*, *03*(11), 588–594.

Jensen, D., & Campbell, J. (2019). The Case for a Digital Ecosystem for the Environment. Technical Report, Governing Consortium, March 2019, 4-37.

Kraus, S., Filser, M., O'Dwyer, M., & Shaw, E. (2014). Social Entrepreneurship: An Exploratory Citation Analyses. *Review of Managerial Science*, *8*(2), 275–292. doi:10.100711846-013-0104-6

Krogstie, J. (2012). *Modeling of Digital Ecosystem. Challenges and Opportunities*. Conference Papier, PRO-VE 2012: Collaborative Networks in the Internet of Services, 137-145.

Mair, J., & Lanuza, I. M. (2006). Social Entrepeneurship Research: A Source of Explanation. Prediction, and Delight. *Journal of World Business*, *41*(1), 36–44. doi:10.1016/j.jwb.2005.09.002

Pasieka, S., Bil, M., Demytrenko, M., & Krasnomovets, V. (2020). Global Transformation of Employment as a Factor of Country's Labor Market Development. Research in World Economy, 11(4), 62-71.

Saebi, T.; Foss, N. J. & Linder, S. (2018). Social Entrepreneurship Research. Past Achievements and Future Promises. *Journal of Management, 45*(1), 70-95.

Scully-Russ, E., & Torraco, R. (2020). The Changing Nature and Organization of Work: An Integrative Review of the Literature. *Human Resource Development Review*, *19*(I), 66–93. doi:10.1177/1534484319886394

KEY TERMS AND DEFINITIONS

Blended Value: A concept that recognises the fundamental connection between financial and social outputs and impacts to create awareness among organizations about the far-reaching scope of their value creation towards a broad stakeholder network.

Digital Ecosystem: Interacting, digitally connected organizations in a self-organizing, demand-driven system that is shaped by the dynamics between the stakeholders, available resources as well as relevant policy.

Fourth Industrial Revolution: The rapid changes in industry, technology and society, made possible by interconnectivity and smart automation.

Social Entrepreneurship: Small and medium-sized enterprises that are orientated towards social problems and pursue social or environmentally oriented goals.

Social Transformation: The change of the society due to technological, economic, and scientific advancements and innovations.

Sustainable Work: The level to which employees are capable and willing to appropriately perform their work in the present and future.

Work Role: A function description that expands to integrate tasks and characteristics, responsibilities and expectations of behaviour as well as future expectations to facilitate the identification of the best fit for the job description and organisation.

Chapter 4
Job Insecurity and Performance:
Contributions for an Integrative Theoretical Framework

Ligia Portovedo
https://orcid.org/0000-0002-0007-9711
University of Minho, Portugal

Ana Veloso
https://orcid.org/0000-0002-2417-2910
University of Minho, Portugal

Miguel Portela
University of Minho, Portugal

ABSTRACT

Based on published literature between 2000 and 2020 and applying a systematic review, the authors reflect on the theoretical bases that describe the effects of psychological moderating and mediating variables in the relationship between job insecurity and performance. An aggregating theoretical model is proposed, anchored on the conservation of resources theory, social exchange theory, and trust to describe the process in which job insecurity impacts performance, through or in the presence of the variables found.

INTRODUCTION

It is true that psychological variables influence performance in the organizational context, for which there is an extensive volume of literature discussing the subject, impossible to describe exhaustively (Colquitt, Scott, & LePine, 2007; Elst, De Cuyper, & De Witte, 2011; Huselid, 1995; Richter, Vander Elst, & De Witte, 2020; Van de Voorde & Boxall, 2014; Veloso, 2007). These psychological variables that literature claims to have an impact on performance are also diverse. For exemple, *organizational commitment* (Colquitt, LePine, Piccolo, Zapata, & Rich, 2012; Riketta, 2002), *trust* (Colquitt et al., 2007;

DOI: 10.4018/978-1-6684-4181-7.ch004

Davis, Schoorman, Mayer, & Tan, 2000; Richter & Näswall, 2019; Vanhala & Dietz, 2019), *psychological capital* (Gao, Wu, Wang, & Zhao, 2020; Probst, Gailey, Jiang, & Bohle, 2017) and *uncertainty* (Colquitt et al., 2012).

Although there are several theories that describe the effects of psychological variables on performance, the need for an integration of these theories remains unattended, in order to allow a more complete understanding of the phenomenon.

The scientific literature has produced studies that describe mediating and moderating variables, using several theoretical models for their understanding. For example, the relationship between *job insecurity (JI)* and *performance*, whose effect is consensual (Cheng & Chan, 2008; Jiang & Lavaysse, 2018; Sverke, Hellgren, & Näswall, 2002), is explained by the authors using different theories, according to the mediating or moderating variables that they test: Niesen reads the mediation of the variable *psychological contract breach* through the Social Exchange Theory (SET) (Niesen, Van Hootegem, Handaja, Battistelli, & De Witte, 2018), Probst uses Conservation of Resources (COR) Theory and SET to understand the moderation of *psychological capital* (Probst et al., 2017) and Wang uses Uncertainty Management Theory (UMT) to frame the results of the *work engagement* mediation (H. J. Wang, Lu, & Siu, 2015). As all of these works test different intermediate variables for the same relationship between *JI* and *performance*, can there be a theoretical framework that integrates the different explanations of the phenomenon?

This chapter explores the possibility of describing a framework that allows theoretical interpretation of empirical research on the impact of JI on performance.

BACKGROUND

In recent decades, the layoffs have become a common practice in companies, as a result of mergers, acquisitions and restructurings. Automation made some functions obsolete and the search for quick profits institutionalized the model of cutting personnel expenses (Greenhalgh & Rosenblatt, 2010; Hirsch & De Soucey, 2006). Although in recent years the practice of downsizing has been less reported to avoid damaging brands with negative press, the "stealth layoff" model adopted by human resource management maintains the same effect of distrust in the psychosocial environment of work contexts (Gandolfi & Littler, 2012).

Job loss is considered a major stressor, and the mere threat of job loss can trigger coping reactions similar to job loss itself (Vander Elst, De Cuyper, Baillien, Niesen, and De Witte, 2016), such as psychological distress, burnout, and depression, leading to reduced productivity, alienation from others, and emotional exhaustion (Hobfoll, 2001).

Economic losses and other consequences of job insecurity have received greater attention in recent decades (Cheng & Chan, 2008), while labor market is undergoing major deregulation and precariousness: layoffs have become easier and new jobs have characteristics of unconventional work, such as part-time, fixed-term and independent work (Kalleberg & Vallas, 2017).

From the individual's point of view, job insecurity affects social identity (Selenko et al., 2017), mental and physical health (Hellgren et al., 1999; Sverke et al., 2002) and well-being (Ogbonnaya, Gahan, & Eib, 2019; Selenko, Mäkikangas, & Stride, 2017; Silla, de Cuyper, Gracia, Peiró, & de Witte, 2009; Van Dick, Ullrich, & Tissington, 2006). It is a stressful event because it diminishes the experience of control

(Elst, De Cuyper, & De Witte, 2011), threatens valuable resources (Hobfoll, Halbesleben, Neveu, & Westman, 2018) and causes a perception of psychological breach of contract (Vander Elst et al., 2016).

Consequences on organizational behavior include decreased job satisfaction (De Cuyper & De Witte, 2006, 2007; De Witte & Näswall, 2003; Hellgren et al., 1999; Sverke et al., 2002; Van Dick et al., 2006), work engagement, organizational commitment, trust (Sverke et al., 2002) and motivation (De Witte & Näswall, 2003; Suifan, 2019).

Job Insecurity has a negative impact on performance (Sverke et al., 2002; Sverke, Låstad, Hellgren, Richter, & Näswall, 2019), innovation (Niesen et al., 2018) and organizational citizenship behaviors (Probst, Gailey, Jiang, & Bohle, 2017; Van Dick et al., 2006). Enhances counterproductive work behaviour (Shoss, 2017) as well as turnover (Richter, Vander Elst, & De Witte, 2020) and turnover intentions (Elst et al., 2011).

As a major source of stress (Vander Elst et al., 2016), JI effects remain relatively stable over time for layoff survivors (Hellgren et al., 1999) and disseminate across the organization by an interpersonal process called crossover that transmits psychological states, resources and experiences to other people in the same social environment (Hobfoll et al., 2018).

Job insecurity is therefore likely to cause individual harm, transmitted by peers to teams and the entire organization. Its effects remain stable over time and have a negative impact on performance, which should motivate human resource management to prevent its development.

It is our purpose to identify empirical literature on the topic and revisit theoretical frameworks used to understand the results. We will limit the scope to literature that explains how the effect of *JI* on *performance* occurs, developing a reflection on the possibility that the theoretical body of trust allows us to integrate the joint understanding of results.

HOW IS THE EFFECT OF JOB INSECURITY PROCESSED ON PERFORMANCE AND HOW THEORY EXPLAINS IT?

Job Insecurity is "the perceived powerlessness to maintain desired continuity in a threatened job situation" (Rosenblatt & Greenhalgh, 1984, p. 438) or the concern about the continued existence of the job in the future (Cheng & Chan, 2008; Sverke et al., 2002).

From studies that explain the process according to which *JI* causes effects on *performance*, using psychological variables with moderation or mediation effects, we have carried out a synthesis of these variables and also of the theoretical frameworks used for its framing.

We have chosen Google Scholar platform to do this research because recent systematic comparison of the performance of 3 academic search engines, Google Scholar (GS), Web of Science (WoS) and Scopus (Martín-Martín et al., 2018), analysing 2.5 million documents, in 252 research areas, concluded that GS is a kind of superset of WoS and Scopus.

Nearly all citations found by WoS (95%) and Scopus (92%) were also found by GS, and in Social Sciences, Business, Economics & Management, unique GS citations surpass 50% of all citations in the area (Martín-Martín et al., 2018), which makes GS the adequate academic search engine to use in this work.

Our search was executed in GS platform, with the following conditions:

- Expression: "Job Insecurity" AND Performance, in the title of the article;
- Empirical articles subject to peer-review, published between 2000 and 2020;

- Written in English, French, Spanish, or Portuguese.

We obtained 95 results. We had eliminated duplicates and other works that did not meet our predefined conditions mentioned above, which resulted in 31 articles presented in Table 1.

We read the articles in full and identified the variables that were studied, the type of relationship between the variables (mediation or moderation) and the theoretical frameworks used to understand the results.

We organized the variables found into 3 subgroups, with the intention of looking for patterns of investigation and use of explanatory theories. One of the defined subgroups is that of performance behaviors, a variable with which job insecurity is related, but which takes on various aspects of performance. The other 2 subgroups, which are the moderation or mediation variables, seek to illustrate antecedents more or less close to performance behaviors. In these two background subgroups, we added:

- **Personality Traits and Perceptions**
    - Personality Traits, that are "internal psychological structures or properties that relate to regularities in behaviour" (Nicholson, 1998, p. 420) and that can predict the development of attitudes (Nicholson, 1998);
    - Perceptions, that are "the result" (VandenBos, 2007, p. 775) of "active cognitive process of selecting, organizing and interpreting the multitude of stimuli that are received" (Nicholson, 1998, p. 409) and that are influenced by internal factors, including personality (Nicholson, 1998), permitting the person "to act in a coordinated manner" (VandenBos, 2007, p. 775).
- **Attitudes and States**
    - Attitudes, that are "a relatively enduring and general evaluation of an object, person, group, issue, or concept" (VandenBos, 2007, p. 88), comprising a "behavioural tendency directed toward specific individuals, groups of individuals, ideas, philosophies, issues or objects" (Nicholson, 1998, p. 20);
    - States, that are "the condition or status of an entity or system at a particular time that is characterized by relative stability of its basic components or elements" (VandenBos, 2007, p. 1026). Job satisfaction, a very present variable in our set of studies, is an attitude (Nicholson, 1998, p. 20; VandenBos, 2007, p. 572) or an affective state (Nicholson, 1998, p. 273), so we decided to add this category.

We found that some of the variables included in the studies belong to one and the same concept. For example, *well-being* integrates *mental health*. Thus, we looked for the definitions of each of the variables to integrate convergent variables in a single concept.

The definitions of the variables were sought in the studies that refer to them, except for *organizational commitment* and *psychological distress*, which were not described and for which we looked for other sources.

We present these definitions in Table 2:

Table 1. Articles, variables and theories

Article	Type of Relation between variables	Mediation or Moderation Variables			Performance Behaviors	Theoretical Framework
		Personality Traits and Perceptions	Attitudes and States			
(Chirumbolo & Areni, 2005)	Moderation		Job Satisfaction		Job Performance	Appraisal Theory
			Organizational Commitment		Job Performance	
(Chirumbolo & Areni, 2010)	Moderation		Need for Closure		Job Performance	No Theory
(König, Debus, Häusler, Lendenmann, & Kleinmann, 2010)	Moderation		Job Satisfaction		Job Performance	COR Theory
			Organizational Commitment			
(Elst et al., 2011)	Mediation	Perceived Control	Psychological Distress			Appraisal Theory
		Perceived Control	Organizational Commitment			
		Perceived Control	Job Satisfaction			
		Perceived Control		Turnover Intentions		
(Schreurs, Emmerik, Gunter, & Germeys, 2012)	Moderation	Supervisor and Coworker Support			Job Performance	Psychological Contract Theory, COR theory
(Piccoli, Setti, Filippi, Argentero, & Bellotto, 2013)	Mediation		Job Satisfaction		Job Performance	SET
			Organizational Commitment			
(Roll, Siu, & Y.W. Li, 2015)	Moderation	Uncertainty Avoidance			Job Performance	No Theory
(H. J. Wang et al., 2015)	Moderation	Organizational Justice			Job Performance	Uncertainty Management Theory
	Mediation		Work Engagement			
(Callea, Urbini, & Chirumbolo, 2016)	Mediation		Organizational Identification		Job Performance	Social Identity Theory, SET
(Vander Elst, De Cuyper, Baillien, Niesen, & De Witte, 2016)	Mediation	Perceived Control			Job Performance	Appraisal Theory
		Psychological Contract Breach				
		Perceived Control			Innovative Work Behaviour	
		Psychological Contract Breach	Emotional Health Complaints			
		Psychological Contract Breach	Physical Health Complaints			
		Psychological Contract Breach	General Strain			
		Psychological Contract Breach	Job Satisfaction			
		Psychological Contract Breach	Organizational Commitment			
		Perceived Control	Job Satisfaction			
		Perceived Control	Organizational Commitment			

continues on following page

Table 1. Continued

Article	Type of Relation between variables	Mediation or Moderation Variables			Performance Behaviors	Theoretical Framework
		Personality Traits and Perceptions	Attitudes and States			
(Mäder & Niessen, 2017)	Mediation		Negative Affect		Job Performance	COR theory
			Negative Work Reflections			
(Piccoli, De Witte, & Reisel, 2017)	Mediation	Psychological Contract Breach			Counterproductive Work Behaviour	Psychological Contract Theory, SET
		Psychological Contract Breach			Organizational Citizenship Behaviour	
		Organizational Justice			Counterproductive Work Behaviour	
		Organizational Justice			Organizational Citizenship Behaviour	
(Probst et al., 2017)	Moderation	Psychological Capital			Job Performance	COR theory, SET
(Selenko, Mäkikangas, & Stride, 2017)	Mediation	Social Identity	Well-being			Social Identity Theory
		Social Identity			Job Performance	
(Bohle, Chambel, Medina, & Da Cunha, 2018)	Mediation		Organizational Commitment		Job Performance	SET
	Moderation		Organizational Support			
(Khan & Ghufran, 2018)	Mediation	Organizational Support			Job Performance	SET
					Organizational Citizenship Behaviour	
(Niesen et al., 2018)	Mediation	Psychological Contract Breach			Innovative Work Behaviour	SET
(Tufail, Sultan, Khalil, & Sahibzada, 2018)	Mediation		Job Satisfaction		Job Performance	Psychological Contract Theory
(Asif, Fiaz, Khaliq, & Nisar, 2019)	Mediation		Organizational Identification		Job Performance	Social Identity Theory
(Guo, Liu, Chu, Ye, & Zhang, 2019)	Moderation	Supervisor and Coworker Support	Job Satisfaction		Safety Performance	COR theory
(Piccoli, Reisel, & Witte, 2019)	Mediation		Organizational Commitment		Job Performance	Appraisal Theory
(Shaikh, Mangi, & Bukhari, 2019)	Mediation	Emotional Intelligence	Intrinsic Motivation		Job Performance	No Theory
(Shin, Hur, Moon, & Lee, 2019)	Mediation		Intrinsic Motivation		Organizational Citizenship Behaviour	Self-Determination Theory

continues on following page

Table 1. Continued

Article	Type of Relation between variables	Mediation or Moderation Variables			Theoretical Framework
		Personality Traits and Perceptions	Attitudes and States	Performance Behaviors	
(Adewale, Dahiru, MukhtarShehu, & Kofar-Mata, 2020)	Mediation	Self-Efficacy		Job Performance	COR Theory
	Moderation	Emotional Intelligence			
(Bibi, 2020)	Mediation		Work Engagement	Job Performance	No Theory
	Moderation	Organizational Justice			
(Darvishmotevali & Ali, 2020)	Moderation	Psychological Capital	Well-being	Job Performance	Appraisal Theory
(Kim & Kim, 2020)	Mediation		Job stress	Job Performance	SET
			Organizational Commitment		
	Moderation	Ethical Leadership			
(Naru & Rehman, 2020)	Mediation		Stress	Job Performance	Person-Environment Fit theory
(Richter et al., 2020)	Mediation		Rumination	Turnover	COR Theory
(Schumacher, Schreurs, De Cuyper, & Grosemans, 2020)	Moderation	Informational Justice		Job Performance	COR Theory
(Shoss, Brummel, Probst, & Jiang, 2020)	Moderation		Job Satisfaction	Counterproductive Work Behaviour	COR Theory
			Job Satisfaction	Turnover Intentions	

Table 2. Variables definitions

Variables	Definition
Counterproductive Work Behaviour	Behaviours that have the potential to be harmful to organizations. (Shoss et al., 2020, p. 304)
Emotional Intelligence	The competency of a person to understand, aware of, and control own emotions in order to understand and recognize the emotions of others. (Shaikh et al., 2019, p. 178)
Ethical Leadership	The demonstration of normatively appropriate conduct through personal actions and interpersonal relationships, and the promotion of such conduct to followers through two-way communication, reinforcement, and decision-making. (Kim & Kim, 2020, p. 3)
General Strain	Well-being - mental and physical health complaints. (Vander Elst et al., 2016, p. 107)
Informational Justice	Employees' perceptions of whether the organisation communicated in an adequate and timely fashion. (Schumacher et al., 2020, p. 2)
Innovative Work Behaviour	The intentional introduction and application within a role, group or organisation of ideas, processes or procedures, new to the relevant unit of adoption, designed to significantly benefit the individual, the group, organisation or wider society. (Niesen et al., 2018, p. 1)
Intrinsic Motivation	Encompasses cognitive (i.e., challenge seeking) and affective (i.e., task enjoyment) components. (Shin et al., 2019, p. 2)
Job Insecurity	Perceived threat of job loss. (Elst et al., 2011, p. 216)
Job Performance	Task performance, contextual performance, counterproductive work behaviour, creativity, and safety compliance. (Sverke, Låstad, Hellgren, Richter, & Näswall, 2019, p. 2)
Job Satisfaction	Internal evaluation of the favourability of one's job (Shoss, 2017, p. 300); work-related well-being (Richter & Näswall, 2019, p. 23).
Need for Closure	Motivated need for certainty, intolerance of ambiguity and preference for predictability. (Chirumbolo & Areni, 2010, p. 195)
Negative Affect	Feeling upset or unpleasantly aroused. (Mäder & Niessen, 2017, p. 234)
Negative Work Reflection	Negative thinking about job-related issues, failures, or negative events at work. (Mäder & Niessen, 2017, p. 235)
Organizational Citizenship Behaviour	The behaviour that helps the organization but not directly in the organization's formal reward system. (Khan & Ghufran, 2018, p. 2)
Organizational Commitment	(a) a desire (affective commitment), (b) a need (continuance commitment), and (c) an obligation (normative commitment) to maintain employment in an organization. (Meyer & Allen, 1991, p. 61)
Organizational Identification	A strategy in which employees feel personal attachments and identity with their organizations. (Asif et al., 2019, p. 178)
Organizational Justice	Organizational justice is concerned with employees' perceptions of how fairly they are treated by the organization. (H. J. Wang et al., 2015, p. 2)
Organizational Support	The dimension in which people believe that their organization considers their contributions and is concerned about their well-being. (Bohle et al., 2018, p. 396)
Perceived Control	The employees' situational appraisal of his or her ability to control the job insecure situation. (Elst et al., 2011, p. 216)
Psychological Capital	A multifaceted construct that consists of four positive personality strengths: self-efficacy, hope, resilience, and optimism. (Probst et al., 2017, p. 2)
Psychological Contract Breach	Contributions of the employee in terms of time, effort, and work attitude, versus promised benefits on the part of the employer, such as salary, appreciation, challenging work, or prospects for promotion. Psychological contract breach occurs when one party perceives another to have broken their promise. (Niesen et al., 2018, p. 3)
Psychological Distress	Opposite to psychological well-being. (Witte, 1999, p. 165)

continues on following page

Table 2. Continued

Variables	Definition
Rumination	The act of repetitively thinking about and dwelling on the insecure future of the job. By studying the relationship between job insecurity and rumination about job insecurity, we highlight the process of stress experiences.(Richter et al., 2020, p. 2)
Safety Performance	Work behaviours that are conducted in accordance with security and safety regulations within the organization. (Sverke et al., 2019, p. 5)
Self-Efficacy	The confidence that individual employee's exhibits in handling organisational related tasks and situations. (Adewale et al., 2020, p. 23)
Social Identity	Define the individual's place in society (…) and also guide their behaviour and evaluations. (Selenko et al., 2017, p. 858)
Social Protection	Social welfare regime and union density. (Sverke et al., 2019, p. 2)
Stress	The insight of an inconsistency between stressors and individual capabilities to fulfil these demands in the job environment. (Naru & Rehman, 2020, p. 310)
Supervisor and Coworker Support	Refer to all behaviours that superiors and colleagues perform to promote employee development. (Guo et al., 2019, p. 292)
Turnover	Changed to a job at another organization during the last year. (Richter et al., 2020, p. 4)
Turnover Intentions	Attitude, intention to quit. (Shoss et al., 2020, p. 298)
Uncertainty Avoidance	The level of stress and anxiety experienced by individuals in response to uncertain situation. (Roll et al., 2015, p. 167)
Well-being	Job satisfaction and mental health (Richter & Näswall, 2019, p. 25); a state of happiness and contentment, with low levels of distress, overall good physical and mental health and outlook, or good quality of life (VandenBos, 2007, p. 1155).
Work Engagement	Work engagement is defined as a persistent, positive, affective motivational state of fulfilment that is characterized by vigour, dedication, and absorption. Vigour refers to working highly energetically. Dedication refers to being strongly involved in work and experiencing a sense of significance, enthusiasm, inspiration, pride, and challenge. Absorption refers to being fully concentrated and happily engrossed in work. Highly engaged employees find their work interesting, meaningful, and energizing and experience positive affect, including happiness, joy, and enthusiasm. Hence, work engagement can be viewed as an active state where an employee experiences positive work-related affect and heightened motivation (H. J. Wang et al., 2015, p. 3).

According to the definition contents, it is possible to aggregate some variables into a single concept, as follows:

- Job satisfaction, general strain, psychological distress, negative affect, negative work relations, stress, job stress, emotional health complaints, physical health complaints and rumination, in the concept of *well-being*;
- Self-efficacy in the concept of *psychological capital*;
- Supervisor and co-worker support and organizational support in the concept of *support*;
- Need for closure and uncertainty avoidance in the concept of *uncertainty avoidance*;
- Job performance, innovative work behaviour, counterproductive work behaviour, organizational citizenship behaviour and safety performance in the concept of *performance*; we opted to add the variables turnover and turnover intentions, since they mean the minimum level of performance.

Aggregating the concepts as described, we obtain the following final variables, ordered by type of mediator / moderator relationship, which we will use from now on (Table 3):

Table 3. Type of relation

Variables	Type of Relation
Intrinsic Motivation	Mediation
Organizational Commitment	Mediation
Organizational Identification	Mediation
Organizational Justice	Mediation
Perceived Control	Mediation
Psychological Capital	Mediation
Psychological Contract Breach	Mediation
Social Identity	Mediation
Support	Mediation
Well-being	Mediation
Work Engagement	Mediation
Organizational Commitment	Moderation
Emotional Intelligence	Moderation
Ethical Leadership	Moderation
Informational Justice	Moderation
Organizational Justice	Moderation
Psychological Capital	Moderation
Support	Moderation
Uncertainty Avoidance	Moderation
Well-being	Moderation

We can illustrate the type of relation within the theoretical body analyzed using Graph 1 representation. Our option for designing moderation variables in the left lies on recent literature pointing out temporal precedence for moderation (Karazsia & Berlin, 2018; Kraemer, Kiernan, Essex, & Kupfer, 2008). In fact, authors argue that when moderation variables moderate an event, they were present before the event occurs and that this time precedence is crucial to distinguish moderation from mediation variables.

In this Figure 1, variables having a negative effect on performance were represented in red. Those that have a positive effect were represented in green.

The variables are aggregated in two sets, representing the moderating variables, on the left, and the mediating variables, positioned between *JI* and *performance*. This positioning intends to map the statistical foundation of the relationship of moderation and mediation. Moderation relationship describes the influence of a variable on the relationship between two others, but it is temporally antecedent to that relationship; in the case of mediation, the mediating variable has an effect temporally after the explanatory variable and it is through it that the effect on the variable of interest is produced (Karazsia & Berlin, 2018).

Figure 1. Variables Effect

According to Graph 1, in the last twenty years, literature has mainly described moderating variables with a positive effect on *performance* (such as *emotional intelligence* and *ethical leadership*) and mediating variables with a negative effect (for instance *intrinsic motivation* and *organizational commitment*).

Table 4. Theories

Appraisal Theory	**COR Theory**	**Person-Environment Fit Theory**	**Psychological Contract Theory**
Organizational Commitment	Emotional Intelligence	Well-being	Organizational Justice
Perceived Control	Informational Justice		Psychological Contract Breach
Psychological Capital	Psychological Capital		Support
Psychological Contract Breach	Support		Well-being
Well-being	Well-being		
Self-Determination Theory	**Social Exchange Theory**	**Social Identity Theory**	**Uncertainty Management Theory**
Intrinsic Motivation	Ethical Leadership	Organizational Identification	Organizational Justice
	Organizational Commitment	Social Identity	Work Engagement
	Organizational Identification	Well-being	
	Psychological Capital		
	Psychological Contract Breach		
	Support		
	Well-being		

To understand these relationships, we identified in the articles, as presented on Table 1, the use of eight theoretical models, for which we list the variables included in the respective studies (Table 4):

Most of the moderating and mediating variables explored to explain the relationship between *JI* and *performance* are framed with the following theories: Appraisal Theory, Conservation of Resources (COR) Theory, Psychological Contract Theory and Social Exchange Theory (table 4). The conceptual scope and the consequent explanatory power of these four theories make them more suitable to explain the complex relationship between the two main variables (*job insecurity* and *performance*), which, as we will see below, is less feasible with the other four theories used, Person-Environment Fit Theory, Self-Determination Theory, Social Identity Theory and Uncertainty Management Theory.

Theoretical Frameworks

We now revisit theories that frame the interpretation that the authors of the aforementioned studies used in their conclusions. We add the theoretical body of Trust, which seems to us to have an integrating potential, since all theories resort, in some way, to this concept.

It is our goal to evidence how these different theories explain the effects on job performance of employees' behaviours and attitudes. All of them use at least a concept that is common to Trust, as we will further argue.

Conservation of Resources Theory (COR), Appraisal Theory (AT) and Person-Environment Fit Theory (P-E Fit)

Conservation of Resources Theory (Hobfoll, 2002) it is a theory that argues that individuals are motivated by the acquisition of new resources and the protection and retention of resources they already have. Resources are defined as "anything perceived by the individual to help attain his or her goals" (Halbesleben, Neveu, Paustian-Underdahl, & Westman, 2014, p. 5) and can be *objects* (physical resources with utilitarian or status function), *conditions* (like marriage, tenure, seniority), *personal characteristics* (orientation towards the world that increases stress resistance) and *energies* (like money, time and knowledge, that help getting other resources) (Hobfoll, 1989).

The loss or threat of loss of resources induces stress that is more salient than the gain of resources, producing a much greater negative emotional impact than the acquisition of resources produces a positive impact.

To acquire resources or to prevent the loss of resources the individual needs to invest resources, hence it is more likely to gain resources for those who already have more resources, and the investment can lead to resource depletion, causing strain and stress, for those who have less resources. For this reason, and also because the resources are organized in groups (caravans), the loss of resources generates a spiral of loss, just as the gain of resources generates a spiral of gains. In fact, if the individual loses his job, he will lose part of the interpersonal relationships that are related to his job, as well as his salary and other benefits. In the same way, getting a job after being unemployed will also bring in several resources at the same time.

An extension of COR Theory states that trust is not a resource, because it is also under the control of another person, but it is used as a sign that the investment of resources will succeed in meeting the goal of obtaining more resources (Halbesleben & Wheeler, 2015).

A competing theory to explain both stress and motivation is Appraisal Theory (Lazarus & Folkman, 1984) which essentially differs from COR theory in that it first understands stress as a result of individual perception and, only secondly, as a result of the requirement of the situation. In fact, Hobfoll points out the importance of the individual's interpretation of the amount of resources he has to face resources gain and retain efforts, but argues that the requirement of the situation, by itself, is directly responsible for the stress response that presents little individual variability and even between cultures (Hobfoll, Halbesleben, Neveu, & Westman, 2018). These arguments make COR theory more suited to the organizational context, than Appraisal Theory (Taris, Schreurs, & Van Iersel-Van Silfhout, 2001), so we follow it in this work.

Person-Environment Fit theory explains stress as a lack of correspondence between the person's characteristics and the demands of the context. More specifically, the theory is divided into two parts: one that focuses on the correspondence between the resources of the context and the motivations, objectives and personal values; another that concerns the correspondence between the requirements of the context and the personal skills and abilities. The subjective evaluation of misfit produces tension and stress (Edwards, Caplan, & Harrison, 1998). The concept of P-E fit was, however, positioned as a resource, with integration in COR theory (Wheeler & Halbesleben, 2009), so we follow COR theory in this theoretical spectrum.

Psychological Contract Theory (PCT)

Psychological Contracts are individual beliefs in a reciprocal obligation between the individual and the organization (Rousseau, 1989, p. 121). It is not about expectations on one's job beyond what is perceived as agreed on topics as work environment or decoration of physical workplace, but specifically about what you will receive in return for complying with obligations (Robinson, 1996). It is the individual's belief that there is an obligation of reciprocity that guides their behavior, but this belief does not affect the behavior of the other party, because it is an individual belief. However, the more explicit and public the contract and the longer the individual's contribution and the organization's reciprocity lasts, the stronger the individual's belief that there is a psychological contract that requires reciprocity (Rousseau, 1989).

Literature distinguishes between transactional and relational psychological contract: the first refers to responsibilities and roles at work and focuses on economic and performance factors; the second refers to long-term relationship and achieves non-economic exchanges. One of the expectations included in the relational contract is job security, in exchange for employee loyalty (Niesen et al., 2018; Richter & Näswall, 2019).

Psychological contract breach is the perception that the other party has failed to fulfill the obligations of the psychological contract (Rousseau, 1989). It is a subjective experience that has negative effects on job satisfaction, organizational commitment and job performance (De Cuyper & De Witte, 2007; Vander Elst et al., 2016).

Trust in the organisation is understood as a prerequisite for a stable psychological contract (Richter & Näswall, 2019).

Social Exchange Theory (SET)

According to Social Exchange Theory (SET) (Blau, 1964), people build relationships at work that are based on material or emotional exchanges and it is these exchanges that are the basis of attitudes such as commitment (Cropanzano & Mitchell, 2005; Cropanzano, Rupp, & Byrne, 2003). These exchange relationships are framed by rules established between those involved, or to which those involved adhere, and with time and repeated favorable exchanges, these relationships evolve towards trust (Cropanzano & Mitchell, 2005; Dirks & Ferrin, 2002).

Social exchanges involve favors that create obligations of reciprocity, which must be fulfilled, although it is not clearly established what obligation is to be fulfilled. The success of several reciprocal exchanges develops trust. This consequence is faster in reciprocal exchange relations, in which no obligation is defined, than in negotiated exchange relations, typical of contracts or businesses, in which is defined what is to be received. The risk and uncertainty are lower in negotiated exchange ratios, but the development of trust is slower, or may never happen, depending on the reliability of the social actors involved (Molm, Takahashi, & Peterson, 2000).

It should be noted that the greater the inequality of exchanges (the more power of one of the players over the other) or the lower the risk of the relationship (more details of the relationship negotiated and defined), the lower the trust generated (Molm et al., 2000). Trust needs a risk factor, in which taking the first step with no guarantee of reciprocity is assessed as proof of good intentions. The negotiated exchange does not create an obligation to reciprocate and closes the relationship in the deal.

An employment contract is a case of a negotiated exchange relationship, in which to time and execution of tasks corresponds a remuneration, among other possible counterparts. However, this relationship corresponds frequently to unequal exchanges, derived from the power that employer has over the employee, and the fact that the employer is less dependent on the employee (he has other employees as an alternative) than the employee is on the employer. Thus, an employment relationship is a situation in which there is a high probability of generating low trust, but this can be increased with a reciprocal exchange relationship, not defined in the employment contract, but performed spontaneously (Molm, 2010).

If predictability of obtaining a reciprocal response is high, that is, if behavior is consistent and allows us to successfully anticipate that a reciprocal response will occur, the greater the trust created (Molm, Schaefer, Collett, Mouvt, & Schfl, 2007).

Normative commitment, induced by social exchange, and uncertainty reduction explains the increased performance that the organizational trust produces (Colquitt et al., 2012).

Trust is, therefore, closely related to social exchanges and consistent and predictable reciprocity.

Social Identity Theory (SIT)

Based on social categorization, Social Identity Theory (SIT) argues that social groups we belong to form a significant part of our self-concept (Van Dick, Ullrich, & Tissington, 2006) and that people strive to maintain or enhance their self-esteem and a positive social identity, which makes them join groups that have positive value connotation; if social identity turns out to be unsatisfactory by individuals evaluation, they leave the group to a more positive one, or try to change their group, acting inside to turn it into a more positively distinct one (Tajfel & Turner, 1986).

Job insecurity also threatens social identity because the group of employees is more socially valued than the unemployed group. This threat has effects on well-being, due to the marginalization the individual anticipates, and on performance, due to the reduction of efforts that exceed the expected (Selenko et al., 2017). In addition to the need of identification with the group of employees, the need for affiliation that organization satisfies also has an impact on well-being, which is deeper the greater the identification with the organization (Van Dick et al., 2006).

The identification of the employee with the work team, with the department, with the job he performs or only with a leader, tends to be generalized to other levels, being able to encompass the entire organization (Ashforth & Johnson, 2001). Identification with the organization is one of the components of the *benevolence* dimension of Trust, as we will see below and was defined in isolation in two multi-dimensional models (Lewicki & Bunker, 1995; Shapiro, Sheppard, & Cheraskin, 1992).

Uncertainty Management Theory (UMT)

Uncertainty Management Theory (UMT) (Lind & van den Bos, 2002) argues that fairness judgments become more salient in an uncertainty context, with fairness decreasing negative affect or increasing positive affect (van den Bos, 2001) and that in situations of job insecurity when information about the organization's trustworthiness is missing, people use data on fairness treatment to form impressions about the organization (Lind & van den Bos, 2002). This means that in an uncertainty environment people are more focused on fairness information and use it to rule emotions, attitudes, and behaviours, reacting particularly well to fair treatment and particularly badly to unfair treatment under uncertainty conditions.

Uncertainty is present in the perception of job insecurity, with effects on well-being (Witte, 1999), in attitudes and performance (Piccoli et al., 2017).

Fairness is one of the components of the *integrity* dimension of trustworthiness (Mayer, Davis, & Schoorman, 1995), which reinforces the suggestion that trust may be the aggregating concept of the interpretation of the effects of job insecurity on attitudes and behaviors, namely job performance.

Self-determination Theory (SDT)

SDT is a theory of motivation, personality development and well-being, centered on three types of psychological needs: autonomy, competence and relatedness (Deci & Ryan, 2008).

Autonomy refers to the need to control one's own choices and to have psychological freedom over how to carry out his activities; Competence indicates the need to experience efficiency and expertise in knowledge; Relatedness refers to connecting with significant people and being accepted as a member of a group.

The theory distinguishes two types of motivation:

- *autonomous motivation*, which includes the intrinsic motivation and the motivation associated with the value of the function, being mainly generated internally.
- *controlled motivation* is regulated externally by incentives and punishments, although part of this regulation of action has been internalized.

The two types of motivation lead to action, but to different experiences: autonomous motivation leads to *volition* and transferring responsibility to oneself; controlled motivation leads to pressure to think and act in a particular way, which is induced by feelings of shame, avoidance and contingent self-esteem.

Literature shows that autonomous motivation is linked to organizational trust (Deci, Olafsen, & Ryan, 2017; Gagné & Deci, 2005; W. T. Wang, 2016) and behavioral trust interacts with basic motivational needs (autonomy, competence and relatedness) to impact work engagement (Heyns & Rothmann, 2018).

Until now, we have highlighted common aspects/concepts of these different theories with Trust theory. Summarizing:

- Conservation of Resources Theory states that trust is used as a sign that the investment of resources will succeed in meeting the goal of obtaining more resources;
- Psychological Contract Theory establishes that trust in the organization is understood as a prerequisite for a stable psychological contract;
- Social Exchange Theory is based on predictability of reciprocal exchange, being predictability a core trust concept;
- Social Identity Theory states that our self-concept includes social groups we belong to and trust encompasses the identification concept;
- Uncertainty Management Theory highlights fairness as a salient feature to deal with uncertainty environments, concept that also included in trust;
- Self-determination Theory links basic psychological needs to trust.

Trust – The Integrating Concept?

As we have seen so far, there are several theories presented by the authors to understand the results of empirical studies that relate *job insecurity* with *performance*, through mediating variables, or in the presence of moderating variables. All these theories are related to trust, which is why we decided to study the topic, with a view to testing it as an integrative concept.

Trust being a concept that:

- emerges from adaptive behaviors and skills in the course of evolution, common to several species of animals (referred to as cooperation) and developed for the survival of individuals (Bateson, 1988);
- that human being is able to decide facial trustworthiness, competence and aggressiveness in 100 milliseconds (Willis & Todorov, 2006) and that decisions of trustworthiness are unconsciously and automatically made in the amygdala brain region (Engell, Haxby, & Todorov, 2007), a part of the brain older than the cortex;
- that research shows the Organizational Trust's connection to various behaviours and attitudes, such as Affective Commitment (Hopkins & Weathington, 2006), Normative Commitment (Colquitt et al., 2012), job satisfaction (Hopkins & Weathington, 2006), Risk Taking (Colquitt et al., 2007), organizational citizenship behaviour (Colquitt et al., 2007), Turnover Intentions (Hopkins & Weathington, 2006), Uncertainty (Colquitt et al., 2012);
- that, in addition to explaining variations in the teams' performance (DeJong, 2016) and organizations (Davis et al., 2000), it explains variations in the Gross Domestic Product (GDP) of countries (Zak & Knack, 2001),

it has the potential to constitute the integrating element of the effect of psychological factors on performance, in an organizational context. As we can see, trust is an ancient phenomenon in the development of the human species and the concept is used in sciences for different purposes.

Human behavior presents details that contributed to individual survival and the evolution of the species. One is the ability to predict the behavior of other individuals, allowing a quicker and more effective reaction to a threat.

Organizational psychology has developed several concepts that are based on this ability to predict the behaviour of others and adapt the response: trust, psychological security, involvement, psychological

Job Insecurity and Performance

contract, empowerment. A recent meta-analysis (Frazier, Fainshmidt, Klinger, Pezeshkan, & Vracheva, 2017) on psychological security explains the difference between trust and other of these concepts (psychological security, empowerment and involvement) as the desire to be vulnerable to the behavior of others, in the case of trust, and to give the benefit of the doubt, in the case of the other concepts. The dichotomous organization of the concepts leads us to the possibility of a gradation between them, where trust would be the next level to the confirmation of characteristics to which, first, we give the benefit of the doubt. In the same sense, literature has pointed out that trust is not a resource but a signal that investment of resources will have success in achieving the individual goals (Halbesleben & Wheeler, 2015) and that perceptions of justice (one of the dimensions of trustworthiness, as we will see further) serve as signal that resource investment is worthy. Justice, determined by attribution processes, influences the level of perceived support from the organization and reduces psychological withdrawal and job burnout (Campbell, Perry, Maertz, Allen, & Griffeth, 2013).

Trust has been defined as willingness to be vulnerable to another person based on the expectation that the other person will act positively (Mayer et al., 1995; Rousseau, Sitkin, Burt, & Camerer, 1998), the expectation that costs and benefits, knowledge of the other, degree of shared values and identity have positive reciprocation (Lewicki, Tomlinson, & Gillespie, 2006) or one's expectations, assumptions, or beliefs about the likelihood that another's future actions will be beneficial, favorable, or at least not detrimental to one's interests (Robinson, 1996, p. 576). Trust needs a history of reciprocity in the social exchange so employees feel the obligation to exchange resources (Kramer, 1999) and evolves in time positively or negatively with upcoming exchanges (Lewicki et al., 2006). Trust evolves also in organization level: the leader's trustful behaviour creates trust in the leader, and that trust in the leader predicts trust in the organization (Legood, Thomas, & Sacramento, 2016).

In a trust relation three parts intervene: the characteristics of a truster, the properties of a trustee and a context in which the relation develops (Hardin, 1996). The characteristics of the truster gave rise to several works and generically analyse the individual propensity to trust. The properties of the trustee, trustworthiness, are the qualities of those who deserve trust (Mayer et al., 1995). Both are necessary to create trust (Mayer et al., 1995), but literature clear support that the best device for creating trust is to establish and support trustworthiness (Hardin, 1996).

In this work, we will only address the qualities of the trustee, which the literature calls trustworthiness.

Trust Theory

Trust is described in literature as a multidimensional concept, which includes cognitive, affective and intentional elements (Lewicki et al., 2006), although several authors point out different dimensions to it.

We identified models that point dimensions for the trustworthiness of a trustee, and it was possible to find ten different models. Models do not have the same number of dimensions and the designations assigned to each dimension are also different.

In the table below, we present the models with each of the dimensions identified by the authors and the description given them respectively. In each of the lines can be found the complete model, and the arrangement in columns that we think best illustrate the coincidence of the contents, supported in the designation attributed by the author and/or in the description that the author gave to it.

Although the model of Clark and Payne is the same as that used by Butler and Cantrell, we decided to consider it in this work, since they tested the possibility of including a new dimension, Respect Shown, that came to verify to be included in the dimensions Consistency, Loyalty and Openness (Clark, Payne,

Journal, & May, 1997). Thus, although the resulting model is the same model of departure, the work of Clark and Payne contributed to confirm the previous model (Butler & Cantrell, 1984), as it had been presented.

It has been consensual for authors that the construction of a trust relationship evolves from a more cognitive stage to a more affective one (Costa, Fulmer, & Anderson, 2017). Shapiro proposes an evolution of deterrence-based trust, knowledge-based trust and identification-based trust (Shapiro et al., 1992); Lewicki and Bunker suggest the same types of trust as Shapiro, but substitute deterrence-based trust for calculus-based trust, following Deutsch (1973) and his argument for calculating the likelihood of consequences that will arise from trust breach or benefits for maintaining expected behaviour (Lewicki & Bunker, 1995); McAllister restricts evolution to cognitive-based trust and affective-based trust (McAllister, 1995).

A less consensual aspect is the distinction between the concepts of trust and distrust (Costa et al., 2017): there are authors who understand that distrust is not only the absence of trust, but the probability of an unpleasant situation occur, predisposing the individual to adopt defensive behaviours (Lewicki, McAllister, & Bies, 1998); others, more recently, understand trust and distrust as the opposite poles of a single scale, with mistrust corresponding to low trust (Pugh, Skarlicki, & Passell, 2003; Schoorman, Mayer, & Davis, 2007).

Some authors point to several dimensions for trustworthiness of a trustee, resulting in several types of trust, capable of existing separately (Clark et al., 1997; Kasperson, Golding, & Tuler, 1992; Mayer et al., 1995; McAllister, 1995; Shapiro et al., 1992; Whitener & Werner, 1998). Relying on someone's competence to perform a task does not mean trusting that the same person will not take advantage of our frailty when it is possible or will always seek to benefit us.

In the following Table 5, we summarize the dimensions found:

We wanted to summarize all the different dimensions identified by the authors, so we decided to compare the descriptions looking for common elements that allowed us to isolate unique concepts.

From the authors' proposals (titles and description), we were able to report on six different dimensions, although none of the authors used more than five dimensions to describe trust. We attribute the identification and description that seemed to best illustrate the content of each dimension.

In the following table 6 we summarize the model that results from this work:

One of the dimensions, *competence*, refers only to the prediction of skills and knowledge to perform a task or fulfill a responsibility successfully. All other dimensions refer to the character of the trustee, which allows to predict its general behavior (Colquitt et al., 2007).

The Relation Between Job Insecurity, Performance and Trust

Job Insecurity undermines employer trust building (Pfeffer, 2007) because *JI* is perceived to be included in the traditional psychological contract, in exchange for employee loyalty (Niesen et al., 2018; Richter & Näswall, 2019). In *JI*, as we saw earlier, the employee's perceptions about downsizing contexts are included, but also about the loss of job quality and the failure to keep promises. Psychological contract breach also appears in the literature as a mediator between trust and performance (Robinson, 1996) and the employer's own behaviour, when it reveals distrust in its employees, generates distrust in them, through reciprocity.

Table 5. Trustworthiness dimensions

Trustworthiness Models	Consistency	Integrity	Openness	Loyalty	Competence
(Butler & Cantrell, 1984, p. 19)	Reliability, predictability and good judgement in handling situations.	Honesty and Truthfulness	Mental accessibility, a willingness to share ideas and information freely.	Benevolent motives, willingness to protect and save face for a person.	Technical and interpersonal knowledge and skills required to do one's job.
(Kasperson et al., 1992, p. 170)	Uncompromised commitment to a mission or goal; Objectivity and fairness in decision processes and the provision of accurate information.	Predictability		Caring	Competence
	Commitment	Expectations fullfilment.		Act in a way that shows concern for and beneficence to trusting individuals.	Technical competency in their mandated area of responsibility.
(Shapiro et al., 1992, pp. 366, 369, 371)	Knowledge-Based Trust	Deterrance-Based Trust		Identification-Based Trust	
	Behaviour predictability based on knowledge and understanding.	Consistency of behaviour; Reliability.		Full internalization of the other's preferences.	
(Lewicki & Bunker, 1995, p. 149,151,153)	Knowledge-Based Trust	Calculus-Based Trust		Identification-Based Trust	
	Grounded on predictability of behaviour	Founded on consistency and on deterrence		Full internalization of the other's desires and intentions	
(McAllister, 1995, pp. 25–26)				Cognitive Trust	Affective Trust
				Reliability, Dependability and Emotional Security	Competence and Responsibility
(Mayer et al., 1995, pp. 717–719)		Integrity		Benevolence	Ability
		Fairness, Justice, Consistency, and Promise fulfilment		Loyalty, Openness, Caring or Supportiveness	Knowledge and Skills

continues on following page

Table 5. Continued

Trustworthiness Models	Trustworthiness Dimensions				
	Reliability			Openness	Concern	Competence
(Mishra, 1996, pp. 6–9)	Expectations about consistent or reliable behaviour				One party believes that it will not be taken unfair advantage of by another	Technical expertise
(Clark et al., 1997, p. 208)	**Consistent Behavior**		Integrity	Honesty	Loyalty	Competence
	Consistency, Fairness, Predictability, Discretion and Good Judgement		Sincerity, Honesty, Truthfulness and Promises' fulfilment		Benevolent motives associated with intentions, motives, shared values and goals; Commitment to and willingness to protect and save face for a person	The technical, interpersonal knowledge and skills required to do one's job, decision making and role performance.
(Whitener & Werner, 1998, pp. 516–517)	**Behavioural Consistency**	Sharing and Delegation of Control	**Behavioural Integrity**	Communication	Demonstration of Concern for Employees Needs	
	Reliability and Predictability	Employees participate in decision; Managers share control	Telling the truth; Keeping promises	Accurate information; Explanations for decisions; Openness	Consideration and sensitivity for employees needs and interests; Acting in a way that protects employees' interests; Refraining from exploiting others for the benefit of one's own interests	
(Dietz & Den Hartog, 2006, p. 560)	Predictability		Integrity		Benevolence	Competence
	Relates specifically to consistency and regularity of behaviour		Involves adherence to a set of principles acceptable to the other party, encompassing honesty and fair treatment, and the avoidance of hypocrisy		Reflects benign motives and a personal degree of kindness toward the other party, and a genuine concern for their welfare	Refers to the other party's capabilities to carry out her/his obligations (in terms of skills and knowledge)

Table 6. Trustworthiness dimensions resume

Trustworthiness Dimensions					
Predictability	**Integrity**	**Delegation**	**Openness**	**Benevolence**	**Competence**
Relates specifically to consistency and regularity of behaviour	Involves adherence to a set of principles acceptable to the other party, encompassing honesty and fair treatment, and the avoidance of hypocrisy	Employees participate in decision; Managers share control	Accurate information; Explanations for decisions; Mental accessibility and availability	Reflects benign motives and a personal degree of kindness toward the other party, and a genuine concern for their welfare	Refers to the other party's capabilities to carry out her/his obligations (in terms of skills and knowledge)

JI has a negative association with trust (Ashford, Lee, & Bobko, 1989; Cheng & Chan, 2008; Richter & Näswall, 2019; Sverke et al., 2002) and trust relates positively to performance (Davis et al., 2000; Mayer & Gavin, 2005; Vanhala & Dietz, 2019; Verburg et al., 2018). Job insecurity has a negative effect on performance via work engagement, but when organizational justice (one of the dimensions of trustworthiness) is low (H. J. Wang et al., 2015). The perception of justice is also generated by the collective distribution of rewards (Pfeffer, 2007), which is higher in private companies than in public ones, and that the authors suggest derives from compensation for greater job insecurity (Monteiro, Portela, & Straume, 2011).

To our knowledge, only a meta-analysis on job insecurity found no significant relationship between trust and performance (Sverke et al., 2002), but this fact was interpreted by the authors as being due to the difficulty in evaluating performance and the consequent use of self-report measures, where respondents tend to overestimate their own performance.

SOLUTIONS AND RECOMMENDATIONS

Resuming the analysis of the variables that we presented at the beginning of this work (figure 1) we propose in this section to discuss all the relations found simultaneously between variables (intrinsic motivation; psychological contract breach; organizational commitment; organizational justice, etc.) both with a mediation and/or moderation effect in performance, using/in the light of the theories that we referred to previously (COR, PCT, SET, SIT, UMT and SDT theories). We will point out as we intent to analyze JI-Performance relation, the minor coverage or some lack of scope of these theories when we look for a more comprehensive theoretical frame on this particular subject.

Finally, we will use *Trust Theory* for this interpretation, as we propose the recognition of Trust as an integrative and useful concept to understand the influence of employees in performance, in particular JI- Performance relation.

Using Conservation of Resources Theory (COR Theory)

In a *JI* context, there is a need to invest resources to prevent job loss. Those who have more resources, such as *emotional intelligence, psychological capital, well-being, organizational justice, support* and *ethical leadership*, are better positioned to gain or retain resources. This is the case with these variables as moderators, which reduce the impact of *JI* on *performance*.

Organizational commitment is not a resource, so it cannot be understood as a moderating variable, in the light of this theory. As a mediating variable, it can be understood as a state that corresponds to a change in resources and that has an impact on performance. The same reasoning is valid for the variables *intrinsic motivation*, *organizational identification*, *work engagement* and even to *well-being*, that is simultaneously a state and a resource (Hobfoll et al., 2018).

Psychological capital, *social identity* and *emotional intelligence* are resources that, in the function of mediating variables are depleted, generating defensive withdrawal for resource conservation.

Organizational justice, *perceived control* and *support*, as part of trust dimensions, may serve as signals that resource loss will not be severe. On the other hand, *psychological contract breach* can be a sign that the loss of resources could be significant, inducing conservation of resources.

Using Psychological Contract Theory

The effect of *psychological contract breach* on *well-being* and performance is immediately understandable through the breach in the expectation of receiving security, in exchange for employee loyalty. The fact that the most serious effects of *JI* on *well-being* are felt by permanent employees can be explained by having more expectations than temporary employees (Cheng & Chan, 2008; De Cuyper & De Witte, 2007; Richter & Näswall, 2019).

The remaining variables do not fit this theory.

Using Social Exchange Theory (SET)

According to SET, the norm of reciprocity encourages a sense of obligation of reciprocity appropriate to the individual's perception of the other's behavior. In the context of *Job Insecurity*, it is expected that employees will lower their efforts and performance will be affected according to this perception of unfair exchange on the part of the organization.

SET was used to interpret variables that are based on perceptions about employer behaviour, such as ethical leadership and *support*, or attitudinal variables, such as *organizational commitment* or *organizational identification*. In the case of personality traits, they are already difficult to explain in light of this theory because they are variables that do not result from organization's behavior, so it is not expected that they will impact performance through the reciprocity mechanism.

However, some researchers reporting the moderation of *psychological capital* (Probst et al., 2017) uses SET to discuss the results, but only the impact of *Job Insecurity* on *Performance*. *Psychological capital* intervenes in the relationship between these two variables with a moderating role and this moderation is interpreted using COR Theory.

Using Social Identity Theory

Job Insecurity affects the *social identity* of the individual by the threat of marginalization in the group of employees, which has more social value than the group of unemployed. Feeling marginalized from a valuable group, the employee is likely to feel less identified with the group of employees and lessen their effort at work. This theory was used to describe the effect of variables such as *social identity* and *organizational identification* (Asif et al., 2019; Selenko et al., 2017), but it doesn't suit personality traits variables like *psychological capital* or *emotional intelligence*.

Using Uncertainty Management Theory (UMT)

This theory allows us to understand the impact of of *uncertainty avoidance* on *well-being* (van den Bos, 2001; Witte, 1999), through the moderation of *fairness*, which when present reduces affective expression (concerns about the possibility of job loss). Here, it was used to interpret the moderating effect of *organizational justice* on the relationship between JI and performance and also the mediating effect of *work engagement* (H. J. Wang et al., 2015). For the same variable, *organizational justice*, Piccoli (Piccoli et al., 2017) uses both SET and Psychological Contract Theory to explain mediation.

Being a theory that requires the presence of *fairness* to be applicable, it does not adapt to the remaining relationships of variables.

Using Self-determination Theory (SDT)

Being a theory of motivation, development and well-being, it is possible to understand the mediating and moderating effect of the variable's *intrinsic motivation* and *work engagement* (need for autonomy) *psychological capital* and *emotional intelligence* (need for competence) in well-*being* and *performance*. Yet the variables, *organizational commitment, organizational identification* and *social identity*, can fit into the concept of *autonomous motivation*. However, the effects of *ethical leadership, informational justice, organizational justice, support, uncertainty avoidance, perceived control* and *psychological contract breach* are not explainable.

What if We Use Trust?

Resuming the analysis of the variables that moderate or mediate the relation between JI and performance, aggregated and represented in Graph 1, we found that some of them correspond to the description of trustworthiness dimensions that resulted from our work (Table 6). Specifically, we compared the variables found in the studies whose description corresponds to the description of the dimensions (see Table 1), concluding that they can be included in the concept of trustworthiness (Table 7).

All other variables remain classified in the types defined above (personality traits and perceptions; attitudes and states), following in our study.

It should be noted that the dimensions of trust that represent the largest number of the above variables (Table 7) are *integrity* and *benevolence*, precisely those that are considered to be the most relevant for employees to develop trust in leaders and in the organization (Krot & Lewicka, 2012; Pirson & Malhotra, 2011).

The remaining variables that didn´t fit *Trustworthiness Dimensions* are: *emotional intelligence, organizational commitment, psychological capital, well-being, social identity* and work *engagement*, i.e., Personality Traits type and States type (see Table 1).

Now, representing the variables by type, we reach the following summary (Graph 2):

Table 7. Integrating variables in trustworthiness dimensions

Trustworthiness Dimensions					
Predictability	**Integrity**	**Delegation**	**Openness**	**Benevolence**	**Competence**
Relates specifically to consistency and regularity of behaviour	Involves adherence to a set of principles acceptable to the other party, encompassing honesty and fair treatment, and the avoidance of hypocrisy	Employees participate in decision; Managers share control	Accurate information; Explanations for decisions; Mental accessibility and availability	Reflects benign motives and a personal degree of kindness toward the other party, and a genuine concern for their welfare	Refers to the other party's capabilities to carry out her/his obligations (in terms of skills and knowledge)
Uncertainty Avoidance	Organizational Justice		Informational Justice	Support	
	Ethical Leadership			Psychological Contract Breach	
				Organizational Identification	
				Perceived Control	

Figure 2. Type of Variables

Keeping the mediating and moderating variables in the position we explained above, we can see that the moderators are mainly of Trustworthiness-type (marked in blue) and Personality Traits-type (in gray); most of the mediating variables are again of Trustworthiness type (in blue) and now also of State-type (in yellow).

Job Insecurity and Performance

When we try to interpret the entire set of variables with the theoretical body of trust, we are immediately faced with moderation variables of personality traits type (such as *emotional intelligence, psychological capital,* etc.), which refer to the employee, and its effect cannot be understood through trust that, to a large extent, is under the control of the trustee. State-type variables (such as *work engagement, organizational commitment,* etc.) as moderators, are also not interpretable, although we can understand them as mediators and as variables of interest, some of them described in literature, like *well-being,* for example (Campbell et al., 2013; Hopkins & Weathington, 2006).

Summarizing the main types of variables, we will have:

Figure 3. Relations between Main Types of Variables

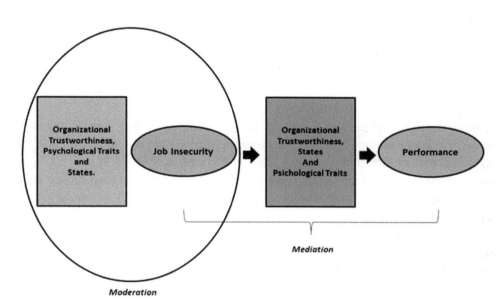

Our option for designing moderation variables in the left lies on recent literature pointing out temporal precedence for moderation (Karazsia & Berlin, 2018; Kraemer, Kiernan, Essex, & Kupfer, 2008), as explained above.

In Graph 3 we find the main types of variables used throughout the analyzed empirical set. We found that the variables that belong to the dimensions of trustworthiness appear as moderators and mediators, which is congruent with the complexity of the concept:

- As a moderator, it works as a signal that allows us to foresee the possibility of success in investing resources to achieve goals (Halbesleben & Wheeler, 2015), a guideline that influences the interpretations of social behaviors (Robinson, 1996) and the expectation of positive reciprocal exchanges (Lewicki et al., 2006) or at least not unfavorable (Robinson, 1996);
- As a mediator, it adapts to reciprocity of social exchanges (Kramer, 1999) and evolves positively or negatively with them (Lewicki et al., 2006), spreading through the various organizational levels (Legood et al., 2016).

This set (Graph 3) can be interpreted as follows:

- Moderation - In the presence of trust (deduced from the trustworthiness dimensions that create trust) and in the presence of personality traits and states, the negative impact of JI on performance will be smaller;
- JI reduces employee trust and employee States and these reduce or worsen performance.

In Graph 2 still appear variables included in personality traits and states among moderating variables included in states, also as mediators. If we retrieve the information from Table 4, we find that the most used theory to explain the effects of personality traits is COR Theory and for States is SET.

Now analyzing the interpretation of all moderating variables in Graph 2 with these two theories, together with the theoretical body of Trust, we will have:

- *Emotional intelligence*, *psychological capital* and *well-being* resources (personal resources type) function as moderators of the relationship between JI and performance, according to COR theory, reducing the impact on stress due to the abundance of resources to invest in process of avoiding job loss or gaining an alternative resource.
- *Ethical leadership, organizational justice, informational justice* and *support* (Trust theory), as moderators, can serve as signals that the investment of resources (COR theory) and the expected exchanges will benefit the employee, or at least, will not harm him (SET);
- *Uncertainty Avoidance*, as a moderator, may mean a sign of imminent trust breach in the employer's predictability of benefiting the employee, or not harming him (SET); it can also be understood as a negative passageway, predictor of a negative spiral, with consequences of work exhaustion (COR theory) (Hobfoll et al., 2018);
- *Organizational commitment*, as a moderator, can be understood as a previous disinvestment of resources in the continuation of employment, making the impact of JI on performance weaker, due to less recruitment of resources to counteract it (COR theory); the only study that works this variable as a moderator (Chirumbolo & Areni, 2005) confirms that the moderating effect only occurs when organizational commitment is low, an effect that disappears when organizational commitment is high.

Such exercise with the mediating variables, results in:

- *Intrinsic motivation, organizational commitment,* and *work engagement* can be understood as the negative effect on States, which results from the perception of JI as unfair in exchange for employee loyalty (SET); simultaneously, they will correspond to the effect of conservation of resources and prevention of loss spirals, divesting in the work relationship/employment (COR theory);
- *Psychological capital, social identity, emotional intelligence* and *well-being* (personal resources type), correspond to the depletion of resources that occurs in an attempt to preserve employment and seek alternatives for earning resources corresponding to the employee's objectives (COR theory);
- *Organizational justice, organizational identification, perceived control, psychological contract breach* and *support* result from the adaptation of these perceptions to the reciprocity of social

exchanges (Trust theory, SET), evolving positively or negatively, according to these exchanges (Trust theory, SET).

FUTURE RESEARCH DIRECTIONS

The evidence collected in literature and shown in this chapter advise JI-Performance researchers to include trust or its various dimensions:

- in cross-sectional studies as a moderating variable;
- in longitudinal studies as both moderating and mediating variable, in order to pursue a better understanding of its influence as a signal of the context in which the relationship occurs, as well as the impact of its evolution, after social exchange events.

This reorientation in the research of the subject could contribute to HRM by pointing out clues to reduce the impact of JI on performance, to avoid the development of JI and also to repair its effects.

CONCLUSION

The relationship between *JI* and *performance* has received the attention of researchers and the phenomenon can be considered well documented (Cheng & Chan, 2008; Jiang & Lavaysse, 2018; Sverke et al., 2002, 2019). In recent years, efforts to clarify the process by which *JI* has an effect on *employee performance* have produced interesting analyses of the effect of mediating and moderating variables, but its full understanding remains to be determined. Concretely, the way in which *JI* influences *performance* has found partial explanations in several studies, through mediating and moderating variables.

The objective of this work was to revisit theories that frame the evidence found in literature on *JI* and *performance*, comprising literature that tests moderating and mediating variables to explain how the effect is produced. Using a systematic review of published literature between 2000 and 2020, we have identified 31 studies that meet our research criteria and summarized the studied variables, explained by the eight theories chosen by the authors of the research to explain the effect.

The second objective was to reflect on the theoretical framework of Trust as a possibility to aggregate the interpretations that have been based on different theories, to understand the results obtained in each work.

We conclude that the interpretation of all the works cited, including all the variables used, is not feasible with any of the theories in isolation, nor with the theoretical body of Trust. However, by adding COR and SET theories to Trust, we were able to analyze the results of all variables simultaneously.

The explanatory capacity of these theories together (COR theory and SET) extends to the entire empirical set, allowing the elimination of other theoretical frameworks, as long as the theoretical body of trust is also added to explain the relationship between *JI* and *performance*. This COR-SET alliance, where resources and social exchanges have well-established explanatory rules, seems to occur under Trust framework, which serves as a signal (Halbesleben & Wheeler, 2015) that allows to foresee the possibility of success in investing resources to achieve goals, inhibiting or disinhibiting resource exchanges, and adapts itself as a signal, after integrate information on social exchanges.

The need to repeat the interaction or observe the behavior of the trustee to create and consolidate trust (Molm, Takahashi, & Peterson, 2003), its role as a marker of expectations (Halbesleben & Wheeler, 2015) and its evolution with experience (Lewicki et al., 2006), suggest the existence of a circuit, which is built and rebuilt.

In schematic representation, the framework for explaining how *JI* impacts *performance* through mediating variables and in the presence of moderating variables, could be described as follows (Graph 4):

Figure 4. Integrative Theoretical Framework

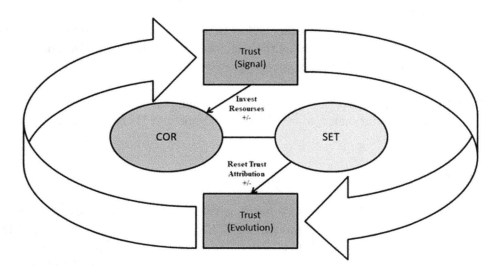

According to literature, trust that can be originated in an exchange relationship stems from the attribution of causality by the truster to the behavior of the trustee and the evaluation that truster makes of trustee's dispositional characteristics, that is, on its trustworthiness (Molm et al., 2003).

Trust attribution seems to work in this relationship between JI and Performance, as has been described in other relationships (Halbesleben & Wheeler, 2015), as a signal to invest or not to invest resources in order to acquire or protect resources, a signal that is confirmed or adapted (in an attribution reset) after verifying exchange fairness. The link between COR and SET has been used in literature, either directly (Probst et al., 2017), either through Psychological Contract Theory, derived from SET (Taris et al., 2001), which may suggest the concentration of future research on the theoretical bases identified in the Integrative Theoretical Framework presented in Graph 4, as we present and argue in this text.

REFERENCES

Adewale, A. A., & Dahiru, I., MukhtarShehu, A., & Kofar-Mata, B. A. (2020). Perceived Job Insecurity and Task Performance among Bank Employees in Nigeria Banking Industry: The Role of Emotional-Intelligence and Self-Efficacy. *Accounting and Taxation Review*, *4*(2), 13–32.

Ashford, S. J., Lee, C., & Bobko, P. (1989). Content, Causes, and Consequences of Job Insecurity: A Theory-Based Measure and Substantive Test. *Academy of Management Journal*, *32*(4), 803–829. doi:10.2307/256569

Ashforth, B. E., & Johnson, S. A. (2001). Social Identity Processes. In Social Identity Processes in Organizational Contexts (Vol. 2, pp. 31–48).

Asif, R., Fiaz, M., Khaliq, Z., & Nisar, S. (2019). Estimating The Mediating Role Of Organizational Identification In Determining The Relationship Between Qualitative Job Insecurity And Job Performance. *Journal of Managerial Sciences*, *13*(3), 175–187.

Bateson, P. (1988). The Biological Evolution of Cooperation and Trust. In D. Gambetta (Ed.), *Trust. Making and breaking Cooperative Relations* (pp. 14–30). Blackwell.

Bibi, A. (2020). Job Insecurity and Job Performance of Nurses in Pakistan: The Roles of Work Engagement and Organizational Justice. *Business Research Review*, *6*(1), 7–20.

Blau, P. M. (1964). *Exchange and power in social life. Exchange and Power in Social Life*. Wiley., doi:10.4324/9780203792643

Bohle, S. A. L., Chambel, M. J., Medina, F. M., & Da Cunha, B. S. (2018). The role of perceived organizational support in job insecurity and performance. *RAE Revista de Administracao de Empresas*, *58*(4), 393–404. doi:10.1590/S0034-759020180405

Butler, J. K., & Cantrell, R. S. (1984). A Behavioral Decision Theory Approach to Modeling. *Clemson University*, *55*(1), 19–28.

Callea, A., Urbini, F., & Chirumbolo, A. (2016). The mediating role of organizational identification in the relationship between qualitative job insecurity, OCB and job performance. *Journal of Management Development*, *35*(6), 735–746. doi:10.1108/JMD-10-2015-0143

Campbell, N. S., Perry, S. J., Maertz, C. P. Jr, Allen, D. G., & Griffeth, R. W. (2013). All you need is. resources: The effects of justice and support on burnout and turnover. *Human Relations*, *66*(6), 759–782. doi:10.1177/0018726712462614

Cheng, G. H. L., & Chan, D. K. S. (2008). Who suffers more from job insecurity? A meta-analytic review. *Applied Psychology*, *57*(2), 272–303. doi:10.1111/j.1464-0597.2007.00312.x

Chirumbolo, A., & Areni, A. (2005). The influence of job insecurity on job performance and absenteeism: The moderating effect of work attitudes. *SA Journal of Industrial Psychology*, *31*(4). Advance online publication. doi:10.4102ajip.v31i4.213

Chirumbolo, A., & Areni, A. (2010). Job insecurity influence on job performance and mental health: Testing the moderating effect of the need for closure. *Economic and Industrial Democracy*, *31*(2), 195–214. doi:10.1177/0143831X09358368

Clark, M. C., Payne, R. L., Journal, S., & May, N. (1997). The Nature and Structure of Workers '. *Trust in Management*, *18*(3), 205–224.

Colquitt, J. A., LePine, J. A., Piccolo, R. F., Zapata, C. P., & Rich, B. L. (2012). Explaining the justice-performance relationship: Trust as exchange deepener or trust as uncertainty reducer? *The Journal of Applied Psychology, 97*(1), 1–15. doi:10.1037/a0025208 PMID:21910516

Colquitt, J. A., Scott, B. A., & LePine, J. A. (2007). Trust, Trustworthiness, and Trust Propensity: A Meta-Analytic Test of Their Unique Relationships With Risk Taking and Job Performance. *The Journal of Applied Psychology, 92*(4), 909–927. doi:10.1037/0021-9010.92.4.909 PMID:17638454

Costa, A. C., Fulmer, C. A., & Anderson, N. R. (2017). Trust in work teams: An integrative review, multilevel model, and future directions. *Journal of Organizational Behavior*, (July). doi:10.1002/job.2213

Cropanzano, R., & Mitchell, M. S. (2005). Social Exchange Theory: An Interdisciplinary Review. *Journal of Management, 31*(6), 874–900. doi:10.1177/0149206305279602

Cropanzano, R., Rupp, D. E., & Byrne, Z. S. (2003). The relationship of emotional exhaustion to work attitudes, job performance, and organizational citizenship behaviors. *The Journal of Applied Psychology, 88*(1), 160–169. doi:10.1037/0021-9010.88.1.160 PMID:12675403

Darvishmotevali, M., & Ali, F. (2020). Job insecurity, subjective well-being and job performance: The moderating role of psychological capital. *International Journal of Hospitality Management, 87*, 102462. doi:10.1016/j.ijhm.2020.102462

Davis, J., Schoorman, F. D., Mayer, R. C., & Tan, H. H. (2000). The Trusted General Manager and Business Unit Performance: Empirical Evidence of a Competitive Advantage. *Strategic Management Journal, 21*(5), 563–576. doi:10.1002/(SICI)1097-0266(200005)21:5<563::AID-SMJ99>3.0.CO;2-0

De Cuyper, N., & De Witte, H. (2007). Job insecurity in temporary versus permanent workers: Associations with attitudes, well-being, and behaviour. *Work and Stress, 21*(1), 65–84. doi:10.1080/02678370701229050

De Witte, H. (1999). Job Insecurity and Psychological Well-being: Review of the Literature and Exploration of Some Unresolved Issues. *European Journal of Work and Organizational Psychology, 8*(2), 155–177. doi:10.1080/135943299398302

De Witte, H., & Näswall, K. (2003). "Objective" vs "subjective" job insecurity: Consequences of temporary work for job satisfaction and organizational commitment in four European countries. *Economic and Industrial Democracy, 24*(2), 149–188. doi:10.1177/0143831X03024002002

Deci, E. L., Olafsen, A. H., & Ryan, R. M. (2017). Self-Determination Theory in Work Organizations: The State of a Science. *Annual Review of Organizational Psychology and Organizational Behavior, 4*(1), 19–43. doi:10.1146/annurev-orgpsych-032516-113108

Deci, E. L., & Ryan, R. M. (2008). Self-Determination Theory : A Macrotheory of Human Motivation, Development, and Health. *Canadian Psychology, 49*(3), 182–185. doi:10.1037/a0012801

DeJong, B. (2016). Team Trust Meta-analysis. *Memory (Hove, England)*. doi:0.1037/1093-4510

Dietz, G., & Den Hartog, D. N. (2006). Measuring trust inside organisations. *Personnel Review, 35*(5), 557–588. doi:10.1108/00483480610682299

Dirks, K. T., & Ferrin, D. L. (2002). Trust in leadership: Meta-analytic findings and implications for research and practice. *The Journal of Applied Psychology*, *87*(4), 611–628. doi:10.1037/0021-9010.87.4.611 PMID:12184567

Edwards, J. R., Caplan, R. D., & Harrison, R. V. (1998). Person-environment fit theory: Conceptual foundations, empirical evidence and directions for future research. In C. L. Cooper (Ed.), *Theories of organizational stress* (pp. 28–67). Oxford University Press., doi:10.1057/9781137310651

Engell, A. D., Haxby, J. V., & Todorov, A. (2007). Implicit trustworthiness decisions: Automatic coding of face properties in the human amygdala. *Journal of Cognitive Neuroscience*, *19*(9), 1508–1519. doi:10.1162/jocn.2007.19.9.1508 PMID:17714012

Frazier, M. L., Fainshmidt, S., Klinger, R. L., Pezeshkan, A., & Vracheva, V. (2017). Psychological Safety: A Meta-Analytic Review and Extension. *Personnel Psychology*, *70*(1), 113–165. doi:10.1111/peps.12183

Gagné, M., & Deci, E. L. (2005). Self-determination theory and work motivation. *Journal of Organizational Behavior*, *26*(4), 331–362. doi:10.1002/job.322

Gandolfi, F., & Littler, C. R. (2012). Downsizing is dead; long live the downsizing phenomenon: Conceptualizing the phases of cost-cutting. *Journal of Management & Organization*, *18*(3), 334–345. doi:10.5172/jmo.2012.18.3.334

Gao, Q., Wu, C., Wang, L., & Zhao, X. (2020). The Entrepreneur's Psychological Capital, Creative Innovation Behavior, and Enterprise Performance. *Frontiers in Psychology*, *11*(July), 1–12. doi:10.3389/fpsyg.2020.01651 PMID:32793048

Greenhalgh, L., & Rosenblatt, Z. (2010). Evolution of research on job insecurity. *International Studies of Management & Organization*, *40*(1), 6–19. doi:10.2753/IMO0020-8825400101

Guo, M., Liu, S., Chu, F., Ye, L., & Zhang, Q. (2019). Supervisory and coworker support for safety: Buffers between job insecurity and safety performance of high-speed railway drivers in China. *Safety Science*, *117*, 290–298. doi:10.1016/j.ssci.2019.04.017

Halbesleben, J. R. B., Neveu, J. P., Paustian-Underdahl, S. C., & Westman, M. (2014). Getting to the "COR": Understanding the Role of Resources in Conservation of Resources Theory. *Journal of Management*, *40*(5), 1334–1364. doi:10.1177/0149206314527130

Halbesleben, J. R. B., & Wheeler, A. R. (2015). To Invest or Not? The Role of Coworker Support and Trust in Daily Reciprocal Gain Spirals of Helping Behavior. *Journal of Management*, *41*(6), 1628–1650. doi:10.1177/0149206312455246

Hardin, R. (1996). Trustworthiness. *Ethics*, *107*(1), 26–42. doi:10.1086/233695

Hellgren, J., Sverke, M., & Isaksson, K. (1999). A Two-dimensional Approach to Job Insecurity: Consequences for Employee Attitudes and Well-being. *European Journal of Work and Organizational Psychology*, *8*(2), 179–195. doi:10.1080/135943299398311

Heyns, M., & Rothmann, S. (2018). Volitional Trust, Autonomy Satisfaction, and Engagement at Work. *Psychological Reports*, *121*(1), 112–134. doi:10.1177/0033294117718555 PMID:28679333

Hirsch, P. M., & De Soucey, M. (2006). Organizational restructuring and its consequences: Rhetorical and structural. *Annual Review of Sociology*, *32*(1), 171–189. doi:10.1146/annurev.soc.32.061604.123146

Hobfoll, S. E. (1989). Conservation of Resources: A New Attempt at Conceptualizing Stress. *The American Psychologist*, *44*(3), 513–524. doi:10.1037/0003-066X.44.3.513 PMID:2648906

Hobfoll, S. E. (2001). The influence of culture, community, and the nested-self in the stress process: Advancing conservation of resources theory. *Applied Psychology*, *50*(3), 337–421. doi:10.1111/1464-0597.00062

Hobfoll, S. E. (2002). Social and Psychological Resources and Adaptation. *Review of General Psychology*, *6*(4), 307–324. doi:10.1037/1089-2680.6.4.307

Hobfoll, S. E., Halbesleben, J., Neveu, J. P., & Westman, M. (2018). Conservation of resources in the organizational context: The reality of resources and their consequences. *Annual Review of Organizational Psychology and Organizational Behavior*, *5*(1), 103–128. doi:10.1146/annurev-orgpsych-032117-104640

Hopkins, S. M., & Weathington, B. L. (2006). The relationships between justice perceptions, trust, and employee attitudes in a downsized organization. *The Journal of Psychology*, *140*(5), 477–498. doi:10.3200/JRLP.140.5.477-498 PMID:17066753

Huselid, M. A. (1995). HRM Article by husalid1995. *The Impact of Human Resource Management Practices on Turnover, Productivity, and Corporate Financial Performance*, *38*(3), 635–672. doi:10.2307/256741

Jiang, L., & Lavaysse, L. M. (2018). Cognitive and Affective Job Insecurity: A Meta-Analysis and a Primary Study. *Journal of Management*, *44*(6), 2307–2342. doi:10.1177/0149206318773853

Kalleberg, A. L., & Vallas, S. P. (2017). Probing precarious work: Theory, research, and politics. *Research in the Sociology of Work*, *31*, 1–30. doi:10.1108/S0277-283320170000031017

Karazsia, B. T., & Berlin, K. S. (2018). Can a Mediator Moderate? Considering the Role of Time and Change in the Mediator-Moderator Distinction. *Behavior Therapy*, *49*(1), 12–20. doi:10.1016/j.beth.2017.10.001 PMID:29405917

Kasperson, R. E., Golding, D., & Tuler, S. (1992). Social Distrust as a Factor in Siting Hazardous Facilities and Communicating Risks. *The Journal of Social Issues*, *48*(4), 161–187. doi:10.1111/j.1540-4560.1992.tb01950.x

Khan, R., & Ghufran, H. (2018). The Mediating Role of Perceived Organizational Support between Qualitative Job Insecurity, Organizational Citizenship Behavior and Job Performance. *Journal of Entrepreneurship & Organization Management*, *07*(1), 1–7. doi:10.4172/2169-026X.1000228

Kim, M. J., & Kim, B. J. (2020). The performance implications of job insecurity: The sequential mediating effect of job stress and organizational commitment, and the buffering role of ethical leadership. *International Journal of Environmental Research and Public Health*, *17*(21), 1–16. doi:10.3390/ijerph17217837 PMID:33114680

König, C. J., Debus, M. E., Häusler, S., Lendenmann, N., & Kleinmann, M. (2010). Examining occupational self-efficacy, work locus of control and communication as moderators of the job insecurity-job performance relationship. *Economic and Industrial Democracy*, *31*(2), 231–247. doi:10.1177/0143831X09358629

Kraemer, H. C., Kiernan, M., Essex, M., & Kupfer, D. J. (2008). How and Why Criteria Defining Moderators and Mediators Differ Between the Baron & Kenny and MacArthur Approaches. *Health Psychology*, *27*(2, SUPPL. 2), S101–S108. doi:10.1037/0278-6133.27.2(Suppl.).S101 PMID:18377151

Kramer, R. M. (1999). Trust and Distrust in Organizations: Emerging Perspectives, Enduring Questions. *Annual Review of Psychology*, *50*(1), 569–598. doi:10.1146/annurev.psych.50.1.569 PMID:15012464

Krot, K., & Lewicka, D. (2012). The Importance of Trust in Manager-Employee Relationships. *International Journal of Electronic Business Management*, *10*(3), 224–233.

Lazarus, R. S., & Folkman, S. (1984). *Stress, Appraisal and Coping*. Springer.

Legood, A., Thomas, G., & Sacramento, C. (2016). Leader trustworthy behavior and organizational trust: The role of the immediate manager for cultivating trust. *Journal of Applied Social Psychology*, *46*(12), 673–686. doi:10.1111/jasp.12394

Lewicki, R. J., & Bunker, B. B. (1995). Trust in relationships: A model of development and decline. *Conflict, Cooperation, and Justice. Essays Inspired by the Work of Morton Deutsch*, (September), 133–173.

Lewicki, R. J., McAllister, D. J., & Bies, R. I. (1998). Trust and distrust: New relationships and realities. *Academy of Management Review*, *23*(3), 438–458. doi:10.2307/259288

Lewicki, R. J., Tomlinson, E. C., & Gillespie, N. (2006). Models of interpersonal trust development: Theoretical approaches, empirical evidence, and future directions. *Journal of Management*, *32*(6), 991–1022. doi:10.1177/0149206306294405

Lind, E., & van den Bos, K. (2002). When fairness works: Toward a general theory of uncertainty management. *Research in Organizational Behavior*, *24*, 181–223. doi:10.1016/S0191-3085(02)24006-X

Mäder, I. A., & Niessen, C. (2017). Nonlinear associations between job insecurity and adaptive performance: The mediating role of negative affect and negative work reflection. *Human Performance*, *30*(5), 231–253. doi:10.1080/08959285.2017.1364243

Martín-Martín, A., Orduña-Malea, E., Thelwall, M., Delgado-López-Cózar, E., Orduna-Malea, E., Thelwall, M., & Delgado López-Cózar, E. (2018). Google Scholar, Web of Science and Scopus: A systematic comparison of citations in 252 subject categories. *Journal of Informetrics*, *12*(4), 1160–1177. doi:10.1016/j.joi.2018.09.002

Mayer, R. C., Davis, J. H., & Schoorman, F. D. (1995). An Integrative Model of Organizational Trust. *Academy of Management Review*, *20*(3), 709–734. doi:10.2307/258792

Mayer, R. C., & Gavin, M. B. (2005). Trust in management and performance: Who minds the shop while the employees watch the boss? *Academy of Management Journal*, *48*(5), 874–888. doi:10.5465/amj.2005.18803928

McAllister, D. J. (1995). Affect- and Cognition-Based Trust As Foundations for Interpersonal Cooperation in Organizations. *Academy of Management Journal*, *38*(1), 24–59. doi:10.2307/256727

Meyer, J. P., & Allen, N. J. (1991). A Three-Component Conceptualization of Organizational Commitment. *Human Resource Management Review*, *1*(1), 61–89. doi:10.1016/1053-4822(91)90011-Z

Mishra, A. K. (1996). Organizational responses to crises: The centrality of trust in organizations. In Trust in Organizations: Frontiers of Theory and Research (pp. 261–287).

Molm, L. D. (2010). The structure of reciprocity. *Social Psychology Quarterly*, *73*(2), 119–131. doi:10.1177/0190272510369079

Molm, L. D., Schaefer, D. R., Collett, J. L., Mouvt, U. D., & Schfl, R. F. R. (2007). The Value of Reciprocity. *Social Psychology Quarterly*, *70*(2), 199–217. doi:10.1177/019027250707000208

Molm, L. D., Takahashi, N., & Peterson, G. (2000). Risk and trust in social exchange: An experimental test of a classical proposition. *American Journal of Sociology*, *105*(5), 1396–1427. doi:10.1086/210434

Molm, L. D., Takahashi, N., & Peterson, G. (2003). In the eye of the beholder: Procedural Justice in Social Exchange. *American Sociological Review*, *68*(1), 128–152. doi:10.2307/3088905

Monteiro, N. P., Portela, M., & Straume, O. R. (2011). Firm Ownership and Rent Sharing. *Journal of Labor Research*, *32*(3), 210–236. doi:10.100712122-011-9109-6

Naru, A. S., & Rehman, A. (2020). Impact of Job Insecurity and Work Overload on Employee Performance With the Mediating Role of Employee Stress: A Case of Pakistan's Fast-food Industry. *International Journal of Human Resource Studies*, *10*(1), 305. doi:10.5296/ijhrs.v10i1.15741

Nicholson, N. (1998). *Encyclopedic Dictionary of Organizational Behavior*. Blackwell.

Niesen, W., Van Hootegem, A., Handaja, Y., Battistelli, A., & De Witte, H. (2018). Quantitative and Qualitative Job Insecurity and Idea Generation: The Mediating Role of Psychological Contract Breach. *Scandinavian Journal of Work and Organizational Psychology*, *3*(1), 3. doi:10.16993jwop.36

Ogbonnaya, C., Gahan, P., & Eib, C. (2019). Recessionary changes at work and employee well-being: The protective roles of national and workplace institutions. *European Journal of Industrial Relations*, *25*(4), 377–393. doi:10.1177/0959680119830885

Pfeffer, J. (2007). Organizational Behavior Perspective. *The Journal of Economic Perspectives*, *21*(4), 115–134. doi:10.1257/jep.21.4.115

Piccoli, B., De Witte, H., & Reisel, W. D. (2017). Job insecurity and discretionary behaviors: Social exchange perspective versus group value model. *Scandinavian Journal of Psychology*, *58*(1), 69–79. doi:10.1111jop.12340 PMID:27925219

Piccoli, B., Reisel, W. D., & De Witte, H. (2019). Understanding the Relationship Between Job Insecurity and Performance : Hindrance or Challenge Effect? *Journal of Career Development*, 1–16. doi:10.1177/0894845319833189

Piccoli, B., Setti, I., Filippi, Z., Argentero, P., & Bellotto, M. (2013). The Influence of Job Insecurity on Task and Contextual Performance: The Mediational Role of Overall Job Attitude. *International Journal of Business Research*, *13*(3), 155–162. doi:10.18374/IJBR-13-3.10

Pirson, M., & Malhotra, D. (2011). Foundations of Organizational Trust: What Matters to Different Stakeholders? *Organization Science*, *22*(4), 1087–1104. doi:10.1287/orsc.1100.0581

Probst, T. M., Gailey, N. J., Jiang, L., & Bohle, S. L. (2017). Psychological capital: Buffering the longitudinal curvilinear effects of job insecurity on performance. *Safety Science, 100*, 74–82. doi:10.1016/j.ssci.2017.02.002

Pugh, S. D., Skarlicki, D. P., & Passell, B. S. (2003). After the Fall: Layoff Victims' Trust and Cynicism in re-Employment. *Journal of Occupational and Organizational Psychology, 76*(2), 201–212. doi:10.1348/096317903765913704

Richter, A., & Näswall, K. (2019). Job insecurity and trust: Uncovering a mechanism linking job insecurity to well-being. *Work and Stress, 33*(1), 22–40. doi:10.1080/02678373.2018.1461709

Richter, A., Vander Elst, T., & De Witte, H. (2020). Job Insecurity and Subsequent Actual Turnover: Rumination as a Valid Explanation? *Frontiers in Psychology, 11*(April), 1–12. doi:10.3389/fpsyg.2020.00712 PMID:32373033

Riketta, M. (2002). Attitudinal Organizational Commitment and Job Performance: a Meta-Analysis. *Journal of Organizatiortal Behavior, 23*(September 2001), 257–266. doi:10.1002/job.141

Robinson, S. L. (1996). Trust and Breach of the Psychological Contract. *Administrative Science Quarterly, 41*(4), 574–599. doi:10.2307/2393868

Roll, L. C., Siu, O.-L., & Li, Y.W., S. (2015). The job insecurity-performance relationship in Germany and China: The buffering effect of uncertainty avoidance. *Human Resources Psychology. Psihologia Resurselor Umane, 13*(2), 165–178.

Rosenblatt, Z., & Greenhalgh, L. (1984). Job Insecurity: Toward Conceptual Clarity. *Academy of Management Review, 9*(3), 438–448. doi:10.2307/258284

Rousseau, D. M. (1989). Psychological and implied contracts in organizations. *Employee Responsibilities and Rights Journal, 2*(2), 121–139. doi:10.1007/BF01384942

Rousseau, D. M., Sitkin, S. B., Burt, R. S., & Camerer, C. (1998). Not so different after all: A cross-discipline view of trust. *Academy of Management Review, 23*(3), 393–404. doi:10.5465/amr.1998.926617

Schoorman, F., Mayer, R. C., & Davis, J. H. (2007). An Integrative Model of Organizational Trust: Past, Present, and Future. *Academy of Management Review, 32*(2), 334–354. doi:10.5465/amr.2007.24348410

Schreurs, B. H. J., Van Emmerik, I. H., Gunter, H., & Germeys, F. (2012). A Weekly Diary Study on the Buffering Role of Social Support in the Relationship Between Job Insecurity and Employee Performance. *Human Resource Management, 51*(2), 259–280. doi:10.1002/hrm.21465

Schumacher, D., Schreurs, B., De Cuyper, N., & Grosemans, I. (2020). The ups and downs of felt job insecurity and job performance: The moderating role of informational justice. *Work and Stress, 0*(0), 1–22. doi:10.1080/02678373.2020.1832607

Selenko, E., Mäkikangas, A., & Stride, C. B. (2017). Does job insecurity threaten who you are? Introducing a social identity perspective to explain well-being and performance consequences of job insecurity. *Journal of Organizational Behavior, 38*(6), 856–875. doi:10.1002/job.2172

Shaikh, S., Mangi, R. A., & Bukhari, N. S. (2019). A Study investigating the empirical relationship of Job insecurity, Job performance and Emotional intelligence. *A mediation analysis*, *13*(2), 177–181. doi:10.24312/19108130223

Shapiro, D. L., Sheppard, B. H., & Cheraskin, L. (1992). Business on a handshake. *Negotiation Journal*, *8*(4), 365–377. doi:10.1111/j.1571-9979.1992.tb00679.x

Shin, Y., Hur, W. M., Moon, T. W., & Lee, S. (2019). A motivational perspective on job insecurity: Relationships between job insecurity, intrinsic motivation, and performance and behavioral outcomes. *International Journal of Environmental Research and Public Health*, *16*(10), 1812. doi:10.3390/ijerph16101812 PMID:31121833

Shoss, M. K. (2017). Job Insecurity: An Integrative Review and Agenda for Future Research. *Journal of Management*, *43*(6), 1911–1939. doi:10.1177/0149206317691574

Shoss, M. K., Brummel, B. J., Probst, T. M., & Jiang, L. (2020). The Joint Importance of Secure and Satisfying Work: Insights from Three Studies. *Journal of Business and Psychology*, *35*(3), 297–316. doi:10.100710869-019-09627-w

Silla, I., de Cuyper, N., Gracia, F. J., Peiró, J. M., & de Witte, H. (2009). Job insecurity and well-being: Moderation by employability. *Journal of Happiness Studies*, *10*(6), 739–751. doi:10.100710902-008-9119-0

Suifan, T. S. (2019). the Effects of Work Environmental Factors on Job Satisfaction: The Mediating Role of Work Motivation. *Business: Theory and Practice*, *20*(0), 456–466. doi:10.3846/btp.2019.42

Sverke, M., Hellgren, J., & Näswall, K. (2002). No security: A meta-analysis and review of job insecurity and its consequences. *Journal of Occupational Health Psychology*, *7*(3), 242–264. doi:10.1037/1076-8998.7.3.242 PMID:12148956

Sverke, M., Låstad, L., Hellgren, J., Richter, A., & Näswall, K. (2019). A meta-analysis of job insecurity and employee performance: Testing temporal aspects, rating source, welfare regime, and union density as moderators. *International Journal of Environmental Research and Public Health*, *16*(14), 2536. Advance online publication. doi:10.3390/ijerph16142536 PMID:31315198

Tajfel, H., & Turner, J. C. (1986). The Social Identity Theory of Intergroup Behavior. In S. Worchel & L. W. Austin (Eds.), Psychology of Intergroup Relations. Chi: Nelson-Hall. doi:10.4135/9781483346274.n163

Taris, T. W., Schreurs, P. J. G., & Van Iersel-Van Silfhout, I. J. (2001). Job stress, job strain, and psychological withdrawal among Dutch university staff: Towards a dual-process model for the effects of occupational stress. *Work and Stress*, *15*(4), 283–296. doi:10.1080/02678370110084049

Tufail, M., Sultan, F., Khalil, S. H., & Sahibzada, S. (2018). Job Insecurity and Job Performance: The Mediating Role of Job Satisfaction. *Abasyn Journal of Social Sciences*, (11), 1–13.

Van de Voorde, K., & Boxall, P. (2014). Individual Well-being and Performance at Work in the Wider Context of Strategic HRM. In *Well-being and Performance at Work: the Role of Context* (pp. 95–111). Psychology Press.

van den Bos, K. (2001). Uncertainty management: The influence of uncertainty salience on reactions to perceived procedural fairness. *Journal of Personality and Social Psychology, 80*(6), 931–941. doi:10.1037/0022-3514.80.6.931 PMID:11414375

Van Dick, R., Ullrich, J., & Tissington, P. A. (2006). Working under a black cloud: How to sustain organizational identification after a merger. *British Journal of Management, 17*(S1, SUPPL. 1), S69–S79. Advance online publication. doi:10.1111/j.1467-8551.2006.00479.x

VandenBos, G. R. (2007). *APA dictionary of psychology. American Psychological Association*. American Psychological Association., doi:10.1037/h0081324

Vander Elst, T., De Cuyper, N., Baillien, E., Niesen, W., & De Witte, H. (2016). Perceived Control and Psychological Contract Breach as Explanations of the Relationships between Job Insecurity, Job Strain and Coping Reactions: Towards a Theoretical Integration. *Stress and Health, 32*(2), 100–116. doi:10.1002mi.2584 PMID:24916812

Vander Elst, T., De Cuyper, N., & De Witte, H. (2011). The role of perceived control in the relationship between job insecurity and psychosocial outcomes: Moderator or mediator? *Stress and Health, 27*(3), 215–227. doi:10.1002mi.1371

Vanhala, M., & Dietz, G. (2019). How Trust in One's Employer Moderates the Relationship Between HRM and Engagement Related Performance. *International Studies of Management & Organization, 49*(1), 23–42. doi:10.1080/00208825.2019.1565092

Veloso, A. L. de O. M. (2007). *O Impacto da Gestão de Recursos Humanos na Performance Organizacional*. Doctoral Dissertation, Universidade do Minho.

Verburg, R. M., Nienaber, A., Searle, R. H., Weibel, A., Den Hartog, D. N., & Rupp, D. E. (2018). The Role of Organizational Control Systems in Employees' Organizational Trust and Performance Outcomes. *Group & Organization Management, 43*(2), 179–206. doi:10.1177/1059601117725191 PMID:29568213

Wang, H. J., Lu, C. Q., & Siu, O. L. (2015). Job insecurity and job performance: The moderating role of organizational justice and the mediating role of work engagement. *The Journal of Applied Psychology, 100*(4), 1249–1258. doi:10.1037/a0038330 PMID:25402953

Wang, W. T. (2016). Examining the Influence of the Social Cognitive Factors and Relative Autonomous Motivations on Employees' Knowledge Sharing Behaviors. *Decision Sciences, 47*(3), 404–436. doi:10.1111/deci.12151

Wheeler, A. R., & Halbesleben, J. R. B. (2009). A Conservation of Resources view of Person-Environment Fit. *Paper Presented at the 3rd Global Fit Conference.*

Whitener, E. M., & Werner, J. O. N. M. (1998). Managers as Initiators of Trust: An Exchange Relationship Framework for Understanding Managerial Trustworthy Behavior. *Academy of Management Review, 23*(3), 513–530. doi:10.2307/259292

Willis, J., & Todorov, A. (2006). First Impressions: Making Up Your Mind After a 100-ms Exposure to a Face. *Psychological Science, 17*(7), 592–598. doi:10.1111/j.1467-9280.2006.01750.x PMID:16866745

Zak, P. J., & Knack, S. (2001). Trust and Growth. *Economic Journal (London)*, *111*(4), 295–321. doi:10.1111/1468-0297.00609

KEY TERMS AND DEFINITIONS

Job Insecurity: The perception that job continuity or job features are threatened.

Mediation: Situation in which the dependent variable is influenced by the independent variable through an intermediate variable.

Moderation: Situation in which the dependent variable is influenced by the independent variable in the presence of another variable.

Performance: The result obtained by the employee executing his job tasks.

Trust: The acceptance of vulnerability to others based on optimistic beliefs about their character, intentions, or ability.

Trustworthiness: The quality of being able to be trusted.

Chapter 5
The Impact of Irregular Schedules on Worker Lives:
Theoretical Considerations and Implications for Practice

Isabel S. Silva
CICS.NOVA, University of Minho, Portugal

Liliana Fernandes
University of Minho, Portugal

Daniela Costa
University of Minho, Portugal

Ana Veloso
https://orcid.org/0000-0002-2417-2910
CICS.NOVA, University of Minho, Portugal

ABSTRACT

In the recent decades, work schedules have diversified, leading to the implementation of different schedules like shift work or irregular hours. This chapter primarily focuses on irregular work schedules, and is structured in three parts. The first part is dedicated to the theoretical framework of the subject, particularly dealing with the main effects of irregular work schedules for the workers. Next, a study carried out in the Portuguese context is presented, where the impacts of irregular work schedules of different types (i.e., depending on their degree of irregularity) on the workers were evaluated, specifically in terms of health, family, and social spheres, as well as satisfaction with work schedule. In general, the results indicate that the greater the irregularity of work schedule, the greater the negative impact on the worker. The third part discusses possible strategies for managing non-standard work schedules by organizations, especially at the level of personnel management.

DOI: 10.4018/978-1-6684-4181-7.ch005

INTRODUCTION

Modern society is constantly changing in terms of economic and productive strategies (e.g., new technologies, market globalization, and information processes) as well as in terms of social organization and individual behavior. Consequently, organizations are faced with the need to extend their working hours to 24 hours a day, 7 days a week, leading to a "24-hour society", which in turn requires a reorganization of work schedules (Costa, 2003). Indeed, over the years, alternative work schedules instead of the standard one, typically considered as working hours from Monday to Friday, from 9:00 am to 5:00 pm, in which people work from 7 to 8 hours daily, have evolved (Costa, 2003; Dhande & Sharma, 2011). In the context of the diversification of working hours, various types of non-standard work schedules have been implemented, as is the case of rotating shift systems or irregular hours. In general, non-standard work schedules tend to be associated with shift work, however they also exist independently, including irregular hours, nights and weekends, among others (Costa, 2016; Li et al., 2014; Perez et al., 2019).

This chapter focuses on irregular working hours. Specifically, it begins by characterizing this type of work schedule as opposed to regular work schedule. It then addresses the main impacts for the worker in terms of health, family and social life, and satisfaction with work schedules. The second topic is dedicated to the presentation of an empirical study carried out in Portugal. It aims to understand the impact of the degree of irregularity in work schedules on the dimensions addressed in the literature review. Based on the previous points, the last part of the chapter is devoted to the discussion of strategies that can be used by both organizations and workers themselves in managing irregular work schedules.

IRREGULAR WORK SCHEDULES

According to Lee et al. (2020), a regular work schedule can be defined as a variable with a fixed daily work period, a fixed weekly work period, a fixed weekly shift, and a fixed start and end time for each shift. That is to say, the duration of working hours as well as the number of days must be the same every week, the weekly shift must be fixed, and the start and end time of each shift must be equally fixed. Thus, irregular working hours were considered those that presented irregularity in any of the previously mentioned criteria, which is the definition that the present investigation will be based on, and which was proposed by the mentioned author. Irregular work schedules are present in several professions, such as railway drivers (Aguirre & Foret, 1994), maritime pilots (Andresen et al., 2007), and bus drivers (Anund et al., 2018) among others.

According to the European Working Conditions Survey, in 2015, it was estimated that 38.9% of Portuguese workers did not have fixed entry and exit times at work, 30.9% of Portuguese workers did not work the same number of hours every week, and 31.5% of Portuguese workers did not work the same number of hours every day (Eurofound, 2015).

Impact on Health

Irregular work schedules can have advantages for workers, among which the greater offer of job opportunities, economic benefits, and greater availability to meet personal needs and preferences stand out (Costa, 2006). However, although non-traditional work schedules can bring advantages, other studies (e.g., Backhaus, 2022) pointed in the opposite direction in terms of workers' health, such as more health complaints or lower well-being. Thus, despite playing a fundamental role in today's society, these work schedules can also represent a threat for workers (Books et al., 2020).

According to the World Health Organization (WHO, 1946), health is not just the absence of disease or infirmity, it is also a state of physical, emotional, and social well-being. According to Presser (1999), non-standard work schedules can have adverse effects on the health and well-being of workers. In the literature review by Wedderburn (2000), because of irregular work schedules and shift work, the presence of stomach problems was reported twice as often compared to day workers. More recently, the results of the study by Books et al. (2020) reinforced such effects, showing that non-fixed work schedules can have a negative impact on several aspects of workers' health, namely physical, psychological, and psychosocial health, as well as their performance at work. According to Satterfield and Dongen (2013), these effects can be explained by insufficient time to sleep and an imbalance in the biological clock among other factors.

According to Aguirre and Forret (1994), workers with more irregular work schedules report a higher frequency of negative judgments in terms of health, namely well-being. More recently, the results of the study by Suleiman et al. (2021) reinforce that long work schedules and irregular work schedules are the biggest obstacles to the well-being of workers. The same study also associated non-standard work schedules to behavioral impacts (poor family and social connections, poor diet, and sleep problems), physical health impacts (exhaustion and excess weight), and prolonged exposure to work (increased stress and increased accidents). Backhaus (2022), using data from the European Working Conditions Survey, found evidence that high working time variability was associated with more sleep problems and psychosomatic complaints in addition to lower well-being and self-reported health perception.

In the study by Lingard and Francis (2005), carried out in an Australian context, the results suggested that the direct relationship between the demands of the work schedules, such as irregular work schedules, and the emotional exhaustion dimension could be better understood as an indirect relationship. In this relationship, the perception that work interferes with the workers' life acts as an important intervening variable between the demands of work schedule and emotional exhaustion. Thus, the demands of work schedules may not directly cause emotional exhaustion, but they can give rise to work-family conflict and consequently lead to emotional exhaustion. The study by Yildirim and Aycan (2008) reinforces these consequences since the results show that work overload and irregular work schedules increase stress, resulting in psychological health problems and negative attitudes towards work.

Impact on Family and Social Life

From a social and family point of view, there are several implications of irregular work schedules for individuals. With the implementation of diversified work schedules, the organization and interaction of work and social times acquired extreme importance, considering that work and non-work (in the family, social, and leisure spheres) are interrelated in the chronometric dimension (i.e., duration of periods of service and duration of free time) as well as the chronological dimension (i.e., position and distribution of different periods) (Costa, 2006). However, in the balance between work and family responsibilities, many workers experience conflict between the two roles (Lee et al., 2022; Lingard & Francis, 2005; Zhao et al., 2021).

In the study by Wight et al. (2008), through a sample of 4000 workers with minor children, the association between non-standard work schedules and family life was analyzed, with positive and negative aspects being reported. On the one hand, parents, particularly males, who worked with non-standard work schedules, spent more time with their children as compared to fathers who worked with conventional work schedules. On the other hand, parents who worked with non-standard work schedules harmed marital relationships and personal leisure time in an endeavor to maximize parental contact. In this regard, Golden (2015) also observed that employees who work on irregular shifts, in contrast to those with more standardized and regular work shifts, experience greater work-family conflict and, sometimes, greater stress at work. In fact, Lee et al. (2022) found that work schedules that occupied "family-friendly" periods such as weekends or evenings were positively correlated with work-family conflict.

Presser (2003) highlighted the fact that working non-standard hours, especially at night, weekends, or in rotating shifts, has an adverse impact on the family, and is associated with higher levels of dissatisfaction and marital instability. More recently, Arlinghaus et al. (2019) showed that the families of workers who work in shifts and in non-standard work schedules are also affected by these. Specifically, they observed that both mothers and fathers who work in the night shift have a higher risk of separation or divorce.

Parental relationships are also affected due to different work schedules. According to Craig and Powell (2011), parents who worked a few hours outside the standard work schedule spent more time on their work and less time on housework, childcare activities, and their children's company as compared to parents who worked on the normal schedule. Over the years, there has been some evidence that shift work by parents is associated with emotional and developmental problems for their children and an increased likelihood of risky behaviors in adolescence (Arlinghaus et al., 2019; Bolino et al., 2021).

Presser (1999) stated that social consequences are the object of less attention in the study, however irregular work schedules can cause significant changes in the structure and stability of family life. Non-standard work schedules, such as night work, long hours, irregular and unpredictable work schedules, and weekends, are commonly associated with reduced social and family well-being. People who work irregular or "atypical" work schedules are often out of touch with society since most family and social activities are organized according to the daytime rhythms of the general population. Work, leisure, and sleep times usually assume different "values" according to social schedules: late afternoon and evening, as well as weekends are the most desirable for social contacts and leisure activities (Costa, 2016). In addition to the weekend being designated as an occasion for recreational and religious activities, the need to stabilize sleep time, due to fatigue caused by shift work, can also be a determining factor in interfering with time for social activities (Dhande & Sharma, 2011).

Satisfaction with Work Schedule

Regarding the impact of irregular work schedules, in particular shift work and night work, in an organizational context, problems have been mentioned mainly in terms of safety and productivity (Folkard & Tucker, 2003). On the other hand, studies that address satisfaction with work schedules are relatively scarce (Prata & Silva, 2013). The study by Andresen et al. (2007), carried out on maritime pilots, showed that non-standard work schedules and irregular work patterns were strong predictors of the stress felt by the worker, which, together with the intervening factors related to work, family, or work environment, tend to reduce job satisfaction. However, the same study showed that despite health problems and reduced quality of life due to atypical work schedules, most workers did not regret their professional choice. Similarly, Simunic and Gregov (2012) studied married nurses with children who worked in four different schedules ("forward rotation with 8-hour morning shifts"—morning, afternoon, night, and a day off; "forward rotation with 12-hour shifts"; "backward rotation with 8-hour shifts"; "8-hour morning shift"). The authors observed that the evaluative cognitive component of job satisfaction was higher in nurses working in the morning shift and lower in nurses on the 12-hour shift. On the other hand, the affective component of life satisfaction was higher in nurses in the morning shift and lower in nurses who work irregularly. However, nurses who work irregular shifts and who have a lower affective component of life satisfaction as compared to other workers, they are generally satisfied with their jobs. More recently, Ingram et al. (2022) found that engagement and job satisfaction could be greater when workers were allocated to their preferred schedules.

STUDY ABOUT IRREGULAR WORK SCHEDULES

In this section, we present a study carried out in Portugal on the impact of irregular working hours. The main objective is to contribute to the understanding of how irregular work schedules of different types (i.e., depending on their degree of irregularity) impact the workers in several areas of their life: family and social spheres, health (at the level of well-being), and general satisfaction with work schedule. The deepening of this theme is even more relevant if we consider its evolution. Indeed, as mentioned by Messenger (2018), there has been a diversification in the organization of working time, towards a move away from the standardized work week consisting of fixed hours of work every day for a fixed number of days.

Method

Participants

The sample consists of 119 participants, divided into four groups. The definition of each group was based on the criteria defined by Lee et al. (2020), as part of their study on irregularity of work schedules. Specifically, the aspects considered were the following: different number of hours of work per week; number of different work days per week; variation in the start and end time of the shifts, this variation being imposed by the shift scale; and shift alternation every week or period longer than one week (e.g., one month). Thus, one of the groups was made up of workers whose working hours only fit into one of the irregular aspects. The second group was made up of workers whose working hours fit into two of the aspects. The third group was made up of workers with a working schedule that included three aspects. Finally, the fourth group was made up of workers whose working hours fit into the four aspects presented to be considered as an irregular work schedule. The constitution of the groups was based on the number of criteria defined in terms of irregularity according to the number of options indicated by the participants. Additionally, in order to have some control mechanism over the constitution of groups, an open question was created at the end of the questionnaire, where participants could make a brief description of their work schedule. In order to facilitate the description, the groups described above will be referred to as Group 1, Group 2, Group 3, and Group 4, respectively.

As can be seen in Table 1, Group 1 consists of 28 participants, of which 57.1% are male. Their ages range from 19 to 62 years (M = 29.25, SD = 9.60), and they are mostly single (64.3%). The most frequent level of education in this group is higher education, with a percentage of 64.3%. It should be noted that for workers in this group, seniority in current work schedule varies from 3 months and 20 years (M = 5.13, SD = 6.10). For Group 2, with 34 workers, the ages are between 18 and 58 years (M = 31.97, SD = 12.21), of which 64.7% are female. Regarding marital status and level of education, 44.1% of the participants are single, and higher education is the most representative level (50%). Regarding the number of years that the workers have been working at the current work schedule, it varies between 1 month and 39 years (M = 5.69, SD = 8.29). Group 3 consists of 48 participants, aged between 19 and 59 years (M = 35.46, SD = 11.58), of which 79.2% are female. In terms of marital status, 41.7% of this group are married. As far as the level of education is concerned, most participants have higher education (85.4%). The workers in this group have been working at the current work schedule for an average of 10 years (M = 9.99, SD = 10.41). The Group 4 consists of 9 participants, of which 55.6% are female, aged between 22 and 46 years (M = 33.78, SD = 10.26). Regarding marital status and level of education, 55.6% of this group are single, and like the other groups, higher education is the most frequent level (77.8%). The seniority of the workers in the current work schedule varies between 1 year and 24 years (M = 9.89, SD = 9.36). In family terms, workers are married or living together for at least one year, and the maximum number of years of union is 36 years (M = 6.13, SD = 9.36). Regarding the household, the number of people varies between one and seven, with 29.4% of the workers reporting two people in this composition.

Table 1. Sociodemographic and professional characterization of workers according to the group and the total sample

Variables	Group 1		Group 2		Group 3		Group 4		Total	
	n	%	n	%	n	%	n	%	n	%
Number of participants	28	23.5	34	28.6	48	40.3	9	7.6	119	100
Gender										
Female	12	42.9	22	64.7	38	79.2	5	55.6	77	64.7
Male	16	57.1	12	35.3	10	20.8	4	44.4	42	35.3
Age M (SD)	29.25 (9.60)		31.97 (12.21)		35.46 (11.58)		33.78 (10.26)		32.87 (11.38)	
Marital status										
Single	18	64.3	15	44.1	19	39.6	5	55.6	57	47.9
Married	7	25	11	32.4	20	41.7	3	33.3	41	34.5
Union	3	10.7	8	23.5	6	12.5	1	11.1	14	15.1
Divorced	--	--	--	--	3	6.3	--	--	3	2.5
Education level										
6th level	--	--	2	5.9	1	2.1	1	11.1	4	3.4
9th level	1	3.6	1	2.9	3	6.3	--	--	5	4.2
12th level	9	32.1	14	41.2	3	6.3	1	11.1	27	22.7
Higher education	18	64.3	17	50	41	85.4	7	77.8	83	69.7
Seniority on the work schedule M (SD)	5.13 (6.10)		5.69 (8.29)		9.99 (10.41)		9.89 (9.36)		7.61 (9.02)	

Note. M = Mean; SD = Standard Deviation.

Measures

In data collection, a research protocol was used that included a sociodemographic and professional questionnaire and several scales to assess well-being, the impact of work schedule on life outside the company, and worker satisfaction with work schedule.

Sociodemographic and Professional Questionnaire

The *sociodemographic and professional data* of the participants were collected through a sociodemographic and professional questionnaire developed within the scope of the present study. This questionnaire contained sociodemographic questions (i.e., age, sex, marital status, education, and seniority at the current time), questions related to the professional situation (i.e., irregular working hours), and questions related to the family situation (e.g., years of marriage).

Personal Well-Being Index

The Portuguese version of the *Personal Well-Being Index* (Pais-Ribeiro & Cummins, 2008) resulted from an adaptation of the comprehensive *Quality of Life Scale* by Cummins et al. (1994) to Portuguese context. This measure aims to measure the subjective well-being of the participants. It is a 7-item scale (e.g., *"How satisfied are you with your health?"*), and the items are answered on a Likert-type scale from "0" (Extremely dissatisfied) to "10" (Extremely satisfied), with a neutral intermediate position. The higher the score obtained on the scale, the greater the perception of well-being. In the study of Pais-Ribeiro and Cummins (2008), the personal well-being scale showed a Cronbach's alpha of 0.81.

Scale on Work Schedule and Life Outside of Work

To understand the influence that work schedules have on the worker's life outside the organization, we used a scale developed by Silva (2007) in the context of an investigation into non-standard work schedules, namely shift work. The instrument consists of six items (e.g., *"Does your work schedule leave you enough time to be with your family and closest friends."*), answered on a 5-point Likert scale (from 1 "Strongly disagree" to 5 "Strongly agree"). Cronbach's alpha was 0.91, which indicates good levels of reliability. The higher the value obtained on the scale, the greater the perception of satisfaction with life outside of work.

General Satisfaction with the Work Schedule

To assess the workers' overall satisfaction with work schedules, a scale developed by Silva (2007) was used. The scale consists of four items (e.g., *"You would recommend your work schedule to a family member or close friend."*), answered on a 5-point Likert scale (from 1 "I totally disagree" to 5 "I totally agree"). As with the other scales, the higher the value obtained on the scale, the greater the satisfaction with work schedule. In the original study, Cronbach's alpha was 0.89.

The protocol ended with an open-ended question where participants could report their experience of working with an irregular work schedule.

Procedure

In the initial phase, a pre-test was carried out with two workers, belonging to the researcher's social network, whose work schedules met the characteristics required in the study. The results of the pre-test led to some changes, essentially in the variable that characterizes working hours to facilitate understanding and avoid ambiguity of answers. For example, initially the following option was placed: *"Non-fixed start and end time of each shift"*, which was later changed to *"Variation in start time and end of shifts, this variation being imposed by the scale of shifts"*. The protocol was drawn up in an online format, using the *Google Forms* tool. The application of the protocol began with the informed consent, where the objectives of the study and the voluntary nature of participation were explained, and the confidentiality of the data collected were guaranteed.

Subsequently, the study was disseminated. In this sense, contacts were established with 12 organizations from various sectors of activity (e.g., industrial sector) in order to detect whether the workers met the inclusion criteria defined in the study. If so, the internal disclosure of the investigation protocol to workers would be requested. However, no response was obtained from these organizations. Given this constraint, we continued the dissemination of the study by establishing contacts with some unions (e.g., nurses, doctors, and police officers). Contact was established through an email, with a brief presentation and explanation of the purpose of the study as well as with the link to the questionnaire. It should be noted that only one of the unions agreed to disseminate the study and the respective questionnaire to its members. However, only 11 responses were obtained. Thus, in order to maximize the number of responses, the dissemination of the study continued on social networks through private groups on Facebook (e.g., groups of firefighters or nurses) and Instagram. This was available online for 3 months (June to September 2022).

Data Analysis

Initially, the sample consisted of 119 participants, divided into four groups according to the irregularity of the work schedule (as described above). However, following the recommendations of Pestana and Gageiro (2008) regarding the minimum number of subjects for the use of the One-Way ANOVA statistical test, it was decided to eliminate Group 4 since it consisted of only 9 participants. For the analysis of quantitative data, the Statistical Package for the Social Sciences program (IBM® SPSS®, version 28.0) was used. The analyses included: i) descriptive analyses (frequencies, means, and standard deviations) for the entire sample; ii) Pearson correlations to assess the associations between the variables under study; and iii) univariate analysis of variance to identify possible differences between different groups of workers with irregular work schedules (one-way ANOVA test). The assumptions underlying the use of this parametric test were previously tested, however the assumption of normality was not fulfilled. In this sense, the alternative strategy proposed by Fife-Schaw (2006) was followed, in which in the case of non-parametric tests and parametric tests report agreement in the results, one can choose to present the results of the parametric tests.

Qualitative data resulting from the answer to the open-ended question were analyzed through content analysis (Bardin, 2016).

Results

Quantitative Analysis

Table 2 presents the mean values and standard deviations for each of the dimensions under analysis according to each group as well as the total sample. The well-being scale is the one with the highest average values, where the averages in Groups 1, 2 and 3 are above the midpoint of the scale (corresponding to 5). On the other hand, the scale of satisfaction with work schedules is the one with the lowest average value, where the averages of all Groups are below the midpoint (corresponding to 3). On the scale of working hours and life outside of work, the means are above the midpoint of the scale in Group 1, but below in Groups 2 and 3 (in this case, the midpoint is also 3).

Considering that one of the objectives of this study is to evaluate the existence of statistically significant differences between the three groups, the parametric test of differences between three or more independent samples, the One-Way ANOVA, was applied. As mentioned earlier, the assumptions for using parametric tests were not met. However, following the recommendations of Fife-Schaw (2006), the results of these tests were reported since both (parametric and non-parametric) tests agreed on the conclusions. Table 2 presents the results of the statistical test as well as the value of the associated significance level.

Table 2. Descriptive measures and comparison of the variables under study according to the groups

Dimension	Group 1 (n=28)		Group 2 (n=34)		Group 3 (n=48)		F
	M	SD	M	SD	M	SD	
Well-being	5.01	2.87	5.12	2.36	5.05	2.47	0.408
Work Schedule and Life Outside of Work	3.18	1.07	2.89	0.86	2.28	0.90	6.332***
Work Schedule Satisfaction	2.96	1.09	2.60	1.06	1.98	0.78	6.571***
Note. M = Mean; SD = Standard Deviation. * $p < .05$. ** $p < .01$. *** $p < .001$							

As indicated by the results obtained, through the one-way ANOVA, there are no statistically significant differences between groups in the well-being dimension (F = 0.408, p = 0.747). On the other hand, in the remaining dimensions, in terms of work schedule and life outside work (F = 6.33, p <0.001) and satisfaction with work schedule (F = 6.57, p <0.001), it was found that there are statistically significant differences according to the different groups. The use of one-way ANOVA shows that there are statistically significant differences between the groups, however it does not specify between which groups statistically significant differences exist. In this sense, to understand which groups presented these differences, the Post-Hoc Bonferroni test was carried out, a test recommended by Pestana and Gageiro (2008) when the number of comparisons is low. Table 3 presents a summary of these comparisons.

Table 3. Synthesis of multiple comparisons between working-hour groups

Dimension	1 vs 2	1 vs 3	2 vs 3
Work schedule and life outside of work	ns	**	**
Work schedule satisfaction	ns	**	**
Note. ns = not significant. * $p < .05$. ** $p < .01$. *** $p < .001$			

Considering the information presented in Tables 2 and 3 and the level of the interface between work schedules and life outside work, there is a perception of lower satisfaction in Group 3 as compared to Groups 1 and 2. That is, as compared to workers in Group 3, workers in Group 1 and Group 2 perceive the interface between their schedule and family life more positively. This dimension was even better evaluated by workers in Group 1 as compared to workers in Group 2, although there were no statistically significant differences. Regarding satisfaction with work schedule, alike the previous dimension, there is a perception of lower satisfaction in Group 3 as compared to the other groups. Specifically, the workers in Group 3, who have more irregular schedule, are less satisfied with their work schedule as compared to those in Groups 1 and 2. Again, Group 1 has greater satisfaction with work schedule as compared to Group 2, although such differences are not statistically significant.

Table 4. Correlational analyzes between dimensions

Dimension	(1)	(2)	(3)
(1) Well-being	-	-	-
(2) Work schedule and life outside of work	.445**	-	-
(3) Work schedule satisfaction	.351**	.779**	-
* $p < .05$. ** $p < .01$. *** $p < .001$			

As complementary analyses, correlation tests were carried out to understand the relationship between the variables under study, namely through Pearson's correlation coefficient. The results presented in Table 4 reveal that well-being is positively correlated with the interface between work schedule and life outside of work ($r = .445$). That is, as workers have a better perception of well-being, they tend to have a better perception of their life outside work schedules. Well-being is also positively correlated with greater satisfaction with the work schedule ($r = .351$). In turn, satisfaction with the work schedule is positively correlated with the interface between work schedule and life outside the company ($r = .779$). That is, as subjects are more satisfied with their work schedule, they are also more satisfied with the interface between work schedules and life outside the company (Table 4).

Qualitative Analysis

The last question in the questionnaire, which was optional, asked workers to comment on their work schedule. In the analysis of the responses obtained, as mentioned earlier, the Content Analysis methodology was used (Bardin, 2016).

A total of 65 participants answered this question, five of which were from Group 4. Since we have not considered this group in terms of quantitative data analysis, we also chose not to consider them in these data. An answer given by the participants ("*The patients*") due to their misunderstanding was also eliminated. Thus, in total, responses from 59 participants (53.64%) were considered. The number of aspects mentioned in the set of subcategories is higher than the number of responses obtained by the participants, given that some workers mentioned more than one aspect in their answer.

Table 5. Frequency of responses obtained in the categories "positive aspects" and "negative aspects" and respective subcategories

1. Positive aspects associated with work schedules (n=17)			
Subcategories (n=17)	Group 1 (n=6)	Group 2 (n=8)	Group 3 (n=3)
1.1 Free time (n=7) "It leaves some free time to be at home, and the fact of working 3 or 4 days and resting helps."	3	2	2
1.2 Variety of tasks (n=1) "The type of work is different while in the morning you do something, at night it is already different."	--	1	--
1.3 Economic aspects (n=1) "Having an extra job (part time), this schedule makes it easier to carry out that same job (...) allows me to raise the standard of living."	--	1	--
1.4 Personal relationships "I even like it to be varied because it also makes me be with different types of people."	--	1	--
1.5 General appreciation of working hours (n=7) "Convenient sometimes."	3	3	1
2. Negative aspects associated with work schedules (n=66)			
Subcategories (n=66)	Group 1 (n=12)	Group 2 (n=22)	Group 3 (n=32)
2.1 Health (n=13) "I feel tired, the time off is never really good for resting."	4	4	5
2.1.1 Sleep (n=5) "I notice the effects mainly on sleep and sleep quality as well."	3	1	1
2.1.2 Psychological level (n=2) "...rest times are short, irregular, which ends up influencing our psyche..."	1	--	1
2.1.3 Physical level (n=1) "Very tiring physically and psychologically."	--	--	1
2.1.4 Well-being (n=1) "Constant rotation between shifts, without resting hours to create wellness routines for mind and body."	--	--	1
2.2 Family life (n=3) "It is very complicated to manage with family life."	--	1	2
2.2.1 Family time (n=5) "I would prefer just the morning shift. At night, I don't have lunch or dinner with the family."	1	3	1
2.2.2 Marital level (n=1) "My work schedule led to the strain on my first marriage, leading to divorce. The constant change meant that my ex-husband was overwhelmed with the responsibilities of the children when they were younger."	--	1	--
2.3 Personal life (n=1) "It's very painful, whether it's just a rest point of view or reconciling with personal life..."	--	--	1
2.4 Social life (n=8) "...difficult management of social use given the rotating schedules."	1	3	4
2.5 Organizational level (n=8) "Extremely unregulated hours and lack of control by the competent authorities."	--	2	6
2.6 General appreciation of working hours (n=18) "Very bad"	2	7	9

The responses of all participants were read, and then categories and subcategories were defined. Two main categories were created: *Positive aspects* and *Negative aspects* associated with work schedules. Subsequently, they were divided into subcategories in order to group the answers given by the participants according to different areas of impact. It should be noted that in each category there is a subcategory called "*General appreciation of working hours*", which corresponds to responses about a general opinion given through an adjective (e.g., "good"), not being specific enough to be grouped into one of the remaining subcategories. Table 5 presents the frequencies obtained in each category and subcategory as well as examples of responses given by workers depending on each group.

In the first category, concerning the positive aspects of working hours, aspects such as the existence of free time, the variety of tasks, the economic aspects, and the personal relationships were mentioned. The workers of Group 2 are the ones who report more positive aspects about irregular work schedules, specifically in terms of free time (e.g., *"It allows me to rest and organize my life outside work, and it also allows me to take more days off, which ends up compensating"*) and the level of general appreciation of working hours (e.g., *"A very nice job"*). On the other hand, the workers in Group 3 are the ones who least mentioned the positive aspects.

In the category of negative aspects, as can be seen in Table 5, the subcategories most impacted by irregular hours were *health* (i.e., sleep, psychological and physical level, and well-being), *family life* (e.g., family time), *social life*, and *organizational level*. Specifically, it is possible to verify that Group 3 workers are the ones who presented the most negative aspects, mostly in terms of health (e.g., *"I feel tired, time off is never really good for resting."*), at the organizational level (e.g., *"...the 35h/week is almost never complied with, I am always left with an overloaded schedule and reduced rest periods"*), and at the level of general appreciation of working hours (e.g., *"Horrible"*). Conversely, the workers in Group 1 are the ones who presented the least negative aspects, highlighting mainly health aspects (e.g., *"I don't like to work in the afternoon shift for a long time, it gets tiring"*).

Discussion

The results of this study reveal that well-being is positively correlated with the interface between work schedules and life outside work as well as the satisfaction with work schedules. These results are in line with the literature, given that according to Schneider and Harknett (2019), associations are estimated between routine instability in work schedules and workers' well-being, increasing conflicts between personal and professional life. Additionally, it was possible to observe that the dimension of family life is also positively correlated with satisfaction with the work schedule, results consistent with other studies (Carneiro & Silva, 2015; Prata & Silva, 2013). According to Prata and Silva (2013), satisfaction with the work schedules is strongly associated with the availability of workers for family and social life, which is one of the predictive factors of satisfaction with the work schedule.

Regarding the results in terms of health, more specifically in terms of well-being, contrary to expectations, no significant differences were found between the three groups with different types of work schedule irregularity. These results somewhat contradict the data obtained by Aguirre and Foret (1994) or by Backhaus (2022), in which higher working time variability was associated with lower levels of well-being. However, in the study of Aguirre and Foret (1994), the comparison was made between workers with irregular work schedules and those with a conventional schedule, not just between different types of irregular work schedules. In this sense, it would be important in future investigations to deepen the analysis of this topic, depending on the different degrees of irregularity.

Regarding work schedules and life outside of work, the results show statistically significant differences between the different groups, with a lower perception of satisfaction being observed at the level of Group 3, the most irregular, as compared to Groups 1 and 2. On the other hand, the workers in Group 1 are the most satisfied with the articulation between their work schedule and their life outside work. These results are consistent with what has been found in the literature, given that the more atypical/non-standard the working time regime, the greater the work-family conflict (Bolino et al., 2021; Zhao et al., 2021). These problems can occur at the level of social time, which is highly valued for family, social, and leisure activities, and ends up being suppressed by atypical work schedules (Arlinghaus et al., 2019).

Regarding satisfaction with the work schedule, the results also show that there is a perception of lower satisfaction in Group 3 as compared to the others. Specifically, workers in Group 3, with a more irregular schedule, revealed greater dissatisfaction when compared to Groups 1 and 2. On the contrary, workers in Group 1 have, on average, greater satisfaction with their work schedule as compared to those in Group 2. In this sense, the results are consistent with the literature, given that, according to Wedderburn (2000), the greater the divergence of a schedule from a standard time, the greater the probability of being negatively evaluated by the workers.

The analysis of the open question in this study corroborated most of the results found. The answers obtained regarding the negative aspects revealed a high impact of irregular work schedules, essentially in the health area. These results are consistent with some studies (Backhaus, 2022; Bannai & Tamakoshi, 2014) that report that employees who work on irregular schedules have more problems in the areas of subjective health status, well-being, and sleep quality. Another of the negative aspects most mentioned by the workers was family life, which could be explained by the lack of time, since it is one of the causes most reported by the workers. As mentioned by Arlinghaus et al. (2019), working time regimes that require shift work or other atypical working hours have significant potential to suppress time that is highly valued for family, social, and leisure activities. On the other hand, regarding the advantages most highlighted by the workers, the existence of free time was the most mentioned. These results are in line with some of the advantages mentioned in the investigation by Carneiro and Silva (2015), namely the possibility of obtaining a more favorable schedule to take care of family or personal projects.

Limitations and Future Studies

In interpreting the results of the empirical part, some limitations must be taken into account. The first limitation concerns the sample size, as well as its characteristics. The study sample is relatively small, with 110 participants. As previously mentioned, the difficulty in obtaining participants who fit into the four groups under study meant that the minimum number of participants to integrate Group 4 was not reached. On the other hand, as the formation of the groups was based on the aspects pointed out by the workers regarding their work schedules, there may have been some bias in their constitution.

In future research, more in-depth studies may be opportune, taking into account the comparison of the four groups according to the different degrees of irregularity, as well as the comparison between these and the normal schedule.

CONCLUSION AND IMPLICATIONS FOR PRACTICE

The organization of working time in modalities such as shift work or irregular schedules, as mentioned earlier, is practically inevitable in modern society. This evidence is even greater when we think of sectors of activity such as the health sector. However, despite the impossibility of eliminating these work schedules, the focus should be on studying means and ways to reduce the implications that these schedules entail for workers and their families and also for organizations. In this sense, in the study by Simunic and Gregov (2012), the authors suggest that organizations could minimize the impacts of irregular shifts through flexibility and scheduling and, consequently, informing workers of the respective work schedules in advance. Similarly, workers can also reduce the adverse effects of these work schedules by maintaining a healthy lifestyle (e.g., healthy diet, physical exercise, and avoiding cigarettes and alcohol) and trying to be more flexible about their priorities. In turn, Yildirim and Aycan (2008) emphasize the importance of reorganizing working conditions in order to reduce excessive workload and irregular working hours, and consequently increase improvements in aspects such as psychological well-being and attitudes towards work (e.g., job satisfaction). According to Shifrin and Michel (2021), concern about measures that decrease workers' health complaints has been increasing, especially after the COVID-19 pandemic. In their meta-analysis, the results pointed to an association between flexible work arrangements and better physical health, less somatic symptoms, and lower absenteeism. In this sense, once again, the importance of flexible working hours is highlighted, and organizations should provide options to workers according to their needs. In terms of strategies, Shifrin and Michel (2021) argued that telecommuting, compressed work weeks, reduced working hours or access to days off can help workers better manage their lives.

The possibility for workers to participate in the management of their own work schedules is also one of the most effective strategies in reducing the impacts of non-standard work schedules as argued by Bolino et al. (2021). For example, in some studies carried out within the research group of the first author (Carneiro & Silva, 2015; Silva & Silva, 2015), the workers' perception of the organization's support in managing their working hours was positively related to their satisfaction with their work schedules and their perception of reconciling their life outside the organization. In sum, the control that the workers may have over their work schedule may lead to better management of their lives and the relationship between work and family life.

REFERENCES

Aguirre, A., & Foret, J. (1994). Irregularity of working hours in railway workers and types of complaints. *International Archives of Occupational and Environmental Health*, *65*(6), 367–371. doi:10.1007/BF00383245 PMID:8034360

Andresen, M., Domsch, M. E., & Cascorbi, A. H. (2007). Working unusual hours and its relationship to job satisfaction: A study of European maritime pilots. *Journal of Labor Research*, *28*(4), 714–734. doi:10.100712122-007-9010-5

Anund, A., Fors, C., Ihlström, J., & Kecklund, G. (2018). An on-road study of sleepiness in split shifts among city bus drivers. *Accident; Analysis and Prevention*, *114*, 71–76. doi:10.1016/j.aap.2017.05.005 PMID:28506403

Arlinghaus, A., Bohle, P., Iskra-Golec, I., Jansen, N., Jay, S., & Rotenberg, L. (2019). Working time society consensus statements: Evidence-based effects of shift work and non-standard working hours on workers, family and community. *Industrial Health*, *57*(2), 184–200. doi:10.2486/indhealth.SW-4 PMID:30700670

Backhaus, N. (2022). Working time control and variability in Europe revisited: Correlations with health, sleep, and well-being. *International Journal of Environmental Research and Public Health*, *19*(22), 14778. doi:10.3390/ijerph192214778 PMID:36429495

Bannai, A., & Tamakoshi, A. (2014). The association between long working hours and health: A systematic review of epidemiological evidence. *Scandinavian Journal of Work, Environment & Health*, *40*(1), 5–18. doi:10.5271jweh.3388 PMID:24100465

Bardin, L. (2016). *Análise de Conteúdo* [Content Analysis]. Edições 70.

Bolino, M. C., Kelemen, T. K., & Matthews, S. H. (2021). Working 9-to-5? A review of research on nonstandard work schedules. *Journal of Organizational Behavior*, *42*(2), 188–211. doi:10.1002/job.2440

Books, C., Coody, L. C., Kauffman, R., & Abraham, S. (2020). Night shift work and its health effects on nurses. *The Health Care Manager*, *36*(3), 122–127. doi:10.1097/HCM.0000000000000297 PMID:32701608

Carneiro, L., & Silva, I. S. (2015). Trabalho por turnos e suporte do contexto organizacional: Um estudo num centro hospitalar [Shift work and organizational support: A study in a hospital]. *International Journal on Working Conditions*, *9*, 142–160.

Costa, G. (2003). Shift work and occupational medicine: An overview. *Occupational Medicine*, *53*(2), 83–88. doi:10.1093/occmed/kqg045 PMID:12637591

Costa, G. (2006). Flexibility of working hours in the 24-hour society. *La Medicina del Lavoro*, *97*(2), 280–287. PMID:17017360

Costa, G. (2016). Introduction to problems of shift work. In I. Iskra-Golec, J. Barnes-Farrell, & P. Bohle (Eds.), *Social and Family Issues in Shift Work and Non Standard Working Hours* (pp. 19–35). Springer International Publishing. doi:10.1007/978-3-319-42286-2_2

Craig, L., & Powell, A. (2011). Non-standard work schedules, work-family balance and the gendered division of childcare. *Work, Employment and Society*, *25*(2), 274–291. doi:10.1177/0950017011398894

Cummins, R. A., McCabe, M. P., Romeo, Y., & Gullone, E. (1994). The Comprehensive Quality of Life Scale: Instrument development and psychometric evaluation on tertiary staff and students. *Educational and Psychological Measurement*, *54*, 372–382. doi:10.1177/0013164494054002011

Dhande, K. K., & Sharma, S. (2011). Influence of shift work in process industry on workers' occupational health, productivity, and family and social life: An ergonomic approach. *Human Factors and Ergonomics in Manufacturing*, *21*(3), 260–268. doi:10.1002/hfm.20231

Eurofound. (2015). *European Working Conditions Survey – Data visualisation*. Eurofund. https://www.eurofound.europa.eu/data/european-working-conditions-survey

Fife-Schaw, C. (2006). Levels of measurement. In G. M. Breakwell, S. Hammond, C. Fife-Schaw, & J. A. Smith (Eds.), Research Methods in Psychology (pp. 50-63). Sage Publications, Inc.

Folkard, S., & Tucker, P. (2003). Shift work, safety, and productivity. *Occupational Medicine*, *53*(2), 95–101. doi:10.1093/occmed/kqg047 PMID:12637593

Golden, L. (2015). Irregular work scheduling and its consequences. *Economic Policy Institute Briefing Paper*, 394.

Ingram, W., Murphy, K. S., & Weinland, J. (2022). The moderating effect of hotel shift work on the relationship between employee work engagement and job satisfaction. *Journal of Human Resources in Hospitality & Tourism*, 1–27. doi:10.1080/15332845.2023.2154029

Lee, W. T., Lim, S. S., Kim, J., Yun, S., Yoon, J. H., & Won, J. U. (2020). Work schedule irregularity and the risk of work-related injury among Korean manual workers. *International Journal of Environmental Research and Public Health*, *17*(20), 1–10. doi:10.3390/ijerph17207617 PMID:33086683

Lee, Y., Lee, S., Kim, Y. J., Kim, Y., Kim, S. Y., & Kang, D. (2022). Relationship between of working hours, weekend work, and shift work and work-family conflicts among Korean manufacturers. *Annals of Occupational and Environmental Medicine*, *34*(1), e20. doi:10.35371/aoem.2022.34.e20 PMID:36147589

Li, J., Johnson, S. E., Han, W. J., Andrews, S., Kendall, G., Strazdins, L., & Dockery, A. (2014). Parents' nonstandard work schedules and child well-being: A critical review of the literature. *The Journal of Primary Prevention*, *35*(1), 53–73. doi:10.100710935-013-0318-z PMID:24014309

Lingard, H., & Francis, V. (2005). Does work-family conflict mediate the relationship between job schedule demands and burnout in male construction professionals and managers? *Construction Management and Economics*, *23*(7), 733–745. doi:10.1080/01446190500040836

Messenger, J. (2018). *Working Time and the Future of Work*. International Labour Organization. https://www.ilo.org/global/topics/future-of-work/publications/research-papers/WCMS_649907/lang--en/index.htm

Pais-Ribeiro, J., & Cummins, R. (2008). O bem-estar pessoal: Estudo de validação da versão portuguesa da escala. [Personal well-being: Validation study of the Portuguese version of the scale] In I. Leal, J. Pais-Ribeiro, I. Silva, & S. Marques (Eds.), *Actas do 7º Congresso Nacional de Psicologia da Saúde* [Proceedings of the 7th National Congress of Health Psychology]. (pp. 505–508). ISPA, https://hdl.handle.net/10216/21065

Perez, J. F., Traversini, V., Fioriti, M., Taddei, G., Montalti, M., & Tommasi, E. (2019). Shift and night work management in European companies. *Calitatea*, *20*(169), 157–165.

Pestana, M. H., & Gageiro, J. N. (2008). *Análise de Dados para Ciências Sociais: A Complementaridade do SPSS* [Data Analysis for Social Sciences: The Complementarity of SPSS]. 5th ed.). Edições Sílabo.

Prata, J., & Silva, I. (2013). Efeitos do trabalho em turnos na saúde e em dimensões do contexto social e organizacional: Um estudo na indústria eletrônica [Shiftwork effects on health and on social and organizational life: A study in the electronics industry]. *Revista Psicologia: Organizações e Trabalho*, *13*(2), 141-154.

Presser, H. B. (1999). Toward a 24-hour economy. *Science*, *284*(5421), 1778–1779. doi:10.1126cience.284.5421.1778

Presser, H. B. (2003). *Working in a 24/7 economy: Challenges for American families*. Russell Sage Foundation.

Satterfield, B. C., & Van Dongen, H. P. A. (2013). Occupational fatigue, underlying sleep and circadian mechanisms, and approaches to fatigue risk management. *Fatigue: Biomedicine, Health & Behavior*, *1*(3), 118–136. doi:10.1080/21641846.2013.798923

Schneider, D., & Harknett, K. (2019). Consequences of routine work-schedule instability for worker health and well-being. *American Sociological Review*, *84*(1), 82–114. doi:10.1177/0003122418823184 PMID:33311716

Silva, H., & Silva, I. S. (2015). Gestão e adaptação aos horários de trabalho: Um estudo de caso no setor hoteleiro [Management and adaptation to work schedule: A case study in the hospitality sector]. *International Journal on Working Conditions*, *9*, 99–116.

Silva, I. S. (2007). *Adaptação ao trabalho por turnos* [Adaptation to shift work] [Doctoral dissertation, University of Minho]. http://hdl.handle.net/1822/7723

Šimunić, A., & Gregov, L. (2012). Conflict between work and family roles and satisfaction among nurses in different shift systems in Croatia: A questionnaire survey. *Archives of Industrial Hygiene and Toxicology*, *63*(2), 189–197. doi:10.2478/10004-1254-63-2012-2159 PMID:22728801

Suleiman, A. O., Decker, R. E., Garza, J. L., Laguerre, R. A., Dugan, A. G., & Cavallari, J. M. (2021). Worker perspectives on the impact of nonstandard workdays on worker and family wellbeing: A qualitative study. *BMC Public Health*, *21*(1), 1–12. doi:10.118612889-021-12265-8 PMID:34879831

Wedderburn, A. (2000). *Shiftwork and Health*. European Foundation for the Improvement of Living and Working Conditions.

Wight, V. R., Raley, S. B., & Bianchi, S. M. (2008). Time for children, one's spouse and oneself among parents who work nonstandard hours. *Social Forces*, *87*(1), 243–271. doi:10.1353of.0.0092

World Health Organization. (1946). *Health and Well-Being*. WHO. https://www.who.int/data/gho/data/major-themes/health-and-well-being

Yildirim, D., & Aycan, Z. (2008). Nurses' work demands and work-family conflict: A questionnaire survey. *International Journal of Nursing Studies*, *45*(9), 1366–1378. doi:10.1016/j.ijnurstu.2007.10.010 PMID:18262529

Zhao, Y., Cooklin, A. R., Richardson, A., Strazdins, L., Butterworth, P., & Leach, L. S. (2021). Parents' shift work in connection with work–family conflict and mental health: Examining the pathways for mothers and fathers. *Journal of Family Issues*, *42*(2), 445–473. doi:10.1177/0192513X20929059

KEY TERMS AND DEFINITIONS

Family and Social Life: Time that the worker spends with his/her family and on social activities.

Flexibility: Working time management strategy provided by the organization that allows the worker to decide certain aspects of his/her work schedule (e.g. start time).

Irregular Work Schedules: Organization of working time that presupposes irregularity in the daily or weekly work period or in the start and end times of shifts.

Job Satisfaction: Satisfaction that the worker expresses with his/her work and its various facets (e.g. working conditions, relationships with colleagues).

Nonstandard Work Schedules: Organization of working time that differs in some respect from the standard work schedule; that is, that it differs from a schedule practiced from Monday to Friday that starts in the morning and ends in the afternoon/evening and rest at the weekend.

Well-Being: Workers' perception of their physical, mental, and social state.

Work-Family Conflict: Conflict that exists between two spheres of the individual's life, work and family.

Work Schedule Management: Policies and practices adopted by the organization in managing the time of its workforce.

Chapter 6
Work Passion and Workaholism:
Antecedents of Psychological Well-Being and Burnout

Joana Vieira dos Santos
https://orcid.org/0000-0003-2612-8056
Psychology Research Centre, University of Algarve, Portugal

Gabriela Gonçalves
University of Algarve, Portugal

Catia Sousa
University of Algarve, Portugal

Alexandra Gomes
University of Algarve, Portugal

ABSTRACT

The passion for work can be a predictor of positive behaviors and attitudes, but can also be negative and harmful to the well-being of employees. The aim of this chapter is to test a model in which workaholism presents itself as the main variable and seeks to analyze antecedents (passion for work) and consequences (burnout and psychological well-being). With a sample of 441 participants from different professional areas, aged between 18 to 63 years (M = 12.47, SD = 1.46), the results show that harmonious work passion contributes to an explanation of workaholism and an individual's well-being. No statistically significant effects were observed on burnout levels. Organizations should seek to foster work environments that favor the harmonious passion of their employees, thus contributing to an increase in their psychological well-being.

DOI: 10.4018/978-1-6684-4181-7.ch006

INTRODUCTION

Workaholism can be defined as working an excessive number of hours and having a compulsion to work (e.g., Salanova et al., 2016). Several predictor variables and outcomes have been pointed out, but the subject is still long overdue for effective intervention designs. In this sense, it is the objective of this study to test a model in which workaholism presents itself as the main variable and seek to analyze antecedents (passion for work) and consequences (burnout and psychological well-being).

Van Beek and colleagues (2012) workaholic employees work hard to preserve and enhance feelings of well-being and self-esteem, and because they personally value the associated outcomes. Workaholic employees are chronically aroused and preoccupied with work. Consequently, they have little time for their spouses, family, and friends, or for leisure activities (Shimazu et al., 2019). The continuous work without sufficient recover opportunities may reduce workaholics' energy resources as time goes by, possibly leading to burnout (Gillet et al., 2017). Since workaholism is also linked to other adverse outcomes it can be considered a "bad" type of heavy work investment (Taris, et al., 2020).

Some studies consider (e.g., Van Beek et al., 2012) that workaholic employees work for instrumental value, so it has been suggested that workaholic employees have a negative self-image and lack self-confidence, leading to a high need to prove themselves at work to achieve a positive self-image (Robinson, 2014). On the other hand, a recent study (Taris, et al., 2020) showed that workaholism promotes introjected regulation and reduces intrinsic motivation across time, as opposed to being an outcome of these individual. Apparently, workaholic employees become more motivated by partially internalized external standards of self-worth and social approval (introjected regulation). So, it highlights the interesting to better understand the relation with work passion, such harmonious as obsessive. Harmonious work passion was associated to work engagement and obsessive work passion was found to be associated with global and specific components of both work engagement and workaholism (Tóth-Király, et al., 2020). According to Vallerand et al. (2003), passion can fuel motivation, improve well-being, and give meaning to everyday life. However, it can also arouse negative emotions, lead to inflexible persistence, and interfere with achieving balance. In this sense, the author proposed a dualistic model of passion for work composed of harmonious passion and obsessive passion. Work passion research most frequently utilizes the dualistic model of passion, which asserts two types of passion that differ based on the internalization of passion into one's identity: harmonious (adaptive) and obsessive (maladaptive) passion (Smith et al., 2022). These two types of passion depend on how the representation of the activity was internalized in the employees´ identity and are associated with different results, as well as with different contextual and dispositional antecedents (Salessi, et al., 2017).

Studies have shown that harmonious passion for work promotes more adaptive results than obsessive passion for various cognitive, affective, and behavioral results (Vallerand, 2008). Individuals with a passion for work have high levels of performance and innovation behaviors at work (Alfrian, 2018; McAllister et al., 2017). There are also some studies (e.g., Birkeland, & Buch, 2015 [citing Liu et al., 2011]; Forest et al., 2011) that specifically point out that harmonious passion contributes to the explanation of high levels of affective commitment.

Thus, it is considered important to know the relationship between passion for work and individual consequences. In this way, the authors seek to analyze passion for work as an antecedent of workaholism and, in terms of consequences, burnout and well-being.

BACKGROUND

Workaholism

The first author to investigate the concept of workaholism was Oates (1971), analyzing that some individuals work regularly above their limits, which could trigger the addition to work – a phenomenon known as workaholism, which means being addicted or dependent on work. Oates (1971) considered that the characteristics of workaholics' behaviors were like any other addition/dependence (e.g., alcoholism). The work developed by this author is considered the basis for workaholism studies; he identified disturbances in the areas of health, happiness, interpersonal relations, and social functioning because of the work addition and the extreme need to work.

In the 1980s, Machlowitz (1980) characterized workaholism as a personality trait that involves an intrinsic desire to work excessively to achieve greater responsibility, opportunities, and recognition at work. She emphasized that the posture of workaholics, expressed in effort and time, represents an extreme involvement with work.

For Shimazu and Schaufeli (2009), workaholism can be conceptualized as an internal force/impulse to which the subject cannot resist, presenting itself as a negative view of the process. Workaholism can be interpreted as an addition, that is, excessive and persistent behavior with negative consequences for the subject (Schaufeli, Taris, & Bakker, 2008). In this perspective, we can distinguish two major dimensions of this construct: working excessively (the behavioral dimension – investing too much time and energy at work; more than expected) and working compulsively (the cognitive dimension – having an uncontrollable impulse to get involved in job issues) (Gorgievski, et al., 2010; Schaufeli et al., 2008; Shimazu, & Schaufeli, 2009). From the perspective of some authors (e.g., Schaufeli, et al., 2009), it is necessary to combine the two dimensions – cognitive and behavioral – so that one can face the situation of true workaholism.

Spence and Robbins (1992) use the workaholic triad to describe the three typical characteristics of a workaholic: 1) pleasure through work; 2) involvement with it (involvement in work) and 3) the feeling of being driven to work. These dimensions give rise to three types of workaholics, namely: 1) workaholics; 2) workaholics and enthusiasts; 3) work enthusiasts. For Gomes (2011) the first ones are characterized by being involved and being very persistent with work, causing them to withdraw little pleasure, leading them to feel depressed when they are not performing professional activities; the second type refers to individuals who get involved with work and derive high satisfaction, however they are not very persistent; finally, the latter type is characterized by having high levels in the three components. Spence and Robbins (1992) characterize workaholics as people who always seek perfection in the performance of their tasks, presenting higher levels of stress and health problems.

Robinson (2014) identified four antecedents of workaholism: 1) environment (e.g. family context in which the individual grows); 2) interconnection between environments (e.g. company requirements for the employee to work too many hours in exchange for financial rewards or recognition); 3) neighborhood and community (e.g. stereotypes supporting positive portraits of workaholics); and (4) culture and societal beliefs (e.g. an economy that requires long hours of work in exchange for a financial situation that enables workers to enjoy an acceptable standard of living). McMillan and O'Driscoll (2006), when studying possible predictors of workaholism, proposed the existence of three antecedents: the drive to work, pleasure taken from work, and an obsessive personality. In turn, the adjacent behaviors associated with workaholism, lead individuals to work anytime and anywhere. These consequences can contribute to a spiraling increase for the workaholic. That is, he/she wants to work even more. Other studies analyzing the possible antecedents of workaholism cover personal demographic characteristics (Burke, et al., 2004; Harpaz, & Snir, 2003; Spence, & Robbins, 1992), personality (Jackson, et al., 2016), and organizational values (Burke, 2000; Schaef, & Fassel, 1988).

In addition to the antecedents of workaholism, several studies have shown that the organizational context plays a prominent role in the development and maintenance of workaholism (e.g., Fassel, 1990; Harpaz, & Snir, 2003), as some organizations have the reputation to be a place where people 'work hard and play hard.'

Regarding the possible consequences of workaholism, some studies have evidenced the relationship between workaholism and negative health and well-being outcomes (e.g., Balducci, et al., 2018). These include outcomes related to work, such as burnout (e.g., Gonçalves, et al., 2017; Schaufeli et al., 2009), or with work-family conflicts (e.g., Pan, 2018; Shkoler, et al., 2017). Studies have proven that workaholic´s social relations are weaker outside the workaholic's context of work, compared to the social relations of the other collaborators (Van Beek, et al., 2012). In addition, workaholism affects not only the individual workaholic himself, but also all those who surround him, not only at work but also in his or her personal life, leading to work-family conflict (e.g., Pan, 2018; Shkoler et al., 2017) and work-family guilt.

Work Passion

Work passion could be described as a strong inclination toward an activity that one likes and considers relevant to invest time and energy into (Vallerand, 2008). In addition, Zigarmi et al. (2009) consider 'an individual´s persistent, emotionally positive, meaning-based, sense of well-being, stemming from reoccurring cognitive and affective appraisals of various job and organizational situations, that result in consistent, constructive, work intentions and behaviors. This process involves: organizational characteristics (e.g., procedural justice, distributive justice, growth, and performance expectations), work characteristics (e.g., work autonomy, variety of tasks, balance of workload, and meaningful work), and relationship characteristics (e.g., feedback, collaboration, relationship with colleagues and leader) (Zigarmi et al., 2009; Nimon, & Zigarmi, 2014). The concept of passion is associated with a strong inclination towards an activity that the individual likes, finds important, and invests time and energy into on a solid and regular basis (Vallerand, 2010).

The positive cognitions of the work environment are positively associated with the satisfaction of psychological needs (Deci, & Ryan, 2000) which, in turn, are positively related to intentions and constructive behaviors, thus reflecting the rise of work passion. Both intentions and constructive behaviors can also be influenced by personal characteristics (e.g., beliefs, values) (Thibault-Landry, et al., 2018).

This process of the internalization of professional activity into the identity of the subject could develop into two different types of passions: a harmonious passion and an obsessive passion (Vallerand, 2010). According to Vallerand et al. (2006), harmonious passion results from the autonomous internalization of the activity, that is, when the subject freely accepts the activity as an important milestone for himself. Harmonious passion is often associated with positive emotions, long periods of concentration, and fluency in production; the activity occupies a significant space, being almost always in harmony with other domains of your life. Individuals 'in love' with their work have a sense of energetic and effective connection with the activities within their companies. They are involved with a sense of importance, inspiration, pride, and dedication. Most people feel excited and enthusiastic when engaged in pleasurable activities, thus affecting their lives in a positive way. In this sense, many investigations into passion reveal that this can positively affect several important outcomes such as psychological well-being, relationship and performance, positive emotions, and, above all, the individual's physical well-being (Vallerand, 2010) and flexible persistence (Chichekian, & Vallerand, 2022).

Alternatively, obsessive passion results from a persistent fixation of the activity and the becomes internalized into the subject's identity (Vallerand, 2010). In this type of passion, the activity controls the person, often provoking personal and behavioral conflicts. However, the person takes pleasure in what he is accomplishing because the work is a part of his own identity, resulting in a persistent fixation of the activity, often giving rise to feelings of social acceptance and self-esteem (Vallerand, & Houlfort, 2003). Obsessive passion is often associated with a controlled internalization, described as a feeling of social acceptance and self-esteem that are related to the individual's work or activity (Vallerand et al., 2007). People who experience this kind of passion feel compelled to practice it as an internal force that controls them; they are in search of feelings of social acceptance or self-esteem. In this sense the obsessive passion may prevent the individual from concentrating on their work by giving rise to negative feelings or experiences. (Vallerand et al, 2010). Individuals with obsessive passion display a rigid persistence toward activity that they love (Vallerand & Rahimi, 2022)

Previous studies show that a harmonious work passion contributes to the experience of more positive emotions, so it could improve the relationship between an individual and their work in a positive way, such as his work involvement and their pleasure.

Hypothesis One: Harmonious work passion contributes to an explanation of workaholism involvement.

Burnout

In an opposite way, Maslach and Jackson (1981) argue that when the individual believes that it is their work that 'makes a difference' and gives purpose to their life, then when they fail in this area they may be at risk for burnout. Maslach, et al., (2001) analyzed this concept because of the work context and the relationship that the individual establishes with the work. For these authors, burnout should be considered as an extension of occupational stress and is the result of a long-term process in which the worker feels that his resources to deal with the demands of the situation are already exhausted. Regarding the causes of burnout, the studies of Maslach and Jackson (1981) are the most thorough in this area. According to the authors, the continuous work of individuals who are constantly in suffering, whether it be psychological, physical, or social, can cause chronic stress and be tiring, contributing to the increase of burnout. It is characterized by fatigue, which is accompanied by suffering, reduced motivation, and by the development of dysfunctional behaviors within the workplace. (Schaufeli, et al., 2003).

In the same line of thought as Maslach (1993), the greater the distance between the individual and work, the higher the risk of developing this syndrome. Work often isolates people and causes conflict that, if left unresolved, can become chronic and destructive of interpersonal relationships within the workplace, thereby increasing feelings of frustration, anxiety, disrespect, and diminish the feeling of companionship between colleagues in situations of stress or difficulty (Maslach, & Leiter, 1997).

Inspired by the work of Maslach and Jackson (1981), Shirom and Melamed (2006) presented a new concept of burnout called the Shirom-Melamed Effort Measure (SMBM). Theoretically, the SMBM was based on the Hobfoll (1989, 1998) Conservation Resources Theory. According to this theory (Hobfoll, 1989, 1998), stress at work occurs when individuals feel threatened in relation to the loss of resources, when they lose them or when they are unable to recover them. According to these authors, burnout is an affective state characterized by a feeling of physical, emotional exhaustion and cognitive energies (Shirom & Melamed, 2006). It is, therefore, a consequence of prolonged exposure to chronic stress, manifested by the gradual depletion over time of individuals' intrinsic energy resources, leading to feelings of emotional exhaustion, physical tiredness, and cognitive tiredness. Burnout, therefore, represents a combination of physical fatigue, emotional exhaustion, and cognitive fatigue, three closely interrelated factors (Hobfoll & Shirom, 2000) that can be represented by a single burnout score. Physical fatigue alludes to feelings of tiredness and low energy levels when performing daily tasks at work. Emotional exhaustion occurs when individuals feel powerless to empathize with clients or coworkers and lack the energy to invest in relationships with others at work. Cognitive fatigue is related to reduced mental agility and slower thinking capacity (Shirom & Melamed, 2005).

Clearly, obsessive work passion could contribute to the emotional destructiveness of individual relations at workplace.

Hypothesis Two: Obsessive work passion contributes to emotional exhaustion.

Psychological Well-Being

Although happiness has a significant impact on people's daily lives, it is not simply a function of the material wealth of an individual. Studies have shown that the increase in the wealth of each is not directly related to the increase in happiness (Diener, & Biswas-Diener, 2008). According to Ryan and Deci (2001), there are two theoretical perspectives on the psychological well-being (PWB), eudemonic perspective and hedonic perspective: the first is reached individually, as a whole, according to the individual and subjective life course, often through a personal process of constant search of goals to achieve. The second perspective is found at certain times and circumstances of well-being (illness, physical, emotional, or psychological pain).

Hypothesis Three: Workaholism involvement contributes to the psychological well-being of individuals.

Working off previous studies developed in the theme of workaholism and psychological well-being, the main goal of this study is to achieve a better understanding on how positive work passion (the 'harmonious') could contribute to the explanation of positive work variables (e.g., work involvement, drive, and psychological well-being). Alternatively, negative work passion (the 'obsessive') may contribute to burnout, specifically in the emotional dimension (emotional exhaustion).

METHODOLOGY

Sample

The sample of this sample was non-probabilistic, composed by 441 employees from different professional areas (health institutions, educational institutions, commercials, financial systems, etc.), recruited by convenience. Respondents were informed of the anonymous and confidential nature of the data collected, and it was noted that their participation was voluntary and that there were no rewards for participation. All incomplete or incorrectly completed questionnaires were discarded.

The sample was mainly composed of females (n = 332; 75.3%). Their ages ranged from 18 to 68 years (M=25.86; SD=10.86). 243 (55.1%) had higher education degree. Most of them (n = 256; 58.0%) were employees with indefinite contracts and did not hold management position (n = 371; 84.1%).

Instruments

Work Passion Scale. The scale used in this study is from the Portuguese version of Work Passion Scale (Gonçalves, et al., 2014). The scale is composed of fourteen items and has two subscales: the subscale of harmonious passion (items 1 to 7), and the subscale of obsessive passion (items 8 to 14) (Vallerand & Houlfort, 2003). Concerning the subscale of harmonious passion, we have, for example, 'this activity allows me to live a variety of experiences,' and for the subscale of obsessive passion we have 'my state of mind depends on my ability to perform this activity.' This scale can be adapted to any type of activity that will be evaluated according to a 7-point Likert scale (1 – Strongly Disagree to 7 – Strongly Agree). It has no items reversed. The adaptation for the Portuguese population presented a Cronbach alpha above .70 and an alpha of .92 and .93 for harmonious passion and obsessive passion, respectively.

Workaholism Battery (WorkBat). For this study to evaluate the workaholic profile, we used the Portuguese version of WorkBat (Santos et al., 2018), originally developed by Spence and Robbins (1992). It is a scale composed of 25 items that evaluate three dimensions: psychological involvement with work (8 items, e.g. item 1 'When I have free time I like to relax and do nothing important'); internal compulsion to work (7 items, e.g. item 11 'I feel the duty to work hard even when it is not pleasant'); and pleasure derived from work (10 items, e.g. item 22 'I lose track of time when I am involved in a project'). Questions are rated on a 7-point Likert scale (1 – strongly disagree to 7 – strongly agree) and items 1, 2, 3 and 21 are reversible.

Burnout Inventory (SMBM). Originally developed by Shirom and Melamed (2006), this scale consists of fourteen items through three distinct subscales, namely, physical fatigue, emotional exhaustion, and cognitive fatigue. In the physical fatigue dimension, we have, for example, 'I feel tired' in the emotional exhaustion dimension we have as example 'I have difficulty concentrating,' and in the dimension of cognitive fatigue we have 'I feel unable to be sensitive to the needs of my work colleagues and customers.'

General Health Questionnaire (GHQ). This scale of psychological well-being was originally developed by Goldberg and Williams (1988). It is a one-dimensional scale consisting of twelve items, three of which are inverted. As an example of reversed items, we have item 2 'Lost hours of sleep due to concerns and item 5 'He felt constantly under pressure.' On the other hand, we have 9 items with a non-reversible direction (e.g., item 8 'was able to address their problems;' item 1 'You have been able to focus on what you do').

The questionnaire also has some questions to obtain demographic information, including gender, age, school year, and number of retentions on previous school years.

Data Collection Procedures

Data was collected using a self-report questionnaire.

Data Analysis

Data was analyzed with IBM SPSS 20.0 and AMOS 20.0. The psychometric properties of the questionnaire were studied by: a) descriptive statistics, which included computing the averages, standard deviations, skewness, and kurtosis whenever appropriate; b) Pearson's correlation coefficients for each scale that composed the questionnaire; c) hierarchical multiple regression; and d) structural equation modeling using maximum likelihood estimation, considering a robust method when the data does not follow a multivariate normal distribution (Schermelleh-Engel, et al., 2003), which did occur in this study.

The assumption of Tabachnick and Fidell (2014) to perform a hierarchical regression was guaranteed.

RESULTS

The purpose of this study was to establish a theoretical model detailing the relations between the different variables that were analyzed. The proposed model considers workaholism as the main variable and then analyses antecedents (work passion) and consequences (burnout and psychological well-being).

Descriptive Statistics

The means and standard deviations, skewness, and kurtosis for the different variables can be observed on Table 1.

Table 1. Descriptive statistics

	M	SD	Skewness	Kurtosis
Work Passion: Harmonious	**4.95**	1.38	-0.44	0.01
Work Passion: Obsessive	2.89	1.41	0.58	-0.38
Workaholism: Involvement	**4.39**	0.98	0.09	-0.08
Workaholism: Drive	3.99	1.37	0.10	0.38
Workaholism: Pleasure	3.79	1.05	0.28	-0.31
Burnout: Physical fatigue	3.45	3.44	0.50	-0.61
Burnout: Cognitive fatigue	2.73	2.73	0.83	-0.094
Burnout: Emotional exhaustion	2.27	2.26	1.33	1.12
Psychological Well-being	**4.17**	4.17	0.31	-1.00

Work involvement has a high mean of 4.39. According to McMillan (2002), despite Spence and Robbins (1992) consider the WI in all forms of workaholism, its specific role is no clear-cut (McMillan et al., 2002, p. 358). Work enjoyment has a mean of 3.79, this value is not consistent with any conceptualization of workaholism involving low enjoyment is contentious. The work drive mean is higher than central point meaning the participants feels compelled or driven to work because of their inner pressures. Those observed highest scores on three components of workaholism, not the standard one (high work involvement, high work drive and lower work enjoyment) are more consistent to the happy workaholic (scores highly on both drive and enjoyment). Nevertheless, despite the observed means are in three components of workaholism higher than the central point of the scale, the highest ones are work involvement and work drive. So, we decided to use the separate three components of this triad, to deep and better understand the relations between the concepts under study.

The highest values are observed in harmonious work passion, workaholism involvement, and psychological well-being. Regarding psychological well-being, it was changed to the positive way to be at the same direction as the other, so 'highest' means highest experience of psychological well-being.

Harman's Single Factor Test

Two criteria can lead to the presence of common method variance, if (a) a single strong factor emerges from an exploratory factor analysis or (b) a first factor accounts for the majority of the variance in the variables (Malhotra, Kim, & Patil, 2006; Podsakoff et al., 2003). According to Kock (2020), Harman's single factor test is sometimes performed via a principal components analysis, and other times via an exploratory factor analysis; the latter is generally seen as more appropriate, so it was the performed in this study.

There is no problem with common method bias in this data since the total variance extracted by one factor is 36.646%, so less the recommended threshold of 50%.

Pearson's Correlation Statistics

The highest correlations are between each scale dimension (Table 2).

Table 2. Pearson's correlation statistics

	1	2	3	4	5	6	7	8	9
1. Work Passion: Harmonious	1	.445**	.101*	.104*	.507**	-.252**	-.265**	-.234**	.079
2. Work Passion: Obsessive		1	.228**	.300**	.431**	.002	.052	.080	.023
3. Workaholism: Involvement			1	.407**	.197**	.100*	.146**	.078	.438**
4. Workaholism: Drive				1	.282**	.193**	.179**	.152**	.007
5. Workaholism: Pleasure					1	-.229**	-.139**	-.037	.193
6. Burnout: Physical fatigue						1	.695**	.503**	.001
7. Burnout: Cognitive fatigue							1	.640**	-.043
8. Burnout: Emotional exhaustion								1	.081
9. Psychological Well-being									1

Regressions

Regarding harmonious work passion, it contributes to the explanation of workaholism involvement ($B = .101$; $t = 2.119$; $p = .035$; $r^2 = 10\%$) and workaholism pleasure ($B = .104$; $t = 2.179$; $p = .030$; $r^2 =$

6%). In the other way, when analyzing the explanation of obsessive work passion to burnout (emotional exhaustion), the effect is not statistically significant ($B = .080$; $t = 1.674$; $p = .094$; $r^2 = 4\%$).

As observed, the harmonious work passion is the work passion dimension with the highest mean in our study and has the most explanation power, so we developed a hierarchical regression in order to better observe its effects in variable studies.

Table 3 shows the three models explaining psychological well-being. The first considers only the harmonious work passion (r^2 1%; $p = .654$), the second adds the workaholism dimensions (r^2 51%; $p = .000$), and the third adds the burnout dimensions (r^2 54%; $p = .122$).

Table 3. Hierarchal multiple regression to explain psychological wellbeing

		B	t	p
1	Harmonious Work Passion	.081	.453	.654
2	Harmonious Work Passion	.003	-.017	.986
	Workaholism Involvement	.597	2.983	**.006**
	Workaholism Drive	-.158	-.979	.335
	Workaholism Pleasure	.307	1.349	.187
3	Harmonious Passion	-.169	-.725	.475
	Workaholism Involvement	.742	3.200	**.004**
	Workaholism Drive	-.130	-.761	.453
	Workaholism Pleasure	.362	1.400	.173
	Burnout: Physical fatigue	-.135	-.594	.557
	Burnout: Physical fatigue	-.209	-.700	.490
	Burnout: Emotional exhaustion	.054	.202	.841

Our data suggest that the involvement of Workaholism has a strong effect on psychological well-being.

Confirmatory Factor Analysis for the Model

In this section, our goal was to establish a model to explain the associations between the variables under study, starting both from their theoretical principles and the relations between the different variables. Inferential statistics, namely regression analysis, allowed us to construct a predictive model we assessed using structural equations. The degree of the model's goodness of fit was studied with the aid of different parameters. The ratio between chi-square statistic and the distribution's degrees of freedom was $X^2/df = 1.686$. The comparative fit index (CFI) and the goodness of fit index (GFI) were, respectively, 0.946 and 0.985, showing a good model fit (Bentler, 1992; Joreskog, 1996). Concerning error assessment, the literature suggests that the Standardised Root Mean Square Residual (SRMSR) and the Root Mean Square Error of Approximation (RMSEA) should be below 0.05 to verify a good model fit, while values between 0.05 and 0.08 represent a reasonable fit (Browne, & Cudeck, 1993; MacCallum, Browne, & Sugawara, 1996). The SMRSM in our model was 0.009 and the RMSEA was 0.030, which may allow us to infer a good model fit.

DISCUSSION

The present study illustrates the applicability of the employee work passion appraisal model to the field of work and the relevance of harmonious passion in explaining positive organizational results, such as psychological well-being.

The results show dimension of harmonious passion has higher levels compared to those recorded for the obsessive passion dimension. Also, regarding workaholism, the positive dimension, involvement, has the higher observed level. The observed mean of psychological well-being is above the central point. It is interesting to relate these results to the Hofstede model in which Portugal, being a more feminine country, has citizens tend to value equality, solidarity, quality in their professional life (Hofstede, 2022), and the balance between family and work (Hofstede, 2011). In this sense, the results obtained may be related to the cultural dimension of femininity, as individuals in love harmoniously with their work are able to balance their work activity with the remaining aspects of their life (e.g., hobbies, friends, family).

The results support the first hypothesis (H1: Harmonious work passion contributes to that explanation of workaholism involvement. Harmonious passion develops when an activity is autonomously internalized in the individual's identity (Marsh et al., 2013) and when it is freely chosen as highly important to you (Vallerand and Houlfort, 2003). In this sense, driven by their interests, the individual selects an activity to get involved in (Lalande et al., 2015).

The same does not happen for obsessively passionate subjects, where work occupies a disproportionate space in their life and conflicts with other aspects (Vallerand & Houlfort, 2003). The results could not support the second hypothesis (H2: Obsessive work passion contributes to emotional exhaustion). A possible explanation could be because the levels of obsessive work passion are not so high in our sample, as well the levels of burnout. This could be a more readily observed relation in masculine cultures (Hofstede, 2011).

The third hypothesis was also confirmed by results (H3: Workaholism involvement contributes to the psychological well-being of individuals). Considering the above, we believe that high-functioning individuals work in environments that make them probably feel an inherent pleasure in being involved in work, in such a way that they invest time and energy in accomplishing it, without it coming into conflict with personal life. This increases the involvement of the employees in other activities, which are not formally prescribed, and develops the emotional bond to their organization.

Despite the dualistic work passion model used, the major results in our study, hierarchical regressions, and the confirmatory model, are related to the harmonious passion. According to a meta-analysis about passion at work and individual and work outcomes (Pollack, et al., 2020), the findings relating to harmonious passion are consistent, in that it is positively related to various types of affects, psychological states, attitudes, and behaviors.

Considering that an organization requires human capital to achieve its business objectives; companies, which offer a better quality of life to their employees, must promote a harmonious passion for work (Forest et al., 2011). According to McAllister et al. (2017), it may be possible to identify and select employees who are passionate about their work (through the recruitment and selection process) and develop the passion of employees already belonging to the organization. Considering this, organizations with favorable work environments will probably have greater strength to attract and retain valuable employees (Permarupan, et al., 2013) – who present, for example, passion for their work. If our natural tendency is to perform gratifying, personally meaningful, and absorbing activities more frequently and for longer in our daily experiences (Rosa, & Vianello, 2020), then such could be observed in our work activities as well.

The present study contributes to the discussion in workaholism triad analysis, considering the separate analysis and the showed importance of work involvement. In future other studies should be performed to better understand each dimension of workaholism and their efficacy in predicting productivity. As far as this study could allow to understand the harmonious passion are related to work involvement and both positively contributes to psychological well-being. Should a positive relation to work mitigate the negative impact of workaholism and promote a positive work involvement which allow a positive well-being? Our results indicate so, highlighting the importance for harmonious passion. Human Resources Managers could be the important key in promoting this type of passion on employees´, by developing environment who potentiate harmonious passion they are promoting healthy workplaces with healthy employees. The importance of this type of passion was patent in the power to mitigate the possible negative impact of workaholism and, in other hand, promote a positive way of work involment which are positively related to well-being.

ACKNOWLEDGMENT

This work was funded by national funds through FCT - Fundação para a Ciência e a Tecnologia - as part the project CIP - Refª UID/PSI/04345/2020».

REFERENCES

Alfrian, F. D. (2018). Does spirituality at work has an impact on the relationship between passion and innovative behavior of employee? *RJOAS*, *6*(78), 106–111. doi:10.18551/rjoas.2018-06.11

Balducci, C., Avanzi, L., & Fraccaroli, F. (2018). The individual costs of workaholism: An analysis based on multisource and prospective data. *Journal of Management*, *44*(7), 2961–2986. doi:10.1177/0149206316658348

Bentler, P., & Bonett, D. (1980). Significance tests and goodness of fit in the analysis of covariance structures. *Psychological Bulletin*, *88*(3), 588–606. doi:10.1037/0033-2909.88.3.588

Bentler, P. M. (1992). On the fit of models to covariances and methodology to the Bulletin. *Psychological Bulletin*, *112*(3), 400–404. doi:10.1037/0033-2909.112.3.400 PMID:1438635

Birkeland, I. K., & Buch, R. (2015). The dualistic model of passion for work: Discriminate and predictive validity with work engagement and workaholism. *Motivation and Emotion*, *39*(3), 392–408. doi:10.100711031-014-9462-x

Browne, M. W., & Cudeck, R. (1993). Alternative ways of assessing model fit. In K. Bollen & J. Long (Eds.), *Testing structural equation models* (pp. 445–455). Sage.

Burke, R. (2000). Workaholism in organizations: Psychological and physical wellbeing consequences. *Stress Medicine*, *16*(1), 11–16. doi:10.1002/(SICI)1099-1700(200001)16:1<11::AID-SMI825>3.0.CO;2-U

Burke, R. (2008). Work motivations, satisfactions, and health: Passion versus addiction. In R. Burke & C. Cooper (Eds.), *The Long Working Hours Culture. Causes, Consequences and Choices* (pp. 227–251). Emerald.

Burke, R., Oberklaid, F., & Burgess, Z. (2004). Workaholism among Australian women psychologists: Antecedents and consequence. *Women in Management Review*, *19*(5), 252–259. doi:10.1108/09649420410545971

Chichekian, T., & Vallerand, R. J. (2022). Passion for science and the pursuit of scientific studies: The mediating role of rigid and flexible persistence and activity involvement. *Learning and Individual Differences*, *93*, 102104. doi:10.1016/j.lindif.2021.102104

Deci, E. L., & Ryan, R. M. (2000). The "what" and "why" of goal pursuits: Human needs and the self-determination of behavior. *Psychological Inquiry*, *11*(4), 227–268. doi:10.1207/S15327965PLI1104_01

Diener, E., & Biswas-Diener, R. (2008). *Happiness: Unlocking the mysteries of psychological wealth*. Blackwell Publishing., doi:10.1002/9781444305159

Fassel, D. (1990). *Working ourselves to death: The high costs of workaholism, the rewards of recovery*. Harper Collins.

Forest, J., Mageau, G. A., Sarrazin, C., & Morin, E. M. (2011). "Work is my passion": The different affective, behavioural, and cognitive consequences of harmonious and obsessive passion toward work. *Canadian Journal of Administrative Sciences/Revue Canadienne des Sciences de l'Administration*, *28*(1), 27–40. doi:10.1002/cjas.170

Gillet, N., Morin, A. J. S., Cougot, B., & Gagné, M. (2017). Workaholism profiles: Associations with determinants, correlates, and outcomes. *Journal of Occupational and Organizational Psychology*, *90*(4), 559–586. doi:10.1111/joop.12185

Goldberg, D., & Williams, P. (1988). *A user's guide to the General Health Questionnaire*. NFER.

Gonçalves, G., Brito, F., Sousa, C., Santos, J., & Sousa, A. (2017). Workaholism and burnout: Antecedents and effects. In P. M. Arezes, J. S. Baptista, M. P. Barroso, P. Carneiro, P. Cordeiro, N. Costa, R. B. Melo, A. S. Miguel, & G. Perestrelo (Eds.), *Occupational Safety and Hygiene, V* (pp. 53–57). Taylor & Francis Group. doi:10.1201/9781315164809-11

Gonçalves, G., Orgambídez-Ramos, A., Ferrão, M., & Parreira, T. (2014). Adaptation and Initial Validation of the Passion Scale in a Portuguese Sample. *Escritos de Psicologia*, *7*(2), 19–27. doi:10.24310/espsiescpsi.v7i2.13255

Gorgievski, M., Bakker, A., & Schaufeli, W. (2010). Work engagement and workaholism: Comparing the self-employed and salaried employees. *The Journal of Positive Psychology*, *5*(1), 83–96. doi:10.1080/17439760903509606

Harpaz, I., & Snir, R. (2003). Workaholism: Its definition and nature. *Human Relations*, *56*(3), 291–319. doi:10.1177/0018726703056003613

Hofstede, G. (2011). Dimensionalizing cultures: The Hofstede model in context. *Online Readings in Psychology and Culture*, *2*(1), 1–26. doi:10.9707/2307-0919.1014

Hofstede (2022). *Country Comparison*. Hofstede. https://www.hofstede-insights.com/country-comparison/portugal/

Jackson, S. S., Fung, M.-C., Moore, M.-A. C., & Jackson, C. J. (2016). Personality and Workaholism. *Personality and Individual Differences*, *95*, 114–120. doi:10.1016/j.paid.2016.02.020

Joreskog, K. G. (1996). Testing a simple structure hypothesis in factor analysis. *Psychometrika*, *31*(2), 165–178. doi:10.1007/BF02289505 PMID:5222205

Lalande, D., Vallerand, R. J., Lafrenière, M. A. K., Verner-Filion, J., Laurent, F. A., Forest, J., & Paquet, Y. (2015). Obsessive passion: A compensatory response to unsatisfied needs. *Journal of Personality*, *85*(2), 163–178. doi:10.1111/jopy.12229 PMID:26385633

Maccallum, R. C., Browne, M. W., & Sugawara, H. M. (1996). Power analysis and determination of size sample for covariance structure modeling. *Psychological Methods*, *1*(2), 130–149. doi:10.1037/1082-989X.1.2.130

Machlowitz, M. (1980). *Workaholics: Living with them, working with them*. Addison-Wesley.

Marsh, H. W., Vallerand, R. J., Lafrenière, M.-A. K., Parker, P., Morin, A. J. S., Carbonneau, N., Jowett, S., Bureau, J. S., Fernet, C., Guay, F., Salah Abduljabbar, A. S., & Paquet, Y. (2013). Passion: Does one scale fit all? Construct validity of two-factor passion scale and psychometric invariance over different activities and languages. *Psychological Assessment*, *25*(3), 796–809. doi:10.1037/a0032573 PMID:23647035

Maslach, C. (1993). Burnout: A multidimensional perspective. In W. B. Schaufeli, C. Maslach, & T. Marek (Eds.), *Professional burnout: Recent developments in theory and research* (pp. 19–32). Taylor & Francis.

Maslach, C., & Jackson, S. E. (1981). The measurement of experienced burnout. *Journal of Organizational Behavior*, *2*(2), 99–113. doi:10.1002/job.4030020205

Maslach, C., & Leiter, M. P. (1997). *The truth about burnout*. Jossey-Bass.

Maslach, C., Schaufeli, W. B., & Leiter, M. P. (2001). Job burnout. *Annual Review of Psychology*, *52*(1), 397–422. doi:10.1146/annurev.psych.52.1.397 PMID:11148311

McAllister, C. P., Harris, J. N., Hochwarter, W. A., Perrewé, P. L., & Ferris, G. R. (2017). Got resources? A multi-sample constructive replication of perceived resource availability's role in work passion–job outcomes relationships. *Journal of Business and Psychology*, *32*(2), 147–164. doi:10.100710869-016-9441-1

McMillan, L. H. W., & O'Driscoll, M. P. (2006). Exploring new frontiers to generate an integrated definition of workaholism. In R. J. Burke (Ed.), *Research Companion to Working Time and Work Addiction* (pp. 89–107). Edward Elgar Publishing Limited. doi:10.4337/9781847202833.00012

Nimon, K., & Zigarmi, D. (2014). The work cognition inventory: Initial evidence of construct validity for the revised form. *Journal of Career Assessment*, *23*(1), 117–136. doi:10.1177/1069072714523241

Oates, W. (1971). *Confessions of a Workaholic: The Facts about Work Addiction*. World Publishing.

Pan, S. Y. (2018). Do workaholic hotel supervisors provide family supportive supervision? A role identity perspective. *International Journal of Hospitality Management*, *68*, 59–67. doi:10.1016/j.ijhm.2017.09.013

Peirperl, M., & Jones, B. (2001). Workaholics or overworkers: Productivity or pathology? *Group & Organization Management, 26*(3), 369–393. doi:10.1177/1059601101263007

Permarupan, P. Y., Saufi, R. A., Kasim, R. S. R., & Balakrishnan, B. K. (2013). The impact of organizational climate on employee's work passion and organizational commitment. *Procedia: Social and Behavioral Sciences, 107*, 88–95. doi:10.1016/j.sbspro.2013.12.403

Pollack, J., Ho, V., O'Boyle, E., & Kirkman, B. (2020). Passion at work: A meta-analysis of individual work outcomes. *Journal of Organizational Behavior, 41*(4), 1–21. doi:10.1002/job.2434

Robinson, B. E. (2014). *Chained to the desk: A guidebook for workaholics, their partners and children and the clinicians who treat them* (3rd ed.). New York University Press.

Rosa, A., & Vianello, M. (2020). Linking calling with workaholism: Examining obsessive and harmonious passion as mediators and moderators. *Journal of Career Assessment, 28*(4), 1–19. doi:10.1177/1069072720909039

Ryan, R. M., & Deci, E. L. (2001). On happiness and human potentials: A review of research on hedonic and eudaimonic well-being. *Annual Review of Psychology, 52*(1), 141–166. doi:10.1146/annurev.psych.52.1.141 PMID:11148302

Salanova, M., López-González, A. A., Llorens, S., Líbano, M., Vicente-Herrero, M. T., & Tomás-Salvá, M. (2016). Your work may be killing you! Workaholism, sleep problems and cardiovascular risk. *Work and Stress, 30*(3), 228–242. doi:10.1080/02678373.2016.1203373

Salessi, S., Omar, A., & Vaamonde, J. D. (2017). Conceptual considerations of work passion. *Ciencias Psicológicas (Montevideo), 11*(2), 165–178. doi:10.22235/cp.v11i2.1488

Santos, J., Sousa, C., Sousa, A., Figueiredo. L., & Gonçalves, G. (2018). Psychometric evidences of the workaholism battery in a Portuguese sample. *Journal of Spatial and Organizational Dynamics – Human Factors in Safety and Health in the Workplace, 6*(1), 40–51.

Schaef, A. W., & Fassel, D. (1988). *The addictive organization*. Harper & Row.

Schaufeli, W., Bakker, A., van der Heijden, M., & Prins, J. (2009). Workaholism, burnout and well-being among junior doctors: The mediating role of role conflict. *Work and Stress, 23*(2), 155–172. doi:10.1080/02678370902834021

Schaufeli, W. B., & Buunk, B. P. (2003). Burnout: An overview of 25 years of research and theorizing. The Handbook of Work and Health Psychology, 2(1), 282–424. doi:10.1002/0470013400.ch19

Schaufeli, W. B., Taris, T. W., & Bakker, A. B. (2008). It takes two to tango: Workaholism is working excessively and working compulsively. In R. J. Burke & C. L. Cooper (Eds.), *The long work hour's culture: Causes, consequences and choices* (pp. 203–226). Emerald.

Schermelleh-Engel, K., Moosbrugger, H., & Müller, H. (2003). Evaluating the fit of structural equation models: Test of significance and descriptive goodness-of-fit measures. *Methods of Psychological Research Online, 8*(2), 23–74. https://www.dgps.de/fachgruppen/methoden/mpr-online/issue20/

Shimazu, A., Balducci, C., & Taris, T. (2019). Workaholism: about the concept, its antecedents, consequences, and prevention. In T. Taris, M. Peeters, & H. De Witte (Eds.), *The Fun and Frustration of Modern Working Life* (pp. 164–176). Pelckmans.

Shimazu, A., & Schaufeli, W. (2009). Is workaholism good or bad for employee wellbeing? The distinctiveness of workaholism and work engagement among Japanese employees. *Industrial Health*, *47*(5), 495–502. doi:10.2486/indhealth.47.495 PMID:19834258

Shirom, A., & Melamed, S. (2006). A comparison of the construct validity of two burnout measures in two groups of professionals. *International Journal of Stress Management*, *13*(2), 176–200. doi:10.1037/1072-5245.13.2.176

Shkoler, O., Rabenu, E., Vasiliu, C., Sharoni, G., & Tziner, A. (2017). Organizing the confusion surrounding workaholism: New structure, measure, and validation. *Frontiers in Psychology*, *8*, 1803. doi:10.3389/fpsyg.2017.01803 PMID:29097989

Smith, R. W., Min, H., Ng, M. A., Haynes, N. J., & Clark, M. A. (2022). A Content Validation of Work Passion: Was the Passion Ever There? *Journal of Business and Psychology*, 1–23. doi:10.100710869-022-09807-1

Spence, J., & Robbins, A. (1992). Workaholism: Definition, measurement, and preliminary results. *Journal of Personality Assessment*, *58*(1), 160–178. doi:10.120715327752jpa5801_15 PMID:16370875

Tabachnick, G., & Fidell, L. (2014). *Using Multivariate Statistics* (6th ed.). Pearson.

Taris, T., van Beek, I., & Schaufeli, W. (2020). The Motivational Make-Up of Workaholism and Work Engagement: A Longitudinal Study on Need Satisfaction, Motivation, and Heavy Work Investment. *Frontiers in Psychology*, *11*(1419), 1–17. doi:10.3389/fpsyg.2020.01419 PMID:32714248

Thibault-Landry, A., Egan, R., Crevier-Braud, L., Manganelli, L., & Forest, J. (2018). An empirical investigation of the employee work passion appraisal model using self-determination theory. *Advances in Developing Human Resources*, *20*(2), 148–168. doi:10.1177/1523422318756636

Tóth-Király, I., Morin, A., & Salmela-Aro, K. (2020). A longitudinal perspective on the associations between work engagement and workaholism. *Work and Stress*, 1–29. doi:10.1080/02678373.2020.1801888

Vallerand, R., & Rahimi, S. (2022). On the passion scale: Theory, Research and Psychometric Properties. In W. Ruch, A. Bakker, L. Tay, & F. Gander (Eds.), *Handbook of Positive Psychology Assessment* (pp. 248–272). Hogrefe Publishing.

Vallerand, R. J. (2008). On the psychology of passion: In search of what makes people's lives most worth living. *Canadian Psychology*, *49*(1), 1–13. doi:10.1037/0708-5591.49.1.1

Vallerand, R. J. (2010). On passion for life activities: The Dualistic Model of Passion. In M. P. Zanna (Ed.), (pp. 97–193). Advances in Experimental Social Psychology. Academic Press.

Vallerand, R. J., & Houlfort, N. (2003). Passion at work: Toward a new conceptualization. In S. W. Gilliland, D. D. Steiner, & D. P. Skarlicki (Eds.), *Emerging Perspective on Values in Organizations* (pp. 175–204). Information Age Publishing.

Vallerand, R. J., Paquet, Y., Philippe, F. L., & Charest, J. (2010). On the role of passion for work in burnout: A process model. *Journal of Personality*, *78*(1), 289–312. doi:10.1111/j.1467-6494.2009.00616.x PMID:20433620

Vallerand, R. J., Rousseau, F. L., Grouzet, F. M. E., Dumais, A., Grenier, S., & Blanchard, C. B. (2006). Passion in sport: A look at determinants and affective experiences. *Journal of Sport & Exercise Psychology*, *28*(4), 454–478. doi:10.1123/jsep.28.4.454

Vallerand, R. J., Salvy, S. J., Mageau, G. A., Elliot, A. J., Denis, P. L., Grouzet, F. M., & Blanchard, C. (2007). On the role of passion in performance. *Journal of Personality*, *75*(5), 505–533. doi:10.1111/j.1467-6494.2007.00447.x PMID:17489890

Van Beek, I., Hu, Q., Schaufeli, W., Taris, T., & Schreurs, B. (2012). For fun, love, or money: What drives workaholic, engaged, and burned-out employees at work? *Applied Psychology*, *61*(1), 30–55. doi:10.1111/j.1464-0597.2011.00454.x

Zigarmi, D., Galloway, F. J., & Roberts, T. P. (2018). Work locus of control, motivational regulation, employee work passion, and work intentions: An empirical investigation of an appraisal model. *Journal of Happiness Studies: An Interdisciplinary Forum on Subjective Well-Being*, *19*(1), 231–256. doi:10.100710902-016-9813-2

Zigarmi, D., Nimon, K., Houson, D., Witt, D., & Diehl, J. (2009). Beyond engagement: Toward a framework and operational definition for employee work passion. *Human Resource Development Review*, *8*(3), 300–326. doi:10.1177/1534484309338171

KEY TERMS AND DEFINITIONS

Burnout: Is characterized by fatigue, which is accompanied by suffering, reduced motivation, and by the development of dysfunctional behaviors within the workplace.

Harmonious passion: Autonomous internalization of the activity, occupies a significant space, being almost always in harmony with other domains of your life.

Obsessive passion: Results from a persistent fixation of the activity and the becomes internalized into the subject's identity.

Well-being: Could be considered a core feature of mental health and may be defined as including hedonic (enjoyment) and eudaimonic (meaning) happiness, as well as resilience (e.g., coping, emotion regulation, healthy problem solving).

Work Compulsively: Could be considered a cognitive dimension of workaholism, characterized by having an uncontrollable impulse to get involve in job issues and tasks.

Work excessively: Could be considered a behavioral dimension of workaholism, characterized by investing too much time and energy at work.

Work Passion: A strong inclination toward an activity that likes and considers relevant to invest time and energy.

Workaholism: An internal force/impulse to work an excessive number of hours and having a compulsion to work.

Chapter 7
Workplace Ostracism and Subjective Well-Being:
A Reflection on Understanding the Experiences of Syrian Asylum Seekers in Turkey

Basak Ucanok Tan
https://orcid.org/0000-0002-4025-1707
Istanbul Bilgi University, Turkey

Fatma Nur Bayır
https://orcid.org/0000-0002-9598-1029
United Work, Turkey

ABSTRACT

There is growing recognition that better adaptation and settlement is achieved amongst refugees when they obtain meaningful and humane employment in the host country. However, asylum seekers face significant barriers to not only finding work, but also experience difficulties integrating into the workplace and face discrimination at work. Such discrimination may take the form of ostracism and is likely to lead to decreased identification with the employing organization along with colleagues and supervisors. The current chapter is thus a non-systematic review of the literature on workplace ostracism and calls for immediate discussion on refugee and asylum seekers' work experiences, and how neglect and discriminatory practices may lead to undesirable work outcomes and socio-cultural integration problems.

INTRODUCTION

The struggle for human rights in the Middle Eastern and North African region, which was ignited by the Arab Spring, turned into a civil war in Syria in 2011. The conflict has caused many Syrians to lose their lives and forced others to seek asylum in nearby countries (Akar & Erdoğdu, 2019). The vast ma-

DOI: 10.4018/978-1-6684-4181-7.ch007

jority of these refugees preferred migrating to Turkey (Öztürk & Timuçin, 2021) both because it is the closest border country to Syria and that it applied an open-door policy (Akar & Erdoğdu, 2019). Since April 2011, the number of Syrian citizens entering Turkey has increased steadily (Öztürk & Timuçin, 2021). As a border neighbor, Turkey, which was most affected by the civil war in Syria, has become the country hosting the largest refugee population in the world today (Alptekin, Ulutaş Akçay & Gündüz Ustabaşı, 2018). United Nations reported that 3.67 million Syrian citizens were officially registered by Turkey (UNHCR, 2021).

The open-door policy has been seen as a "humanitarian discourse" concerning the admission and accommodation of Syrian refugees. "Turkey's policies have been broadly acclaimed and well-received both domestically and internationally. The open-door policy was neither criticized nor questioned" (Sert & Danış, 2020). "Initially, Syrians were seen as guests because the war would end, and they would return to their own country. But in 2014 they were given temporary protection status. The 'Temporary Protection Status' granted to 3.65 million people can be defined as Turkey's way of defining refugee rights based on ambiguity, uncertainty and unpredictable living conditions. At the same time, the European Union made an agreement with Turkey allowing Syrians to stay in Turkey. Thus, Syrian refugees were prevented from going to European countries to seek asylum, which meant, as the crisis in Syria continues, there is neither a return option nor the possibility of resettlement in a safe European country. All this means that Syrian refugees are "now" permanently settling in Turkey" (Sert & Danış, 2020).

To elaborate on the context of Syrian asylum seekers in Turkey and to frame and clarify their status, it is critical to distinguish them from immigrants. As defined in the 1951 Refugee Convention, a refugee is "someone who is unable or unwilling to return to their country of origin owing to a well-founded fear of being persecuted for reasons of race, religion, nationality, membership of a particular social group, or political opinion" (UNHCR, 2022a). According to the UNHCR, a person who seeks asylum "is some- one whose request for sanctuary has yet to be processed" (UNHCR, 2022b). Although there is no internationally accepted legal definition of a migrant (Amnesty International, 2022), most agencies center on framing migrants to be people staying outside their country of origin, who are not asylum-seekers or refugees. Some migrants leave their country because they want to work, study, or join family others feel they must leave because of poverty, political unrest, gang violence, natural disasters or other serious circumstances that exist there. Recent research suggests that refugees and people seeking asylum suffer from educational disadvantages, mental health issues and further marginalization especially after the COVID-19 pandemic (Mupenzi et al., 2020; Rees & Fisher, 2020).

To better frame Syrian asylum-seekers experiences and to reflect on their work-related conditions, it is important to understand the policies with regards to their socio-economic, educational and health conditions in Turkey.

THE BACKGROUND OF SYRIAN REFUGEE POLICY IN TURKEY

In Turkey, public services such as health and education have been stretched by the refugee influx, and this negatively affected the quality of life in the country as well (Akar & Erdoğdu, 2019). Initially the influx was assumed to be a temporary phenomenon, and Syrian refugees were seen as "guests" and warmly welcomed. However, after 2014–2015, the positive atmosphere began to gradually erode, and refugees were perceived by Turkish citizens as "overstaying guests." The Syrian refugee policy shifted from a short-term protection and humanitarian assistance to longer-term social and economic integration. This strain has aggravated socio-economic and political tensions in Turkey (Özçürümez Bilgili, 2018).

The refugee policy in Turkey mostly includes providing for basic services for survival and lacks psychological support for the trauma caused by the war and displacement. Being a refugee means to be displaced suddenly and often violently which means to be marked by trauma that is reflected beyond post-traumatic stress disorder (PTSD). Trauma creates a situation where people feel deep helplessness and have an experience of being abandoned by all good and helping objects (Özçürümez Bilgili, 2018). Massive events, like war and terror attacks, increase the risk of mental trauma because of the increase in stressful events that go beyond ordinary daily life (e.g., physical injury, abuse, and deprivation of needs) (Şar, 2017). The anxiety caused by such trauma may be expressed as dissociated states of mind, as bodily pains and other somatic dysfunctions, overwhelming thoughts and feelings, behavioral tendencies etc. (Varvin, 2017). For Syrians, leaving their own country and trying to adapt to a new realm of existence brings about problems such as work, shelter, language, and education. Under the precarious conditions of being a refugee, many asylum seekers must maintain their physical, moral, and psychological integrity and provide for the family's basic material needs for safety, shelter, nutrition, activity, and health.

Labor market integration deserves special attention since the participation of refugees in the local labor force holds a critical role. Less effective adaptation of refugees to the labor market increases both individual and societal costs. Although many people tend to see refugees as a burden, refugees can provide a larger talent pool for the host economy and be able to make an active contribution to the host community (Akar & Erdoğdu, 2019).

The number of work permits granted to Syrians is very low due to major weaknesses and a lack of incentives (İçduygu & Diker, 2017). According to the latest DGMM figures, there are more than 1.7 million (61% of the total) Syrians of working age (between 15 and 65) in Turkey. Yet, only 1% of the total working-age population has been granted work permits according to the Ministry of Labor and Social Security (İçdugu & Diker, 2017). The socio-economic conditions surrounding Syrian refugees pose a great threat to both their well-being and their integration into the local system. Those refugees who have succeeded to enter the labor market also suffer from negative perceptions of the recipient populations. The majority of the Syrian asylum seekers work in blue-collar jobs, due to their socioeconomic status, skill level, language capability, and other psychosocial factors (Bennett, Scornaiencki, Brzozowski, Denis, & Magalhaes, 2012). The skills profile of Syrian refugees remains an overarching obstacle to their access to formal employment opportunities (Kayaoglu & Erdogan, 2019). Overall, the level of education and of Turkish command are the two main determinants of access to reliable employment for Syrians.

REFLECTIONS ON THE EXPERIENCES OF SYRIAN ASYLUM SEEKERS IN TURKEY

To understand the experiences and realities of Syrian asylum seekers in Turkey this section outlines the socio-cultural and economic constraints that surround the Syrian people. It was indicated earlier in the chapter that the number of Syrians migrating to Turkey increased tremendously since 2014. Almost 80 percent of the Syrians came directly from their own means through irregular crossings from the border. As it is frequently encountered in immigration cases, it was mainly based on compatriot ties. The Syrians settled primarily in the neighborhoods of their fellow countrymen in the form of large groups in tribes (Alptekin, Ulutaş Akçay & Gündüz Ustabaşı, 2018). The integration of the large groups of Syrian asylum seekers is a complex, highly ambiguous and problematic process for the host countries. The integration concept may be defined according to different actors' interests and values (Castles, Korac, Vasta, & Vertovec, 2002; Penninx & Garcés-Mascareñas, 2016; Spencer & Cooper, 2006) and thus requires change in the relationship between the migrant and the receiving society along different dimensions, whether structural, social, or personal (Kappa, 2019).

Integration is a highly vague concept and there is no single definition. It is a concept that includes the rights of (compulsory) immigrants, settlement processes and legal regulations. Main "rights" (employment, housing, education, health), "social connections" (social bridges, social bonds, social connections), "facilitators" (language and cultural knowledge, security, and stability) and "determinants" (rights and citizenship) are grouped under four main headings (Ward et al., 2020). It emphasizes the development of social relations between immigrants and the communities they migrated to, the sense of belonging to the community they migrated to, and the importance of access to rights and resources such as education, work, and housing (Şimşek, 2019). One of the main pillars of refugee integration is attainment of secure status. In the case of Syrian refugees, the fact that their status is not permanent – they are under temporary protection – affects the integration processes negatively. To support a sustainable life for the refugees, Turkey is trying to establish integration programs similar to that of those implemented in Europe (Şimşek, 2019).

Studies show that the greater cultural and social similarity between people, the faster the adaptation and integration takes place (Budyta-Budzyńska, 2011). Turkish and Syrian people have their own unique lifestyles, social norms (children work in some family instead of their parents, living and walking as a group, to divorce with a single word, women's begging for help, etc.) and habits (food, cleaning, dressing, etc.). The attitudes and behaviors of the Syrians residing in the ghettos, peculiar to marginalized groups, are somewhat disturbed (such as verbal abuse, not obeying the apartment rules, making noise, being prone to violence, stealing). The encounters with the Syrian asylum seekers are frequently shaped by prejudice among the public that the state pays special attention to Syrians in Turkey. The public's reaction is that the state does not allocate an additional budget for Syrians in social assistance, and that Syrians work in business lines with low wages, and the illusion that the state grants privileges to Syrians. Also, Turkish citizens receiving social assistance think that they are being limited from their own budgets because too much aid is given to Syrians. Sometimes irresponsible media broadcasts (where Syrians get free help, their children study at our universities without taking the exam, etc.) are also effective in the formation of such prejudices.

The majority of local people's attitudes towards Syrian refugees are unwelcoming. Negative attitudes and complaints come to the fore. Undoubtedly, the reasons such as the fact that Syrians live in large groups in unhygienic environments, low levels of education, lack of qualifications, upset the Turkish population and reinforce the prejudice regarding Syrian asylum seekers in the region (Alptekin et al., 2018). Asylum seekers' acceptance in the receiving country is also affected by the stereotypical prejudice that the media conveys to the public. Bowes et al. (2009: 25) argue that media and political stereotypes portray asylum seekers as burdensome competitors for the economic benefit of some sort or another.

According to Alptekin and colleagues (2018), the biggest barrier to social cohesion is language problems. Those Syrian's who are fluent in Turkish can be integrated into the socio-cultural, work, and educational life in Turkey (Alptekin, Ulutaş Akçay & Gündüz Ustabaşı, 2018).

Another major problem that prohibits work-life integration is the entry barrier in the traditional professions of even the high-skilled Syrians. One of the reasons, behind this disconnect, is the fact that Syrians not only left their homes but also their diplomas behind as they fled the war (Alptekin et al.,

2018). After resettlement, they get stuck in unemployment or jobs that do not match their qualifications (Bygnes, 2021). Most Syrians did not have alternatives to working in inhumane conditions; they were not only under-paid but were forced to work in unskilled jobs.

Precarious socio-economic conditions have taken a huge toll on asylum seekers' even for those who have had the opportunity to be integrated into the system (Akar & Erdogdu, 2019; Crawley, 2021; Ertörer, 2021). The next section of the chapter aims to contemplate on the subjective well-being and workplace ostracism experiences of asylum seekers.

SUBJECTIVE WELL-BEING AND THE EXPERIECES OF REFUGEES

A good working definition of subjective well-being is "the experience of joy, contentment, or positive well-being, combined with a sense that one's life is good, meaningful, and worthwhile" (Lyubomirsky, 2013, p. 32). The line of study on subjective well-being, refers to it as:

The scientific analysis of how people evaluate their lives—both at the moment and for longer periods such as for the past year [including] people's emotional reactions to events, their moods, and judgments they form about their life satisfaction, fulfillment, and satisfaction with domains such as marriage and work (Diener, Oishi, & Lucas, 2003, p. 404).

Subjective well-being (SWB) is a psychological construct concerned not with what people have or what happens to them but with how they think about and feel about what they have and what happens to them (Maddux, 2018). The study of subjective well-being makes a distinction between the objective conditions of someone's life and that person's subjective evaluations of and feelings about his or her life. Plenty of relatively rich, healthy people may be miserable, and plenty of relatively poor or unhealthy people may lead lives of meaning and joy (Myers, 2000).

Research in the field of subjective well-being is of particular relevance to the study of refugees' assessment of life in their host country as it helps to examine the psychological consequences of migration experiences (Jibeen, 2019). The experiences of immigrants and how they manage their lives in migrant-receiving societies have been extensively studied by scholars in the past decades (Alexander et al., 2021; Carlson & Güler, 2018; Güler & Yıldırım, 2022; Shiromohammadi et al., 2022; Yoon et al., 2020). However, in Turkey, still very little is known about the subjective well-being and the work-related experiences of forcibly displaced Syrians.

Some of the studies on subjective well-being of refugees, have found that cultural integration increases SWB when acculturating to the new culture of the host country (Berry and Hou, 2016; Dimitrova et al., 2016; Güngör & Bornstein, 2013; Wu et al., 2018); whereas marginalization is negatively associated with SWB (Jetten et al., 2015; Nguyen & Benet-Martínez, 2013). Knappert et al. (2018) showed that Syrians who reside in Turkey face several forms of discrimination including being treated unfairly, isolated, rejected, abused, and frustrated at work which in turn decreases their subjective well-being (Güler & Yıldırım, 2022).

These studies are in line with the assertion by Shirmohammadi, et al. (2022) indicating that a refugee status can be an important source of inequality for well-being at work. In their evaluation of the literature on blue-collar immigrants work experiences; Shirmohammadi et al. (2022) identified reviews highlighting the prevalence of occupational injuries and fatalities among immigrants, and their increased likelihood of experiencing poor work conditions, such as exposure to workplace hazards, lack of safety standards and training, healthcare support, and compensation for workplace injury (Hargreaves et al., 2019; Moyce & Schenker, 2018; Sterud et al., 2018). So, irrespective of their host country, most refugees who have no other option to work in blue-collar jobs comprise a highly vulnerable sub-set of employees (McGahan, 2020). Employment undertaken by refugees in such conditions are more likely to be low paid, physically, or emotionally demanding (e.g., construction work or homecare), carried out in harsh working environments (e. g., extreme temperatures or dangerous products and processes, such as the use of hazardous chemicals), and isolated locations (e.g., farms) (Moyce & Schenker, 2018).

Thus, the refugee's subjective well-being is impacted as much by their host country context as by their respective work and nonwork conditions, individual skills and competencies, or other psychological and physical factors. In this respect, Shirmohammadi et al., (2022) emphasizes the use of conservation of resources theory (COR) to understand the well-being of vulnerable populations (Hobfoll, 2012). The central tenet of the COR theory is that employees who lose personal resources (e.g., cognitive, emotional, and material) due to broader life events are more vulnerable to further resource loss. Since refugees' experience loss of personal resources (e.g., status, cultural knowledge, sense of belonging, and social networks), they are more likely to experience further resource loss due to stress at work or to other nonwork factors (Mahmud, Alam, & Hartel, 2014). In contrast, resource gain occurs when an employee has the required resources to overcome their work and life stressors or when they can build additional personal resources to do so (Hobfoll, 2011). COR theory also presumes that resource loss is more powerful than resource gain, and because stress occurs when resources are threatened with loss or are lost, for individuals with fewer resources, loss can increase exponentially (Hobfoll, 1989). Therefore, to obtain desired outcomes, such as well-being an effective management of resources is necessary (Hobfoll et al., 2018, p. 104).

Among the resources that immigrants perceive as highly predictive of their subjective well-being were listed as social connections and emotional support by friends, family, or social support group (Hall, Pangan, et al., 2019; Leung & Tang, 2018; Shirmohammadi et al., 2022). The presence of social connections is indeed an important predictor for subjective well-being and meaning in life. The absence of these connections, exemplified by loneliness, social exclusion, or ostracism, can be devastating to one's well-being (see Williams 2007, 2012). Social ties and connections are in a sense the life jacket of individuals such as the refugees who are experiencing major difficulties. In a meta-analysis by Holt-Lundstad, Smith and Layton (2010) those individuals with strong social relationships had a 50% greater likelihood of survival compared to those with poor or insufficient social relationships. According to Williams (2009) the deleterious consequences of interpersonal social exclusion can be particularly threatening for marginalized social groups, such as prisoners, homeless people, and immigrants, who are pervasively exposed to persistent exclusion (Williams, 2009). Social exclusion – being kept apart from others physically (e.g., social isolation) or emotionally (e.g., social rejection; Riva & Eck, 2016) impairs self-esteem, self-regulation, cognitive ability and induces negative emotions, meaninglessness, and suicidal thoughts (Baumeister, Twenge, & Nuss, 2002; Chen, Poon, DeWall, & Jiang, 2020; Gerber & Wheeler, 2009). On the physical level, social exclusion can generate acute negative physiological responses and increase the risk to suffer from cardiovascular, respiratory conditions, and mental health disorders (Aldridge et al., 2018; Jin & Josephs, 2016; Marunicci et. al., 2022).

Ostracism, just like social exclusion is a painful event that the majority of individuals experience in minimal forms daily and often in meaningfully important forms at least once in their lives (Nezlek et al., 2012; Wesselmann et al., 2021; Williams, 2007a). Ostracism can be psychologically harmful to the target, leading to impaired self-regulation (Baumeister et al., 2005; Oaten et al., 2008), self-perceived dehumanization (Bastian & Haslam, 2010), and decreased cognitive ability (Baumeister et al. 2002), and provokes immediate negative physiological responses (Dickerson & Kemeny, 2004; Gunnar et al., 2003; Josephs et al., 2012; Moor et al., 2010).

OSTRACISM AND ITS IMPACT ON REFUGEE GROUPS

Ostracism occurs in a myriad of cultures and contexts among humans (Williams & Nida, 2011). Contemporary social psychological research on ostracism has defined it as "being ignored or excluded" by others (Ren, Hales & Williams, 2016). Ostracism is sometimes confused with other concepts like "exclusion and rejection." These concepts seem somewhat similar, but have slight differences in meaning (Hitlan et al., 2015). Wesselman et al. (2021) have distinguished these concepts from one another as follows; rejection is an explicit declaration that the target is not wanted; social exclusion is when the target is kept apart from others; and, finally, ostracism is when the target is ignored and excluded by others (Williams, 2007b).

The Temporal Need-Threat Model of Ostracism (Williams, 2009) can help explain how the negative and detrimental effects of social exclusion and ostracism may impact asylum seekers. According to the temporal need-threat model, individuals' responses to social exclusion and ostracism occur in three subsequent temporal stages. In the reflexive stage, victims experience negative emotions and hurt feelings that signal the threat to four fundamental human needs harmed by social exclusion: the need for belonging, self-esteem, control, and meaningful existence. In the following stage, the reflective stage, people appraise the characteristics of the excluding situations, and they enact coping behaviors aimed at recovering satisfaction of the threatened needs. People would reestablish inclusion via prosocial behaviors, regain control and recognition via aggressive behaviors, or as more recently proposed, prevent further social exclusion experiences via solitude seeking (Ren, Wesselmann, & van Beest, 2020). The last stage of the model focuses on persistent social exclusion. Individuals who experience social exclusion for prolonged periods should unavoidably enter the resignation stage, characterized by feelings of depression, alienation, unworthiness, and helplessness (Marunicci et al., 2022). The prediction from this is that persistent social exclusion and ostracism leads people to self-isolate (Williams, 2009). If exclusion persists over time, people learn that exclusion is unavoidable. They consequently give up any attempt to reconnect with others. Their chronically frustrated needs turn into chronic feelings of depression, alienation, unworthiness, and helplessness.

Refugees and immigrants are among the social groups excluded from society (Strang & Ager, 2010). Social exclusion of refugees occurs on multiple levels of the system, ranging from the sociopolitical and economic levels to the inter-personal ones. The exclusion from political rights prevents them from participating in a society's social and cultural life, relegating them to a marginalized position (Ager & Strang, 2008). At the socio-economic level, Esses (2020) reviewed that immigrants' societal discrimination may include employment and housing. Moreover, inadequate economic support from the host countries alongside policies that prevent immigrants and refugees from working jeopardize their economic development (Allsopp, Sigona, & Phillimore, 2014). Also, refugees are at risk of being excluded at the intergroup and interpersonal levels. The national majority groups' prejudice can turn into discriminating, dehumanizing, and aggressive behaviors towards these groups (Esses, Medianu, & Lawson, 2013). Among other threats, refugees are at risk of being mistreated at work, excluded in the school settings, and ignored during conversations (Asendorpf & Motti-Stefanidi, 2017; Dotan-Eliaz, Sommer, & Rubin, 2009). In response, excluded groups may feel rejected, uprooted, and chronically thwarted in the satisfaction of their basic needs with severe health repercussions (Echterhoff et al., 2020; Li, Liddell, & Nickerson, 2016; Hynie, 2018).

WORKPLACE OSTRACISM AND ITS EFFECTS ON EMPLOYEES

One of the contexts in which ostracism is a prevalent phenomenon is the workplace (Fox and Stallworth, 2005). Being isolated by others and excluded from group interactions is a painful experience (Çelik & Koşar, 2015; Fiset, Hajj & Vongas, 2017; Gerber & Wheeler, 2014; Legate et al., 2013; Nezlek et al., 2012). Workplace ostracism takes place whenever an individual or group, the 'ostracizer,' neglects to take actions that engage another employee, the 'ostracize,' when it is customary and suitable to do so (Robinson et al., 2013). Ostracism is low in behavioral intensity; however, even if it is a subtle form of mistreatment, growing evidence has demonstrated that being denied social connection either by an individual or a group leads to harmful outcomes for the victim (Williams, 2007a; Eisenberger, 2015; O'Reilly et al., 2015). Thus, negative emotional states emerge because of ostracism, such as alienation, depression, helplessness, and worthlessness. Exposure to such behaviors leads to increased stress, anxiety, burnout, social isolation, social separation, emotional exhaustion, and job dissatisfaction in the long run. Also, the excluded person may experience an existential questioning, pain, sadness, anxiety, fear, lack of self-efficacy, self-esteem, and self-control (Ball, 2011; Çelik & Koşar, 2015; Liu & Xia, 2016; Nezlek et al., 2012). Studies have shown that people exposed to even minimal levels of ostracism experience a significant decrease in their belongingness to and identification with their organization/social group (Akın et al., 2016; Ferris et al., 2008; Nezlek et al., 2012).

In the workplace ostracism can present itself as the avoidance of eye contact, leaving the room when the ostracize enters, or failing to respond to greetings (Williams, 2007a; Robinson et al., 2013; Zhu et al., 2017), being silent and unresponsive to an individual who is being ignored (Williams, 2007b); shunning, overlooking and isolating the ostracize from others (Gerber & Wheeler, 2014; Halis & Demirel, 2016; Robinson et al., 2013; Yaakobi, 2017).

Experiencing ostracism on the job has not only consequences for the employee's psychological well-being, but also their ability to function at work (Robinson & Schabram, 2017). The study by Yoo and Lee (2018) on Korean employees showed that exposure to bullying and ostracism decreases subjective well-being and quality of life; and increases psychological distress (Liu et al., 2013; Yoo & Lee, 2018). It was found that ostracism caused psychological distress among employees and negative financial impact for the organization or workplace. Individuals who are exposed to workplace ostracism have a lower level of commitment to their profession, work, colleagues, managers, and organizations (Halis & Demirel, 2016).

According to belongingness theory (Baumeister & Leary, 1995), individuals strive to be accepted and to gain a sense of belonging. Through omission of inaction, workplace ostracism serves as negative feedback and thus damages the victim's sense of belonging. Moreover, workplace ostracism can bring social pain and generate negative effects (Ferris et al., 2008; Robinson et al., 2013). Workplace ostracism can also require the victim to exert more effort in dealing with interpersonal demands, which can make the individual "feel drained and overwhelmed by their work" (Wilk and Moynihan, 2005, p. 917) and emotionally exhausted. Thus, ostracism is a painful and costly experience and those who are exposed to such behaviors in the workplace are prone to greater stress (e.g., Cohen et al., 1983; DeLongis, Folkman, & Lazarus, 1988). Feelings of loneliness and social isolation following discrimination and exclusion are risk factors that threaten psychological well-being (Başaran, 2021).

SYRIAN ASYLUM SEEKERS' WORK EXPERIENCES: A FINAL REMARK

It has been documented that many Syrians are exposed to exploitation due to overwork, low wages, and lack of safe working conditions (İçduygu & Şimşek, 2016). Those who work long hours and excessively are less socially connected with members of the host community because of isolation (Şimşek, 2020).

In Gürlek's (2021) recent study Syrians exposed to workplace ostracism displayed counter-productive work behaviors (CWB). Exclusion and ostracism are known to increase specifically deviant behaviors of immigrants (Mazzoni et al., 2020; Walsh et al., 2019). Syrians exposed to workplace ostracism tend to displace their aggressive impulse arising from the negative experiences against an alternative target instead of the actual one (i.e., co-workers, managers; basically, whom the ostracizers are). When individuals experience ostracism, they may be reluctant to express themselves and voice their concerns due to the fear of reprisal and in turn may experience greater stress and decrease in well-being at work (Gürlek, 2021).

Under the umbrella of social identity research there is a sizeable body of work that has explored how members of different groups react to and treat one another (Scott & Duffy, 2015). This subset of research argues that individuals seek membership in groups that reinforce their self-concept (e.g., shared values, attitudes, beliefs). The process by which they identify those groups due to self-perceived similarities is known as social categorization (Turner, 1985). The resulting body of work from this perspective has consistently demonstrated that individuals favor members of their own group over those in out groups (i.e., ingroup bias) and, thus, are potentially untrusting, hostile, or aggressive toward those viewed as threatening or different (Abrams & Hogg, 2006; Hogg & Terry, 2000). Scott and Duffy (2015) contend that in-group bias likely plays a role in determining who becomes the ostracized target. The Syrian asylum seekers in this case, as indicated earlier in the chapter, are perceived as the out-group in majority of the workplaces in Turkey due to differences in their value and belief orientations (Erdogan, 2020). As self-categorization theory contends, when asylum seekers are labelled as the "out-group" they are potentially perceived to be untrusting, aggressive, hostile, undeserving by the members of the in-group. Thus, the asylum seekers are more likely to be excluded and ostracized in the workplaces that they find employment. The issue of exclusion in the workplace coupled with the more macro-level problems that the asylum seekers must endure, multiplies their troubles (i.e. Gürlek, 2021). The conservation of resources theory explained in the previous section contends that, as the problems asylum seekers must overcome multiply, their ability and skills to cope with such burden becomes inadequate (see Shirmohammadi, et al., 2021). This in turn depletes the individual and decreases their well-being. This equation clearly signals the importance of creating intervention mechanisms in the workplace, so that these individuals will be equipped to counter the vast number of challenges that surround them. We understand that positive interventions are needed to promote resiliency and healthy coping skills for the Syrians in reducing the ostracism they encounter in the workplace.

We also must note that workplace interventions may not be sufficient to completely equip the refugees that seek shelter in host countries. It is well documented that refugees who experienced/witnessed traumatic events have significantly lower life satisfaction than other migrants (Bilen & Kıran, 2020; Giesebrecht, et al., 2022; Theisen-Womerslay, 2021). The position of the individual in society, life events, quality of life, personal abilities/skills, and experience are all determinants of subjective well-being. Experiencing/witnessing potentially traumatic events is an important risk factor that leads to deterioration of mental health and decreased well-being (Bilen & Kıran, 2020). Recent studies support the negative relationship between well-being and refugees' exposure to traumatic events. For example, studies on the well-being of refugees in the Netherlands (Sleijpen et al., 2016), in Korea (Palmer et al., 2019) and on Palestinian children exposed to military violence and to missile attacks (Veronese et al., 2017) all found decreased life satisfaction and increased stress (Borho et al., 2020).

This chapter portrays the complex web of macro and micro level phenomena that create causal mechanisms leading to the degradation of the subjective well-being of Syrian asylum seekers in Turkey. There is uncertainty around the specific causes of exclusion and ostracism asylum seekers are exposed to. Most likely, these changes are caused by the large, rapid influx of asylum seekers, who are perceived to be out-siders and pose a threat to the order of the society (Bjanesoy, 2019; İçdugu & Diker, 2017). These issues regarding the public perception of Syrian asylum seekers along with interventions that will help equip Syrian's has to be tackled with immediacy by the governmental and non-governmental bodies.

IMPLICATIONS AND SUGGESTIONS FOR PRACTICE

Employers who hire refugees should be mindful of the importance of work in the lives of these individuals. The refugees who are trying to cope with the traumatic experiences of fleeing the war and the challenges associated with integration, struggle to meet their basic needs and to sustain their well-being. Impaired psychosocial and occupational functionality in turn would be expected to endanger subjective well-being and life satisfaction (Bilen & Kıran, 2020). Şimşek's research (2019) on Syrian asylum seekers in Istanbul, highlight that access to basic rights is the primary concern for these people. From the point of view of Syrians, integration can be achieved through having access to the job market, increased safety standards, transitioning from temporary protection to a permanent status, being able to settle down, secure legal status and belonging to the society (Şimşek, 2019). The ambiguity surrounding their status (not receiving permanent status) damages their sense of belonging and increases anxiety, stress, endangering their well-being. Having work permits, citizenship rights and other legal rights form the basis of their integration (Şimşek, 2018).

Employers may use interventions such as small consumption loans, deposit waivers, and temporary housing solutions to allow refugees to afford and live in suitable housing. Other solutions to help reduce stressors may include ensuring reasonable work hours, having appropriate rest periods, taking breaks during the day, and having time off to spend with family and friends, rotating job tasks to add skill variety, and increasing their level of autonomy and control over their job duties (Shirmohammadi, et. al., 2022).

Language has also been indicated as a barrier that the asylum seekers encounter (Jibeen, 2019; Shiromohammadi, et al., 2022). It is one of the most important factors in establishing professional and private relations and enables integration of the individual into the society (Sarmini et al., 2020). In tackling the issues surrounding workplace integration of asylum seekers, practices revolving around improving organizational socialization process is of paramount importance. Organizational socialization is 'the process by which an individual acquires the social knowledge and skills necessary to assume an organizational role' (Van Maanen & Schein, 1979, p. 211). This process includes the internalization of corporate norms and values as well as the acquisition of job-specific knowledge, skills, and abilities (Feldman, 1981).

The socialization process produces invaluable long-term outcomes, such as individuals' role clarity, role orientation, task mastery, job satisfaction, organizational commitment, and workplace well-being (Bauer et al., 2007; Saks et al., 2007). In this respect co-workers and managers hold an important function as socialization agents (e.g., Cooper et al., 2021).

Tharenou and Kulik (2020), based on a literature review on the socialization of skilled migrants, suggested that organizations adopt measures designed to manage newcomers' expectations and to foster their relationships with managers and co-workers. Immigrants when they enter the workforce are less familiar with local workplace norms (Zikic, 2015), and thus have greater difficulty building relationships with other organizational members (Malik & Manroop, 2017). There are a number of best practice reports and guidelines (Szkudlarek, 2019) that recommend measures such as cultural and language training, mentorship programs and initiatives to facilitate the creation of social networks. They also indicate that managers, co-workers, and the refugees themselves are willing to invest extra-time and energy into the onboarding process.

The literature began underlining a variety of practices that organizations can adopt to foster refugees' organizational socialization and development (see Gericke et al., 2018). Employers may support the integration of their refugee workers by giving advice, offering language translation, or acting as cultural ambassadors who familiarize the refugees with the country. Other studies point to the conditions of refugees, indicating that many refugees strive to learn at work and display an 'extreme will to adapt' (Ponzoni et al., 2017) or gratitude towards the employer (Ortlieb et al., 2021), whereas they do not know their rights at work and do not dare to speak up if they feel mistreated (Kosny et al., 2020).

Regarding formal measures, Ortlieb and Ressi (2022) found that although training and checklists provide newcomers with important information and orientation at earlier socialization stages, it is especially important to avoid false promises. Since organizational rules may be difficult to convey in seminars, practitioners should foster frequent interaction between newcomers and organizational incumbents, through working side-by-side, to provide newcomers with the opportunity during everyday work to obtain knowledge about informal rules and to form realistic expectations. According to Ortlieb and Ressi (2022) in efforts to create structure and to search jointly for possible solutions when expectations are not met, refugees may feel they are being treated unfairly or that development plans need to be adjusted. Such conversations in the apprenticeship programs are crucial because refugees may not be able to learn everything at once at the beginning of their apprenticeships. Rather, they need more opportunity for step-by-step learning, including continuous adaptations and reflections. Likewise, they may need extra room for developing resilience capabilities and coping strategies for dealing with time pressures at work (Kunzelmann & Rigotti, 2021).

Therefore, to facilitate the asylum seekers transition to a settled order, transparent and rapid asylum procedures should be ensured. Furthermore, refugees need more contact with whom they can talk about their work and learn from their experiences, so politicians and managerial decision-makers should create spaces where they can meet. Examples might include mentorship programs or the support of volunteer initiatives in community centers. However, Risberg and Romani (2021) underline that there is also the danger that locals urge immigrants to become 'normal' citizens and workers like themselves, therefore volunteers need help to recognize the value of diversity, to avoid producing additional tensions.

In conclusion, employers along with other regulatory authorities can make a major contribution to the challenge of refugee integration. Offering refugees stable jobs, training and opportunity for career development helps them become economically independent, meet locals, improve their language and cultural skills as well as increase self-esteem and self-reliance (Ager & Strang, 2008).

REFERENCES

Abrams, D., & Hogg, M. A. (2006). *Social identifications: A social psychology of intergroup relations and group processes*. Routledge. doi:10.4324/9780203135457

Ager, A., & Strang, A. (2008). Understanding integration: A conceptual framework. *Journal of Refugee Studies*, *21*(2), 166–191. doi:10.1093/jrs/fen016

Akar, S., & Erdoğdu, M. M. (2019). Syrian refugees in Turkey and integration problem ahead. *Journal of International Migration and Integration*, *20*(3), 925–940. doi:10.100712134-018-0639-0

Akın, A., Uysal, R., & Akın, Ü. (2016, Mart). Ergenler için Ostracism (sosyal dışlanma) Ölçeğinin Türkçe'ye uyarlanması. *Kastamonu Eğitim Dergisi, 24*(2), 895-904. https://dergipark.org.tr/tr/pub/kefdergi/issue/22590/241325

Alexander, N., Mathilde, S., & Øivind, S. (2021). Post-migration stressors and subjective well-being in adult Syrian refugees resettled in Sweden: A gender perspective. *Frontiers in Public Health*, *9*, 717353. doi:10.3389/fpubh.2021.717353 PMID:34568258

Allsopp, J., Sigona, N., & Phillimore, J. (2014). Poverty among refugees and asylum seekers in the UK. An evidence and policy review. *IRiS Working Paper Series*, *1*, 1–46.

Alptekin, K., Ulutaş Akçay, D., & Gündüz Ustabaşı, D. (2018). Konya'da geçici koruma altında yaşayan Suriyeliler üzerine bir çalışma. *Sosyal Politika Çalışmaları Dergisi, 40*(2), 87-114. https://dergipark.org.tr/tr/download/article-file/561584

Amnesty International. (2022). *Home*. Amnesty International. https://www.amnesty.org/en/what-we-do/refugees-asylum-seekers-and-migrants/.

Asendorpf, J. B., & Motti-Stefanidi, F. (2017). A longitudinal study of immigrants' peer acceptance and rejection: Immigrant status, immigrant composition of the classroom, and acculturation. *Cultural Diversity & Ethnic Minority Psychology*, *23*(4), 486–498. doi:10.1037/cdp0000155 PMID:28394167

Bansak, K., Hainmueller, J. & Hangartner, D. (2016). How economic, humanitarian, and religious concerns shape European attitudes toward asylum seekers. *Science, 354* (6309)-217-222. doi:10.1126/science.aag2147

Başaran, K. D. (2021). Peer bullying effects on psychological wellbeing of Syrian immigrant children: A literature review from Turkey, Lebanon, and Jordan. *Sosyal Çalışma Dergisi, 5*(2), 245-257. https://dergipark.org.tr/pub/scd/issue/67855/978783

Bauer, T. N., Bodner, T., Erdogan, B., Truxillo, D. M., & Tucker, J. S. (2007). Newcomer adjustment during organizational socialization: A meta-analytic review of antecedents, outcomes, and methods. *The Journal of Applied Psychology*, *92*(3), 707–721. doi:10.1037/0021-9010.92.3.707 PMID:17484552

Baumeister, R. F., & Leary, M. R. (1995). The need to belong desire for interpersonal attachments as a fundamental human motivation. *Psychological Bulletin*, *117*(3), 497–529. doi:10.1037/0033-2909.117.3.497 PMID:7777651

Baumeister, R. F., Twenge, J. M., & Nuss, C. K. (2002). Effects of social exclusion on cognitive processes: Anticipated aloneness reduces intelligent thought. *Journal of Personality and Social Psychology*, *83*(4), 817–827. doi:10.1037/0022-3514.83.4.817 PMID:12374437

Bennett, K. M., Scornaiencki, J. M., Brzozowski, J., Denis, S., & Magalhaes, L. (2012). Immigration and its impact on daily occupations: A scoping review. *Occupational Therapy International*, *19*(4), 185–203. doi:10.1002/oti.1336 PMID:22987528

Bilen, D., & Kıran, B. (2020). Investigation of Post-Traumatic Stress Disorder and life satisfaction levels according to how Syrian refugees experience various traumatic experiences. *International Journal of Scientific Research*, *15*(26), 397–3987. doi:10.26466/opus.658813

Bjånesøy, L. L. (2019). Effects of the Refugee Crisis on Perceptions of Asylum Seekers in Recipient Populations. *Journal of Refugee Studies*, *32*(1), 219–237. doi:10.1093/jrs/fey070

Boho, A., Viazminsky, A., Morawa, E., Schmitt, G. M., Georgiadou, E., & Erim, Y. (2020). The prevalence and risk factors for mental distress among Syrian refugees in Germany: A register-based follow-up study. *BMC Psychiatry*, *20*(362), 362. doi:10.118612888-020-02746-2 PMID:32641014

Bowes, A., Ferguson, I., & Sim, D. (2009). Asylum policy and asylum experiences: Interactions in a Scottish context. *Ethnic and Racial Studies*, *32*(1), 23–43. doi:10.1080/01419870701722570

Budyta-Budzyńska, M. (2011). Adaptation, integration, assimilation: An attempt at a theoretical approach. *Warsaw Collegium Civitas*. http://migracje. civitas. edu. pl/migracje/images/pdf_eng.

Carlson, E., & Güler, A. (2018). Cultural involvement and preference in immigrant acculturation. *Journal of International Migration and Integration*, *19*(3), 625–647. doi:10.100712134-018-0554-4

Castles, S., Korac, M., Vasta, E., & Vertovec, S. (2002). Integration: Mapping the field, report of a project by the University of Oxford Centre for Migration and Policy Research and Refugee Studies Centre. *Integration Research and Statistics Service* (IRSS), *Home Office online report 28/03*.

Chen, Z., Poon, K. T., DeWall, C. N., & Jiang, T. (2020). Life lacks meaning without acceptance: Ostracism triggers suicidal thoughts. *Journal of Personality and Social Psychology*, *119*(6), 1423–1443. doi:10.1037/pspi0000238 PMID:32118466

Chung, Y. W. (2018). Workplace ostracism and workplace behaviors: A moderated mediation model of perceived stress and psychological empowerment. *Anxiety, Stress, and Coping*, *31*(3), 304–317. doi:10.1080/10615806.2018.1424835 PMID:29325438

Colic-Peisker, V. (2009). Visibility, settlement success and life satisfaction in three refugee communities in Australia. *Ethnicities*, *9*(2), 175–199. doi:10.1177/1468796809103459

Colic-Peisker, V., & Tilbury, F. (2006). Employment niches for recent refugees: Segmented labour market in twenty-first century Australia. *Journal of Refugee Studies*, *19*(2), 203–229. doi:10.1093/jrs/fej016

Cooper, D., Rockmann, K. W., Moteabbed, S., & Thatcher, S. M. B. (2021). Integrator or gremlin? Identity partnerships and team newcomer socialization. *Academy of Management Review*, *46*(1), 128–146. doi:10.5465/amr.2018.0014

Crawley, H. (2021). The Politics of Refugee Protection in a (Post)COVID-19 World. *Social Sciences*, *10*(3), 81. doi:10.3390ocsci10030081

DeLongis, A., Folkman, S., & Lazarus, R. S. (1988). The impact of daily stress on health and mood: Psychological and social resources as mediators. *Journal of Personality and Social Psychology*, *54*(3), 486–495. doi:10.1037/0022-3514.54.3.486 PMID:3361420

Diener, E., & Biswas-Diener, R. (2008). *Happiness: Unlocking the mysteries of psychological wealth.* Wiley/Blackwell. doi:10.1002/9781444305159

Diener, E., Oishi, S., & Lucas, R. E. (2003). Personality, culture, and subjective well- being: Emotional and cognitive evaluations of life. *Annual Review of Psychology*, *54*(1), 403–425. doi:10.1146/annurev.psych.54.101601.145056 PMID:12172000

Diener, E., Pressman, S. D., Hunter, J., & Delgadillo-Chase, D. (2017). If, why, and when subjective well-being influences health, and future needed research. *Applied Psychology. Health and Well-Being*, *9*(2), 133–167. doi:10.1111/aphw.12090 PMID:28707767

Dotan-Eliaz, O., Sommer, K. L., & Rubin, Y. S. (2009). Multilingual groups: Effects of linguistic ostracism on felt rejection and anger, coworker attraction, perceived team potency, and creative performance. *Basic and Applied Social Psychology*, *31*(4), 363–375. doi:10.1080/01973530903317177

Echterhoff, G., Hellmann, J. H., Back, M. D., Kartner, J., Morina, N., & Hertel, G. (2020). Psychological antecedents of refugee integration (PARI). *Perspectives on Psychological Science*, *15*(4), 856–879. doi:10.1177/1745691619898838 PMID:32392450

Eid, M., & Larsen, R. J. (Eds.). (2008). *The science of subjective well-being.* Guilford Press.

Erdoğan, M. M. (2020). "Securitization from Society" and "Social Acceptance": Political Party-Based Approaches in Turkey to Syrian Refugees. *Uluslararası İlişkiler Dergisi*, *17*(68), 73–92.

Ertorer, S. E. (2021). Asylum regimes and refugee experiences of precarity: The case of Syrian refugees in Turkey. *Journal of Refugee Studies*, *34*(3), 2568–2592. doi:10.1093/jrs/feaa089

Esses, V. M. (2020). Prejudice and discrimination toward immigrants. *Annual Review of Psychology*, *72*(1), 503–531. doi:10.1146/annurev-psych-080520-102803 PMID:32916080

Esses, V. M., Medianu, S., & Lawson, A. S. (2013). Uncertainty, threat, and the role of the media in promoting the dehumanization of immigrants and refugees. *The Journal of Social Issues*, *69*(3), 518–536. doi:10.1111/josi.12027

Fiset, J., Al Hajj, R., & Vongas, J. G. (2017). Workplace ostracism seen through the lens of power. *Frontiers in Psychology*, *8*, 1528. doi:10.3389/fpsyg.2017.01528 PMID:28928702

Gerber, J., & Wheeler, L. (2009). On being rejected: A meta-analysis of experimental research on rejection. *Perspectives on Psychological Science*, *4*(5), 468–488. doi:10.1111/j.1745-6924.2009.01158.x PMID:26162220

Gerber, J., & Wheeler, L. (2009). On being rejected: A meta-analysis of experimental research on rejection. *Perspectives on Psychological Science*, *4*(5), 468–488. doi:10.1111/j.1745-6924.2009.01158.x PMID:26162220

Gerber, J. P., & Wheeler, L. (2014). Clarifying the relationship between ostracism and relational devaluation. *The Journal of Social Psychology*, *154*(1), 14–27. doi:10.1080/00224545.2013.826619 PMID:24689334

Gericke, D., Burmeister, A., Löwe, J., Deller, J., & Pundt, L. (2018). How do refugees use their social capital for successful labor market integration? An exploratory analysis in Germany. *Journal of Vocational Behavior*, *105*, 46–61. doi:10.1016/j.jvb.2017.12.002

Giesebrecht, J., Grupp, F., Reich, H., Weise, C., & Mewes, R. (2022). Relations between criteria for somatic symptom disorder and quality of life in asylum seekers living in Germany. *Journal of Psychosomatic Research*, *160*, 110977. doi:10.1016/j.jpsychores.2022.110977 PMID:35803108

Halis, M., & Demirel, Y. (2016, Ocak). Sosyal desteğin örgütsel soyutlama (dışlama) etkisi. *Kastamonu Üniversitesi İktisadi ve İdari Bilimler Fakültesi Dergisi*, *11*. https://dergipark.org.tr/tr/download/article-file/309391

Hall, B. J., Pangan, C. A. C., Chan, E. W., & Huang, R. L. (2019). The effect of discrimination on depression and anxiety symptoms and the buffering role of social capital among female domestic workers in Macao, China. *Psychiatry Research*, *271*, 200–207. doi:10.1016/j.psychres.2018.11.050 PMID:30500710

Hargreaves, S., Rustage, K., Nellums, L. B., McAlpine, A., Pocock, N., Devakumar, D., Aldridge, R. W., Abubakar, I., Kristensen, K. L., Himmels, J. W., Friedland, J. S., & Zimmerman, C. (2019). Occupational health outcomes among international migrant workers: A systematic review and meta-analysis. *The Lancet. Global Health*, *7*(7), e872–e882. doi:10.1016/S2214-109X(19)30204-9 PMID:31122905

Hobfoll, S. E. (2011). Conservation of resource caravans and engaged settings. *Journal of Occupational and Organizational Psychology*, *84*(1), 116–122. doi:10.1111/j.2044-8325.2010.02016.x

Hobfoll, S. E. (2012). Conservation of resources and disaster in cultural context: The caravans and passageways for resources. *Psychiatry*, *75*(3), 227–232. doi:10.1521/psyc.2012.75.3.227 PMID:22913498

Hobfoll, S. E., Halbesleben, J., Neveu, J. P., & Westman, M. (2018). Conservation of resources in the organizational context: The reality of resources and their consequences. *Annual Review of Organizational Psychology and Organizational Behavior*, *5*(1), 103–128. doi:10.1146/annurev-orgpsych-032117-104640

Hogg, M. A., & Terry, D. J. (2000). The dynamic, diverse, and variable faces of organizational identity. *Academy of Management Review*, *25*(1), 150–152. doi:10.5465/amr.2000.27711645

Holt-Lunstad, J., Smith, T. B., & Layton, J. B. (2010). Social relationships and mortality risk: A meta-analytic review. *PLoS Medicine*, *7*(7), e1000316. doi:10.1371/journal.pmed.1000316 PMID:20668659

Hynie, M. (2018). The social determinants of refugee mental health in the post-migration context: A critical review. *Canadian Journal of Psychiatry*, *63*(5), 297–303. doi:10.1177/0706743717746666 PMID:29202665

İçduygu, A., & Şimşek, D. (2016). Syrian refugees in Turkey: Toward integration policies. *Turkish Policy Quarterly*, *15*(3), 59–69.

Jackson, S., & Bauder, H. (2014). Neither temporary, nor permanent: The precarious employment experiences of refugee claimants in Canada. *Journal of Refugee Studies, 27*(3), 360–381. doi:10.1093/jrs/fet048

Kappa, K. (2019). The social integration of asylum seekers and refugees: An interactional perspective. *Journal of Immigrant & Refugee Studies, 17*(3), 353–370. doi:10.1080/15562948.2018.1480823

Kayaoglu, A., & Erdogan, M. M. (2019, February). Labor market activities of Syrian refugees in Turkey. *Economic Research Forum (ERF)*.

Kosny, A., Yanar, B., Begum, M., Al-khooly, D., Premji, S., Lay, M. A., & Smith, P. M. (2020). Safe employment integration of recent immigrants and refugees. *Journal of International Migration and Integration, 21*(3), 807–827. doi:10.100712134-019-00685-w

Kunzelmann, A., & Rigotti, T. (2021). How time pressure is associated with both work engagement and emotional exhaustion: The moderating effects of resilient capabilities at work. *German Journal of Human Resource Management, 35*(3), 309–336. doi:10.1177/2397002220952741

Leung, D. D. M., & Tang, E. Y. T. (2018). Correlates of life satisfaction among Southeast Asian foreign domestic workers in Hong Kong: An exploratory study. *Asian and Pacific Migration Journal, 27*(3), 368–377. doi:10.1177/0117196818789736

Li, S. S. Y., Liddell, B. J., & Nickerson, A. (2016). The relationship between post- migration stress and psychological disorders in refugees and asylum seekers. *Current Psychiatry Reports, 18*(9), 1–9. doi:10.100711920-016-0723-0 PMID:27436307

Liu, H., & Xia, H. (2016). Workplace ostracism: A review and directions for future research. *Journal of Human Resource and Sustainability Studies, 4*(03), 197–201. doi:10.4236/jhrss.2016.43022

Liu, J., Kwan, H. K., Lee, C., & Hui, C. (2013, January). Work-to-family spillover effects on workplace ostracism: The role of work-home segmentation preferences. *Human Resource Management, 52*(1), 75–93. doi:10.1002/hrm.21513

Lyubomirsky, S. (2013). *The myths of happiness: What should make you happy, but doesn't, what shouldn't make you happy, but does*. Penguin Press.

Lyubomirsky, S., King, L., & Diener, E. (2005). The benefits of frequent positive affect: Does happiness lead to success? *Psychological Bulletin, 131*(6), 803–855. doi:10.1037/0033-2909.131.6.803 PMID:16351326

Maddux, J. E. (2018). *Subjective well-being and life satisfaction: An introduction to conceptions, theories, and measures*. Routledge/Taylor & Francis Group.

Mahmud, S., Alam, Q., & Härtel, C. (2014). Mismatches in skills and attributes of immigrants and problems with workplace integration: A study of IT and engineering professionals in Australia. *Human Resource Management Journal, 24*(3), 339–354. doi:10.1111/1748-8583.12026

Mazzoni, D., Pancani, L., Marinucci, M., & Riva, P. (2020). The dual path of the rejection (dis)identification model: A study on adolescents with a migrant background. *European Journal of Social Psychology, 50*(4), 799–809. doi:10.1002/ejsp.2672

McGahan, A. M. (2020). Immigration and impassioned management scholarship. *Journal of Management Inquiry*, *29*(1), 111–114. doi:10.1177/1056492619877617

Moyce, S. C., & Schenker, M. (2018). Migrant workers and their occupational health and safety. *Annual Review of Public Health*, *39*(1), 351–365. doi:10.1146/annurev-publhealth-040617-013714 PMID:29400993

Mupenzi, A., Mude, W., & Baker, S. (2020). Reflections on COVID-19 and impacts on equitable participation: The case of culturally and linguistically diverse migrant and/or refugee (CALDM/R) students in Australian higher education. *Higher Education Research & Development*, *39*(7), 1337–1341. doi:10.1080/07294360.2020.1824991

Myers, D. G. (2000). The funds, friends, and faith of happy people. *The American Psychologist*, *55*(1), 56–57. doi:10.1037/0003-066X.55.1.56 PMID:11392866

Özçürümez Bilgili, S. (2018). International protection and psychosocial support services. In Forced migration and social trauma: interdisciplinary perspectives from Psychoanalysis, Psychology, Sociology and Politics (pp. 9-17). Routledge. doi:10.4324/9780429432415-3

Öztürk, L., & Timuçin, E. D. (2021). Emek piyasası ve ekonomik dışlanma: Adıyaman ilinde Suriyeli göçmenler örneği. *Ekev Akademi Dergisi*, *25*(85), 227–246. doi:10.17753/Ekev1796

Palmer, B. W., Friend, S., Huege, S., Mulvaney, M., Badawood, A., Almaghraby, A., & Lohr, J. B. (2019). Aging and trauma: Post Traumatic Stress Disorder among Korean War veterans. *Federal Practitioner*, *36*(12), 554–562. https://www.ncbi.nlm.nih.gov/pmc/articles/PMC6913617/ PMID:31892780

Penninx, R., & Garcés-Mascareñas, B. (2016). The concept of integration as an analytical tool and as a policy concept. In *Integration processes and policies in Europe* (pp. 11–29). Springer. doi:10.1007/978-3-319-21674-4_2

Ponzoni, E., Ghorashi, H., & van der Raad, S. (2017). Caught between norm and difference: Narratives on refugees' inclusion in organizations. *Equality, Diversity and Inclusion*, *36*(3), 222–237. doi:10.1108/EDI-11-2015-0093

Rees, S., & Fisher, J. (2020). COVID-19 and the mental health of people from refugee backgrounds. *International Journal of Health Services*, *50*(4), 415–417. doi:10.1177/0020731420942475 PMID:32669034

Ren, D., Wesselmann, E. D., & van Beest, I. (2020). Seeking solitude after being ostracized: A replication and beyond. *Personality and Social Psychology Bulletin*. doi:10.1177/0146167220928238 PMID:32515281

Risberg, A. & Romani, L. (2021). Underemploying highly skilled migrants: An organizational logic protecting corporate 'normality'. *Human Relations*. . doi:10.1177/00187267211992854

Riva, P., & Eck, J. (2016). The many faces of social exclusion. In P. Riva & J. Eck (Eds.), *Social exclusion: Psychological approaches to understanding and reducing its impact* (pp. ix–xv). Springer International., doi:10.1007/978-3-319-33033-4

Robinson, S., & Schabram, K. (2016). Workplace ostracism. In *Ostracism, exclusion, and rejection* (pp. 234–249). Routledge.

Saks, A. M., Uggerslev, K. L., & Fassina, N. E. (2007). Socialization tac- tics and newcomer adjustment: A meta-analytic review and test of a model. *Journal of Vocational Behavior*, *70*(3), 413–446. doi:10.1016/j.jvb.2006.12.004

Şar, V. (2017). Savaş ve terör yaşantılarında travma ve stres. *Okmeydanı Tıp Dergisi, 33*(Ek sayı),114-120. doi:10.5222/otd.2017.114

Sarmini, I., Topçu, E. & Scharbrodt, O. (2020). Integrating Syrian refugee children in Turkey: The role of Turkish language skills (A case study in Gaziantep). *International Journal of Education research Open, 1*. doi:10.1016/j.ijedro.2020.100007

Scott, K. L., & Duffy, M. K. (2015). Antecedents of workplace ostracism: new directions in research and intervention. In *Mistreatment in organizations*. Emerald Group Publishing Limited. doi:10.1108/S1479-355520150000013005

Sert, D. Ş., & Danış, D. (2020). Framing Syrians in Turkey: State control and no crisis discourse. *International Migration (Geneva, Switzerland)*, *59*(1), 197–214. doi:10.1111/imig.12753

Şimşek, D. (2018). Refugee integration, migration policies and social class: The case of Syrian refugees in Turkey. *Sosyal Politika Çalışmaları Dergisi 18*(40).

Şimşek, D. (2019). Integration of Syrian refugees in Turkey: Challenges and opportunities. Journal of Research in Economics. *Politics & Finance*, *4*(2), 172–187.

Şimşek, D. (2020). Integration processes of Syrian refugees in Turkey: 'Class-based integration'. *Journal of Refugee Studies*, *33*(3), 537–554. doi:10.1093/jrs/fey057

Sleijpen, M., Haagen, J., Mooren, T., & Kleeber, R. J. (2016). Growing from experience: An exploratory study of posttraumatic growth in adolescent refugees. *European Journal of Psychotraumatology*, *7*(1), 28698. doi:10.3402/ejpt.v7.28698 PMID:26886487

Spencer, S., & Cooper, B. (2006). Social integration of migrants in Europe: A review of the European literature 2000-2006. *Gaining from migration (A joint European Commission/Organisation for Economic Co-operation and Development project of July 2007)*.

Sterud, T., Tynes, T., Mehlum, I. S., Veiersted, K. B., Bergbom, B., Airila, A., Johansson, B., Brendler-Lindqvist, M., Hviid, K., & Flyvholm, M. A. (2018). A systematic review of working conditions and occupational health among immigrants in Europe and Canada. *BMC Public Health*, *18*(1), 1–15. doi:10.118612889-018-5703-3 PMID:29925349

Szkudlarek, B. (2019) Engaging business in refugee employment: The employers' perspective. Sydney.

Theisen-Womersley, G. (2021). Prevalence of PTSD Among Displaced Populations—Three Case Studies. In *Trauma and Resilience Among Displaced Populations* (pp. 67–82). Springer. doi:10.1007/978-3-030-67712-1_3

UNHCR. (2022a). *Asylum seekers*. UNHCR. https://www.unhcr.org/tr/en/asylum-seekers

UNHCR. (2022b). *What is a refugee?* UNHCR. https://www.unhcr.org/what-is-a-refugee.html

Van Maanen, J., & Schein, E. H. (1979). Toward a theory of organizational socialization. In B. M. Staw (Ed.), *Research in organizational behavior* (Vol. 1, pp. 209–264). JAI Press.

Varvin, S. (2017). Our Relations to Refugees: Between Compassion and Dehumanization. *American Journal of Psychoanalysis*, 77(4), 1–19. doi:10.105711231-017-9119-0 PMID:29085057

Veronese, G., Pepe, A., Jaradah, A., Al Muranak, F., & Hamdouna, H. (2017). Modelling life satisfaction and adjustment to trauma in children exposed to ongoing military violence: An exploratory study in Palestine. *Child Abuse & Neglect*, 63, 61–72. doi:10.1016/j.chiabu.2016.11.018 PMID:27907846

Walsh, S. D., Tartakovsky, E., & Shifter-David, M. (2019). Personal values and immigrant group appraisal as predictors of voluntary contact with immigrants among majority students in Israel. *International Journal of Psychology*, 54(6), 731–738. doi:10.1002/ijop.12531 PMID:30238966

Ward, M., Poleacovschi, C., Faust, K. M., Weems, C. F., & Gabiam, N. (2020). Evaluating the role of infrastructure components and demographics on social capital in refugee camps. *Journal of Management Engineering*, 36(3), 04020007. doi:10.1061/(ASCE)ME.1943-5479.0000754

Williams, K. D. (2009). Ostracism: A temporal need-threat model. Advances in Experimental Social Psychology, 41, 275–314. doi: (08)00406–1 doi:10.1016/S0065–2601

Williams, K. D., & Nida, S. A. (2011). Ostracism: Consequences and coping. *Current Directions in Psychological Science*, 20(2), 71–75. doi:10.1177/0963721411402480

Yoo, G., & Lee, S. (2018). It doesn't end there: Workplace Bullying, work-to-family conflict, and employee well-being in Korea. *International Journal of Environmental Research and Public Health*, 15(7), 1548. doi:10.3390/ijerph15071548 PMID:30037131

Yoon, M. S., Feyissa, I. F., & Jung, E. H. (2020). The Long Way to Refugee Status Acquisition and Mental Health in Post-Migration: Based on Asylum Seekers and Refugees in South Korea. *The Psychiatric Quarterly*, 91(2), 403–416. doi:10.100711126-020-09714-9 PMID:31950331

Youssef, C. M., & Luthans, F. (2007). Positive organizational behavior in the workplace: The impact of hope, optimism, and resilience. *Management Department Faculty Publications*, 36(5), 774–800. doi:10.1177/0149206307305562

Zikic, J. (2015). Skilled migrants' career capital as a source of competi- tive advantage: Implications for strategic HRM. *International Journal of Human Resource Management*, 26(10), 1360–1381. doi:10.1080/09585192.2014.981199

Chapter 8
Environment of Inclusion and Diversity Management on Perceived Diversity Climate

Stephen Deepak
Kristu Jayanti College, India

Syed Khalid Perwez
Vellore Institute of Technology, India

ABSTRACT

Diversity at the workplace refers to the environment where individuals from different social backgrounds work together to pursue organizational goals. It is often difficult for individuals to accept members who belong to a different country, culture, religion, and other backgrounds. To manage this, organizations must encourage a climate that appreciates diversity and fosters inclusivity. Diversity climate in organizations is an indication of the extent that working individuals in organizations appreciate diversity related management policies, practices, and action plans aimed to accommodate everyone equally. Employees experience a sense of inclusion when their feelings of uniqueness and belongingness are addressed by the firm's inclusive initiatives making them contribute to the objectives of the organization. This study conceptually provides a theoretical understanding that inclusion and diversity management positively influences the perceived diversity climate which in turn motivates employees towards higher organizational performance.

INTRODUCTION

Workforce diversity is a reality today as the world has shrunk into a global village becoming a melting point for people of all ages, genders, abilities, social and culture backgrounds, religions, sexualities, and lifestyles to come together and work for a common purpose. This transformation is due to the rapid changes witnessed over the last two decades in the political economic, technological and socio culture spheres. This has necessitated a heterogeneous workforce that in turn creates a different climate that needs to be understood by the organizations and must strive to provide opportunities equally for all individuals.

Diversity earlier was restricted to differences in physical, gender, ethnic and religious characteristics but today it covers attitudes, lifestyles, generational cohorts, disabilities and sexual preferences. It covers visible and invisible attributes of people. Diversity becomes evident in organizations in the way employees think, feel and behave with respect to work, performance, satisfaction and contribution to growth in the organization (Hays-Thomas and Bendick 2013). Interpersonal relationships of people reflect their perceptions, values and behaviours that emanate from the beliefs they hold and the backgrounds they come from. Managing these employees requires a good understanding of their diverse backgrounds (Jeffery Sanchez-Burks and Michal E. Mor Barak, 2005). It is an absolute necessity in globalized markets to address and accommodate the requirements of diverse employees. If a firm fails to do so, it is branded to be non-competitive in today's context (Sharbari Saha, Dewpha Mukherjee Patra, 2008). Firms need to bring in inclusive practices to make employees from diverse backgrounds to become a part of the organization, as it is a natural tendency for members of the same background to group themselves as one unit and disassociate themselves from others belonging to other backgrounds (Mor Barak, 2000). It is imperative for firms in this generation to understand the serious need to address diversity and use it to gain competitive advantage (Kreitz, 2008). Firms that manage diversity well are able to see results from employees in the form of creativity, decision making, skill transfer, energy and motivation (Qasim, 2017)

REVIEW OF LITERATURE: DIVERSITY CLIMATE AND MANAGEMENT

Diversity Climate refers to the environment employees experience in their organizations as a result of diversity and inclusive practices implemented by them. Diversity Climate will be perceived to be positive if the organization accommodates heterogeneous groups, addresses diversity issues and creates an inclusive climate (Hyde and Hopkins, 2004). This will be evident through the firm's human resource policies that strive to integrate the minority and diverse members into organizational activities. This climate is perceived at three levels, at the individual level it is addressed by the biases and prejudices that individuals experience, at the group level it refers to the perceptions of conflict within and between groups composed of diverse members and at the organization level includes the organization culture, human resource policies and decision making where efforts are made to involve members from diverse communities (Cox, 1994). Diversity issues cannot be managed unless firms take a policy stand to ring in efforts to promote diversity and inclusiveness. Diversity Management has been defined as gathering necessary knowledge and skills to articulate the differences appropriately and adequately. It also requires one to have a creative attitude to see situations from different perspectives without possessing a prejudice (Ting-Toomey and Chung, 2005). Diversity management actions at the workplace have both positive and negative outcomes (Chrobot-Mason & Aramovich, 2013). How employees perceive outcomes depends on the work environment and the manner in which diversity is comprehensively managed (Chrobot-Mason & Aramovich, 2013). Employees who perceive that the organization is affirmative in its diversity and inclusive measures demonstrate loyalty, innovativeness and are attached to the organization (Ivancevich & Gilbert, 2000; Robinson & Dechant, 1997). Affirmative diversity actions were found to result in organizational commitment, empowerment and job satisfaction (Wolfson et.al, 2011). Workers today prefer working in organizations that regard diversity and respect differences that employees bring to their work groups. Diversity can be understood under four dimensions: a) Diversity as a construct of similarity and difference b) as shared resources and representations during social and verbal interactions c) to view intercultural negotiations emphasising on mediation and translation d) to know the interplay of power and intercultural contexts of organizations, (Kundu and Mor, 2017). Identifying, recognizing and understanding these differences are important if organizations are keen on utilizing the unique advantages that diverse individuals bring to the organization.

Firms must make efforts to initiative practices that promote diversity and make employees from all walks of life feel inclusive. The actions they enable must strive to promote equality and proactively engage the social, cultural and ethnic diversity of employees. Firms need to manage diversity with a conscious plan and action. Managing diversity originates from the affirmative actions and equal employment laws and guidelines (Kelly & Dobbin, 1998; Thomas, 1992; Yakura, 1996) It does not just include efforts taken to improve racial and ethnic representation of the minorities but makes sustained efforts to create an environment that is conductive for all to work comfortably in the organization (Thomas, 1992). These efforts create a climate where employers become aware of the differences diversity brings in and hence utilizes their abilities and potentials towards organizational activities. (Emico & Eunmi, 2009). Diversity Management encompasses the initiatives and practices followed by the organization that brings feelings of equality, respect, appreciation and engagement among the members of the organization belonging to either majority or minority groups. (Thomas, 1990; Gao and He, 2017; Valentine and Godkin, 2017). These initiatives and practices strike a balance between majority and minority workers ensuring a climate of fairness and trust (Muhr et.al,2012), (Knoppers et.al, 2015). When organizations strive to accept employees as they are and makes efforts to create a climate of fairness it results in positive organizational outcomes such as Job satisfaction, organization citizenship behaviours, loyalty, trust and employee performance (Alas and Mousa, 2016). Research also has demonstrated Diversity management's initiatives on outcomes such as employee wellbeing (Mor Barak and Levin, 2002) employee turnover (Mor Barak and Cherin, 1998) employee's financial rewards (Light, 2008) responsible leadership and organizational commitment (Mousa, 2017). Hence, Organizations must consciously design work systems and environments that make individuals from diverse social backgrounds to be included and enable them to contribute meaningfully towards the organization.

Diversity and Inclusion

Inclusion is defined as the extent or degree to which an individual is accepted and treated as one among them by the groups in the work system (Pelled, Ledford, and Mohrman, 1999). It also refers to the removal of obstacles to allow for full participation and contribution by the employees. (Roberson, 2006). Lirio et al. (2008) state that inclusion as an employee experience of belongingness and inclusivity where employee contributions are valued daily by their organizations. (Avery, McKay, Wilson, and Volpone, 2008) believe that an inclusive organization allows members to use their individual talents to contribute towards the mission and operations of the organization. (Wasserman, Gallegos, and Ferdman, 2008) define inclusion as a culture where members of all social backgrounds have a chance to present themselves, have a voice to be heard and appreciated and involve in the primary activities with the rest of the workforce. Holvino, Ferdman, and Merrill-Sands, (2004) explain that an inclusive organization is one where the diversity of knowledge and perspectives of the members from different groups are brought to pursue the organizations strategy, work processes, management decisions, core operations and value systems of the organization. Inclusion refers to the extent to which individuals are allowed to involve and fully contribute to the organizations functions (Miller, 1998). It is a feeling where an employee is treated well and accepted as an insider in the organization and is allowed to access information, use resources, have good relationships with superiors and fellow workers and participate in decision making activities of the organization (Mor Barak, 2000).

From the definitions cited above two dimensions are distinctly clear, one being the approach for belongingness and the other being the approach for distinctiveness.

Researchers on Inclusion opine that though pioneering work on inclusion has been done by scholars like Mor Barak and Brewer, inclusion as a concept needs deeper understanding as there is no consensus in terms of its construct. One approach of Inclusion has been understood from the Optimal Distinctiveness Theory of Brewer (1991). Brewer states that there is a prevailing tension in the individual for a feeling of validation and similarity on one hand and the need to express uniqueness and individuality on the other. Hence individuals try to balance these two tensions optimally through inclusion to the groups they belong to. In order for individuals to establish strong and stable interpersonal relationships it is fundamental for them to belong to a group and find social identities by joining those groups for acceptance by its members and avoid isolation by them (Baumeister & Leary, 1995). (Pickett, Silver, & Brewer, 2002) state that Individuals who belong to a group display similar characteristics as its group members and show favouritism by them (Turner, 1975) Further, inclusive members enjoy the support, trust and cooperation of the group (Brewer, 2007). Sometimes, if the members become too similar and lack any uniqueness, it triggers a need for category membership to enable members to establish a distinction from the other group members. Members in a group always look to satisfy the dual needs for belongingness and uniqueness (Pickett, Bonner, and Coleman (2002) when both needs are difficult to be met, they choose to pick any one depending on the group context

A culture or climate of Inclusion is said to exist when people of all social identities get opportunities to present themselves, have their voices heard and appreciated and able to engage in activities as part of the collective workforce (Wasserman et.al, 2008). Firms can take full advantage when leaders in the organization experience a feeling of inclusiveness individuals feel truly inclusive only when they experience the same in their interactions with leaders, managers, peer members and the organization as a whole (Bailinson et.al, Mckinsey report, 2020). Promoting Inclusiveness in hiring, promotion, development and leadership by organizations contributes to 30% higher revenue per employee and increased profitability than competitors. Teams with diverse individuals can fully contribute if the firm encourages an inclusive environment. Inclusive organizations have witnessed positive team performances, greater innovativeness, increased creativity, higher employee engagement, higher productivity, lower attrition and increased employee retention. (Deloitte Research Report, 2012) Inclusive organizations are multicultural, in which the diversity of its members shape the strategy, work, values, norms and management of work activities (Holvino et.al, 2004) in which members feel free to speak and participate in decision processes (Detert and Burris, 2007) and make contributions that receive appreciation from their superiors (Nembhard and Edmonson, 2006)

PURPOSE OF THE STUDY

The motive of the study is to conceptually understand the role of inclusion and diversity management as researchable constructs and study their influence on perceived diversity climate. A distinct clarity based on review of literature was required to understand this distinction. Studies on the subject of Diversity have pointed out to the variables that create differences but not many studies have covered inclusion.

This study is follows the Optimal Distinctiveness theory that addresses the twin needs of belongingness and uniqueness among individuals at the workplace. Organizations have Diversity management policies that addresses diversity but may not do enough to include the dimension of inclusion. Diversity studies have focussed on demographic variables and not emphasized enough on integrating employees and empowering them to contribute through inclusion.

Firms could be satisfied following a policy of giving representation to the minority groups unrepresented in the past and employees may be working there without a sense of uniqueness and belongingness. This would lead to a complete failure in the diversity management initiative. Hence, there is a need to study inclusion as part of diversity management. This study specifically brings about a strong theoretical connection between Inclusion, Diversity Management and Perceived Diversity Climate.

Methodology

The article has been prepared through the systematic review of literature approach mining though 80 research articles on Diversity and Inclusiveness. The article has constructed a narrative to highlight the emergence of Diversity, the prevalence of the diversity climate, need for diversity management and inclusivity in organizations. Articles have been reviewed to frame the theoretical hypothesis to construct a linkage between Inclusion and Diversity Management with Perceived Diversity Climate and Organization Performance.

HYPOTHESES

H1: Diversity Management Practices Positively Influence Perceived Diversity Climate

Employees are aware about their diversity and choose to work in organizations that regard diversity and respect the differences employees bring to the organization (Kundu and Mor, 2017). Firms are consciously making an effort to attract the best of talent to make sure they stay competitive in the industry and market. Organizations in the west have the experience of implementing Diversity and affirmative actions that strives to provide equal opportunity and ensures fairness to the minorities (Selden and Selden, 2001; Ashkali and Groenveld, 2015) and seen in practices such a hiring, developing and retaining employees with differences (Ely and Thomas, 2001; Nishii, 2013). This has resulted in employees perceiving their organizations as employee friendly and develop a positive perception towards it. A positive diversity climate creates an environment conducive for employee and organizational growth. In this regard, firms are creating, reviewing and updating diversity related policies to make them inclusive and acceptable to all. These initiatives ensure an environment that allows its employees to experience justice, tolerance, respect, providing equal opportunity to all regardless of whether they belong to a majority or a minority category (Healy et.al, 2010). Diversity climate improves when firms take proactive measures to promote diversity by recognizing demographic differences such as age, gender, religion, ethnicity, religion and education.(Kundu and Mor, 2017) The goal must be to ensure that diversity management practices create a climate that welcomes individual uniqueness and appreciates differences (Thomas, 1990). Creating or adapting policies to make it diversity friendly is not an easy task as it results in changes in the organization's values, culture and traits (Celik et al, 201, Sore et al, 2011, Mousa 2018a, Mousa 2018b, Mousa et al 2019). Diversity climate of the firm consciously adapts and customizes policies in the organization that makes employees feel involved, engaged, accepted and develop a sense of belongingness (Mousa, 2019).

H2: Inclusion Positively Affects and Influences Diversity Management Practices

Inclusion is referred as a climate where employees are made to experience a feeling of uniqueness and belongingness to the organization they work. Inclusion must be a part of diversity management policy, as the outcome of any diversity program is to make employees experience acceptance and utilize his or her unique abilities irrespective of the differences they are categorized with. A policy of Inclusion enables every employee to be a part of the mission and function of the organization (Avery et.al, 2008).

Organizations must take efforts to make the workforce diverse and workplaces inclusive. Diversity management strategies are implemented in organizations to achieve this noble goal and these efforts alone are not sufficient to achieve them (Sabharwal, 2014). Inclusion in workplaces are supported by good leaders and empowered employees will organizations see gainful results. Studies on the status of inclusion reveals that a significant number of employees in the workforce feel excluded (Prasad, 2001) revealing that organizations have not yet reached a full diversity status. Diversity and Inclusion strategies, highlight an employer's brand by appealing to the best talent in the labour market. If firms lack sincerity in diversity implementation and do not demonstrate promises made to the labour market it can result in negative consequences (Hays-Thomas and Bendick, 2013). Diversity management for some organizations remains a rhetoric far from reality and whether minority groups are truly represented and whether they have a voice is something that requires examination if firms are to be called truly inclusive. Measures taken by the firm must not be merely doing a lip service but must be perceived as fairly working for the inclusivity of all. Diversity management ensures that all employees have an equal chance and opportunity as others in accessing organization's resources (Buttner et al., 2010; Mousa, 2017a), hence designing a Diversity management program that is acceptable to all is difficult as every organization would have its own values, culture and different demographic profiles among employees (Mor Bark and Levin. 2002), Jin et al (2017). Hence it is better to have a Diversity policy that is acceptable in different scenarios and assimilates the cultures followed by the employees (Andrews, 2005), (Pitts, 2005).

H3: Climate of Inclusion Positively Enhances Perceptions of Perceived Diversity Climate

Inclusion creates an experience where an employee feels that he or she has been treated with respect and fairness and experiences a sense of value and belongingness. Employees feel inclusive at two levels. The first level is based on equality and participation where employees compare their pay, rewards and other outcomes with others. The second level is based on the feeling where the employee understands that his or her uniqueness is recognized by the members of the work group and organization and they have a voice or can raise issues on organizational matters (Deloitte Research Report, 2012)

Employee's perceptions of inclusion is based on a degree of their experiences of uniqueness and belongingness on the Inclusion – Exclusion continuum. When an employee experiences high level of uniqueness and belongingness he or she feels included as an insider on par with the other members in the group contrary to employee's experiences of low sense of uniqueness and belongingness and feel like an outsider excluded. Employees may experience high belongingness but low uniqueness leading to a state of assimilation. In this context, the employee is treated as an insider only when they adhere to group norms or the dominant culture, underplaying their uniqueness. When employees experience a high sense of uniqueness and low sense of belongingness it results in a state of differentiation where the employee is treated for his or her uniqueness but is not made to feel as an insider by the work group and the organization. (Shore et.al 2011).

H4: Perceptions of Inclusion and Diversity Management Positively Influences Organizational Performance

Diversity can be harnessed through the process of Inclusion where employees feel valued and develop affiliation to the organization. This is possible when organizations make an effort to recognize differences by valuing them and take initiatives to create an atmosphere of inclusion. Diversity and Inclusion process is truly understood and experienced when employees are treated with fairness, if this experience is not truly felt by the employees, it would mean the firm has failed to ensure an inclusive climate in the organization. Diversity related initiatives help the firm gain not only a public image and but also result in economic gains. Firms in turn also would gain acceptance, respect and loyalty of the employees in the process. A Deloitte survey report reveals that if only 10% of employees feel included it would result in an increase in attendance among employees equal to one day per employee per year. The report also stated that when employees felt included business performances increased due to the ability of the employees to innovate, respond to customer requirements and collaborate with team members (Deloitte Research Report, 2012)

Firms need to consciously move away from merely doing diversity based recruitment and training but look at ways to encompass diversity in holistic ways. It must focus on acceptance and integration by overcoming perceptions, biases and differences both conscious and unconscious and address diversity related issues as soon as they crop up. It is possible when diversity measures are not centred on demographic differences but are inclusive in all respects. When employees experience inclusion they bring themselves wholly towards contributing to the organization participating in creativity, innovation and problem solving

SCOPE FOR FUTURE RESEARCH

Perceived Diversity Climate can be understood by studying the inclusion dimension in diversity management practices as diversity management without inclusion is not adequate enough to serve the purpose. This study has provided a theoretical support to the constructs. Empirical studies on the given constructs using a demographic dimension, comparative organizational context, different cultural setting, majority or minority dominated work centres could be explored for future research. Inclusion literature is limited and constructs are being developed, future research could focus on contributing to inclusive measures in process and outcomes.

Future research can attempt to study the role of the supervisor or leader in implementing these policies and practices as line managers are instrumental in making these policies reach subordinates. Perceptions of uniqueness and belongingness with an understanding of fairness and justice will be of importance to gauge perceptions at the individual, group and organizational level. Past studies on diversity have highlighted a different attitude and behaviour for leaders dealing with diversity, hence a diversity leadership style where diversity guidelines and policies are implemented to fulfil the minority groups needs to be researched. If a leader is not just confined to implementing diversity related action plans but is willing to strive to recognise individual uniqueness and engages with the subordinates will increase their esteem as insiders. What leadership style or behaviour would be right? Should the leader be a diversity leader or an inclusive leader or an ethical leader? The attitude and behavioural dimension can be explored to study the definite role played by leaders who adopt these behaviours and styles?

DISCUSSION AND CONCLUSION

The study on Perceived Diversity Climate evokes a lot of interest among scholars as the nature of diversity varies across organizations, cultures and nationalities. With a changing labour market that is influenced by globalization the differences in diversity have increased manifold making organizations think of strategies to understand, manage and leverage diversity. Firms have been adding diversity strategies in recruitment, selection, training and development, promotions, pay and rewards structures, team composition, assignment of responsibilities and decision making to ensure there is equal representation of the non-traditional groups (Deloitte Research Report, 2012). Firms in the west have used affirmative actions and equal opportunity laws to ensure diversity implementation but in many countries in Asia, Africa and other continents diversity measures are still a far call. Many countries like India are multi - cultural and managing diversity within the country itself could be a challenge and any diversity measure could leave some other groups feeling discriminated.

Hence a cautious and a multi-pronged approach is needed to manage diversity well. In the same breath, diversity measures adopted by firms often lack inclusiveness in them leading to a perception that diversity measures are more for compliance than implemented in spirit. diversity policy and measures are managerial actions that seek to provide equal opportunities that would have all groups of workers represented but inclusion goes a step further to have the employees experience a sense of uniqueness and belongingness in equal measure (Sabharwal, 2014),. Firms have to create diversity and inclusion measures that incorporate assimilation and differentiation in them to enable employees feel as insiders and contribute wholly to the organization's goals.(Shore et.al, 2011). Inclusion and diversity management practices can positively influence the perceived diversity climate in the organization through which meaningful contributions can be leveraged in achieving organizational performances and outcomes.

REFERENCES

Alas, R., & Mousa, M. (2016). Cultural diversity and business schools' curricula: A case from Egypt. *Problems and Perspectives in Management*, *14*(2), 130–137. doi:10.21511/ppm.14(2-1).2016.01

Andrews, R., Boyne, G. A., Meier, K. J., O'Toole, L. J. Jr, & Walker, R. M. (2005). Representative bureaucracy, organizational strategy, and public service performance: An empirical analysis of English local government. *Journal of Public Administration: Research and Theory*, *15*(2), 489–504. doi:10.1093/jopart/mui032

April, K., Katoma, V., & Peters, K. (2009). Critical effort and leadership in specialised virtual networks. *Annual Review of High Performance Coaching & Consulting*, *1*(1), 187–215.

Ashikali, T., & Groeneveld, S. (2015). Diversity management for all? An empirical analysis of diversity management outcomes across groups. *Personnel Review*, *44*(5), 757–780. doi:10.1108/PR-10-2014-0216

Avery, D. R., McKay, P. F., Wilson, D. C., & Volpone, S. (2008). *Attenuating the effect of seniority on intent to remain: The role of perceived inclusiveness*. Paper presented at the meeting of the Academy of Management, Anaheim, CA.

Avery, D. R., McKay, P. F., Wilson, D. C., & Volpone, S. (2008, August). Attenuating the effect of seniority on intent to remain: The role of perceived inclusiveness. In meeting of the Academy of Management, Anaheim, CA.

Bailinson, P., Decherd, W., Ellsworth, D., & Guttman, M. "Understanding organizational barriers to a more inclusive workplace" https://www.mckinsey.com/business-functions/organization/our-insights/understanding-organizational-barriers-to-a-more-inclusive-workplace

Barak, M. (2000). Beyond affirmative action: Toward a model of diversity and organizational inclusion. *Administration in Social Work*, *23*(3/4), 47–68.

Baumeister, R. F., & Leary, M. R. (1995). The need to belong: Desire for interpersonal attachments as a fundamental human motivation. *Psychological Bulletin*, *117*(3), 497–529. doi:10.1037/0033-2909.117.3.497 PMID:7777651

Booysen, L. (2007). Managing cultural diversity: A south African perspective. In K. April & M. Shockley (Eds.), Diversity in Africa: The coming of age of a continent (pp. 51–92). New York, NY: Palgrave. doi:10.1057/9780230627536_5

Brewer, M. B. (1991). The social self: On being the same and different at the same time. *Personality and Social Psychology Bulletin*, *17*(5), 475–482. doi:10.1177/0146167291175001

Brewer, M. B. (2007). The importance of being we: Human nature and intergroup relations. *The American Psychologist*, *62*(8), 728–738. doi:10.1037/0003-066X.62.8.728 PMID:18020737

Buttner, E. H., Lowe, K. B., & Billings-Harris, L. (2010). Diversity climate impact on employee of color outcomes: Does justice matter? *Career Development International*, *15*(3), 239–258. doi:10.1108/13620431011053721

Celik, S., Ashikali, T., & Groeneveld, S. (2011). De invloed van diversiteitsmanagement op de binding van werknemers in de publieke sector. De rol van transformationeel leiderschap. (The binding effect of diversity management on employees in the Dutch public sector. The role of transformational leadership). *Tijdschrift voor HRM*, *14*(4), 32–53.

Chin, J. L. (Ed.). (2009). *The psychology of prejudice and discrimination: A revised and condensed edition*. ABC-CLIO.

Chrobot-Mason, D., & Aramovich, N. P. (2013). The psychological benefits of creating an affirming climate for workplace diversity. *Group & Organization Management*, *38*(6), 659–689. doi:10.1177/1059601113509835

Cox, T. H. Jr. (1994). *Cultural diversity in organizations: Theory, research, & practice*. Berrett-Koehler.

Daya, P. (2014). Diversity and inclusion in an emerging market context, equality diversity and inclusion. *International Journal (Toronto, Ont.), 33*(3), 293–308.

Daya, P. (2014). Diversity and inclusion in an emerging market context. *Equality, Diversity and Inclusion, 33*(3), 293–308. doi:10.1108/EDI-10-2012-0087

Deloitte. (2011). Only skin deep? Reexamining the business case for diversity. Deloitte.

Detert, J. R., & Burris, E. R. (2007). Leadership behavior and employee voice: Is the door really open? *Academy of Management Journal, 50*(4), 869–884. doi:10.5465/amj.2007.26279183

Ely, R. J., & Thomas, D. A. (2001). Cultural diversity at work: The effects of diversity perspectives on work group processes and outcomes. *Administrative Science Quarterly, 46*(2), 229–273. doi:10.2307/2667087

Ferdman, M., & Sagiv, L. (2012). Diversity in organizations and cross-cultural work psychology: What if they were more connected? *Industrial and Organizational Pyschology, 5*(3), 323–345. doi:10.1111/j.1754-9434.2012.01455.x

Gao, Y., & He, W. (2017). Corporate social responsibility and employee organizational citizenship behavior: The pivotal roles of ethical leadership and organizational justice. *Management Decision, 55*(2), 294–309. doi:10.1108/MD-05-2016-0284

Saumya Goyal, (Aug 2009) "Diversity at Workplace" HRM Review

Hays-Thomas, R., & Bendick, M. Jr. (2013). Professionalizing diversity and inclusion practice: Should voluntary standards be the chicken or the egg? *Industrial and Organizational Psychology: Perspectives on Science and Practice, 6*(3), 193–205. doi:10.1111/iops.12033

Healy, G., Kirton, G., & Noon, M. (2010). *Equality. Palgrave Macmillan.* Inequalities and Diversity.

Holvino, E., Ferdman, B. M., & Merrill-Sands, D. (2004). Creating and sustaining diversity and inclusion in organizations: Strategies and approaches.

Hyde, C. A., & Hopkins, A. (2004). Diversity climates in human service agencies: An exploratory assessment. *Journal of Ethnic & Cultural Diversity in Social Work, 13*(2), 25–43. doi:10.1300/J051v13n02_02

Jin, M., Lee, J., & Lee, M. (2017). Does leadership matter in diversity management? Assessing the relative impact of diversity policy and inclusive leadership in the public sector. *Leadership and Organization Development Journal, 38*(2), 303–319. doi:10.1108/LODJ-07-2015-0151

Kelly, E., & Dobbin, F. (1998). How Affirmative Action Became Diversity Management: Employer Response to Antidiscrimination Law, 1961 to 1996. *American Behavioral Scientist, 41*(7), 960–984. https://doi.org/10.1177/0002764298041007008.

Knoppers, A., Claringbould, I., & Dortants, M. (2015). Discursive managerial practices of diversity and homogeneity. *Journal of Gender Studies, 24*(3), 259–274. doi:10.1080/09589236.2013.833086

Kreitz, P. A. (2008). Best practices for managing organizational diversity. *Journal of Academic Librarianship, 34*(2), 101–120. doi:10.1016/j.acalib.2007.12.001

Kundu, S. C., & Mor, A. (2017). Workforce diversity and organizational performance: A study of IT industry in India. *Employee Relations*, *39*(2), 160–183. doi:10.1108/ER-06-2015-0114

Light, P. C. (2008). A government ill executed: The depletion of the federal service. *Public Administration Review*, *68*(3), 413–419. doi:10.1111/j.1540-6210.2008.00878.x

Lirio, P., Lee, M. D., Williams, M. L., Haugen, L. K., & Kossek, E. E. (2008). The inclusion challenge with reducedload professionals: The role of the manager. *Human Resource Management*, *47*(3), 443–461. doi:10.1002/hrm.20226

Magoshi, E., & Chang, E. (2009). Diversity management and the effects on employees' organizational commitment: Evidence from Japan and Korea [January.]. *Journal of World Business, Elsevier*, *44*(1), 31–40. doi:10.1016/j.jwb.2008.03.018

Miller, F. A. (1998). Miller, "Strategic culture change: The door to acheiving high performance and inclusion. *Public Personnel Management*, *27*(2), 151–160. doi:10.1177/009102609802700203

Mor Barak, M. E. (2000). Beyond affirmative action: Toward a model of diversity and organizational inclusion. *Administration in Social Work*, *23*(3-4), 47–68. doi:10.1300/J147v23n03_04

Mor Barak, M. E. (2005). *Managing diversity: Toward a globally inclusive workplace*. Sage.

Mor Barak, M. E., & Cherin, D. A. (1998). A tool to expand organizational understanding of workforce diversity: Exploring a measure of inclusion-exclusion. *Administration in Social Work*, *22*(1), 47–64. doi:10.1300/J147v22n01_04

Mor Barak, M. E., Cherin, D. A., & Berkman, S. (1998). Organizational and personal dimensions in diversity climate: Ethnic and gender differences in employee perceptions. *The Journal of Applied Behavioral Science*, *34*(1), 82–104. doi:10.1177/0021886398341006

Mor Barak, M. E., & Levin, A. (2002). Outside of the corporate mainstream and excluded from the work community: A study of diversity, job satisfaction and well-being. *Community Work & Family*, *5*(2), 133–157. doi:10.1080/13668800220146346

Mousa, M. (2017). Responsible leadership and organizational commitment among physicians: Can inclusive diversity climate enhance the relationship. *Journal of Intercultural Management*, *9*(2), 103–141. doi:10.1515/joim-2017-0010

Mousa, M. (2018a). Inspiring work-life balance: Responsible leadership among female pharmacists in the Egyptian health sector. *Entrepreneurial Business and Economics Review*, *6*(1), 71–90. doi:10.15678/EBER.2018.060104

Mousa, M. (2018b). The effect of cultural diversity challenges on organizational cynicism dimensions: A study from Egypt. *Journal of Global Responsibility*, *9*(3), 133–155. doi:10.1108/JGR-06-2017-0037

Mousa, M., & Ayoubi, R. (2019a). Inclusive/exclusive talent management, responsible leadership and organizational downsizing: A study among academics in Egyptian business schools. *Journal of Management Development*, *38*(2), 87–104. doi:10.1108/JMD-11-2018-0325

Muhr, S. L., Pedersen, M., & Alvesson, M. (2012). Workload, aspiration and fun: Problems of balancing self-exploitation and self-exploration in work life. *Research in the Sociology of Organizations, 37*, 193–220. doi:10.1108/S0733-558X(2013)0000037011

Nembhard, M., & Edmonson, A. C. (2006). Making it safe: The effects of leader inclusiveness and professional status on psychological safety and improvement efforts in health care teams. *Journal of Organizational Behavior, 27*(7), 941–966. doi:10.1002/job.413

Nishii, L. (2013). The benefits of climate for inclusion for gender diverse groups. *Academy of Management Journal, 56*(6), 1754–1774. doi:10.5465/amj.2009.0823

Pelled, L. H., Ledford, G. E., & Mohrman, S. A. (1999). Demographic dissimilarity and workplace inclusion. *Journal of Management Studies, 36*(7), 1013–1031. doi:10.1111/1467-6486.00168

Pickett, C. L., Bonner, B. L., & Coleman, J. M. (2002). Motivated self-stereotyping: Heightened assimilation and differentiation needs result in increased levels of positive and negative self-stereotyping. *Journal of Personality and Social Psychology, 82*(4), 543–562. doi:10.1037/0022-3514.82.4.543 PMID:11999923

Pickett, C. L., Silver, M. D., & Brewer, M. B. (2002). The impact of assimilation and differentiation needs on perceived group importance and judgments of group size. *Personality and Social Psychology Bulletin, 28*(4), 546–558. doi:10.1177/0146167202287011

Pitts, D. (2005). Diversity, representations, and performance: Evidence about race and ethnicity in public organizations. *Journal of Public Administration: Research and Theory, 15*(4), 615–631. doi:10.1093/jopart/mui033

Prasad, A. (2001). Prasad, "Understanding workplace empowerment as inclusion. *The Journal of Applied Behavioral Science, 37*(1), 51–69. doi:10.1177/0021886301371004

Roberson, Q. M. (2006). Disentangling the meanings of diversity and inclusion in organizations. *Group & Organization Management, 31*(2), 212–236. doi:10.1177/1059601104273064

Roosevelt, T. R. (1990). From affirmative action to affirming diversity. *Harvard Business Review, 68*(2), 107–117. PMID:10106515

Sabharwal, M. (2014). Is diversity management sufficient? Organizational inclusion to further performance. *Public Personnel Management, 43*(2), 197–217. doi:10.1177/0091026014522202

Shore, L. M., Randel, A. E., Chung, B. G., Dean, M. A., Ehrhart, K. H., & Singh, G. (2011). Inclusion and diversity in work groups: A review and model for future research. *Journal of Management, 37*(4), 1262–1289. doi:10.1177/0149206310385943

Shore, M., Randel, A. E., Chung, B. G., Dean, M. A., Ehrhart, K. H., & Singh, G. (2011). Inclusion and diversity in work groups: A review and model for future research. *Journal of Management, 37*(4), 1262–1289. doi:10.1177/0149206310385943

Thomas, D. A., & Ely, R. J. (1996). Making differences matter. *Harvard Business Review, 74*(5), 79–90.

Thomas, R. R. Jr. (1990). From affirmative action to affirming diversity. *Harvard Business Review, 2*, 107–117. PMID:10106515

Thomas, R. R. Jr. (1992). Managing diversity: A conceptual framework. In S. E. Jackson (Ed.), *The professional practice series. Diversity in the workplace: Human resources initiatives* (pp. 306–317). Guilford Press.

Thomas, R. R. Jr, & Woodruff, M. I. (1999). *Building a House for Diversity*. American Management Association.

Ting-Toomey, Stella, and Leeva C. Chung. *Understanding intercultural communication*. New York: oxford university Press, 2005.

Turner, J. C. (1975). Social comparison and social identity: Some prospects for intergroup behavior. *European Journal of Social Psychology*, *5*(1), 5–34. doi:10.1002/ejsp.2420050102

Valentine, S., & Godkin, L. (2017). Banking employees' perceptions of corporate social responsibility, value-fit commitment, and turnover intentions: Ethics as social glue and attachment. *Employee Responsibilities and Rights Journal*, *29*(2), 51–71. doi:10.100710672-017-9290-8

van Dijk, H., van Engen, M., & Paauwe, J. (2012). Reframing the business case for diversity: A values and virtues perspective [macmillan]. *Journal of Business Ethics*, *111*(1), 73–84. doi:10.100710551-012-1434-z

Wah, L. (1999). Diversity at Allstate. *Management Review*, *88*(7), 24–30. doi:10.1057/9780230627536_5

Wasserman, I. C., Gallegos, P. V., & Ferdman, B. M. (2008). Dancing with resistance: Leadership challenges in fostering a culture of inclusion. In K. M. Thomas (Ed.), *Diversity resistance in organizations: 175-200*. Taylor & Francis Group/Lawrence Erlbaum.

Wasserman, I. C., Gallegos, P. V., & Ferdman, B. M. (2008). Dancing with resistance. *Diversity resistance in organizations*, 175-200.

Yakura, E. K. (1996). *Managing Diversity* (E. E. Kossek & S. A. Lobel, Eds.). Blackwell Publishers LTD.

Chapter 9
The Effect of Gender Diversity and Locus of Control on Employee Sustainability:
The Mediating Effect of Equity and Engagement — A Comparative Study Between Lebanon and Europe

Khodor Shatila

https://orcid.org/0000-0002-1580-121X

IProCares International Research Center, Lebanon

ABSTRACT

Workplaces in Lebanon have a wide range of diversity, including cultural, linguistic, and religious diversity, which all contribute to a better work environment for everyone. Women in Lebanon have not been able to fully exploit the basic right granted to them because of a variety of financial difficulties, stereotypes, and hidden discrimination. Data had been collected using survey distributed among 300 respondents; only 257 respondents filled the questionnaires maintaining 80% response rate. The data had been analyzed using SPSS to evaluate the mediating effect of equity and engagement on the relationship of gender diversity and locus of control on employee performance. The findings stated that the perception of gender diversity in the workplace is expected to enhance feelings of adequacy, empowerment, and physical and emotional well-being, has empirically supported a positive relationship between perceived gender diversity and employees performance. In the workplace, job equality has a significant impact on the performance of employees.

DOI: 10.4018/978-1-6684-4181-7.ch009

INTRODUCTION

Workplaces in Lebanon have a wide range of diversity, including cultural, linguistic, and religious diversity, which all contribute to a better work environment for everyone. Women in Lebanon have not been able to fully exploit the basic right granted to them because of a variety of financial difficulties, stereotypes, and hidden discrimination. In the World Economic Forum's Global Gender Gap Report, which ranks countries based on their ability to bridge the gender gap on four key factors, Lebanon scored 105th, which is the lowest among the Middle Eastern states. Due to the problems they face, women's job development is more complicated than that of males, according to the findings of Chrobot-Mason & Aramovich (2013). Discrimination in the workplace hurts employees' mental health and their ability to succeed in their jobs. The researchers are trying to find out whether there are differences in perceived diversity practices and workplace psychological safety for diverse groups according to Kobayashi et al. (2018). Employee contextual performance is also examined about fair representation, development opportunities, gender diversity, and psychological safety.

Kobayashi et al. (2018) used factor analysis, correlations, analyses of variance, and regression analysis to look at the Indian private banking industry's n = 536 employees. In terms of fair representation and development opportunities and the promotion of gender diversity, the statistics demonstrate that there are variations in gender diversity. Perceived equality and development prospects and psychological safety had a negative correlation with contextual performance. Gender diversity promotion techniques were not associated with contextual performance. Employees who feel safe and secure in their employment are more likely to be aggressive and less likely to engage in additional work activities (Gallego-Sosa et al., 2020). They used SPSS software to analyze employees' perceptions, behavior, and performance to help managers make better decisions for their workers, promote business growth, effective human resources, and management, as well as foster healthy and collaborative workplaces in private banks and other organizations.

Employer Branding and Company Development Strategy

There are several benefits to adhering to the workplace sustainable development principles. Young professionals who are just starting in their professions might provide valuable insight for businesses. Generation Z's perspectives on sustainable development and the gender of those who participated in the poll are being investigated by Rehman et al, (2020). Data had been collected using a survey from 291 students from Polish universities and colleges. Sustainable development efforts have been shown to boost the number of people who want to work for a company that implements such initiatives. Generation Z's perceptions have a direct effect on the value of branding and sustainable development activities by firms. Females put greater importance on environmental issues than men, and as a consequence, they are more inclined to advocate for laws that support sustainable development.

Gender Diversity and Locus of Control and Mediation of Work Engagement in Employee Well-being

Increasingly, Japanese businesses are worried about their workers' health and the long-term sustainability of potential employees. Promoting human sustainability and well-being in areas like work-life balance, adaptability, and gender diversity is difficult in large enterprises (Mousa et al., 2020). To get a better understanding of this problem, researchers interviewed twelve managers from eight prominent Japanese corporations and industries. Some of the issues that arise in promoting employee well-being include resources, family, stakeholders, and partners; meritocracy versus gender equality; indirect discrimination due to uneven care commitments and external limits on work hours; a probable link between personal and business success were also discovered. To maintain employee welfare and human sustainability as a goal for Japanese firms, he argued that Japanese organizations would have to face internal and external difficulties.

Researchers such as Galletta et al. (2021) are interested in finding out whether job engagement functions as a mediator between the components of perceived gender equality and control over work-related well-being measured through optimism, general satisfaction with life, and work, and executive burnout. A personal survey technique was used to interview 373 managers (both men and women) from Japanese industrial and service businesses. This study's focus is on how perceived gender equality affects workplace motivation and well-being, and how it might be operationalized. Conceptualization of well-being may help us better understand the expanding idea of well-being, which incorporates both positive and negative aspects according to Agarwal (2016). Gender equality is not only beneficial to workers' well-being but also has practical implications for talent management and job satisfaction.

Assessing the Effect of Perceived Diversity Practices and Psychological Safety on Contextual Performance for Sustainable Workplace

Prejudice in the workplace may hurt employees' mental health and their ability to perform at their best. Workplace diversity practices such as equitable representation and development modifications and gender diversity promotion are the focus of the study of Sulea et al. (2012). The study also investigates the link between employee contextual performance and equitable representation and growth opportunities, gender diversity promotion, and psychological safety. An Indian private banking sector sample size of (n = 536) was analyzed using statistical approaches, including factor analysis, correlations, and analysis of variance. For equal representation and development opportunities, and gender diversity promotion, the data showed inequalities in diversity of gender and tenure (Sulea et al., 2012). Employee contextual performance was negatively correlated with equal representation and development possibilities, as well as psychological safety. No correlation between gender diversity promotion strategies and contextual performance was found either. Unlike previous researches, the findings suggested that excessive psychological safety, equality in representation, and development opportunities to have workforce diversity disengage people from future work behavior. Analysis of employees' perception, behavior, and performance using SPSS software will aid managers in making better decisions for their employees; promoting business growth; effective human resources and management; and establishing a healthy and sustainable work environment in private banks and similar organizations according to Chrobot-Mason & Aramovich (2013).

METHODOLOGY

The participants will be drawn from a stratified random sample of managers from the public and commercial sectors in Lebanon and the European Union. Researchers plan to contact the human resources department of a national bank or insurance firm operating in Lebanon's capital city, Beirut, and other European Union nations. In Lebanon and the European Union, the service sector will be represented by these groups. The participants will be chosen at random from a list of corporate managers. They will all gather at the same time and place. Data would be collected using a personal survey technique because of the sensitivity of the topic of gender equality in the workplace, which was time-consuming and expensive but provided various advantages. Using SPSS for data analysis the research will evaluate the impact of gender diversity and locus of control on the relationship between these two characteristics, as well as the mediating influence of employee well-being.

Research Model

Referring to the above figure, the following is the research model which will be implemented in the research and it is made up of the independent variables which are Gender Diversity and Locus of Control, mediators which include Equity and Engagement and the dependent variable which is Employee Productivity. The following section will elaborate more on the research model including the scale that had been used.

Figure 1. Research Model

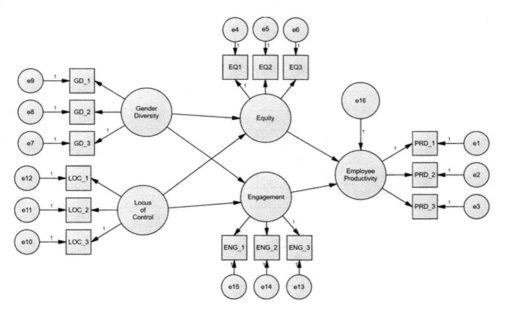

Measures

Standardized measures were used to gather data on the variables under investigation. In addition to indigenous measurements, additional measurements were adapted and used. Results of validity and reliability testing for each of the measures are summarized in the following table.

The scale of Galbreath (2018) had been used for attitudes toward gender diversity. A total of 48 males and females from Lebanese manufacturing and service sectors were surveyed, as well as 190 and 353 persons from the EU's manufacturing and service industries. For social desirability, the scale of Galbreath

(2018) had been used and it included 77 items on a scale ranging from 1 (Never) to 6 (Always), and the Cronbach alpha of this scale is 0.933.

Engagement survey by Alazzani et al. (2017a) has 17 questions and six response options, which range from 1 (never) to 6 (always/every day). Three subscales are used to measure the degree of engagement, which are vigor, dedication, and absorption, and Cronbach's alpha of this scale was 0.937.

The Locus of Control (LOC) scale developed by Blouch & Azeem (2019) included 10 statements; the respondent must choose the one that best conveys what he or she is thinking about locus of control. This scale has a Cronbach alpha of 0.668.

The Alazzani et al. (2017b) Employee Productivity comprises 28 questions to measure executive burnout on five main characteristics - uncertainty, inadequacy and discontent, and helplessness - as well as depersonalization and physical and emotional exhaustion. The Cronbach's alpha of the scale was 0.910.

Descriptive Statistics for Gender, Age and Locus of Control

Referring to the above descriptive statistics, it can be noted that Lebanese females, which fall under the age category of 20-29 years old, scored a mean of 0.0996, and those who fall under the age category of 30-39 years old scored a mean of 0.1230, and females, which fall under the age category of 40-49 scored a mean of 0.0936.

Table 1. Descriptive statistics for gender, age and locus of control

Report					
Locus of Control					
Country of origin	Gender	Age	Mean	N	Std. Deviation
Lebanon	Female	20-29	.0996	59	.03544
		30-39	.1230	38	.03622
		40-49	.0936	15	.03720
		Total	.3162	112	.03779
	Male	20-29	.0894	23	.03957
		30-39	.1352	13	.02959
		40-49	.0932	6	.04940
		Total	.3178	42	.04096
Europe	Female	20-29	.1099	18	.03828
		30-39	.1136	22	.03027
		40-49	.1254	21	.03317
		Total	.3489	61	.03469
	Male	20-29	.1954	12	.03194
		30-39	.1162	17	.03362
		40-49	.1020	13	.02384
		Total	.4136	42	.03311

As for the males in Lebanon, those who fall under the age range of 20-29 years old scored a mean of 0.0894, and those who fall in the age range of 0.1352 and at last males who fall under the age category of 40-49 years old scored a mean of 0.0932.

It can be noted that males in Lebanon that fall under the age range of 30-39 years old tend to have higher locus of control than females in the Lebanese companies.

However, European females, which fall under the age range of 20-29 years old, scored a mean of 0.1099, those who fall under the age range of 30-39 years old scored a mean of 0.1136, and at last the European females, which fall under the age range of 40-49 years old, scored a mean of 0.1254.

At last, it can be noted that European males which fall under the age range of 20-29 years old, scored a mean of 0.1954, those who fall under the age range of 30-39 years old scored a mean of 0.1162, and at last the European males, which fall under the age range of 40-49 years old, scored a mean of 0.1020.

Referring to the descriptive statistics, it can be noted that European males which falls under the age range of 20-29 years old scored the highest mean among European Youths which is 0.1954 and this depends on the workplace culture and their ability to be creative and innovative in the workplace and have the ability to control their workplace decisions.

Descriptive Statistics for Gender, Age and Engagement

Referring to the above descriptive statistics, it can be noted that Lebanese females, which fall under the age category of 20-29 years old, scored a mean of 0.0944, and those who fall under the age category of 30-39 years old scored a mean of 0.0930, and females, which fall under the age category of 40-49 scored a mean of 0.0996.

As for the males in Lebanon, those who fall under the age range of 20-29 years old scored a mean of 0.0986, and those who fall in the age range of 0.0998 and at last males who fall under the age category of 40-49 years old scored a mean of 0.0972.

It can be noted that males in Lebanon that fall under the age range of 30-39 years old tend to have higher engagement rate than females in the Lebanese companies.

However, European females, which fall under the age range of 20-29 years old, scored a mean of 0.0929, those who fall under the age range of 30-39 years old scored a mean of 0.0952, and at last the European females, which fall under the age range of 40-49 years old, scored a mean of 0.1034.

At last, it can be noted that European males which fall under the age range of 20-29 years old, scored a mean of 0.1009, those who fall under the age range of 30-39 years old scored a mean of 0.1000, and at last the European males, which fall under the age range of 40-49 years old, scored a mean of 0.9325.

Referring to the descriptive statistics, it can be noted that European males which falls under the age range of 20-29 years old scored the highest mean among European Youths which is 0.1009 and this depends on the workplace culture and their ability to be creative and innovative in the workplace and have the ability to control their workplace decisions and they are freshly educated and motivated to be engaged in the workplace and to share their ideas and knowledge to boost productivity.

Table 2. Descriptive statistics for gender, age and engagement

Report					
Engagement					
Country of origin	Gender	Age	Mean	N	Std. Deviation
Lebanon	Female	20-29	.0944	59	.01374
		30-39	.0930	38	.01834
		40-49	.0996	15	.01140
		Total	.0946	112	.01488
	Male	20-29	.0986	23	.01806
		30-39	.0998	13	.01407
		40-49	.0992	6	.01480
		Total	.0981	42	.01860
Europe	Female	20-29	.0929	18	.01232
		30-39	.0952	22	.00810
		40-49	.1034	21	.01248
		Total	.1012	61	.01668
	Male	20-29	.1009	12	.02132
		30-39	.1000	17	.01242
		40-49	.9325	13	.00747
		Total	.1118	42	.01292

Descriptive Statistics for Gender, Age and Productivity

Referring to the above descriptive statistics, it can be noted that Lebanese females, which fall under the age category of 20-29 years old, scored a mean of 0.1088, and those who fall under the age category of 30-39 years old scored a mean of 0.1014, and females, which fall under the age category of 40-49 scored a mean of 0.1052.

As for the males in Lebanon, those who fall under the age range of 20-29 years old scored a mean of 0.1193, and those who fall in the age range of 0.1040 and at last males who fall under the age category of 40-49 years old scored a mean of 0.1083.

It can be noted that males in Lebanon that fall under the age range of 20-29 years old tend to have higher productivity rate than females in the Lebanese companies.

However, European females, which fall under the age range of 20-29 years old, scored a mean of 0.1148, those who fall under the age range of 30-39 years old scored a mean of 0.1129, and at last the European females, which fall under the age range of 40-49 years old, scored a mean of 0.1221.

At last, it can be noted that European males which fall under the age range of 20-29 years old, scored a mean of 0.1267, those who fall under the age range of 30-39 years old scored a mean of 0.1072, and at last the European males, which fall under the age range of 40-49 years old, scored a mean of 0.1230.

Table 3. Descriptive statistics for gender, age and productivity

Report					
Productivity					
Country of origin	Gender	Age	Mean	N	Std. Deviation
Lebanon	Female	20-29	.1088	59	.02231
		30-39	.1014	38	.02616
		40-49	.1052	15	.03371
		Total	.1121	112	.02517
	Male	20-29	.1193	23	.02721
		30-39	.1040	13	.02222
		40-49	.1083	6	.03971
		Total	.1103	42	.02772
Europe	Female	20-29	.1148	18	.02342
		30-39	.1129	22	.01710
		40-49	.1221	21	.02456
		Total	.1167	61	.02322
	Male	20-29	.1267	12	.01773
		30-39	.1072	17	.01698
		40-49	.1230	13	.01691
		Total	.1097	42	.01684

Referring to the descriptive statistics, it can be noted that European males which falls under the age range of 20-29 years old scored the highest mean among European Youths which is 0.1267 and this depends on the workplace culture, their engagement and ability to be creative since they are freshly educated and motivated to be engaged in the workplace and to share their ideas and knowledge to boost productivity

Regression One: The Effect of Gender Diversity and Locus of Control on Employee Productivity

It can be noted from the above model summary that Lebanon scored R (0.265) and R^2 (0.070) and Europe scored R (0.373) and R^2 (0.139) which means that as shown in this model the relationship between gender diversity, locus of control and performance is higher in Europe than in Lebanon.

Referring to the above regression analysis, it can be noted that in Lebanon, Gender Diversity scored a P (0.00) < 0.05, and T (4.307) > 2 and Beta (0.314) and Locus of Control scored a P (0.002) < 0.05 and T (3.127) > 2 and Beta (0.228) which means that there is a positive significant relationship between gender diversity and locus of control (independent variables) with employees productivity (Dependent variable) and by that the following equation can be developed:

Productivity = 0.217 Gender Diversity + 0.228 Locus of Control

Table 4. Relationship between gender diversity, locus of control and productivity

Model Summary					
Country of origin	Model	R	R Square	Adjusted R Square	Std. Error of the Estimate
Lebanon	1	.265a	.070	.055	.02010
Europe	1	.373a	.139	.129	.02410
a. Predictors: (Constant), Gender Diversity, Locus of Control and Performance					

Coefficientsa							
Country of origin	Model		Unstandardized Coefficients		Standardized Coefficients	t	Sig.
			B	Std. Error	Beta		
Lebanon	1	(Constant)	.077	.009		8.593	.000
		Gender Diversity	.259	.060	.217	4.307	.000
		Locus of Control	.152	.049	.228	3.127	.002
Europe	1	(Constant)	.077	.010		7.554	.000
		Gender Diversity	.158	.066	.314	2.385	.019
		Locus of Control	.142	.055	.233	2.561	.012
a. Dependent Variable: Productivity							

This means that

- For every 1-unit increase in gender diversity, the productivity in Lebanese companies tend to be affected by 21.7 units.
- For every 1-unit increase in locus of control, the productivity in Lebanese companies tend to be affected by 22.8 units.

However, as for Europe it can be noted that Gender Diversity scored a P (0.019) < 0.05, and T (2.385) > 2 and Beta (0.217) and Locus of Control scored a P (0.012) < 0.05 and T (2.561) > 2 and Beta (0.233) which means that there is a positive significant relationship between gender diversity and locus of control (independent variables) with employees productivity (Dependent variable) and by that the following equation can be developed:

Productivity = 0.314 Gender Diversity + 0.233 Locus of Control

This means that

- For every 1-unit increase in gender diversity, the productivity in European companies tend to be affected by 31.4 units.
- For every 1-unit increase in locus of control, the productivity in European companies tend to be affected by 23.3 units

It can be concluded from this regression analysis that both gender diversity and locus of control tends to affect the employees performance in a positive way, but it can be noted that Gender diversity in European countries (Beta = 314) is higher than that in Lebanon (Beta = 21.7) which means that gender diversity in European culture tends to impact the workplace performance than the Lebanese culture.

Furthermore, the locus of control in European countries (Beta = 0.233) is greater than the Beta of Lebanon (Beta = 0.228) which means that in European countries, the workplace tends to be affected more by the locus of control and by that employees are trained to take their decisions in the workplace to ensure a reliable performance.

Referring to the mentioned results, the following hypothesis can be validated:

H1: There is a positive significant relationship between gender diversity and employee productivity.
H2: There is a positive significant relationship between locus of control and employee productivity

Regression two: Mediation Effect of Equity on the relationship between Gender Diversity, Locus of Control and Productivity

Referring to the above regression analysis, it can be noted that in Lebanon, Gender Diversity scored a P (0.00) < 0.05, and T (4.189) > 2 and Beta (0.240) and Locus of Control scored a P (0.007) < 0.05 and T (2.743) > 2 and Beta (0.245) and the mediator equity scored a P (0.041) < 0.05 and T (2.461) > 2 and Beta (.118), which means that equity mediates the relationship between gender diversity and locus of control and employees productivity and by that the following equation can be developed:

Productivity = 0.240 Gender Diversity + 0.245 Locus of Control + 0.118 Equity

This means that

- For every 1-unit increase in gender diversity, the productivity in Lebanese companies tend to be affected by 24 units.
- For every 1-unit increase in locus of control, the productivity in Lebanese companies tend to be affected by 24.5 units.
- For every 1-unit increase in equity, the productivity in Lebanese companies tend to be affected by 11.8 units.

However, as for Europe it can be noted that Gender Diversity scored a P (0.011) < 0.05, and T (2.580) > 2 and Beta (0.310) and Locus of Control scored a P (0.006) < 0.05 and T (2.776) > 2 and Beta (0.300) and equity scored P (0.014), T (2.488) and Beta (0.230) which means that equity mediates the relationship between gender diversity and locus of control and employees productivity in European Countries and by that the following equation can be developed:

Productivity = 0.310 Gender Diversity + 0.277 Locus of Control + 0.230 equity

Table 5. Mediation effect of equity on the relationship between gender diversity, locus of control and productivity

Model Summary					
Country of origin	Model	R	R Square	Adjusted R Square	Std. Error of the Estimate
Lebanon	1	.283a	.080	.058	.20017
Europe	1	.374a	.140	.124	.20016

a. Predictors: (Constant), Equity, Gender Diversity, Locus of Control

Coefficientsa							
Country of origin	Model		Unstandardized Coefficients		Standardized Coefficients	t	Sig.
			B	Std. Error	Beta		
Lebanon	1	(Constant)	.079	.011		7.263	.000
		Gender Diversity	.256	.061	.240	4.189	.000
		Locus of Control	.164	.060	.245	2.743	.007
		Equity	.123	.050	.118	2.461	.041
Europe	1	(Constant)	.084	.012		7.109	.000
		Gender Diversity	.175	.068	.310	2.580	.011
		Locus of Control	.183	.066	.300	2.776	.006
		Equity	.107	.043	.230	2.488	.014

a. Dependent Variable: Productivity

This means that

- For every 1-unit increase in gender diversity, the productivity in European companies tend to be affected by 31 units.
- For every 1-unit increase in locus of control, the productivity in European companies tend to be affected by 27.6 units
- For every 1-unit increase in equity, the productivity in European companies tend to be affected by 23 units

It can be concluded from this regression analysis that equity mediates the relationship between gender diversity, locus of control and performance in both countries, but it can be noted that equity in European countries (Beta = .230) is higher than that in Lebanon (Beta =.118) which means that equity in European workplace tends to mediate the relationship between gender diversity, locus of control and employees performance more than the Lebanese culture.

Furthermore, it can be noticed that the R in regression two (.283) for Lebanon and (.374) in Europe increased from that of regression one (.265) for Lebanon and (.373) for Europe which means that equity plays an important role in mediating the relationship among the variables.

Referring to the mentioned results, the following hypothesis can be validated:

H3: Equity mediates the relationship between gender diversity, locus of control and employee productivity.

Regression Three: Mediation Effect of Engagement on the relationship between Gender Diversity, Locus of Control and Productivity

Referring to the above regression analysis, it can be noted that in Lebanon, Gender Diversity scored a P (0.00) < 0.05, and T (3.878) > 2 and Beta (0.207) and Locus of Control scored a P (0.032) < 0.05 and T (2.160) > 2 and Beta (0.162) and the mediator engagement scored a P (0.004) < 0.05 and T (2.894) > 2 and Beta (.218), which means that engagement mediates the relationship between gender diversity and locus of control and employees productivity and by that the following equation can be developed:

Productivity = 0.207 Gender Diversity + 0.162 Locus of Control + 0.218 Engagement

Table 6. Mediation effect of engagement on the relationship between gender diversity, locus of control and productivity

Model Summary					
Country of origin	Model	R	R Square	Adjusted R Square	Std. Error of the Estimate
Lebanon	1	.268a	.072	.049	.02017
Europe	1	.426a	.182	.166	.02318

a. Predictors: (Constant), Engagement, Gender Diversity, Locus of Control

Coefficientsa							
Country of origin	Model		Unstandardized Coefficients		Standardized Coefficients	T	Sig.
			B	Std. Error	Beta		
Lebanon	1	(Constant)	.051	.013		4.072	.000
		Gender Diversity	.232	.060	.207	3.878	.000
		Locus of Control	.108	.050	.162	2.160	.032
		Engagement	.349	.121	.218	2.894	.004
Europe	1	(Constant)	.074	.014		5.437	.000
		Gender Diversity	.151	.068	.280	2.206	.029
		Locus of Control	.133	.060	.218	2.228	.028
		Engagement	.153	.029	.391	5.275	.004

a. Dependent Variable: Productivity

This means that

- For every 1-unit increase in gender diversity, the productivity in Lebanese companies tend to be affected by 20.7 units.
- For every 1-unit increase in locus of control, the productivity in Lebanese companies tend to be affected by 16.2 units.
- For every 1-unit increase in equity, the productivity in Lebanese companies tend to be affected by 21.8 units.

However, as for Europe it can be noted that Gender Diversity scored a P (0.029) < 0.05, and T (2.206) > 2 and Beta (0.280) and Locus of Control scored a P (0.028) < 0.05 and T (2.228) > 2 and Beta (0.218) and engagement scored P (0.004), T (5.275) and Beta (0.391) which means that engagement mediates the relationship between gender diversity and locus of control and employees productivity in European Countries and by that the following equation can be developed:

Productivity = 0.280 Gender Diversity + 0.218 Locus of Control + 0.391 equity

This means that

- For every 1-unit increase in gender diversity, the productivity in European companies tend to be affected by 28 units.
- For every 1-unit increase in locus of control, the productivity in European companies tend to be affected by 21.8 units
- For every 1-unit increase in equity, the productivity in European companies tend to be affected by 39.1 units

It can be concluded from this regression analysis that engagement mediates the relationship between gender diversity, locus of control and performance in both countries, but it can be noted that equity in European countries (Beta = .391) is higher than that in Lebanon (Beta =.218) which means that engagement in European workplace tends to mediate the relationship between gender diversity, locus of control and employees performance more than the Lebanese culture.

Furthermore, it can be noticed that the R in regression three (.268) for Lebanon and (.426) in Europe increased from that of regression one (.265) for Lebanon and (.373) for Europe which means that engagement plays an important role in mediating the relationship among the variables.

Referring to the mentioned results, the following hypothesis can be validated:

H4: Engagement mediates the relationship between gender diversity, locus of control and employee productivity.

DISCUSSION AND IMPLICATIONS

Relationship Between Gender Diversity and Employee Productivity

The findings stated that the perception of gender diversity in the workplace is expected to enhance feelings of adequacy, empowerment, and physical and emotional well-being, has empirically supported a positive relationship between perceived gender diversity and employees performance. It is more probable that employees who feel treated properly in the workplace will put out their best efforts and experience less stress than their counterparts who do not according to the study of Dongrey & Rokade (2021). To satisfy the demands of globalization, today's workplace would have a higher degree of intercultural interaction among its varied workforce. Workers from all over the world don't want a solitary existence; they want to be part of a global economy so that they may make a greater contribution. As a result, firms must diversify in all ways conceivable, notably in terms of employee diversity, in order to stay competitive on the global commercial stage. Employer diversity is an asset that has to be used in order to maintain a competitive edge. For this reason, managers of today and tomorrow must be able to recognize how to implement organizational changes and development that can accommodate a multicultural environment in order to retain and attract employees in order to achieve the common goal of any organization, profit maximization through better employee performance at the macro level. Using data from an empirical investigation, this article examines how gender diversity in the workplace affects workers' performance.

Relationship Between Locus of Control and Employee Productivity

An employee's internal locus of control and work engagement are linked (vigor, dedication, and absorption). Internal locus of control is associated with more involvement in one's work and a greater feeling of well-being at the workplace for those who have it. As a result, people who have an internal center of control are less likely to experience burnout and tends to be retained to the organization they work in. Furthermore, the findings of this study have a significant influence on future gender-based research. People who have an internal locus of control (LOC) are better able to deal with stressful situations and rate themselves more highly, both of which have been linked to better performance and work satisfaction in a previous study by Dongrey & Rokade (2021). The service sector in Lebanon and Europe is a focus of this study's locus of control (LOC) and employee performance section. An inferential research in the form of a survey was undertaken to better understand the relationship between LOC and employee performance. Following the Likert scale, respondents filled out closed-ended questionnaires based on the instructions provided inside the questionnaire. In both Lebanese and European firms, the survey's participants are in positions of management at all levels, from the top down. Employees were given 300 questionnaires, and 257 of them were completed properly and returned, resulting in an overall response rate of 80%. The findings of this study suggest that the link between Locus of control and employee performance is medium and does not show adequate proof, however the association between employee organizational commitment and employee performance is significant and does exhibit evidence. An internal locus of control (ILC) employee believes in the importance of organizational commitment, while an external locus of control (ELC) employee believes in the importance of organizational commitment. Since locus of control may be changed with adequate training, it is the manager's primary obligation to help their staff understand and shape their locus of control.

Equity Mediates the Relationship Between Gender Diversity, Locus of Control and Employee Productivity

The research suggests a link between job satisfaction and a positive perception of gender equality. According to this study, which was based on the work engagement hypothesis proposed by Rzemieniak & Wawer (2021), the degree to which employees believe their workplaces are gender-equal is a significant predictor of their level of engagement at work. Gender equality perceptions are also influenced by employees' sense of control, according to research from the perception of gender equality.

In the workplace, job equality has a significant impact on the performance of employees. Other aspects of an employee's motivation to succeed were emphasized, but little was said about the impact of employment equality and perceived fairness on an employee's performance. To better understand how gender diversity and locus of control influence employee performance, this research uses equity as a mediator and a dependent variable to examine how a company's perception of equality affects that of its employees. It concludes that job equality has a significant impact on employee morale and performance by reviewing previous studies and literature. That's why the article says leaders and organizations should constantly make sure there is justice and fairness in decision-making at all levels, so that employees may feel comfortable and secure.

Engagement Mediates the Relationship Between Gender Diversity, Locus of Control and Employee Productivity

Gender diversity, locus of control, and employee productivity will be examined in this research to see whether employee engagement may mitigate the link between these factors. Results demonstrated that work engagement is a mediating factor in this connection, highlighting the necessity of providing workers with enough resources so that they are motivated to succeed in their employment. Women who have a strong work ethic are more satisfied with life and job than those who don't. According to the findings, work engagement acts as a mediator between perceived gender equality, internal locus of control (independent variables), and employee well-being. Employee happiness, in turn, may reduce the risk of executive burnout by increasing employee engagement and giving employees a stronger feeling of ownership over their work. The findings of this study aligns with the findings of Gallego-Sosa et al. (2020)

Implications

Organizational strategies for hiring and training and development, pay, and promotion must be implemented to ensure that the perception of gender equality remains. When workers are treated with professionalism and kindness in the workplace, productivity soars and morale soars. There should be a consideration for the national and cultural settings while implementing gender equality laws and practices. Human resource development and employee engagement initiatives should be designed to guarantee that employees (particularly women) may fulfill their full potential and love their work. Gender equity efforts and gender-sensitive inputs in educational programs must be implemented if gender equity concepts are to be passed on to future generations. Several countries have worked with the International Centre for Research on Women to develop and implement a curriculum for 12- to 14-year olds. Similar techniques may be employed to enhance gender equality in places with a high degree of gender discrimination. Young people may be successfully taught about women's equality by using audiovisual and social media. Gender equality in the workplace can only be achieved by the correct rules, practices, and acceptable perception and attitude modifications that enterprises must apply to establish a humane society.

CONTRIBUTIONS

As a starting point for future research, scholars may draw on this study's findings on gender equality in the workplace. This study might be useful in a variety of contexts where gender disparity is a problem. Accordingly, research on women has concentrated on work-family conflict, commitment, and supervisory support rather than equity because of the difficulties in identifying it

Gender equality in the workplace and an internal locus of control have been shown to increase job satisfaction, according to new research. Employee satisfaction and well-being will increase as a result of increased job participation, which will benefit both the company and its workers.

This study contributes to the growing body of research on employee well-being in positive psychology. Scientists looked at three variables to better comprehend the concept of employee well-being: optimism, contentment with one's life and job, and dissatisfaction (executive burnout). A whole new perspective on employee well-being has emerged as a consequence of this research.

Academics and practitioners are paying increasing attention to well-being as a result of the stressful work environment and the associated turbulence in the economy, which affects workers in general and makes women employees more vulnerable. Policy decisions based on the study's results on the elements that impact employee pleasure at work might increase employee well-being. According to the self-interest hypothesis, workers' behavior is affected by personal gains to maximize the utility of their actions. When it comes to increasing productivity, organizations usually focus on male and female workers equally, even though women may be an invaluable resource when treated fairly. Work-family initiatives have been shown to have a positive effect on a company's reputation and popularity. Female talent management has been shown to assist firms to enhance their image and reputation, which is why it is a justifiable investment for many businesses. Gender-specific theories of work satisfaction and motivation might be developed using the data.

REFERENCES

Agarwal, U. A. (2016). Examining perceived organizational politics among Indian managers: Engagement as mediator and locus of control as moderator. *The International Journal of Organizational Analysis*, *24*(3), 415–437. doi:10.1108/IJOA-07-2014-0786

Alazzani, A., Hassanein, A., & Aljanadi, Y. (2017a). Impact of gender diversity on social and environmental performance: Evidence from Malaysia. *Corporate Governance (Bingley)*, *17*(2), 266–283. doi:10.1108/CG-12-2015-0161

Alazzani, A., Hassanein, A., & Aljanadi, Y. (2017b). Impact of gender diversity on social and environmental performance: Evidence from Malaysia. *Corporate Governance (Bingley)*, *17*(2), 266–283. doi:10.1108/CG-12-2015-0161

Blouch, R., & Azeem, M. F. (2019). Effects of perceived diversity on perceived organizational performance: Mediating role of perceived organizational justice. *Employee Relations*, *41*(5), 1079–1097. doi:10.1108/ER-05-2018-0150

Chrobot-Mason, D., & Aramovich, N. P. (2013). The Psychological Benefits of Creating an Affirming Climate for Workplace Diversity. *Group & Organization Management*, *38*(6), 659–689. doi:10.1177/1059601113509835

Dongrey, R., & Rokade, V. (2021). Assessing the effect of perceived diversity practices and psychological safety on contextual performance for sustainable workplace. *Sustainability (Switzerland)*, *13*(21), 11653. doi:10.3390u132111653

Galbreath, J. (2018). Is Board Gender Diversity Linked to Financial Performance? The Mediating Mechanism of CSR. *Business & Society*, *57*(5), 863–889. doi:10.1177/0007650316647967

Gallego-Sosa, C., Fernández-Torres, Y., & Gutiérrez-Fernández, M. (2020). Does gender diversity affect the environmental performance of banks? *Sustainability (Switzerland)*, *12*(23), 1–15. doi:10.3390u122310172

Galletta, S., Mazzù, S., Naciti, V., & Vermiglio, C. (2021). Gender diversity and sustainability performance in the banking industry. *Corporate Social Responsibility and Environmental Management*. Advance online publication. doi:10.1002/csr.2191

Kobayashi, K., Eweje, G., & Tappin, D. (2018). Employee wellbeing and human sustainability: Perspectives of managers in large Japanese corporations. *Business Strategy and the Environment*, *27*(7), 801–810. doi:10.1002/bse.2032

Mousa, M., Massoud, H. K., & Ayoubi, R. M. (2020). Gender, diversity management perceptions, workplace happiness and organisational citizenship behaviour. *Employee Relations*, *42*(6), 1249–1269. doi:10.1108/ER-10-2019-0385

Rehman, S., Orij, R., & Khan, H. (2020). The search for alignment of board gender diversity, the adoption of environmental management systems, and the association with firm performance in Asian firms. *Corporate Social Responsibility and Environmental Management*, *27*(5), 2161–2175. doi:10.1002/csr.1955

Rzemieniak, M., & Wawer, M. (2021). Employer branding in the context of the company's sustainable development strategy from the perspective of gender diversity of generation Z. *Sustainability (Switzerland)*, *13*(2), 1–25. doi:10.3390u13020828

Sulea, C., Virga, D., Maricutoiu, L. P., Schaufeli, W., Zaborila Dumitru, C., & Sava, F. A. (2012). Work engagement as mediator between job characteristics and positive and negative extra role behaviors. *Career Development International*, *17*(3), 188–207. doi:10.1108/13620431211241054

Chapter 10
Gender Diversity Management in the Labor Market:
The Integration of Trans People

José Baptista
ISCSP, Universidade de Lisboa, Portugal

Dália Costa
ISCSP, Universidade de Lisboa, Portugal

Sónia P. Gonçalves
https://orcid.org/0000-0003-3704-2995
ISCSP, Universidade de Lisboa, Portugal

ABSTRACT

Managing diversity in the labor market means adopting flexible management measures that recognize and respect each workers individuality, taking into account that everyone works differently but allowing for everyone to feel recognised, valued, and safe. Within the very broad issue of diversity in human resources, this chapter means to focus on transgender people, often forgotten when discussing this issue. The main goal of this piece of work is to bring this very timely issue to the discussion lineup - not only for research purposes, but for organizations and society as a whole.

INTRODUCTION

Managing diversity in the labor market means adopting flexible management measures that recognize and respect each workers individuality, considering that everyone works differently but allowing for everyone to feel recognised, valued, and safe (Fleury, 2000; Kim, 2006).

DOI: 10.4018/978-1-6684-4181-7.ch010

Within the very broad issue of diversity in Human Resources, this chapter means to focus on transgender people - hereinafter referred to as inclusively as trans people - often forgotten when discussing this issue (Baggio, 2017). The term trans describes all those who, in some way, do not determine their gender identity by the gender assigned at birth (Winter et al., 2016).

LGBT - *Lesbian, Gay, Bissexual and Trans* – specific experiences have been studied in different areas (e.g. Bauerband, Teti & Velicer, 2019; Meyer, 1995; Rumens, 2017), however, studies that focus soley on trans people are scarce, so this chapter aims to be a contribution to increase this area of knowledge, since the existing literature is very recent, little recognized, sporadic and intermittent (Hines & Santos, 2018).

In Portuguese context, research is concentrated around three main clusters: (1) activism and legal issues; (2) sociocultural representations; and (3) issues related to health (Hines & Santos, 2018). In this sense, this chapter is relevant and a precursor in studying the access of these people to employment and integration into the labor market, contributing to the study of Human Resources Development Policies.

The small number of trans people in the labor market is worrying, as it prevents the establishment of a collective force that leads all stakeholders towards change and towards a better integration of diversity and the reduction of precarious and discriminatory professional experiences (Barclay & Scot, 2006).

The following chapter aims to bring this very timely issue to the discussion lineup - not only for research purposes, but also for organizations and society as a whole. In broader terms, the core question that serves as a starting point is: what do we know about the current situation of trans people in the labor market? Therefore, assuming that human capital is leveled, it is important to understand the existence of mechanisms that reproduce gender stereotypes and their effects, allowing organizations to not integrate trans people among its workers. The aim is to analyze the adversities experienced by trans people in the labor market, including access to an organization for the attainment of a profession.

Mapping the structure of the chapter, it is composed as follows: an introduction about diversity management in organizations, discussing the pros and cons; a deep dive in gender diversity and trans people, with some historical and legal context (including the Portuguese context); an extensively take on transphobia, prejudice and discrimination against trans people, and how the organizations can integrate them in the labour market; and a final section with general remarks. At the end, the bibliographical references used for this chapter are provided.

DIVERSITY MANAGEMENT IN ORGANIZATIONS

Organizations can look at diversity through different paradigms: (1) moral paradigm; (2) social necessity; or (3) as a competitive advantage. Furthermore, when analyzing from a diversity point of view, there are three types of organizations: (1) the monolithic organization - with a homogeneous workforce, providing equally homogeneous culture and practices; (2) the plural organization - with a heterogeneous workforce, trying to act in accordance with laws and public policies that promote equality in the workplace, with the aim of preventing discrimination in the workplace; and (3) the multicultural organization - valuing cultural differences and equally incorporating all collaborators (Cox, 1994; Cox, 2001; Rawat & Basergekar, 2016).

In recent years, organizations have started to recognize the need to endorse diversity management measures (Rawat & Basergekar, 2016). They often adopt a vision of homogeneity in their day-to-day, dealing with the existing diversity as something that is diffused, assuming that all individuals separate or are able to separate their personal characteristics, traits and interests from their professional ones

(Saraiva & Irigaray, 2009). This view is limited, as it has already been proven that people do not reveal detachment between who they are in their personal lives and who they are in their professional roles, so it is important to manage people and their diferences well (Saraiva & Irigaray, 2009).

Diversity management in an organizational environment is an attempt to proactively respond to the growing diversification of the workforce and the need for competitiveness, with diversity being something that adds competitive value to organizations, making it beneficial to manage it well (Fleury, 2000; Kim, 2006; Saraiva & Irigaray, 2009).

A diverse workforce reflects the changing world and job market in which we operate and managing diversity is an increasing challenge felt by organizations, where the constant shifts in organizational culture and in personal beliefs of each employee lead the organizational world to be increasingly concerned with this particular topic. This diverse workforce is influenced by many factors, such as demographic variations; diversity types; the level of pressure for diversity to exist; the mergers and acquisitions that take place in the organizational world; the global job market; the laws of local governments; or competitiveness (Kim, 2006).

The main objective of the diversity management is to conduct labor relations, employment practices and the internal composition of the workforce, in an attempt to increase the attraction and retention of the best talents in minority groups. In a broader sense, it also tries to face social inequalities (Alves & Galeão-Silva, 2004; Fleury, 2000).

In an organizational context, it is more important to manage heterogeneity (translated into diversity) than homogeneity of employees and this management should take place through inclusive human resources policies included in the recruitment processes of each organization, as well as through investment in training and communication (Fleury, 2000; Kim, 2006).

As a starting point, it is also important to underline the difference between just having diversity or managing this diversity, as an organization can have a very diverse workforce and not manage it well. It is also important to emphasize the difference between appreciating and valuing diversity and managing it well (Kim, 2006).

Positives Aspects of Diversity Management

There is no consensus regarding a correlation between diversity management and organizational results, as positive elements and less positive elements or limitations - brought forward. From a positive management of diversity perspective, three principles are important for organizations: flexibility, creativity and responsiveness. Organizations that have these values adopt a broader management perspective and look at diversity as something positive and not as a drawback (Kim, 2006).

Diversity management is endorsed as something positive, with two main arguments. The first is the organizations' internal programs aimed at diversity as being socially fairer (based on meritocracy and not favoritism); and the second one is the fact that good management of organizational diversity leads to the increase of competitive advantage, which may boost organizations performances due to a positive influence of multicultural environment (Alves & Galeão-Silva, 2004).

The main benefits of managing organizational diversity are: the creation of new ideas – a homogeneous workforce is less prone to new ideas or creative solutions, solutions that can bring immense organizational benefits; improvements in organization growth – good diversity management will help organizations compete in international markets; enhancement of an organization's image – a favorable organizational vision will help to attract investors, customers and employees; and hiring valuable human resources – organizations that want to survive and prosper will have to hire a diverse workforce that includes minorities (Kim, 2006).

Diversity management will allow organizations to compete in international markets in a positive way, generating new ideas, improving their performance and their image in the market, as well as hiring valuable human resources. Not all organizations will benefit from a diverse workforce, but only those that learn to manage it well (Kim, 2006).

Constraints of Diversity Management

Although there is currently a greater concern regarding the potential benefits and limitations of diversity management, some organizations do not accomplish the best results. This may be justified by limited knowledge of the theory regarding this subject, an incorrect diagnosis of the problem or skepticism from employees in relation to diversity programs and their effectiveness (Alves & Galeão-Silva, 2004; Kim, 2006).

The main obstacles when managing diversity can be classified according to four paradigms: (1) resistance - not recognizing diversity as something positive; (2) discrimination/injustice - considering that differences cause problems; (3) access/legitimacy - failing to recognize that diversity creates opportunities; and (4) learning/effectiveness - considering that both diversity and similarities create opportunities (Kim, 2006).

Incorrect diversity management will have an impact on the lack of available opportunities for workers to develop skills and increase motivation to carry out their professional tasks, thus decreasing their satisfaction, performance and productivity. If diversity exposes negative results within the organization, this can be amended through a change in organizational culture, a receptiveness to change and a lot of learning (Kim, 2006).

Unfortunately, companies' rethoric, sometimes also expressed in organizational policies, becomes ineffective mainly due to prejudices, stereotypes and discrimination present and rooted in employees, associated with a certain permissiveness and a lack of sense of diversity from a management level. This translates into associations regulated by pro-diversity policies that end up not applying these in the day to day functioning of the organization (Kim, 2006; Saraiva & Irigaray, 2009).

GENDER DIVERSITY AND TRANS PEOPLE

Gender is one of the main elements of human identity (Moolchaem, 2015) and gender equality should always be promoted to include gender diversity, as it will benefit and enrich the concept (Saleiro, 2017). As many societies are making legal progress to embrace gender equality, many companies are still lagging in this process. Among those who lead, for the most, gender equality refers to equality in opportunities for man and women.

The term trans describes all those who somehow do not determine their gender identity by the gender assigned at birth (Winter et. al., 2016) or do not conform to the gender roles and behaviors associated with an assigned gender (Costa & Davies, 2012). It refers to all those who have non-normative gender imagine, self presentation and practices and whose gender identified at birth is an incorrect description of who they are or how they identify (Cobb & McKenzie-Harris, 2019; Nadal et al., 2012).

On the other hand, cisgender (or just cis) refers to all those who do not identify as trans and/or have a gender experience consistent with the gender identified at birth (Bauerband et al., 2019). When analyzing the origin of the words, the prefix "cis" designates something that remains, which when associated with gender means the gender identity remains constant and stable from birth. In turn, "trans" means change or transformation, symbolizing the gender that is not congruent with the gender identified at birth (Almeida & Vasconcellos, 2018).

The term transgender was first used by activist Virgina Prince to distinguish those who did not undergo a gender reassignment surgery from those who did - so-called post-op transsexuals. The distinction between the terms "transsexual" and "transgender" is related to the fact that, in the first case, the person changes their anatomy to match their gender identity (including medical and surgical procedures) and, in the second case, the person undergoes a social transition and lives acording to their gender identity, regardless of their anatomy. Despite this, the term "trans" (the one used in this chapter) is a broad term and is considered more inclusive, encompassing both of the previous terms (Beauregard et. al., 2021; Cobb & McKenzie-Harris, 2019).

Being a trans person is not the same as being intersex. An intersex person has an atypical development with respect to some or all aspects of their biological sex (chromosomal, hormonal, gonadal or genital), whereas a trans person identifies in a way that it does not coincide with their biological sex (Winter et al., 2016). Being trans pertains to personal identity and is not related to sexual orientation, that is, to whom these people feel attracted (Winter et al., 2016). Trans people have very different experiences, whether it be regarding gender issues or sexual orientation issues, and there is no equal experience that encompasses all people (Dargie et al., 2014). Within the LGBT community, trans people can sometimes feel excluded, as despite having a non-normative gender identity, they may or may not identify themselves as heterosexual people (Collins et. al., 2015).

Another important term to be included in this chapter is "transition", which refers to the process of altering gender roles and expectations associated with the gender assigned at birth to the gender with which the person truly identifies, thus aligning their outward appearance and their behaviors with their true gender identity. This process may (not necessarily) include changes in name, clothing, legal documentation and body - through hormones or surgery (Austin, 2016). It is important to emphasize that this transition process may or may not involve physical changes in the body (Dargie et al., 2014). During this transition period, many trans people disclose difficulties such as the loss of family relationships and friendships, lack of support or even dismissal from their workplaces and also a lack of support from educational and health institutions (Moolchaem et al., 2015).

Trans People: Historial Context

The history of trans people in society is not recent and dates back more than three thousand years – being one of the first known trans figures in history Hatshepsut, who ruled Egypt in the 15th century BC. In the 16th and 17th centuries, European colonizers reported gender fluid practices in indigenous people and forced them to abandon these practices. In 1755, actress Charlotte Clarke assumed her trans identity, becoming one of the first trans icons in history. Years later, in 1930, painter Lily Elbe became the first trans person to undergo gender reassignment surgery (Cobb & McKenzie-Harris, 2019).

During the 1990s, the term trans was included in the acronym LGB - lesbian, gay and bisexual, becoming LGBT - lesbian, gay, bisexual and trans. Currently, the acronym LGBT has evolved to be more inclusive, now being LGBTQIA+ - lesbian, gay, bisexual, trans, queer, intersex, asexual and a + that encompasses all other sexual orientations and diverse gender identities (Cobb & McKenzie-Harris, 2019).

In Europe the estimation is that between 30.000 to 1.5 million people do not identify with the gender assigned to them at birth (Amnesty International, 2014). It is also estimated that the trans community represents about 2% to 3% of the entire LGBT community, but there are no solid numbers. Indeed, these numbers will only exist when the enormous oppression experienced by these people comes to an end and there is a safe environment in society that allows everyone to assume their true gender identity (Burdge, 2007).

Trans People: Legal framework

In the Portuguese context, LGBT issues gained visibility from the 1990s onwards, as a side effect of the struggles against AIDS - Acquired Immunodeficiency Syndrome. This movement was possible due to depathologization, on a medical level, and to decriminalization, on a legal level (Vale de Almeida, 2010).

In 1973, the American Psychiatric Association (APA) removed homosexuality from the list of pathologies and in 1981 the Parliamentary Assembly of the Council of Europe adopted a recommendation condemning all legal and social discrimination against homosexuals. Only in 1982 was the punishment of homosexuality between adults removed from the Penal Code in Portugal. In 1989, Denmark becomes the first country to legalize registered partnerships between same-sex couples and in Portugal the law was approved in 2010 (Vale de Almeida, 2010).

The World Health Organization (WHO) cease to consider homosexuality a disease only on May 17th, 1990, making this date the International Day to Fight Homophobia. As for Transsexuality, only on June 18th, 2018, was it no longer classified by the WHO as a mental disorder, equated with depression or schizophrenia and began to be considered a condition related to sexual health, together with conditions such as erectile dysfunction or premature ejaculation. There is still a way to go – just like for homosexuality – for it not to be considered a disease or sexual health condition (Leal & Oliveira, 2020).

In 1992, the ECHR - European Court of Human Rights recognized that a state's refusal to accept gender change in official documents requested by a trans person is a violation of the European Convention on Human Rights. Despite this, almost 30 years later there are still trans people in Europe who experience difficulties with this process (Amnesty International, 2014).

In 1995 the prohibition of sex reassignment surgeries was removed from the Medical Association Ethics Code, as up the this point these surgeries were considered illicit and unethical (article 55). Since this change there was an exception for subjects diagnosed with gender dysphoria or transsexuality - unless they were married people (Hines & Santos, 2018).

Since 1996, trans people in the EU - European Union have been legally protected from direct or indirect discrimination in employment, vocational training, promotions and working conditions (Whittle & Turner, 2017).

The trans rights activist movement in Portugal started to strength, particularly after the murder of Gisberta Salce Júnior, a trans woman assassinated in 2006 in the Porto region. This event brought media attention to the violence suffered by trans people and the lack of legal protection. In 2007, the Penal Code was amended and included hate crimes due to sexual orientation as an aggravating factor (article 132) – but not gender identity (along with race, religion, political choices, ethnic origin or nationality and gender). Although gender identity was not included, this represents an advance for LGBT rights in Portugal (Hines & Santos, 2018).

Hate crimes and murders of trans people are a growing reality: between October 1st, 2019, and September 30, 2020, 350 trans people were murdered around the world (11 in Europe), 6% more than in 2019 and of these deaths 98% were trans women or transfeminine (Transrespect versus Transphobia Worldwide, 2020).

In 2011, the Portuguese Parliament approved a Gender Identity Law (Law No. 7/2011) which allowed trans persons with Portuguese nationality and of legal age (over 18) to change their sex and first name in the Civil Registry. Since 2012, the Student Statue in Portugal has included a category of non-discrimination based on the concept of "gender identity" (Law No. 51/2012 art. 7, 1a), but there are still several measures that can be implemented.

Regarding education, the State must guarantee the enactment of measures in the educational system (at all levels of education and study phases) which promote the right to self determine gender identity and expression and the right to each person's sexual characteristics protection. Educational establishments must guarantee the necessary conditions so that everyone feels respected according to their gender identity and expression (Law No. 38/2018).

According to Law No. 38/2018 of August 7th, the right to self-determine gender identity and expression and the right to each person's sexual characteristics protection is established and any type of discrimination, both direct and indirect based on these is prohibited. The practice of any discriminatory act gives the injured party the right to compensation.-

In 2018, the National Strategy for Equality and Non-Discrimination – Portugal + Equal (ENIND) was also drawn up, defining strategic and specific objectives for non-discrimination based on sex and the equality between men and women, domestic and gender violence and combating discrimination based on sexual orientation, gender identity and expression and sexual characteristics (Resolution of the Council of Ministers No. 61/2018).

In the labor context, direct or indirect discrimination based on sexual orientation, stating that no worker or job candidate can be privileged, benefited, harmed, deprived of any right or exempt from any duty due to (among others) their sexual orientation and gender, is explicitly prohibited by the new Labor Code (approved by the law No. 99/2003 and regulated by Law No. 35/2004). Despite this legal progression and the policy improvements, Portugal still does not have specific laws and consequences for discrimination of trans people and trans workers, so there is still nothing very clear and defined and there is much ambiguity in this field.

Transphobia: Prejudice and Discrimination against Trans People

In the social system, majority groups, that is, those who have historically obtained economic and power advantages, coexist with minority groups (Fleury, 2000). Both minority and majority individuals demonstrate prejudices and discriminatory attitudes that reveal difficulty respecting differences and diversity (Saraiva & Irigaray, 2009).

Prejudice is not always explicitly present, and recently, visible and explicit prejudice has decreased, but unconscious and unintentional prejudice persists, as there is not always an individual perception of existing internal prejudices (Di Marco et al., 2016; Dovidio, 2001). Transphobia is the name associated with prejudice specifically related to gender identity, which includes fear, hatred, disgust and harmful treatment towards trans people (Almeida & Vasconcellos, 2018; Worthen, 2016). Transphobia derives from the hetero-cis-normative system of which today's society is part of a hierarchical system where cisgender and heterosexual people are privileged, and people perceived as non-cisgender and non-heterosexual suffer prejudice and discrimination (Worthen, 2016).

The fact that gender is still interpreted as something binary in many aspects of society leads many people to be unaware of the existence of trans people. Prejudice - associated with ignorance of what it means to be trans - is expressed by discrimination in diverse forms, both in direct, conscious, aggressive and explicit discrimination, as well as through subtle, unconscious or micro-aggression discrimination, which are not always very visible (Di Marco et al. al., 2016; Nadal et al., 2012; Nadal et al., 2014).

Considering subtle discrimination or microaggressions, we must highlight: the use of transphobic or gender-incorrect language; the assumption of universal experience as a trans person; exoticization/fetishization; discomfort or disapproval of the trans individual's experience; excessive support for binary and normative gender culture and behaviors; transphobia denial; assumption of sexual pathology or abnormality; physical threats or harassment; and microaggressions from family (Nadal et al., 2012). There should be laws and policies to avoid and prevent these micro-aggressions, to safeguard trans people from these situations. Professionals such as educators, doctors, psychologists, among others, should be trained to implement these policies and be able to competently work with the trans population (Nadal et al., 2012).

Trans people face systematic oppression and devaluation as a result of social stigma, often finding themselves with less legal protection than the rest of society, exposed to discrimination, harassment and violence, with difficult access to health care, education and social aid, as well as subject to numerous challenges in their intimate relationships (Bockting et al., 2013; Levitt & Ippolito, 2014; Rudin et al., 2015).

Because of the discrimination, exclusion, discomfort and violence, trans people are devalued, tend to experience psychological and emotional suffering and experience multiple discriminations, affecting their well-being and health. This can translate into feelings of despair, shame, low self-esteem, anxiety, frustration, isolation, sadness, depression or sometimes suicidal thoughts or other destructive behaviors such as substance abuse, risky sexual behavior or sex work (Barclay & Scot, 2006; Moolchaem et al., 2015; Nadal et al., 2014). Trans people also have difficulties gaining trust and acceptance from their peers, facing rejection which is justified due to biological and physical differences, as well as different experiences and socialization processes (Barclay & Scot, 2006).

In Portugal, the only document reporting LGBT complaints is the Annual Report from the Discrimination Observatory against LGBTI+ people, which aims to disclose complaints about situations of discrimination and/or violence based on sexual orientation, identity and gender expression or sexual characteristics throughout each year. In 2019, of the 171 complaints of hate crimes and discrimination that took place during that year, 29.71% involved transphobia, with some of these complaints occurring in a work environment (ILGA Portugal, 2020).

Integration of Trans People in the Labor Market

The experiences of LGBT people have been studied, however, trans people are underrepresented and receive little attention in scientific literature, with an absence of influential narratives where trans people are recognized (and with whom they identify) in today's society as social agents with a prominent role (Santos, 2020; Wada et al., 2019). Even within the LGBT community, there are different patterns of prejudice. For example, the risk of a trans worker to lose their job is three times higher when compared to a gay worker or a lesbian worker (Gut et al., 2018).

We must recognize that only recently trans people are understood and studied beyond pathological and medical frames and in their everyday experiences, mainly due to the contribution of social movements and trans academics themselves, especially from the 1990s onwards (Saleiro, 2017). Despite the public awareness on the existence of trans people in society, there are not many publications about labor market and management of these people in organizations. Finding a job is challenging for a trans person and, if they reach this goal, they experience different forms of discrimination, such as transphobia, either in the form of jokes, or of inappropriate language or even harassment. Adding to this, the inexistence or lack of adequacy of labor policies and/or laws that protect them makes this process of inclusion into the labor market even more complicated (Barclay & Scot, 2006; Bockting et. al, 2016; Nadal et. al., 2014).

In Portugal, there are few published articles whose goal is to understand and situate trans people in a work context. All the issues related to discrimination at work based on sexual orientation, gender identity or expression still needs to be observed accounting the right-wing dictatorial regime in the recent history of the country (1926-1974) as well as a secular Judeo-Christian matrix influencing culture and generating effects on job precariousness (Hines & Santos, 2018).

The literature places trans people in four clusters in work environments: (1) pre-career - articles on a more personal, educational approach and on the social experiences they go through and that will affect their careers; (2) the search for work - literature about looking for a job or career, often focused on people in the post-transition period; (3) careers in general - articles on issues that already situate trans people in a professional and career environment, excluding issues of job search and transition; and (4) transition in the workplace - literature that directly relates to issues of trans workers in transition (McFadden & Crowley-Henry, 2016).

The talent and contributions of trans workers are sometimes left unnoticed or underutilized if these workers do not meet traditional standards – often defined by and for cisgender people. This employment system built with a majority of cisgender, heterosexual and white men in mind leads to trans workers being ignored in terms of promotions or access to career development opportunities (Collins et. al., 2015). Reformulation of the competence standards expected from employees is very important as these standards are often associated with and based on gender issues, thus invalidating the perspectives and experiences of trans people (Collins et al., 2015).

In the labor market, the discrimination of and experienced by trans people is multidimensional and utterly systemic, since in today's society there are higher levels of unemployment and poverty amongst trans people when compared to cis-gender people; institutional, when working in organizations without anti-discrimination policies; and interpersonal, when discriminated and/or harassed by strangers or co-workers (Almeida & Vasconcellos, 2018; Nadal et al., 2012; Nadal et al., 2014).

Thus, trans people face numerous challenges in the labor market related to their physical and psychological health, and also associated with their well-being and safety at work (Beauregard et. al., 2021). Furthermore, workplace discrimination will also affect the economic well-being of these people since being trans can also influence someone's salary (Collins et al., 2015; Davidson, 2016). Often, they are not even recognized as an employment possibility given the enormous marginalization they suffer, often guided to undervalued jobs, entry or low-level job opportunities or seen as only having career options and livelihoods in the sex industry and prostitution - which will expose them to numerous risks, such as physical and emotional violence, substance abuse or risky sexual behavior (Dias & Bernardineli, 2016; Nadal et al., 2014; Ozturk & Tatlib, 2015).

Trans people face numerous oppressions and prejudices in different dimentions of life, whether it be in school, within family or in the community, which will affect their experiences in the labor market and their careers (Wada et. al., 2019). Thus, it is challenging for a trans person to find a job due to the different forms of discrimination they experience, such as transphobia, jokes, inappropriate language or even harassment, making it difficult to remain employed under these conditions (Barclay & Scot, 2006; Bockting et. al, 2016; Nadal et. al., 2014). Even before entering the labor market, trans people already experience the lack of opportunities due to the reported difficulties in accessing education, where they end up skipping school or even giving up entirely when faced with discrimination and prejudice. Thus, the lack of access to education, the lack of policies to defend and include them, and the lack of detailed information that supports trans students in an accessible and available way will determine the future success of their careers and may lead to less access to professional opportunities (Collins et al., 2015; Dias & Bernardineli, 2016; McFadden & Croewley-Henry, 2016).

During recruitment and selection processes, trans people report three main issues. First of all, they feel under-represented and anticipate stigma when looking at company websites, social network and other resources; secondly, they experience fear about being exposed or discriminated against when filling out application forms and having to explain incompatibilities in curriculum and references; and, finally, they have to manage the conflict between being exposed or not referring to or discriminating against their trans identity while in interview processes, assessment centers or other selection tools, which are in themselves challenging (Beauregard et. al., 2021).

In order to present all their experience and skills acquired throughout their career, trans people often feel the need to reveal their trans identity to the potential employer during the recruitment and selection process, at the risk of suffering prejudice and stigma and discarding the possibility of a fresh start with their true gender expression (McFadden & Crowley-Henry, 2016). Even after joining an organization, they continue to deal with discrimination - in promotions, performance appraisals or even dismissals. In addition, they also find themselves informally discriminated against due to bullying or violence which impacts their careers and leads to psychological damage (Collins et al., 2015).

Trans workers need specific and appropriate support and policies from organizations to avoid the perpetuation of prejudiced attitudes both vertically (hierarchical superiors) and horizontally (co-workers). Some guidelines have been developed in an attempt to minimize discrimination felt in the workplace, such as: raising awareness about the topic (through training or just through sharing information); changes in dress code policies; time available to deal with issues related to the transition of trans people; creation of confidentiality policies; and changes in the use of certain facilities, such as bathrooms (Barclay & Scot, 2006; Dias & Bernardineli, 2016). When discrimination happens and/or when policies and guidelines are disrespected, management should take serious and disciplinary action to condemn these attitudes, thus promoting an idea that prejudice and transphobic actions will not be accepted (Nadal et al., 2014).

It is important to recognize that on the one hand, trans people face several problems regarding their acceptance, either by employers and in society in general and, on the other hand, employers must be aware of this obstacle, which causes these people to often feel unsafe or unwelcome. Organizations must also understand that acceptance and inclusion must be put in place to try to minimize these problematic issues (Barclay & Scot, 2006; Davis, 2009).

Due to fear of prejudice, a lot of trans workers hide their gender identity in a professional context. According to the European Union Agency for Fundamental Rights, that number is around 46% (FRA, 2014). Organizations should be inclusive of all trans workers, both those who prefer silence and to not reveal their gender identity or their previous gender presentation and those who voluntarily talk about their gender identity and make their own voice heard (Beauregard et al., 2016).

The discrimination of trans people in the labor market may lead to low numbers in organizations, absenteeism, low morale, reduced productivity, conflicts and may even lead to risky behavior such as unemployment, sex work and prostitution, substance abuse, or even damage to mental health, leading to depression or suicidal ideation (Barclay & Scot, 2006; Nadal et al., 2012; Nadal et al., 2014).

The professional environment is the context where (in Europe) the highest levels of discrimination are reported by trans people, not only when searching for a job search but also in the workplace and visible also in the unemployment levels. More than one in three people feel discriminated against for being trans when looking for a job (37%) and about a quarter of these people feel discriminated against in their workplace (29%). In Portugal, the numbers are slightly lower, 17% and 16%, acknowleging that the Portuguese sample for this study was small – less than 30 subjects (FRA, 2014). According to the 2019 Social Indicators Report of the Organization for Economic Cooperation and Development (OECD), only 40% of respondents were comfortable with having a trans co-worker (OECD, 2019).

CONCLUSION

The literature clearly has established a lot of evidence on how difficult and challenging can be for a trans person to find a job and to remain employed (e.g. Beauregard et. al., 2021; Davidson, 2016). It is now urgent that the organizations, but also society as a whole truly understand the importance of acceptance and inclusion of LGBT workers, specifically trans workers, aknowledging that a diverse worforce is a reflection of a chaning world and job market. The benefits of workplace diversity are huge and translate into gains in productivity related to personal and social well-being (Barclay & Scot, 2006; Davis, 2009; Kim, 2006).

Since not all organizations benefit from a diverse workforce, but only those that learn how to manage the diversity in a positive way, the organizations who are able to integrate and manage gender diversity (including trans people) will have a lot of benefits, such as generating new ideas, improving their performance and their image in the market, as well as hiring valuable human resources (Kim, 2006). Nonetheless, companies' rethoric are sometimes ineffective mainly due to prejudices, stereotypes and discrimination deeply rooted in the employees (Kim, 2006; Saraiva & Irigaray, 2009).

In Portugal, still without specific laws and consequences for discrimination of trans people and trans workers, there is a long way to go in terms of trans and gender diversity integration in modern organizations. With this chapter, we aim to raise awareness for this important topic, highlighting the importance of specific and appropriate support and policies to avoid the perpetuation of discrimination and prejudice both vertically and horizontally against trans people in the workplace (Barclay & Scot, 2006; Dias & Bernardineli, 2016).

REFERENCES

Almeida, C., & Vasconcellos, V. (2018). Transexuais: Transpondo barreiras no mercado de trabalho em Sao Paulo? *Revista Direito GV*, *14*(2), 303–333. doi:10.1590/2317-6172201814

Alves, M., & Galeão-Silva, L. (2004). A Crítica da Gestão da Diversidade nas Organizações. *RAE - Revista de Administração de Empresas, 44* (3), 20-29.

Amnesty International. (2014). *The State decides who I am: Lack of recognition for transgender people.* Amnesty. International. https://www.es.amnesty.org/uploads/media/The_state_decide_who_I_am._Febrero_201 4.pdf

Austin, A. (2016). "There I am": A grounded theory study of young adults navigating a transgender or gender nonconforming identity within a context of oppression and invisibility. *Sex Roles, 75*(5-6), 215–230. doi:10.100711199-016-0600-7

Baggio, M. (2017). About the relation between transgender people and the organizations: New subjects for studies on organizational diversity. *REGE - Revista de Gestão, 24*(4), 360-370. doi:10.1016/j.rege.2017.02.001

Barclay, J., & Scott, L. (2006). Transsexuals and workplace diversity. *Personnel Review, 35*(4), 487–502. doi:10.1108/00483480610670625

Bauerband, L., Teti, M., & Velicer, W. (2019). Measuring Minority Stress: Invariance of a Discrimination and Vigilance Scale Across Transgender and Cisgender LGBQ Individuals. *Psychology and Sexuality, 10*(1), 17–30. doi:10.1080/19419899.2018.1520143

Beauregard, T., Arevshatian, L., Booth, J., & Whittle, S. (2016). Listen carefully: Transgender voices in the workplace. *International Journal of Human Resource Management, 29*(5), 857–884. doi:10.1080/09585192.2016.1234503

Beauregard, T., Booth, J., & Whiley, L. (2021). Transgender employees: Workplace impacts on health and well-being. In J. Hassard & L. D. Torres (Eds.), *Aligning perspectives in gender mainstreaming: Gender, health, safety and wellbeing* (pp. 177–196). Springer. doi:10.1007/978-3-030-53269-7_10

Bockting, W., Coleman, E., Deutsch, M., Guillamon, A., Meyer, I., Meyer, W., Reisner, S., Sevelius, J., & Ettner, R. (2016). Adult development and quality of life of transgender and gender nonconforming people. *Current Opinion in Endocrinology, Diabetes, and Obesity, 23*(2), 188–197. doi:10.1097/MED.0000000000000232 PMID:26835800

Bockting, W., Miner, M., Swinburne Romine, R., Hamilton, A., & Coleman, E. (2013). Stigma, mental health, and resilience in an online sample of the US transgender population. *American Journal of Public Health, 103*(5), 943–951. doi:10.2105/AJPH.2013.301241 PMID:23488522

Burdge, B. (2007). Bending gender, ending gender: Theoretical foundations for social work practice with the transgender community. *Social Work, 52*(3), 243–250. doi:10.1093w/52.3.243 PMID:17850032

Cobb, J., & McKenzie-Harris, M. (2019). "And Justice for All"... Maybe: Transgender Employee Rights in America. *ABA JournaL of Labor & Employment Law, 34*(91), 91–111.

Collins, J., McFadden, C., Rocco, T., & Mathis, M. (2015). The problem of transgender marginalization and exclusion. *Human Resource Development Review, 14*(2), 205–226. doi:10.1177/1534484315581755

Costa, P., & Davies, M. (2012). Portuguese adolescents' attitudes toward sexual minorities: Transphobia, homophobia, and gender role beliefs. *Journal of Homosexuality*, *59*(10), 1424–1442. doi:10.1080/009 18369.2012.724944 PMID:23153027

Cox, T. (1994). *Cultural Diversity in Organizations: Theory, Research & Practice*. Berrett Koehler.

Cox, T. (2001). *Creating a Multicultural Organization: A Strategy for Capturing the Power of Diversity*. Jossey-Koehler.

Dargie, E., Blair, K., Pukall, C., & Coyle, S. (2014). Somewhere under the rainbow: Exploring the identities and experiences of trans persons. *The Canadian Journal of Human Sexuality*, *23*(2), 60–74. doi:10.3138/cjhs.2378

Davidson, S. (2016). Gender inequality: Nonbinary transgender people in the workplace. *Cogent Social Sciences*, *2*(1), 1236511. doi:10.1080/23311886.2016.1236511

Davis, D. (2009). Transgender issues in the workplace: HRD's newest challenge/opportunity. *Advances in Developing Human Resources*, *11*(1), 109–120. doi:10.1177/1523422308329189

Di Marco, D., López-Cabrera, R., Arenas, A., Giorgi, G., Arcangeli, G., & Mucci, N. (2016). Approaching the discriminatory work environment as stressor: The protective role of job satisfaction on health. *Frontiers in Psychology*, *7*. doi:10.3389/fpsyg.2016.01313 PMID:27625625

Dias, J., & Bernardineli, M. (2016). O Transexual e o Direito de Acesso ao Mercado de Trabalho: Do Preconceito a Ausência de Oportunidades. *Revista de Gênero. Sexualidade e Direito*, *2*(2), 243. doi:10.26668/2525-9849/Index_Law_Journals/2016.v2i2.1376

Dovidio, J. F. (2001). On the nature of contemporary prejudice: The third wave. *The Journal of Social Issues*, *57*(4), 829–849. doi:10.1111/0022-4537.00244

Fleury, M. (2000). Gerenciando a diversidade cultural: Experiências de empresas Brasileiras. *Revista de Administração de Empresas*, *40*(3), 18–25. doi:10.15900034-75902000000300003

FRA - European Union Agency for Fundamental Rights. (2014). *Being Trans in the European Union Comparative Analysis of EU LGBT Survey Data*. Publications Office of the European Union.

Gut, T., Arevshatian, L., & Beauregard, T. (2018). HRM and the case of transgender workers: A complex landscape of limited HRM "know how" with some pockets of good practice. *Human Resource Management International Digest*, *26*(2), 7–11. doi:10.1108/HRMID-06-2017-0121

Hines, S., & Santos, A. C. (2018). Trans* policy, politics and research: The UK and Portugal. *Critical Social Policy*, *38*(1), 35–56. doi:10.1177/0261018317732880

Kim, B. (2006). Managing Workforce Diversity. *Journal of Human Resources in Hospitality & Tourism*, *5*(2), 69–90. doi:10.1300/J171v05n02_05

Leal, C., & Oliveira, B. (2020). O Direito à Identidade de Gênero e Políticas Públicas de Trabalho: Pelas Garantia do Mínimo Existencial para a População Trans no Brasil. *Revista Brasileira de Estudos Jurídicos*, *15*(1), 64–93.

Levitt, H., & Ippolito, M. (2014). Being transgender. *Psychology of Women Quarterly, 38*(1), 46–64. doi:10.1177/0361684313501644 PMID:25089681

McFadden, C., & Crowley-Henry, M. (2016). A Systematic Literature Review on Trans* Careers and Workplace Experiences. In T. Köllen (Ed.), *Sexual Orientation and Transgender Issues in Organizations.* Springer. doi:10.1007/978-3-319-29623-4_4

Meyer, I. (1995). Minority stress and mental health in gay men. *Journal of Health and Social Behavior, 36*(1), 38. doi:10.2307/2137286 PMID:7738327

Moolchaem, P., Liamputtong, P., O'Halloran, P., & Muhamad, R. (2015). The lived experiences of transgender persons: A meta-synthesis. *Journal of Gay & Lesbian Social Services, 27*(2), 143–171. doi:10.1080/10538720.2015.1021983

Nadal, K., Davidoff, K., & Fujii-Doe, W. (2014). Transgender Women and the Sex Work Industry: Roots in Systemic, Institutional, and Interpersonal Discrimination. *Journal of Trauma & Dissociation, 15*(2), 169–183. doi:10.1080/15299732.2014.867572 PMID:24313294

Nadal, K., Skolnik, A., & Wong, Y. (2012). Interpersonal and Systemic Microaggressions Toward Transgender People: Implications for Counseling. *Journal of LGBT Issues in Counseling, 6*(1), 55–82. doi:10.1080/15538605.2012.648583

OECD. (2019). *Society at a Glance 2019: OECD Social Indicators.* OECD Publishing. doi:10.1787oc_glance-2019-

Ozturk, M., & Tatli, A. (2015). Gender identity inclusion in the workplace: Broadening diversity management research and practice through the case of transgender employees in the UK. *International Journal of Human Resource Management, 27*(8), 781–802. doi:10.1080/09585192.2015.1042902

Portugal, I. L. G. A. (2020). *Relatório Anual 2019 - Discriminação Contra Pessoas LGBTI+.* Ilga-portugal.pt. https://ilga-portugal.pt/ficheiros/pdfs/observatorio/ILGA_Relatorio_Discriminacao_2019.pdf

Rawat, P., & Basergekar, P. (2016). Managing Workplace Diversity: Performance of Minority Employees. *Indian Journal of Industrial Relations, 51*(3), 488–501.

Rudin, J., Yang, Y., Ruane, S., Ross, L., Farro, A., & Billing, T. (2015). Transforming attitudes about transgender employee rights. *Journal of Management Education, 40*(1), 30–46. doi:10.1177/1052562915609959

Rumens, N. (2017). Queering lesbian, gay, bisexual and transgender identities in human resource development and management education contexts. *Management Learning, 48*(2), 227–242. doi:10.1177/1350507616672737

Saleiro, S. (2017). Diversidade de género na infância e na educação: Contributos para Uma escola sensível ao (trans)género. *ex aequo - Revista da Associação Portuguesa de Estudos sobre as Mulheres,* (36). doi:10.22355/exaequo.2017.36.09

Santos, A. (2020). From villain to hero: Trans men and non-binary persons as care providers in Southern Europe. *International Journal of Care and Caring, 11-15.* doi:10.1332/239788220X16051223899742

Saraiva, L., & Irigaray, H. (2009). Políticas de Diversidade nas Organizações. *RAE – Revista de Administração de Empresas, 49* (3), 337-348.

Transrespect versus Transphobia Worldwide. (2020, November 11). *TMM Update Trans Day of Remembrance 2020 [Press release].* Transrespect. https://transrespect.org/en/tmm-update-tdor-2020/

Vale de Almeida, M. (2010). O Contexto LGBT em Portugal. In Nogueira, C. & Oliveira, J., Estudo sobre a discriminação em função da orientação sexual e da identidade de género (pp. 45-94). Lisboa: Comissão para a Cidadania e a Igualdade de Género.

Wada, K., McGroarty, E., Tomaro, J., & Amundsen-Dainow, E. (2019). Affirmative career counselling with transgender and gender nonconforming clientes: A social justice perspective. *Canadian Journal of Counselling and Psychotherapy, 53*(3), 255–275.

Whittle, S., & Turner, L. (2017). *Trans-inclusive Workplaces – Guidelines for Employers and Businesses.* Transgender Europe.

Winter, S., Diamond, M., Green, J., Karasic, D., Reed, T., Whittle, S., & Wylie, K. (2016). Transgender people: Health at the margins of society. *Lancet, 388*(10042), 390–400. doi:10.1016/S0140-6736(16)00683-8 PMID:27323925

Worthen, M. (2016). Hetero-cis–normativity and the gendering of transphobia. *International Journal of Transgenderism, 17*(1), 31–57. doi:10.1080/15532739.2016.1149538

Chapter 11
Work Identity, Meaning, and Meaningfulness of Work in the Immigration Context:
Systematic Literature Review

Silvana Curvello de Cerqueira Campos
Universidade Federal da Bahia, Brazil

Sônia Maria Guedes Gondim
Universidade Federal da Bahia, Brazil

Juliana Paranhos Moreno Batista
Universidade Federal da Bahia, Brazil

ABSTRACT

The objective of this chapter is to find evidence of empiric relations among work identity, meaning and meaningfulness of work in the immigration context. The method used was systematic literature review, adopting PRISMA recommendations. The following database has been consulted: Scopus, Web of Science, SciELO, PsycInfo and Lilacs. Empiric articles available between 2010 and 2020 have been used, with work identity, meaning and meaningfulness of work, immigration and immigrant descriptors in Portuguese and English. Data was analyzed with thematic content analysis. Results show twenty-seven articles have been found. The created categories considered each construct separately, being three for work identity, two for meaning of work, and none for meaningfulness of work. The main conclusions were that work identity in a host country depends a lot of the environment characteristics, institutional recognition and social status, and on immigrant personal characteristics. In addition, the type of career favors or hinders redefinition of work identity.

DOI: 10.4018/978-1-6684-4181-7.ch011

Work Identity, Meaning, and Meaningfulness of Work in the Immigration Context

INTRODUCTION

Immigration is the inward movement of people from one country to another, in a permanent or temporary way, to work and/or live (Guizardi, 2019). Generally, a phenomenon of ascension and as an answer, in part, to poverty and lack of professional opportunities in economically-peripheral countries (Oliveira, 2017); they were 173 million in year 2000, 220 million in 2010, 258 million in 2017 and 272 million in 2019 (United Nations [UN], 2020).

Despite the positive aspects of immigration, such as access to better life conditions and job, the immigrant may experience sensation of strangeness for leaving a social familiar environment (Caligiuru & Bonache, 2016). This condition may cause a change in personal and social identity, which vary according to time and context of insertion (Carvalho & Bridi, 2015). One social identity probably affected by the immigration is the work identity. It can also be understood as a way of acting in the world, endowing the work, and not necessarily the profession, with meaning and meaningfulness (Teodorescu, 2015).

Due to the fact that work identity is an element that changes according to time and space (Carvalho & Bridi, 2015), modifications in it rebound in the attribution given to the meaning and meaningfulness of work, and the contrary is also true. In a first exploratory review of national and international literature, it was not found any study which related these constructs in the context of immigration in an integrated and direct way, despite the fact that the concepts are very close and interrelated. The studies dealt with these phenomena separately, such as resignification of work identity in the immigration process (Oliveira et al., 2015), and meaning of work in the view of immigrant groups domiciled in Brazil (Comin & Pauli, 2018). Studies focusing on immigrants' personal identity (Borba, 2008) and their difficulties to obtain social support in the immigration country (Medina & Posso, 2011) have been found. Other studies address the precarious work conditions endured by immigrants in the United States (Romero, 2013), the profile of developed activities (Cassel et al., 2005), latin immigration in the USA and the process of violation of work rights (Bustamante, 2011).

Therefore, given the lack of national and international studies that relate the researched constructs and immigration, the objective of this systematic review was to find evidence of empiric relations among work identity, meaning and meaningfulness of work in the context of immigration. Systematic literature reviews are secondary studies which, parting from a well-defined research question, have the objective of identifying, choosing, analyzing and summarizing important primary studies available in scientific literature (Galvão & Pereira, 2014).

BACKGROUND

The term "work identity" is defined as a kind of social identity that poses work in a central position for an individual self-description (Mcnulty & Brewster, 2017; Moura & Silva, 2019). It is an expression that enhances the scope of identity at work, which refers to the way the individual builds himself/herself from work (Dickie, 2003; Dutton et al., 2010), because it places work as a central element in self-concept, and not only as an aspect of personal self-description (Brown, 2019; Corlett et al., 2017; Miscenko & Day, 2016).

Work identity maintains close relation with other kinds of social identity, such as occupational identity (Kirpal, 2004), organizational identity (Gjerde & Alvesson, 2020) and professional identity (Caza &

Creary, 2016). These approaches reveal how challenging it is to understand the value assigned to work without considering career or profession (Bitencourt et al., 2011).

Professional identity is considered a kind of group or company identity, related to career (Gomes et al., 2013), formed from the feeling of belonging to a professional or occupational group and the choice of an area (Rossit et al., 2018). It is also a result of sharing knowledge and rules established by formation, certification and professional regulation organs (Reeves, 2016).

Some researchers, however, consider that work identity is not reduced to professional identity only, but a lot wider for it is supported by the quality of relations stablished with work (Bentley at al., 2019). It is a result of the identification of workers with their labor, responsibilities, workmates and employers (Fouche et al., 2017; Sui & Humphreys, 2017).

Associated to work identity, the concepts of meaning and meaningfulness of work play a special role in the agenda of work psychology researchers, highlighting three aspects of phenomena understanding (Bendassolli & Gondim, 2014; Rosso et al., 2010; Silva & Tolfo, 2011). In the first aspect, meaning and meaningfulness are distinguished (Borges, 1999; Borges et al., 2008; Hackman & Oldham, 1975). In the second one, they are treated as synonyms or complements (Borges & Barros, 2015; Borges et al., 2008; Cavalheiro, 2010; Lips-Wiersma & Morris, 2009; Morin, 2001; Pratt & Ashforth, 2003). In some studies, for example, meaningfulness of work is considered a component of meaning of work (Bispo & Dourado, 2013; Lemos et al., 2015; Morin, 2001; M*eaning of Working Research Team* [MOW], 1987). Last, in the third aspect, the concepts are treated as different ones, but interrelated (Bendassolli & Gondim, 2014; Silva & Tolfo, 2011; Rosso et al., 2010).

Inserted in the second aspect, the MOW movement (1987), was responsible for popularizing the expression *Meaningfulness of Work* in in the academic environment, considering it a component of meaning of work and defining it as a dynamic multifaceted phenomenon, socially shared and constructed in the relation of individuals with the work world. The research involved approximately 14.000 workers from eight countries (Germany, Belgium, USA, Netherlands, England, Israel, Yugoslavia and Japan).

Nonetheless, researchers who treat meaning and meaningfulness of work as distinct, non-overlapped concepts, despite the fact that it is difficult to distinguish them, criticize such perspective (Bendassolli & Gondim, 2014; Rosso et al., 2010). In the international literature, the meaningfulness of work is considered a group of beliefs understood over the years about what work is, whereas meaning of work, despite closely related to meaningfulness of work, mentions reinterpretation assigned by each individual to the value of work based on their personal experience (Rosso et al., 2010). Similar understanding may be found in national literature among researchers who add a third axis to the other two: psychologic function of work, defined as the process of subject construction in the intertwined game of meaningfulness and meaning mediated by work (Bendassolli & Gondim, 2014).

However, these three constructs must be understood in an interrelated way, because according to the literature, the meaning and meaningfulness of work help in the construction of the work identity (Marcelino & Cavalcante, 2012; Reis & Puente-Palácios, 2019; Salas et al., 2015). The relationship between identity, meaning and meaningfulness of work can be metaphorized in the figure of a gear, in which its components act in an interrelated way and the function of one impacts on the dynamics of the others.

In addition, they are constructs that change according to time and context (Rossit et al., 2018). A hypothesis could be that if immigration is a new context for many people, immigrant goes through more challenging changes in his/her work identity, meaning and meaningfulness of work when he/she leaves his/her country, where work identity would be more defined, looking for new opportunities in a foreign country.

Work Identity, Meaning, and Meaningfulness of Work in the Immigration Context

These reviews also allowed researchers to respond in terms of quality and quantity about the scientific knowledge that is being produced in a specific field of study (Sampaio & Mancini, 2007). Therefore, proposing systematic review about this theme would bring contributions to the field, offering a more defined overview of how work identity, meaning and meaningfulness of work have been operationalized in empiric studies with immigrant groups.

MAIN FOCUS OF THE CHAPTER

Issues, Controversies, Problems

This review of literature has the following research question as guideline: "What are the empiric relations among identity, meaning and meaningfulness of work in the context of immigration available in national and international literature?"

The present review has followed recommendations of PRISMA *(Preferred Reporting items for Systematic Review and Meta-Analysis)* (Moher et al., 2009) that may be accessed at http://www.prisma-statement.org/. This research was registered in the *International Prospective Register of Ongoing Systematic Reviews* (Prospero) database under number CRD42022296385.

Criteria of Inclusion and Exclusion

Table 1 presents the main indicators of inclusion and exclusion used in the selection of articles.

Table 1. Criteria of inclusion and exclusion

	Inclusion	Exclusion
Criteria of Selection	Articles in English and Portuguese	Review of literature, thesis, dissertations, theoretical essays, books and book chapters, documents and comments about articles
	Adult and active participants in the job market	Articles which did not refer to the context of immigration, investigated constructs and/or did not refer to the professional activity of the immigrant, but to other contexts of their lives (students; children/teenagers' parent-child relation; racial, transgenerational and national identity, prison, psychopathology, mental health, political, resignation, sports and other contexts)

Source: Author's elaboration

Articles which did not refer to the context of immigration, investigated constructs and/or did not refer to the professional activity of the immigrant, but to other contexts of their lives (students; children/teenagers' parent-child relation; racial, transgenerational and national identity, prison, psychopathology, mental health, political, resignation, sports and other contexts)

The time frame was established from 2010 and 2020, thus, 11 years. The reason for that period lies on the fact that in the last 10 years there has been an increase of 20% in the migratory process, jumping from 220 million to 272 million in 2019 (UN, 2020), generating a necessity of update in the literature about the subject.

Furthermore, in the year 2020 a serious world health crisis emerged with the Coronavirus Disease-19 (COVID-19), creating consequences in the way of working and in work relations that are still being studied. This health crisis has affected economy, causing dismissal (Costa, 2020), which led to a major problem for immigrants, who were outside their countries and, most of the times, without work policies that protected their jobs. In the United States, for example, one of the first measures of the American government was to prohibit renewal or concession of work visa for immigrants (Loweree et al., 2020; Mendes & Brasil, 2020).

Research Strategy

Keywords selected for the search of studies were: *work identity, meaning of work, meaningfulness of work, immigration* and *immigrant*. The words in Portuguese and English were combined with Boolean operators "AND" and "OR", defining the following string: "identidade de trabalho AND sentido do trabalho AND significado do trabalho AND imigração" **OR** "identidade de trabalho AND sentido do trabalho AND significado do trabalho AND imigrante" **OR** "*work identity* AND *meaning of work* AND *meaningfulness of work* AND *immigration*" **OR** "*work identity* AND *meaning of work* AND *meaningfulness of work* AND *immigrant*".

The search occurred between the months of July and December, year 2020, in the following databases: *Scopus, PsycINFO*, developed and maintained by the *American Psychological Association* (APA), *Web of Science, Scientific Electronic Library Online (Scielo)* and Literatura Latino-Americana em Ciências da Saúde (Health Science Latin-American Literature - Lilacs). These databases are available to higher education institutions through journals portal of Coordenação de Aperfeiçoamento de Pessoal de Ensino Superior (Higher Education Personal Improvement Coordination – CAPES), linked to the Brazilian Ministry of Education.

The database was chosen due to the quantity and quality of published articles, as well as the diversity of addressed areas, for the proposed review of literature considers the interest in the theme by interdisciplinary fields. According to the search criteria of each database, the search was made by "title" and "subject" in *Web of Science,* and by "title" and "keywords" in the other databases. Two researchers acted independently through the whole process of search in the databases, and in subsequent stages, with the objective of guaranteeing more precision in the selection and analysis of studies.

Selection of Studies

The first step was to use a string in each database to identify and select the studies. In the first general search, no article relating the three constructs together in the context of immigration was found 1.194 articles related to only one or two constructs. At the end of the selection, 140 texts were selected, removing articles based on the criteria of exclusion. Among the 140 articles, 13 were from *Scielo,* 84 from Web of Science, 26 from Scopus, 11 from *PsycINFO* and 6 from Lilacs; all referring to only one construct.

For the stage of selection of the 140 studies, three steps were followed: assessment of titles (step 1), assessment of abstracts (step 2) and the full reading of selected articles (step 3). At the end of each step, the two researchers gathered and, based on the defined selection criteria, registered whether they agreed or not on the inclusion of the study. Table 2 specifies the first two steps, quantity of articles and their respective database.

Table 2. Steps 1 and 2 of article selection by construct and database

DATABASE	Steps (1 – Reading of Title; 2 – Reading of Abstract)	CONSTRUCT			
		Work identity	Meaning of work	Meaningfulness of work	TOTAL
Scielo	Step 1	4	5	0	9
	Step 2	1	1	0	2
Web of Science	Step 1	32	21	0	53
	Step 2	8	8	0	16
Scopus	Step 1	5	2	1	8
	Step 2	5	0	1	6
PsycINFO	Step 1	5	0	1	6
	Step 2	2	0	0	2
Lilacs	Step 1	5	0	0	5
	Step 2	1	0	0	1
TOTAL	Step 1	51	28	2	81
	Step 2	17	9	1	27

Source: Author's ellaboration

In the third and last step of selection, it was checked if any other article would be excluded. All were used, summing up 27.

Data Extraction

Both researchers used individual Excel sheets to extract data from each study whose information can be found in Table 3. The formulary of extraction contained three groups of information: a) characteristics of identification (code assigned to the article, title, year, database and journal of publication, authors and their academic background, country of origin, nationality of the immigrant, country of immigration, investigated central construct, objective); b) methodologic characteristics (research draft, nature of research, strategy of data analysis, sample, instruments) and c) characteristics of content (relations sought in the results of studies)

Methodologic Quality Assessment

After data extraction, a methodologic quality assessment was made based on elements described in the article: a) participants: size and gender of sample; b) methodological design: time strategy of data collection (longitudinal/transversal) and nature of research (qualitative/quantitative); c) instruments: detailing; d) procedures of data analysis: detailing. The criterion of methodologic defined was for the study to have, at least, three elements described and according to Table 3. Most of the studies matched the criteria, except for Rosenbaum (2016), which did not define the size of sample.

Results

Table 3 summarizes information of the 27 final articles, including elements of methodologic quality assessment: 17 about work identity, 9 about meaning of work and 1 about meaningfulness of work.

In the following stage, individually, the researchers created the categories and, after common understanding, labeled them. For categorization, the thematic content analysis was used, following the steps of pre-analysis, material exploration and treatment of results parting from inference and interpretation of concepts and propositions, in which similar or thematically close studies are grouped (Bardin, 2011). The choice of this data analysis technique was based on recommendation extracted from Soares et al. (2014), which signalizes that the data analysis of a literature review needs to consider elements and themes that compare the studies.

The first three categories created were about the 17 articles of work identity: "Relation among individual and contextual factors and work identity" (Category 1), "Breaks in professional identity and the impacts in work identity" (Category2) and "Centrality of work identity" (Category 3).

The first category, **"Relation among individual and contextual factors and work identity"**, with 11 studies, rests on the assumption that reconstruction of work identity of immigrants depends on their individual characteristics (two studies) and on environmental factors of the new context (9 studies) (for example, characteristics of new work, informal jobs, underemployment, work environment, etc.), which can act in a favorable or unfavorable way, influencing on how work identity is built or reconstructs itself in this new context.

Among the studies that address contextual elements, 4 emphasize the unfavorable interference and 5 emphasize the favorable interference of these factors in the (re)construction of work identity. The unfavorable aspects mentioned were: informal work (Bonizzoni, 2016; Roberman, 2013; Showers, 2018) or the work environment (Nordstrom, 2020). In relation to informal work, despite the fact that 3 studies mentioned investigate people of different nationalities (Germany, Africa and Italy), the conclusion was similar: this kind of work perpetuates marginalization of immigrants and acts as an obstacle for the sense of belonging to the new country.

This interferes negatively in the reconstruction of work identity, undermining it, contributing to a superficial relation with work and decrease of its importance in their lives. As for the work environment, there is the study of Nordstrom (2020), which presents the following examples of environmental challenges that a swedish teacher faces while acting in a school in Australia: students diversity, difficulty with local language, insufficient qualification and discrimination.

Concerning the 5 studies which addressed the favorable interference of environmental factors, one covers the importance of working (Yijälä & Luoma, 2019) and the other covers institutional recognition (Shan & Guo, 2013). The other 3 address domestic work performed by female immigrants (Carpenedo & Nardi, 2013; Cheng, 2013; Tedesco, 2014). In the study of Yijälä and Luoma (2019), the focus was on long-term adaptation of Iraqi with high level of education who signed up for international protection in Finland. Results indicate that, despite the difficulties faced in the beginning of asylum procedure, working acted positively for their welfare and became a facilitator for acculturation, with the establishment of social networks, sense of group purpose, maintenance of work identity and cultural capital accumulation.

The same way, Shan e Guo (2013), exploring how differences in Canadian job market acted in the work identity of Chinese engineer immigrants, concluded that in the context of globalization, the immigrants work identity depends a lot on the institutional recognition, which affects directly their opportunities and job status.

Work Identity, Meaning, and Meaningfulness of Work in the Immigration Context

Table 3. *Characteristics of article identification*

Code	Author(s)	Construct	Year	Title	Participants	Objective	Design	Nature	Instrument	Data Analysis	Database	Journal	Origin of the study	Nacionality / Destination (Immigrant)	Area of Science
1	Saksvik et al.,	Work Identity	2010	Identity, Over-Commitment, Work Environment, and Health Outcomes among Immigrant Workers	924 workers of food and drink industry, being 84 immigrants several nationalities (mixed sample)	**Establishing relations**	Transversal	Quantitative	Questionaire	Descriptive Statistics	Web of Science	**Journal of Identity and Migration Studies**	Poland	Mixed nationalities/ Norway	Phylosophy
2	Abramova	Meaning of Work	2011	Making Meaning of Work: Uncovering the Complexity of Immigrant Experience in a Multicultural Landscape	A white woman of education field	**Descriptive**	Transversal	Qualitative	Semi-structured interview	Narrative Analysis	Web of Science	**Multicultural Perspectives**	USA	Rússia /USA	Phylosophy
3	Stebleton	Meaning of Work	2012	The Meaning of Work for Black African Immigrant Adult College Students	Seven black African immigrants	**Descriptive**	Transversal	Qualitative	Semi-structured interview	Narrative Analysis	Web of Science	**Journal of Career Development**	USA	South Africa/ USA	Business
4	Carpenedo & Nardi	Work identity	2013	Mulheres Brasileiras na divisão internacional do trabalho reprodutivo: construindo subjetividade(s)	Eight Brazilian women living and working illegally in Paris as housekeepers, maids and babysitters	**Descriptive**	Transversal	Qualitative	Semi-structured interview	Content Analysis	Web of Science	**Revista de Estudios Sociales**	Spain	Brazil /France	Sociology
5	Cheng	Work identity	2013	Rethinking differences and inequality at the age of globalization	45 Polish immigrants (female) who work as housekeeper in the USA	**Descriptive**	Transversal	Qualitative	Semi-structured interview	Content Analysis	Scopus	**Equality, Diversity and Inclusion: An International Journal**	USA	Poland /USA	Sociology
6	González	Meaning of Work	2013	Mujeres migrantes cuidadoras en flujos migratorios sur y sur- norte: expectativas, experiências valoraciones	67 people (39 in Spain and 28 in Chile) (Mixed sample)	**Establishing relations**	Transversal	Qualitative	Semi-structured interview	Content Analysis	Scielo	**Revista Latinoamericana**	Chile	Spain /Chile	Psychology
7	Joseph	Work identity	2013	(Re)negotiating cultural and work identities pre and post-migration: Malaysian migrant women in Australia	6 female immigrants from Malaysia who work in the Australian educational context	**Establishing relations**	Transversal	Qualitative	Semi-structured interview	Content Analysis	Scopus	**Women's Studies International Forum**	Australia	Malaysia / Australia	Sociology

continues on following page

Table 3. Continued

Code	Author(s)	Construct	Year	Title	Participants	Objective	Design	Nature	Instrument	Data Analysis	Database	Journal	Origin of the study	Nacionality / Destination (Inmigrant	Area of Science
8	Roberman	Work identity	2013	All That is Just Ersatz: The Meaning of Work in the Life of Immigrant Newcomers	40 Russians (between 35 and 55 years old) (mixed sample)	Descriptive	Longitudinal	Qualitative	Semi-structured interview	Content Analysis	Web of Science	Ethos	Germany	Russia / Germany	Sociology
9	Saksvik et al.,	Work identity	2013	Migrant Labor in the Workforce	779 workers of the cleaning sector in Poland, being 125 immigrants from different countries (mixed sample)	Establishing Relations	Transversal	Quantitative	Questionaire	Correlation	Web of Science	Journal of Identity and Migration Studies	Poland	Different nationalities/ Poland	Philosophy
10	Shan & Guo	Work identity	2013	Learning as sociocultural practice: Chinese immigrant professionals negotiating differences and identities in the Canadian labor market	16 Chinese immigrants, engineer, in three Canadian (Toronto, Calgary and Edmonton) Mixed sample)	Descriptive	Longitudinal	Qualitative	Semi-structured interview	Content Analysis	Web of Science	Comparative Education	Canada	China / Canada	Education
11	Tedesco	Work identity	2014	Casamentos mistos: novas sociabilidades e quadros coletivos. Aspectos da imigraçãode brasileiras na Itália	Seven Brazilian immigrants, housekeepers in Italy (2 in Milan, 3 Brescia and 2 in Verona)	Descriptive	Transversal	Qualitative	Semi-structured interview	Content Analysis	Scielo	Female studies	Brazil	Brazil / Italy	Sociology
12	Oliveira et al.	Work identity	2015	Ressignificação da identidade no processo de imigração haitianazuma pesquisa numa cidade do Sul do Brasil	Seven Haitian immigrants living in Balneario Camburiú (male)	Descriptive	Transversal	Qualitative	Semi-structured interview	Content Analysis	PsycINFO	Revista Brasileira de Tecnologias Sociais	Brazil	Haiti /Brasil	Sociology
13	Zikic & Richardson	Work identity	2015	What happens when you can't be who you are: Professional identity at the institutional periphery	32 doctors and 26 IT professionals de (mixed sample)	Establishing Relations	Longitudinal	Qualitative	Semi-structured interview	Narrative analysis	Web of Science	Human Relations	Canada	Different nationalities / Canada	Psychology
14	Rosenbaum	Meaning of work	2016	Todos sacrifican: immigrant organizing and the meanings of (domestic) work	Group of housekeepers and Sparkle and Shine Cooperative	Descriptive	Transversal	Qualitative	Semi-structured interview	Narrative analysis	Web of Science	The Journal of Labor and Society	USA	Different nationalities / USA	Business

continues on following page

Work Identity, Meaning, and Meaningfulness of Work in the Immigration Context

Table 3. Continued

Code	Author(s)	Construct	Year	Title	Participants	Objective	Design	Nature	Instrument	Data Analysis	Database	Journal	Origin of the study	Nacionality / Destination /Immigrant	Area of Science
15	Välipakka al.,	Meaningfulness of work	2016	Experiencing Cultural Contact at Work: An Exploration of Immigrants' Perceptions of Work in Finland	12 Polish workers in Finland (mixed sample)	**Descriptive**	Transversal	Qualitative	Semi-structured interview -	Narrative analysis	Scopus	**Journal of Business Ethics**	Finland	Poland / Finland	Psychology
16	Yu	Meaning of work	2016	Immigrant workers responses to stigmatized work: Constructing dignity through moral reasoning	Two groups of low-income immigrant workers: the first group formed by 18 cleaning workers in office buildings and the second one with 37 nursing assistants Haitians (mixed sample)	**Establishing relations**	Transversal	Qualitative	Semi-structured interview	Narrative analysis	Web of Science	**Journal of Industrial Relations**	USA	Different nationalities / USA	Business
17	Bonizzoni	Work identity	2017	The shifting boundaries of (un)documentedness: a gendered understanding of migrants' employment-based legalization pathways in Italy	Immigrants of different nationalities 17 women e 18 men)	**Descriptive**	Transversal	Qualitative	Semi-structured interview	Content Analysis	Scopus	**Ethnic and racial studies**	Italy	Various / Italy	Sociology
18	Coelho & Cézar	Work identity	2017	O sabiá e sua memória de elefante	1 immigrant, male, 78 years old, businessman, from Tanzania	**Establishing Relations**	Transversal	Qualitative	Open interview	Content Analysis	Lilacs	**Mental**	Brazil	Tanzania / Brazil	Psychology
19	Sigad	Meaning of work	2017	The meaning of work among immigrants living in poverty in Israel: Replanting roots of belonging: Meaning of work among Israeli immigrants living in poverty	80 immigrants (mixed sample)	**Establishing Relations**	Transversal	Qualitative	Semi-structured interview	Content Analysis	Web of Science	**International Journal of Social Welfare**	Israel	Ethiopia, Síria, Argentina / Israel	Sociology
20	Sharabi	Meaning of work	2017	Ethno-religious groups work values and ethics: the case of Jews, Muslims and Christians in Israel	898 Jews, 215 Muslims e 103 Christians (mixed sample)	**Establishing Relations**	Transversal	Qualitative	Questionnaire	Correlation	Web of Science	**International Review of Sociology**	Israel	Palestina / Israel	Sociology

continues on following page

Work Identity, Meaning, and Meaningfulness of Work in the Immigration Context

Table 3. Continued

Code	Author(s)	Construct	Year	Title	Participants	Objective	Design	Nature	Instrument	Data Analysis	Database	Journal	Origin of the study	Nacionality / Destination (Immigrant	Area of Science
21	Trindade	Work identity	2017	Trabalho é vida e vida é trabalho!": escrita de si e imigração polonesa, a memória, o esquecimento e a identidade na narrativa de um intelectual imigrante	1 immigrant, intellectual, Polish emigrated from Brazil	**Descriptive**	Transversal	Qualitative	Observation	Content Analysis	Web of Science	**MÉTIS:história &cultura**	Brazil	Poland / Brazil	History
22	Comin & Pauli	Meaning of work	2018	The meaning of work, organizational socialization and work context: the perspective of migrant workers	186 Haitian immigrants, Senegalese, from Bangladesh and Ghanaian (mixed sample)	**Establishing relations**	Transversal	Quantitative	Semi-structured interview	Correlation	Web of Science	**RAM**	Brazil	Haiti / Brazil	Business
23	Showers	Work identity	2018	Learning to care: work experiences and identity formation among African immigrant care workers in the US	23 immigrants from Sierra Leone in Africa (11 female and 12 male)	**Descriptive**	Longitudinal	Mixed	Semi-structured interview / Questionnaire	Content Analysis	Web of Science	**International Journal of Care and Caring**	USA	South África / USA	Business
24	Tu et al.,	Meaning of work	2018	Realities of the American dream: Vocational experiences and intersecting invisibility of low-income Chinese immigrant laborers	17 low-income Chinese immigrants (mixed sample)	**Establishing relations**	Longitudinal	Qualitative	Semi-structured interview -	Content Analysis	Web of Science	**Journal of Vocational Behavior**	USA	China / USA	Business
25	Yijälä & Luoma	Work identity	2019	The Importance of Employment in the Acculturation Process of Well-Educated Iraqis in Finland: A Qualitative Follow-up Study	7 Iraqi immigrants in Finland (3 women and 4 men) well educated and English speakers	**Descriptive**	Longitudinal	Qualitative	Semi-structured interview	Content Analysis	Scopus	**Refugee Survey Quarterly**	Finland	Iraq /Finland	Sociology
26	Dal Forno et al.,	Work identity	2020	O Trabalho como Potencialidade Subjetiva na Experiência Migratória	1 Haitian immigrant from Brazil	**Descriptive**	Longitudinal	Qualitative	Semi-structured interview	Content Analysis	PsycINFO	**Estudos e Pesquisas em Psicologia**	Brazil	Haiti / Brazil	Psychology
27	Nordstrom	Work identity	2020	Teaching in the periphery: Teacher identity in community language schools	1 teacher from an English course in a Swedish community, living in Australia	**Descriptive**	Transversal	Qualitative	Semi-structured interview	Content Analysis	Scopus	**Teaching and Teacher Education**	Australia	Sweden / Australia	Education

Source: Author

Work Identity, Meaning, and Meaningfulness of Work in the Immigration Context

Immigrants manage their work identity according to the social and cultural status granted to them in host society. The more recognized it is, the more favorably organized is their work identity, namely, acquiring more value.

In turn, among the 3 studies which address the optics of domestic work, two of them concluded that, despite the fact that domestic immigrants felt discriminated due to social devaluation of this type of work, being employed granted them empowerment and maintenance of dignity (Carpenedo & Nardi, 2013; Cheng, 2013). The conclusion of Cheng (2013) was that white immigrants suffer less prejudice when compared to immigrants of other ethnicities/skin color. Thus, perception of less social discrimination influences on the strengthening of reconstructed work identity.

The second study about domestic workers portrayed Brazilian immigrants in Paris (Carpenedo & Nardi, 2013), and stated that the positive relation with domestic work is a consequence of precariousness and economic instability experienced before in Brazil. In other words, even if they performed a socially-devaluated work, when they compared the different realities of life in France and in Brazil, there was a positive balance related to the new country. That said, the new work identity is strengthened because they were able to negotiate advantageous labor agreements which increased life quality of such, as above-average daily rates, and flexible labor agreements (idiosyncratic agreements).

Finally, the third study about Brazilian domestic workers depicted a different focus compared to the other two (Tedesco, 2014). Despite having arrived in Italy to do domestic work, this fact was only a bridge, because they married a member of the employer's family. In this new condition, the immigrants engaged other professional activities, such as working in their husband's company, demonstrating change in professional identity, yet preserving work identity, because working continued being valued.

Still about the first category, but leaving the axis if environmental factors, there are the personal factors (for example, commitment) which interfere on the formation of work identity. Such axis gathers two studies that compare immigrant and native workers in relation to the way they understood their work identity and the influence of such perception in their health (Saksvik et al., 2010; Saksvik et al., 2013). The perception of stress and poor health was more prevalent among immigrants in the study of Saksvik et al. (2010).

On the other hand, in Saksvik et al. (2013), natives as well as immigrants understood stress and mental health equally. The results of both studies revealed that the immigrants show higher levels of commitment compared to natives.

Therefore, commitment, understood as the active bond related to intentions reserved for the organization, such as intentions of extra effort, permanence and rewards (Carvalho et al., 2011), worked as a barrier for the escalade of stress and health problems among immigrants, playing an important role in the way how work identity was constructed. Probably, if the worker is committed to the organization, more is his affective relationship with the institution, which will make he shows higher levels of positive moods, achievement and satisfaction in several dimensions and less stress at work.

The second category ("Breaks in professional identity and the impacts on work identity"), groups the 4 studies about immigrants who break the links with the professional career they had in the home country. However, depending on the personal resources available and on the opportunities found, such break can have more or less impact on the reconstruction of work identity.

Two studies are about less-impacting breaks (Dal Forno et al., 2020; Joseph, 2013). The first one discussed the reconstruction of work identity among women from Malaysia who had a solid career, and who migrated to Australia (Joseph, 2013). In the beginning, most of them went backwards in their career when they got involved in activities out of their work area, but it allowed them to engage in a new social environment, flexibility in the exercise of work identity and creation of survival strategies in the construction of meaningful lives. This initial setback was considered necessary for a future progress in their career.

The second study in this category was about a haitian immigrant who performed his activity in Brazil, as a teacher (Dal Forno et al., 2020). This immigrant put his professional identity on suspension at first. However, that fact of knowing he could move on his profession impacted positively in the search of reconstruction of his work identity, enhancing it. In this study it was demonstrated how working in another country allows the immigrant to reconstruct his/her work identity in a positive way, which is considered important in human life.

However, there are dysfunctional impacts in the interruption of professional identity (Oliveira et al., 2015; Zikic & Richardson, 2015), such as the case of doctors and professionals of IT (Zikic & Richardson, 2015). The results signaled that the level of demand and requirements that each immigrant needs to match to perform their profession legally strongly interferes in how work identity is shaped. IT professionals do not need to validate their diploma, thus employers can hire them without this requirement, which provides them more autonomy, enhancement and professional improvement.

In turn, in the field of medical science, rules are more complex, which causes many workers to abandon that career, leading them to less adaptive ways of reconstruction of work identity, with possibility of identity crisis.

The fourth and last study belonging to this category, which refers to more challenging aspects, aimed at understanding how redefinition of work identity of seven haitian immigrants with specific professional qualifications (language and computing teacher, businessmen and goldsmith), in the city of Balneário Camboriú, in Santa Catarina (Oliveira et al., 2015) occurs. The result pointed out that some immigrants may temporarily perform different activities, connected to low-qualification informal jobs, being underemployed, still willing to get a job compatible to the profession they had before. This break rebounds in the structuration of work identity, inasmuch as working remains important, yet, it becomes vital that this job is one that explores the potential of that immigrant.

Finally, the third category ("**Centrality of** work identity") includes two studies. One about a Polish immigrant (Trindade, 2017) and the other about a Tanzanian (Coelho & Cézar, 2017), both living in Brazil. The conclusion reveals that being employed, especially in the same professional area, is essential for structuration of work identity due to the centrality that both work and profession had for those subjects.

Table 4 summarizes the categories of work identity presenting on the following information of studies: author/year, definition of construct, objectives, most relevant results/conclusions.

The identity of work finds obstacles in its reconstruction because these immigrants face barriers as the fact that they only work in informal jobs

Working is a facilitator of welfare, acculturation, and reconstruction of identity of work

The subject demonstrated valuation of the profession of scientist and professor, which strengthened his work identity in the new

Concerning the construct meaning of work, two categories were found: "Positive redefinition of meaning of work" and "Negative redefinition of meaning of work". The first category (**"Positive redefinition of meaning of work"**) gathers six studies which indicate that meaning of work goes through a positive process of redefinition (Abramova, 2011; Comin & Pauli, 2018; Sharabi, 2017; Stebleton, 2012; Tu et al., 2018; Yu, 2016).

Table 4. Categorization of studies about work identity

Author / Year	Definition of Construct	Objective(s)	Result(s)
Category 1 Relation among contextual and individual factors and identity of work			
Saksvik et al., 2010	No definition	To compare native immigrant workers in Poland in various factors related to perception of their work identity anchored in psychosocial environment of work and the result of these factors in stress at work and in subjective health	Immigrant workers have more excessive commitment, more mental health problems and more stress at work than native workers, what affects redefinition of work identity
Carpenedo & Nardi, 2013	Definition not mentioned	To understand the way by which Brazilian female workers deal with the immigration process	The performing of an informal devalued activity is not an obstacle for those immigrants to find ways to structure a new work identity even more strengthened and well-structured than the one they had in Brazil, through establishment of flexible work agreements and with good income.
Cheng, 2013	Definition not mentioned	to examine if the migratory experience of white Polish women is better due to the color of skin	Despite having better migratory experience if compared to immigrants of other ethnicities, Polish domestic workers consider that domestic worker faces social discrimination, but construct their work identity in a positive way to neutralize negative images upon them and their work.
Roberman, 2013	Defines only meaning of work as something that goes beyond its material and economic dimensions and as a value assigned to work (Grint 2005)	To assess how Russian immigrants reconstruct their work identity being obligated to survive with alternative informal jobs in Germany	The immigrants consider that informal jobs undermine them and difficult their recognition by natives, which interferes negatively in reconstruction of work identity
Saksvik et al., 2013	Identity is defined as the ideas about who the human being is and to which groups he belongs (Jenkins, 2008).	To compare immigrant workers and native workers in Poland in various factors related to perception of their work identity anchored in their psychosocial work environment and the result of these factors in the stress at work and in subjective health	Immigrant workers have more excessive commitment, more mental health problems and more stress at work than native workers, what affects reconfiguration of identity of work. However, mental health problems were not greater among immigrants. Excessive commitment was seen as a barrier to avoid health problem
Shan & Guo, 2013	The construction of identity happens in a private social context (Handley et al. 2007).	To investigate work identity of a specific group of workers, Chinese engineers in the USA.	Work identity of immigrants depends a lot on institutional recognition, which affects directly their opportunities and work status
Tedesco, 2014	Definition not mentioned	To analyze if work identity of Brazilians who migrate to Italy to work as domestic workers, but end up marring a member of the employer's family change due to marriage.	Even with the change of status within that family, these women continued considering work as something important for the structure of their identity.
Showers, 2018	Definition not mentioned	Investigating the work experience in a group of black African immigrants in public attendance sector	
Yijälä & Luoma, 2019	Definition not mentioned	Investigating the role of work in the process of acculturation of Iraqi immigrants in Finland	

continues on following page

Table. Continued

Author / Year	Definition of Construct	Objective (s)	Result (s)
Nordstrom, 2020	Definition not mentioned	Exploring experience and challenges of a teacher in a public language school in Australia	The structuration of their identity of work was weakened due to contextual elements (e.g. their difficulty to speak the local language)
Category 2 Breaks in professional identity the impacts on identity of work			
Joseph, 2013	Definition not mentioned	To understand reconstruction of work identity of female Immigrants with high qualification from Malaysia to Australia	Among cultural restrictions and opportunities, Malaysian women learned how to create strategies, survive and construct significant lives as immigrant females in Australia strengthening the work identity.
Zikic & Richardson, 2015	Definition not mentioned	To theorize how people out of the organization, with established professional identities, respond to institutional requirements and, specifically, to the pre-entry scripts in the new host country	Work identity is influenced by formal requirements, such as diploma validation so that the immigrant can perform his/her work in the new country.
Oliveira et al., 2015	Definition not mentioned	To understand how the process of redefinition of work identity occurs among Haitian immigrants living in the city of Balneário Camboriu, in the state of Santa Catarina	The immigrants, in general, perform activities that are different from the ones they did in their home country for a long period, willing to find a better work, which is compatible with the profession they had before, so that the identity is successfully restructured.
Dal Forno et al., 2020	The work is, for Dejours (2011), a central element in the promotion of psychic development and constitution of identity	To discuss about the role of professional work before impasses of migratory living of Haitians in Brazil	Working in a different country allows the immigrant to reconstruct in a positive way his/her work identity, because, despite being initially suspended, the stimulus to improve their career was a positive one.
Category 3 The Centrality of work identity			
Trindade, 2017	Definition not mentioned	Analyzing the discourse of retirement of Biezanko, addressing the importance of work identity in this context	
Coelho & Cézar, 2017	Identity is linked to doing; the activity is, understanding that the work was essential for aged 78, in the structuring of his above all, naming. It is by acting, by doing identity and adaptation to the new country that someone becomes something (Ciampa, 1989)	Analyzing labor experience of a Tanzanian businessman, established in his home country, Brazilian soil for more than 40 years	

Source: Author

Two studies address the relation between meaning of work and the practice of informal work, examining how immigrants with low salaries construct dignity in their work and life (Stebleton, 2012; Yu, 2016). The conclusion was that even exercising socially devalued work, such activity is important for guaranteeing social mobility in the new country, acquiring meaning.

Focusing in Chinese and Russian immigrant, two other studies address the change in the meaning of work by reducing importance given to money and cultivating a more pleasant relation with work (Abramova, 2011; Tu et al., 2018). In the study of Tu et al. (2018), the participants started giving more importance to family and community rather than work. In Abramova (2011), results signaled how much a collaborative dialogue between an immigrant teacher, highly motivated and in search of success, and a truly interested school administration may help improve teacher-student relation.

The fifth study (Comin & Pauli, 2018), shows that the meaning of work for immigrant subjects would be directly related to work organization, because the more affinity between present profession and the one they had before, the more redefinition of meaning turns up more positive, becoming a source of self-esteem, dignity and sense of usefulness. The sixth and last study belonging to this category brought a comparative perspective, using the instrument MOW (1987) to investigate meaning of work among Jews, Arabs, Muslims and Christians in Israel, pointing out ethical similarities and differences at work (Sharabi, 2017). The results indicated more similarity between Christians and Jews than between Christians and Muslims, whereas the main differences were noticed between Jews and Muslims.

Christians and Jews showed greater need to establish relationship with other people than Muslims and such need is positively related to the income among the three religious' groups. Christians need more interpersonal relationships. Muslims presented more centrality of work and it seems to vary according to the place of residence. The ones who lived in rural areas and small cities have more centrality if compared to the ones in the cities, and the same happens with Christians.

Different from the previous one, the second category (**"Negative redefinition of meaning of work"**), with three studies, points out factors that act negatively in the meaning given to work by the immigrant (González, 2013; Rosenbaum, 2016; Sigad, 2017). All of them focused on informal work, being two of them about domestic work (González, 2013; Rosenbaum, 2016), converging to the conclusion that informal work has little recognition and value, but represents source of income. Thus, the new meaning of work is confused with the need of subsistence, against immigrants will. In the host country, they worked not only to get by, but also to maintain self-esteem. When they need to work only to get by, work loses capacity to contribute to personal and emotional development.

Finally, as for the construct meaningfulness of work, only 1 study was found (Välipakka et al., 2016), whose objective was to investigate the meaningfulness of work for Polish workers in Finland, examining how immigrants' perception of work is shaped by their daily intercultural interactions at work. The results of such analysis reveal that work has unique meaningfulness and is a fundamental factor for adaptation and integration of immigrants in the Finland society. Work may help stop the exclusion of immigrants from the community and make them become part of it. Furthermore, work shapes the identity of immigrants, impacting on how they see and value themselves as immigrants and as individuals.

Table 5. *Categorization of studies about meaning of work*

Author/Year	Definition of Construct	Objetive (s)	Result(s)
Category 1 "Positive redefinition of meaning of work"			
Stebleton, 2012	Definition not mentioned	Exploring the meaning of work for sub-Saharan blacks who have informal jobs.	Meaning of work changes, allowing mobility to the immigrant.
Yu, 2016	Definition not mentioned	Examining the meaning of work for education professional (teachers) who speak Russian in a school community.	Present discoveries reveal that immigrants go through a process of reconciliation with their initial will of social mobility, reformulating the meaning of work in their lives.
Abramova, 2011	Meaning of work plays the role of instrumental character of an economic dimension, providing people with basic survival needs. However, as non-economic dimension, it provides satisfaction, relationship, occupation and usefulness. (Morin, 2001)	Investigating the meaning of work for a Russian teacher in the USA	Meaning of work was linked to financial reward before, but, after moving to a new country and based on this new perspective of relation with the school, it started to be linked to source of pleasure.
Tu et al., 2018	The measure of valued result is based on typology of six general meanings: status and prestige, income, time absorption, interesting contacts, service to society and interest and satisfaction (Kaplan & Tausky, (974)	Investigating the intersection of multiple identities of subordinated groups who address this vulnerable population and the impact on professional experience.	Before, the work for immigrants was related to financial condition, but with immigration, its importance was reduced and started to be linked to family and personal life appreciation.
Comin & Pauli, 2018		Relating meaning of work with the organization of work performed by the immigrant.	A organização do trabalho interfere no sentido dado ao novo trabalho, podendo mudar a depender da atividade profissional que ele exerce no novo país.
Sharabi, 2017		Investigating the meaning of work between Jews and Arabs (Muslims and Christians) in Israel and trying to explain the similarities and differences of ethics at work among these religious immigrants. For that, the instrument used has origin on MOW (1987)	As result it was found that despite the fact that Judaism, Christianism, and Islamism have similar values about MOW (1987), the 'people from 3 religious' groups in Israel have different dimensions of MOW (1987) (excluding norms of obligation and rights).
Category 2 "Negative Redefinition of meaning of work"			
González, 2013	Definition not mentioned	Investigating comparatively two migratory flows about expectations and motivations that shape the standards of migration of female subjects in relation to domestic work and how meaning of work is structured in this context.	Results found allow one to state that domestic work. Despite the fact that it produces social profitability, it presents a considerable recognition deficit, and this interferes in the meaning work starts to have in the life of that immigrant.
Sigad, 2017	Definition not mentioned	Analyzing the interaction of work, immigration and poverty among immigrants working in Israel.	The immigrant that moves to escape the situation of poverty changes radically the meaning of work, because work starts to be more linked to survival than it was in their home country.
Rosenbaum, 2016	Definition not mentioned	Analyzing the interaction of work, immigration and poverty in Israel and the potential meanings assigned to work.	The immigrant that performs domestic work has the meaning of work changed because labor starts to be more linked to survival.

Source: Author

SOLUTIONS AND RECOMMENDATIONS

This review aimed at answering the following research question: what are the empiric relations among work identity, meaning of work and meaningfulness of work in the context of immigration available in national and international literature? Despite the fact that it was not found any article that related the three constructs together in the context of immigration (because the authors chose one or another construct as central), relations among them appeared in the studies, present in the alternation of use and in concept overlapping.

Among the nine studies about meaning of work, three of them treated meaning and meaningfulness as synonyms (Comin & Pauli, 2018; Sharabi, 2017; Stebleton, 2012). Researchers of MOW (1987) treat meaningfulness of work as a component of meaning of work (Morin, 2001). Thus, possibly in the study of Sharabi (2017), which is based on the MOW *(1987)* and on Comin e Pauli (2018), which uses as referential the framing given by Morin (2001), these two concepts may have been understood as synonyms or equivalent.

Another indication showing lack of concept demarcation is found in the study of Stebleton (2012). The article was found when meaningfulness of work was used as search word. However, by reading the article, one can notice it is a study about meaning of work.

Also, the only article about meaningfulness of work alternated the terms *meaningfulness* and *meaning of work* as if they were synonyms (Välipakka et al., 2016). Possibly the lack of concept demarcation between the two concepts may explain the reduced number of articles about meaningfulness of work. In the literature, there are researchers who affirm that not always these concepts are separated (Bendassolli & Gondim, 2014a; Silva & Tolfo, 2011), because several perspectives deal with both terms as one phenomenon only (Borges & Barros, 2015; Cavalheiro, 2010). Yet, there are authors who distinguish theoretically the differences, considering meaning as an individual production, whereas meaningfulness is a result of collective learning incorporated in the process of socialization (Rosso et al., 2010).

Another element that aroused attention was the conception of constructs: only eight articles did it. It seems to suggest that the concepts of meaning and meaningfulness of work can do without conceptual demarcation, being presented as intuitive constructs.

The same conclusion was found in the studies of work identity, where among the 17 studies, only one defined the construct explicitly (Coelho & Cézar, 2017). For example, three studies presented definition of social identity (Saksvik et al., 2013; Saksvik et al., 2010; Shan & Guo, 2013) and engaged more in the concept of work, than in the concept of work identity (Dal Forno et al., 2020).

Another proof of imprecision of the constructs is in the conceptual overlapping between work identity and professional identity, alternating their use in the same text (Bonizzoni, 2016; Cheng, 2013; Nordstrom, 2020; Oliveira et al., 2015; Showers, 2018; Tedesco, 2014; Trindade, 2017; Yijälä & Luoma, 2019; Zikic & Richardson, 2015). Work identity and professional identity are types of social identity (Byron & Cranfford, 2012) and, in several moments, they are concepts that overlap in the literature, in which authors treat both as being the same (Bitencourt et al., 2011; Caza & Creary, 2016; Machado, 2003). However, there are researchers that separate them stating that professional identity involves the inclusion in a group with specific professional activity, whereas work identity does not depend on the professional group it is inserted (Gomes et al., 2013). The important question is the symbolic bond with work and how much the characteristic of work valuation is incorporated to self-concept. Thus, these data lead one to conclude how much work identity and professional identity are interrelated, difficult to demarcate the concept. This may have contributed for the exclusion from the review of studies about professional identity, which were not included in the search, but could approach the theme work identity.

Another aspect that calls the attention is the nationality of the immigrant. Among the 27 studies, only two were Brazilian (Carpenedo & Nardi, 2013; Tedesco, 2014). There are more than four million of Brazilians living abroad, among which around 2 million living in the USA (Ministério das Relações Exteriores Brasileiro [MRE] (2020) and in 2021, another 130.000 left the country seeking new professional opportunities, with the USA continuing to be the main destination (Oliveira et al., 2019). The theme also seems to interest other countries, more than Brazil, because 21 were international authors (78%), seven Americans (26%) and six national (22%).

As for the design of the research, only seven of them were longitudinal. Studies with this design are not very used for investigate work identity, meaning and meaningfulness of work among immigrants, despite being a process of adaptation in a new country. In addition, work identity is related to work experience, direct or indirect, throughout life (Rossit et al., 2018; Teodorescu, 2015), and it is recognized that there are changes over live. It is not a hermetic process noticeable with only one temporal cut, supported by only one observation or captured only by self-report (Kohlsdorf & Junior, 2017). This fact, combined with the fact that meaning and meaningfulness of work depend on a dialectic relation with reality for their construction (Rosso et al., 2010), reaffirm the importance of time while assessing these constructs. The longitudinal studies help capturing changes in meaning and meaningfulness of work over time, bringing information about how determined groups and occupations build their collective view about work and also how the processes of influence by meanings is developed (Abbad & Carlotto, 2016; Bendassolli & Gondim, 2014).

In relation to the nature of the data, 85% of the studies (n=23) used the qualitative methodology. Possibly, it is due to the complex and multi-faceted nature of the phenomenon, which requires idiographic approach in order to understand its specificities (Almeida et al., 2019). Qualitative methods may allow greater approximation to the subject and to the construction of meaning and meaningfulness of work, done through researcher observation, reflection of research subject and methodologies of data collection, such as narrative interview (Bendassolli & Gondim, 2014).

Immigration is an interdisciplinary context of study, emphasized by areas of the selected articles 'authors. Ten studies were in the field of Sociology (n=10; 37%), whereas only five (18%) were in the field of Psychology.

Another interesting result is that, despite most of publications (n=14; 52%) are dated from the last five years (between 2016 and 2020), none of them approached the effects of COVID-19 on the relation of the immigrant with his/her work. COVID-19 may bring a complicating factor to the studies about the theme, what shows that, maybe, it is important to relate meaning, meaningfulness and identity after COVID-19. As for the demographic characteristic of gender, five studies were about male subjects (18.5%), five about female subjects (18.5%) and 17 of both genders (63%).

One of the points to highlight is that the focus of the studies is on the immigrant himself/herself, not on the family members who follow them in the migratory process, for example, wives (Lee & Qomariyah, 2015). Many of these wifes leave their professional lives behind to follow their husbands and, if they want to go back to work, they will need to reconsider and plan their professional journey. Accordingly, such wife may have to deal with a feeling of cultural incapacity (Martins & Souza, 2015), associated with an intrapsychic imbalance (Piaget, 1978), which influence in self-perception of the world and how to position in it. Possibly, the constructs of work identity, meaning and meaningfulness of work go through changes over the migratory experience, for they are a phenomenon sensible to time and context in which it is inserted (Rossit et al., 2018).

The reviewed studies show that environmental and individual factors interfere in the process of reconstruction of work identity in a new country (Dal Forno et al., 2020; Joseph, 2013; Oliveira et al., 2015; Zikic & Richardson, 2015). Immigrants interrupt their professional life in order to dive into a new universe. Such break may have considerable impacts since some immigrants cannot remain in the same profession in the new country, what may cause a crisis in professional identity and in work identity. One of the reasons why they are not able to achieve such goal involve legal issues to regularize the profession in the new country, for example medical professionals, who need to go through a long time-consuming process, not to mention the high costs to revalidate their diplomas (Zikic & Richardson, 2015).

Thus, considering the process that the immigrant faces to reconstruct work identity, meaning and meaningfulness of work, it is notorious that the difficulties are inherent to all of them, regardless their nationality or country where they are moving to. The immigrant always goes through a transition process, for the change of residence means, most of the times, leaving a social environment, what may interfere in their personal and/or social identity, including work identity (Caligiuri & Bonache, 2016; Mcnulty & Brewster, 2017). It is also important to understand the singularity of each process. Since meaning and meaningfulness of work are components which help in the construction of work identity (Marcelino & Cavalcante, 2012; Reis & Puente-Palácios, 2019, Salas et al., 2015), it becomes relevant to develop more studies that approach this relation in the context of immigration.

FUTURE RESEARCH DIRECTIONS

More studies about the theme open ways for the organizations to encourage, create or improve programs of socialization among immigrant workers in the companies, aiming at a better adaptation to the new country, and their families, as well as providing tools for workers in the company to deal with diversity, encouraging parsimonious environment of collaboration and empathy. Another important contribution would be in the field of national public policies, so that the countries may create guidelines to facilitate the flow of information and development of competences necessary for the immigrant to have conditions to enter the work market in the new country.

However, this review of literature has its limitations. Due to imprecision and overlapping of concepts, some important studies may not have been selected in the process article search. Another limitation is because review and meta-analysis studies were excluded from the selection, even if they were consulted. The focus relied on empiric studies only.

CONCLUSION

Considering the results, one can affirm that this systematic review achieved its objective because evidence of empiric relations between work identity, meaning and meaningfulness of work in the context of immigration was found. Therefore, some final considerations deserve highlighting. The first one is the need of new empiric researches that approach simultaneously work identity, meaning and meaningfulness of work in the context of immigration due to the interdependence among these constructs and confirmation that the reviewed studies only deal with one or two of these constructs.

The second conclusion is that, considering conceptual overlapping between meaning and meaningfulness of work, the new studies should choose a theoretical clipping which takes into consideration the singularity of these constructs, dealing with them inside their specificities, as proposed by Bendassolli e Gondim (2014) e Rosso et al. (2010). The same way it is important to contemplate studies that differ work identity and professional identity, because despite conceptual overlapping found in many articles, there are researchers who investigate the difference between the terms (Byron & Crafford, 2012; Gomes et al., 2013).

The third conclusion was the prevalence of cross–sectional studies, pointing to the necessity of more longitudinal studies that consider the passing of time in the impact of immigration over potential meanings, meaningfulness and work identities of immigrants. Furthermore, one may suggest that more Brazilian researchers engage in the understanding the reasons why Brazilian immigrate to other countries. Among these Brazilians, considering the little number of studies, there is the family of such immigrants, including their wives that, many times, give up their professional lives to follow their husbands or families.

The fourth conclusion, which already sets a limitation of this study, is that immigration comes out as an interdisciplinary field with economic, social, psychological, historical and political impacts. Considering the importance of meaning, meaningfulness and work identity for Psychology, it would be advisable the elaboration of more studies, bearing in mind that only five articles in this field of study were found. Additionally, there is the necessity of studies that try to capture the effects in times of sanitary measures to contain COVID-19, which spread all over the world, affecting work significantly in the first months of year 2020. The crisis caused by the pandemic created unemployment, especially for immigrants, many times without any work-protection policies (Costa, 2020). The period of review, between 2016 and 2020, certainly limited the inclusion of studies that addressed the influence of COVID-19 in work life of the immigrant, mainly the impact on work identity, meaning and meaningfulness of work. Another limitation refers to the conceptual imprecision and overlapping, which may have left out some important studies not selected in the article search process.

REFERENCES

Abbad, G. S., & Carlotto, M. S. (2016). Analyzing challenges associated with the adoption of longitudinal studies in Work and Organizational Psychology. *Revista Psicologia Organizações e Trabalho*, *16*(4), 340–348. doi:10.17652/rpot/2016.4.12585

Abramova, I. (2011). Making Meaning of Work: Uncovering the Complexity of Immigrant Experience in a Multicultural Landscape. *Multicultural Perspectives*, *13*(4), 209–214. doi:10.1080/15210960.2011.616833

Almeida, S. R., Penso, M. A., & Freitas, L. G. (2019). Identidade docente com foco no cenário de pesquisa: Uma revisão sistemática. *Educação em Revista*, *35*, 15–35. doi:10.1590/0102-4698204516

Bardin, L. (2011). *Análise de conteúdo,* 70. Edições.

Bendassolli, P., & Gondim, S. M. G. (2014). Significados, sentidos e função psicológica do trabalho: Discutindo essa tríade conceitual e seus desafios metodológicos. *Avances en Psicología Latinoamericana*, *32*(1), 131–147. doi:10.12804/apl32.1.2014.09

Bentley, S., Peters, K., Haslam, S., & Greenaway, K. (2019). Construction at Work: Multiple Identities Scaffold Professional Identity Development in Academia. *Frontiers in Psychology*, *10*, 628. https:// doi:10.3389/fpsyg.2019.00628

Bispo, D. A., Dourado, D. C. P., & Amorim, M. F. C. L. (2013). Possibilidade de dar sentido ao trabalho além do difundido pela lógica do mainstream: Um estudo com indivíduos que atuam no âmbito do movimento hip hop. *Organizações & Sociedade*, *20*(67), 717–731. doi:10.1590/S1984-92302013000400007

Bitencourt, B. M., Gallon, S., Batista, M. K., & Piccinini, V. C. (2011). Para além do tempo de emprego: o sentido do trabalho no processo de aposentadoria. *Revista de Ciências da Administração*, *13*(31), 30-57. https:// doi:10.5007/2175-8077.2011v13n31p30

Bonizzoni, P. (2016). The shifting boundaries of (un)documentedness: A gendered understanding of migrants' employment-based legalization pathways in Italy. *Ethnic and Racial Studies*, *40*(10), 1–20. doi:10.1080/01419870.2016.1229488

Borba, D. (2008). *Individuação e expatriação: resiliência da esposa acompanhante* [Dissertação de Mestrado, Pontifícia Universidade Católica de São Paulo, São Paulo, Brasil].

Borges, L. O. (1999). As concepções do trabalho: Um estudo de análise de conteúdo de dois periódicos de circulação nacional. *Revista de Administração Contemporânea*, *3*(3), 81–107. doi:10.1590/S1415-65551999000300005

Borges, L. O., Alves-Filho, A., & Tamayo, A. (2008). Motivação e significado do trabalho. In *M. M. M. Siqueira (Org.), Medidas do comportamento organizacional: ferramentas de diagnóstico e de gestão* (pp. 215–248). Artmed.

Borges, L. O., & Barros, S. C. (2015). Inventário de significado do trabalho para trabalhadores de baixa instrução. In K. PuentePalácios & A. L. A. Peixoto (Orgs.). Ferramentas de diagnóstico para organizações e trabalho (pp. 232-260). Artmed.

Brown, A. D. (2019). Identities in Organization Studies. *Organization Studies*, *40*(1), 7–22. doi:10.1177/0170840618765014

Bustamante, A. V. (2011). Physicians cite hurdles ranging from lack of coverage to poor communication in providing high-quality care to latinos. *Health Affairs*, *30*(10), 191–199. doi:10.1377/hlthaff.2011.0344 PMID:21976336

Byron, A., & Crafford, A. (2012). Identity at work: Exploring strategies for Identity Work. *SA Journal of Industrial Psychology*, *38*(1), 120–131. doi:10.4102ajip.v38i1.904

Caligiuri, P., & Bonache, J. (2016). Evolving and enduring challenges in global mobility. *Journal of World Business*, *51*(1), 127–141. doi:10.1016/j.jwb.2015.10.001

Carpenedo, M., & Nardi, H. C. (2013). Mulheres Brasileiras na divisão internacional do trabalho reprodutivo: Construindo subjetividade(s). *Revista de Estudios Sociales*, (45), 96–109. doi:10.7440/res45.2013.08

Carvalho, P., Alves, F. J. O., Peixoto, A. L. A., & Bastos, A. V. B. (2011). Comprometimento afetivo, de continuação e entrincheiramento organizacional: Estabelecendo limites conceituais e empíricos. *Psicologia: Teoria e Prática*, *13*(2), 127–141.

Carvalho, V., & Bridi, M. A. (2015). Trabalho e desigualdade: A terceirização e seus impactos sobre os trabalhadores. *Revista da ABET, 14*(1), 99–113.

Cassel, D. K., Moreira, G. S., & Ziliotto, D. M. (2005). A imigração alemã e a concepção de trabalho no Vale dos Sinos. *Revista Prâksis, 1*(2), 57–62.

Cavalheiro, G. (2010*). Sentidos atribuídos ao trabalho por profissionais afastados do ambiente laboral em decorrência de depressão* [Dissertação de mestrado, Universidade Federal de Santa Catarina, Florianópolis, SC].

Caza, B., & Creary, S. (2016). The construction of professional identity. *Perspectives on Contemporary Professional Work, 1*(2), 259-285. https:// doi:10.4337/9781783475582.00022

Cheng, S. (2013). Rethinking differences and inequality at the age of globalization: A case study of white immigrant domestic workers in the global city of Chicago. *Equality, 32*(6), 537–556. doi:10.1108/EDI-07-2012-0059

Coelho, M. P., & Cézar, M. A. (2017). O sabiá e sua memória de elefante. *Mental (Barbacena), 11*(21), 396–410.

Comin, L. C., & Pauli, J. (2018). The Meaning Of Work, Organizational Socialization And Work Context: The Perspective Of Migrant Workers. *Revista de Administração Mackenzie,* 19(spe). doi:10.1590/1678-6971/eramd180088

Corlett, S., Coupland, C., McInnes, P., & Sheep, M. (2017). Exploring the registers of identity research. *International Journal of Management Reviews, 17,* 409-412. https:// doi:10.1111/ijmr.12080

Costa, S. S. (2020). Pandemia e desemprego no Brasil. *Revista de Administração Pública, 54*(4), 969–978. doi:10.1590/0034-761220200170

Dal Forno, C., Canabarro, R., & Macedo, M. (2020). O Trabalho como Potencialidade Subjetiva na Experiência Migratória. *Estudos e Pesquisas em Psicologia, 20*(1), 309–329. doi:10.12957/epp.2020.50836

Dickie, V. A. (2003). Establishing Worker Identity: A Study of People in Craft Work. *Am J Occup, 57*(3), 250–261. doi:10.5014/ajot.57.3.250 PMID:12785663

Dutton, J., Roberts, L., & Bednar, J. (2010). Pathways for Positive Identity Construction at Work: Four Types of Positive Identity and the Building of Social Resources. *Academy of Management Review, 35.* https:// doi:10.5465/AMR.2010.48463334

Fouche, E., Rothmann, S., & Van der Vtver, C. (2017). Antecedents and outcomes of meaningful work among schoolteachers. *Journal of Industrial Psychology, 43*(0), 1-10. https:// doi:10.4102/sajip.v43i0.1398

Galvão, T. F., & Pereira, M. G. (2014). Revisões sistemáticas da literatura: Passos para sua elaboração. *Epidemiologia e Serviços de Saúde: Revista do Sistema Unico de Saúde do Brasil, 23*(1), 183–184. doi:10.5123/S1679-49742014000100018

Gjerde, S., & Alvesson, M. (2020). Sandwiched: Exploring role and identity of middle managers in the genuine middle. *Human Relations, 73*(1), 124–151. doi:10.1177/0018726718823243

Gomes, P. M. S., Ferreira, C. P. P., Pereira, A. L., & Batista, P. M. F. (2013). A identidade profissional do professor: Um estudo de revisão sistemática. *Revista Brasileira de Educação Física e Esporte*, *27*(2), 247–267. doi:10.1590/S1807-55092013000200009

González, E. A. (2013). Mujeres migrantes cuidadoras en flujos migratorios sur-sur y sur-norte: Expectativas, experiencias y valoraciones. *Polis*, *12*(35), 35–62. doi:10.4067/S0718-65682013000200003

Guizardi, M. L. (2019). The Age of Migration Crisis. *Tempo*, *25*, 577–598. doi:10.1590/tem-1980-542x2019v250303

Hackman, J., & Oldhan, G. (1975). Development of job diagnostic survey. *The Journal of Applied Psychology*, *60*(2), 159–170. doi:10.1037/h0076546

Joseph, C. (2013). (Re)negotiating cultural and work identities pre and post-migration: Malaysian migrant women in Australia. *Women's Studies International Forum*, *36*, 27–36. doi:10.1016/j.wsif.2012.10.002

Kirpal, S. (2004) 'Researching work identities in European context'. *Career Development International*, *9* (3), 199–221. https:// doi:10.1108/13620430410535823

Kohlsdorf, M., & Junior, A. D. C. (2017). O autorrelato na pesquisa em psicologiada saúde: desafios metodológicos. *Psicologia Argumento*, *27*, 131-142. https:// doi:10.7213/psicolargum.v27i57.19763

Lee, L., & Qomariyah, A. (2015). Exploring Expatriate Adjustment from Expatriate's Intelligence and Family Adaptability: A meta-Analytic Approach. *International J. Soc. Sci. & Education*, *5*, 374–398. doi:10.1177/1470595819836688

Lemos, A. H., Cavazotte, F. S. C., & Souza, D. O. S. (2015). De empregado a empresário: mudanças no sentido do trabalho para empreendedores. *Revista Pensamento Contemporâneo em Administração*, *11*(5),103-115. https:// doi:10.12712/rpca.v11i5.836

Lips-Wiersma, M., & Morris, L. (2009). Discriminating between 'meaningful work' and the 'management of meaning'. *Journal of Business Ethics*, *88*(3), 491–511. doi:10.100710551-009-0118-9

Loweree, J., Reichlin-Melnick, A., & Ewing, W. (May, 2020). *The Impact of COVID-19 on Noncitizens and Across the U.S. Immigration System*. American Immigration Council. https://www.americanimmigrationcouncil.org/research/impact-covid-19-us-immigration-system

Machado, H. V. (2003). A identidade e o contexto organizacional: perspectivas de análise. *Revista de Administração Contemporânea*, *7*(spe), 51-73. doi:10.1590/S1415-65552003000500004

Marcelino, P., & Cavalcante, S. (2012). Por uma definição de terceirização. *Caderno CRH*, *25*(65), 331–346. doi:10.1590/S0103-49792012000200010

Martins, D., & Sousa, A. (2015). *La adaptación intercultural de la familia como factor de éxito en las misiones internacionales de expatriados portugueses*. [Dissertação de mestrado, Instituto Politécnico do Porto, Porto, Portugal].

Mcnulty, Y., & Brewster, C. (2017). Theorizing the meaning(s) of 'expatriate': Establishing boundary conditions for business expatriates. *International Journal of Human Resource Management*, *28*(1), 27–61. doi:10.1080/09585192.2016.1243567

Medina, C., & Posso, C. (2011). South American immigrants in the USA. *Journal of Economic Studies (Glasgow, Scotland), 40*(2), 255–279. doi:10.1108/01443581311283709

Mendes, A. A., & Brasil, D. R. (2020). A Nova Lei de Migração Brasileira e sua Regulamentação da Concessão de Vistos aos Migrantes. *Sequência (Florianópolis), 84*(84), 64–88. doi:10.5007/2177-7055.2020v43n84p64

Ministério das Relações Exteriores. Secretaria de Assuntos e Soberania Nacional e Cidadania (2020). *Comunidade Brasileira no Exterior (Estimativas 2020).*

Miscenko, D., & Day, D. (2016). Identity and identification at work. *Organizational Psychology Review, 6*(3), 215–247. doi:10.1177/2041386615584009

Moher, D., Liberati, A., Tetzlaff, J., & Altman, D. G.The PRISMA Group. (2009). Preferred reporting items for systematic reviews and meta-analyses: The PRISMA Statement. *PLoS Medicine, 6*(7), e1000097. doi:10.1371/journal.pmed.1000097 PMID:19621072

Morin, E. M. (2001). Os sentidos do trabalho. *Revista de Administração de Empresas*, 41(3), 8-19. https:// doi// doi:10.1590/S0034-75902001000300002

Moura, A. O. R., & Silva, L. C. O. (2019). Centralidade do trabalho, metas e realização profissional: intersecções entre trabalho e carreira. *Revista De Administração Mackenzie*, 20(1), 150-200. https://Dx.Doi.Org/10.1590/1678-6971/Eramg190087

MOW. (1987). *Meaning of Work International Research Team. The meaning of work.* Academic Press.

Nordstrom, J. (2020). Teaching in the periphery: Teacher identity in community language schools. *Teaching and Teacher Education, 96*(2), 121–130. doi:10.1016/j.tate.2020.103192

Oliveira, A. T. R. (2017). Nova lei brasileira de migração: Avanços, desafios e ameaças. *Revista Brasileira de Estudos de Populacao, 34*(1), 171–179. doi:10.20947/S0102-3098a0010

Oliveira, H. N., Silva, C. A. M., & Oliveira, A. T. R. (2019). Imigração internacional: Uma alternativa para os impactos das mudanças demográficas no Brasil? *Revista Brasileira de Estudos de Populacao, 36*, 10–20. doi:10.20947/S0102-3098a0076

Oliveira, M. R., Junior, J. S., Benfica, V. B. M., & Royer, A. S. S. (2015). Ressignificação da identidade no processo de imigração haitiana: Uma pesquisa numa cidade do Sul do Brasil. *Revista Brasileira de Tecnologias Sociais, 2*(2), 145–159. doi:10.14210/rbts.v2n2.p145-159

Piaget, J. (1978). La equilibración de las estructuras cognitivas. Problema central del desarrollo. Madrid: Siglo XXI.

Pratt, M. G., & Ashforth, B. E. (2003). Fostering meaningfulness in working and at work. In K. S. Cameron, J. E. Dutton, & R. E. Quinn (Eds.), *Positive organizational scholarship* (pp. 309–327). Berrett-Koehler.

Reeves, S. (2016). Ideas for the development of the interprofessional education and practice field: an update. *J Interprof Care, 30*(4), 405-7. https:// doi:10.1080/13561820.2016.1197735

Reis, D. P., & Puente-Palacios, K. (2019). Team effectiveness: The predictive role of team identity. *Management Journal, 54*(2), 141–153. doi:10.1108/RAUSP-07-2018-0046

Roberman, S. (2013). All That is Just Ersatz: The Meaning of Work in the Life of Immigrant Newcomers. *Ethos (Berkeley, Calif.)*, *41*(1), 1–23. doi:10.1111/etho.12000

Romero, J. G. (2013). What circumstances lead a government to promote brain drain? *Journal of Economics*, *108*(2), 173–202. doi:10.100700712-012-0272-x

Rosenbaum, S. (2016). Todos Sacrifican: Immigrant Organizing and the Meanings of (Domestic) Work. *Working USA*, *19*(2), 187–206. doi:10.1111/wusa.12236

Rossit, R. A. S., Freitas, M. A. O., Batista, S. H. S. S., & Batista, N. A. (2018). Construção da identidade profissional na Educação Interprofissional em Saúde: Percepção de egressos. Interface (Botucatu). *Interface: Comunicacao, Saude, Educacao*, *32*(1, suppl 1), 399–410. doi:10.1590/1807-57622017.0184

Rosso, B., Dekas, K., & Wrzesniewski, A. (2010). On the meaning of work: A theoretical integration and review. *Research in Organizational Behavior*, *30*, 91–127. doi:10.1016/j.riob.2010.09.001

Saksvik, P., Dahl-Jorgensen, C., Eiken, T., & Tvedt, S. (2010). Identity, Over-Commitment, Work Environment, and Health Outcomes among Immigrant Workers. *Journal of Identity and Migration Studies*, *4*, 50-60. https:// doi:10.3390/ijerph17228616

Saksvik, P., Dahl-Jorgensen, C., & Tvedt, S. (2013). Migrant Labor in the Workforce. *JIMS*, *7*, 95–110. doi:10.1177/0022185618824137

Salas, E., Shuffler, M. L., Thayer, A. L., Bedwell, W. L., & Lazarra, E. H. (2015). Understanding and improving teamwork in organizations: A scientifically based practical guide. *Human Resource Management*, *54*(4), 599–622. doi:10.1002/hrm.21628

Sampaio, R. F., & Mancini, M. C. (2007). Estudos de revisão sistemática: Um guia para síntese criteriosa da evidência científica. *Brazilian Journal of Physical Therapy*, *11*(1), 83–89. doi:10.1590/S1413-35552007000100013

Shan, H., & Guo, S. (2013). Learning as sociocultural practice: Chinese immigrant professionals negotiating differences and identities in the Canadian labor market. *Comparative Education*, *49*(1), 190–199. doi:10.1080/03050068.2012.740218

Sharabi, M. (2017). Ethno-religious groups work values and ethics: The case of Jews, Muslims and Christians in Israel. *International Review of Sociology*, *28*(1), 1–22. doi:10.1080/03906701.2017.1385226

Showers, F. (2018). Learning to care: Work experiences and identity formation among African immigrant care workers in the US. *International Journal of Care and Caring*, *2*(1), 7–25. doi:10.1332/2397 88218X15187914933434

Sigad, L., Eisikovits, Z., Strier, R., & Buchbinder, E. (2017). The meaning of work among immigrants living in poverty in Israel: Replanting roots of belonging: Meaning of work among Israeli immigrants living in poverty. *International Journal of Social Welfare*, *27*(2), 11–20. doi:10.1111/ijsw.12282

Silva, N., & Tolfo, S. R. (2011). Felicidade, Bem-estar e Assédio Moral: paradoxos e tensões nas organizações da atualidade. In L. Leopold (Ed.), *Fagúndez, D.; Sobreba, N. (Orgs.). Investigaciones e intervenciones innovadoras en el campo de la psicología de las organizaciones y el trabajo: el estado del arte* (pp. 2247–2260). Psicolibros Universitareo – Conitriun.

Soares, C. B., Hoga, L. A. K., Peduzzi, M., Sangaleti, C., Yonekura, T., Silva, D. R., & Audebert, D. (2014). Revisão integrativa: Conceitos e métodos utilizados na enfermagem. *Rev. esc. Enferm*, *48*(2). Advance online publication. doi:10.1590/S0080-623420140000200020

Stebleton, M. (2012). The Meaning of Work for Black African Immigrant Adult College Students. *Journal of Career Development*, *39*(1), 50–75. doi:10.1177/0894845309358888

Sui, J., & Humphreys, G. W. (2017). Aging enhances cognitive biases to friends but not the self. *Psychon. Bull*, *24*, 2021–2030. https:// doi:10.3758/s13423-017-1264-1

Tedesco, J. C. (2014). Casamentos mistos: Novas sociabilidades e quadros coletivos. Aspectos da imigração de brasileiras na Itália. *Revista Estudos Feministas*, *22*(1), 115–133. doi:10.1590/S0104-026X2014000100007

Teodorescu, M. (2015). Herminia Ibarra: Working Identity, Your Personal Story, Strategies for Reinventing Your Career. *An extended book review*. https:// doi:10.13140/RG.2.1.4872.5920

Trindade, R.T.Z. (2017). Trabalho é vida e vida é trabalho!": escrita de si e imigração polonesa, a memória, o esquecimento e a identidade na narrativa de um intelectual imigrante. *Métis: história & cultura*. *16*(31), 173-193

Tu, M.-C., Zhou, S., Wong, S. N., & Okazaki, S. (2018). Realities of the American dream: Vocational experiences and intersecting invisibility of low-income Chinese immigrant laborers. *Journal of Vocational Behavior*, *113*, 1–29. doi:10.1016/j.jvb.2018.10.009

United Nations. (2020). Secretaria de imigração. *Relatório de migração global 2020*. Caderno: Migrantes e refugiados.

Välipakka, H., Zeng, C., Lahti, M., & Croucher, S. (2016). Experiencing Cultural Contact at Work: An Exploration of Immigrants' Perceptions of Work in Finland. In S. Shenoy-Packer & E. Gabor (Eds.), *Immigrant Workers and Meanings of Work: Communicating Life and Career Transitions* (pp. 21–32). Peter Lang.

Yijälä, A., & Luoma, T. (2019). The Importance of Employment in the Acculturation Process of Well-Educated Iraqis in Finland: A Qualitative Follow-up Study. *Refugee Survey Quarterly*, *38*(3), 314–340. doi:10.1093/rsq/hdz009

Yu, K.-H. (2016). Immigrant workers responses to stigmatized work: Constructing dignity through moral reasoning. *The Journal of Industrial Relations*, *58*(5), 571–588. Advance online publication. doi:10.1177/0022185615609204

Zikic, M., & Richardson, J. (2015). What happens when you can't be who you are: Professional identity at the institutional periphery. *Human Relations*, *69*(1), 139–168. doi:10.1177/0018726715580865

KEY TERMS AND DEFINITIONS

Immigration: Movement of people from one country to another, in a permanent or temporary way, to work and/or live

Meaning of Work: Mentions reinterpretation assigned by each individual to the value of work based on their personal experience.

Meaningfulness of Work: Group of beliefs understood over the years about what work is, whereas meaning of work

PRIMA: Preferred Reporting Items for Systematic Review and Meta-Analysis

Professional Identity: Kind of group or company identity, related to career, formed from the feeling of belonging to a professional or occupational group and the choice of an area.

Systematic Review: Secondary study which, parting from a well-defined research question, have the objective of identifying, choosing, analyzing and summarizing important primary studies available in scientific literature.

Work Identity: Kind of social identity that poses work in a central position for an individual self-description.

Chapter 12
Flexibility of Work During the Pandemic:
The Cases of Portugal and Greece

Özgün Sarımehmet Duman
https://orcid.org/0000-0001-9882-2544
Hacettepe University, Turkey

ABSTRACT

Economic recovery programmes implemented in Portugal and Greece during the Eurozone crisis prioritised atypical forms of work to increase the efficiency and productivity of labour. Just after they exited their structural adjustment programmes, there happened the COVID-19 outbreak with further challenges to their economic wellbeing and labour-capital relations. This chapter aims to comparatively analyse the labour market indicators in flexible forms of work before and during the pandemic. It argues that the economic policies implemented during the COVID-19 crisis had initially aimed to contain the adverse effects of the pandemic on societies, by simply limiting the contagion among individuals. With their widespread coverage, COVID-19 measures tended to sustain the already-in-place flexibilisation policies with increasing numbers in part-time and temporary employment relations. In this respect, COVID-19 practices in the labour market simply consolidated the economic recovery policies implemented in the post-crisis years in Portugal and Greece.

INTRODUCTION

Global economy has gone through important transitions in the past several decades. The need for a change in economic policy based on the falling rates of profits (Bullock & Yaffe, 1988; Savran, 1988; Wright, 1988) from the early 1970s and the end of bipolar world in the 1980s have introduced neoliberal economic values as the hegemonic policies (Harvey, 2005) in the developed and the developing world. 20th century global capitalist relations of production have been consolidated over the principles of international trade, transnational production, and global division of labour (O'Brian & Williams, 2016). This change has intensified the competition among national economies, industries, and firms. Capital has inclined

DOI: 10.4018/978-1-6684-4181-7.ch012

towards more inclusive surplus-value strategies and strengthened the discipline mechanisms on labour (Bonefeld, 1996). Hence, the conflict between capital and labour on the extraction of surplus-value has been carried to the global platform.

As the national and regional economies have become comparatively more interdependent in time, recent economic crises such as 1994 Mexican crisis, 1997 Asian crisis, 2001 Argentinian crisis had great impacts on global markets. Likewise, 2008 global economic crisis, originated in the US mortgage market, had important repercussions on national economies all over the globe. It also posed a severe challenge for the EU and its member states in the form of the Eurozone crisis (Sarımehmet Duman, 2014; Ioannou, Leblond, & Niemann, 2015; Warren, 2017).

The European Commission introduced new mechanisms in the failing countries, with a specific focus on economic restructuring to improve economic indicators. The European Stability Mechanism (ESM) strengthened the relationship between structural adjustment programmes and conditionalities (Sarımehmet Duman, 2020). There existed a direct correlation between conditionalities put forward for the release of loans to bailout economies and implementation of structural adjustment policies in the European periphery. These conditionalities mainly involved reforms to restructure the production relations with mechanisms to increase efficiency and productivity of labour (ESM, 2017). Peripheral economies, especially the bailout countries benefited from the ESM such as Ireland, Cyprus, Portugal, and Greece, implemented comprehensive reforms aiming to increase the flexibility of work, and hence, to bring their levels of competitiveness to the level of core economies. These reforms had important repercussions on deregulation of production relations and structurally changed the relationship between labour and capital. Thus, the aim of the ESM had gone beyond improving the economic indicators and meant to have long-term structural effects on these economies. The bailout countries started to restructure their productive markets towards the target of boosting competitiveness (Sarımehmet Duman, 2020).

Just after the bailout countries exited their structural adjustment programmes, there happened the SARS-CoV-2 (COVID-19) outbreak with further challenges to economic wellbeing. COVID-19 started to spread through the world from December 2019, and took markets and societies under its influence from February 2020. World Health Organization (WHO) called this new situation as a 'pandemic', which generated a big challenge for countries in economic, political, and social terms.

The COVID-19 crisis had important implications on the labour market. Quarantine policies spread the implementation of atypical forms of work such as short-time and part-time work, telework, temporary work and subcontracted work (ILO, 2020). These flexible forms of work caused increasing number of job losses and further limited the labour's social benefits (Sankaran, 2020). In that respect, COVID-19 labour policies functioned to consolidate the post-crisis flexibilisation processes with further adjustments in production relations. Although the post-COVID-19 flexibilisation happened as an unexpected imperative on the economy, it continued the post-crisis labour policies in the European periphery.

This paper aims to critically evaluate the move towards labour market flexibility in the first quarters of COVID-19 crisis in two bailout countries that had exited their structural adjustment programmes under the ESM just before the pandemic: Portugal and Greece. First, it offers an inquiry into flexibilisation of production relations in Portugal and Greece to present how their post-crisis labour markets reflected economic restructuring, i.e., increasing efficiency and productivity of labour. This analysis allows to monitor the levels of flexibility in the labour market in Portugal and Greece once they had faced the COVID-19 outbreak.

On this basis, the paper presents a comparative inquiry into the key indicators of labour market flexibility, that is, telework, short-time and part-time work, temporary work, and subcontracted work, during two consecutive crises: Eurozone economic crisis and the COVID-19 crisis. It discusses how Portugal and Greece *faced* and *responded* the COVID-19 crisis in terms of their labour market flexibility. The paper argues that the ESM programmes had increased the levels of flexibility in the labour markets in Portugal and Greece during their recovery from the Eurozone crisis. Moreover, labour market flexibility has started to be consolidated due to the economic policies implemented during the COVID-19 crisis in Portugal and Greece.

A BRIEF REVIEW OF THE LITERATURE: THE POLITICAL ECONOMY OF THE PANDEMIC

COVID-19 posed a real challenge for the world market, generating significant complications in health sector, production relations, labour market and international trade networks. These diverse challenges have also had a reflection in the discipline of international political economy in academic terms. Research outputs mainly included micro and macroeconomic activities (Jomo & Chowdhury, 2020; Lipscy, 2020; Campbell-Verduyn et al., 2021), trade (Baldwin & Weder di Mauro, 2020; Gruszczynski, 2020; Vidya & Prabheesh, 2020; Espitia et al., 2022), globalisation (Campbell-Verduyn & Roozendaal, 2020; Song & Zhou, 2020; Delios et al., 2021), supply chains (Gunessee & Subramanian, 2020; Ivanov, 2020; Butt, 2021; Chowdhury et al., 2021; Goel et al., 2021), labour markets and distribution of wealth (Anderton et al., 2020; Birinci et al., 2020; Lee et al., 2020; Drela et al., 2021). Research in social sciences also included publications on public health, management of the health crisis, international governance, gender inequalities, education policies, media, sustainability, and environmental impacts (Azcona et al., 2020; Bellini et al., 2020; Carvalho et al., 2021; DeSalvo et al., 2021; Ranjbari et al., 2021; Smith et al., 2021; Sousa-Uva et al., 2021; Santos et al., 2022).

Despite the increasing impact of COVID-19 related research in the scholarly world, flexibilisation of work remained rather understudied within the discipline of international political economy. Limited research on labour flexibility included Allen & Orifici, 2021; Feregrino Basurto, 2021; Hansen et al., 2021; Lirios, 2021; and Quazada et al., 2021. Some research on flexibilisation of work focused on specific countries such as Slovenia, China and Kosovo, or specific issues such as gender and climate change including Gashi et al., 2022; Ren et al., 2021; Štebe & Vovk, 2021; and Uršič, 2021. There were also a few publications on flexibilisation policies in Portuguese (Shaaban et al., 2020; Andrade & Lousã, 2021; and Lopes & Carreira, 2021;) and Greek (Katris, 2021 and Timokleia et al., 2021) labour markets, as well as some cross-country analyses including Portugal and Greece (Youmni & Cheikh, 2020; Kapitsinis, 2020; Kapitsinis et.al., 2020; and Kapitsinis & Sykas, 2021).

This paper aims to fill the gap in the literature by presenting a comparative analysis of the levels of flexibilisation in two bailout countries, i.e., Portugal and Greece. It initially presents a comparative outline of how Portugal and Greece had responded the devastating effects of the Eurozone crisis in the previous decade. It offers an inquiry into the coverage of structural adjustment programmes Portugal and Greece implemented under the ESM and assesses the scope of conditionalities on flexibility of work. Based on this background, the paper aims to outline the impact of the Covid-19 crisis on the flexibility of work. To serve this purpose, it comparatively evaluates key labour market indicators, that is, labour cost, real labour productivity per person, annual net earnings, part-time employment, and temporary employment, during the implementation of the bailout programmes and the first quarters of COVID-19. It argues that flexibilisation policies had been in increase during the implementation of the ESM programme and started to consolidate in the first year of the COVID-19 crisis in both Portugal and Greece.

FROM THE EUROZONE CRISIS TO THE PANDEMIC: FLEXIBILITY OF WORK IN THE EUROPEAN PERIPHERY

Diffusion of the global economic crisis to the Eurozone unveiled the flaws of tight economic integration in the European Union. Peripheral economies started to have serious economic difficulties, including balance of payments problems. Due to significant imbalances in the Eurozone, economic recovery policies prioritised mechanisms to bring core and peripheral economies to similar levels of productivity and competitiveness. The European Commission operationalised the ESM to provide financial assistance to the failing economies. ESM agendas included rescue packages, austerity measures and structural adjustment programmes. The ESM granted liquidity assistance in the form of structural adjustment programmes, which put conditionalities for the release of loans with the aim of economic restructuring (Sawicki, 2012; Sarımehmet Duman, 2020).

Among many other measures such as restoring public finances and financial sustainability, enhancing growth, promoting competitiveness and investment, and strengthening banks' liquidity and capital, structural adjustment programmes included labour market reforms that strikingly changed the labour and capital relations. These reforms mainly involved removal of labour market regulations and promotion of flexibilisation policies, i.e., atypical forms of work, contracting out, part-time work, temporary work, and telework. In this respect, the economic crisis generated a legitimate imperative to implement structural adjustment programmes, mainly including policy tools for restructuring production relations.

Flexibilisation of work aimed to increase profitability and competitiveness of peripheral economies, putting the "burden of adjustment" on labour's shoulders within "the regions with lower competitiveness and greater deficits, with swingeing cuts and painful austerity" (Varoufakis & Holland, 2012, p. 241). This policy was a strategic move to restructure the economies, bringing a striking change in labour's levels of efficiency and productivity "to increase competitiveness of both individual capitals and national markets in the global market" (Sarımehmet Duman, 2020, p. 133).

Starting from March 2020, COVID-19 pandemic started to take global markets under influence and rapidly spread among the markets. This quick flow was due to the world's "more interdependent and integrated" structure (van Barneveld et.al., 2020, p. 143) since the introduction of neoliberal policies in the 1980s and their consolidation in the early 2000s. The increasing trends in global air transport, rise in mobility and the growth of urbanised areas occurred to be the key drivers of the spread of the disease (Kapitsinis, 2020, p. 1029). Tightly connected international trade networks, transnational production processes and global division of labour played a significant role on the diffusion of this unique economic crisis throughout the world. Hence, it is plausible to argue that COVID-19 further highlighted the economic interdependency among markets, with certain implications on global supply chains, facing the global markets with significant slowdown in production processes.

The COVID-19 outbreak had three interlinked ways to affect the markets: demand perspective, supply perspective and the global financial system (Kousi et al., 2021, p. 8). On the demand side, the crisis resulted in a deceleration in exports and decrease in consumption and investment. On the supply side, disturbances in the global supply chains caused business closures and impeded the control on the crisis.

Finally, on the financial system side, the COVID-19 outbreak complicated the financial conditions for banks, businesses, and households.

Economic strategies, policies and measures have resulted in extensive outcomes for the global market. Flaws in the production processes at domestic levels have had important reflections on global supply chains – market access to certain goods and services was interrupted. The COVID-19 pandemic was reported as "highly asymmetric" (Lopes & Carreira, 2021, p. 2), with evidence from "the most vulnerable countries, and segments of the workforce being hardest hit" (Fana, et al., 2020, p. 392). As this economic bottleneck further disclosed the domestic and global inequalities and imbalances, there existed the necessity to execute diverse measures to keep the economies on track.

Governments responded the COVID-19 crisis with two correlated mechanisms to contain the adverse effects of the pandemic on societies. First, there appeared a need to control the pandemic with certain mechanisms to limit the contagion among workers. Quarantine practices that were coherent with their economic specificities such as the scale of the economy, sectoral differences, and national wealth aimed to reduce the density of workers in workplaces and lessen the risks of infection. Second, there was the necessity to overcome or limit the negative effects of the shortcomings in the market. It was perceived crucial to prevent any ruptures in supply chains, and to respond people's daily needs to nondurables and hygienic products by simply continuing production processes. These two mechanisms merged in increasing the flexibility of labour markets with atypical practices of telework, short-time and part-time work, temporary work, and subcontracted work. In other words, public health strategies implemented to contain the adverse effects of the pandemic were reinforced by flexibilisation policies in the labour market.

Diverse levels of economic development faced countries with changing quarantine policies, support mechanisms and subsidies in various sectors (Birinci et al., 2021, p. 2), unveiling global divergences as well as intra-class imbalances (Sokol & Pataccini, 2020). Workflow increased in some sectors and decreased in some others. The implications of COVID-19 policies were "unequal among social classes, with the poorest being the hardest hit" (Kapitsinis et al., 2020, p. 1). Blue-collar workers stayed in production lines whereas white-collar workers skipped to home-office practices. Moreover, these practices generated different results for people and societies depending on their gender, age, and citizenship (van Barneveld et al., 2020, p. 134). Hence, labour's struggle with the pandemic passed beyond surviving the health crisis and turned into a battle in the changing conditions of the labour market.

International Labour Organization (ILO) estimated that the pandemic could lead to the loss of 25 million jobs worldwide, which is much greater than the 2008 global economic crisis (ILO, 2020). It was also argued that the increase in the unemployment rate and hence job insecurity would "inevitably lead to losses in workers' income and a consequent fall in the consumption of goods and services" (Almeida & Santos, 2020, p. 995). In most cases, employment protection policies proved to be insufficient especially among young people, whose problems were rather acute even before 2020 (Kapitsinis et al., 2020, p. 11). In this respect, the COVID-19 pandemic deepened social inequalities, putting young people into a more vulnerable position under short-term and seasonal employment relations (Tidey, 2020).

The COVID-19 pandemic revealed the fatal consequences of "the sharp rise in economic inequality, the concentration of wealth in fewer and fewer hands and the increasing precarity of labour" (Sell, 2020, p. 152). The spread of the atypical forms of work and the flexibilisation policies in production processes increased poverty and the rate of unregistered economy in the global market (Lee et al., 2020, pp. 13-14). The spread of job losses in the labour market narrowed down the social security policies and carried atypical working relations to the status of the 'new normal' (Sankaran, 2020, p. 91).

The COVID-19 crisis also had important implications on the fragile economies of the Eurozone, which had exited their structural adjustment programmes a short time prior to the pandemic. Before a real economic recovery could be achieved in the Eurozone, markets were deeply shaken by economic scarcities, global supply chain problems and ruptures in international trade networks. As a quick response, bailout countries have implemented further measures to adjust their production processes to the new rules of the game – quarantine practices. Labour market policies, including flexibilisation of work, have been executed to handle the devastating economic effects of COVID-19.

Portugal

Portugal struggled with the implications of the Eurozone crisis due to its "long period of weak economic growth", accompanied by low interest rates, high wage growth and debt, and low productivity levels (ESM, 2020d). As a response to its devastating effects on the economy, Portugal received €52 billion loans from the European Financial Stability Facility (EFSF) and an additional €26 billion from the IMF until 2014.

The EFSF structural adjustment programme mainly included fiscal consolidation policies with revenue-raising and expenditure-reducing measures, amendments in the financial sector for liquidity issues, and structural reforms to address "external and internal imbalances and to raise potential growth" by labour market reforms and liberalisation of services (ESM, 2014, p. 5). Portugal's adjustment programme involved 1993 conditionalities, 118 of which were directly linked to structural reforms to deal with the problems of competitiveness. These reforms introduced changes in the management of state-owned enterprises, public sector expenditure, market liberalisation to boost competition, privatisation, and decentralisation (ESM, 2020b).

Portugal implemented comprehensive structural reforms and had a clean exit from the programme with GDP growth reaching 1.2% and budget deficit decreasing to 4% in 2014 (ESM, 2014, p. 6). However, 2019 Annual Report indicated that the economic indicators worsened towards the end of the 2010s with moderate growth, increased trade deficit and fiscal deficit going above the target (ESM, 2019, p. 29). In overall, the Report concluded that "Portugal's high public debt burden remains an important vulnerability" (ESM, 2019, p. 29).

The COVID-19 crisis came shortly after the recent recovery from the economic crisis that Portugal "went through strict fiscal austerity" (Shaaban et al., 2020, p. 1). Upon the first signs of COVID-19 in Portugal, the government declared a state of emergency on March 18, to be renewed in the following months. It adopted extraordinary measures "in the form of restrictions over domestic and international movements and the application of social distancing rules" to "contain the transmission of the virus" and "prevent the expansion of the disease" (Shaaban et al., 2020, p. 2). Economic indicators worsened due to restrictive measures. GDP fell by 7.6% in 2020 and registered numbers of unemployed reached at a rate of 7.5% in January 2021 with almost 100 thousand increase (Ferreira, 2021). Negative employment trends from the first quarter of 2020 worsened the economic situation in Portugal (Kapitsinis, 2021, p. 7).

Portuguese government also introduced comprehensive measures in the labour market. It regulated atypical forms of work by practices such as reduction of the normal working time and suspension of employment contracts based on employers' demand (Carvalho Martins, 2020, pp. 2-3). These regulations also meant to rule out any allusions on job losses by prohibiting dismissals, but allowed the termination of contracts, which left employers with room for manoeuvre to secure capital accumulation during the COVID-19 crisis. Temporary workers became more vulnerable in the labour market – they were made redundant or dismissed permanently due to COVID-19 measures. Short-term unemployment rate skyrocketed to 45% in 2020 and converted into long-term unemployment, increasing it to 32% between April 2020 and April 2021 (Ferreira, 2021).

As another dimension of flexible work, Portugal mastered the practice of telework during the one-decade-long economic crisis and got ready to adapt teleworking as a response to the pandemic (Gonçalves et al., 2021). The government made teleworking mandatory, as a flexible working type alternative to the on-site mode. "Performing work in a remote location or far from central offices or production facilities" (Gupta et al., 1995; Bentley et al., 2016, cited in Andrade & Lousã, 2021, p. 1), telecommuting revealed "role overload, after-hours work-related technology use, and low job autonomy accounted for the prediction of work-family conflict" in Portugal (Andrade & Lousã, 2021, p. 9). Telework brought flexibility in the workplace as well as on the schedule, bringing "inter-role conflicts" in the family, "negative impacts on work-life balance" and "extension of working hours" (Andrade & Lousã, 2021, pp. 3-4). It generated asymmetrical implications on Portuguese labour market depending on gender, age, geographic regions, and sectors of activity (Almeida & Santos, 2020, pp. 9990-1000).

Greece

Greece was severely hit by the Eurozone crisis. Economic recovery process incorporated three structural adjustment programmes under consecutive mechanisms: (i) bilateral Greek Loan Facility (€52.9 billion), (ii) the EFSF (€141.8 billion), and (iii) the ESM (€61.9 billion). Greece received a total amount of €288.7 billion to improve its financial indicators and generate economic restructuring.

The Greek economy was defined by its major structural problems such as "long-standing financial, economic, and structural weaknesses" (ESM, 2020a, p. 13), "wage rises outpac[ing] productivity gains" and inability "to compete with other countries" (ESM, 2020c). ESM programme mainly included policies to restore the sustainability of Greek public finances, financial viability, growth, competitiveness, investment potential and the wellbeing of the public sector (ESM, 2018, p. 2). Among others, the objectives of growth and competitiveness contained major reforms in the labour market to extend atypical forms of work and deregulation practices. 147 of 4542 conditionalities were related to measures taken for economic restructuring to fuel competitiveness under the category of structural labour market policies. These reforms mainly included regulations on collective bargaining processes, restrictions in regulated professions, privatisation, and liberalisation.

During the implementation of structural adjustment programmes, Greece agreed to execute comprehensive labour market reforms, including privatisations, regulations to attract investment and support job creation, removal of administrative barriers to competition, liberalisations in employment protection legislation, amendments in industrial policies (industrial action and collective dismissals), and extension of temporary employment practices (ESM, 2020b). Despite the discernible gap between the undertakings and implementations of structural reforms, it would be plausible to argue that economic recovery process restructured Greek market in various respects.

During the decade-long recovery process, economy had a growing tendency – budget deficit reached to a surplus of 0.6% and current account deficit fell to -0.9% in 2017 (ESM, 2018, p. 1). The healthcare system underwent "a series of structural and efficiency-oriented reforms" (Kousi et al., 2021, p. 3). By means of these reforms cutting public spending on social services, Greece reached its fiscal target for the fifth consecutive year and had steady growth at 1.9% in 2019. 2019 Annual Report affirmed that reform policies decreased public expenditure with lower levels of spending in public investment, but further actions were needed to "safeguard financial stability" (ESM, 2019, pp. 24-26).

There existed a striking change in production relations based on the spread of atypical forms of work in the labour market. Unemployment rate decreased due to increase in labour demand, which was mainly bred by part-time and temporary employment practices (Hazakis, 2021, p. 10). This proved that flexible forms of work gained prevalence in the Greek labour market during the economic recovery. It was stated in the 2019 Annual Report that Greek economy had taken an important step in structural transition, which was to be advanced through productivity mechanisms in the labour market (ESM, 2019, p. 26).

Greece was one of the first countries adopting restrictive measures against the spread of the virus and its implications on the economy. Greek government introduced a complete prohibition on public movement in March to slow down the contagion. Legislations included the closure of certain areas of the country, school closures and termination of educational facilities, extension of parental leave practices, lockdown and interruption of business operations, atypical working practices, suspension of employment contracts in line with no dismissals policy, and termination of social security rights (Bakirtzi, 2020). The government introduced fiscal measures to support households and businesses against the devastating effects of the COVID-19 crisis (Hazakis, 2021, p. 2).

As Greek economy was recovering from a long period of deep recession due to the economic crisis (Kousi et al., 2021, p. 2), the COVID-19 pandemic posed a real challenge to its fiscal balance, production relations and monetary operations. This had important repercussions on outputs and trade flows, employment, and poverty (Hazakis, 2021, pp. 9-10). As tourism was a major industry in the country, travel restrictions hit the economy significantly (Kousi et al., 2021, p. 13).

Low-income families suffering from high poverty rates during the Eurozone crisis were particularly affected by the pandemic (OECD, 2021, p. 138). Total employment declined 2.8% in the second quarter of 2020 and 1.1% in the third quarter of 2020, compared to the same period of the previous year (Kapitsinis, 2021, p. 4). Unemployment strikingly increased, especially effecting female and young workers in the labour market (Katris, 2021, p. 8). In sum, it is plausible to argue that increasing unemployment, undeclared work, and flexible forms of work in line with decreasing female and full-time employment significantly changed production relations in Greece.

FLEXIBILITY OF WORK BEFORE AND DURING THE PANDEMIC: A COMPARATIVE ANALYSIS

Both Portugal and Greece exited their structural adjustment programmes a short while before the start of the COVID-19 outbreak. This had certain implications on their way of handling the pandemic in terms of the introduction of restrictive measures, including labour market reforms. Hence, it is important to discuss how Portugal and Greece *faced* and *responded* the COVID-19 outbreak in terms of their levels of flexibility in the labour market.

This section comparatively analyses labour cost, labour productivity and annual net earnings before and during the pandemic. The comparison of flexibility with indicators available in part-time employment, temporary employment and their ratio in full employment provides a solid basis to discuss the scale of the tendency towards atypical forms of work in Portugal and Greece during the COVID-19 crisis.

Figure 1. Labour cost before the pandemic (2016=100)
Source: OECD, 2021b.

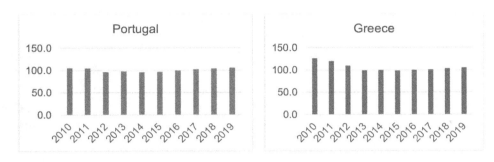

As shown in Figure 1, the increasing trend in labour cost from the early 2000s reached a pre-crisis peak around 2008 in Portugal and around 2010 in Greece. Under the influence of structural adjustment programmes, it had a declining tendency until 2016. Taking the year of 2016 as equal to 100, the figure shows that labour cost had a slight increase between 2016 and 2019. It can be argued that Portugal and Greece had a significant decline in their labour costs during the implementation of structural adjustment programmes. In Portugal, labour costs started to have an upward trend once it exited its structural adjustment programmes. As Greece probably had the firmest programme, labour cost had a prominent decrease during the initial years of the programme and only a minor increase in the following years.

Figure 2. Labour cost during the pandemic
Source: OECD, 2021b.

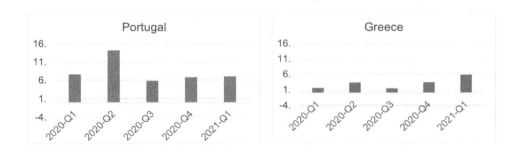

Labour cost had a sharp increase in both Portugal and Greece in the second quarter of 2020 (Figure 2). It then significantly declined between the second and the third quarters, but a steady increase started from the third quarter onwards.

Labour productivity is another key element of the labour market. Taking the year of 2010 as equal to 100 (Figure 3), this data outlines that labour productivity was very steady with very minor fluctuations in Portugal and Greece until early 2020. With the pandemic, the decline from 2019 to 2020 was 105.0 to 98.7 in Portugal and 87.5 to 81.4 in Greece.

Figure 3. Labour productivity before and during the pandemic (2010=100)
Source: OECD, 2021b.

Figure 4. Annual net earnings before and during the pandemic
Source: OECD, 2021b.

Pushing wages down is a major policy effecting the labour markets. Annual net earnings had slightly fluctuated during the crisis management years, with a tendency to increase in Portugal and to decrease in Greece (Figure 4). Under the influence of the pandemic in 2020, annual net earnings vaguely increased in Portugal and further decreased in Greece. Based on this, it can be argued that the COVID-19 pandemic did not have a major impact on earnings.

Part-time employment and temporary employment are both important forms of flexibilisation. As shown in Figure 5, Portugal had a sharp peak in the first year of its programme, but this increase then sloped down towards the end of the decade. Similarly, temporary employment also had an increasing tendency in the pre-crises years until a downward movement started with the emergence of the crisis. Part-time employment had an increasing tendency even in the pre-crisis years and gained pace in Greece during the adjustment programmes. Number of people employed as part-time almost had around 30% increase. Greece had an enormous upsurge from 2010 to 2019.

A comparison of part time and temporary employment to full employment rate between 2011 and 2019 indicates that part time employment had an increasing tendency in both countries even when full employment was in decline (Figure 5). Likewise, increase in full employment during the adjustment programmes had a reflection on atypical forms of work.

COVID-19 pandemic had important implications on employment rate and atypical forms of work. As seen in Figure 6, full employment rate had a decline in the second quarter of 2020, which seemed to recover in the following quarters until 2021. Strikingly, employment rate had another wave of decline in the first quarter of 2021. Part-time employment had a continuous decrease in Portugal and Greece.

Temporary employment sharply fell in the second quarter of 2020, but an increasing tendency was seen in the following quarters in Portugal. It had a decline in 2020 and started to recover in 2021 in Greece.

Figure 5. Employment, part-time employment, and temporary employment rates before the pandemic
Source: OECD, 2021b.

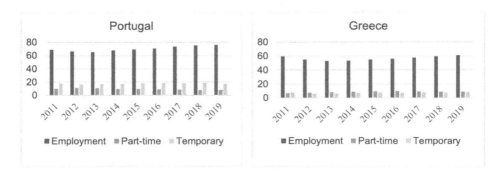

Figure 6. Employment, part-time employment, and temporary employment rates during the pandemic
Source: OECD, 2021b.

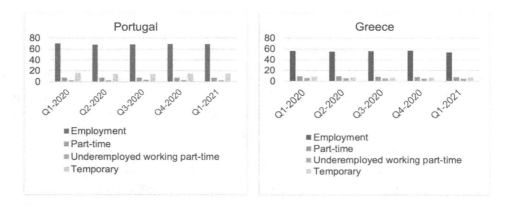

When it comes to the share of atypical forms of work within employment (Figure 7), the sharp negative change in full employment rate also had reflections on part-time and temporary employment in Portugal. All three indicators turned positive in the third quarter of 2020. Despite an increase in the percentage of change in full employment in the fourth quarter, it is shown that the change in part-time employment stayed negative. Temporary employment, on the other hand, had a significant increase in the fourth quarter.

As also shown in Figure 7, the percentage of change in temporary employment was much bigger than the percentage of change in full employment in Greece in the second quarter of 2020. When the change in full employment turned positive in the third quarter indicating that employment rate started to recover, the change in part-time employment sharply increased. Whereas full time employment worsened in the first quarter of 2021, both part-time and temporary employment started to recover.

Figure 7. % change in employment, part-time employment, and temporary employment rates during the pandemic
Source: OECD, 2021b.

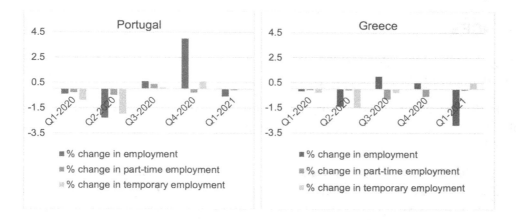

CONCLUSION

This paper analysed the implications of COVID-19 on employment relations in two peripheral countries of the Eurozone, i.e., Portugal and Greece, which had long years of economic recovery after the Eurozone crisis and exited their structural adjustment programmes a short while before the COVID-19 outbreak. It broadly covered the economic background of the recovery policies in the earlier decade in Portugal and Greece. To serve this, it analysed the key parameters of production relations and flexible forms of work to outline the frame of economic transformation. The paper claimed that the economic recovery programmes mainly intended comprehensive restructuring in the labour market not only to increase productivity, efficiency, and competitiveness of these economies, but also to adjust weaker Eurozone economies to a higher standard.

The paper argued that Portugal and Greece encountered the COVID-19 outbreak under the implications of structural adjustment programmes, which generated significant flexibilisation in employment relations. The COVID-19 crisis brought additional measures, such as quarantine practices, encouraging short-time, part-time and temporary employment as well as telework and subcontracted work. In the second quarter of 2020, labour cost had a sharp increase whereas full-time, part-time and temporary employment declined in both Portugal and Greece. A steady recovery in labour cost and employment rates started from the third quarter of 2020 onwards. Despite an increase in the percentage of change in full employment in the fourth quarter, the change in part-time employment stayed negative. Temporary employment, on the other hand, had a significant increase in the fourth quarter.

The paper concludes that the economic policies implemented during the COVID-19 crisis had initially aimed to contain the adverse effects of the pandemic on societies, by simply limiting the contagion among individuals. With their widespread coverage, COVID-19 measures tended to sustain the already-in-place flexibilisation policies with increasing numbers in part-time and temporary employment relations. In this respect, COVID-19 practices in the labour market simply consolidated the economic recovery policies implemented in the post-crisis years in Portugal and Greece. It would be interesting to conduct further research on future developments in labour market flexibility to present a deeper analysis on its implications on the relationship between labour and capital.

REFERENCES

Allen, D., & Orifici, A. (2021). Home Truths: What did Covid-19 Reveal About Workplace Flexibility. *Australian Journal of Labour Law*, *34*(1&2), 77–94.

Almeida, F., & Santos, J. D. (2020). The effects of COVID-19 on job security and unemployment in Portugal. *The International Journal of Sociology and Social Policy*, *40*(9/10), 995–1003. doi:10.1108/IJSSP-07-2020-0291

Anderton, R., Botelho, V., Consolo, A. da Silva, A.D., Foroni, C., Mohr, M., & Vivian, L. (2020). The impact of the COVID-19 pandemic on the euro area labour market. *ECB Economic Bulletin*, 8.

Andrade, C., & Lousã, E. P. (2021). Telework and Work–Family Conflict during COVID-19 Lockdown in Portugal: The Influence of Job-Related Factors. *Administrative Sciences*, *11*(3), 1–14. doi:10.3390/admsci11030103

Azcona, G., Bhatt, A., Davies, S. E., Harman, S., Smith, J., & Wenham, C. (2020). Spotlight on gender, COVID-19 and the SDGs: will the pandemic derail hard-won progress on gender equality? Spotlight on the SDGs. UN Women, New York.

Bakirtzi, E. (2020). COVID-19 and Labour Law: Greece. *Italian Labour Law e-Journal,* Special Issue 1(13), 1-4.

Baldwin, R., & Weder di Mauro, B. (Eds.). (2020). *Economics in the Time of COVID-19*. London: Centre for Economic Policy Research (CEPR) Press. https://voxeu.org/content/economics-time-covid-19

Bellini, M. I., Pengel, L., Potena, L., & Segantini, L. (2020). COVID-19 and education: Restructuring after the pandemic. *Transplant International*, *34*(2), 220–223. doi:10.1111/tri.13788 PMID:33205410

Birinci, S., Karahan, F., Mercan, Y., & See, K. (2021). Labor market policies during an epidemic. *Journal of Public Economics*, *194*, 1–15. doi:10.1016/j.jpubeco.2020.104348

Bonefeld, W. (1996). Monetarism and Crisis. In W. Bonefeld & J. Holloway (Eds.), *Global Capital, National State and the Politics of Money* (pp. 35–68). Macmillan. doi:10.1007/978-1-349-14240-8_3

Bullock, P., & Yaffe, D. (1988). Inflation, the Crisis and the Post-War Boom. In N. Satlıgan & S. Savran (Eds.), *Crisis of the World Capitalism* (pp. 223–291). Alan Press. (in Turkish)

Butt, A. S. (2021). Strategies to mitigate the impact of COVID-19 on supply chain disruptions: A multiple case analysis of buyers and distributors. *International Journal of Logistics Management*. doi:10.1108/IJLM-11-2020-0455

Campbell-Verduyn, M., Metinsoy, S., Linsi, L., & Brandi, C. (Eds.). (2021). *Special Collection: Global Political Economy of COVID-19*. Global Perspectives.

Campbell-Verduyn, M., & van Roozendaal, G. (2020). The Covid-19 Pandemic: Continuity and Change in the International Political Economy. *Globalisation Studies Groningen.* https://research.rug.nl/en/publications/the-covid-19-pandemic-continuity-and-change-in-the-international-

Carvalho, V., Rita, R., & Chambel, M. J. (2021). Teleworkers' flourishing during COVID-19 lockdown: The work-family relationship. *Occupational and Environmental Medicine, 78*(1).

Carvalho Martins, D. (2020). COVID-19 and Labour Law: Portugal. *Italian Labour Law e-Journal, 1*(13), 1-4.

Chowdhury, P., Paul, S. K., Kaisar, S., & Moktadir, A. (2021). COVID-19 pandemic related supply chain studies: A systematic review. *Transportation Research Part E, Logistics and Transportation Review, 148*, 1–26. doi:10.1016/j.tre.2021.102271 PMID:33613082

Delios, A., Perchthold, G., & Capri, A. (2021). Cohesion, COVID-19 and contemporary challenges to globalization. *Journal of World Business, 56*(3), 1–8. doi:10.1016/j.jwb.2021.101197

DeSalvo, K., Hughes, Bç, Bassett, M., Benjamin, G., Fraser, M., Galea, S., & Gracia, J.N. (2021) Public Health COVID-19 Impact Assessment: Lessons Learned and Compelling Needs. *NAM Perspect.*

Drela, K., Malkowska, A., Bera, A., & Tokarz-Kocik, A. (2021). Instruments for Managing the EU Labour Market in the Face of the COVID-19 Crisis. *European Research Studies, 24*(1), 984–998. doi:10.35808/ersj/2006

ESM. (2014). *Conclusion of EFSF financial assistance programme for Portugal: an overview.* ESM. https://www.esm.europa.eu/sites/default/files/portugal_exit_pppresentation.pdf

ESM. (2017). *Lending Toolkit.* ESM. https://www.esm.europa.eu/assistance/lending-toolkit

ESM. (2018). *Conclusion of ESM programme for Greece: an overview.* ESM. https://www.esm.europa.eu/sites/default/files/greece_programme_conclusion_presentation.pdf

ESM. (2019). *Annual Report.* ESM. https://www.esm.europa.eu/sites/default/files/esm-annual-report-2019.pdf

ESM. (2020a). *Lessons from Financial assistance to Greece.* ESM. https://www.esm.europa.eu/sites/default/files/lessons-financial-assistance-greece.pdf

ESM. (2020b). *Conditionality.* ESM. https://www.esm.europa.eu/assistance/programme-database/conditionality

ESM. (2020c). *Greece emerges from crisis.* ESM. https://www.esm.europa.eu/assistance/greece#bringing_greece_back_to_growth

ESM. (2020d). Portugal regained economic footing. https://www.esm.europa.eu/assistance/portugal

Espitia, A., Mattoo, A., Rocha, N., Ruta, M., & Winkle, D. (2022). Pandemic trade: COVID-19, remote work and global value chains. Invited Review. *World Economy, 45*(2), 561–589. doi:10.1111/twec.13117 PMID:33821085

Fana, M., Pérez, S. T., & Fernández-Macías, E. (2020). Employment impact of Covid-19 crisis: From short term effects to long terms prospects. *Economia e Politica Industriale, 47*(3), 391–410. doi:10.100740812-020-00168-5

Feregrino Basurto, M. (2021). Labor Flexibility, Teleworking and Covid-19. *Tendencias, 22*(2), 371–395. doi:10.22267/rtend.212202.181

Ferreira, P. (2021). *The impact of the COVID-19 crisis on labour markets around the world: The case of Portugal.* ILO. https://www.ilo.org/wcmsp5/groups/public/---ed_emp/documents/presentation/wcms_797054.pdf

Gashi, A., Kutllovci, E., & Zhushi, G. (2022). E-work evaluation through work–life balance, job effectiveness, organizational trust and flexibility: Evidence from Kosovo during COVID-19. *Employee Relations, 44*(2), 371–385. doi:10.1108/ER-04-2021-0136

Goel, R. K., Saunoris, J. W., & Goel, S. S. (2021). Supply chain performance and economic growth: The impact of COVID-19 disruptions. *Journal of Policy Modeling, 43*(2), 298–316. doi:10.1016/j.jpolmod.2021.01.003

Gonçalves, S. P., Santos, J. V., Silva, I. S., Veloso, A., Brandão, C., & Moura, R. (2021). COVID-19 and People Management: The View of Human Resource Managers. *Administrative Sciences, 11*(3), 1–13. doi:10.3390/admsci11030069

Gruszczynski, L. (2020). The COVID-19 Pandemic and International Trade: Temporary Turbulence or Paradigm Shift? *European Journal of Risk Regulation, 11*(2), 337-342.

Gunessee, S., & Subramanian, N. (2020). Ambiguity and its coping mechanisms in supply chains lessons from the Covid-19 pandemic and natural disasters. *International Journal of Operations & Production Management, 40*(7/8), 1201–1223. doi:10.1108/IJOPM-07-2019-0530

Hansen, B., Sabia, J. J., & Schaller, J. (2021). Schools, Job Flexibility, and Married Women's Labor Supply: Evidence from the Covid-19 Pandemic. *Working Paper 29660.* https://www.nber.org/papers/w29660

Harvey, D. (2005). *A Brief History of Neoliberalism.* Oxford University Press. doi:10.1093/oso/9780199283262.001.0001

Hazakis, K.J. (2021). Is there a way out of the crisis? Macroeconomic challenges for Greece after the Covid-19 pandemic. *European Politics and Society,* 1-15.

ILO. (2020). *Almost 25 million jobs could be lost worldwide as a result of COVID-19, says ILO.* ILO. https://www.ilo.org/global/about-the-ilo/newsroom/news/WCMS_738742/lang--en/index.htm

Ivanov, D. (2020). Predicting the impacts of epidemic outbreaks on global supply chains: A simulation-based analysis on the coronavirus outbreak (COVID-19/SARS-CoV-2) case. *Transportation Research Part E, Logistics and Transportation Review, 136,* 1–14. doi:10.1016/j.tre.2020.101922 PMID:32288597

Jomo, K. S., & Chowdhury, A. (2020). COVID-19 Pandemic Recession and Recovery. *Development, 63*(2-4), 226–237. doi:10.105741301-020-00262-0 PMID:33223764

Kapitsinis, N. (2020). The underlying factors of the COVID-19 spatially uneven spread. Initial evidence from regions in nine EU countries. *Regional Science Policy and Practice*, *12*(6), 1027–1045. doi:10.1111/rsp3.12340

Kapitsinis, N., Saroukou, A., Sykas, G., Psarologos, D., Kanelleas, A., Voulgaris, D., Gourzis, K., & Gialis, S. (2020). An overview of the Covid-19 effects on employment during 2020. Evidence from Cyprus, France, Spain, Greece, Italy, Malta, Croatia and Portugal. *Technical Report*, University of Aegean/YOUTH Share - Coronavirus Response & Labour Statistics.

Kapitsinis, N., & Sykas, G. (2021). A brief overview on the uneven impact of the Covid-19 pandemic on employment, 2020Q2 and 2020Q3: Evidence from Cyprus, France, Spain, Greece, Italy, Malta, Croatia and Portugal. *Technical Report*, University of Aegean/YOUTH Share - Coronavirus Response & Labour Statistics.

Katris, C. (2021). Unemployment and COVID-19 Impact in Greece: A Vector Autoregression (VAR) Data Analysis. *Engineering Proceedings*, *5*(41), 1–11.

Kousi, T., Mitsi, L. C., & Simos, J. (2021). The Early Stage of COVID-19 Outbreak in Greece: A Review of the National Response and the Socioeconomic Impact. *International Journal of Environmental Research and Public Health*, *18*(322), 1–17. doi:10.3390/ijerph18010322 PMID:33406780

Lee, S., Schmidt-Klau, D., & Verick, S. (2020). The Labour Market Impact of the COVID-19: A Global Perspective. *The Indian Journal of Labour Economics*, *63*(S1), 11–15. doi:10.100741027-020-00249-y PMID:33041544

Lipscy, P. Y. (2020). COVID-19 and the Politics of Crisis. *International Organization*, *74*(S1), 98–127. doi:10.1017/S0020818320000375

Lirios, C. G. (2021). Climate and Labor Flexibility Again Covid-19. *Jurnal Office*, *7*(1), 55–70.

Lopes, A.S., & Carreira, P. (2021). Covid-19 Impact on Job Losses in Portugal: Who are the Hardest-hit? *International Journal of Manpower*.

O'Brian, R., & Williams, R. (2016). *Global Political Economy: Evolution & Dynamics*. Palgrave.

OECD. (2021a). *Timeline*. OECD. http://www.oecd.org/60-years/timeline/#selectorBlock

OECD. (2021b). *Statistics*. OECD. https://stats.oecd.org/

Quazada, A. N., Lirios, C. G., & Sánchez, A. S. (2021). Review of Labor Flexibility in the Covid-19 Era. *Ingenio Libre*, *9*(19): 1-25. https://revistas.unilibre.edu.co/index.php/inge_libre/article/view/8406/7459

Ranjbari, M., Esfandabadi, Z. S., Zanetti, M. C., Scagnelli, S. D., Siebers, P. O., Aghbashlo, M., Peng, W., Quatraro, F., & Tabatabaei, M. (2021). Three pillars of sustainability in the wake of COVID-19: A systematic review and future research agenda for sustainable development. *Journal of Cleaner Production*, *297*, 1–23. doi:10.1016/j.jclepro.2021.126660 PMID:34785869

Ren, M., Wang, B., & Rasell, M. (2021). Flexibility and Professionalisation: Reflections on Adaptions by Social Work Services in China during COVID-19. *Practice*, *34*(2), 87–101. doi:10.1080/09503153.2021.1998413

Sankaran, K. (2020). Emerging Perspectives in Labour Regulation in the Wake of Covid-19. *The Indian Journal of Labour Economics*, *63*(1), 91–95. doi:10.100741027-020-00262-1 PMID:32921941

Santos, A., Chambel, M.J., & Carvalho, V.S. (2022). 'With a little help...': Supervisor support, work-life balance, and wellbeing among Portuguese employees on telework due to COVID-19. *Cualquier forma de reproducción, distribución, comunicación pública o transformación de esta obra sólo puede ser realizada con la autorización de sus coordinadores* 48.

Sarımehmet Duman, Ö. (2014). The rise and consolidation of neoliberalism in the European Union: A comparative analysis of social and employment policies in Greece and Turkey. *European Journal of Industrial Relations*, *20*(4), 367–382. doi:10.1177/0959680113520274

Sarımehmet Duman, Ö. (2020). ESM as a Strategy for Fuelling Competitiveness: Economic Restructuring in Bailout Countries. In M. M. Erdoğdu, H. Merritt, & A. C. Garcia (Eds.), *Global Inequalities and Polarization* (pp. 132–151). IJOPEC Publication.

Savran, S. (1988). Preface: The Crisis, Restructuring of the Capital, and Neoliberalism. In N. Satlıgan & S. Savran (Eds.), *Crisis of the World Capitalism* (pp. 19–65). Alan Press. (in Turkish)

Sawicki, J. (2012). Preserving EMU Depends on Success of ESM in Solving the Debt Crisis. *Gospodarka Narodowa*, *10*(254), 1–22. doi:10.33119/GN/100993

Sell, S. K. (2020). What COVID-19 Reveals About Twenty-First Century Capitalism: Adversity and Opportunity. *Development*, *63*(2-4), 150–156. doi:10.105741301-020-00263-z PMID:33173259

Shaaban, A. N., Peleteiro, B., & Martins, M. R. O. (2020). COVID-19: What Is Next for Portugal? *Frontiers in Public Health*, 1–8. PMID:32974253

Smith, J., Davies, S. E., Feng, H., Gan, C. C. R., Grepin, K. A., Harman, S., Herten-Crabb, A., Morgan, R., Vandan, N., & Wenham, C. (2021). More than a public health crisis: A feminist political economic analysis of COVID-19. *Global Public Health: An International Journal for Research, Policy and Practice*, *16*(8-9), 1364–1380. doi:10.1080/17441692.2021.1896765 PMID:33705248

Sokol, M., & Pataccini, L. (2020). Winners and Losers in Coronavirus Times: Financialisation, Financial Chains and Emerging Economic Geographies of the Covid-19 Pandemic. *Journal of Economic and Human Geography*, *111*(3), 401–415. doi:10.1111/tesg.12433 PMID:32834148

Song, L., & Zhou, Y. (2020). The COVID-19 Pandemic and Its Impact on the Global Economy: What Does It Take to Turn Crisis into Opportunity? *China & World Economy*, *28*(4), 1–25. doi:10.1111/cwe.12349

Sousa-Uva, M., Sousa-Uva, A., & Serranheira, F. (2021). Telework during the COVID-19 epidemic in Portugal and determinants of job satisfaction: A cross-sectional study. *BMC Public Health*, *21*(1), 1–11. doi:10.118612889-021-12295-2 PMID:34865641

Štebe, J., & Vovk, T. (2021). Gender inequality on display in the flexibilisation of employment during the covid-19 crisis in Slovenia. *Teorija in Praksa*, 576–597. doi:10.51936/tip.58.specialissue.576-597

Tidey, A. (2020). COVID-19 creating 'lockdown generation' as young workers take the biggest hit. *Euronews*. https://www.euronews.com/2020/05/28/covid-19-creating-lockdown-generation-as-young-workers-take-the-biggest-hit

Timokleia Kousi, T., Mitsi, L.-C., & Simos, J. (2021). The Early Stage of COVID-19 Outbreak in Greece: A Review of the National Response and the Socioeconomic Impact. *International Journal of Environmental Research and Public Health*, *18*(322), 1–18. PMID:33406780

Uršič, M. (2021). The Covid-19 Pandemic Continuing the Processes of the Flexibilisation and Precarisation of Working Conditions in Creative Professions in Slovenia. *Teorija in Praksa*, *58*(3), 762–784.

van Barneveld, K., Quinlan, M., Kriesler, P., Junor, A., Baum, F., Chowdhury, A., Junankar, P. N. R., Clibborn, S., Flanagan, F., Wright, C., Friel, S., Halevi, J., & Rainnie, A. (2020). The COVID-19 Pandemic: Lessons on Building more Equal and Sustainable Societies. *Economic and Labour Relations Review*, *31*(2), 133–157. doi:10.1177/1035304620927107

Varoufakis, Y., & Holland, S. (2012). A Modest Proposal for Resolving the Eurozone Crisis. *Inter Economics*, *4*(4), 240–247. doi:10.100710272-012-0424-9

Vidya, C.T., & Prabheesh, K.P. (2020). Implications of COVID-19 Pandemic on the Global Trade Networks. *Emerging Markets Finance and Trade*, 56(10), Special Issue: Research on Pandemics, 2408-2421.

Wright, E. O. (1988). Alternative Perspectives in Marxist Theory of Accumulation. In N. Satlıgan & S. Savran (Eds.), *Crisis of the World Capitalism* (pp. 172–218). Alan Press. (in Turkish)

Youmni, A., & Cheikh, M. (2020). Exploring Causal relationship between risk factors and vulnerability to COVID-19 Cases of Italy, Spain, France, Greece, Portugal, Morocco and South Africa. medRxiv, 1-13. doi:10.1101/2020.06.24.20139121

KEY TERMS AND DEFINITIONS

COVID-19: SARS-CoV-2 pandemic generating a big challenge for countries in economic, political, and social terms.

European Stability Mechanism (ESM): Financial assistance mechanism operationalised by the European Commission to assist failing economies with rescue packages, austerity measures and structural adjustment programmes during the Eurozone crisis.

Eurozone crisis: Reflection of the 2008 global economic crisis on the Eurozone, uncovering the asymmetries between the core and peripheral countries.

Flexibility: Implementation of atypical forms of work such as short-time, part-time and temporary work, as well as telework and home-office practices.

Labour: Key agent of the production process; workers' input.

Pandemic: SARS-CoV-2 disease being epidemic throughout the world.

Work: The way labour engages into the production process.

Chapter 13
Levers of Control and Employee Groupwork to Develop a Novel Strategy in the Post-COVID-19 Era

Marco Borria
Ca' Foscari University of Venice, Italy

Maurizio Massaro
Ca' Foscari University of Venice, Italy

Carlo Bagnoli
Ca' Foscari University of Venice, Italy

ABSTRACT

Since the onset of the COVID-19 pandemic, businesses are competing in an unknown, ever-changing environment. This turbulence generates new forms of uncertainty and risks that not only affect business performance but also the wellbeing of employees. Groupwork as a management control system can support business risk reduction and increase employee wellbeing. However, while groupwork can help companies develop a novel strategy apt to face unprecedented competitive scenarios, it can also bring new challenges in terms of practical organization and efficiency. Moving from this premise, the chapter will discuss how groupwork can be used as a management control system using the levers of control lens. Opportunities and challenges both for businesses and employee wellbeing will be discussed.

INTRODUCTION

COVID-19 poses turbulent problems to organisations and governments. Originally developed in physics, the turbulence concept has been used in social sciences to describe increasing levels of organizational complexity and unpredictability on a global scale (Ansell et al., 2021; Radford, 1978). Experts failed

DOI: 10.4018/978-1-6684-4181-7.ch013

Levers of Control and Employee Groupwork to Develop a Novel Strategy in the Post-COVID-19 Era

to foresee the pandemic whereas responses of governments centred around lockdown measures that disrupted society and the economy. The concept of environmental turbulence, featuring uncertainty and unpredictability (Calantone et al., 2003; Ho & Plewa, 2020; Wu et al., 2021), has also been employed to encompass market turbulence (Ch'ng et al., 2021; Christopher & Lee, 2004) and technological turbulence (Lichtenthaler, 2009). We can argue that the pandemic has changed the rules of the game for most marketplaces companies operate in today. This increased the risks for organisations, facing unprecedented operating conditions. However, the crisis demands businesses to develop new strategies and decisions that adequately address an ever-changing environment.

The objectives of this conceptual chapter are to review and argue that groupwork of employees may help companies develop more updated control systems in such turbulent environment and help them formulate emerging strategies that are compatible with the rapidly changing environment in which they operate. In order to accomplish such objectives, we will i) introduce the relevance of groupwork in the current external and internal environments featuring the post-pandemic era, ii) apply Simons' (1995) Levers of Control framework to the case of using groupwork as a management control system, and iii) highlight the risks and pitfalls of groupwork from an analytic perspective.

BACKGROUND

Returning to work in an office environment has a strategic impact (Klimczuk et al., 2021). Flexible work-from-home setups have sometimes been the only way around the restrictions imposed by the pandemic. In psychiatrist Wilfred Bion's terms, a relationship exists between raw thinking or feeling and the process of more elaborated thinking. This is what he called the "container" concept (Ogden, 2004): a process which allows the analysand to express their unprocessed thoughts and find words for them through the working of a containing function. Today, the containing function of the organisation is at risk in that its boundaries are no longer clearly defined, hence the process of elaborating thoughts out of raw feelings might be in jeopardy. This means raised levels of anxiety and unprocessed thinking for people which may threaten the groups they belong to. Whatever organisations and governments will decide to do with the work set-up situation in the time to come, companies are left dealing with the transition. Turbulence has been brought from outside the organisation to within the organisation. With turbulence come risks, anxiety, and uncertainty.

We have been presented with an idea of the "new normal". This reflects the wish for things to go back the way they were before. However, until December 2021, the end of the pandemic was still not observed yet. The most that we seemed to be able to hope for was a status change from pandemic to endemic, meaning we are going to be living aside the disease for years to come (Tayag, 2021).

Many people enacted forms of protest towards the measures that have being taken: some refused to be vaccinated, some argued against COVID passes, others protested against mandatory jabs (The Guardian, 2021). Yet, businesses were caught in the middle of such protest. They were forced to expect employees to comply with the restrictions and the measures set up by the government, yet they were facing the brunt of their same employees' discontent.

Due to the pandemic, business risks and uncertainty have increased (Sharma et al., 2020). Such features need to be addressed by companies. We can envisage external sources of risks from disruptive events such as the outbreak of the virus or the spreading of its strains bringing consequences to the company. Threats of new lockdowns, restrictions to movement and to business. These affect how companies can survive in their natural environment. We can also envisage internal sources of risks generated by the difficult experiences that employee bring to the workplace. Evidence shows that symptoms of anxiety and depression, together with self-reported stress are associated with COVID-19 (Rajkumar, 2020). Companies are affected by the increased difficulties experienced by their employees. On the one hand, Platts et al.'s (2022) cross-sectional study with 623 participants found that, out of the 81% of respondents working from home, mental distress such as stress, burnout, sleep trouble, and depressive symptoms were most acutely experienced by those with previous mental health conditions, female participants, under 45 subjects, those working from home part-time and having two dependants whilst men reported greater work-life balance issues. Mun et al.'s (2022) systematic literature review found that the overall wellbeing of employees has been threatened by work conditions that have shifted during the COVID-19 pandemic from commuting to telework. On the other hand, Davidsen and Petersen's (2021) found from 1.328 self-reporting Faroese employees that whilst mental wellbeing stayed on average level in April and May 2020, during lock-down, the COVID-19 outbreak significantly worsened work-related commitment, ability, satisfaction, and work-family life.

During the second world war the British Army invested heavily in the prevention and treatment of psychiatric illness among its soldiers. Both psychiatrists Bion and S. H. Foulkes worked at the Northfield military psychiatric hospital and developed their own forms of group psychotherapy with the aim of returning soldiers to wellbeing and to the front (Thalassis, n.d.). In Foulkes' (2018) tradition, on the one hand, the group is seen as an object to which members' projections, or the attribution of their own inner characteristics, affects, and impulses (*APA Dictionary of Psychology*, n.d.), latch onto. In Bion's (2003) tradition, on the other hand, the very belief that a group existed as a separate object from its individual members, was part of a regressive illusion (Nitsun, 2014). By "regressive" we mean it enacts a lower state of cognitive, emotional, or behavioral functioning for the individual or the group (*APA Dictionary of Psychology*, n.d.).

RUNNING GROUPS IN BUSINESS

It is not practical for managers, nor it is viable, to roll out psychotherapy group programmes without specific clinical needs as a blanket policy within companies. However, George and Baker (2011) suggested creating group experiences which they defined as "True North Groups" and "consist[s] of six to eight people who meet on a regular basis to share their personal challenges and discuss important questions in their lives" (p. 17). These are not psychotherapy groups; they are more like peer groups without any hierarchy. They are grounded in confidentiality, and they foster the development of personal leadership by creating a support team around their members. They are based on openness and intimacy and can be single-gendered or mixed-gendered. The benefit of such groups lies in the power of conversation that helps members develop as human beings and as professionals. It is, however, an intimate setting where the atmosphere is relaxed, safe, non-competitive, and conducive to sharing. These groups are an example of groupwork which could be deployed across and within organisations.

Along similar lines, Groysberg and Halperin (2022) highlight the benefits of small peer groups both within the same organization and across different companies. They suggest paying attention to the group composition, the principles for participation, the meeting structure, its processes and content, and the use of flexible technologies. Among the examples of peer group taking place within the same companies they list in-organization groups as part of a leadership-development program, e.g., Arts' Xcelerators program for high-potential leaders, and in-organization company-wide groups, e.g., Spitfire Strategies' "peer pods" of seven to 10 people each.

These groups can be viewed as applications of so-called "experiential" groups (Ohrt et al., 2014), described by Stein (1998) as groups running without any tasks other than to understand group processes themselves in the "here and now". Members are therefore meeting without an agenda, yet they are free to interact with each other on whatever topic of their liking. Luke and Kiweewa (2010) view participation in experiential groups "to facilitate the development of . . . personal growth and awareness" (p. 365). We are not recommending here to run psychotherapy groups but to value and roll out forms of groupwork of various kinds which could present companies with invaluable benefits at a time of crisis. Even if the groups a company is running have a task and they are not "pure" experiential groups, they can still benefit members and companies according to the features that we are about to describe.

Groupwork as Viable Forms of Management Control Systems in Response to the Pandemic

One of the most frequently adopted frameworks of management control systems (Martyn et al., 2016; Massaro et al., 2019) is Simons' (1995) Levers Of Control (LOCs) framework. These include: (a) beliefs systems, (b) boundary systems, (c) diagnostic systems, and (d) interactive control system. Groupwork offers members and their companies features that are compatible with all such management control systems. Furthermore, groupwork may also implement efficient and effective levers of control. It makes use of the resources available within the firm, the only cost being time subject to how the groupwork is structured. If an overt business task is assigned to the group, the appearance of saving time and money will make such group look more cost effective. If no task is assigned to the group and the group is run as an experiential one, participants will have the opportunity to familiarise themselves more with group process and develop more self-awareness. In any case groups are efficient and effective if compared to recourse to individual interventions as demonstrated by the successful comparison of group versus individual psychotherapy in the clinical literature (McRoberts et al., 1998). In particular, group psychotherapy has recently been shown to generate positive outcomes for anxiety and depression (Barkowski et al., 2020; Martin et al., 2021) and a recent meta-analysis of 42 Randomized Control Trials published from 1990 to 2018 (Janis et al., 2021) demonstrated the efficacy of group therapy for depression and bipolar disorder.

Belief systems are organizational statements that are related to the core values of an organization and its strategy. They are meant to inspire and drive the behaviour of personnel towards the goals that are part of the company's strategy. They are based on core values, which are the motives that are meant to drive people's action (Simons, 1995).

Groupwork allows members to share and discuss around their core values. If members feel safe enough within the group, they will start sharing their own personal views on the firm's policy, the environment, actions and on the setting that surrounds them. The sharing of members' views will provide management with an incredible opportunity to compare the members' values with the organisation's core values and establish whether they are aligned, or whether any discrepancy exists. If the core values of the firm are not aligned with those of the group members, this could lead to different courses of action. On the one hand, management would want to explore more fully where the members stand on their inner motives and provide them with the time and the space to elaborate on their thinking. On the other hand, this would be an opportunity to place into question the company's core values and check whether they are up to date with the time and social *milieu* in which it operates. In other words, groupwork, we argue, could provide an opportunity for management to listen to their people and check whether any risks exist from a misalignment of values between the organisation and its employees as stakeholders.

Groups can be homogeneous or heterogeneous with regard to any specific parameter. For example, in relation to gender, we could have male or female groups. However homogeneous we intend our groups to be, members will be always confronted with differences from other group members. This is a very important yet difficult part of the group process dynamics. Confronting members with differences can result into the group splitting into little subgroups or allow for members to work creatively with difference and enable diversity to contribute to their joint discussion. Working with difference is not easy, it can be threatening. Meeting someone who has a different worldview compared to ours can make us feel as if our ideas, opinion, and ultimately worldview are worthless. It can trigger negative emotions that, on a conscious or unconscious level, can lead to attacking others and engaging into conflict. If the facilitation of the group allows for different views to co-exist within the same group, then we can see how the need for consistency and coherence is temporarily dispensed with in the group dynamics to make space for something new to happen. This "something new" could lead to generate new thoughts and ideas that may creatively address a novel environment. When we speak of group environment, we mean both the *internal* environment made up by the group members within its setting, but also the *external* environment made up by the external setting within which the group takes place. It is in such regard that the group's creativity function becomes particularly relevant as it allows to address external stimuli in novel ways. This could be fruitful at a time of global pandemic such as COVID-19 when we need new, creative responses to a risky, threatening, and uncertain external environment. Groups, leveraging their diversity and creativity resources, can provide such novel responses.

Boundary systems provide the limits within which it is safe to act from an organizational perspective given the risks that face the organisation both from outside and from within the company. Examples of boundary systems can be codes of conduct, which set the ground rules for the behaviour of employees in a specific domain (Simons, 1995).

Groups can constitute effective boundary systems in at least two ways: i) by providing insight into risks that were not previously foreseen, and ii) by providing psychological containment to their members and their conversation. Allowing members to freely discuss among themselves can help identifying risks for them and the companies, which were not previously foreseen. Again, such risks can originate from inside or outside of the organisation. It is however crucial, at time of turbulence, for management to be able to listen to any potential risk or threat facing the company. Groups, we argue, could provide management with this function.

Furthermore, the group itself is regulated by ground rules such as the time, length, and place of meeting; confidentiality; safety issues; etc. In psychoanalysis, the analysand is confronted with elements which they meet with regularity and provide the so-called "setting" for the meeting: "regular appointments, fixed length of sessions, the respective position of couch and armchair, limitation of communication to a verbal level, free association, the ending of the session, regular breaks, means of payment, etc." (Green, 1975, p. 10). The group's ground rules will turn the group itself into a physical and psychological space akin to a "setting" in its own rights. Within such group setting members will feel safe enough to voice their views and express their concerns, for example, on how the company or the external environment are evolving. In this respect, the group setting will function as a boundary system itself which will protect members and their organisation from potential risks arising from inside and outside. Feeling safe in a group setting may mean that members form attachment bonds to each other and become stronger as teams for the benefit of the company they work for (George & Baker, 2011; Groysberg & Halperin, 2022).

Diagnostic control systems are used to "monitor organizational outcomes and correct deviations from pre-set standards of performance" (Simons, 1995, p. 59). The key concept here is the presence of a feedback loop between performance, measurement of variance to key performance variables, and adjustment. In a turbulent environment such as the one we live in today it is exceedingly difficult to have the time to wait for such a feedback loop to take place. It might be too late by the time a negative performance occurs hence the need to pre-empt any negative variance. In addition to that, key performance variables are not to be taken by default. In a challenging environment such as the one created by COVID-19 it is not clear which are the most relevant key performance variables to measure performance against. To the limit of the paradox, it could be the case that the company is measuring variance against traditional key performance variables in a successful way and yet fail in the short-term competition. This might be due to the fact that when we measure the variance against key performance variables, we already have a set idea of what the competitive environment will look like. Yet, in the current scenario such is not the case any longer. What we need is the input of human intelligence in both the feedback system of diagnostic controls and in the setting of key performance variables.

Groupwork allows for the provision of a rich form of intelligence. By working in an unstructured way, groups provide up-to-date insight on the current environment the company is competing in. This means that the group can highlight quickly and effectively what the critical variables are in the context of an environment dominated by COVID-19 and report discrepancies between actual performance and such variables. This will allow the company to swiftly identify the factors potentially undermining current and future performance and quickly act on them. The group will provide material which will alert the company of current, potential, and future threats before management has had the chance to get to know about them. Such is the potential of the group as diagnostic control systems in that it allows for the control feedback loop to be revised and adapted to the current turbulent environment. The use of groups as diagnostic control systems, we argue, may allow management to pre-empt negative variance in the business performance at a time of high turbulence.

Interactive control systems collect the information through a bottom-up approach in the presence of strategic uncertainties. They constitute a form of intelligence which will lead management to gather and ponder over added information in the search of the best course of action. Today more than ever we live in uncertain environments. Through dialogue, exchanges, and relationships, groupwork can be a powerful form of interactive control systems. It is not possible to know in advance what the outcome of a group will be and this is due to its creative potential. Similarly, this makes groups the most suitable means to deal with strategic uncertainties and gather novel forms of intelligence. Different people will bring different experiences and the meeting of such differences through conversation will lead to novel insight for members, the group, and their organization. Management will then be able to capitalise on such insight, use it to revise the current company strategy, and develop novel directions of action. This is only possible thanks to the information that comes from group members. In this regard, it is fair to say that the group will function as interpretative of the current competitive environment with levels of efficiency and effectiveness which are higher than any formalised strategy-making process. The opportunity will arise for management to develop novel strategies which are more apt to deal with a changing environment.

The Challenging Aspects of Groupwork

Groups are not an all-good modality neither for their members nor for the organizations to which they belong. There are many examples of impaired dynamics to watch for and here we will review a few which can affect groups as management control systems. Such dysfunctional dynamics can hinder the potential of the group, prevent them from doing their work and from attaining the objectives for which they were formed. Given the analytical dimension of the group experience we described above, out of the many forms of dysfunctional group forces we will limit ourselves to reviewing those that have been put forward by analytical writers or those compatible with such approach.

Wilfred Bion (2003) compared the functioning of the so-called "work group" with those groups which are dominated by dysfunctional dynamics which he called "basic assumptions". They are featured in "basic assumption groups", to be contrasted with the work group itself. The main basic assumptions that Bion formulated were: i) dependency, ii) fight or flight, and iii) pairing. Now we will review the main features of those groups to raise awareness of their existence and their impact on the organisations which they form.

The basic assumption of dependency influences how the group will depend on a leader in its thinking and feeling. How it will be swayed by such a leader in its functioning. This is a threat to the autonomy of both the individual members and the group as a whole. It is a threat to the group in that it will impede the ability for the group to originate new thinking. The generation of new thinking was one of the key features why we recommended using groups as management control systems. If the group falls prey to such a basic assumption, then the thinking and the feeling will depend on what has been conveyed by the leader. Hence creativity will be hampered and there will be little point in using the group as a form of intelligence on values, critical performance variables, or strategic uncertainties. This is because the group will end up putting forward what is already known by the managers and will not add anything new. It is a powerful threat to group functioning in organisations. Finding their justification in the presence of a hierarchy, groups will end up limiting what members will have to say or to add to the discussion. It follows that such a dynamic will make the group and the organisation blind to the environment in which they compete.

Adorno et al. (2019) in their construction of the "F" scale for the measurement of the Authoritarian Personality included the feature of Authoritarian Submission, defined as "Submissive, uncritical attitude towards idealized moral authorities of the ingroup" (p. 381). Many decades have passed since the introduction of the Authoritarian Personality concept, yet Bob Altemeyer (2007) still includes a high degree of submissiveness to the authority as a core feature of Right-Wing Authoritarians. As with totalitarian regimes and totalitarian groups, submissive members will tend to accept what has been conveyed by the authority without reviewing it with their critical minds. Such lack of critical thinking represents one of the major threats to organizations and their strategic functioning (Altemeyer, 2007).

The basic assumptions are regressive dynamics for the group. The regressive dynamic of fight-or-flight might be described by the tendency in the group to feel as if its main purpose were to attack or flight from the attacks of a common enemy. Such tendency is both truly relevant in the current context as is harmful. Since the inception of the COVID pandemic the disease has been described as an enemy and the public discourse has verted around the war metaphor. This is not without any reason. The disruption of ordinary activities caused by the pandemic, the massive involvement of the pharmaceutical industry in the response, the public intervention of the state in terms of subsidies and financial aids for companies and the population, the restrictions to the circulation of people are all factors that resemble those of wartime. Even us authors in our above description of the origin of group therapy have mentioned the Northfield experiments during the Second World War.

So, is the virus the real enemy to fight? While this might be a realistic metaphor on some level, we must be aware of the impact that such form of thinking will bear on groups as management control systems within organisations. The fight-or-flight basic assumption will act as a catalyst for group thinking and will focus the group attention on the response to the virus while leaving other sides of the external and internal reality unattended. When we speak of reality, we must differentiate the reality of the external world, such as the riots happening on the street, the reality of the internal world of individuals, such as the way the virus is represented in the mind of each one of us, and the reality of the group representations where the internal worlds of individuals will meet and may find meaning. The risk in a fight-or-flight group is that any instance of external reality will be co-opted into a schematic dynamic by which everything must be for or against us. Such a way of thinking is very limiting because it will easily discount the novelty that any idea could bring to the group discussion and to the group strategy. Thus, managers will fail to see the novelty of a new event or phenomenon by simply classifying their appearance in for-or-against-us terms. This will take attention away from opportunities for novel response to the competitive environment. It will restrict, we argue, management's freedom of movement in the formulation of a novel, more apt strategy for facing turbulence.

The basic assumption of pairing can be described by the regressive tendency to the emergence of a pair of people who monopolise the conversation with the phantasy (the unconscious fantasy) of generating a new leader. Not only is this basic assumption threatening to the existing hierarchy of the firm, but it hampers the thinking of the group as a whole. People will be drawn in as spectators to the show that a pair of people will be putting on hence members will be silenced in their thinking. This constitutes a restriction of the thinking and the feeling capacity of the group as a whole and will affect: i) the functioning of the group as effective management control systems, and ii) the breadth and depth of the strategy management will produce with the aid of the group. If the unconscious expectation is that the pair will produce a new leader, this might reveal some levels of frustration with the current management as well as the unwillingness of members to do any thinking. It is more tempting to delegate the dialectical work to the pairing couple than for members to expose themselves and contribute with their ideas and observations. Concurrently, any frustration with the current situation, which might feature problems with the external reality, the group functioning, or management, will feed into an unrealistic hope for a future leader who will come and solve all the problems of the group. Such unrealistic hope is a problem for the company because it will act as an empty buffer whilst groupwork will be suspended and no real progress will be made (Bion, 2003).

In the review of his clinical experience Nitsun (2014) elaborated the concept of the "anti-group" to summarise all the forces that get in the way of the functioning of a group as an experience. Starting from questioning whether the group is a on object or a regressive representation in people's mind, as Bion argued, Nitsun is aware that the practice of groupwork is quite different from the theory. There could be fears, anxieties, people dropping out and other expressions of difficulty for the group to come together as an experience. He named these forces the "anti-group" and would make use of such an element to explain all the destructive forces at play in the running of a group. There could be rivalry, aggression, and so forth. On an epistemological level, we find the opposition between constructive and destructive forces slightly weak because it is based on a dichotomised view of the world in polar opposites or opposed forces. Nitsun seems to be aware of this criticism and refers back to Freud's dualism of eros vs. death instincts. Yet, this does not resolve the question of how to position the anti-group in the contemporary epistemological debate. One could argue that group forces might be more or less destructive on a gradient and that ultimately the emergence of destructive outcomes would have to be judged and described as such by the participants or the managers running the group. Nonetheless, the concept of the anti-group is particularly useful in explaining the sources of everything that does not work in a group through recourse to a unitary concept. From a practical perspective one could see the appeal of recognising the anti-group at work in a group and learn to work with that. This is to prevent the negative outcomes of destructiveness from occurring in the group. The major features of the anti-group are dominated by hostility, anger, aggression and "the destructive aspect of groups that threatens the integrity of the group" (Nitsun, 1991, p. 7).

Adorno et al. (2019) defined ethnocentrism in general terms as the attribution of more value to the in-group vs. the out-group: "Most essentially, outgroups are seen as *threatening* and *power-seeking* . . . Ethnocentric ideology regarding ingroups shows similar trends, though often in an opposite direction, to that regarding outgroups. The ingroups are conceived of as superior in morality, ability, and general development" (Adorno et al., 2019, pp. 281-282). Such is the preference for the group to which we belong over the groups that are external in our experience. This could apply to groups running from different departments within the same company to the opposition of groups and different organisations on the whole, to racism, and discrimination. How can ethnocentrism undermine the functioning of a group as a management control system? On a cognitive level, it could generate bias in framing the group in relation to the competition. It could lead to gross underestimations or overestimations of the group's resources which could cause damage on a strategic level. Furthermore, it could lead to a certain kind of blindness in assessing internal and external risks. If we unfairly believe that our organization is stronger than competitors, this could lead to take on too many risks or challenges.

On an emotional level, ethnocentrism could fuel aggression and tension towards features which are "foreign" to those representing the group. Such feelings could threaten the cohesiveness, the unity of the group, and of the organisation as a whole.

Scapegoating represents the phenomenon by which an individual group member is made to represent all the negative material circulating in the group. All the aggression and the dysfunctional material is projected onto one individual member who is then seen as different from everyone else. Their features of difference are to be despised by the group up to the point when such individual(s) might be even expelled from the group itself. Scapegoating creates a false sense of social reality and affects the way that a company can compete effectively in its own business environment. Through scapegoating, the problems lying at the heart of the projective process is not solved, it is only shifted to a convenient subject. Therefore, even if the subject has been expelled by the group, the group is left with all the material that caused the problem in the first instance. Furthermore, something must be said about the relationship between difference and scapegoating. Scapegoating is based on projected difference. Yet, all projections need to find a suitable host to latch onto. And such suitability might be generated by the differences that members bring to the group. Hence it is quite common that group members who are different from the others in some regard end up being scapegoated. This results from a failure in recognising difference as a resource rather than a threat. We are here arguing that when difference is not recognised as a resource it becomes a hindrance and therefore a threat to the group functioning, potentially leading to the expulsion of the member carrying such difference. What is the impact of scapegoating onto groups as management control systems? The identification of a member as scapegoat does not solve the problems that the group is facing. On the contrary, finding a scapegoat provides the illusion of having solved the problem. Yet it leaves the group dealing with its own dysfunctional aspects. On an ethical level, it is a highly despisable outcome because it mistreats people as victims for something they are not responsible.

CONCLUSION

Groupwork can help companies navigate these challenging times if deployed as management control systems (Simons, 1995). As belief systems groups help the company checking the alignment between its core values and those of the environment and their employees; as boundary systems they help the company contain risks and uncertainty; as interactive control systems they provide the company with the intelligence to develop a novel and up to date strategy; as diagnostic control systems they can pre-empt negative variance and identify more representative key performance variables. However, groups are not to be intended as all-good modalities. Groups have pitfalls and managers need to be watchful and ready to timely recognise their dysfunctional elements. Through dependency, the group can become over-reliant on its leaders and fail to do any work; through fight-or-flight the group can catalyse all its energy against an imagined enemy and ignore most of the reality of the company environment; through pairing the group might delegate the thinking to a couple of people hoping that they will generate the new leader; anti-group forces might be at play when they threaten the integrity of the group; ethnocentrism might lead to the overvaluation of the ingroup at the expense of outgroups and the external environment; finally, scapegoating might prompt to identify a member or a subgroup as carrying all the negative features that other members do not like to see in themselves.

Despite its resulting and unintentional complexity, this is hoped to be a balanced picture of groups and their function as management control systems. On such balance, groups may offer the resources to develop a novel strategy in turbulent times and help contain the risks from the external and internal environments, including those related to the employee wellbeing.

REFERENCES

Adorno, T., Frenkel-Brenswik, E., & Levinson, D. (2019). *The authoritarian personality*. https://books.google.com/books?hl=it&lr=&id=SUmHDwAAQBAJ&oi=fnd&pg=PR23&dq=adorno+the+authoritarian+personality&ots=z_TV8ZCIff&sig=bLjdzeEI31bSEG-yKfl8_LTIHUM

AltemeyerB. (2007). *The authoritarians*. https://theauthoritarians.org/options-for-getting-the-book/

Ansell, C., Sørensen, E., & Torfing, J. (2021). The COVID-19 pandemic as a game changer for public administration and leadership? The need for robust governance responses to turbulent problems. *Public Management Review*, 23(7), 949–960. doi:10.1080/14719037.2020.1820272

APA Dictionary of Psychology. (n.d.). APA. https://dictionary.apa.org/

Barkowski, S., Schwartze, D., Strauss, B., Burlingame, G. M., & Rosendahl, J. (2020). Efficacy of group psychotherapy for anxiety disorders: A systematic review and meta-analysis. *Psychotherapy Research*, 30(8), 965–982. doi:10.1080/10503307.2020.1729440 PMID:32093586

Bion, W. (2003). *Experiences in groups: And other papers*. Taylor and Francis. https://api.taylorfrancis.com/content/books/mono/download?identifierName=doi&identifierValue=10.4324/9780203359075&type=googlepdf

Calantone, R., Garcia, R., & Dröge, C. (2003). The effects of environmental turbulence on new product development strategy planning. *Journal of Product Innovation Management*, *20*(2), 90–103. doi:10.1111/1540-5885.2002003

Ch'ng, P.-C., Cheah, J., & Amran, A. (2021). Eco-innovation practices and sustainable business performance: The moderating effect of market turbulence in the Malaysian technology industry. *Journal of Cleaner Production*, *283*, 124556. doi:10.1016/j.jclepro.2020.124556

Christopher, M., & Lee, H. (2004). Mitigating supply chain risk through improved confidence. *International Journal of Physical Distribution & Logistics Management*, *34*(5), 388–396. doi:10.1108/09600030410545436

Davidsen, A. H., & Petersen, M. S. (2021). The impact of covid-19 restrictions on mental well-being and working life among faroese employees. *International Journal of Environmental Research and Public Health*, *18*(9), 4775. doi:10.3390/ijerph18094775 PMID:33947133

Foulkes, S. H. (2018). Introduction to group-analytic psychotherapy*. *Foundations of Group Analysis for the Twenty-First Century*, 9–16. 1 doi:0.4324/9780429474903-2/INTRODUCTION-GROUP-ANALYTIC-PSYCHOTHERAPY-FOULKES

George, B., & Baker, D. (2011). *True north groups: A powerful path to personal and leadership development*. Berrett-Koehler Publishers.

Green, A. (1975). The analyst, symbolization and absence in the analytic setting (on changes in analytic practice and analytic experience). *The International Journal of Psycho-Analysis*, *56*(1), 1–22. PMID:1158564

Groysberg, B., & Halperin, R. R. (2022). How to Get the Most out of Peer Support Groups: A guide to benefits and best practices. *Harvard Business Review*, 131–141.

Ho, J., & Plewa, C. (2020). Recipes for new product success: The interplay between orientations and environmental turbulence. *Journal of Business and Industrial Marketing*, *35*(8), 1345–1357. doi:10.1108/JBIM-08-2019-0387

Janis, R. A., Burlingame, G. M., Svien, H., Jensen, J., & Lundgreen, R. (2021). Group therapy for mood disorders: A meta-analysis. *Psychotherapy Research*, *31*(3), 342–358. doi:10.1080/10503307.2020.1817603 PMID:32930060

Klimczuk, A., Belzunegui-Eraso, A., Beno, M., & Hvorecky, J. (2021). Data on an Austrian Company's Productivity in the Pre-Covid-19 Era, During the Lockdown and After Its Easing: To Work Remotely or Not? *Frontiers in Communication*, *1*, 641199. Www.Frontiersin.Org. doi:10.3389/fcomm.2021.641199

Lichtenthaler, U. (2009). Outbound open innovation and its effect on firm performance: Examining environmental influences. *R & D Management*, *39*(4), 317–330. doi:10.1111/j.1467-9310.2009.00561.x

Luke, M., & Kiweewa, J. M. (2010). Personal growth and awareness of counseling trainees in an experiential group. *Journal for Specialists in Group Work*, *35*(4), 365–388. doi:10.1080/01933922.2010.514976

Martin, E., Byrne, G., Connon, G., & Power, L. (2021). An exploration of group cognitive analytic therapy for anxiety and depression. *Psychology and Psychotherapy: Theory, Research and Practice*, *94*(S1). doi:10.1111/papt.12299 PMID:32981230

Martyn, P., Sweeney, B., & Curtis, E. (2016). Strategy and control: 25 years of empirical use of Simons' Levers of Control framework. *Journal of Accounting and Organizational Change*, *12*(3), 281–324. doi:10.1108/JAOC-03-2015-0027

Massaro, M., Moro, A., Aschauer, E., & Fink, M. (2019). Trust, control and knowledge transfer in small business networks. *Review of Managerial Science*, *13*(2), 267–301. doi:10.100711846-017-0247-y

McRoberts, C., Burlingame, G. M., & Hoag, M. J. (1998). Comparative efficacy of individual and group psychotherapy: A meta-analytic perspective. *Group Dynamics*, *2*(2), 101–117. doi:10.1037/1089-2699.2.2.101

Mun, S., Moon, Y., Kim, H., & Kim, N. (2022). Current Discussions on Employees and Organizations During the COVID-19 Pandemic: A Systematic Literature Review. *Frontiers in Psychology*, *13*, 848778. doi:10.3389/fpsyg.2022.848778 PMID:35496177

Nitsun, M. (1991). Fernando Arroyave Memorial Prize Essay: The Anti-Group: Destructive Forces in the Group and their Therapeutic Potential. *Group Analysis*, *24*(1), 7–20. doi:10.1177/0533316491241003

Nitsun, M. (2014). *The Anti-Group*. The Anti-Group., doi:10.4324/9781315745510

Ogden, T. H. (2004). On holding and containing, being and dreaming. *The International Journal of Psycho-Analysis*, *85*(6), 1349–1364. doi:10.1516/T41H-DGUX-9JY4-GQC7 PMID:15801512

Ohrt, J. H., Prochenko, Y., Stulmaker, H., Huffman, D., Fernando, D., & Swan, K. (2014). An Exploration of Group and Member Development in Experiential Groups. *Journal for Specialists in Group Work*, *39*(3), 212–235. doi:10.1080/01933922.2014.919047

Platts, K., Breckon, J., & Marshall, E. (2022). Enforced home-working under lockdown and its impact on employee wellbeing: A cross-sectional study. *BMC Public Health*, *22*(1), 199. Advance online publication. doi:10.118612889-022-12630-1 PMID:35093054

Radford, K. J. (1978). Decision-making in a turbulent environment. *The Journal of the Operational Research Society*, *29*(7), 677–682. doi:10.1057/jors.1978.144

Rajkumar, R. P. (2020). COVID-19 and mental health: A review of the existing literature. *Asian Journal of Psychiatry*, *52*, 102066. doi:10.1016/j.ajp.2020.102066 PMID:32302935

Sharma, P., Leung, T. Y., Kingshott, R. P. J., Davcik, N. S., & Cardinali, S. (2020). Managing uncertainty during a global pandemic: An international business perspective. *Journal of Business Research*, *116*, 188–192. doi:10.1016/j.jbusres.2020.05.026 PMID:32501304

Simons, R. (1995). *Levers of control: How managers use innovative control systems to drive strategic renewal*. Harvard Business School Press.

Stein, M. (1998). Projective identification in management education. *Journal of Managerial Psychology*, *13*(8), 558–566. doi:10.1108/02683949810244938

Tayag, Y. (2021, December 5). From pandemic to endemic: this is how we might get back to normal. *The Guardian*.

Thalassis, N. (n.d.). Soldiers in Psychiatric Therapy. *The Case of Northfield Military Hospital, 1942-1946*. doi:10.1093hm/hkm040 PMID:18605333

The Guardian. (2021, November 23). The Guardian view on Europe's Covid protests: treat with care. *The Guardian*.

Wu, X., Li, S., Xu, N., Zhang, W., & Wu, D. (2021). User participation depth and innovation performance of Internet companies: The moderating effect of environmental turbulence. *Technology Analysis and Strategic Management*, 1–14. doi:10.1080/09537325.2021.2008893

Chapter 14
Chess as a Way of Inclusion of Prisoners:
A Portuguese Experience

Eduardo Tomé
Universidade Lusófona de Humanidades e Tecnologias, Portugal

Cátia Godinho
https://orcid.org/0000-0002-7836-0802
GOVCOPP Research Centre, Universidade de Aveiro, Portugal

António José F. Lopes
Academia de Xadrez de Gaia, Portugal

ABSTRACT

This paper describes a Portuguese ongoing experience of policies aiming at including people in society and ultimately in the labour market, promoting sustainability in wellbeing. Namely, if focuses on the teaching of chess to prisoners in Portuguese jails, and the following participation of these prisoners in championships as the first Hybrid European Championship for Prisoners held in October of 2021. the authors base the study in theories about social inclusion and relate them to chess. Then they explain in detail experiences dealing with the inclusion of chess in society. Furthermore, they explain the Portuguese case. The chapter concludes that chess has been a very interesting tool for the social integration of prisoners in Portugal as well as in other countries. Therefore, the experience is worth being pursued and developed worldwide.

INTRODUCTION

Chess is considered to be one of the most fascinating table games that exist. Its origins are legendary – it would have been invented in Antiquity for a King who would have been tired of wars, and who could not pay the inventor the sum he demanded (Dodona, 2021). Chess evolved in the Middle Ages – and in

DOI: 10.4018/978-1-6684-4181-7.ch014

the Renaissance the two first chess books were written by a Portuguese (Damião, 1512), and by a Spanish monk (Lopez de Segura, 1561) Long time considered as a luxury for very intelligent people, chess became a sport with official champions since the end of the 19th century (Winter, 2021).

Nowadays chess is considered both a sport (Chess and Technology, 2015), a science (Chess and Science, 2021) and even a form of art (Humble, 1993, McDonald, 2013) or all of them as the same time (Fine, 2015). First, chess is a sport, because millions of registered players enter official championships every year under the umbrella of the International Chess Federation (FIDE) (FIDE, 2021); to those should be added the millions of amateurs that each day practice in online platforms like chess.com or lichess (Chess.com 2021, Lichess 2021); chess is played at different speeds (classic, rapid, blitz) and there are World Championships for the three categories (Fide, 2021). Secondly, chess is a science, because it has not only rules, but even a very developed theory (Šahovski Informator, 2021); in fact since the 1980s chess began to be played by computers, a goal aimed at by Alan Turing some decades before (Turing, 2016; Stezano, 2018); the "silicone monsters" first won a controversial match against a World Champion in 1996, (Newborn, 1997); afterwards the potency of the Artificial Intelligence grew, and nowadays the the Stockfish program (Stockfish, 2021) and Alphazero program (Sadler, 2019) seem to be the most advanced machines in the theory of chess; world class players use computer programs to enhance their knowledge and skills about chess (Kalinin, 2017). Thirdly, chess is an art, because every game is a collection of moves, and all those moves are options for creation; novices are usually very creative, and they lose a lot; therefore experienced players tend to follow more reliable and known lines of play; but, it is always possible to find a new move or to improve a previous studied position – and this possibility of creativity makes every game a constant surprise (Kasparov, 2018). It is said that "the player who loses is in many cases the one that does the last big mistake" (Tartakover, 2021) but this usually happens because the opposite side has been playing good and creative moves that provoke and induce the decisive mistake. All in all, even if computers may have changed the game, they did not change the players, who are as human and creative and able of art as ever (Metcalfe, 2021).

As it will be seen in this chapter, chess is also a set of rules, and an has educative meaning. In this chapter we try to analyse if chess can be used as a tool for social integration. In order to answer to that research question the chapter is composed the following four sections: Theoretical Background, Methods and Data, Collection, Results and Discussion. This will be a exploratory study, based in interviews with experts and participants, from which some preliminary results and an instrument to be implemented are derived.

THEORETICAL BACKGROUND

On Social Integration and Chess

It is well known that when someone is jailed, the rehabilitation and integration after prison may be helped or hindered by the experience the prisoner has during the jail term (Hoskins and Cobina, 2020). This means that if there is no practice of support, the individual will leave the prison with lower social skills then he entered, and as a consequence will most likely become a re-incident; furthermore, as humans are "social animals", if no alternative form of socialization is granted to the prisoners, they will tend to develop social contacts with their fellow inmates in a way that prisons will become "des-educational" institutions, in which bad habits, and negative values will pass from inmate to inmate; if this "vicious cycle" happens, the person will leave the prison even more "marginal" to the society than he or she entered, and the jail term would have ended des-educating and wronging the individual and not educating or in any form correcting himself (Foucault, 1975 and Guilford, 2019). Quite unfortunately, there are many examples of situations in which prisons ended up alienating or excluding the persons or even their close families (Murray, 2007). Therefore, it is quite important that prisons provide in-mates with some form of activity that may help their inclusion in the society after ending the jail term (Esteban and al, 2014; Pearson and al, 2002). Many diverse experiences have been tried, from teaching a job to develop an occupation inside (Hecker and Kuehn, 2019) or outside the jail (Santiago Quintal, 2021), to making the prisoner having a part in the management of the prison (Bishop, 2006), developing gardening skills (Harta and Reisner, 2021) or reading (Koman and Yee, 2021). As a general idea, if some positive social practice is developed and encouraged, it is possible that that practice will benefit the individual in the long run, and the after serving its term, the person will enjoy a positive life afterwards. It is in this context that chess may make a difference.

On Personality Traits and Chess

Personality may be described by a Five Factor Model (Rothman and Coetzer, 2003) composed namely by Openness to experience, Conscientiousness, Extraversion, Agreeableness and Neuroticism. Increased aggression and antisocial behaviour have been found to be associated with low Agreeableness, low Conscientiousness, and high Neuroticism (Dam and al, 2018). Dam and al, 2018 found that violent offenders scored significantly lower on Agreeableness, including the subfacets Trust, Altruism, and Compliance; also, within the violent offender group, Agreeableness was negatively associated with trait aggression, while Neuroticism, including the subfacets Angry Hostility and Impulsivity, was positively associated with both trait aggression and mental distress. Therefore, is seems that prisoners tend to have lower levels of Trust, Altruism and Compliance than non-prisoners and also higher levels of Angry Hostility and Impulsivity.

Chess may be a way to control Impulsivity. Chess is a game full of rules. Indeed, artificial intelligence-based computers might fulfil the dream of "cracking the chess code" and finding the "best way" or "the golden rule" to play the game (He. 2022); therefore to win in chess one has to control his or her emotions – indeed a game may be lost with a mistake and a lapse of concentration. Finally, chess is a game that has to be played with civility: there are dress code issues (FIDE. 2013), and players have to behave in respectful manner, handshaking before and after the game (Ganguly, 2021) – some notable incidents between chess players have been well documented labelled very negatively (Chessnews, 2008).

Also, chess is a form on confronting issues of Hostility and particularly of Angry Hostility. Chess is a combat, and no one likes to lose a game, even if it is played in a friendly mode – therefore to play chess one has to deal with "sore losers" issues which are very close to "Angry Hostility" issues. Chess is a way to learn how to lose, and to understand why we lose. Understanding defeats and coping with them is one of the best ways of maturing, and maturing is a decisive step to inclusion. Prisoners are people that may be trapped in a vicious cycle of personal and social defeats: understanding those defeats and coping with them may be the way to achieve victory in the future and to go from exclusion to inclusion and from a vicious cycle to a virtuous one.

Chess may also be a way to increase Compliance. Chess is a set of rules, about the pieces, and there are also social rules to play chess. Also, it is very difficult to cheat in chess – moves are written down, if not recorded, and any wrongly played move may be denounced to umpires; modern technologies made cheating possible and examples exist but are denounced (Doggers, 2015). Therefore, in chess, wining outside the rules is impossible. And consequently, Compliance is a consequence of playing chess.

Also, chess may enhance the levels of Trust, in two ways. First chess may increase one's Trust in her or himself because to win it is needed to be better than the opponent, making better moves or at least to making less mistakes. Second Chess may increase your trust in society because the game has stable rules and gives a sensation of stability to those that play it often. Finally, to learn chess one has to play a lot and to discuss with other fellow players; therefore, the Chess learning curve requires high levels of social Trust, which may help to increase the Trust of players.

Finally, even regarding Altruism, the cooperation that is needed to learn chess means that prisoners may have their levels of Altruism increased if they learn how to play better. Crucially even if Chess is a individual sport, to grow as a player cooperation and therefore Altruism are essential. The best world players achieve their major conquests with a team of advisers (so called "seconds"). The importance of the "seconds" is so high, that very recently a player (Daniil Dubov) was banned from playing in Russian national team, after it appeared that he was part of the team of Magnus Carlsen, the world champion, who beat the Russian player Ian Nepomniachtchi (Chess News, 2021 b)

Summing up on a Theoretical Model

We do not consider chess will change the prisoners Personality, but the believe that chess will changes their Behaviour, by having an impact in the five Personality traits we described. Therefore, we believe the psychological improvement derived from chess may have a positive social impact. That social impact is reflected in better and deeper socialization. That socialization will last after the moment the individual leaves prison and will lead to inclusion, employment, and well-being. Therefore, the possibility of chess contributing to inclusion is intuitively possible and theoretically grounded. As a consequence, we present the following theoretical model, defining chess as a tool for an inclusive policy for prisoners:

Teaching Chess --) Learning Chess --) Playing Chess --)

Psychological Effects ----)

Less Impulsivity (focus) Less Hostility (Chanel anger) More Compliance More Trust More Altruism ---) Change in Behaviour --) More Socialization ----) Leaving prison --) More Inclusion ---) Employment and Well being

In the next sections we will explain how this model has been put in place, in Portugal

KNOWN EXPERIENCES

The International Federation of Chess (FIDE) and the Cook County Sheriff Office, with sponsorship of Anatoly Karpov (12th World Chess Champion) created the Chess for Freedom Programme (Chess for Freedom, 2021) which started in May 2021 This programme was created after the big success of chess among inmates all over the world in countries such as United States of America, Russia, England, Brazil, Italy, Spain and even Portugal since 2012. The American case is very famous (International Chess Federation 2021a) Portugal, Spain, Russia, Armenia, United States of America and 26 more countries participated in First Intercontinental Online Chess Championship for prisoner on October 21 2021 (International Chess Federation 2021b and Chessbase, 2021). At the same time in England Carl

Chess as a Way of Inclusion of Prisoners

Portsman developed the Chess in Prison initiative (Mokal, 2018) from which he originated the book" Chess Behind Bars" (Portman, 2017).

METHODS AND DATA COLLECTION

Within this context, the Portuguese Chess Federation developed a partnership with the Portuguese Prisons Directorate, in order to teach chess to prisoners. The program has been ongoing since 2015. This activity is the specific focus of the chapter.

Phase 1: The Interview

Data were collected in two phases. First in November 2021 and December 2021 we interviewed Chess International Master António Frois, who in 2017 had visited a Portuguese prison and taught chess to the prisoners. We made a semi-structured interview. The main questions addressed in the interviews were the following:

1. How is Chess a tool for the integration of a prisoner in society?
2. This sport is attributed the quality of helping to control anxiety and aggression. What characteristics of chess promote the development of this self-control?
3. Is teaching chess to a captive citizen more demanding than teaching a freed citizen? If yes, what are the differences?
4. What evaluation has been made of this experience? Are there changes in the behaviour of prisoners who engage in this sport?

We did content analysis to the interview report, and we present it below.

Phase 2: Questionnaire and Journal Articles

We then developed a questionnaire within the setting of a 5 points Likert Scale, that is presented in section "Future studies" of this chapter, we believed could be useful to find the prisoners' opinion about the project. Unfortunately, even if we contacted the President of the Portuguese Chess Federation, we were not able to find answers.

Finally, we were able to find the written opinions of International Chess Master Antonio Frois, (Frois, 2019) one administrator (Reis, 2019), and two prisoners (Silva, 2019 and Semana, 2019) in a chess review of 2019. We used it as a base for the next section. The analysis of the texts was done in May 2022.

We did content analysis to the four texts.

We present the results of our analysis in the next pages of the chapter.

RESULTS

The Interview

Playing the Game

The specialist Antonio Fróis went to Paços de Ferreira, in north of Portugal, prison to teach chess to the prisoners, as a Portuguese master of chess. He explains that most of the prisoners had a clear expertise of the sport and he tried to make the games more difficult to test their skills.

About Order

António Fróis advocates that even when we put the pieces on the table we are already organizing and develop tools to social life. Every piece in chess has an order and a mission, as in a feudal society. In fact the chess board includes a social organization.

About Life

Futhermore, If we think about chess, as a strategic game it is not difficult to compare it with living our life: we have ways to win and we have ways to deal with failure. Here is one of the main reasons why this sport should be used in prisons to promote the rehabilitation of prisoners: António Fróis thinks that chess gives prisoners a way to be prepared for everything, meaning routines but also unexpected surprises when going out from jail to live a free life. Furthermore, according to Antonio Frois, we have a chessboard (which we can compare it with a city) with 64 squares (we can see them as streets), eight pieces (we can see them as city authorities) and eight paws (the citizens). As in society, we can observe a hierarchy. And in fact, in terms of hierarchy, there is the King, the Queen, the Tower, (representing the major weapons and most power full classes) the Bishop (in ancient times also called the Vizier), the Horse (representing the Infantry), and finally the pawns – representing the anonymous persons. According to Antonio Frois, even Garry Kasparov, a famous world chess champion, and probably the best-known chess player, compares chess to life. According to Kasparov, "our confidence level is reflected in how we move and talk, not just by what we say, but how we say it" (Kasparov, 2006. 197). This thought can be used as in chess as in day-to-day life, in an organized society. As in chess, "taking control" in life is crucial because it gives you power. Kasparov (2006) describes "empowerment" as a crucial concept in personal and professional lives. According to Kasparov, "when we feel in control, we are literally stronger" (Kasparov p.202, 2006).

About Strategies in Life

The experience of teaching chess in prisons is much more than a game or a hobby. It also can develop cognitive skills, as well as strategic thoughts, and tools to use in day-to-day life. Antonio Frois defends that chess prepares prisoners, unconsciously, to the community and society life, respecting the rules and hierarchy. At the same time, chess appears to be indifferent from their reality. As Fernando Pessoa, a Portuguese poet, wrote, mentioning indifference, "players ignore the outside noise"/ "everything that is serious no matters to us". (Reis, 2022) Therefore, chess appears in prisons as a hobby but also as a way of thinking about strategies of life.

Creativity and Aggressiveness

The perception of emotional control is a great feeling for those we live in prison and could be seen as a way of resocialization. According to Frois: Chess awakens the creative ability and logical/mathematical reasoning, which helps anyone find tools for their everyday life. In this context, a very important aspect is the issue of "decision-making. In any chess match a player on the first move has 20 different ways to do it, but in each game, you can only choose one! So, in one hand, as in our life, chess helps us to reflect on decision-making and bear the consequences of those same decisions". On the other hand, chess has an important mission controlling aggressiveness: According to Frois:

Aggressiveness is channelled to the search for the creativity of plays and reasoning, and even the question of lines: in chess there are lines, columns, and diagonals and 6 pieces with different movements.

The Texts

Here we summarize the ideas expressed in journal articles from 2019 by an administrator of the prison, Mr Reis, the main "change agent", Mr. Frois, and two prisoners that were involved in the experience, Mr Silva and Mr. Semana.

The Administrator

Master António Frois run a Workshop on Chess for Prisoners in Paços de Ferreira Jail on November 30th, 2018 (Reis, 2019). All the participants prisoners already new chess; prisoners were so eager to play that the meeting began with a "simultaneous" match so that each one could play with the Master as soon as possible; prisoners could show their skills and see the complexity of having to play an adversary of Master quality; it was evident for the Master that the prisoners were no beginners, but players with practice and study. After that there was a challenge of solving "mate in two" problems. Finally, there was a discussion on world champions, the functioning of tournaments and the ELO system. It was an enriching afternoon that should be repeated (Reis, 2019)

The Chess Master

I and my colleague Ruben Freitas, arrived at 20 past 1 pm and were received by lecturer Mr Miguel Lapa (Frois, 2019). The prisoners were quite excited with chess, because it allows them to do some extraordinary things in the difficult times they are having; the session was expected to last for one hour and lasted more than two hours (Frois, 2019). First, I gave a simul; then we discussed decision making and I mentioned Kasparov (2006), a fantastic book because, precisely it helps explaining how strategic thinking in chess may help day to day decisions; then Ruben and I played again with the prisoners – they were so "hungry for chess" it could have lasted much more time (Frois, 2019). Finally, in a very moving moment the prisoners offered a book of poems they made. These are the experiences that show what really matters in life

The Prisoners

I always loved strategy games, with tactics, that made me calculate (Silva, 2019); when I entered prison I played daily droughts, cards and domino, to keep the mind busy and to forget a bit where I was; after a while I did not enjoy the games anymore. Then one day in a class of Information Technology I found chess in a Windows file. I started by moving a pawn. I had no idea how complex it was, even If I had heard about it for long. The pieces looked like an old army, from Antiquity battles. The board had and epic beauty. I was conquered. I used my technology classes to play. I bought a board in a home visit. I began to play with fellow prisoners. Then I was transferred to Paços de Ferreira jail, and I met "the chess group". Here the level was much higher, but we studied and learnt. I was very well received and matured as a player. The group was my family. Everything I am as player is because of that group, found in the most improbable of places. It was the best thing that happened to me in prison. I am about to leave jail, but I know chess made me and helped me grow and will remain in my life.

Chess is extremely complex (Semana, 2019), and there are many parallels with life that must be taken into consideration: there is a beginning, equal and fair, and after each player seeks to capture the opposite king. Each piece has its own way to move and value in this strategy and a pawn may have more value than the Queen. There is some magic in being attacked by multiple moves, and to have mental discipline to avoid moves that lead to disaster – as in life, perhaps? In life we have to make choices, some easier than others. It may be a surprise, but while in jail, we seek to improve our capacity of choice, our evolution and discipline. In black and white piece, we discover yin e o yang, the Good and the Bad, and from that struggle we find balance. Chess is an entertaining battlefield that improves our capacities of reasoning. The most important characteristic for success, inside and outside the board is Know yourself, profit from your strengths and hide your weaknesses. This sounds like a cliché, but if one uses it as a rule, we will have success. Also important are discipline, capacity of calculation, nerves of steel, patience. I like to make sacrifices of pieces in order to win; sacrifices in chess as in life are dangerous – one miss may lead to defeat. The logic sequence that leads a player to recognize capabilities and liabilities is the same we should use for our continuous development as persons. Other important aspect is how to deal with complex situations; as humans, we tend to rush things; in chess we learn to plan in anticipation, to forecast the moves of the opponent and to prepare a trap, in order to gain advantage; and transposing to life we must ponder what can go well and band, minimizing unnecessary risks and only then act. Chess is much more than a game. It is a philosophy of life. If help us to grow as persons. It is a lesson on how to use scarce resources, material or time. Regardless different learning capabilities, hard work, will power and dedication make anyone improve. If you do not know how to play, start today; to win the first game is fantastic but to see the world as a chess player is beyond words. In jail, where there is no freedom, we find it in the only place where we will never be prisoners – our mind.

DISCUSSION

The information exposed in section 5 broadly supports the theoretical ideas exposed in section 2. Namely:

- both players highlighted the importance of chess as a way of growing as a person. This idea has also been advocated by national federations, in order to create classes of chess in the primary

Chess as a Way of Inclusion of Prisoners

schools – the question of those classes being mandatory being very problematic however (Jerrim and al, 2016).
- Chess is seen also as a way of controlling impulsivity by the players and the Master, because otherwise, the matches will be all lost.
- Chess is all about confronting hostility, because as in any sport, but particularly in this one that is silent and intellectual, the win can only be attained if hostility is fought and won over.
- Compliance is essential for the victory, because any foul play will lead to defeat.
- Finally, trust also is increased because players have to trust themselves, the opponent and the organizers, in order to play-

Some additional may be made. As expressed by António Frois in the follow up of the interview, the question of altruism, is very interesting because we cannot grow, in chess and in life, if we do not share our knowledge. Also, about the rules – in competition it is forbidden to interfere in another's player game, and only the player can call the arbiter in case of fault by the adversary – and this helps one learning how to fight for our own rights. On impulsivity, sometimes we decide too quickly, sometimes too slow, and the clock helps us to decide how to play well and fast! About creativity, sometimes the most obvious play is not the best – it is good to the creative to find the "truth of the position". One example shown by Master António Frois in Paços de Ferreira show this eloquently: White pawn in a7, pawn in c7 and King in c6. Black King in a7. Solution, mate in two, is promote c8 as Rook because as Queen, the Black King is stalemate.

These simple findings base the possibility of creating a large program to support chess in prisons in Portugal. The involvement of the chess federation and of the prisons' management would be primordial. The possibility of causing a positive impact in the prisoner's well-being and integration process is clear, given what was described in the previous pages. The question of mandatory participation could be debated; prisoners also have free will and may refuse to participate, but some type of "merit good" formula might be found for this case (Musgrave, 1987). Also, more workshops should be organized, now that the pandemic of COVID-19 is being more controlled. Also, when those workshops happen, scholars should be informed so that a more accurate and deep scientific assessment of the experience could be carried out.

This chapter as the limitation of having a very small, even if important and relevant sample of respondents. In the future we would like to enlarge the scope of the analysis. If the number of participants becomes large enough and they are monitored after learning the game and after serving sentence long enough, it will be likely be possible to pass from a well based intuition, as we have now, to a strongly defined policy of inclusion; when that happens, chess Masters like Antonio Frois, administrators like, Mr Reis, and two prisoners like Mr. Silva and Mr. Semana will find they contributed to something bigger than just chess, they helped the Portuguese society.

FUTURE RESEARCH DIRECTIONS

As a suggestion for further study, we would like to be able to send the following questionnaire in 5 points Likert Scale, from 1 totally disagree to 5 totally agree to the prisoners that studied chess in Portugal. The questions would be the following:

1. Chess Is important in my everyday life.
2. The practice of chess is important in my relations with the other inmates.
3. Other than a hobby, chess is important to me.
4. In chess I learn to have more order in my life.
5. Chess is a representation of society.
6. Chess is a representation of life.
7. With chess I learn to lose and win with ethics.
8. With chess I learn to deal with failures.
9. Chess makes me learn strategy.
10. Chess makes me develop cognitive skills.
11. With chess I become more focused.
12. With chess I reflect strategically about the life outside the prison.
13. Chess makes me be more creative.
14. Chess makes me be more aggressive.
15. Chess increases my creativity.
16. With Chess I increase the control of my emotions.
17. With chess I learn skills that I can use in a context of freedom.

These questions follow the model described in Figure 1. Namely the first four questions are about the importance of the game for the prisoner, the next two about the meaning of chess for the prisoners, and the other remaining eleven about the consequences of playing chess for the prisoner.

As another suggestion for further research, we would like to confirm the utility of the survey by comparing its results with the results of the inmates' history following release using data from DGRSP.

CONCLUSION

Chess is a game, an art and science. Chess entertains, educates and makes players grow as persons. Prisoners have difficulties, that may be addressed through and by chess. In 2015 Portugal began to support chess for prisoners, mostly in Paços de Ferreira. In 2018 a Workshop was held. After interviewing the International Master that managed the workshop and reading four accounts in a chess magazine from the chess Master, the prison administrator and two players we found that, by and large the expectations were met, and that chess effectively helped integrating those players.

REFERENCES

Semana, A. (2019). Xadrez, Jogo e Estratégia. Gaya Chess, (5), 8.

Bishop, N. (2006). Prisoner Participation in Prison Management. *Champ pénal/Penal field (Vol. 3)*. https://journals.openedition.org/champpenal/487

Silva, C. (2019). *Xadrez, Vida e Prisão Gaya Chess*. Gaya Chess, (5), 9.

Chess and Science. (2021). *Science and Chess*. https://www.chess-science.com/en/chess-and-science/

Chess and Technology. (2015). Ten Reasons why Chess is a Sport. *Chess and Technology.* https://londonchessconference.com/a-question-of-sport/.

Chess for Freedom. (2021). *About the Chess for Freedom program.* Chess for freedom. https://chessforfreedom.fide.com/

Chess News. (2008). Short-Cheparinov handshake game ends 1-0. *Chess News.* https://en.chessbase.com/post/short-cheparinov-handshake-game-ends-1-0

Chess News. (2021b). Dubov faces criticism in Russia after working for Carlsen. Chess News. https://en.chessbase.com/post/dubov-faces-criticism-in-russia

Chessbase (2021). Teams from 31 countries to participate in Championship for Prisoners. *Chess Base.* https://en.chessbase.com/post/championship-for-prisoners-2021-fide.

Chess.com. (2021). *Homepage.* Chess.com. https://www.chess.com/today

Dam, V., Hjord, L., Da Cunha-Bang, S., Sestoft Knudsen, D., & Stenbæk, D. (2018, March). Five-factor personality is associated with aggression and mental distress in violent offenders. *European Neuropsychopharmacology, 28*(Supplement 1), S35–S36. doi:10.1016/j.euroneuro.2017.12.061

Damião, P. (1512). *Questo libro e da imparare giocare a scachi et de li partiti.*

Dodona. (2021). On the origins of chess. *Dodna.* https://dodona.ugent.be/en/exercises/11405563/

Doggers, P. (2015). Sebastien Feller Can Play Chess Again. *Chess.com.* https://www.chess.com/news/view/sebastien-feller-can-play-chess-again-2037.

Esteban, F., Alós, R., Jódar, P., & Miguélez, F. (2014). 'Ex-inmates' job placement. a qualitative approach | [La inserción laboral de ex reclusos. Una aproximación cualitativa]. *Revista Espanola de Investigaciones Sociologicas, 145*(1), 181–204.

FIDE. (2013). *Fide Dress Code Policy: Help Chess By Wearing Proper Attire.* FIDE. https://www.fide.com/images/stories/NEWS_2013/FIDE/Proposal_of_Ms._B._Marinello_in_respect_of_the_dress_code.pdf

FIDE. (2021). *International Chess Federation – Homepage.* FIDE. https://www.fide.com/ .

Fine, G. (2015). *Players and Pawns - How Chess Builds Community and Culture.* Chicago University Press. doi:10.7208/chicago/9780226265032.001.0001

Foucault, M. (1975). *Surveiller et Punir.* Gallimard.

Frois, A. (2019). Workshops no Estabelecimento Prisional de Paços de Ferreira, Gaya Chess, N5. Pag 7.

Ganguly, P. (2021) Why Do Chess Players Shake Hands? (Explained!) https://chessdelta.com/why-do-chess-players-shake-hands/

Gifford, B. (2019). Prison crime and the economics of incarceration. *Stanford Law Review, 71*(1), 71–135.

Harta, F. B., & Reisner, M. (2021). More than just a gardening program – Using horticultural therapy and mindfulness practice to promote health and connection for incarcerated individuals and those preparing to re-enter their communities. *Acta Horticulturae,* (1330), 41–47. doi:10.17660/ActaHortic.2021.1330.6

He, W. (2022).. . *Computer Games Based on Artificial Intelligence Lecture Notes on Data Engineering and Communications Technologies*, *85*, 847–851.

Hecker, I., & Kuehn, D. (2019). Apprenticeship and the Justice System Adapting a Proven Training Model to Serve People in Prison. *Urban Institute*. https://www.urban.org/sites/default/files/publication/99822/apprenticeship_and_the_justice_system_0.pdf

Hoskins, K. M., & Cobbina, J. E. (2020, July). It Depends on the Situation: Women's Identity Transformation in Prison, Jail, and Substance Abuse Treatment Settings –. *Feminist Criminology*, *15*(3), 340–3581. doi:10.1177/1557085119878268

Humble, P. N. (1993, January). Chess as an art form. *British Journal of Aesthetics*, *33*(1), 59–66. doi:10.1093/bjaesthetics/33.1.59

Informator, Š. (2021). *Encyclopaedia of Chess Openings*.

International Chess Federation. (2021a). *Chess in prisons: The Cook County case*. FIDE. https://www.fide.com/news/1027.

International Chess Federation. (2021b). *Intercontinental Online Chess Championship for Prisoners announced*. FIDE. https://www.fide.com/news/1191

Jerrim, J., Macmillan, L., Micklewright, J., Sawtell, M., & Wiggins, M. (2016). *Chess in Schools: Evaluation Report and Executive Summary. Education Endowment Foundation*. ERIC.

Kalinin A. (2017). *Chess Training for Candidate Masters: Accelerate Your Progress by Thinking for Yourself*. New In Chess.

Kasparov, G. (2006). *How life imitates chess*. William Heinemann Ltd.

Kasparov, G. (2018). *Deep Thinking: Where Machine Intelligence Ends and Human Creativity Begins*. John Murray Press.

Koman, R.N. & Yee, M.S. (2021). Reading between the bars: Evaluating probation, remodelling offenders, and reducing recidivism. *British Journal of Community Justice 17*(2), 134-149.

Lichess. (2021). *Homepage*. Lichess. https://lichess.org/.

Lopez de Segura, R. (1561). *Libro de la invencion liberal y arte del juego del axedrez*.

McDonald, N. (2013). *Chess: The Art of Logical Thinking: From the First Move to the Last*. Batsford.

Metcalfe, T. (2021). Oh, the humanity: Chess computers changed the game, but not the players. *NBC News*. https://www.nbcnews.com/tech/tech-news/world-chess-championship-computers-push-limits-humanity-shines-rcna8282

Murray, J. (2007). The cycle of punishment: Social exclusion of prisoners and their children. *Criminology & Criminal Justice, 7*(1), 55-81. doi:10.1177/1748895807072476

Musgrave, R. (1987). Merit Goods. *The New Palgrave: A Dictionary of Economics, (vol. 3)*, 452-53.

Newborn, M. (1997). *Kasparov versus Deep Blue: Computer Chess Comes of Age Softcover reprint of the original* (1st ed. 1997). Edition Springer. doi:10.1007/978-1-4612-2260-6

Pearson, F.S., Lipton, D.S., Cleland, C.M., Yee, D.S. (2002) The effects of behavioral/cognitive-behavioral programs on recidivism. *Crime and Delinquency 48*(3), pp. 476-496

Portman, C. (2017). Chess Behind Bars. Quality Chess, UK.

Quintal, S. (2021, April-June). The (Un) Feasibility Of Education And Work As Instruments For The Release Of Justice Individuals. Eccos -. *Revista Científica (Maracaibo)*, (57), 1–19.

Reis, R. (2022). *Ricardo Reis Ouvi contar que outrora, quando a Pérsia*. Arquivo Pessoa. http://arquivo-pessoa.net/textos/2974

Reis, S. (2019). Workshops no Estabelecimento Prisional de Paços de Ferreira. Gaya Chess, (5), 7.

Rothmann, S., & Coetzer, E. P. (2003, October 24). The big five personality dimensions and job performance. *SA Journal of Industrial Psychology*, 29(1). doi:10.4102ajip.v29i1.88

Sadler, M. & Regan N. (2019). *Game Changer: AlphaZero's Groundbreaking Chess Strategies and the Promise of AI*. New in Chess.

Stezano, M. (2018). In 1950, Alan Turing Created a Chess Computer Program That Prefigured A.I. *History.com*. https://www.history.com/news/in-1950-alan-turing-created-a-chess-computer-program-that-prefigured-a-i

Stockfish (2021). *Homepage*. Stock Fish Chess. https://stockfishchess.org/

Tartakover, S. (2021). *Victory goes to the player who makes the next-to-last mistake*. FunSAAZ. https://funsaaz.com/quotes/victory/victory-goes-to-the-player-who-makes-the-next-to-last-mistake/

Turing, S. (2016). *Alan M Turing*. Centenary Edition Cambridge University Press.

Winter, E. (2021). Early Uses of 'World Chess Champion.' *Chess History*. https://www.chesshistory.com/winter/extra/champion.html

KEY TERMS AND DEFINITIONS

Chess: A millenary game.
Chess Master: A person that gained a national or international recognition.
Creativity: The possibilities of doing original things.
Inclusion: A process by which somebody successfully is integrated in society.
Learning: A process by which somebody becomes competent in an activity.
Prisoner: A person that lost liberty due to crime.
Strategy: A way of acting within a long term objective, not to be confounded with tactics which is the set of small steps necessary to put to strategy in place.

Compilation of References

Abbad, G. S., & Carlotto, M. S. (2016). Analyzing challenges associated with the adoption of longitudinal studies in Work and Organizational Psychology. *Revista Psicologia Organizações e Trabalho*, *16*(4), 340–348. doi:10.17652/rpot/2016.4.12585

ABERC. (n.d.). *Mercado Real*. [Real Market]. ABERC. https://www.aberc.com.br/mercado-real/

Abramova, I. (2011). Making Meaning of Work: Uncovering the Complexity of Immigrant Experience in a Multicultural Landscape. *Multicultural Perspectives*, *13*(4), 209–214. doi:10.1080/15210960.2011.616833

Abrams, D., & Hogg, M. A. (2006). *Social identifications: A social psychology of intergroup relations and group processes*. Routledge. doi:10.4324/9780203135457

Acemoglu, D., & Restrepo, P. (2018). The Race between Man and Machine: Implications of Technology for Growth, Factor Shares, and Employment. *The American Economic Review*, *108*(6), 1488–1542. doi:10.1257/aer.20160696

Adebanjo, D., Teh, P.-L., & Ahmed, P. (2016). The impact of external pressure and sustainable management practices on manufacturing performance and environmental outcomes. *International Journal of Operations & Production Management*, *36*(9), 995–1013. doi:10.1108/IJOPM-11-2014-0543

Adewale, A. A., & Dahiru, I., MukhtarShehu, A., & Kofar-Mata, B. A. (2020). Perceived Job Insecurity and Task Performance among Bank Employees in Nigeria Banking Industry: The Role of Emotional- Intelligence and Self-Efficacy. *Accounting and Taxation Review*, *4*(2), 13–32.

Adorno, T., Frenkel-Brenswik, E., & Levinson, D. (2019). *The authoritarian personality*. https://books.google.com/books?hl=it&lr=&id=SUmHDwAAQBAJ&oi=fnd&pg=PR23&dq=adorno+the+authoritarian+personality&ots=z_TV8ZCIff&sig=bLjdzeEI31bSEG-yKfl8_LTIHUM

Affonso, C. (2005). Nutrição, Prevenção e Qualidade de Vida. In A. Gonçalves, G. Gutierrez, & R. Vilarta (Orgs.), Gestão da Qualidade de Vida na Empresa (p. 141–146). IPES Editorial.

Agarwal, U. A. (2016). Examining perceived organizational politics among Indian managers: Engagement as mediator and locus of control as moderator. *The International Journal of Organizational Analysis*, *24*(3), 415–437. doi:10.1108/IJOA-07-2014-0786

Ager, A., & Strang, A. (2008). Understanding integration: A conceptual framework. *Journal of Refugee Studies*, *21*(2), 166–191. doi:10.1093/jrs/fen016

Aguirre, A., & Foret, J. (1994). Irregularity of working hours in railway workers and types of complaints. *International Archives of Occupational and Environmental Health*, *65*(6), 367–371. doi:10.1007/BF00383245 PMID:8034360

Compilation of References

Akar, S., & Erdoğdu, M. M. (2019). Syrian refugees in Turkey and integration problem ahead. *Journal of International Migration and Integration*, *20*(3), 925–940. doi:10.100712134-018-0639-0

Akın, A., Uysal, R., & Akın, Ü. (2016, Mart). Ergenler için Ostracism (sosyal dışlanma) Ölçeğinin Türkçe'ye uyarlanması. *Kastamonu Eğitim Dergisi, 24*(2), 895-904. https://dergipark.org.tr/tr/pub/kefdergi/issue/22590/241325

Alas, R., & Mousa, M. (2016). Cultural diversity and business schools' curricula: A case from Egypt. *Problems and Perspectives in Management*, *14*(2), 130–137. doi:10.21511/ppm.14(2-1).2016.01

Alazzani, A., Hassanein, A., & Aljanadi, Y. (2017a). Impact of gender diversity on social and environmental performance: Evidence from Malaysia. *Corporate Governance (Bingley)*, *17*(2), 266–283. doi:10.1108/CG-12-2015-0161

Alexander, N., Mathilde, S., & Øivind, S. (2021). Post-migration stressors and subjective well-being in adult Syrian refugees resettled in Sweden: A gender perspective. *Frontiers in Public Health*, *9*, 717353. doi:10.3389/fpubh.2021.717353 PMID:34568258

Alfrian, F. D. (2018). Does spirituality at work has an impact on the relationship between passion and innovative behavior of employee? *RJOAS*, *6*(78), 106–111. doi:10.18551/rjoas.2018-06.11

Allen, D., & Orifici, A. (2021). Home Truths: What did Covid-19 Reveal About Workplace Flexibility. *Australian Journal of Labour Law*, *34*(1&2), 77–94.

Allsopp, J., Sigona, N., & Phillimore, J. (2014). Poverty among refugees and asylum seekers in the UK. An evidence and policy review. *IRiS Working Paper Series*, *1*, 1–46.

Almeida, C., & Vasconcellos, V. (2018). Transexuais: Transpondo barreiras no mercado de trabalho em Sao Paulo? *Revista Direito GV*, *14*(2), 303–333. doi:10.1590/2317-6172201814

Almeida, F., & Santos, J. D. (2020). The effects of COVID-19 on job security and unemployment in Portugal. *The International Journal of Sociology and Social Policy*, *40*(9/10), 995–1003. doi:10.1108/IJSSP-07-2020-0291

Almeida, S. R., Penso, M. A., & Freitas, L. G. (2019). Identidade docente com foco no cenário de pesquisa: Uma revisão sistemática. *Educação em Revista*, *35*, 15–35. doi:10.1590/0102-4698204516

Alptekin, K., Ulutaş Akçay, D., & Gündüz Ustabaşı, D. (2018). Konya'da geçici koruma altında yaşayan Suriyeliler üzerine bir çalışma. *Sosyal Politika Çalışmaları Dergisi, 40*(2), 87-114. https://dergipark.org.tr/tr/download/article-file/561584

AltemeyerB. (2007). *The authoritarians.* https://theauthoritarians.org/options-for-getting-the-book/

Alves, M., & Galeão-Silva, L. (2004). A Crítica da Gestão da Diversidade nas Organizações. *RAE - Revista de Administração de Empresas, 44* (3), 20-29.

Amelia, A. (2018). *Employer branding: When HR is the new marketing.* Penerbit Buku Kompas.

Amil, S., Lemieux, I., Poirier, P., Lamarche, B., Després, J.-P., & Alméras, N. (2021). Targeting Diet Quality at the Workplace: Influence on Cardiometabolic Risk. *Nutrients*, *13*(2283), 2283. doi:10.3390/nu13072283 PMID:34209458

Amnesty International. (2014). *The State decides who I am: Lack of recognition for transgender people*. Amnesty. International. https://www.es.amnesty.org/uploads/media/The_state_decide_who_I_am._Febrero_201 4.pdf

Amnesty International. (2022). *Home*. Amnesty International. https://www.amnesty.org/en/what-we-do/refugees-asylum-seekers-and-migrants/.

Anderton, R., Botelho, V., Consolo, A. da Silva, A.D., Foroni, C., Mohr, M., & Vivian, L. (2020). The impact of the COVID-19 pandemic on the euro area labour market. *ECB Economic Bulletin*, *8*.

Andrade, C., & Lousã, E. P. (2021). Telework and Work–Family Conflict during COVID-19 Lockdown in Portugal: The Influence of Job-Related Factors. *Administrative Sciences*, *11*(3), 1–14. doi:10.3390/admsci11030103

Andresen, M., Domsch, M. E., & Cascorbi, A. H. (2007). Working unusual hours and its relationship to job satisfaction: A study of European maritime pilots. *Journal of Labor Research*, *28*(4), 714–734. doi:10.100712122-007-9010-5

Andrews, R., Boyne, G. A., Meier, K. J., O'Toole, L. J. Jr, & Walker, R. M. (2005). Representative bureaucracy, organizational strategy, and public service performance: An empirical analysis of English local government. *Journal of Public Administration: Research and Theory*, *15*(2), 489–504. doi:10.1093/jopart/mui032

Ansell, C., Sørensen, E., & Torfing, J. (2021). The COVID-19 pandemic as a game changer for public administration and leadership? The need for robust governance responses to turbulent problems. *Public Management Review*, *23*(7), 949–960. doi:10.1080/14719037.2020.1820272

Anund, A., Fors, C., Ihlström, J., & Kecklund, G. (2018). An on-road study of sleepiness in split shifts among city bus drivers. *Accident; Analysis and Prevention*, *114*, 71–76. doi:10.1016/j.aap.2017.05.005 PMID:28506403

APA Dictionary of Psychology. (n.d.). APA. https://dictionary.apa.org/

April, K., Katoma, V., & Peters, K. (2009). Critical effort and leadership in specialised virtual networks. *Annual Review of High Performance Coaching & Consulting*, *1*(1), 187–215.

Araújo, M. da P. N. (2002). *Avaliação do Programa de Alimentação do Trabalhador: um estudo da evolução normativa e do acesso de trabalhadores e empresas baianas* [Dissertação de Mestrado em Nutrição, Repositório Institucional da Universidade Federal da Bahia]. https://repositorio.ufba.br/handle/ri/11163

Arlinghaus, A., Bohle, P., Iskra-Golec, I., Jansen, N., Jay, S., & Rotenberg, L. (2019). Working time society consensus statements: Evidence-based effects of shift work and non-standard working hours on workers, family and community. *Industrial Health*, *57*(2), 184–200. doi:10.2486/indhealth.SW-4 PMID:30700670

Asendorpf, J. B., & Motti-Stefanidi, F. (2017). A longitudinal study of immigrants' peer acceptance and rejection: Immigrant status, immigrant composition of the classroom, and acculturation. *Cultural Diversity & Ethnic Minority Psychology*, *23*(4), 486–498. doi:10.1037/cdp0000155 PMID:28394167

Ashford, S. J., Lee, C., & Bobko, P. (1989). Content, Causes, and Consequences of Job Insecurity: A Theory-Based Measure and Substantive Test. *Academy of Management Journal*, *32*(4), 803–829. doi:10.2307/256569

Ashforth, B. E., & Johnson, S. A. (2001). Social Identity Processes. In Social Identity Processes in Organizational Contexts (Vol. 2, pp. 31–48).

Ashikali, T., & Groeneveld, S. (2015). Diversity management for all? An empirical analysis of diversity management outcomes across groups. *Personnel Review*, *44*(5), 757–780. doi:10.1108/PR-10-2014-0216

Asif, R., Fiaz, M., Khaliq, Z., & Nisar, S. (2019). Estimating The Mediating Role Of Organizational Identification In Determining The Relationship Between Qualitative Job Insecurity And Job Performance. *Journal of Managerial Sciences*, *13*(3), 175–187.

Attanasio, G., Battistella, C., & Preghenella, N. (2021). *Sustainable Value and Stakeholders: a Conceptual Framework from Multiple Case Studies*. Paper presented at the International Forum on Knowledge Asset Dynamics (IFKAD), Rome, Italy.

Austin, A. (2016). "There I am": A grounded theory study of young adults navigating a transgender or gender nonconforming identity within a context of oppression and invisibility. *Sex Roles*, *75*(5-6), 215–230. doi:10.100711199-016-0600-7

Compilation of References

Austin, J., Stevenson, H., & Wei-Skillern, J. (2006). Social and commercial entrepreneurship: Same, different, or both? *Entrepreneurship Theory and Practice, 30*(1), 1–22. doi:10.1111/j.1540-6520.2006.00107.x

Avery, D. R., McKay, P. F., Wilson, D. C., & Volpone, S. (2008*). Attenuating the effect of seniority on intent to remain: The role of perceived inclusiveness.* Paper presented at the meeting of the Academy of Management, Anaheim, CA.

Avery, D. R., McKay, P. F., Wilson, D. C., & Volpone, S. (2008, August). Attenuating the effect of seniority on intent to remain: The role of perceived inclusiveness. In meeting of the Academy of Management, Anaheim, CA.

Azcona, G., Bhatt, A., Davies, S. E., Harman, S., Smith, J., & Wenham, C. (2020). Spotlight on gender, COVID-19 and the SDGs: will the pandemic derail hard-won progress on gender equality? Spotlight on the SDGs. UN Women, New York.

Backhaus, N. (2022). Working time control and variability in Europe revisited: Correlations with health, sleep, and well-being. *International Journal of Environmental Research and Public Health, 19*(22), 14778. doi:10.3390/ijerph192214778 PMID:36429495

Baggio, M. (2017). About the relation between transgender people and the organizations: New subjects for studies on organizational diversity. *REGE - Revista de Gestão, 24*(4), 360-370. doi:10.1016/j.rege.2017.02.001

Bailinson, P., Decherd, W., Ellsworth, D., & Guttman, M. "Understanding organizational barriers to a more inclusive workplace" https://www.mckinsey.com/business-functions/organization/our-insights/understanding-organizational-barriers-to-a-more-inclusive-workplace

Bakirtzi, E. (2020). COVID-19 and Labour Law: Greece. *Italian Labour Law e-Journal,* Special Issue 1(13), 1-4.

Bakker, A. B., & Demerouti, E. (2007). The job demands-resources model: State of the art. *Journal of Managerial Psychology, 22*(3), 309–328. doi:10.1108/02683940710733115

Balducci, C., Avanzi, L., & Fraccaroli, F. (2018). The individual costs of workaholism: An analysis based on multisource and prospective data. *Journal of Management, 44*(7), 2961–2986. doi:10.1177/0149206316658348

Baldwin, R., & Weder di Mauro, B. (Eds.). (2020). *Economics in the Time of COVID-19*. London: Centre for Economic Policy Research (CEPR) Press. https://voxeu.org/content/economics-time-covid-19

Bandoni, D. H., Brasil, B. G., & Jaime, P. C. (2006). Programa de Alimentação do Trabalhador: representações sociais de gestores locais Workers' Food Program: local managers' social representations. *Revista de Saude Publica, 40*(5), 837–842. doi:10.1590/S0034-89102006000600013 PMID:17301905

Bannai, A., & Tamakoshi, A. (2014). The association between long working hours and health: A systematic review of epidemiological evidence. *Scandinavian Journal of Work, Environment & Health, 40*(1), 5–18. doi:10.5271jweh.3388 PMID:24100465

Bansak, K., Hainmueller, J. & Hangartner, D. (2016). How economic, humanitarian, and religious concerns shape European attitudes toward asylum seekers. *Science, 354* (6309)-217-222. doi:10.1126/science.aag2147

Barak, M. (2000). Beyond affirmative action: Toward a model of diversity and organizational inclusion. *Administration in Social Work, 23*(3/4), 47–68.

Barclay, J., & Scott, L. (2006). Transsexuals and workplace diversity. *Personnel Review, 35*(4), 487–502. doi:10.1108/00483480610670625

Bardin, L. (1977). Análise de Conteúdo. In L. Edições 70 (Ed.), *Revista Educação, 22*(37). http://books.google.com/books?id=AFpxPgAACAAJ%5Cnhttp://cliente.argo.com.br/~mgos/analise_de_conteudo_moraes.html#_ftn1

Bardin, L. (2011). *Análise de conteúdo,* 70. Edições.

Bardin, L. (2016). *Análise de Conteúdo* [Content Analysis]. Edições 70.

Barkowski, S., Schwartze, D., Strauss, B., Burlingame, G. M., & Rosendahl, J. (2020). Efficacy of group psychotherapy for anxiety disorders: A systematic review and meta-analysis. *Psychotherapy Research*, *30*(8), 965–982. doi:10.1080/10503307.2020.1729440 PMID:32093586

Barrington-Leigh, C., & Escande, A. (2018). Measuring Progress and Well-Being: A Comparative Review of Indicators. *Social Indicators Research*, *135*(3), 893–925. doi:10.100711205-016-1505-0

Barros, F., Zilveti, F., Isabella, G., Carvalho, H., Marques, J., Guilhoto, J., & Mazzon, J. (2016). *40 anos do Programa de Alimentação do Trabalhador: conquistas e desafios da política nutricional com foco em desenvolvimento econômico e social*. (J. Mazzon (org.)). Blucher.

Başaran, K. D. (2021). Peer bullying effects on psychological wellbeing of Syrian immigrant children: A literature review from Turkey, Lebanon, and Jordan. *Sosyal Çalışma Dergisi*, *5*(2), 245-257. https://dergipark.org.tr/pub/scd/issue/67855/978783

Bateson, P. (1988). The Biological Evolution of Cooperation and Trust. In D. Gambetta (Ed.), *Trust. Making and breaking Cooperative Relations* (pp. 14–30). Blackwell.

Batista Filho, M., & Rissin, A. (2003). A transição nutricional no Brasil: Tendências regionais e temporais. *Cadernos de Saude Publica*, *19*(suppl.1), 181–191. https://doaj.org/article/1988797ea06e4cfb8f4fac9687292f2a. doi:10.1590/S0102-311X2003000700019

Bauerband, L., Teti, M., & Velicer, W. (2019). Measuring Minority Stress: Invariance of a Discrimination and Vigilance Scale Across Transgender and Cisgender LGBQ Individuals. *Psychology and Sexuality*, *10*(1), 17–30. doi:10.1080/19419899.2018.1520143

Bauer, T. N., Bodner, T., Erdogan, B., Truxillo, D. M., & Tucker, J. S. (2007). Newcomer adjustment during organizational socialization: A meta-analytic review of antecedents, outcomes, and methods. *The Journal of Applied Psychology*, *92*(3), 707–721. doi:10.1037/0021-9010.92.3.707 PMID:17484552

Baumeister, R. F., & Leary, M. R. (1995). The need to belong desire for interpersonal attachments as a fundamental human motivation. *Psychological Bulletin*, *117*(3), 497–529. doi:10.1037/0033-2909.117.3.497 PMID:7777651

Baumeister, R. F., Twenge, J. M., & Nuss, C. K. (2002). Effects of social exclusion on cognitive processes: Anticipated aloneness reduces intelligent thought. *Journal of Personality and Social Psychology*, *83*(4), 817–827. doi:10.1037/0022-3514.83.4.817 PMID:12374437

Beauregard, T., Arevshatian, L., Booth, J., & Whittle, S. (2016). Listen carefully: Transgender voices in the workplace. *International Journal of Human Resource Management*, *29*(5), 857–884. doi:10.1080/09585192.2016.1234503

Beauregard, T., Booth, J., & Whiley, L. (2021). Transgender employees: Workplace impacts on health and well-being. In J. Hassard & L. D. Torres (Eds.), *Aligning perspectives in gender mainstreaming: Gender, health, safety and wellbeing* (pp. 177–196). Springer. doi:10.1007/978-3-030-53269-7_10

Bellini, M. I., Pengel, L., Potena, L., & Segantini, L. (2020). COVID-19 and education: Restructuring after the pandemic. *Transplant International*, *34*(2), 220–223. doi:10.1111/tri.13788 PMID:33205410

Bendassolli, P., & Gondim, S. M. G. (2014). Significados, sentidos e função psicológica do trabalho: Discutindo essa tríade conceitual e seus desafios metodológicos. *Avances en Psicología Latinoamericana*, *32*(1), 131–147. doi:10.12804/apl32.1.2014.09

Bennett, K. M., Scornaiencki, J. M., Brzozowski, J., Denis, S., & Magalhaes, L. (2012). Immigration and its impact on daily occupations: A scoping review. *Occupational Therapy International*, *19*(4), 185–203. doi:10.1002/oti.1336 PMID:22987528

Bentler, P. M. (1992). On the fit of models to covariances and methodology to the Bulletin. *Psychological Bulletin*, *112*(3), 400–404. doi:10.1037/0033-2909.112.3.400 PMID:1438635

Bentler, P., & Bonett, D. (1980). Significance tests and goodness of fit in the analysis of covariance structures. *Psychological Bulletin*, *88*(3), 588–606. doi:10.1037/0033-2909.88.3.588

Bentley, S., Peters, K., Haslam, S., & Greenaway, K. (2019). Construction at Work: Multiple Identities Scaffold Professional Identity Development in Academia. *Frontiers in Psychology*, *10*, 628. https:// doi:10.3389/fpsyg.2019.00628

Berntson, E., Sverke, M., & Marklund, S. (2006). Predicting perceived employability: Human capital or labor market opportunities? *Economic and Industrial Democracy*, *27*(2), 223–244. doi:10.1177/0143831X06063098

Berrill, J., Cassells, D., O'Hagan-Luff, M., & Stel, A. van. (2020). *The Relationship Between Financial Distress and Well-Being : Exploring the role of self-employment*. Sage. doi:10.1177/0266242620965384

Bezerra, I. W. L. (2015). *Avaliação da Efetividade do Programa de Alimentação do Trabalhador*. Universidade Federal do Rio Grande do Norte.

Bezerra, J. M., Matos, M. F., Oliveira, E. de S., & Costa, A. M. M. (2020). valiação da adesão do programa de alimentação do trabalhador: Uma revisão integrativa. *Research. Social Development*, *9*(5), 9–25.

Bibi, A. (2020). Job Insecurity and Job Performance of Nurses in Pakistan: The Roles of Work Engagement and Organizational Justice. *Business Research Review*, *6*(1), 7–20.

Bilen, D., & Kıran, B. (2020). Investigation of Post-Traumatic Stress Disorder and life satisfaction levels according to how Syrian refugees experience various traumatic experiences. *International Journal of Scientific Research*, *15*(26), 397–3987. doi:10.26466/opus.658813

Bion, W. (2003). *Experiences in groups: And other papers*. Taylor and Francis. https://api.taylorfrancis.com/content/books/mono/download?identifierName=doi&identifierValue=10.4324/9780203359075&type=googlepdf

Birinci, S., Karahan, F., Mercan, Y., & See, K. (2021). Labor market policies during an epidemic. *Journal of Public Economics*, *194*, 1–15. doi:10.1016/j.jpubeco.2020.104348

Birkeland, I. K., & Buch, R. (2015). The dualistic model of passion for work: Discriminate and predictive validity with work engagement and workaholism. *Motivation and Emotion*, *39*(3), 392–408. doi:10.100711031-014-9462-x

Bishop, N. (2006). Prisoner Participation in Prison Management. *Champ pénal/Penal field* (Vol. 3). https://journals.openedition.org/champpenal/487

Bispo, D. A., Dourado, D. C. P., & Amorim, M. F. C. L. (2013). Possibilidade de dar sentido ao trabalho além do difundido pela lógica do mainstream: Um estudo com indivíduos que atuam no âmbito do movimento hip hop. *Organizações & Sociedade*, *20*(67), 717–731. doi:10.1590/S1984-92302013000400007

Bitencourt, B. M., Gallon, S., Batista, M. K., & Piccinini, V. C. (2011). Para além do tempo de emprego: o sentido do trabalho no processo de aposentadoria. *Revista de Ciências da Administração*, *13*(31), 30-57. https:// doi:10.5007/2175-8077.2011v13n31p30

Bjånesøy, L. L. (2019). Effects of the Refugee Crisis on Perceptions of Asylum Seekers in Recipient Populations. *Journal of Refugee Studies*, *32*(1), 219–237. doi:10.1093/jrs/fey070

Blau, P. M. (1964). *Exchange and power in social life. Exchange and Power in Social Life*. Wiley., doi:10.4324/9780203792643

Blouch, R., & Azeem, M. F. (2019). Effects of perceived diversity on perceived organizational performance: Mediating role of perceived organizational justice. *Employee Relations*, *41*(5), 1079–1097. doi:10.1108/ER-05-2018-0150

Bockting, W., Coleman, E., Deutsch, M., Guillamon, A., Meyer, I., Meyer, W., Reisner, S., Sevelius, J., & Ettner, R. (2016). Adult development and quality of life of transgender and gender nonconforming people. *Current Opinion in Endocrinology, Diabetes, and Obesity*, *23*(2), 188–197. doi:10.1097/MED.0000000000000232 PMID:26835800

Bockting, W., Miner, M., Swinburne Romine, R., Hamilton, A., & Coleman, E. (2013). Stigma, mental health, and resilience in an online sample of the US transgender population. *American Journal of Public Health*, *103*(5), 943–951. doi:10.2105/AJPH.2013.301241 PMID:23488522

Bohle, S. A. L., Chambel, M. J., Medina, F. M., & Da Cunha, B. S. (2018). The role of perceived organizational support in job insecurity and performance. *RAE Revista de Administracao de Empresas*, *58*(4), 393–404. doi:10.1590/S0034-759020180405

Boho, A., Viazminsky, A., Morawa, E., Schmitt, G. M., Georgiadou, E., & Erim, Y. (2020). The prevalence and risk factors for mental distress among Syrian refugees in Germany: A register-based follow-up study. *BMC Psychiatry*, *20*(362), 362. doi:10.118612888-020-02746-2 PMID:32641014

Bolino, M. C., Kelemen, T. K., & Matthews, S. H. (2021). Working 9-to-5? A review of research on nonstandard work schedules. *Journal of Organizational Behavior*, *42*(2), 188–211. doi:10.1002/job.2440

Bonefeld, W. (1996). Monetarism and Crisis. In W. Bonefeld & J. Holloway (Eds.), *Global Capital, National State and the Politics of Money* (pp. 35–68). Macmillan. doi:10.1007/978-1-349-14240-8_3

Bonizzoni, P. (2016). The shifting boundaries of (un)documentedness: A gendered understanding of migrants' employment-based legalization pathways in Italy. *Ethnic and Racial Studies*, *40*(10), 1–20. doi:10.1080/01419870.2016.1229488

Books, C., Coody, L. C., Kauffman, R., & Abraham, S. (2020). Night shift work and its health effects on nurses. *The Health Care Manager*, *36*(3), 122–127. doi:10.1097/HCM.0000000000000297 PMID:32701608

Booysen, L. (2007). Managing cultural diversity: A south African perspective. In K. April & M. Shockley (Eds.), Diversity in Africa: The coming of age of a continent (pp. 51–92). New York, NY: Palgrave. doi:10.1057/9780230627536_5

Borba, D. (2008). *Individuação e expatriação: resiliência da esposa acompanhante* [Dissertação de Mestrado, Pontifícia Universidade Católica de São Paulo, São Paulo, Brasil].

Borges, L. O., & Barros, S. C. (2015). Inventário de significado do trabalho para trabalhadores de baixa instrução. In K. PuentePalácios & A. L. A. Peixoto (Orgs.). Ferramentas de diagnóstico para organizações e trabalho (pp. 232-260). Artmed.

Borges, L. O. (1999). As concepções do trabalho: Um estudo de análise de conteúdo de dois periódicos de circulação nacional. *Revista de Administração Contemporânea*, *3*(3), 81–107. doi:10.1590/S1415-65551999000300005

Borges, L. O., Alves-Filho, A., & Tamayo, A. (2008). Motivação e significado do trabalho. In *M. M. M. Siqueira (Org.), Medidas do comportamento organizacional: ferramentas de diagnóstico e de gestão* (pp. 215–248). Artmed.

Bornstein, D. (2007). *How to change the world: Social entrepreneurs and the power of new ideas*. Penguin Books.

Bowes, A., Ferguson, I., & Sim, D. (2009). Asylum policy and asylum experiences: Interactions in a Scottish context. *Ethnic and Racial Studies*, *32*(1), 23–43. doi:10.1080/01419870701722570

Brewer, M. B. (1991). The social self: On being the same and different at the same time. *Personality and Social Psychology Bulletin*, *17*(5), 475–482. doi:10.1177/0146167291175001

Brewer, M. B. (2007). The importance of being we: Human nature and intergroup relations. *The American Psychologist*, *62*(8), 728–738. doi:10.1037/0003-066X.62.8.728 PMID:18020737

Brown, A. D. (2019). Identities in Organization Studies. *Organization Studies*, *40*(1), 7–22. doi:10.1177/0170840618765014

Browne, M. W., & Cudeck, R. (1993). Alternative ways of assessing model fit. In K. Bollen & J. Long (Eds.), *Testing structural equation models* (pp. 445–455). Sage.

Brunetti, F., Matt, D. T., Bonfanti, A., De Longhi, A., Pedrini, G., & Orzes, G. (2020). Digital transformation challenges: Strategies emerging from a multi-stakeholder approach. *The TQM Journal*, *32*(4), 697–724. doi:10.1108/TQM-12-2019-0309

Budyta-Budzyńska, M. (2011). Adaptation, integration, assimilation: An attempt at a theoretical approach. *Warsaw Collegium Civitas*. http://migracje. civitas. edu. pl/migracje/images/pdf_eng.

Bullock, P., & Yaffe, D. (1988). Inflation, the Crisis and the Post-War Boom. In N. Satlıgan & S. Savran (Eds.), *Crisis of the World Capitalism* (pp. 223–291). Alan Press. (in Turkish)

Burdge, B. (2007). Bending gender, ending gender: Theoretical foundations for social work practice with the transgender community. *Social Work*, *52*(3), 243–250. doi:10.1093w/52.3.243 PMID:17850032

Burke, R. (2000). Workaholism in organizations: Psychological and physical wellbeing consequences. *Stress Medicine*, *16*(1), 11–16. doi:10.1002/(SICI)1099-1700(200001)16:1<11::AID-SMI825>3.0.CO;2-U

Burke, R. (2008). Work motivations, satisfactions, and health: Passion versus addiction. In R. Burke & C. Cooper (Eds.), *The Long Working Hours Culture. Causes, Consequences and Choices* (pp. 227–251). Emerald.

Burke, R., Oberklaid, F., & Burgess, Z. (2004). Workaholism among Australian women psychologists: Antecedents and consequence. *Women in Management Review*, *19*(5), 252–259. doi:10.1108/09649420410545971

Bustamante, A. V. (2011). Physicians cite hurdles ranging from lack of coverage to poor communication in providing high-quality care to latinos. *Health Affairs*, *30*(10), 191–199. doi:10.1377/hlthaff.2011.0344 PMID:21976336

Bustos, A. (2021). *El futuro del trabajo y cómo prepararnos para afrontarlo* (Issue March). Research Gate. https://www.researchgate.net/profile/Alfonso-Bustos/publication/350043257_El_futuro_del_trabajo_y_como_prepararnos_para_afrontarlo/links/604d1e7e92851c2b23c90685/El-futuro-del-trabajo-y-como-prepararnos-para-afrontarlo.pdf

Butler, J. K., & Cantrell, R. S. (1984). A Behavioral Decision Theory Approach to Modeling. *Clemson University*, *55*(1), 19–28.

Butt, A. S. (2021). Strategies to mitigate the impact of COVID-19 on supply chain disruptions: A multiple case analysis of buyers and distributors. *International Journal of Logistics Management*. doi:10.1108/IJLM-11-2020-0455

Buttner, E. H., Lowe, K. B., & Billings-Harris, L. (2010). Diversity climate impact on employee of color outcomes: Does justice matter? *Career Development International*, *15*(3), 239–258. doi:10.1108/13620431011053721

Byron, A., & Crafford, A. (2012). Identity at work: Exploring strategies for Identity Work. *SA Journal of Industrial Psychology*, *38*(1), 120–131. doi:10.4102ajip.v38i1.904

Calantone, R., Garcia, R., & Dröge, C. (2003). The effects of environmental turbulence on new product development strategy planning. *Journal of Product Innovation Management*, *20*(2), 90–103. doi:10.1111/1540-5885.2002003

Caldas, L. M. R. Jr. (1995). *O combustível da empresa moderna*. Inovação Empresarial.

Caligiuri, P., & Bonache, J. (2016). Evolving and enduring challenges in global mobility. *Journal of World Business*, *51*(1), 127–141. doi:10.1016/j.jwb.2015.10.001

Callea, A., Urbini, F., & Chirumbolo, A. (2016). The mediating role of organizational identification in the relationship between qualitative job insecurity, OCB and job performance. *Journal of Management Development*, *35*(6), 735–746. doi:10.1108/JMD-10-2015-0143

Campbell, N. S., Perry, S. J., Maertz, C. P. Jr, Allen, D. G., & Griffeth, R. W. (2013). All you need is. resources: The effects of justice and support on burnout and turnover. *Human Relations*, *66*(6), 759–782. doi:10.1177/0018726712462614

Campbell-Verduyn, M., & van Roozendaal, G. (2020). The Covid-19 Pandemic: Continuity and Change in the International Political Economy. *Globalisation Studies Groningen*. https://research.rug.nl/en/publications/the-covid-19-pandemic-continuity-and-change-in-the-international-

Campbell-Verduyn, M., Metinsoy, S., Linsi, L., & Brandi, C. (Eds.). (2021). *Special Collection: Global Political Economy of COVID-19*. Global Perspectives.

Canella, D. S., Bandoni, D. H., & Jaime, P. C. (2011). Densidade energética de refeições oferecidas em empresas inscritas no programa de alimentação do Trabalhador no município de São Paulo. *Revista de Nutrição*, *24*(5), 715–724. doi:10.1590/S1415-52732011000500005

Carlson, E., & Güler, A. (2018). Cultural involvement and preference in immigrant acculturation. *Journal of International Migration and Integration*, *19*(3), 625–647. doi:10.100712134-018-0554-4

Carneiro, L., & Silva, I. S. (2015). Trabalho por turnos e suporte do contexto organizacional: Um estudo num centro hospitalar [Shift work and organizational support: A study in a hospital]. *International Journal on Working Conditions*, *9*, 142–160.

Carpenedo, M., & Nardi, H. C. (2013). Mulheres Brasileiras na divisão internacional do trabalho reprodutivo: Construindo subjetividade(s). *Revista de Estudios Sociales*, (45), 96–109. doi:10.7440/res45.2013.08

Carvalho Martins, D. (2020). COVID-19 and Labour Law: Portugal. *Italian Labour Law e-Journal, 1*(13), 1-4.

Carvalho, P., Alves, F. J. O., Peixoto, A. L. A., & Bastos, A. V. B. (2011). Comprometimento afetivo, de continuação e entrincheiramento organizacional: Estabelecendo limites conceituais e empíricos. *Psicologia: Teoria e Prática*, *13*(2), 127–141.

Carvalho, V., & Bridi, M. A. (2015). Trabalho e desigualdade: A terceirização e seus impactos sobre os trabalhadores. *Revista da ABET*, *14*(1), 99–113.

Carvalho, V., Rita, R., & Chambel, M. J. (2021). Teleworkers' flourishing during COVID-19 lockdown: The work-family relationship. *Occupational and Environmental Medicine*, *78*(1).

Cassel, D. K., Moreira, G. S., & Ziliotto, D. M. (2005). A imigração alemã e a concepção de trabalho no Vale dos Sinos. *Revista Prâksis*, *1*(2), 57–62.

Castles, S., Korac, M., Vasta, E., & Vertovec, S. (2002). Integration: Mapping the field, report of a project by the University of Oxford Centre for Migration and Policy Research and Refugee Studies Centre. *Integration Research and Statistics Service* (IRSS), *Home Office online report 28/03*.

Cavalheiro, G. (2010). *Sentidos atribuídos ao trabalho por profissionais afastados do ambiente laboral em decorrência de depressão* [Dissertação de mestrado, Universidade Federal de Santa Catarina, Florianópolis, SC].

Compilation of References

Caza, B., & Creary, S. (2016). The construction of professional identity. *Perspectives on Contemporary Professional Work*, *1*(2), 259-285. https:// doi:10.4337/9781783475582.00022

Celik, S., Ashikali, T., & Groeneveld, S. (2011). De invloed van diversiteitsmanagement op de binding van werknemers in de publieke sector. De rol van transformationeel leiderschap. (The binding effect of diversity management on employees in the Dutch public sector. The role of transformational leadership). *Tijdschrift voor HRM*, *14*(4), 32–53.

CGU. (2017). *RELATÓRIO Nº 201702245*. CGU. https://eaud.cgu.gov.br/relatorios/download/11004.pdf

Ch'ng, P.-C., Cheah, J., & Amran, A. (2021). Eco-innovation practices and sustainable business performance: The moderating effect of market turbulence in the Malaysian technology industry. *Journal of Cleaner Production*, *283*, 124556. doi:10.1016/j.jclepro.2020.124556

Chartered Institute of Personnel and Development. (2019). *Health and Wellbeing Survey Report*. CIPD. https://www.cipd.co.uk/Images/health-and-well-being-at-work-2019.v1_tcm18-55881.pdf

Chell, E. (2007). Social enterprise and entrepreneurship: Towards a convergent theory of the entrepreneurial process. *International Small Business Journal*, *25*(1), 5–26. doi:10.1177/0266242607071779

Cheng, G. H. L., & Chan, D. K. S. (2008). Who suffers more from job insecurity? A meta-analytic review. *Applied Psychology*, *57*(2), 272–303. doi:10.1111/j.1464-0597.2007.00312.x

Cheng, S. (2013). Rethinking differences and inequality at the age of globalization: A case study of white immigrant domestic workers in the global city of Chicago. *Equality*, *32*(6), 537–556. doi:10.1108/EDI-07-2012-0059

Chen, Z., Poon, K. T., DeWall, C. N., & Jiang, T. (2020). Life lacks meaning without acceptance: Ostracism triggers suicidal thoughts. *Journal of Personality and Social Psychology*, *119*(6), 1423–1443. doi:10.1037/pspi0000238 PMID:32118466

Chess and Science. (2021). *Science and Chess*. https://www.chess-science.com/en/chess-and-science/

Chess and Technology. (2015). Ten Reasons why Chess is a Sport. *Chess and Technology*. https://londonchessconference.com/a-question-of-sport/.

Chess for Freedom. (2021). *About the Chess for Freedom program*. Chess for freedom. https://chessforfreedom.fide.com/

Chess News. (2008). Short-Cheparinov handshake game ends 1-0. *Chess News*. https://en.chessbase.com/post/short-cheparinov-handshake-game-ends-1-0

Chess News. (2021b). Dubov faces criticism in Russia after working for Carlsen. Chess News. https://en.chessbase.com/post/dubov-faces-criticism-in-russia

Chess.com. (2021). *Homepage*. Chess.com. https://www.chess.com/today

Chessbase (2021). Teams from 31 countries to participate in Championship for Prisoners. *Chess Base*. https://en.chessbase.com/post/championship-for-prisoners-2021-fide.

Chichekian, T., & Vallerand, R. J. (2022). Passion for science and the pursuit of scientific studies: The mediating role of rigid and flexible persistence and activity involvement. *Learning and Individual Differences*, *93*, 102104. doi:10.1016/j.lindif.2021.102104

Chin, J. L. (Ed.). (2009). *The psychology of prejudice and discrimination: A revised and condensed edition*. ABC-CLIO.

Chirumbolo, A., & Areni, A. (2005). The influence of job insecurity on job performance and absenteeism: The moderating effect of work attitudes. *SA Journal of Industrial Psychology*, *31*(4). Advance online publication. doi:10.4102ajip.v31i4.213

Chirumbolo, A., & Areni, A. (2010). Job insecurity influence on job performance and mental health: Testing the moderating effect of the need for closure. *Economic and Industrial Democracy*, *31*(2), 195–214. doi:10.1177/0143831X09358368

Chowdhury, P., Paul, S. K., Kaisar, S., & Moktadir, A. (2021). COVID-19 pandemic related supply chain studies: A systematic review. *Transportation Research Part E, Logistics and Transportation Review*, *148*, 1–26. doi:10.1016/j.tre.2021.102271 PMID:33613082

Christopher, M., & Lee, H. (2004). Mitigating supply chain risk through improved confidence. *International Journal of Physical Distribution & Logistics Management*, *34*(5), 388–396. doi:10.1108/09600030410545436

Chrobot-Mason, D., & Aramovich, N. P. (2013). The psychological benefits of creating an affirming climate for workplace diversity. *Group & Organization Management*, *38*(6), 659–689. doi:10.1177/1059601113509835

Chung, Y. W. (2018). Workplace ostracism and workplace behaviors: A moderated mediation model of perceived stress and psychological empowerment. *Anxiety, Stress, and Coping*, *31*(3), 304–317. doi:10.1080/10615806.2018.1424835 PMID:29325438

Clark, M. C., Payne, R. L., Journal, S., & May, N. (1997). The Nature and Structure of Workers'. *Trust in Management*, *18*(3), 205–224.

Cobb, J., & McKenzie-Harris, M. (2019). "And Justice for All"... Maybe: Transgender Employee Rights in America. *ABA JournaL of Labor & Employment Law*, *34*(91), 91–111.

Coelho, M. P., & Cézar, M. A. (2017). O sabiá e sua memória de elefante. *Mental (Barbacena)*, *11*(21), 396–410.

Cohen, E., Taylor, S., & Muller-Camen, M. (2012). *Effective Practice Guidelines Series HRM's Role in Corporate Social and Environmental Sustainability*. HRM. https://www.shrm.org/hr-today/trends-and-forecasting/special-reports-and-expert-views/Documents/Corporate-Social-Environmental-Sustainability.pdf

Colic-Peisker, V. (2009). Visibility, settlement success and life satisfaction in three refugee communities in Australia. *Ethnicities*, *9*(2), 175–199. doi:10.1177/1468796809103459

Colic-Peisker, V., & Tilbury, F. (2006). Employment niches for recent refugees: Segmented labour market in twenty-first century Australia. *Journal of Refugee Studies*, *19*(2), 203–229. doi:10.1093/jrs/fej016

Collins, J., McFadden, C., Rocco, T., & Mathis, M. (2015). The problem of transgender marginalization and exclusion. *Human Resource Development Review*, *14*(2), 205–226. doi:10.1177/1534484315581755

Colombo, E., Mercorio, F., & Mezzanzanica, M. (2019). AI meets labor market: Exploring the link between automation and skills. *Information Economics and Policy*, *47*, 27–37. doi:10.1016/j.infoecopol.2019.05.003

Colquitt, J. A., LePine, J. A., Piccolo, R. F., Zapata, C. P., & Rich, B. L. (2012). Explaining the justice-performance relationship: Trust as exchange deepener or trust as uncertainty reducer? *The Journal of Applied Psychology*, *97*(1), 1–15. doi:10.1037/a0025208 PMID:21910516

Colquitt, J. A., Scott, B. A., & LePine, J. A. (2007). Trust, Trustworthiness, and Trust Propensity: A Meta-Analytic Test of Their Unique Relationships With Risk Taking and Job Performance. *The Journal of Applied Psychology*, *92*(4), 909–927. doi:10.1037/0021-9010.92.4.909 PMID:17638454

Columbia University. (n.d.). *Content Analysis*. Columbia University. https://www.publichealth.columbia.edu/research/population-health-methods/content-analysis

Comin, L. C., & Pauli, J. (2018). The Meaning Of Work, Organizational Socialization And Work Context: The Perspective Of Migrant Workers. *Revista de Administração Mackenzie*, 19(spe). doi:10.1590/1678-6971/eramd180088

Cooper, D., Rockmann, K. W., Moteabbed, S., & Thatcher, S. M. B. (2021). Integrator or gremlin? Identity partnerships and team newcomer socialization. *Academy of Management Review*, *46*(1), 128–146. doi:10.5465/amr.2018.0014

Corlett, S., Coupland, C., McInnes, P., & Sheep, M. (2017). Exploring the registers of identity research. *International Journal of Management Reviews*, *17*, 409-412. https:// doi:10.1111/ijmr.12080

Cortelazzo, L., Bruni, E., & Zamperie, R. (2019). The Role of Leadership in a Digitalized World: A Review. *Front Psychology*, *10*(1938), 1–21.

Costa, A. C., Fulmer, C. A., & Anderson, N. R. (2017). Trust in work teams: An integrative review, multilevel model, and future directions. *Journal of Organizational Behavior*, (July). doi:10.1002/job.2213

Costa, G. (2003). Shift work and occupational medicine: An overview. *Occupational Medicine*, *53*(2), 83–88. doi:10.1093/occmed/kqg045 PMID:12637591

Costa, G. (2006). Flexibility of working hours in the 24-hour society. *La Medicina del Lavoro*, *97*(2), 280–287. PMID:17017360

Costa, G. (2016). Introduction to problems of shift work. In I. Iskra-Golec, J. Barnes-Farrell, & P. Bohle (Eds.), *Social and Family Issues in Shift Work and Non Standard Working Hours* (pp. 19–35). Springer International Publishing. doi:10.1007/978-3-319-42286-2_2

Costa, P., & Davies, M. (2012). Portuguese adolescents' attitudes toward sexual minorities: Transphobia, homophobia, and gender role beliefs. *Journal of Homosexuality*, *59*(10), 1424–1442. doi:10.1080/00918369.2012.724944 PMID:23153027

Costa, S. S. (2020). Pandemia e desemprego no Brasil. *Revista de Administração Pública*, *54*(4), 969–978. doi:10.1590/0034-761220200170

Cox, T. (1994). *Cultural Diversity in Organizations: Theory, Research & Practice*. Berrett Koehler.

Cox, T. (2001). *Creating a Multicultural Organization: A Strategy for Capturing the Power of Diversity*. Jossey-Koehler.

Cox, T. H. Jr. (1994). *Cultural diversity in organizations: Theory, research, & practice*. Berrett-Koehler.

Craig, L., & Powell, A. (2011). Non-standard work schedules, work-family balance and the gendered division of childcare. *Work, Employment and Society*, *25*(2), 274–291. doi:10.1177/0950017011398894

Crawley, H. (2021). The Politics of Refugee Protection in a (Post)COVID-19 World. *Social Sciences*, *10*(3), 81. doi:10.3390ocsci10030081

Cropanzano, R., & Mitchell, M. S. (2005). Social Exchange Theory: An Interdisciplinary Review. *Journal of Management*, *31*(6), 874–900. doi:10.1177/0149206305279602

Cropanzano, R., Rupp, D. E., & Byrne, Z. S. (2003). The relationship of emotional exhaustion to work attitudes, job performance, and organizational citizenship behaviors. *The Journal of Applied Psychology*, *88*(1), 160–169. doi:10.1037/0021-9010.88.1.160 PMID:12675403

Cummins, R. A., McCabe, M. P., Romeo, Y., & Gullone, E. (1994). The Comprehensive Quality of Life Scale: Instrument development and psychometric evaluation on tertiary staff and students. *Educational and Psychological Measurement*, *54*, 372–382. doi:10.1177/0013164494054002011

Curtin, R. T., Davidson, R., & Paul, D. (2018). Panel Study of Entrepreneurial Dynamics, PSED II, United States, 2005-2011: Version 1 [Data set]. Inter-University Consortium for Political and Social Research. doi:10.3886/ICPSR37202.V1 da Silva, T. (2005). Pensando a Gestão Estratégica, Saúde e a Qualidade de Vida. In A. Gonçalves, G. L. Gutierrez, & R. Vilarta (Orgs.), Gestão da Qualidade de Vida na Empresa (p. 147–152). IPES Editorial.

Dacin, P. A., Dacin, M. T., & Matear, M. (2010). Social entrepreneurship: Why we don't need a new theory and how we move forward from here. *The Academy of Management Perspectives*, *24*(3), 37–57.

Dal Forno, C., Canabarro, R., & Macedo, M. (2020). O Trabalho como Potencialidade Subjetiva na Experiência Migratória. *Estudos e Pesquisas em Psicologia*, *20*(1), 309–329. doi:10.12957/epp.2020.50836

Damião, P. (1512). *Questo libro e da imparare giocare a scachi et de li partiti*.

Dam, V., Hjord, L., Da Cunha-Bang, S., Sestoft Knudsen, D., & Stenbæk, D. (2018, March). Five-factor personality is associated with aggression and mental distress in violent offenders. *European Neuropsychopharmacology*, *28*(Supplement 1), S35–S36. doi:10.1016/j.euroneuro.2017.12.061

Dargie, E., Blair, K., Pukall, C., & Coyle, S. (2014). Somewhere under the rainbow: Exploring the identities and experiences of trans persons. *The Canadian Journal of Human Sexuality*, *23*(2), 60–74. doi:10.3138/cjhs.2378

Darvishmotevali, M., & Ali, F. (2020). Job insecurity, subjective well-being and job performance: The moderating role of psychological capital. *International Journal of Hospitality Management*, *87*, 102462. doi:10.1016/j.ijhm.2020.102462

Davidsen, A. H., & Petersen, M. S. (2021). The impact of covid-19 restrictions on mental well-being and working life among faroese employees. *International Journal of Environmental Research and Public Health*, *18*(9), 4775. doi:10.3390/ijerph18094775 PMID:33947133

Davidson, S. (2016). Gender inequality: Nonbinary transgender people in the workplace. *Cogent Social Sciences*, *2*(1), 1236511. doi:10.1080/23311886.2016.1236511

Davis, D. (2009). Transgender issues in the workplace: HRD's newest challenge/opportunity. *Advances in Developing Human Resources*, *11*(1), 109–120. doi:10.1177/1523422308329189

Davis, J., Schoorman, F. D., Mayer, R. C., & Tan, H. H. (2000). The Trusted General Manager and Business Unit Performance: Empirical Evidence of a Competitive Advantage. *Strategic Management Journal*, *21*(5), 563–576. doi:10.1002/(SICI)1097-0266(200005)21:5<563::AID-SMJ99>3.0.CO;2-0

Daya, P. (2014). Diversity and inclusion in an emerging market context, equality diversity and inclusion. *International Journal (Toronto, Ont.)*, *33*(3), 293–308.

Daya, P. (2014). Diversity and inclusion in an emerging market context. *Equality, Diversity and Inclusion*, *33*(3), 293–308. doi:10.1108/EDI-10-2012-0087

De Cuyper, N., & De Witte, H. (2007). Job insecurity in temporary versus permanent workers: Associations with attitudes, well-being, and behaviour. *Work and Stress*, *21*(1), 65–84. doi:10.1080/02678370701229050

de Paula, C. L. C., & Dias, J. C. R. (2017). Avaliação do consumo alimentar e perfil nutricional de colaboradores atendidos por uma Unidade de Alimentação e Nutrição (UAN). *Revista Ciências Nutricionais Online*, *1*(1), 11–20. https://unifafibe.com.br/revistasonline/arquivos/cienciasnutricionaisonline/sumario/46/27032017152056.pdf

De Witte, H. (1999). Job Insecurity and Psychological Well-being: Review of the Literature and Exploration of Some Unresolved Issues. *European Journal of Work and Organizational Psychology*, *8*(2), 155–177. doi:10.1080/135943299398302

De Witte, H., & Näswall, K. (2003). "Objective" vs "subjective" job insecurity: Consequences of temporary work for job satisfaction and organizational commitment in four European countries. *Economic and Industrial Democracy*, *24*(2), 149–188. doi:10.1177/0143831X03024002002

Deci, E. L., Olafsen, A. H., & Ryan, R. M. (2017). Self-Determination Theory in Work Organizations: The State of a Science. *Annual Review of Organizational Psychology and Organizational Behavior*, *4*(1), 19–43. doi:10.1146/annurev-orgpsych-032516-113108

Deci, E. L., & Ryan, R. M. (2000). The "what" and "why" of goal pursuits: Human needs and the self-determination of behavior. *Psychological Inquiry*, *11*(4), 227–268. doi:10.1207/S15327965PLI1104_01

Deci, E. L., & Ryan, R. M. (2008). Self-Determination Theory : A Macrotheory of Human Motivation, Development, and Health. *Canadian Psychology*, *49*(3), 182–185. doi:10.1037/a0012801

Decreto nº 10.854, de 10 de novembro da Presidência da República do Brasil, Pub. L. No. Diário Oficial da União-Seção 1-11/11/202; Edição 212 Seção 1;Página 3 (2021). https://www.in.gov.br/en/web/dou/-/decreto-n.10.854-de-10-de-novembro-de-2021-359085615

Decreto nº 349, de 21 de novembro da Presidência da República do Brasil, Pub. L. No. Diário Oficial da União-Seção 1-22/11/1991, Página 26443 (1991).

Decreto nº 77.116, de 6 de fevereiro de 1976. da Presidência da República do Brasil, Pub. L. No. Diário Oficial da União-Seção 1-6/2/1976, Página 1745 (1976). https://www2.camara.leg.br/legin/fed/decret/1970-1979/decreto-77116-6-fevereiro-1976-425734-publicacaooriginal-1-pe.html

Decreto nº 78.676, de 08 de novembro da Presidência da República do Brasil, Pub. L. No. Diário Oficial da União-Seção 1-9/11/1976, Página 14807 (1976). https://www2.camara.leg.br/legin/fed/decret/1970-1979/decreto-78676-8-novembro-1976-427964-publicacaooriginal-1-pe.html

DeJong, B. (2016). Team Trust Meta-analysis. *Memory (Hove, England)*. doi:0.1037/1093-4510

Delios, A., Perchthold, G., & Capri, A. (2021). Cohesion, COVID-19 and contemporary challenges to globalization. *Journal of World Business*, *56*(3), 1–8. doi:10.1016/j.jwb.2021.101197

Deloitte. (2011). Only skin deep? Reexamining the business case for diversity. Deloitte.

DeLongis, A., Folkman, S., & Lazarus, R. S. (1988). The impact of daily stress on health and mood: Psychological and social resources as mediators. *Journal of Personality and Social Psychology*, *54*(3), 486–495. doi:10.1037/0022-3514.54.3.486 PMID:3361420

Departamento Intersidical de Estatística e Estudos Socioeconômicos (DIEESE). (2013). *Relatório Final sobre o Programa de Alimentação do Trabalhador*. PAT.

DeSalvo, K., Hughes, Bç, Bassett, M., Benjamin, G., Fraser, M., Galea, S., & Gracia, J.N. (2021) Public Health COVID-19 Impact Assessment: Lessons Learned and Compelling Needs. *NAM Perspect*.

Detert, J. R., & Burris, E. R. (2007). Leadership behavior and employee voice: Is the door really open? *Academy of Management Journal*, *50*(4), 869–884. doi:10.5465/amj.2007.26279183

Dhande, K. K., & Sharma, S. (2011). Influence of shift work in process industry on workers' occupational health, productivity, and family and social life: An ergonomic approach. *Human Factors and Ergonomics in Manufacturing*, *21*(3), 260–268. doi:10.1002/hfm.20231

Di Marco, D., López-Cabrera, R., Arenas, A., Giorgi, G., Arcangeli, G., & Mucci, N. (2016). Approaching the discriminatory work environment as stressor: The protective role of job satisfaction on health. *Frontiers in Psychology*, *7*. doi:10.3389/fpsyg.2016.01313 PMID:27625625

Dias, J., & Bernardineli, M. (2016). O Transexual e o Direito de Acesso ao Mercado de Trabalho: Do Preconceito a Ausência de Oportunidades. *Revista de Gênero. Sexualidade e Direito*, *2*(2), 243. doi:10.26668/2525-9849/Index_Law_Journals/2016.v2i2.1376

Dickie, V. A. (2003). Establishing Worker Identity: A Study of People in Craft Work. *Am J Occup*, *57*(3), 250–261. doi:10.5014/ajot.57.3.250 PMID:12785663

Diener, E., & Biswas-Diener, R. (2008). *Happiness: Unlocking the mysteries of psychological wealth*. Blackwell Publishing., doi:10.1002/9781444305159

Diener, E., Oishi, S., & Lucas, R. E. (2003). Personality, culture, and subjective well- being: Emotional and cognitive evaluations of life. *Annual Review of Psychology*, *54*(1), 403–425. doi:10.1146/annurev.psych.54.101601.145056 PMID:12172000

Diener, E., Pressman, S. D., Hunter, J., & Delgadillo-Chase, D. (2017). If, why, and when subjective well-being influences health, and future needed research. *Applied Psychology. Health and Well-Being*, *9*(2), 133–167. doi:10.1111/aphw.12090 PMID:28707767

Dietz, G., & Den Hartog, D. N. (2006). Measuring trust inside organisations. *Personnel Review*, *35*(5), 557–588. doi:10.1108/00483480610682299

Dirks, K. T., & Ferrin, D. L. (2002). Trust in leadership: Meta-analytic findings and implications for research and practice. *The Journal of Applied Psychology*, *87*(4), 611–628. doi:10.1037/0021-9010.87.4.611 PMID:12184567

Dobni, C. B. (2008). The DNA of innovation. *The Journal of Business Strategy*, *29*(2), 43–50. doi:10.1108/02756660810858143

Docherty, P., Kira, M., & Shani, A. B. (2009). What the world needs now is sustainable work systems. In P. Docherty, M. Kira, & A. B. Shani (Eds.), *Creating sustainable work systems: Developing social sustainability* (pp. 1–32). Routledge.

Dodona. (2021). On the origins of chess. *Dodna*. https://dodona.ugent.be/en/exercises/11405563/

Doggers, P. (2015). Sebastien Feller Can Play Chess Again. *Chess.com*. https://www.chess.com/news/view/sebastien-feller-can-play-chess-again-2037.

Dolphin, T. (Ed.). (2015). *Technology, Globalisation and the future of work in Europe: Essays on employment in a digitised economy*. Institute for Public Policy Research. https://www.ippr.org/publications/technology-globalisation-and-the-future-of-work-in-europe

Dongrey, R., & Rokade, V. (2021). Assessing the effect of perceived diversity practices and psychological safety on contextual performance for sustainable workplace. *Sustainability (Switzerland)*, *13*(21), 11653. doi:10.3390u132111653

Dotan-Eliaz, O., Sommer, K. L., & Rubin, Y. S. (2009). Multilingual groups: Effects of linguistic ostracism on felt rejection and anger, coworker attraction, perceived team potency, and creative performance. *Basic and Applied Social Psychology*, *31*(4), 363–375. doi:10.1080/01973530903317177

Dovidio, J. F. (2001). On the nature of contemporary prejudice: The third wave. *The Journal of Social Issues*, *57*(4), 829–849. doi:10.1111/0022-4537.00244

Drela, K., Malkowska, A., Bera, A., & Tokarz-Kocik, A. (2021). Instruments for Managing the EU Labour Market in the Face of the COVID-19 Crisis. *European Research Studies*, *24*(1), 984–998. doi:10.35808/ersj/2006

Durand, M., & Boarini, R. (2016). Well-Being as a Business Concept. *Humanistic Management Journal*, *1*(1), 127–137. doi:10.100741463-016-0007-1

Compilation of References

Dutton, J., Roberts, L., & Bednar, J. (2010). Pathways for Positive Identity Construction at Work: Four Types of Positive Identity and the Building of Social Resources. *Academy of Management Review*, 35. https:// doi:10.5465/AMR.2010.48463334

Echterhoff, G., Hellmann, J. H., Back, M. D., Kartner, J., Morina, N., & Hertel, G. (2020). Psychological antecedents of refugee integration (PARI). *Perspectives on Psychological Science*, 15(4), 856–879. doi:10.1177/1745691619898838 PMID:32392450

Edelman. (2019). 2019 Edelman Trust Barometer Global Report. In *Edelman Trust Barometer*. https://cms.edelman.com/sites/default/files/2017-03/2009-Trust-Barometer-Global-Deck.pdf

Edelman. (2020). *Edelman Trust Barometer 2020*. Edelman.

Edwards, J. R., & Billsberry, J. (2010). Testing a multidimensional theory of person-environment fit. *Journal of Managerial Issues*, 22, 476–493. https://www.jstor.org/stable/25822526

Edwards, J. R., Caplan, R. D., & Harrison, R. V. (1998). Person-environment fit theory: Conceptual foundations, empirical evidence and directions for future research. In C. L. Cooper (Ed.), *Theories of organizational stress* (pp. 28–67). Oxford University Press., doi:10.1057/9781137310651

Ehnert, I., Parsa, S., Roper, I., Wagner, M., & Muller-Camen, M. (2016). Reporting on sustainability and HRM : A comparative study of sustainability reporting practices by the world's largest companies. *International Journal of Human Resource Management*, 27(1), 88–108. doi:10.1080/09585192.2015.1024157

Eid, M., & Larsen, R. J. (Eds.). (2008). *The science of subjective well-being*. Guilford Press.

Elkington, J. (2018). 25 Years Ago I Coined the Phrase "Triple Bottom Line." Here's Why It's Time to Rethink It. *Harvard Business Review*. https://hbr.org/2018/06/25-years-ago-i-coined-the-phrase-triple-bottom-line-heres-why-im-giving-up-on-it

Elkington, J. (1997). *Cannibals with Forks: The Triple Bottom Line of 21st Century Business*. Capstone Publishing.

Ely, R. J., & Thomas, D. A. (2001). Cultural diversity at work: The effects of diversity perspectives on work group processes and outcomes. *Administrative Science Quarterly*, 46(2), 229–273. doi:10.2307/2667087

Emerson, J. (2003). The blended value proposition: Integrating social and financial returns. *California Management Review*, 45(4), 35–51. doi:10.2307/41166187

Engell, A. D., Haxby, J. V., & Todorov, A. (2007). Implicit trustworthiness decisions: Automatic coding of face properties in the human amygdala. *Journal of Cognitive Neuroscience*, 19(9), 1508–1519. doi:10.1162/jocn.2007.19.9.1508 PMID:17714012

Erdoğan, M. M. (2020). "Securitization from Society" and "Social Acceptance": Political Party-Based Approaches in Turkey to Syrian Refugees. *Uluslararası İlişkiler Dergisi*, 17(68), 73–92.

Ertorer, S. E. (2021). Asylum regimes and refugee experiences of precarity: The case of Syrian refugees in Turkey. *Journal of Refugee Studies*, 34(3), 2568–2592. doi:10.1093/jrs/feaa089

ESM. (2014). *Conclusion of EFSF financial assistance programme for Portugal: an overview*. ESM. https://www.esm.europa.eu/sites/default/files/portugal_exit_pppresentation.pdf

ESM. (2017). *Lending Toolkit*. ESM. https://www.esm.europa.eu/assistance/lending-toolkit

ESM. (2018). *Conclusion of ESM programme for Greece: an overview*. ESM. https://www.esm.europa.eu/sites/default/files/greece_programme_conclusion_presentation.pdf

ESM. (2019). *Annual Report*. ESM. https://www.esm.europa.eu/sites/default/files/esm-annual-report-2019.pdf

ESM. (2020a). *Lessons from Financial assistance to Greece*. ESM. https://www.esm.europa.eu/sites/default/files/lessons-financial-assistance-greece.pdf

ESM. (2020b). *Conditionality*. ESM. https://www.esm.europa.eu/assistance/programme-database/conditionality

ESM. (2020c). *Greece emerges from crisis*. ESM. https://www.esm.europa.eu/assistance/greece#bringing_greece_back_to_growth

ESM. (2020d). Portugal regained economic footing. https://www.esm.europa.eu/assistance/portugal

Espitia, A., Mattoo, A., Rocha, N., Ruta, M., & Winkle, D. (2022). Pandemic trade: COVID-19, remote work and global value chains. Invited Review. *World Economy*, *45*(2), 561–589. doi:10.1111/twec.13117 PMID:33821085

Esses, V. M. (2020). Prejudice and discrimination toward immigrants. *Annual Review of Psychology*, *72*(1), 503–531. doi:10.1146/annurev-psych-080520-102803 PMID:32916080

Esses, V. M., Medianu, S., & Lawson, A. S. (2013). Uncertainty, threat, and the role of the media in promoting the dehumanization of immigrants and refugees. *The Journal of Social Issues*, *69*(3), 518–536. doi:10.1111/josi.12027

Esteban, F., Alós, R., Jódar, P., & Miguélez, F. (2014). 'Ex-inmates' job placement. a qualitative approach | [La inserción laboral de ex reclusos. Una aproximación cualitativa]. *Revista Espanola de Investigaciones Sociologicas*, *145*(1), 181–204.

Estrin, S., Mickiewicz, T., & Stephan, U. (2013). Entrepreneurship, Social Capital, and Institutions: Social and Commercial Entrepreneurship across Nations. *Entrepreneurship Theory and Practice*, *37*(3), 479–504. doi:10.1111/etap.12019

Eurofound. (2015). *European Working Conditions Survey – Data visualisation*. Eurofund. https://www.eurofound.europa.eu/data/european-working-conditions-survey

European Commission. (2010). *Psychosocial risks and health effects of restructuring*. EC. https://www.google.com/url?sa=t&rct=j&q=&esrc=s&source=web&cd=&cad=rja&uact=8&ved=2ahUKEwiE7KatwOr0AhV7Q_EDHT34DqwQFnoECAgQAQ&url=https%3A%2F%2Fec.europa.eu%2Fsocial%2FBlobServlet%3FdocId%3D6245%26langId%3Den&usg=AOvVaw22OtHLcxEg4sZ2xJsmrYCw

European Commission. (2020). *Commission staff working document-Digital Education action Plan 2021-2027 Resetting education and training for the digital age* (SWD No. 2020, 209 final). EC. https://ec.europa.eu/education/sites/default/files/document-library-docs/deap-swd-sept2020_en.pdf

Fana, M., Pérez, S. T., & Fernández-Macías, E. (2020). Employment impact of Covid-19 crisis: From short term effects to long terms prospects. *Economia e Politica Industriale*, *47*(3), 391–410. doi:10.100740812-020-00168-5

Fassel, D. (1990). *Working ourselves to death: The high costs of workaholism, the rewards of recovery*. Harper Collins.

Ferdman, M., & Sagiv, L. (2012). Diversity in organizations and cross-cultural work psychology: What if they were more connected? *Industrial and Organizational Pyschology*, *5*(3), 323–345. doi:10.1111/j.1754-9434.2012.01455.x

Feregrino Basurto, M. (2021). Labor Flexibility, Teleworking and Covid-19. *Tendencias*, *22*(2), 371–395. doi:10.22267/rtend.212202.181

Ferreira, P. (2021). *The impact of the COVID-19 crisis on labour markets around the world: The case of Portugal*. ILO. https://www.ilo.org/wcmsp5/groups/public/---ed_emp/documents/presentation/wcms_797054.pdf

FIDE. (2013). *Fide Dress Code Policy: Help Chess By Wearing Proper Attire*. FIDE. https://www.fide.com/images/stories/NEWS_2013/FIDE/Proposal_of_Ms._B._Marinello_in_respect_of_the_dress_code.pdf

Compilation of References

FIDE. (2021). *International Chess Federation – Homepage*. FIDE. https://www.fide.com/ .

Fife-Schaw, C. (2006). Levels of measurement. In G. M. Breakwell, S. Hammond, C. Fife-Schaw, & J. A. Smith (Eds.), Research Methods in Psychology (pp. 50-63). Sage Publications, Inc.

Fine, G. (2015). *Players and Pawns - How Chess Builds Community and Culture*. Chicago University Press. doi:10.7208/chicago/9780226265032.001.0001

Fiset, J., Al Hajj, R., & Vongas, J. G. (2017). Workplace ostracism seen through the lens of power. *Frontiers in Psychology*, *8*, 1528. doi:10.3389/fpsyg.2017.01528 PMID:28928702

Fleury, M. (2000). Gerenciando a diversidade cultural: Experiências de empresas Brasileiras. *Revista de Administração de Empresas*, *40*(3), 18–25. doi:10.15900034-75902000000300003

Folkard, S., & Tucker, P. (2003). Shift work, safety, and productivity. *Occupational Medicine*, *53*(2), 95–101. doi:10.1093/occmed/kqg047 PMID:12637593

Food and Agrivulture Organization of the Unided Nations (FAO). (n.d.). *Insegurança Alimentar e Covid-19 no Brasil*. [Food Insecurity and Covid-19 in Brazil].

Forest, J., Mageau, G. A., Sarrazin, C., & Morin, E. M. (2011). "Work is my passion": The different affective, behavioural, and cognitive consequences of harmonious and obsessive passion toward work. *Canadian Journal of Administrative Sciences/Revue Canadienne des Sciences de l'Administration*, *28*(1), 27–40. doi:10.1002/cjas.170

Foucault, M. (1975). *Surveiller et Punir*. Gallimard.

Fouche, E., Rothmann, S., & Van der Vtver, C. (2017). Antecedents and outcomes of meaningful work among schoolteachers. *Journal of Industrial Psychology*, *43*(0), 1-10. https:// doi:10.4102/sajip.v43i0.1398

Foulkes, S. H. (2018). Introduction to group-analytic psychotherapy*. *Foundations of Group Analysis for the Twenty-First Century*, 9–16. 1 doi:0.4324/9780429474903-2/INTRODUCTION-GROUP-ANALYTIC-PSYCHOTHERAPY-FOULKES

FRA - European Union Agency for Fundamental Rights. (2014). *Being Trans in the European Union Comparative Analysis of EU LGBT Survey Data*. Publications Office of the European Union.

Frazier, M. L., Fainshmidt, S., Klinger, R. L., Pezeshkan, A., & Vracheva, V. (2017). Psychological Safety: A Meta-Analytic Review and Extension. *Personnel Psychology*, *70*(1), 113–165. doi:10.1111/peps.12183

Freeman, R. E. (1984). *Strategic management: A stakeholder approach*. Pitman.

Frois, A. (2019). Workshops no Estabelecimento Prisional de Paços de Ferreira, Gaya Chess, N5. Pag 7.

Fugate, M., Kinicki, A. J., & Ashforth, B. E. (2004). Employability: A psycho-social construct,its dimensions, and applications. *Journal of Vocational Behavior*, *65*(1), 14–38. doi:10.1016/j.jvb.2003.10.005

Gagné, M., & Deci, E. L. (2005). Self-determination theory and work motivation. *Journal of Organizational Behavior*, *26*(4), 331–362. doi:10.1002/job.322

Galbreath, J. (2018). Is Board Gender Diversity Linked to Financial Performance? The Mediating Mechanism of CSR. *Business & Society*, *57*(5), 863–889. doi:10.1177/0007650316647967

Gallego-Sosa, C., Fernández-Torres, Y., & Gutiérrez-Fernández, M. (2020). Does gender diversity affect the environmental performance of banks? *Sustainability (Switzerland)*, *12*(23), 1–15. doi:10.3390u122310172

Galletta, S., Mazzù, S., Naciti, V., & Vermiglio, C. (2021). Gender diversity and sustainability performance in the banking industry. *Corporate Social Responsibility and Environmental Management*. Advance online publication. doi:10.1002/csr.2191

Galvão, T. F., & Pereira, M. G. (2014). Revisões sistemáticas da literatura: Passos para sua elaboração. *Epidemiologia e Serviços de Saúde: Revista do Sistema Unico de Saúde do Brasil, 23*(1), 183–184. doi:10.5123/S1679-49742014000100018

Gandolfi, F., & Littler, C. R. (2012). Downsizing is dead; long live the downsizing phenomenon: Conceptualizing the phases of cost-cutting. *Journal of Management & Organization, 18*(3), 334–345. doi:10.5172/jmo.2012.18.3.334

Ganguly, P. (2021) Why Do Chess Players Shake Hands? (Explained!) https://chessdelta.com/why-do-chess-players-shake-hands/

Gao, Q., Wu, C., Wang, L., & Zhao, X. (2020). The Entrepreneur's Psychological Capital, Creative Innovation Behavior, and Enterprise Performance. *Frontiers in Psychology, 11*(July), 1–12. doi:10.3389/fpsyg.2020.01651 PMID:32793048

Gao, Y., & He, W. (2017). Corporate social responsibility and employee organizational citizenship behavior: The pivotal roles of ethical leadership and organizational justice. *Management Decision, 55*(2), 294–309. doi:10.1108/MD-05-2016-0284

García-Morales, V. J., Martín-Rojas, R., & Garde-Sánchez, R. (2020). How to Encourage Social Entrepreneurship Action? Using Web 2.0 Technologies in Higher Education Institutions. *Journal of Business Ethics, 161*(2), 329–350. doi:10.100710551-019-04216-6

Gartner. (2020). *Gartner Identifies Three Dimensions That Define The New Employer-Employee Relationship*. https://www.gartner.com/en/newsroom/press-releases/2020-10-13-gartner-identifies-three-dimensions-that-define-the-new-employer-employee-relationship

Gashi, A., Kutllovci, E., & Zhushi, G. (2022). E-work evaluation through work–life balance, job effectiveness, organizational trust and flexibility: Evidence from Kosovo during COVID-19. *Employee Relations, 44*(2), 371–385. doi:10.1108/ER-04-2021-0136

Gebauer, J., Schirmer, H., Fels, M., Lange, F., & Meyer, N. (Eds.). (2013). Unternehmerisch und verantwortlich wirken? Forschung an der Schnittstelle von Corporate Social Responsibility und Social Entrepreneurship. IÖW, Institut für ökologische Wirtschaftsforschung.

George, B., & Baker, D. (2011). *True north groups: A powerful path to personal and leadership development*. Berrett-Koehler Publishers.

Gerber, J. P., & Wheeler, L. (2014). Clarifying the relationship between ostracism and relational devaluation. *The Journal of Social Psychology, 154*(1), 14–27. doi:10.1080/00224545.2013.826619 PMID:24689334

Gerber, J., & Wheeler, L. (2009). On being rejected: A meta-analysis of experimental research on rejection. *Perspectives on Psychological Science, 4*(5), 468–488. doi:10.1111/j.1745-6924.2009.01158.x PMID:26162220

Gericke, D., Burmeister, A., Löwe, J., Deller, J., & Pundt, L. (2018). How do refugees use their social capital for successful labor market integration? An exploratory analysis in Germany. *Journal of Vocational Behavior, 105*, 46–61. doi:10.1016/j.jvb.2017.12.002

Giannetti, B. F., Agostinho, F., Almeida, C. M. V. B., & Huisingh, D. (2015). A review of limitations of GDP and alternative indices to monitor human wellbeing and to manage eco-system functionality. *Journal of Cleaner Production, 87*(1), 11–25. doi:10.1016/j.jclepro.2014.10.051

Compilation of References

Giesebrecht, J., Grupp, F., Reich, H., Weise, C., & Mewes, R. (2022). Relations between criteria for somatic symptom disorder and quality of life in asylum seekers living in Germany. *Journal of Psychosomatic Research*, *160*, 110977. doi:10.1016/j.jpsychores.2022.110977 PMID:35803108

Gifford, B. (2019). Prison crime and the economics of incarceration. *Stanford Law Review*, *71*(1), 71–135.

Gillet, N., Morin, A. J. S., Cougot, B., & Gagné, M. (2017). Workaholism profiles: Associations with determinants, correlates, and outcomes. *Journal of Occupational and Organizational Psychology*, *90*(4), 559–586. doi:10.1111/joop.12185

Gjerde, S., & Alvesson, M. (2020). Sandwiched: Exploring role and identity of middle managers in the genuine middle. *Human Relations*, *73*(1), 124–151. doi:10.1177/0018726718823243

Global Entrepreneurship Monitor. (n.d.). *Entrepreneurial behaviour and attitudes*. GEM Global Entrepreneurship Monitor. https://www.gemconsortium.org/data/sets

Goel, R. K., Saunoris, J. W., & Goel, S. S. (2021). Supply chain performance and economic growth: The impact of COVID-19 disruptions. *Journal of Policy Modeling*, *43*(2), 298–316. doi:10.1016/j.jpolmod.2021.01.003

Goldberg, D., & Williams, P. (1988). *A user's guide to the General Health Questionnaire*. NFER.

Golden, L. (2015). Irregular work scheduling and its consequences. *Economic Policy Institute Briefing Paper*, 394.

Gollan, P. J. (2000). *Human Resources, Capabilities And Sustainability*. London School of Economics. https://www.agrh.fr/assets/actes/2000gollan038.pdf

Gomes, P. M. S., Ferreira, C. P. P., Pereira, A. L., & Batista, P. M. F. (2013). A identidade profissional do professor: Um estudo de revisão sistemática. *Revista Brasileira de Educação Física e Esporte*, *27*(2), 247–267. doi:10.1590/S1807-55092013000200009

Gonçalves, G., Brito, F., Sousa, C., Santos, J., & Sousa, A. (2017). Workaholism and burnout: Antecedents and effects. In P. M. Arezes, J. S. Baptista, M. P. Barroso, P. Carneiro, P. Cordeiro, N. Costa, R. B. Melo, A. S. Miguel, & G. Perestrelo (Eds.), *Occupational Safety and Hygiene, V* (pp. 53–57). Taylor & Francis Group. doi:10.1201/9781315164809-11

Gonçalves, G., Orgambídez-Ramos, A., Ferrão, M., & Parreira, T. (2014). Adaptation and Initial Validation of the Passion Scale in a Portuguese Sample. *Escritos de Psicologia*, *7*(2), 19–27. doi:10.24310/espsiescpsi.v7i2.13255

Gonçalves, S. P., Santos, J. V., Silva, I. S., Veloso, A., Brandão, C., & Moura, R. (2021). COVID-19 and People Management: The View of Human Resource Managers. *Administrative Sciences*, *11*(3), 1–13. doi:10.3390/admsci11030069

González, E. A. (2013). Mujeres migrantes cuidadoras en flujos migratorios sur-sur y sur-norte: Expectativas, experiencias y valoraciones. *Polis*, *12*(35), 35–62. doi:10.4067/S0718-65682013000200003

Gorgievski, M., Bakker, A., & Schaufeli, W. (2010). Work engagement and workaholism: Comparing the self-employed and salaried employees. *The Journal of Positive Psychology*, *5*(1), 83–96. doi:10.1080/17439760903509606

Gratton, L. (2011). *The shift: The future of work is already here*. HarperCollins Publisher.

Green, A. (1975). The analyst, symbolization and absence in the analytic setting (on changes in analytic practice and analytic experience). *The International Journal of Psycho-Analysis*, *56*(1), 1–22. PMID:1158564

Greenhalgh, L., & Rosenblatt, Z. (2010). Evolution of research on job insecurity. *International Studies of Management & Organization*, *40*(1), 6–19. doi:10.2753/IMO0020-8825400101

Groysberg, B., & Halperin, R. R. (2022). How to Get the Most out of Peer Support Groups: A guide to benefits and best practices. *Harvard Business Review*, 131–141.

Gruszczynski, L. (2020). The COVID-19 Pandemic and International Trade: Temporary Turbulence or Paradigm Shift? *European Journal of Risk Regulation*, *11*(2), 337-342.

Guilherme, R. C., Canuto, R., Clark, S. G. F., de Vasconcelos, F. N., Padilha, V. M., & Tavares, F. C. de L. P., Pessoa, R. F. de M., & de Lira, P. I. C. (2019). Worker's nutrition: An evaluation in industries in North-Eastern Brazil. *Ciencia & Saude Coletiva*, *25*(10), 4013–4020. doi:10.1590/1413-812320202510.29512018

Guizardi, M. L. (2019). The Age of Migration Crisis. *Tempo*, *25*, 577–598. doi:10.1590/tem-1980-542x2019v250303

Gunessee, S., & Subramanian, N. (2020). Ambiguity and its coping mechanisms in supply chains lessons from the Covid-19 pandemic and natural disasters. *International Journal of Operations & Production Management*, *40*(7/8), 1201–1223. doi:10.1108/IJOPM-07-2019-0530

Guo, M., Liu, S., Chu, F., Ye, L., & Zhang, Q. (2019). Supervisory and coworker support for safety: Buffers between job insecurity and safety performance of high-speed railway drivers in China. *Safety Science*, *117*, 290–298. doi:10.1016/j.ssci.2019.04.017

Gut, T., Arevshatian, L., & Beauregard, T. (2018). HRM and the case of transgender workers: A complex landscape of limited HRM "know how" with some pockets of good practice. *Human Resource Management International Digest*, *26*(2), 7–11. doi:10.1108/HRMID-06-2017-0121

Hackman, J., & Oldhan, G. (1975). Development of job diagnostic survey. *The Journal of Applied Psychology*, *60*(2), 159–170. doi:10.1037/h0076546

Halbesleben, J. R. B., Neveu, J. P., Paustian-Underdahl, S. C., & Westman, M. (2014). Getting to the "COR": Understanding the Role of Resources in Conservation of Resources Theory. *Journal of Management*, *40*(5), 1334–1364. doi:10.1177/0149206314527130

Halbesleben, J. R. B., & Wheeler, A. R. (2015). To Invest or Not? The Role of Coworker Support and Trust in Daily Reciprocal Gain Spirals of Helping Behavior. *Journal of Management*, *41*(6), 1628–1650. doi:10.1177/0149206312455246

Halis, M., & Demirel, Y. (2016, Ocak). Sosyal desteğin örgütsel soyutlama (dışlama) etkisi. *Kastamonu Üniversitesi İktisadi ve İdari Bilimler Fakültesi Dergisi*, *11*. https://dergipark.org.tr/tr/download/article-file/309391

Hall, B. J., Pangan, C. A. C., Chan, E. W., & Huang, R. L. (2019). The effect of discrimination on depression and anxiety symptoms and the buffering role of social capital among female domestic workers in Macao, China. *Psychiatry Research*, *271*, 200–207. doi:10.1016/j.psychres.2018.11.050 PMID:30500710

Hansen, B., Sabia, J. J., & Schaller, J. (2021). Schools, Job Flexibility, and Married Women's Labor Suppy: Evidence from the Covid-19 Pandemic. *Working Paper 29660*. https://www.nber.org/papers/w29660

Hardin, R. (1996). Trustworthiness. *Ethics*, *107*(1), 26–42. doi:10.1086/233695

Hargreaves, S., Rustage, K., Nellums, L. B., McAlpine, A., Pocock, N., Devakumar, D., Aldridge, R. W., Abubakar, I., Kristensen, K. L., Himmels, J. W., Friedland, J. S., & Zimmerman, C. (2019). Occupational health outcomes among international migrant workers: A systematic review and meta-analysis. *The Lancet. Global Health*, *7*(7), e872–e882. doi:10.1016/S2214-109X(19)30204-9 PMID:31122905

Harpaz, I., & Snir, R. (2003). Workaholism: Its definition and nature. *Human Relations*, *56*(3), 291–319. doi:10.1177/0018726703056003613

Harta, F. B., & Reisner, M. (2021). More than just a gardening program – Using horticultural therapy and mindfulness practice to promote health and connection for incarcerated individuals and those preparing to re-enter their communities. *Acta Horticulturae*, (1330), 41–47. doi:10.17660/ActaHortic.2021.1330.6

Harvey, D. (2005). *A Brief History of Neoliberalism.* Oxford University Press. doi:10.1093/oso/9780199283262.001.0001

Hays-Thomas, R., & Bendick, M. Jr. (2013). Professionalizing diversity and inclusion practice: Should voluntary standards be the chicken or the egg? *Industrial and Organizational Psychology: Perspectives on Science and Practice*, 6(3), 193–205. doi:10.1111/iops.12033

Hazakis, K.J. (2021). Is there a way out of the crisis? Macroeconomic challenges for Greece after the Covid-19 pandemic. *European Politics and Society,* 1-15.

Healy, G., Kirton, G., & Noon, M. (2010). *Equality. Palgrave Macmillan.* Inequalities and Diversity.

Hecker, I., & Kuehn, D. (2019). Apprenticeship and the Justice System Adapting a Proven Training Model to Serve People in Prison. *Urban Institute.* https://www.urban.org/sites/default/files/publication/99822/apprenticeship_and_the_justice_system_0.pdf

Hedge, J. W. (2008). Strategic human resource management and the older worker. *Journal of Workplace Behavioral Health*, 23(1-2), 109–123. doi:10.1080/15555240802189513

Hellgren, J., Sverke, M., & Isaksson, K. (1999). A Two-dimensional Approach to Job Insecurity: Consequences for Employee Attitudes and Well-being. *European Journal of Work and Organizational Psychology*, 8(2), 179–195. doi:10.1080/135943299398311

He, W. (2022)... *Computer Games Based on Artificial Intelligence Lecture Notes on Data Engineering and Communications Technologies*, 85, 847–851.

Heyns, M., & Rothmann, S. (2018). Volitional Trust, Autonomy Satisfaction, and Engagement at Work. *Psychological Reports*, 121(1), 112–134. doi:10.1177/0033294117718555 PMID:28679333

Hines, S., & Santos, A. C. (2018). Trans* policy, politics and research: The UK and Portugal. *Critical Social Policy*, 38(1), 35–56. doi:10.1177/0261018317732880

Hirsch, P. M., & De Soucey, M. (2006). Organizational restructuring and its consequences: Rhetorical and structural. *Annual Review of Sociology*, 32(1), 171–189. doi:10.1146/annurev.soc.32.061604.123146

Hobfoll, S. E. (1989). Conservation of Resources: A New Attempt at Conceptualizing Stress. *The American Psychologist*, 44(3), 513–524. doi:10.1037/0003-066X.44.3.513 PMID:2648906

Hobfoll, S. E. (2001). The influence of culture, community, and the nested-self in the stress process: Advancing conservation of resources theory. *Applied Psychology*, 50(3), 337–421. doi:10.1111/1464-0597.00062

Hobfoll, S. E. (2002). Social and Psychological Resources and Adaptation. *Review of General Psychology*, 6(4), 307–324. doi:10.1037/1089-2680.6.4.307

Hobfoll, S. E. (2011). Conservation of resource caravans and engaged settings. *Journal of Occupational and Organizational Psychology*, 84(1), 116–122. doi:10.1111/j.2044-8325.2010.02016.x

Hobfoll, S. E. (2012). Conservation of resources and disaster in cultural context: The caravans and passageways for resources. *Psychiatry*, 75(3), 227–232. doi:10.1521/psyc.2012.75.3.227 PMID:22913498

Hobfoll, S. E., Halbesleben, J., Neveu, J. P., & Westman, M. (2018). Conservation of resources in the organizational context: The reality of resources and their consequences. *Annual Review of Organizational Psychology and Organizational Behavior*, 5(1), 103–128. doi:10.1146/annurev-orgpsych-032117-104640

Hofstede (2022). *Country Comparison.* Hofstede. https://www.hofstede-insights.com/country-comparison/portugal/

Hofstede, G. (2011). Dimensionalizing cultures: The Hofstede model in context. *Online Readings in Psychology and Culture*, *2*(1), 1–26. doi:10.9707/2307-0919.1014

Hogg, M. A., & Terry, D. J. (2000). The dynamic, diverse, and variable faces of organizational identity. *Academy of Management Review*, *25*(1), 150–152. doi:10.5465/amr.2000.27711645

Ho, J., & Plewa, C. (2020). Recipes for new product success: The interplay between orientations and environmental turbulence. *Journal of Business and Industrial Marketing*, *35*(8), 1345–1357. doi:10.1108/JBIM-08-2019-0387

Holt-Lunstad, J., Smith, T. B., & Layton, J. B. (2010). Social relationships and mortality risk: A meta-analytic review. *PLoS Medicine*, *7*(7), e1000316. doi:10.1371/journal.pmed.1000316 PMID:20668659

Holvino, E., Ferdman, B. M., & Merrill-Sands, D. (2004). Creating and sustaining diversity and inclusion in organizations: Strategies and approaches.

Hopkins, S. M., & Weathington, B. L. (2006). The relationships between justice perceptions, trust, and employee attitudes in a downsized organization. *The Journal of Psychology*, *140*(5), 477–498. doi:10.3200/JRLP.140.5.477-498 PMID:17066753

Horne, R., Fien, J., Beza, B. B., & Nelson, A. (2016). *Sustainability Citizenship in Cities*. Routledge.

Hoskins, K. M., & Cobbina, J. E. (2020, July). It Depends on the Situation: Women's Identity Transformation in Prison, Jail, and Substance Abuse Treatment Settings –. *Feminist Criminology*, *15*(3), 340–3581. doi:10.1177/1557085119878268

Hronová, Š., & Špaček, M. (2021). Sustainable HRM practices in corporate reporting. *Economies*, *9*(2), 75. doi:10.3390/economies9020075

Humble, P. N. (1993, January). Chess as an art form. *British Journal of Aesthetics*, *33*(1), 59–66. doi:10.1093/bjaesthetics/33.1.59

Huselid, M. A. (1995). HRM Article by husalid1995. *The Impact of Human Resource Management Practices on Turnover, Productivity, and Corporate Financial Performance*, *38*(3), 635–672. doi:10.2307/256741

Hyde, C. A., & Hopkins, A. (2004). Diversity climates in human service agencies: An exploratory assessment. *Journal of Ethnic & Cultural Diversity in Social Work*, *13*(2), 25–43. doi:10.1300/J051v13n02_02

Hynie, M. (2018). The social determinants of refugee mental health in the post-migration context: A critical review. *Canadian Journal of Psychiatry*, *63*(5), 297–303. doi:10.1177/0706743717746666 PMID:29202665

IBGE. (1977). *Estudo Nacional da Despesa Familiar (ENDEF): Tabelas de Composição dos Alimentos*. IBGE.

İçduygu, A., & Şimşek, D. (2016). Syrian refugees in Turkey: Toward integration policies. *Turkish Policy Quarterly*, *15*(3), 59–69.

ILO. (2020). *Almost 25 million jobs could be lost worldwide as a result of COVID-19, says ILO*. ILO. https://www.ilo.org/global/about-the-ilo/newsroom/news/WCMS_738742/lang--en/index.htm

INE. (2017). *ÍNDICE DE BEM ESTAR 2004-2016*. INE. https://www.ine.pt/xportal/xmain?xpid=INE&xpgid=ine_publicacoes&PUBLICACOESpub_boui=313010615&PUBLICACOESmodo=2

INE. (n.d.). *O que é o Índice de Bem-estar?* INE. https://www.ine.pt/xportal/xmain?xpid=INE&xpgid=ine_indbemestar&xlang=pt

Informator, Š. (2021). *Encyclopaedia of Chess Openings*.

Ingram, W., Murphy, K. S., & Weinland, J. (2022). The moderating effect of hotel shift work on the relationship between employee work engagement and job satisfaction. *Journal of Human Resources in Hospitality & Tourism*, 1–27. doi:10.1080/15332845.2023.2154029

International Chess Federation. (2021a). *Chess in prisons: The Cook County case*. FIDE. https://www.fide.com/news/1027.

International Chess Federation. (2021b). *Intercontinental Online Chess Championship for Prisoners announced*. FIDE. https://www.fide.com/news/1191

Ivanov, D. (2020). Predicting the impacts of epidemic outbreaks on global supply chains: A simulation-based analysis on the coronavirus outbreak (COVID-19/SARS-CoV-2) case. *Transportation Research Part E, Logistics and Transportation Review*, *136*, 1–14. doi:10.1016/j.tre.2020.101922 PMID:32288597

Jackson, S. S., Fung, M.-C., Moore, M.-A. C., & Jackson, C. J. (2016). Personality and Workaholism. *Personality and Individual Differences*, *95*, 114–120. doi:10.1016/j.paid.2016.02.020

Jackson, S., & Bauder, H. (2014). Neither temporary, nor permanent: The precarious employment experiences of refugee claimants in Canada. *Journal of Refugee Studies*, *27*(3), 360–381. doi:10.1093/jrs/fet048

Janis, R. A., Burlingame, G. M., Svien, H., Jensen, J., & Lundgreen, R. (2021). Group therapy for mood disorders: A meta-analysis. *Psychotherapy Research*, *31*(3), 342–358. doi:10.1080/10503307.2020.1817603 PMID:32930060

Janssen, O. (2000). Job demands, perceptions of effort-reward fairness and innovative work behaviour. *Journal of Occupational and Organizational Psychology*, *73*(3), 287–302. doi:10.1348/096317900167038

Jarden, R. J., Sandham, M., Siegert, R. J., & Koziol-Mclain, J. (2018). Quality appraisal of workers' wellbeing measures: A systematic review protocol. *Systematic Reviews*, *7*(1), 1–5. doi:10.118613643-018-0905-4 PMID:30572952

Javed, A., Yasir, M., & Majid, A. (2019). Is Social Entrepreneurship a Panacea for Sustainable Enterprise Development? *Pakistan Journal of Commerce and Social Sciences*, *13*(1), 29.

Jerrim, J., Macmillan, L., Micklewright, J., Sawtell, M., & Wiggins, M. (2016). *Chess in Schools: Evaluation Report and Executive Summary*. Education Endowment Foundation. ERIC.

Jiang, L., & Lavaysse, L. M. (2018). Cognitive and Affective Job Insecurity: A Meta-Analysis and a Primary Study. *Journal of Management*, *44*(6), 2307–2342. doi:10.1177/0149206318773853

Jin, M., Lee, J., & Lee, M. (2017). Does leadership matter in diversity management? Assessing the relative impact of diversity policy and inclusive leadership in the public sector. *Leadership and Organization Development Journal*, *38*(2), 303–319. doi:10.1108/LODJ-07-2015-0151

Jomo, K. S., & Chowdhury, A. (2020). COVID-19 Pandemic Recession and Recovery. *Development*, *63*(2-4), 226–237. doi:10.105741301-020-00262-0 PMID:33223764

Joreskog, K. G. (1996). Testing a simple structure hypothesis in factor analysis. *Psychometrika*, *31*(2), 165–178. doi:10.1007/BF02289505 PMID:5222205

Joseph, C. (2013). (Re)negotiating cultural and work identities pre and post-migration: Malaysian migrant women in Australia. *Women's Studies International Forum*, *36*, 27–36. doi:10.1016/j.wsif.2012.10.002

Kac, G., & Velásquez-Meléndez, G. (2003). A transição nutricional e a epidemiologia da obesidade na América Latina The nutritional transition and the epidemiology of obesity in Latin America. *Cadernos de Saude Publica*, *19*(suppl 1), S4–S5. doi:10.1590/S0102-311X2003000700001 PMID:12886430

Kainzbauer, A., & Rungruang, P. (2019). Science mapping the knowledge base on sustainable human resource management, 1982-2019. *Sustainability (Switzerland)*, *11*(14), 3938. doi:10.3390u11143938

Kalinin A. (2017). *Chess Training for Candidate Masters: Accelerate Your Progress by Thinking for Yourself.* New In Chess.

Kalleberg, A. L., & Vallas, S. P. (2017). Probing precarious work: Theory, research, and politics. *Research in the Sociology of Work*, *31*, 1–30. doi:10.1108/S0277-283320170000031017

Kamau, J. W., Schader, C., Biber-Freudenberger, L., Stellmacher, T., Amudavi, D. M., Landert, J., Blockeel, J., Whitney, C., & Borgemeister, C. (2022). A holistic sustainability assessment of organic (certified and non-certified) and non-organic smallholder farms. *Environment, Development and Sustainability*, *24*(5), 6984–7021. doi:10.100710668-021-01736-y

Kapitsinis, N., & Sykas, G. (2021). A brief overview on the uneven impact of the Covid-19 pandemic on employment, 2020Q2 and 2020Q3: Evidence from Cyprus, France, Spain, Greece, Italy, Malta, Croatia and Portugal. *Technical Report*, University of Aegean/YOUTH Share - Coronavirus Response & Labour Statistics.

Kapitsinis, N., Saroukou, A., Sykas, G., Psarologos, D., Kanelleas, A., Voulgaris, D., Gourzis, K., & Gialis, S. (2020). An overview of the Covid-19 effects on employment during 2020. Evidence from Cyprus, France, Spain, Greece, Italy, Malta, Croatia and Portugal. *Technical Report,* University of Aegean/YOUTH Share - Coronavirus Response & Labour Statistics.

Kapitsinis, N. (2020). The underlying factors of the COVID-19 spatially uneven spread. Initial evidence from regions in nine EU countries. *Regional Science Policy and Practice*, *12*(6), 1027–1045. doi:10.1111/rsp3.12340

Kappa, K. (2019). The social integration of asylum seekers and refugees: An interactional perspective. *Journal of Immigrant & Refugee Studies*, *17*(3), 353–370. doi:10.1080/15562948.2018.1480823

Karazsia, B. T., & Berlin, K. S. (2018). Can a Mediator Moderate? Considering the Role of Time and Change in the Mediator-Moderator Distinction. *Behavior Therapy*, *49*(1), 12–20. doi:10.1016/j.beth.2017.10.001 PMID:29405917

Kasparov, G. (2018). *Deep Thinking: Where Machine Intelligence Ends and Human Creativity Begins.* John Murray Press.

Kasparov, G. (2006). *How life imitates chess*. William Heinemann Ltd.

Kasperson, R. E., Golding, D., & Tuler, S. (1992). Social Distrust as a Factor in Siting Hazardous Facilities and Communicating Risks. *The Journal of Social Issues*, *48*(4), 161–187. doi:10.1111/j.1540-4560.1992.tb01950.x

Katris, C. (2021). Unemployment and COVID-19 Impact in Greece: A Vector Autoregression (VAR) Data Analysis. *Engineering Proceedings*, *5*(41), 1–11.

Kayaoglu, A., & Erdogan, M. M. (2019, February). Labor market activities of Syrian refugees in Turkey. *Economic Research Forum (ERF)*.

Kelly, E., & Dobbin, F. (1998). How Affirmative Action Became Diversity Management: Employer Response to Antidiscrimination Law, 1961 to 1996. *American Behavioral Scientist*, *41*(7), 960–984. https://doi.org/10.1177/0002764298041007008.

Khan, R., & Ghufran, H. (2018). The Mediating Role of Perceived Organizational Support between Qualitative Job Insecurity, Organizational Citizenship Behavior and Job Performance. *Journal of Entrepreneurship & Organization Management*, *07*(1), 1–7. doi:10.4172/2169-026X.1000228

Kim, B. (2006). Managing Workforce Diversity. *Journal of Human Resources in Hospitality & Tourism*, *5*(2), 69–90. doi:10.1300/J171v05n02_05

Compilation of References

Kim, M. J., & Kim, B. J. (2020). The performance implications of job insecurity: The sequential mediating effect of job stress and organizational commitment, and the buffering role of ethical leadership. *International Journal of Environmental Research and Public Health*, *17*(21), 1–16. doi:10.3390/ijerph17217837 PMID:33114680

Kirpal, S. (2004) 'Researching work identities in European context'. *Career Development International*, *9*(3), 199–221. https:// doi:10.1108/13620430410535823

Klimczuk, A., Belzunegui-Eraso, A., Beno, M., & Hvorecky, J. (2021). Data on an Austrian Company's Productivity in the Pre-Covid-19 Era, During the Lockdown and After Its Easing: To Work Remotely or Not? *Frontiers in Communication*, *1*, 641199. Www.Frontiersin.Org. doi:10.3389/fcomm.2021.641199

Knoppers, A., Claringbould, I., & Dortants, M. (2015). Discursive managerial practices of diversity and homogeneity. *Journal of Gender Studies*, *24*(3), 259–274. doi:10.1080/09589236.2013.833086

Kobayashi, K., Eweje, G., & Tappin, D. (2018). Employee wellbeing and human sustainability: Perspectives of managers in large Japanese corporations. *Business Strategy and the Environment*, *27*(7), 801–810. doi:10.1002/bse.2032

Kohlsdorf, M., & Junior, A. D. C. (2017). O autorrelato na pesquisa em psicologia da saúde: desafios metodológicos. *Psicologia Argumento*, *27*, 131-142. https:// doi:10.7213/psicolargum.v27i57.19763

Koman, R.N. & Yee, M.S. (2021). Reading between the bars: Evaluating probation, remodelling offenders, and reducing recidivism. *British Journal of Community Justice 17*(2), 134-149.

König, C. J., Debus, M. E., Häusler, S., Lendenmann, N., & Kleinmann, M. (2010). Examining occupational self-efficacy, work locus of control and communication as moderators of the job insecurity-job performance relationship. *Economic and Industrial Democracy*, *31*(2), 231–247. doi:10.1177/0143831X09358629

Kosny, A., Yanar, B., Begum, M., Al-khooly, D., Premji, S., Lay, M. A., & Smith, P. M. (2020). Safe employment integration of recent immigrants and refugees. *Journal of International Migration and Integration*, *21*(3), 807–827. doi:10.100712134-019-00685-w

Kossek, E. E., & Ollier-Malaterre, A. (2020). Desperately seeking sustainable careers: Redesigning professional jobs for the collaborative crafting of reduced-load work. *Journal of Vocational Behavior*, *117*, 103315. doi:10.1016/j.jvb.2019.06.003

Kousi, T., Mitsi, L. C., & Simos, J. (2021). The Early Stage of COVID-19 Outbreak in Greece: A Review of the National Response and the Socioeconomic Impact. *International Journal of Environmental Research and Public Health*, *18*(322), 1–17. doi:10.3390/ijerph18010322 PMID:33406780

Kowalski, T. H. P., & Loretto, W. (2017). Well-being and HRM in the changing workplace. *International Journal of Human Resource Management*, *28*(16), 2229–2255. doi:10.1080/09585192.2017.1345205

KPMG. (2020). *The time has come: The KPMG Survey of Sustainability Reporting 2020*. KPMG. https://home.kpmg/xx/en/home/insights/2020/11/the-time-has-come-survey-of-sustainability-reporting.html

Kraemer, H. C., Kiernan, M., Essex, M., & Kupfer, D. J. (2008). How and Why Criteria Defining Moderators and Mediators Differ Between the Baron & Kenny and MacArthur Approaches. *Health Psychology*, *27*(2, SUPPL. 2), S101–S108. doi:10.1037/0278-6133.27.2(Suppl.).S101 PMID:18377151

Kramer, R. M. (1999). Trust and Distrust in Organizations: Emerging Perspectives, Enduring Questions. *Annual Review of Psychology*, *50*(1), 569–598. doi:10.1146/annurev.psych.50.1.569 PMID:15012464

Kreitz, P. A. (2008). Best practices for managing organizational diversity. *Journal of Academic Librarianship*, *34*(2), 101–120. doi:10.1016/j.acalib.2007.12.001

Kristof-Brown, A. L., Zimmerman, R. D., & Johnson, E. C. (2005). Consequences of individuals' fit at work: A meta-analysis of person-job, person-organization, person-group, and person-supervisor fit. *Personnel Psychology*, *58*(2), 281–342. doi:10.1111/j.1744-6570.2005.00672.x

Krot, K., & Lewicka, D. (2012). The Importance of Trust in Manager-Employee Relationships. *International Journal of Electronic Business Management*, *10*(3), 224–233.

Kuleta-Hulboj, M. (2016). The global citizen as an agent of change: Ideals of the global citizen in the narratives of polish NGO employees. *The Journal for Critical Education Policy Studies*, *14*(3), 220–250.

Kundu, S. C., & Mor, A. (2017). Workforce diversity and organizational performance: A study of IT industry in India. *Employee Relations*, *39*(2), 160–183. doi:10.1108/ER-06-2015-0114

Kunzelmann, A., & Rigotti, T. (2021). How time pressure is associated with both work engagement and emotional exhaustion: The moderating effects of resilient capabilities at work. *German Journal of Human Resource Management*, *35*(3), 309–336. doi:10.1177/2397002220952741

Lalande, D., Vallerand, R. J., Lafrenière, M. A. K., Verner-Filion, J., Laurent, F. A., Forest, J., & Paquet, Y. (2015). Obsessive passion: A compensatory response to unsatisfied needs. *Journal of Personality*, *85*(2), 163–178. doi:10.1111/jopy.12229 PMID:26385633

Lassen, A. AV, T., Trolle, E., Elsig, M., & Ovesen, L. (2004). Successful strategies to increase the consumption of fruits and vegetables: results from the Danish "6 a day" Work-site Canteen Model Study. In Public health nutrition, 7(2), 263–270. doi:10.1079/PHN2003532

Lazarus, R. S., & Folkman, S. (1984). *Stress, Appraisal and Coping*. Springer.

Leal, C., & Oliveira, B. (2020). O Direito à Identidade de Gênero e Políticas Públicas de Trabalho: Pelas Garantia do Mínimo Existencial para a População Trans no Brasil. *Revista Brasileira de Estudos Jurídicos*, *15*(1), 64–93.

Leduc, S., & Liu, Z. (2021). *Robots or Workers? A Macro Analysis of Automation and Labor Markets*. Federal Reserve Bank of San Francisco.

Lee, L., & Qomariyah, A. (2015). Exploring Expatriate Adjustment from Expatriate's Intelligence and Family Adaptability: A meta-Analytic Approach. *International J. Soc. Sci. & Education*, *5*, 374–398. doi:10.1177/1470595819836688

Lee, S., Schmidt-Klau, D., & Verick, S. (2020). The Labour Market Impact of the COVID-19: A Global Perspective. *The Indian Journal of Labour Economics*, *63*(S1), 11–15. doi:10.100741027-020-00249-y PMID:33041544

Lee, W. T., Lim, S. S., Kim, J., Yun, S., Yoon, J. H., & Won, J. U. (2020). Work schedule irregularity and the risk of work-related injury among Korean manual workers. *International Journal of Environmental Research and Public Health*, *17*(20), 1–10. doi:10.3390/ijerph17207617 PMID:33086683

Lee, Y., Lee, S., Kim, Y. J., Kim, Y., Kim, S. Y., & Kang, D. (2022). Relationship between of working hours, weekend work, and shift work and work-family conflicts among Korean manufacturers. *Annals of Occupational and Environmental Medicine*, *34*(1), e20. doi:10.35371/aoem.2022.34.e20 PMID:36147589

Legood, A., Thomas, G., & Sacramento, C. (2016). Leader trustworthy behavior and organizational trust: The role of the immediate manager for cultivating trust. *Journal of Applied Social Psychology*, *46*(12), 673–686. doi:10.1111/jasp.12394

Lei n° 6.321, de 14 de abril de 1976 da Presidencia da República do Brasil, Pub. L. No. Diário Oficial da União-Seção 1-19/4/1976, Página 4895 (1976). https://www.planalto.gov.br/ccivil_03/leis/l6321.htm

Leichenko, R., & Silva, J. A. (2014). Climate change and poverty: Vulnerability, impacts, and alleviation strategies. *Wiley Interdisciplinary Reviews: Climate Change*, *5*(4), 539–556. doi:10.1002/wcc.287

Lemos, A. H., Cavazotte, F. S. C., & Souza, D. O. S. (2015). De empregado a empresário: mudanças no sentido do trabalho para empreendedores. *Revista Pensamento Contemporâneo em Administração*, *11*(5),103-115. https:// doi:10.12712/rpca.v11i5.836

Leung, D. D. M., & Tang, E. Y. T. (2018). Correlates of life satisfaction among Southeast Asian foreign domestic workers in Hong Kong: An exploratory study. *Asian and Pacific Migration Journal*, *27*(3), 368–377. doi:10.1177/0117196818789736

Levitt, H., & Ippolito, M. (2014). Being transgender. *Psychology of Women Quarterly*, *38*(1), 46–64. doi:10.1177/0361684313501644 PMID:25089681

Lewicki, R. J., & Bunker, B. B. (1995). Trust in relationships: A model of development and decline. *Conflict, Cooperation, and Justice. Essays Inspired by the Work of Morton Deutsch*, (September), 133–173.

Lewicki, R. J., McAllister, D. J., & Bies, R. I. (1998). Trust and distrust: New relationships and realities. *Academy of Management Review*, *23*(3), 438–458. doi:10.2307/259288

Lewicki, R. J., Tomlinson, E. C., & Gillespie, N. (2006). Models of interpersonal trust development: Theoretical approaches, empirical evidence, and future directions. *Journal of Management*, *32*(6), 991–1022. doi:10.1177/0149206306294405

Li, W., Badr, Y., & Biennier, F. (2012). Digital ecosystems: challenges and prospects. *Proceedings of the international conference on management of Emergent Digital EcoSystems*, ACM. https://dl.acm.org/doi/pdf/10.1145/2457276.2457297

Lichess. (2021). *Homepage*. Lichess. https://lichess.org/.

Lichtenthaler, U. (2009). Outbound open innovation and its effect on firm performance: Examining environmental influences. *R & D Management*, *39*(4), 317–330. doi:10.1111/j.1467-9310.2009.00561.x

Light, P. C. (2008). A government ill executed: The depletion of the federal service. *Public Administration Review*, *68*(3), 413–419. doi:10.1111/j.1540-6210.2008.00878.x

Li, J., Johnson, S. E., Han, W. J., Andrews, S., Kendall, G., Strazdins, L., & Dockery, A. (2014). Parents' nonstandard work schedules and child well-being: A critical review of the literature. *The Journal of Primary Prevention*, *35*(1), 53–73. doi:10.100710935-013-0318-z PMID:24014309

Limongi-França, A. C. (1996). *Indicadores empresariais de qualidade de vida no trablaho: Esforço empresarial e satisfação dos empregados no ambiente de manufaturas com cetificação ISO 9000*. FEA / USP.

Lind, E., & van den Bos, K. (2002). When fairness works: Toward a general theory of uncertainty management. *Research in Organizational Behavior*, *24*, 181–223. doi:10.1016/S0191-3085(02)24006-X

Lingard, H., & Francis, V. (2005). Does work-family conflict mediate the relationship between job schedule demands and burnout in male construction professionals and managers? *Construction Management and Economics*, *23*(7), 733–745. doi:10.1080/01446190500040836

Lipscy, P. Y. (2020). COVID-19 and the Politics of Crisis. *International Organization*, *74*(S1), 98–127. doi:10.1017/S0020818320000375

Lips-Wiersma, M., & Morris, L. (2009). Discriminating between 'meaningful work' and the 'management of meaning'. *Journal of Business Ethics*, *88*(3), 491–511. doi:10.100710551-009-0118-9

Lirio, P., Lee, M. D., Williams, M. L., Haugen, L. K., & Kossek, E. E. (2008). The inclusion challenge with reducedload professionals: The role of the manager. *Human Resource Management*, *47*(3), 443–461. doi:10.1002/hrm.20226

Lirios, C. G. (2021). Climate and Labor Flexibility Again Covid-19. *Jurnal Office*, *7*(1), 55–70.

Li, S. S. Y., Liddell, B. J., & Nickerson, A. (2016). The relationship between post- migration stress and psychological disorders in refugees and asylum seekers. *Current Psychiatry Reports*, *18*(9), 1–9. doi:10.100711920-016-0723-0 PMID:27436307

Liu, H., & Xia, H. (2016). Workplace ostracism: A review and directions for future research. *Journal of Human Resource and Sustainability Studies*, *4*(03), 197–201. doi:10.4236/jhrss.2016.43022

Liu, J., Kwan, H. K., Lee, C., & Hui, C. (2013, January). Work-to-family spillover effects on workplace ostracism: The role of work-home segmentation preferences. *Human Resource Management*, *52*(1), 75–93. doi:10.1002/hrm.21513

Lopes, A.S., & Carreira, P. (2021). Covid-19 Impact on Job Losses in Portugal: Who are the Hardest-hit? *International Journal of Manpower*.

Lopez de Segura, R. (1561). *Libro de la invencion liberal y arte del juego del axedrez*.

Loweree, J., Reichlin-Melnick, A., & Ewing, W. (May, 2020). *The Impact of COVID-19 on Noncitizens and Across the U.S. Immigration System*. American Immigration Council. https://www.americanimmigrationcouncil.org/research/impact-covid-19-us-immigration-system

Luís, S., & Silva, I. (2022). Humanizing sustainability in organizations: a place for workers' perceptions and behaviors in sustainability indexes? *Sustainability: Science. Practice and Policy*, *18*(1), 371–383. doi:10.1080/15487733.2022.2068751

Luke, M., & Kiweewa, J. M. (2010). Personal growth and awareness of counseling trainees in an experiential group. *Journal for Specialists in Group Work*, *35*(4), 365–388. doi:10.1080/01933922.2010.514976

Lyubomirsky, S. (2013). *The myths of happiness: What should make you happy, but doesn't, what shouldn't make you happy, but does*. Penguin Press.

Lyubomirsky, S., King, L., & Diener, E. (2005). The benefits of frequent positive affect: Does happiness lead to success? *Psychological Bulletin*, *131*(6), 803–855. doi:10.1037/0033-2909.131.6.803 PMID:16351326

Maccallum, R. C., Browne, M. W., & Sugawara, H. M. (1996). Power analysis and determination of size sample for covariance structure modeling. *Psychological Methods*, *1*(2), 130–149. doi:10.1037/1082-989X.1.2.130

Machado, H. V. (2003). A identidade e o contexto organizacional: perspectivas de análise. *Revista de Administração Contemporânea*, *7*(spe), 51-73. doi:10.1590/S1415-65552003000500004

Machlowitz, M. (1980). *Workaholics: Living with them, working with them*. Addison-Wesley.

Maddux, J. E. (2018). *Subjective well-being and life satisfaction: An introduction to conceptions, theories, and measures*. Routledge/Taylor & Francis Group.

Mäder, I. A., & Niessen, C. (2017). Nonlinear associations between job insecurity and adaptive performance: The mediating role of negative affect and negative work reflection. *Human Performance*, *30*(5), 231–253. doi:10.1080/08959285.2017.1364243

Magoshi, E., & Chang, E. (2009). Diversity management and the effects on employees' organizational commitment: Evidence from Japan and Korea [January.]. *Journal of World Business, Elsevier*, *44*(1), 31–40. doi:10.1016/j.jwb.2008.03.018

Mahmud, S., Alam, Q., & Härtel, C. (2014). Mismatches in skills and attributes of immigrants and problems with workplace integration: A study of IT and engineering professionals in A ustralia. *Human Resource Management Journal*, *24*(3), 339–354. doi:10.1111/1748-8583.12026

Compilation of References

Marcelino, P., & Cavalcante, S. (2012). Por uma definição de terceirização. *Caderno CRH*, *25*(65), 331–346. doi:10.1590/S0103-49792012000200010

Marsh, H. W., Vallerand, R. J., Lafrenière, M.-A. K., Parker, P., Morin, A. J. S., Carbonneau, N., Jowett, S., Bureau, J. S., Fernet, C., Guay, F., Salah Abduljabbar, A. S., & Paquet, Y. (2013). Passion: Does one scale fit all? Construct validity of two-factor passion scale and psychometric invariance over different activities and languages. *Psychological Assessment*, *25*(3), 796–809. doi:10.1037/a0032573 PMID:23647035

Martin, E., Byrne, G., Connon, G., & Power, L. (2021). An exploration of group cognitive analytic therapy for anxiety and depression. *Psychology and Psychotherapy: Theory, Research and Practice*, *94*(S1). doi:10.1111/papt.12299 PMID:32981230

Martínez-Garcia, E., Sorribes, J., & Celma, D. (2018). Sustainable Development through CSR in Human Resource Management Practices: The Effects of the Economic Crisis on Job Quality: Sustainable development: economic crisis and job quality. *Corporate Social Responsibility and Environmental Management*, *25*(4), 441–456. doi:10.1002/csr.1471

Martín-Martín, A., Orduña-Malea, E., Thelwall, M., Delgado-López-Cózar, E., Orduna-Malea, E., Thelwall, M., & Delgado López-Cózar, E. (2018). Google Scholar, Web of Science and Scopus: A systematic comparison of citations in 252 subject categories. *Journal of Informetrics*, *12*(4), 1160–1177. doi:10.1016/j.joi.2018.09.002

Martins, D., & Sousa, A. (2015). *La adaptación intercultural de la familia como factor de éxito en las misiones internacionales de expatriados portugueses*. [Dissertação de mestrado, Instituto Politécnico do Porto, Porto, Portugal].

Martyn, P., Sweeney, B., & Curtis, E. (2016). Strategy and control: 25 years of empirical use of Simons' Levers of Control framework. *Journal of Accounting and Organizational Change*, *12*(3), 281–324. doi:10.1108/JAOC-03-2015-0027

Maslach, C. (1993). Burnout: A multidimensional perspective. In W. B. Schaufeli, C. Maslach, & T. Marek (Eds.), *Professional burnout: Recent developments in theory and research* (pp. 19–32). Taylor & Francis.

Maslach, C., & Jackson, S. E. (1981). The measurement of experienced burnout. *Journal of Organizational Behavior*, *2*(2), 99–113. doi:10.1002/job.4030020205

Maslach, C., & Leiter, M. P. (1997). *The truth about burnout*. Jossey-Bass.

Maslach, C., Schaufeli, W. B., & Leiter, M. P. (2001). Job burnout. *Annual Review of Psychology*, *52*(1), 397–422. doi:10.1146/annurev.psych.52.1.397 PMID:11148311

Massaro, M., Moro, A., Aschauer, E., & Fink, M. (2019). Trust, control and knowledge transfer in small business networks. *Review of Managerial Science*, *13*(2), 267–301. doi:10.100711846-017-0247-y

Mayer, R. C., Davis, J. H., & Schoorman, F. D. (1995). An Integrative Model of Organizational Trust. *Academy of Management Review*, *20*(3), 709–734. doi:10.2307/258792

Mayer, R. C., & Gavin, M. B. (2005). Trust in management and performance: Who minds the shop while the employees watch the boss? *Academy of Management Journal*, *48*(5), 874–888. doi:10.5465/amj.2005.18803928

Mazur, B., & Walczyna, A. (2020). *Bridging Sustainable Human Resource Management and Corporate Sustainability*. Sustainability., doi:10.3390u12218987

Mazzon, J. A. (1992). PAT – Programa de Alimentação do Trabalhador. Uma avaliação histórica e impactos socioeconômicos (2o ed). São Paulo: Abrh; Assert; Aberc; Abracesta.

Mazzon, J. A. (1996). PAT - Programa de Alimentação do Trabalhador - 20 Anos de desenvolvimento: uma avaliação histórica e impactos socioeconômicos (1o ed). Abrh; Assert; Aberc; Abracesta.

Mazzon, J. A. (2001). Programa de Alimentação do Trabalhador - 25 anos de contribuições ao desenvolvimento do Brasil (1o ed). FIA - USP.

Mazzon, J. A. (2006). PAT - Programa de Alimentação do Trabalhador: 30 anos de contribuições ao desenvolvimento do Brasil (1o ed). FIA-USP.

Mazzoni, D., Pancani, L., Marinucci, M., & Riva, P. (2020). The dual path of the rejection (dis) identification model: A study on adolescents with a migrant background. *European Journal of Social Psychology*, *50*(4), 799–809. doi:10.1002/ejsp.2672

McAllister, C. P., Harris, J. N., Hochwarter, W. A., Perrewé, P. L., & Ferris, G. R. (2017). Got resources? A multi-sample constructive replication of perceived resource availability's role in work passion–job outcomes relationships. *Journal of Business and Psychology*, *32*(2), 147–164. doi:10.100710869-016-9441-1

McAllister, D. J. (1995). Affect- and Cognition-Based Trust As Foundations for Interpersonal Cooperation in Organizations. *Academy of Management Journal*, *38*(1), 24–59. doi:10.2307/256727

McDonald, N. (2013). *Chess: The Art of Logical Thinking: From the First Move to the Last*. Batsford.

McFadden, C., & Crowley-Henry, M. (2016). A Systematic Literature Review on Trans* Careers and Workplace Experiences. In T. Köllen (Ed.), *Sexual Orientation and Transgender Issues in Organizations*. Springer. doi:10.1007/978-3-319-29623-4_4

McGahan, A. M. (2020). Immigration and impassioned management scholarship. *Journal of Management Inquiry*, *29*(1), 111–114. doi:10.1177/1056492619877617

McMillan, L. H. W., & O'Driscoll, M. P. (2006). Exploring new frontiers to generate an integrated definition of workaholism. In R. J. Burke (Ed.), *Research Companion to Working Time and Work Addiction* (pp. 89–107). Edward Elgar Publishing Limited. doi:10.4337/9781847202833.00012

Mcnulty, Y., & Brewster, C. (2017). Theorizing the meaning(s) of 'expatriate': Establishing boundary conditions for business expatriates. *International Journal of Human Resource Management*, *28*(1), 27–61. doi:10.1080/09585192.2016.1243567

McRoberts, C., Burlingame, G. M., & Hoag, M. J. (1998). Comparative efficacy of individual and group psychotherapy: A meta-analytic perspective. *Group Dynamics*, *2*(2), 101–117. doi:10.1037/1089-2699.2.2.101

McSweeney, M. J. (2020). Returning the 'social' to social entrepreneurship: Future possibilities of critically exploring sport for development and peace and social entrepreneurship. *International Review for the Sociology of Sport*, *55*(1), 3–21. doi:10.1177/1012690218784295

Medina, C., & Posso, C. (2011). South American immigrants in the USA. *Journal of Economic Studies (Glasgow, Scotland)*, *40*(2), 255–279. doi:10.1108/01443581311283709

Meister, J. (2021). *The Future Of Work Is Employee Well-Being*. https://www.forbes.com/sites/jeannemeister/2021/08/04/the-future-of-work-is-worker-well-being/?sh=4d7124984aed

Mendes, A. A., & Brasil, D. R. (2020). A Nova Lei de Migração Brasileira e sua Regulamentação da Concessão de Vistos aos Migrantes. *Sequência (Florianópolis)*, *84*(84), 64–88. doi:10.5007/2177-7055.2020v43n84p64

Messenger, J. (2018). *Working Time and the Future of Work*. International Labour Organization. https://www.ilo.org/global/topics/future-of-work/publications/research-papers/WCMS_649907/lang--en/index.htm

Metcalfe, T. (2021). Oh, the humanity: Chess computers changed the game, but not the players. *NBC News.* https://www.nbcnews.com/tech/tech-news/world-chess-championship-computers-push-limits-humanity-shines-rcna8282

Meyer, I. (1995). Minority stress and mental health in gay men. *Journal of Health and Social Behavior*, *36*(1), 38. doi:10.2307/2137286 PMID:7738327

Meyer, J. P., & Allen, N. J. (1991). A Three-Component Conceptualization of Organizational Commitment. *Human Resource Management Review*, *1*(1), 61–89. doi:10.1016/1053-4822(91)90011-Z

Miller, F. A. (1998). Miller, "Strategic culture change: The door to acheiving high performance and inclusion. *Public Personnel Management*, *27*(2), 151–160. doi:10.1177/009102609802700203

Ministério das Relações Exteriores. Secretaria de Assuntos e Soberania Nacional e Cidadania (2020). *Comunidade Brasileira no Exterior (Estimativas 2020).*

Miscenko, D., & Day, D. (2016). Identity and identification at work. *Organizational Psychology Review*, *6*(3), 215–247. doi:10.1177/2041386615584009

Mishra, A. K. (1996). Organizational responses to crises: The centrality of trust in organizations. In Trust in Organizations: Frontiers of Theory and Research (pp. 261–287).

Mohamed, N. (2020). Takeaways On The Importance of Entrepreneurship. *Duke Sanford.* https://dcid.sanford.duke.edu/importance-of-entrepreneurship/.

Moher, D., Liberati, A., Tetzlaff, J., & Altman, D. G.The PRISMA Group. (2009). Preferred reporting items for systematic reviews and meta-analyses: The PRISMA Statement. *PLoS Medicine*, *6*(7), e1000097. doi:10.1371/journal.pmed.1000097 PMID:19621072

Mohrman, S. A., & Worley, C. G. (2010). The organizational sustainability journey. *Organizational Dynamics*, *39*(4), 289–294. doi:10.1016/j.orgdyn.2010.07.008

Molm, L. D. (2010). The structure of reciprocity. *Social Psychology Quarterly*, *73*(2), 119–131. doi:10.1177/0190272510369079

Molm, L. D., Schaefer, D. R., Collett, J. L., Mouvt, U. D., & Schfl, R. F. R. (2007). The Value of Reciprocity. *Social Psychology Quarterly*, *70*(2), 199–217. doi:10.1177/019027250707000208

Molm, L. D., Takahashi, N., & Peterson, G. (2000). Risk and trust in social exchange: An experimental test of a classical proposition. *American Journal of Sociology*, *105*(5), 1396–1427. doi:10.1086/210434

Molm, L. D., Takahashi, N., & Peterson, G. (2003). In the eye of the beholder: Procedural Justice in Social Exchange. *American Sociological Review*, *68*(1), 128–152. doi:10.2307/3088905

Monteiro, N. P., Portela, M., & Straume, O. R. (2011). Firm Ownership and Rent Sharing. *Journal of Labor Research*, *32*(3), 210–236. doi:10.100712122-011-9109-6

Moolchaem, P., Liamputtong, P., O'Halloran, P., & Muhamad, R. (2015). The lived experiences of transgender persons: A meta-synthesis. *Journal of Gay & Lesbian Social Services*, *27*(2), 143–171. doi:10.1080/10538720.2015.1021983

Mor Barak, M. E. (2005). *Managing diversity: Toward a globally inclusive workplace.* Sage.

Mor Barak, M. E., & Cherin, D. A. (1998). A tool to expand organizational understanding of workforce diversity: Exploring a measure of inclusion-exclusion. *Administration in Social Work*, *22*(1), 47–64. doi:10.1300/J147v22n01_04

Mor Barak, M. E., Cherin, D. A., & Berkman, S. (1998). Organizational and personal dimensions in diversity climate: Ethnic and gender differences in employee perceptions. *The Journal of Applied Behavioral Science*, *34*(1), 82–104. doi:10.1177/0021886398341006

Mor Barak, M. E., & Levin, A. (2002). Outside of the corporate mainstream and excluded from the work community: A study of diversity, job satisfaction and well-being. *Community Work & Family*, *5*(2), 133–157. doi:10.1080/13668800220146346

Moreira, S., Vasconcelos, L., & Santos, C. S. (2017). Sustainability of green jobs in Portugal: A methodological approach using occupational health indicators. *Journal of Occupational Health*, *59*(5), 374–384. doi:10.1539/joh.17-0045-RA PMID:28794392

Morin, E. M. (2001). Os sentidos do trabalho. *Revista de Administração de Empresas*, 41(3), 8-19. https://doi//doi:10.1590/S0034-75902001000300002

Moura, A. O. R., & Silva, L. C. O. (2019). Centralidade do trabalho, metas e realização profissional: intersecções entre trabalho e carreira. *Revista De Administração Mackenzie*, 20(1), 150-200. https://Dx.Doi.Org/10.1590/1678-6971/Eramg190087

Mousa, M. (2017). Responsible leadership and organizational commitment among physicians: Can inclusive diversity climate enhance the relationship. *Journal of Intercultural Management*, *9*(2), 103–141. doi:10.1515/joim-2017-0010

Mousa, M. (2018a). Inspiring work-life balance: Responsible leadership among female pharmacists in the Egyptian health sector. *Entrepreneurial Business and Economics Review*, *6*(1), 71–90. doi:10.15678/EBER.2018.060104

Mousa, M. (2018b). The effect of cultural diversity challenges on organizational cynicism dimensions: A study from Egypt. *Journal of Global Responsibility*, *9*(3), 133–155. doi:10.1108/JGR-06-2017-0037

Mousa, M., & Ayoubi, R. (2019a). Inclusive/exclusive talent management, responsible leadership and organizational downsizing: A study among academics in Egyptian business schools. *Journal of Management Development*, *38*(2), 87–104. doi:10.1108/JMD-11-2018-0325

Mousa, M., Massoud, H. K., & Ayoubi, R. M. (2020). Gender, diversity management perceptions, workplace happiness and organisational citizenship behaviour. *Employee Relations*, *42*(6), 1249–1269. doi:10.1108/ER-10-2019-0385

MOW. (1987). *Meaning of Work International Research Team. The meaning of work*. Academic Press.

Moyce, S. C., & Schenker, M. (2018). Migrant workers and their occupational health and safety. *Annual Review of Public Health*, *39*(1), 351–365. doi:10.1146/annurev-publhealth-040617-013714 PMID:29400993

Muhr, S. L., Pedersen, M., & Alvesson, M. (2012). Workload, aspiration and fun: Problems of balancing self-exploitation and self-exploration in work life. *Research in the Sociology of Organizations*, *37*, 193–220. doi:10.1108/S0733-558X(2013)0000037011

Mun, S., Moon, Y., Kim, H., & Kim, N. (2022). Current Discussions on Employees and Organizations During the COVID-19 Pandemic: A Systematic Literature Review. *Frontiers in Psychology*, *13*, 848778. doi:10.3389/fpsyg.2022.848778 PMID:35496177

Mupenzi, A., Mude, W., & Baker, S. (2020). Reflections on COVID-19 and impacts on equitable participation: The case of culturally and linguistically diverse migrant and/or refugee (CALDM/R) students in Australian higher education. *Higher Education Research & Development*, *39*(7), 1337–1341. doi:10.1080/07294360.2020.1824991

Murray, J. (2007). The cycle of punishment: Social exclusion of prisoners and their children. *Criminology & Criminal Justice,* *7*(1), 55-81. doi:10.1177/1748895807072476

Musgrave, R. (1987). Merit Goods. *The New Palgrave: A Dictionary of Economics, (vol. 3)*, 452-53.

Myers, D. G. (2000). The funds, friends, and faith of happy people. *The American Psychologist*, *55*(1), 56–57. doi:10.1037/0003-066X.55.1.56 PMID:11392866

Nadal, K., Davidoff, K., & Fujii-Doe, W. (2014). Transgender Women and the Sex Work Industry: Roots in Systemic, Institutional, and Interpersonal Discrimination. *Journal of Trauma & Dissociation*, *15*(2), 169–183. doi:10.1080/15299732.2014.867572 PMID:24313294

Nadal, K., Skolnik, A., & Wong, Y. (2012). Interpersonal and Systemic Microaggressions Toward Transgender People: Implications for Counseling. *Journal of LGBT Issues in Counseling*, *6*(1), 55–82. doi:10.1080/15538605.2012.648583

Nahas, M. V. (2001). *Atividade física, saúde e qualidade de vida: conceitos e sugestões para um estilo de vida ativo* (2ª). Midiograf.

Nangoy, R., Mursitama, T. N., Setiadi, N. J., & Pradipto, Y. D. (2020). Creating sustainable performance in the fourth industrial revolution era: The effect of employee's work well-being on job performance. *Management Science Letters*, 1037–1042. doi:10.5267/j.msl.2019.11.006

Naru, A. S., & Rehman, A. (2020). Impact of Job Insecurity and Work Overload on Employee Performance With the Mediating Role of Employee Stress: A Case of Pakistan's Fast-food Industry. *International Journal of Human Resource Studies*, *10*(1), 305. doi:10.5296/ijhrs.v10i1.15741

Nembhard, M., & Edmonson, A. C. (2006). Making it safe: The effects of leader inclusiveness and professional status on psychological safety and improvement efforts in health care teams. *Journal of Organizational Behavior*, *27*(7), 941–966. doi:10.1002/job.413

Newborn, M. (1997). *Kasparov versus Deep Blue: Computer Chess Comes of Age Softcover reprint of the original* (1st ed. 1997). Edition Springer. doi:10.1007/978-1-4612-2260-6

Nicholls, A. (2010). The Legitimacy of Social Entrepreneurship: Reflexive Isomorphism in a Pre-Paradigmatic Field. *Entrepreneurship Theory and Practice*, *4*(34), 611–633. doi:10.1111/j.1540-6520.2010.00397.x

Nicholson, N. (1998). *Encyclopedic Dictionary of Organizational Behavior*. Blackwell.

Niesen, W., Van Hootegem, A., Handaja, Y., Battistelli, A., & De Witte, H. (2018). Quantitative and Qualitative Job Insecurity and Idea Generation: The Mediating Role of Psychological Contract Breach. *Scandinavian Journal of Work and Organizational Psychology*, *3*(1), 3. doi:10.16993jwop.36

Nimon, K., & Zigarmi, D. (2014). The work cognition inventory: Initial evidence of construct validity for the revised form. *Journal of Career Assessment*, *23*(1), 117–136. doi:10.1177/1069072714523241

Nishii, L. (2013). The benefits of climate for inclusion for gender diverse groups. *Academy of Management Journal*, *56*(6), 1754–1774. doi:10.5465/amj.2009.0823

Nitsun, M. (1991). Fernando Arroyave Memorial Prize Essay: The Anti-Group: Destructive Forces in the Group and their Therapeutic Potential. *Group Analysis*, *24*(1), 7–20. doi:10.1177/0533316491241003

Nitsun, M. (2014). *The Anti-Group*. The Anti-Group., doi:10.4324/9781315745510

Nordstrom, J. (2020). Teaching in the periphery: Teacher identity in community language schools. *Teaching and Teacher Education*, *96*(2), 121–130. doi:10.1016/j.tate.2020.103192

O'Brian, R., & Williams, R. (2016). *Global Political Economy: Evolution & Dynamics*. Palgrave.

Oates, W. (1971). *Confessions of a Workaholic: The Facts about Work Addiction*. World Publishing.

Object Management Group. (n.d.). Unified Modeling Language, v2.5.1. *Unified Modeling Language*, 796.

OCDE. (n.d.). *What's the Better Life Index?* OCDE. https://www.oecdbetterlifeindex.org/about/better-life-initiative/

Ochoa, P., Lepeley, M.-T., & Essens, P. (2018). *Wellbeing for Sustainability in the Global Workplace*. Routledge. doi:10.4324/9780429470523

OECD. (2013). *OECD Guidelines on Measuring Subjective Well-being*. https://www.oecd-ilibrary.org/economics/oecd-guidelines-on-measuring-subjective-well-being_9789264191655-en

OECD. (2017). *OECD Guidelines on Measuring the Quality of the Working Environment*. OECD. doi:10.1787/9789264278240-

OECD. (2019). *Society at a Glance 2019: OECD Social Indicators*. OECD Publishing. doi:10.1787oc_glance-2019-

OECD. (2020). *Putting people's well-being at the top of the agenda*. OECD. https://www.oecd.org/wise/Peoples-well-being-at-the-top-of-the-agenda-WISE-mission.pdf

OECD. (2021a). *Timeline*. OECD. http://www.oecd.org/60-years/timeline/#selectorBlock

OECD. (2021b). *Statistics*. OECD. https://stats.oecd.org/

OECD. (n.d.-a). *Measuring Business Impacts on People's Well-being and Sustainability*. OECD. https://www.oecd.org/investment/measuring-business-impacts-on-peoples-well-being.htm

OECD. (n.d.-b). *What's the Better Life Index?* OECD. https://www.oecdbetterlifeindex.org/about/better-life-initiative/

Ogbonnaya, C., Gahan, P., & Eib, C. (2019). Recessionary changes at work and employee well-being: The protective roles of national and workplace institutions. *European Journal of Industrial Relations*, *25*(4), 377–393. doi:10.1177/0959680119830885

Ogden, T. H. (2004). On holding and containing, being and dreaming. *The International Journal of Psycho-Analysis*, *85*(6), 1349–1364. doi:10.1516/T41H-DGUX-9JY4-GQC7 PMID:15801512

Ohrt, J. H., Prochenko, Y., Stulmaker, H., Huffman, D., Fernando, D., & Swan, K. (2014). An Exploration of Group and Member Development in Experiential Groups. *Journal for Specialists in Group Work*, *39*(3), 212–235. doi:10.1080/01933922.2014.919047

Oliveira, A. T. R. (2017). Nova lei brasileira de migração: Avanços, desafios e ameaças. *Revista Brasileira de Estudos de Populacao*, *34*(1), 171–179. doi:10.20947/S0102-3098a0010

Oliveira, H. N., Silva, C. A. M., & Oliveira, A. T. R. (2019). Imigração internacional: Uma alternativa para os impactos das mudanças demográficas no Brasil? *Revista Brasileira de Estudos de Populacao*, *36*, 10–20. doi:10.20947/S0102-3098a0076

Oliveira, M. R., Junior, J. S., Benfica, V. B. M., & Royer, A. S. S. (2015). Ressignificação da identidade no processo de imigração haitiana: Uma pesquisa numa cidade do Sul do Brasil. *Revista Brasileira de Tecnologias Sociais*, *2*(2), 145–159. doi:10.14210/rbts.v2n2.p145-159

Özçürümez Bilgili, S. (2018). International protection and psychosocial support services. In Forced migration and social trauma: interdisciplinary perspectives from Psychoanalysis, Psychology, Sociology and Politics (pp. 9-17). Routledge. doi:10.4324/9780429432415-3

Öztürk, L., & Timuçin, E. D. (2021). Emek piyasası ve ekonomik dışlanma: Adıyaman ilinde Suriyeli göçmenler örneği. *Ekev Akademi Dergisi, 25*(85), 227–246. doi:10.17753/Ekev1796

Ozturk, M., & Tatli, A. (2015). Gender identity inclusion in the workplace: Broadening diversity management research and practice through the case of transgender employees in the UK. *International Journal of Human Resource Management, 27*(8), 781–802. doi:10.1080/09585192.2015.1042902

Pais-Ribeiro, J., & Cummins, R. (2008). O bem-estar pessoal: Estudo de validação da versão portuguesa da escala. [Personal well-being: Validation study of the Portuguese version of the scale] In I. Leal, J. Pais-Ribeiro, I. Silva, & S. Marques (Eds.), *Actas do 7º Congresso Nacional de Psicologia da Saúde* [Proceedings of the 7th National Congress of Health Psychology]. (pp. 505–508). ISPA, https://hdl.handle.net/10216/21065

Palmer, B. W., Friend, S., Huege, S., Mulvaney, M., Badawood, A., Almaghraby, A., & Lohr, J. B. (2019). Aging and trauma: Post Traumatic Stress Disorder among Korean War veterans. *Federal Practitioner, 36*(12), 554–562. https://www.ncbi.nlm.nih.gov/pmc/articles/PMC6913617/ PMID:31892780

Pan, S. Y. (2018). Do workaholic hotel supervisors provide family supportive supervision? A role identity perspective. *International Journal of Hospitality Management, 68*, 59–67. doi:10.1016/j.ijhm.2017.09.013

Parmar, B. L., Freeman, R. E., Harrison, J. S., Wicks, A. C., Purnell, L., & De Colle, S. (2010). Stakeholder theory: The state of the art. *The Academy of Management Annals, 4*(1), 403–445. doi:10.5465/19416520.2010.495581

Pearson, F.S., Lipton, D.S., Cleland, C.M., Yee, D.S. (2002) The effects of behavioral/cognitive-behavioral programs on recidivism. *Crime and Delinquency 48*(3), pp. 476-496

Pegado, P. (1995). *Saúde e Produtividade. Revista Proteção, 44*. VII.

Peirperl, M., & Jones, B. (2001). Workaholics or overworkers: Productivity or pathology? *Group & Organization Management, 26*(3), 369–393. doi:10.1177/1059601101263007

Pelled, L. H., Ledford, G. E., & Mohrman, S. A. (1999). Demographic dissimilarity and workplace inclusion. *Journal of Management Studies, 36*(7), 1013–1031. doi:10.1111/1467-6486.00168

Penninx, R., & Garcés-Mascareñas, B. (2016). The concept of integration as an analytical tool and as a policy concept. In *Integration processes and policies in Europe* (pp. 11–29). Springer. doi:10.1007/978-3-319-21674-4_2

Perez, J. F., Traversini, V., Fioriti, M., Taddei, G., Montalti, M., & Tommasi, E. (2019). Shift and night work management in European companies. *Calitatea, 20*(169), 157–165.

Permarupan, P. Y., Saufi, R. A., Kasim, R. S. R., & Balakrishnan, B. K. (2013). The impact of organizational climate on employee's work passion and organizational commitment. *Procedia: Social and Behavioral Sciences, 107*, 88–95. doi:10.1016/j.sbspro.2013.12.403

Pestana, M. H., & Gageiro, J. N. (2008). *Análise de Dados para Ciências Sociais: A Complementaridade do SPSS* [Data Analysis for Social Sciences: The Complementarity of SPSS]. 5th ed.). Edições Sílabo.

Peters, V., Engels, J. A., de Rijk, A. E., & Nijhuis, F. J. N. (2015). Sustainable employability in shiftwork: Related to types of work schedule rather than age. *International Archives of Occupational and Environmental Health, 88*(7), 881–893. doi:10.100700420-014-1015-9 PMID:25578669

Pfeffer, J. (2007). Organizational Behavior Perspective. *The Journal of Economic Perspectives, 21*(4), 115–134. doi:10.1257/jep.21.4.115

Phillips, W., Lee, H., Ghobadian, A., O'Regan, N., & James, P. (2015). Social Innovation and Social Entrepreneurship. *Group & Organization Management*, *40*(3), 428–461. doi:10.1177/1059601114560063

Piaget, J. (1978). La equilibración de las estructuras cognitivas. Problema central del desarrollo. Madrid: Siglo XXI.

Piccoli, B., De Witte, H., & Reisel, W. D. (2017). Job insecurity and discretionary behaviors: Social exchange perspective versus group value model. *Scandinavian Journal of Psychology*, *58*(1), 69–79. doi:10.1111jop.12340 PMID:27925219

Piccoli, B., Reisel, W. D., & De Witte, H. (2019). Understanding the Relationship Between Job Insecurity and Performance : Hindrance or Challenge Effect? *Journal of Career Development*, 1–16. doi:10.1177/0894845319833189

Piccoli, B., Setti, I., Filippi, Z., Argentero, P., & Bellotto, M. (2013). The Influence of Job Insecurity on Task and Contextual Performance: The Mediational Role of Overall Job Attitude. *International Journal of Business Research*, *13*(3), 155–162. doi:10.18374/IJBR-13-3.10

Pickett, C. L., Bonner, B. L., & Coleman, J. M. (2002). Motivated self-stereotyping: Heightened assimilation and differentiation needs result in increased levels of positive and negative self-stereotyping. *Journal of Personality and Social Psychology*, *82*(4), 543–562. doi:10.1037/0022-3514.82.4.543 PMID:11999923

Pickett, C. L., Silver, M. D., & Brewer, M. B. (2002). The impact of assimilation and differentiation needs on perceived group importance and judgments of group size. *Personality and Social Psychology Bulletin*, *28*(4), 546–558. doi:10.1177/0146167202287011

Pîroșcă, G. I., Șerban-Oprescu, G. L., Badea, L., Stanef-Puică, M.-R., & Valdebenito, C. R. (2021). Digitalization and Labor Market—A Perspective within the Framework of Pandemic Crisis. *Journal of Theoretical and Applied Electronic Commerce Research*, *16*(7), 2843–2857. doi:10.3390/jtaer16070156

Pirson, M., & Malhotra, D. (2011). Foundations of Organizational Trust: What Matters to Different Stakeholders? *Organization Science*, *22*(4), 1087–1104. doi:10.1287/orsc.1100.0581

Pitts, D. (2005). Diversity, representations, and performance: Evidence about race and ethnicity in public organizations. *Journal of Public Administration: Research and Theory*, *15*(4), 615–631. doi:10.1093/jopart/mui033

Platts, K., Breckon, J., & Marshall, E. (2022). Enforced home-working under lockdown and its impact on employee wellbeing: A cross-sectional study. *BMC Public Health*, *22*(1), 199. Advance online publication. doi:10.118612889-022-12630-1 PMID:35093054

Pohlan, L. (2019). Unemployment and social exclusion. *Journal of Economic Behavior & Organization*, *164*, 273–299. doi:10.1016/j.jebo.2019.06.006

Política Nacional de Saúde e Segurança no Trabalho, (2004). http://www.prevideenciasocial.gov.br/arquivos/office/3_081014-105206-701.pdf

Pollack, J., Ho, V., O'Boyle, E., & Kirkman, B. (2020). Passion at work: A meta-analysis of individual work outcomes. *Journal of Organizational Behavior*, *41*(4), 1–21. doi:10.1002/job.2434

Ponzoni, E., Ghorashi, H., & van der Raad, S. (2017). Caught between norm and difference: Narratives on refugees' inclusion in organizations. *Equality, Diversity and Inclusion*, *36*(3), 222–237. doi:10.1108/EDI-11-2015-0093

Portaria Interministerial 66, de 25 de agosto do Gabinete do Ministro, Pub. L. No. Diário Oficial da União-Seção 1-n° 165; 28/08/2006 Pag. 153/154 (2006). https://www.gov.br/trabalho-e-previdencia/pt-br/servicos/empregador/programa-de-alimentacao-do-trabalhador-pat/arquivos-legislacao/portarias-interministeriais/pat_portaria_interministerial_66_2006.pdf

Compilation of References

Portaria Interministerial nº 05, de 30 de novembro do Ministério do Trabalho e Previdência/Gabinete do Ministro, Pub. L. No. Diário Oficial da União 03/12/1999 (1999). https://www.gov.br/trabalho-e-previdencia/pt-br/servicos/empregador/programa-de-alimentacao-do-trabalhador-pat/arquivos-legislacao/portarias-interministeriais/pat_portaria_interministerial_05_1999_atualizada.pdf

Portman, C. (2017). Chess Behind Bars. Quality Chess, UK.

Portugal, I. L. G. A. (2020). *Relatório Anual 2019 - Discriminação Contra Pessoas LGBTI+*. Ilga-portugal.pt. https://ilga-portugal.pt/ficheiros/pdfs/observatorio/ILGA_Relatorio_Discriminacao_2019.pdf

Prasad, A. (2001). Prasad, "Understanding workplace empowerment as inclusion. *The Journal of Applied Behavioral Science*, *37*(1), 51–69. doi:10.1177/0021886301371004

Prata, J., & Silva, I. (2013). Efeitos do trabalho em turnos na saúde e em dimensões do contexto social e organizacional: Um estudo na indústria eletrônica [Shiftwork effects on health and on social and organizational life: A study in the electronics industry]. *Revista Psicologia: Organizações e Trabalho*, *13*(2), 141–154.

Pratt, M. G., & Ashforth, B. E. (2003). Fostering meaningfulness in working and at work. In K. S. Cameron, J. E. Dutton, & R. E. Quinn (Eds.), *Positive organizational scholarship* (pp. 309–327). Berrett-Koehler.

Presser, H. B. (1999). Toward a 24-hour economy. *Science*, *284*(5421), 1778–1779. doi:10.1126cience.284.5421.1778

Presser, H. B. (2003). *Working in a 24/7 economy: Challenges for American families*. Russell Sage Foundation.

Probst, T. M., Gailey, N. J., Jiang, L., & Bohle, S. L. (2017). Psychological capital: Buffering the longitudinal curvilinear effects of job insecurity on performance. *Safety Science*, *100*, 74–82. doi:10.1016/j.ssci.2017.02.002

Puciato, D., Rozpara, M., Bugdol, M., & Gorgoń, B. M. (2022). Socio - economic correlates of quality of life in single and married urban individuals : A Polish case study. *Health and Quality of Life Outcomes*, *20*(1), 1–16. doi:10.118612955-022-01966-2 PMID:35366910

Pugh, S. D., Skarlicki, D. P., & Passell, B. S. (2003). After the Fall: Layoff Victims' Trust and Cynicism in re-Employment. *Journal of Occupational and Organizational Psychology*, *76*(2), 201–212. doi:10.1348/096317903765913704

Qasim, M. (2017). Sustainability and Wellbeing: A Scientometric and Bibliometric Review of the Literature. *Journal of Economic Surveys*, *31*(4), 1035–1061. doi:10.1111/joes.12183

Quazada, A. N., Lirios, C. G., & Sánchez, A. S. (2021). Review of Labor Flexibility in the Covid-19 Era. *Ingenio Libre*, *9*(19): 1-25. https://revistas.unilibre.edu.co/index.php/inge_libre/article/view/8406/7459

Quintal, S. (2021, April-June). The (Un) Feasibility Of Education And Work As Instruments For The Release Of Justice Individuals. Eccos -. *Revista Científica (Maracaibo)*, (57), 1–19.

Radford, K. J. (1978). Decision-making in a turbulent environment. *The Journal of the Operational Research Society*, *29*(7), 677–682. doi:10.1057/jors.1978.144

Rajkumar, R. P. (2020). COVID-19 and mental health: A review of the existing literature. *Asian Journal of Psychiatry*, *52*, 102066. doi:10.1016/j.ajp.2020.102066 PMID:32302935

Randev, K. K., & Jha, J. K. (2019). *Sustainable Human Resource Management : A Literature-based Introduction*. Sage. doi:10.1177/2631454119873495

Ranjbari, M., Esfandabadi, Z. S., Zanetti, M. C., Scagnelli, S. D., Siebers, P. O., Aghbashlo, M., Peng, W., Quatraro, F., & Tabatabaei, M. (2021). Three pillars of sustainability in the wake of COVID-19: A systematic review and future research agenda for sustainable development. *Journal of Cleaner Production*, *297*, 1–23. doi:10.1016/j.jclepro.2021.126660 PMID:34785869

Rasche, A., Morsing, M., & Moon, J. (2017). The Changing Role of Business in Global Society: CSR and Beyond. In Cambridge University Press (Ed.), *Corporate Social Responsibility Strategy, Communication, Governance*.

Raulio, S., Roos, E., & Prättälä, R. (2010). School and workplace meals promote healthy food habits. In *Public health nutrition*, *13*(6A), 987–992. doi:10.1017/S1368980010001199

Raulio, S., Roos, E., Ovaskainen, M.-L., & Prättälä, R. (2009). Food use and nutrient intake at worksite canteen or in packed lunches at work among Finnish employees. *Journal of Foodservice*, *20*(6), 330–341. https://doi.org/10.1111/j.1748-0159.2009.00157.x

Rawat, P., & Basergekar, P. (2016). Managing Workplace Diversity: Performance of Minority Employees. *Indian Journal of Industrial Relations*, *51*(3), 488–501.

Rede, P. E. N. S. A. N. (2021). VIGISAN: Inquérito Nacional sobre Insegurança Alimentar no Contexto da Pandemia da Covid-19 no Brasil. In Rede PENSSAN. Rede Pensan.

Rees, S., & Fisher, J. (2020). COVID-19 and the mental health of people from refugee backgrounds. *International Journal of Health Services*, *50*(4), 415–417. doi:10.1177/0020731420942475 PMID:32669034

Reeves, S. (2016). Ideas for the development of the interprofessional education and practice field: an update. *J Interprof Care*, *30*(4), 405-7. https:// doi:10.1080/13561820.2016.1197735

Rehman, S., Orij, R., & Khan, H. (2020). The search for alignment of board gender diversity, the adoption of environmental management systems, and the association with firm performance in Asian firms. *Corporate Social Responsibility and Environmental Management*, *27*(5), 2161–2175. doi:10.1002/csr.1955

Reis, R. (2022). *Ricardo Reis Ouvi contar que outrora, quando a Pérsia*. Arquivo Pessoa. http://arquivopessoa.net/textos/2974

Reis, S. (2019). Workshops no Estabelecimento Prisional de Paços de Ferreira. Gaya Chess, (5), 7.

Reis, D. P., & Puente-Palacios, K. (2019). Team effectiveness: The predictive role of team identity. *Management Journal*, *54*(2), 141–153. doi:10.1108/RAUSP-07-2018-0046

Ren, D., Wesselmann, E. D., & van Beest, I. (2020). Seeking solitude after being ostracized: A replication and beyond. *Personality and Social Psychology Bulletin*. doi:10.1177/0146167220928238 PMID:32515281

Ren, M., Wang, B., & Rasell, M. (2021). Flexibility and Professionalisation: Reflections on Adaptions by Social Work Services in China during COVID-19. *Practice*, *34*(2), 87–101. doi:10.1080/09503153.2021.1998413

Rhee, C. S., Woo, S., Yu, S.-J., & Rhee, H. (2021). Corporate Social Responsibility and Sustainable Employability: Empirical Evidence from Korea. *Sustainability*, *13*(14), 8114. doi:10.3390u13148114

Richter, A., & Näswall, K. (2019). Job insecurity and trust: Uncovering a mechanism linking job insecurity to well-being. *Work and Stress*, *33*(1), 22–40. doi:10.1080/02678373.2018.1461709

Richter, A., Vander Elst, T., & De Witte, H. (2020). Job Insecurity and Subsequent Actual Turnover: Rumination as a Valid Explanation? *Frontiers in Psychology*, *11*(April), 1–12. doi:10.3389/fpsyg.2020.00712 PMID:32373033

Compilation of References

Riketta, M. (2002). Attitudinal Organizational Commitment and Job Performance: a Meta-Analysis. *Journal of Organizatiortal Behavior, 23*(September 2001), 257–266. doi:10.1002/job.141

Risberg, A. & Romani, L. (2021). Underemploying highly skilled migrants: An organizational logic protecting corporate 'normality'. *Human Relations.* . doi:10.1177/0018726721992854

Riva, P., & Eck, J. (2016). The many faces of social exclusion. In P. Riva & J. Eck (Eds.), *Social exclusion: Psychological approaches to understanding and reducing its impact* (pp. ix–xv). Springer International., doi:10.1007/978-3-319-33033-4

Roberman, S. (2013). All That is Just Ersatz: The Meaning of Work in the Life of Immigrant Newcomers. *Ethos (Berkeley, Calif.), 41*(1), 1–23. doi:10.1111/etho.12000

Roberson, Q. M. (2006). Disentangling the meanings of diversity and inclusion in organizations. *Group & Organization Management, 31*(2), 212–236. doi:10.1177/1059601104273064

Robinson, B. E. (2014). *Chained to the desk: A guidebook for workaholics, their partners and children and the clinicians who treat them* (3rd ed.). New York University Press.

Robinson, S. L. (1996). Trust and Breach of the Psychological Contract. *Administrative Science Quarterly, 41*(4), 574–599. doi:10.2307/2393868

Robinson, S., & Schabram, K. (2016). Workplace ostracism. In *Ostracism, exclusion, and rejection* (pp. 234–249). Routledge.

Roll, L. C., Siu, O.-L., & Li, Y.W., S. (2015). The job insecurity-performance relationship in Germany and China: The buffering effect of uncertainty avoidance. *Human Resources Psychology. Psihologia Resurselor Umane, 13*(2), 165–178.

Romero, J. G. (2013). What circumstances lead a government to promote brain drain? *Journal of Economics, 108*(2), 173–202. doi:10.100700712-012-0272-x

Roosevelt, T. R. (1990). From affirmative action to affirming diversity. *Harvard Business Review, 68*(2), 107–117. PMID:10106515

Rosa, A., & Vianello, M. (2020). Linking calling with workaholism: Examining obsessive and harmonious passion as mediators and moderators. *Journal of Career Assessment, 28*(4), 1–19. doi:10.1177/1069072720909039

Rosenbaum, S. (2016). Todos Sacrifican: Immigrant Organizing and the Meanings of (Domestic) Work. *Working USA, 19*(2), 187–206. doi:10.1111/wusa.12236

Rosenblatt, Z., & Greenhalgh, L. (1984). Job Insecurity: Toward Conceptual Clarity. *Academy of Management Review, 9*(3), 438–448. doi:10.2307/258284

Rossit, R. A. S., Freitas, M. A. O., Batista, S. H. S. S., & Batista, N. A. (2018). Construção da identidade profissional na Educação Interprofissional em Saúde: Percepção de egressos. Interface (Botucatu). *Interface: Comunicacao, Saude, Educacao, 32*(1, suppl 1), 399–410. doi:10.1590/1807-57622017.0184

Rosso, B., Dekas, K., & Wrzesniewski, A. (2010). On the meaning of work: A theoretical integration and review. *Research in Organizational Behavior, 30*, 91–127. doi:10.1016/j.riob.2010.09.001

Rothmann, S., & Coetzer, E. P. (2003, October 24). The big five personality dimensions and job performance. *SA Journal of Industrial Psychology, 29*(1). doi:10.4102ajip.v29i1.88

Roundy, P. T. (2017). Social entrepreneurship and entrepreneurial ecosystems: Complementary or disjoint phenomena? *International Journal of Social Economics, 44*(9), 1252–1267. doi:10.1108/IJSE-02-2016-0045

Rousseau, D. M. (1989). Psychological and implied contracts in organizations. *Employee Responsibilities and Rights Journal*, *2*(2), 121–139. doi:10.1007/BF01384942

Rousseau, D. M., Sitkin, S. B., Burt, R. S., & Camerer, C. (1998). Not so different after all: A cross-discipline view of trust. *Academy of Management Review*, *23*(3), 393–404. doi:10.5465/amr.1998.926617

Rudin, J., Yang, Y., Ruane, S., Ross, L., Farro, A., & Billing, T. (2015). Transforming attitudes about transgender employee rights. *Journal of Management Education*, *40*(1), 30–46. doi:10.1177/1052562915609959

Rumens, N. (2017). Queering lesbian, gay, bisexual and transgender identities in human resource development and management education contexts. *Management Learning*, *48*(2), 227–242. doi:10.1177/1350507616672737

Ruževičius, J. (2014). Quality of life and of working life: conceptions and research. *17th Toulon-Verona International Conference, May*, 317–334. https://citeseerx.ist.psu.edu/viewdoc/download?doi=10.1.1.829.6991&rep=rep1&type=pdf

Ryan, R. M., & Deci, E. L. (2001). On happiness and human potentials: A review of research on hedonic and eudaimonic well-being. *Annual Review of Psychology*, *52*(1), 141–166. doi:10.1146/annurev.psych.52.1.141 PMID:11148302

Rzemieniak, M., & Wawer, M. (2021). Employer branding in the context of the company's sustainable development strategy from the perspective of gender diversity of generation Z. *Sustainability (Switzerland)*, *13*(2), 1–25. doi:10.3390u13020828

S&P Global. (2021). *Dow Jones Sustainability Indices components*. S&P Global. https://www.spglobal.com/esg/csa/csa-resources/dow-jones-sustainability-indices-components-bh19

Sabharwal, M. (2014). Is diversity management sufficient? Organizational inclusion to further performance. *Public Personnel Management*, *43*(2), 197–217. doi:10.1177/0091026014522202

Sadler, M. & Regan N. (2019). *Game Changer: AlphaZero's Groundbreaking Chess Strategies and the Promise of AI*. New in Chess.

Sadri, S., & Jayashree, S. (2013). *Human Resources Management in Modern India (concepts and cases)*. Himalaya Publishing Co.

Saks, A. M., Uggerslev, K. L., & Fassina, N. E. (2007). Socialization tac- tics and newcomer adjustment: A meta-analytic review and test of a model. *Journal of Vocational Behavior*, *70*(3), 413–446. doi:10.1016/j.jvb.2006.12.004

Saksvik, P., Dahl-Jorgensen, C., Eiken, T., & Tvedt, S. (2010). Identity, Over-Commitment, Work Environment, and Health Outcomes among Immigrant Workers. *Journal of Identity and Migration Studies*, *4*, 50-60. https:// doi:10.3390/ijerph17228616

Saksvik, P., Dahl-Jorgensen, C., & Tvedt, S. (2013). Migrant Labor in the Workforce. *JIMS*, *7*, 95–110. doi:10.1177/0022185618824137

Salanova, M., López-González, A. A., Llorens, S., Líbano, M., Vicente-Herrero, M. T., & Tomás-Salvá, M. (2016). Your work may be killing you! Workaholism, sleep problems and cardiovascular risk. *Work and Stress*, *30*(3), 228–242. doi:10.1080/02678373.2016.1203373

Salas, E., Shuffler, M. L., Thayer, A. L., Bedwell, W. L., & Lazzara, E. H. (2015). Understanding and improving teamwork in organizations: A scientifically based practical guide. *Human Resource Management*, *54*(4), 599–622. doi:10.1002/hrm.21628

Saleiro, S. (2017). Diversidade de género na infância e na educação: Contributos para Uma escola sensível ao (trans)género. *ex aequo - Revista da Associação Portuguesa de Estudos sobre as Mulheres*, (36). doi:10.22355/exaequo.2017.36.09

Compilation of References

Salessi, S., Omar, A., & Vaamonde, J. D. (2017). Conceptual considerations of work passion. *Ciencias Psicológicas (Montevideo)*, *11*(2), 165–178. doi:10.22235/cp.v11i2.1488

Sampaio, R. F., & Mancini, M. C. (2007). Estudos de revisão sistemática: Um guia para síntese criteriosa da evidência científica. *Brazilian Journal of Physical Therapy*, *11*(1), 83–89. doi:10.1590/S1413-35552007000100013

Sankaran, K. (2020). Emerging Perspectives in Labour Regulation in the Wake of Covid-19. *The Indian Journal of Labour Economics*, *63*(1), 91–95. doi:10.100741027-020-00262-1 PMID:32921941

Santos, A., Chambel, M.J., & Carvalho, V.S. (2022). 'With a little help...': Supervisor support, work-life balance, and wellbeing among Portuguese employees on telework due to COVID-19. *Cualquier forma de reproducción, distribución, comunicación pública o transformación de esta obra sólo puede ser realizada con la autorización de sus coordinadores* 48.

Santos, J., Sousa, C., Sousa, A., Figueiredo. L., & Gonçalves, G. (2018). Psychometric evidences of the workaholism battery in a Portuguese sample. *Journal of Spatial and Organizational Dynamics – Human Factors in Safety and Health in the Workplace, 6*(1), 40–51.

Santos, L. M. P., & Araújo, M. da P. N., Martins, M. C., Veloso, I. S., Assunção, M. P., & Santos, S. M. C. dos. (2007). Avaliação de políticas públicas de segurança alimentar e combate à fome no período 1995-2002: 2 - the Workers' Nutriti. *Cadernos de Saúde Pública*, *23*(8), 1931–1945. doi:10.1590/S0102-311X2007000800020

Santos, A. (2020). From villain to hero: Trans men and non-binary persons as care providers in Southern Europe. *International Journal of Care and Caring*, *11-15*. doi:10.1332/239788220X16051223899742

Şar, V. (2017). Savaş ve terör yaşantılarında travma ve stres. *Okmeydanı Tıp Dergisi, 33*(Ek sayı),114-120. doi:10.5222/otd.2017.114

Saraiva, L., & Irigaray, H. (2009). Políticas de Diversidade nas Organizações. *RAE – Revista de Administração de Empresas, 49* (3), 337-348.

Sarımehmet Duman, Ö. (2014). The rise and consolidation of neoliberalism in the European Union: A comparative analysis of social and employment policies in Greece and Turkey. *European Journal of Industrial Relations*, *20*(4), 367–382. doi:10.1177/0959680113520274

Sarımehmet Duman, Ö. (2020). ESM as a Strategy for Fuelling Competitiveness: Economic Restructuring in Bailout Countries. In M. M. Erdoğdu, H. Merritt, & A. C. Garcia (Eds.), *Global Inequalities and Polarization* (pp. 132–151). IJOPEC Publication.

Sarmini, I., Topçu, E. & Scharbrodt, O. (2020). Integrating Syrian refugee children in Turkey: The role of Turkish language skills (A case study in Gaziantep). *International Journal of Education research Open, 1*. doi:10.1016/j.ijedro.2020.100007

Satterfield, B. C., & Van Dongen, H. P. A. (2013). Occupational fatigue, underlying sleep and circadian mechanisms, and approaches to fatigue risk management. *Fatigue: Biomedicine, Health & Behavior*, *1*(3), 118–136. doi:10.1080/21641846.2013.798923

Saumya Goyal, (Aug 2009) "Diversity at Workplace" HRM Review

Savran, S. (1988). Preface: The Crisis, Restructuring of the Capital, and Neoliberalism. In N. Satlıgan & S. Savran (Eds.), *Crisis of the World Capitalism* (pp. 19–65). Alan Press. (in Turkish)

Sawicki, J. (2012). Preserving EMU Depends on Success of ESM in Solving the Debt Crisis. *Gospodarka Narodowa*, *10*(254), 1–22. doi:10.33119/GN/100993

Schaef, A. W., & Fassel, D. (1988). *The addictive organization*. Harper & Row.

Scharpe, K., & Wunsch, M. (n.d.). *Social Entrepreneuship Netzwerk Deutschland e.V. (SEND)*. 92.

Schaufeli, W. B., & Buunk, B. P. (2003). Burnout: An overview of 25 years of research and theorizing. The Handbook of Work and Health Psychology, 2(1), 282–424. doi:10.1002/0470013400.ch19

Schaufeli, W. B., Taris, T. W., & Bakker, A. B. (2008). It takes two to tango: Workaholism is working excessively and working compulsively. In R. J. Burke & C. L. Cooper (Eds.), *The long work hour's culture: Causes, consequences and choices* (pp. 203–226). Emerald.

Schaufeli, W., Bakker, A., van der Heijden, M., & Prins, J. (2009). Workaholism, burnout and well-being among junior doctors: The mediating role of role conflict. *Work and Stress*, *23*(2), 155–172. doi:10.1080/02678370902834021

Schermelleh-Engel, K., Moosbrugger, H., & Müller, H. (2003). Evaluating the fit of structural equation models: Test of significance and descriptive goodness-of-fit measures. *Methods of Psychological Research Online*, *8*(2), 23–74. https://www.dgps.de/fachgruppen/methoden/mpr-online/issue20/

Schlogl, L., & Sumner, A. (2018). The Rise of the Robot Reserve Army: Automation and the Future of Economic Development, Work, and Wages in Developing Countries. SSRN *Electronic Journal*. doi:10.2139/ssrn.3208816

Schneider, D., & Harknett, K. (2019). Consequences of routine work-schedule instability for worker health and well-being. *American Sociological Review*, *84*(1), 82–114. doi:10.1177/0003122418823184 PMID:33311716

Schoorman, F., Mayer, R. C., & Davis, J. H. (2007). An Integrative Model of Organizational Trust: Past, Present, and Future. *Academy of Management Review*, *32*(2), 334–354. doi:10.5465/amr.2007.24348410

Schotanus-Dijkstra, M., Pieterse, M. E., Drossaert, C., Westerhof, G. J., de Graaf, R., ten Have, M., Walburg, J. A., & Bohlmeijer, E. T. (2016). What factors are associated with flourishing? Results from a large representative national sample. *Journal of Happiness Studies*, *17*(4), 1351–1370. doi:10.100710902-015-9647-3

Schreurs, B. H. J., Van Emmerik, I. H., Gunter, H., & Germeys, F. (2012). A Weekly Diary Study on the Buffering Role of Social Support in the Relationship Between Job Insecurity and Employee Performance. *Human Resource Management*, *51*(2), 259–280. doi:10.1002/hrm.21465

Schumacher, D., Schreurs, B., De Cuyper, N., & Grosemans, I. (2020). The ups and downs of felt job insecurity and job performance: The moderating role of informational justice. *Work and Stress*, *0*(0), 1–22. doi:10.1080/02678373.2020.1832607

Scott, K. L., & Duffy, M. K. (2015). Antecedents of workplace ostracism: new directions in research and intervention. In *Mistreatment in organizations*. Emerald Group Publishing Limited. doi:10.1108/S1479-355520150000013005

Selenko, E., Mäkikangas, A., & Stride, C. B. (2017). Does job insecurity threaten who you are? Introducing a social identity perspective to explain well-being and performance consequences of job insecurity. *Journal of Organizational Behavior*, *38*(6), 856–875. doi:10.1002/job.2172

Sell, S. K. (2020). What COVID-19 Reveals About Twenty-First Century Capitalism: Adversity and Opportunity. *Development*, *63*(2-4), 150–156. doi:10.105741301-020-00263-z PMID:33173259

Semana, A. (2019). Xadrez, Jogo e Estratégia. Gaya Chess, (5), 8.

Semeijn, J. H., Van Dam, K., Van Vuuren, T., & Van der Heijden, B. I. J. M. (2015). Sustainable labor participation and sustainable careers. In A. VosDe, A., Van der Heijden, B. (Eds.), The handbook of research on sustainable careers. Cheltenham: Edward Elgar Publishing.

Sert, D. Ş., & Danış, D. (2020). Framing Syrians in Turkey: State control and no crisis discourse. *International Migration (Geneva, Switzerland)*, *59*(1), 197–214. doi:10.1111/imig.12753

Shaaban, A. N., Peleteiro, B., & Martins, M. R. O. (2020). COVID-19: What Is Next for Portugal? *Frontiers in Public Health*, 1–8. PMID:32974253

Shaikh, S., Mangi, R. A., & Bukhari, N. S. (2019). A Study investigating the empirical relationship of Job insecurity, Job performance and Emotional intelligence . *A mediation analysis*, *13*(2), 177–181. doi:10.24312/19108130223

Shain, M., & Kramer, D. M. (2004). Health promotion in the workplace: Framing the concept; reviewing the evidence. *Occupational and Environmental Medicine*, *61*(7), 643–648. https://doi.org/10.1136/oem.2004.013193

Shan, H., & Guo, S. (2013). Learning as sociocultural practice: Chinese immigrant professionals negotiating differences and identities in the Canadian labor market. *Comparative Education*, *49*(1), 190–199. doi:10.1080/03050068.2012.740218

Shapiro, D. L., Sheppard, B. H., & Cheraskin, L. (1992). Business on a handshake. *Negotiation Journal*, *8*(4), 365–377. doi:10.1111/j.1571-9979.1992.tb00679.x

Sharabi, M. (2017). Ethno-religious groups work values and ethics: The case of Jews, Muslims and Christians in Israel. *International Review of Sociology*, *28*(1), 1–22. doi:10.1080/03906701.2017.1385226

Sharma, P., Leung, T. Y., Kingshott, R. P. J., Davcik, N. S., & Cardinali, S. (2020). Managing uncertainty during a global pandemic: An international business perspective. *Journal of Business Research*, *116*, 188–192. doi:10.1016/j.jbusres.2020.05.026 PMID:32501304

Sheel, S., Sindhwani, D. B. K., Goel, S., & Pathak, S. (2012). *Quality of work life, employee performance and career growth opportunities: a literature review*, *2*, 10.

Shimazu, A., Balducci, C., & Taris, T. (2019). Workaholism: about the concept, its antecedents, consequences, and prevention. In T. Taris, M. Peeters, & H. De Witte (Eds.), *The Fun and Frustration of Modern Working Life* (pp. 164–176). Pelckmans.

Shimazu, A., & Schaufeli, W. (2009). Is workaholism good or bad for employee wellbeing? The distinctiveness of workaholism and work engagement among Japanese employees. *Industrial Health*, *47*(5), 495–502. doi:10.2486/indhealth.47.495 PMID:19834258

Shinwell, M., & Shamir, E. (2018). *Measuring the impact of businesses on people's well-being and sustainability: Taking stock of existing frameworks and initiatives*. OECD.

Shin, Y., Hur, W. M., Moon, T. W., & Lee, S. (2019). A motivational perspective on job insecurity: Relationships between job insecurity, intrinsic motivation, and performance and behavioral outcomes. *International Journal of Environmental Research and Public Health*, *16*(10), 1812. doi:10.3390/ijerph16101812 PMID:31121833

Shirom, A., & Melamed, S. (2006). A comparison of the construct validity of two burnout measures in two groups of professionals. *International Journal of Stress Management*, *13*(2), 176–200. doi:10.1037/1072-5245.13.2.176

Shkoler, O., Rabenu, E., Vasiliu, C., Sharoni, G., & Tziner, A. (2017). Organizing the confusion surrounding workaholism: New structure, measure, and validation. *Frontiers in Psychology*, *8*, 1803. doi:10.3389/fpsyg.2017.01803 PMID:29097989

Shore, L. M., Randel, A. E., Chung, B. G., Dean, M. A., Ehrhart, K. H., & Singh, G. (2011). Inclusion and diversity in work groups: A review and model for future research. *Journal of Management*, *37*(4), 1262–1289. doi:10.1177/0149206310385943

Shoss, M. K. (2017). Job Insecurity: An Integrative Review and Agenda for Future Research. *Journal of Management*, *43*(6), 1911–1939. doi:10.1177/0149206317691574

Shoss, M. K., Brummel, B. J., Probst, T. M., & Jiang, L. (2020). The Joint Importance of Secure and Satisfying Work: Insights from Three Studies. *Journal of Business and Psychology*, *35*(3), 297–316. doi:10.100710869-019-09627-w

Showers, F. (2018). Learning to care: Work experiences and identity formation among African immigrant care workers in the US. *International Journal of Care and Caring*, *2*(1), 7–25. doi:10.1332/239788218X15187914933434

Sigad, L., Eisikovits, Z., Strier, R., & Buchbinder, E. (2017). The meaning of work among immigrants living in poverty in Israel: Replanting roots of belonging: Meaning of work among Israeli immigrants living in poverty. *International Journal of Social Welfare*, *27*(2), 11–20. doi:10.1111/ijsw.12282

Silla, I., de Cuyper, N., Gracia, F. J., Peiró, J. M., & de Witte, H. (2009). Job insecurity and well-being: Moderation by employability. *Journal of Happiness Studies*, *10*(6), 739–751. doi:10.100710902-008-9119-0

Silva, C. (2019). *Xadrez, Vida e Prisão Gaya Chess*. Gaya Chess, (5), 9.

Silva, I. S. (2007). *Adaptação ao trabalho por turnos* [Adaptation to shift work] [Doctoral dissertation, University of Minho]. http://hdl.handle.net/1822/7723

Silva, H., & Silva, I. S. (2015). Gestão e adaptação aos horários de trabalho: Um estudo de caso no setor hoteleiro [Management and adaptation to work schedule: A case study in the hospitality sector]. *International Journal on Working Conditions*, *9*, 99–116.

Silva, N., & Tolfo, S. R. (2011). Felicidade, Bem-estar e Assédio Moral: paradoxos e tensões nas organizações da atualidade. In L. Leopold (Ed.), *Fagúndez, D.; Sobreba, N. (Orgs.). Investigaciones e intervenciones innovadoras en el campo de la psicología de las organizaciones y el trabajo: el estado del arte* (pp. 2247–2260). Psicolibros Universitareo – Conitriun.

Simons, R. (1995). *Levers of control: How managers use innovative control systems to drive strategic renewal*. Harvard Business School Press.

Şimşek, D. (2018). Refugee integration, migration policies and social class: The case of Syrian refugees in Turkey. *Sosyal Politika Çalışmaları Dergisi 18*(40).

Şimşek, D. (2019). Integration of Syrian refugees in Turkey: Challenges and opportunities. Journal of Research in Economics. *Politics & Finance*, *4*(2), 172–187.

Şimşek, D. (2020). Integration processes of Syrian refugees in Turkey: 'Class-based integration'. *Journal of Refugee Studies*, *33*(3), 537–554. doi:10.1093/jrs/fey057

Šimunić, A., & Gregov, L. (2012). Conflict between work and family roles and satisfaction among nurses in different shift systems in Croatia: A questionnaire survey. *Archives of Industrial Hygiene and Toxicology*, *63*(2), 189–197. doi:10.2478/10004-1254-63-2012-2159 PMID:22728801

Sleijpen, M., Haagen, J., Mooren, T., & Kleeber, R. J. (2016). Growing from experience: An exploratory study of post-traumatic growth in adolescent refugees. *European Journal of Psychotraumatology*, *7*(1), 28698. doi:10.3402/ejpt.v7.28698 PMID:26886487

Smith, J., Davies, S. E., Feng, H., Gan, C. C. R., Grepin, K. A., Harman, S., Herten-Crabb, A., Morgan, R., Vandan, N., & Wenham, C. (2021). More than a public health crisis: A feminist political economic analysis of COVID-19. *Global Public Health: An International Journal for Research, Policy and Practice*, *16*(8-9), 1364–1380. doi:10.1080/17441692.2021.1896765 PMID:33705248

Smith, R. W., Min, H., Ng, M. A., Haynes, N. J., & Clark, M. A. (2022). A Content Validation of Work Passion: Was the Passion Ever There? *Journal of Business and Psychology*, 1–23. doi:10.100710869-022-09807-1

Compilation of References

Soares, C. B., Hoga, L. A. K., Peduzzi, M., Sangaleti, C., Yonekura, T., Silva, D. R., & Audebert, D. (2014). Revisão integrativa: Conceitos e métodos utilizados na enfermagem. *Rev. esc. Enferm*, *48*(2). Advance online publication. doi:10.1590/S0080-623420140000200020

Softgarden. (2019, January 1). *Bewerbungsreport 2019: Wie nehmen Kandidaten aktuell Recruitingprozesse wahr?* Softgarden. https://softgarden.com/de/studie/bewerbungsreport-wie-nehmen-kandidaten-aktuell-recruitingprozesse-wahr/

Sokol, M., & Pataccini, L. (2020). Winners and Losers in Coronavirus Times: Financialisation, Financial Chains and Emerging Economic Geographies of the Covid-19 Pandemic. *Journal of Economic and Human Geography*, *111*(3), 401–415. doi:10.1111/tesg.12433 PMID:32834148

Song, L., & Zhou, Y. (2020). The COVID-19 Pandemic and Its Impact on the Global Economy: What Does It Take to Turn Crisis into Opportunity? *China & World Economy*, *28*(4), 1–25. doi:10.1111/cwe.12349

Sousa-Uva, M., Sousa-Uva, A., & Serranheira, F. (2021). Telework during the COVID-19 epidemic in Portugal and determinants of job satisfaction: A cross-sectional study. *BMC Public Health*, *21*(1), 1–11. doi:10.118612889-021-12295-2 PMID:34865641

Souza, J. (2013). *A gênese do Programa de Incentivo Fiscal à Alimentação do Trabalhador (PIFAT/PAT)*. [Tese de Doutoramento em Saúde Pública, Repositório Institucional da Universidade Federal da Bahia]. https://repositorio.ufba.br/handle/ri/11477

Spence, J., & Robbins, A. (1992). Workaholism: Definition, measurement, and preliminary results. *Journal of Personality Assessment*, *58*(1), 160–178. doi:10.120715327752jpa5801_15 PMID:16370875

Spencer, S., & Cooper, B. (2006). Social integration of migrants in Europe: A review of the European literature 2000-2006. *Gaining from migration (A joint European Commission/Organisation for Economic Co-operation and Development project of July 2007)*.

Štebe, J., & Vovk, T. (2021). Gender inequality on display in the flexibilisation of employment during the covid-19 crisis in Slovenia. *Teorija in Praksa*, 576–597. doi:10.51936/tip.58.specialissue.576-597

Stebleton, M. (2012). The Meaning of Work for Black African Immigrant Adult College Students. *Journal of Career Development*, *39*(1), 50–75. doi:10.1177/0894845309358888

Stein, M. (1998). Projective identification in management education. *Journal of Managerial Psychology*, *13*(8), 558–566. doi:10.1108/02683949810244938

Sterud, T., Tynes, T., Mehlum, I. S., Veiersted, K. B., Bergbom, B., Airila, A., Johansson, B., Brendler-Lindqvist, M., Hviid, K., & Flyvholm, M. A. (2018). A systematic review of working conditions and occupational health among immigrants in Europe and Canada. *BMC Public Health*, *18*(1), 1–15. doi:10.118612889-018-5703-3 PMID:29925349

Stezano, M. (2018). In 1950, Alan Turing Created a Chess Computer Program That Prefigured A.I. *History.com*. https://www.history.com/news/in-1950-alan-turing-created-a-chess-computer-program-that-prefigured-a-i

Stiglitz, J. E., Sen, A., & Fitoussi, J.-P. (2009). *Report by the Commission on the Measurement of Economic Performance and Social Progress*. Europa. https://ec.europa.eu/environment/beyond_gdp/reports_en.html

Stockfish (2021). *Homepage*. Stock Fish Chess. https://stockfishchess.org/

Stone, M., Aravopolou, E., Gerardi, G., Todeva, E., Weinzerl, L., Laughlin, P., & Scott, R. (2017). How platforms are transforming customer information management. *The Bottom Line (New York, N.Y.)*, *30*(3), 216–235. doi:10.1108/BL-08-2017-0024

Strasburg, V. J., & Redin, C. (2014). O Contexto Da Alimentação Institucional Na Saúde Do Trabalhador Brasileiro. *Revista Eletrônica em Gestão, Educação e Tecnologia Ambiental, 18*(0), 127–136. doi:10.5902/2236117013028

Sui, J., & Humphreys, G. W. (2017). Aging enhances cognitive biases to friends but not the self. *Psychon. Bull, 24*, 2021–2030. https:// doi:10.3758/s13423-017-1264-1

Suifan, T. S. (2019). the Effects of Work Environmental Factors on Job Satisfaction: The Mediating Role of Work Motivation. *Business: Theory and Practice, 20*(0), 456–466. doi:10.3846/btp.2019.42

Sulea, C., Virga, D., Maricutoiu, L. P., Schaufeli, W., Zaborila Dumitru, C., & Sava, F. A. (2012). Work engagement as mediator between job characteristics and positive and negative extra role behaviors. *Career Development International, 17*(3), 188–207. doi:10.1108/13620431211241054

Suleiman, A. O., Decker, R. E., Garza, J. L., Laguerre, R. A., Dugan, A. G., & Cavallari, J. M. (2021). Worker perspectives on the impact of nonstandard workdays on worker and family wellbeing: A qualitative study. *BMC Public Health, 21*(1), 1–12. doi:10.118612889-021-12265-8 PMID:34879831

Suleimankadieva, A., Petrov, M., & Kuznetsov, A. (2021). Digital educational ecosystem as a tool for the intellectual capital development. *SHS Web of Conferences, 116*, 00060. 10.1051hsconf/202111600060

Sung, S. H., Seong, J. Y., & Kim, Y. G. (2020). Seeking sustainable development in teams: Towards improving team commitment through person-group fit. *Sustainability, 12*(15), 6033. doi:10.3390u12156033

Sverke, M., Hellgren, J., & Näswall, K. (2002). No security: A meta-analysis and review of job insecurity and its consequences. *Journal of Occupational Health Psychology, 7*(3), 242–264. doi:10.1037/1076-8998.7.3.242 PMID:12148956

Sverke, M., Låstad, L., Hellgren, J., Richter, A., & Näswall, K. (2019). A meta-analysis of job insecurity and employee performance: Testing temporal aspects, rating source, welfare regime, and union density as moderators. *International Journal of Environmental Research and Public Health, 16*(14), 2536. Advance online publication. doi:10.3390/ijerph16142536 PMID:31315198

Szkudlarek, B. (2019) Engaging business in refugee employment: The employers' perspective. Sydney.

Tabachnick, G., & Fidell, L. (2014). *Using Multivariate Statistics* (6th ed.). Pearson.

Tajfel, H., & Turner, J. C. (1986). The Social Identity Theory of Intergroup Behavior. In S. Worchel & L. W. Austin (Eds.), Psychology of Intergroup Relations. Chi: Nelson-Hall. doi:10.4135/9781483346274.n163

Tamrakar, D., Shrestha, A., Karmacharya, B. M., Rai, A., Malik, V., Mattei, J., & Spiegelman, D. (2020). Drivers of healthy eating in a workplace in Nepal: A qualitative study. *BMJ Open, 10*(2). https://doi.org/10.1136/bmjopen-2019-031404

Tang, Y., Shao, Y.-F., Chen, Y.-J., & Ma, Y. (2021). How to Keep Sustainable Development Between Enterprises and Employees? Evaluating the Impact of Person–Organization Fit and Person–Job Fit on Innovative Behavior. *Frontiers in Psychology, 12*, 653534. doi:10.3389/fpsyg.2021.653534 PMID:33995213

Taris, T. W., Schreurs, P. J. G., & Van Iersel-Van Silfhout, I. J. (2001). Job stress, job strain, and psychological withdrawal among Dutch university staff: Towards a dual-process model for the effects of occupational stress. *Work and Stress, 15*(4), 283–296. doi:10.1080/02678370110084049

Taris, T., van Beek, I., & Schaufeli, W. (2020). The Motivational Make-Up of Workaholism and Work Engagement: A Longitudinal Study on Need Satisfaction, Motivation, and Heavy Work Investment. *Frontiers in Psychology, 11*(1419), 1–17. doi:10.3389/fpsyg.2020.01419 PMID:32714248

Compilation of References

Tartakover, S. (2021). *Victory goes to the player who makes the next-to-last mistake*. FunSAAZ. https://funsaaz.com/quotes/victory/victory-goes-to-the-player-who-makes-the-next-to-last-mistake/

Tayag, Y. (2021, December 5). From pandemic to endemic: this is how we might get back to normal. *The Guardian*.

Tedesco, J. C. (2014). Casamentos mistos: Novas sociabilidades e quadros coletivos. Aspectos da imigração de brasileiras na Itália. *Revista Estudos Feministas*, *22*(1), 115–133. doi:10.1590/S0104-026X2014000100007

Teodorescu, M. (2015). Herminia Ibarra: Working Identity, Your Personal Story, Strategies for Reinventing Your Career. *An extended book review*. https:// doi:10.13140/RG.2.1.4872.5920

Thalassis, N. (n.d.). Soldiers in Psychiatric Therapy. *The Case of Northfield Military Hospital, 1942-1946*. doi:10.1093hm/hkm040 PMID:18605333

The Guardian. (2021, November 23). The Guardian view on Europe's Covid protests: treat with care. *The Guardian*.

Theisen-Womersley, G. (2021). Prevalence of PTSD Among Displaced Populations—Three Case Studies. In *Trauma and Resilience Among Displaced Populations* (pp. 67–82). Springer. doi:10.1007/978-3-030-67712-1_3

Theobald, T., & Cooper, C. (2012). The relationship between happiness and wellbeing. In *Doing the Right Thing*. Palgrave Macmillan. doi:10.1057/9780230359017_3

Thibault-Landry, A., Egan, R., Crevier-Braud, L., Manganelli, L., & Forest, J. (2018). An empirical investigation of the employee work passion appraisal model using self-determination theory. *Advances in Developing Human Resources*, *20*(2), 148–168. doi:10.1177/1523422318756636

Thiry-Cherques, H. R. (1991). A guerra sem fim: sobre a produtividade administrativa. *Revista de Administração de Empresas*, *31*(3), 37–46. doi:10.1590/S0034-75901991000300004

Thomas, D. A., & Ely, R. J. (1996). Making differences matter. *Harvard Business Review*, *74*(5), 79–90.

Thomas, R. R. Jr. (1992). Managing diversity: A conceptual framework. In S. E. Jackson (Ed.), *The professional practice series. Diversity in the workplace: Human resources initiatives* (pp. 306–317). Guilford Press.

Thomas, R. R. Jr, & Woodruff, M. I. (1999). *Building a House for Diversity*. American Management Association.

Tidey, A. (2020). COVID-19 creating 'lockdown generation' as young workers take the biggest hit. *Euronews*. https://www.euronews.com/2020/05/28/covid-19-creating-lockdown-generation-as-young-workers-take-the-biggest-hit

Tierney, P., & Farmer, S. M. (2002). Creative self-efficacy: Its potential antecedents and relationship to creative performance. *Academy of Management Journal*, *45*(6), 1137–1148. doi:10.2307/3069429

Ting-Toomey, Stella, and Leeva C. Chung. *Understanding intercultural communication*. New York: oxford university Press, 2005.

Tóth-Király, I., Morin, A., & Salmela-Aro, K. (2020). A longitudinal perspective on the associations between work engagement and workaholism. *Work and Stress*, 1–29. doi:10.1080/02678373.2020.1801888

Transrespect versus Transphobia Worldwide. (2020, November 11*). TMM Update Trans Day of Remembrance 2020 [Press release]*. Transrespect. https://transrespect.org/en/tmm-update-tdor-2020/

Trindade, R.T.Z. (2017). Trabalho é vida e vida é trabalho!": escrita de si e imigração polonesa, a memória, o esquecimento e a identidade na narrativa de um intelectual imigrante. *Métis: história & cultura*. *16*(31), 173-193

Tsai, C. H. (2011). Innovative behaviors between employment modes in knowledge intensive organizations. *International Journal of Humanities and Social Science*, *1*, 153–162.

Tufail, M., Sultan, F., Khalil, S. H., & Sahibzada, S. (2018). Job Insecurity and Job Performance: The Mediating Role of Job Satisfaction. *Abasyn Journal of Social Sciences*, (11), 1–13.

Tu, M.-C., Zhou, S., Wong, S. N., & Okazaki, S. (2018). Realities of the American dream: Vocational experiences and intersecting invisibility of low-income Chinese immigrant laborers. *Journal of Vocational Behavior*, *113*, 1–29. doi:10.1016/j.jvb.2018.10.009

Turing, S. (2016). *Alan M Turing*. Centenary Edition Cambridge University Press.

Turner, J. C. (1975). Social comparison and social identity: Some prospects for intergroup behavior. *European Journal of Social Psychology*, *5*(1), 5–34. doi:10.1002/ejsp.2420050102

UNHCR. (2022a). *Asylum seekers*. UNHCR. https://www.unhcr.org/tr/en/asylum-seekers

UNHCR. (2022b). *What is a refugee?* UNHCR. https://www.unhcr.org/what-is-a-refugee.html

Unified Modeling Language, v2.5.1. (n.d.). *Unified Modeling Language*, 796. UML.

United Nations. (1972). *Stockholm 1972: Declaration of the United Nations Conference on the Human Environment*. UN. https://www.unep.org/Documents.Multilingual/

United Nations. (2020). Secretaria de imigração. *Relatório de migração global 2020*. Caderno: Migrantes e refugiados.

Uršič, M. (2021). The Covid-19 Pandemic Continuing the Processes of the Flexibilisation and Precarisation of Working Conditions in Creative Professions in Slovenia. *Teorija in Praksa*, *58*(3), 762–784.

Valdez-De-Leon, O. (2019). How to Develop a Digital Ecosystem – a Practical Framework. *Technology Innovation Management Review*, *9*(8), 43–54. doi:10.22215/timreview/1260

Vale de Almeida, M. (2010). O Contexto LGBT em Portugal. In Nogueira, C. & Oliveira, J., Estudo sobre a discriminação em função da orientação sexual e da identidade de género (pp. 45-94). Lisboa: Comissão para a Cidadania e a Igualdade de Género.

Valentine, S., & Godkin, L. (2017). Banking employees' perceptions of corporate social responsibility, value-fit commitment, and turnover intentions: Ethics as social glue and attachment. *Employee Responsibilities and Rights Journal*, *29*(2), 51–71. doi:10.100710672-017-9290-8

Välipakka, H., Zeng, C., Lahti, M., & Croucher, S. (2016). Experiencing Cultural Contact at Work: An Exploration of Immigrants' Perceptions of Work in Finland. In S. Shenoy-Packer & E. Gabor (Eds.), *Immigrant Workers and Meanings of Work: Communicating Life and Career Transitions* (pp. 21–32). Peter Lang.

Vallerand, R. J. (2008). On the psychology of passion: In search of what makes people's lives most worth living. *Canadian Psychology*, *49*(1), 1–13. doi:10.1037/0708-5591.49.1.1

Vallerand, R. J. (2010). On passion for life activities: The Dualistic Model of Passion. In M. P. Zanna (Ed.), (pp. 97–193). Advances in Experimental Social Psychology. Academic Press.

Vallerand, R. J., & Houlfort, N. (2003). Passion at work: Toward a new conceptualization. In S. W. Gilliland, D. D. Steiner, & D. P. Skarlicki (Eds.), *Emerging Perspective on Values in Organizations* (pp. 175–204). Information Age Publishing.

Vallerand, R. J., Paquet, Y., Philippe, F. L., & Charest, J. (2010). On the role of passion for work in burnout: A process model. *Journal of Personality*, *78*(1), 289–312. doi:10.1111/j.1467-6494.2009.00616.x PMID:20433620

Compilation of References

Vallerand, R. J., Rousseau, F. L., Grouzet, F. M. E., Dumais, A., Grenier, S., & Blanchard, C. B. (2006). Passion in sport: A look at determinants and affective experiences. *Journal of Sport & Exercise Psychology*, *28*(4), 454–478. doi:10.1123/jsep.28.4.454

Vallerand, R. J., Salvy, S. J., Mageau, G. A., Elliot, A. J., Denis, P. L., Grouzet, F. M., & Blanchard, C. (2007). On the role of passion in performance. *Journal of Personality*, *75*(5), 505–533. doi:10.1111/j.1467-6494.2007.00447.x PMID:17489890

Vallerand, R., & Rahimi, S. (2022). On the passion scale: Theory, Research and Psychometric Properties. In W. Ruch, A. Bakker, L. Tay, & F. Gander (Eds.), *Handbook of Positive Psychology Assessment* (pp. 248–272). Hogrefe Publishing.

van Barneveld, K., Quinlan, M., Kriesler, P., Junor, A., Baum, F., Chowdhury, A., Junankar, P. N. R., Clibborn, S., Flanagan, F., Wright, C., Friel, S., Halevi, J., & Rainnie, A. (2020). The COVID-19 Pandemic: Lessons on Building more Equal and Sustainable Societies. *Economic and Labour Relations Review*, *31*(2), 133–157. doi:10.1177/1035304620927107

Van Beek, I., Hu, Q., Schaufeli, W., Taris, T., & Schreurs, B. (2012). For fun, love, or money: What drives workaholic, engaged, and burned-out employees at work? *Applied Psychology*, *61*(1), 30–55. doi:10.1111/j.1464-0597.2011.00454.x

Van Dam, K. (2004). Antecedents and consequences of employability orientation. European Journal of Work and Organizational Psychology, 13, 29–51.

Van Dam, K., van Vuuren, T., & Kemps, S. (2017). Sustainable employment: The importance of intrinsically valuable work and an age-supportive climate. *International Journal of Human Resource Management*, *28*(17), 2449–2472. https://doi.org/10.1080/09585192.2015.1137607

Van de Voorde, K., & Boxall, P. (2014). Individual Well-being and Performance at Work in the Wider Context of Strategic HRM. In *Well-being and Performance at Work: the Role of Context* (pp. 95–111). Psychology Press.

van den Bos, K. (2001). Uncertainty management: The influence of uncertainty salience on reactions to perceived procedural fairness. *Journal of Personality and Social Psychology*, *80*(6), 931–941. doi:10.1037/0022-3514.80.6.931 PMID:11414375

Van der Klink, J. J. L. (2010). *Duurzaam inzetbaar: werk als waarde. Rapport in opdracht van ZonMw ten behoeve van het programma Participatie en Gezondheid*. Rijksuniversiteit Groningen.

Van Dick, R., Ullrich, J., & Tissington, P. A. (2006). Working under a black cloud: How to sustain organizational identification after a merger. *British Journal of Management*, *17*(S1, SUPPL. 1), S69–S79. Advance online publication. doi:10.1111/j.1467-8551.2006.00479.x

van Dijk, H., van Engen, M., & Paauwe, J. (2012). Reframing the business case for diversity: A values and virtues perspective [macmillan]. *Journal of Business Ethics*, *111*(1), 73–84. doi:10.100710551-012-1434-z

Van Maanen, J., & Schein, E. H. (1979). Toward a theory of organizational socialization. In B. M. Staw (Ed.), *Research in organizational behavior* (Vol. 1, pp. 209–264). JAI Press.

Van Vuuren, T. (2012). Vitality management: One does not need to be ill to get better! *Gedrag en Organisatie*, *25*, 400–418.

VandenBos, G. R. (2007). *APA dictionary of psychology. American Psychological Association*. American Psychological Association., doi:10.1037/h0081324

Vander Elst, T., De Cuyper, N., Baillien, E., Niesen, W., & De Witte, H. (2016). Perceived Control and Psychological Contract Breach as Explanations of the Relationships between Job Insecurity, Job Strain and Coping Reactions: Towards a Theoretical Integration. *Stress and Health*, *32*(2), 100–116. doi:10.1002mi.2584 PMID:24916812

Vander Elst, T., De Cuyper, N., & De Witte, H. (2011). The role of perceived control in the relationship between job insecurity and psychosocial outcomes: Moderator or mediator? *Stress and Health*, *27*(3), 215–227. doi:10.1002mi.1371

Vanhala, M., & Dietz, G. (2019). How Trust in One's Employer Moderates the Relationship Between HRM and Engagement Related Performance. *International Studies of Management & Organization*, *49*(1), 23–42. doi:10.1080/00208825.2019.1565092

Vanin, M., Southier, N., Novello, D., & Francishetti, V. A. (2006). ADEQUAÇÃO NUTRICIONAL DO ALMOÇO DE UMA UNIDADE DE ALIMENTAÇÃO E NUTRIÇÃO DE GUARAPUAVA - PR Lunch nutritional adequacy in a Meal and Nutrition Unit in Guarapuava - PR Resumo. *Revista Sallus-Guarapuava-PR*, *1*(1), 31–38.

Varoufakis, Y., & Holland, S. (2012). A Modest Proposal for Resolving the Eurozone Crisis. *Inter Economics*, *4*(4), 240–247. doi:10.100710272-012-0424-9

Varvin, S. (2017). Our Relations to Refugees: Between Compassion and Dehumanization. *American Journal of Psychoanalysis*, *77*(4), 1–19. doi:10.105711231-017-9119-0 PMID:29085057

Veloso, A. L. de O. M. (2007). *O Impacto da Gestão de Recursos Humanos na Performance Organizacional*. Doctoral Dissertation, Universidade do Minho.

Veloso, I. S. (2005). *Programa de Alimentação do Trabalhador e os efeitos sobre a saúde* [Tese de Doutoramento em Saúde Pública, Repositório Institucional da Universidade Federal da Bahia]. https://repositorio.ufba.br/handle/ri/27084

Veloso, I. S., Santana, V. S., & Oliveira, N. F. (2007). Programas de alimentação para o trabalhador e seu impacto sobre ganho de peso e sobrepeso The Brazilian Workers' Food Program and its impact on weight gain and overweight. *Revista de Saude Publica*, *41*(5), 769–776. https://doi.org/10.1590/S0034-89102007000500011

Verburg, R. M., Nienaber, A., Searle, R. H., Weibel, A., Den Hartog, D. N., & Rupp, D. E. (2018). The Role of Organizational Control Systems in Employees' Organizational Trust and Performance Outcomes. *Group & Organization Management*, *43*(2), 179–206. doi:10.1177/1059601117725191 PMID:29568213

Veronese, G., Pepe, A., Jaradah, A., Al Muranak, F., & Hamdouna, H. (2017). Modelling life satisfaction and adjustment to trauma in children exposed to ongoing military violence: An exploratory study in Palestine. *Child Abuse & Neglect*, *63*, 61–72. doi:10.1016/j.chiabu.2016.11.018 PMID:27907846

Vial, G. (2019). Understanding digital transformation: A review and a research agenda. *The Journal of Strategic Information Systems*, *28*(2), 118–144.

Vidya, C.T., & Prabheesh, K.P. (2020). Implications of COVID-19 Pandemic on the Global Trade Networks. *Emerging Markets Finance and Trade*, 56(10), Special Issue: Research on Pandemics, 2408-2421.

Volini, E., Schwartz, J., Eaton, K., Mallon, D., Van Durme, Y., Hauptmann, M., Scoble-Williams, N., & Poynton, S. (2021). The worker-employer relationship disrupted. In *Deloitte Insights*. https://www2.deloitte.com/us/en/insights/focus/human-capital-trends/2021/the-evolving-employer-employee-relationship.html/#endnote-7

vom Lehn, D. (2020). Digitalization as "an Agent of Social Change" in a Supermarket Chain: Applying Blumer's Theory of Industrialization in Contemporary Society. *Symbolic Interaction*, *43*(4), 637–656. doi:10.1002ymb.502

Wada, K., McGroarty, E., Tomaro, J., & Amundsen-Dainow, E. (2019). Affirmative career counselling with transgender and gender nonconforming clientes: A social justice perspective. *Canadian Journal of Counselling and Psychotherapy*, *53*(3), 255–275.

Walsh, S. D., Tartakovsky, E., & Shifter-David, M. (2019). Personal values and immigrant group appraisal as predictors of voluntary contact with immigrants among majority students in Israel. *International Journal of Psychology*, *54*(6), 731–738. doi:10.1002/ijop.12531 PMID:30238966

Walton, R. E. (1973). Quality of Working Life: What Is It. *Sloan Management Review*, *15*(1), 11–21. https://search.ebscohost.com/login.aspx?direct=true&db=bth&AN=4009978&site=eds-live

Wang, H. J., Lu, C. Q., & Siu, O. L. (2015). Job insecurity and job performance: The moderating role of organizational justice and the mediating role of work engagement. *The Journal of Applied Psychology*, *100*(4), 1249–1258. doi:10.1037/a0038330 PMID:25402953

Wang, W. T. (2016). Examining the Influence of the Social Cognitive Factors and Relative Autonomous Motivations on Employees' Knowledge Sharing Behaviors. *Decision Sciences*, *47*(3), 404–436. doi:10.1111/deci.12151

Ward, M., Poleacovschi, C., Faust, K. M., Weems, C. F., & Gabiam, N. (2020). Evaluating the role of infrastructure components and demographics on social capital in refugee camps. *Journal of Management Engineering*, *36*(3), 04020007. doi:10.1061/(ASCE)ME.1943-5479.0000754

Wasserman, I. C., Gallegos, P. V., & Ferdman, B. M. (2008). Dancing with resistance. *Diversity resistance in organizations*, 175-200.

Wasserman, I. C., Gallegos, P. V., & Ferdman, B. M. (2008). Dancing with resistance: Leadership challenges in fostering a culture of inclusion. In K. M. Thomas (Ed.), *Diversity resistance in organizations: 175-200*. Taylor & Francis Group/Lawrence Erlbaum.

Wedderburn, A. (2000). *Shiftwork and Health*. European Foundation for the Improvement of Living and Working Conditions.

Wheeler, A. R., & Halbesleben, J. R. B. (2009). A Conservation of Resources view of Person-Environment Fit. *Paper Presented at the 3rd Global Fit Conference*.

Whitener, E. M., & Werner, J. O. N. M. (1998). Managers as Initiators of Trust: An Exchange Relationship Framework for Understanding Managerial Trustworthy Behavior. *Academy of Management Review*, *23*(3), 513–530. doi:10.2307/259292

Whittle, S., & Turner, L. (2017). *Trans-inclusive Workplaces – Guidelines for Employers and Businesses*. Transgender Europe.

WHO. (1946). *Constitution of the World Health Organization*.

WHOQOL GROUP. (1994). Development of the WHOQOL: Rationale and Current Status. *International Journal of Mental Health*, *23*(3), 24–56. https://doi.org/10.1080/00207411.1994.11449286

Wight, V. R., Raley, S. B., & Bianchi, S. M. (2008). Time for children, one's spouse and oneself among parents who work nonstandard hours. *Social Forces*, *87*(1), 243–271. doi:10.1353of.0.0092

Williams, K. D. (2009). Ostracism: A temporal need-threat model. Advances in Experimental Social Psychology, 41, 275–314. doi: (08)00406–1 doi:10.1016/S0065–2601

Williams, K. D., & Nida, S. A. (2011). Ostracism: Consequences and coping. *Current Directions in Psychological Science*, *20*(2), 71–75. doi:10.1177/0963721411402480

Willis, J., & Todorov, A. (2006). First Impressions: Making Up Your Mind After a 100-ms Exposure to a Face. *Psychological Science*, *17*(7), 592–598. doi:10.1111/j.1467-9280.2006.01750.x PMID:16866745

Winter, E. (2021). Early Uses of 'World Chess Champion.' *Chess History*. https://www.chesshistory.com/winter/extra/champion.html

Winter, S., Diamond, M., Green, J., Karasic, D., Reed, T., Whittle, S., & Wylie, K. (2016). Transgender people: Health at the margins of society. *Lancet*, *388*(10042), 390–400. doi:10.1016/S0140-6736(16)00683-8 PMID:27323925

World Health Organization. (1946). *Health and Well-Being*. WHO. https://www.who.int/data/gho/data/major-themes/health-and-well-being

Worthen, M. (2016). Hetero-cis–normativity and the gendering of transphobia. *International Journal of Transgenderism*, *17*(1), 31–57. doi:10.1080/15532739.2016.1149538

Wright, P. M., & Nishii, L. H. (2007). Strategic HRM and organizational behavior: Integrating multiple levels of analysis. *CAHRS Working Paper Series*, 468. http://digitilcommons.ilr.cornell.edu/cahrswp/468

Wright, E. O. (1988). Alternative Perspectives in Marxist Theory of Accumulation. In N. Satlıgan & S. Savran (Eds.), *Crisis of the World Capitalism* (pp. 172–218). Alan Press. (in Turkish)

Wu, X., Li, S., Xu, N., Zhang, W., & Wu, D. (2021). User participation depth and innovation performance of Internet companies: The moderating effect of environmental turbulence. *Technology Analysis and Strategic Management*, 1–14. doi:10.1080/09537325.2021.2008893

Yakura, E. K. (1996). *Managing Diversity* (E. E. Kossek & S. A. Lobel, Eds.). Blackwell Publishers LTD.

Yijälä, A., & Luoma, T. (2019). The Importance of Employment in the Acculturation Process of Well-Educated Iraqis in Finland: A Qualitative Follow-up Study. *Refugee Survey Quarterly*, *38*(3), 314–340. doi:10.1093/rsq/hdz009

Yildirim, D., & Aycan, Z. (2008). Nurses' work demands and work-family conflict: A questionnaire survey. *International Journal of Nursing Studies*, *45*(9), 1366–1378. doi:10.1016/j.ijnurstu.2007.10.010 PMID:18262529

Yoo, G., & Lee, S. (2018). It doesn't end there: Workplace Bullying, work-to-family conflict, and employee well-being in Korea. *International Journal of Environmental Research and Public Health*, *15*(7), 1548. doi:10.3390/ijerph15071548 PMID:30037131

Yoon, M. S., Feyissa, I. F., & Jung, E. H. (2020). The Long Way to Refugee Status Acquisition and Mental Health in Post-Migration: Based on Asylum Seekers and Refugees in South Korea. *The Psychiatric Quarterly*, *91*(2), 403–416. doi:10.100711126-020-09714-9 PMID:31950331

Youmni, A., & Cheikh, M. (2020). Exploring Causal relationship between risk factors and vulnerability to COVID-19 Cases of Italy, Spain, France, Greece, Portugal, Morocco and South Africa. medRxiv, 1-13. doi:10.1101/2020.06.24.20139121

Youssef, C. M., & Luthans, F. (2007). Positive organizational behavior in the workplace: The impact of hope, optimism, and resilience. *Management Department Faculty Publications*, *36*(5), 774–800. doi:10.1177/0149206307305562

Yu, K.-H. (2016). Immigrant workers responses to stigmatized work: Constructing dignity through moral reasoning. *The Journal of Industrial Relations*, *58*(5), 571–588. Advance online publication. doi:10.1177/0022185615609204

Zahra, S. A., Newey, L. R., & Li, Y. (2014). On the Frontiers: The Implications of Social Entrepreneurship for International Entrepreneurship. *Entrepreneurship Theory and Practice*, *38*(1), 137–158. https://doi.org/10.1111/etap.12061

Zak, P. J., & Knack, S. (2001). Trust and Growth. *Economic Journal (London)*, *111*(4), 295–321. doi:10.1111/1468-0297.00609

Zhao, Y., Cooklin, A. R., Richardson, A., Strazdins, L., Butterworth, P., & Leach, L. S. (2021). Parents' shift work in connection with work–family conflict and mental health: Examining the pathways for mothers and fathers. *Journal of Family Issues*, *42*(2), 445–473. doi:10.1177/0192513X20929059

Compilation of References

Zigarmi, D., Galloway, F. J., & Roberts, T. P. (2018). Work locus of control, motivational regulation, employee work passion, and work intentions: An empirical investigation of an appraisal model. *Journal of Happiness Studies: An Interdisciplinary Forum on Subjective Well-Being*, *19*(1), 231–256. doi:10.100710902-016-9813-2

Zigarmi, D., Nimon, K., Houson, D., Witt, D., & Diehl, J. (2009). Beyond engagement: Toward a framework and operational definition for employee work passion. *Human Resource Development Review*, *8*(3), 300–326. doi:10.1177/1534484309338171

Zikic, J. (2015). Skilled migrants' career capital as a source of competi- tive advantage: Implications for strategic HRM. *International Journal of Human Resource Management*, *26*(10), 1360–1381. doi:10.1080/09585192.2014.981199

Zikic, M., & Richardson, J. (2015). What happens when you can't be who you are: Professional identity at the institutional periphery. *Human Relations*, *69*(1), 139–168. doi:10.1177/0018726715580865

About the Contributors

Paula Figueiredo has a degree in Economics with a specialization in Human Resources Economics, a Master in Human Resources Management and a PhD in Management. She is currently a professor at higher education institutions, and she has also been the Director of an institution since 2019. Paula has 20 years of experience in the business area with functions of direction, coordination, and consultancy. Throughout her professional experience, she has collaborated on leadership development projects. At the research level, she has developed research on Human Resource Development, more specifically Leadership Development in organizations, with some publications in scientific journals and conferences.

***

Celina Alonso has a Degree and Master in Nutrition from the School of Nutrition of the Federal University of Bahia (1991/2003) where he has been a professor since 1998, and is currently Adjunct Professor IV. She works in the Gastronomy course in the area of Management of Gastronomic Units. She is a Postgraduate in Data Analysis in Social Sciences at ISCTE / Portugal (2021) and in People Management with an Emphasis on Management by Competencies from the School of Administration of UFBA (2018). She is currently pursuing her PhD in Human Resources Development Policies at the Instituto Superior de Ciências Sociais e Políticas (ISCSP) of the University of Lisbon since 2018, where she investigates the impacts of the COVID-19 pandemic on the restaurant sector in Portugal. She works in the areas of Restaurant Management and Human Resource Management (HR) and has publications mainly in the area of HR Management and Food Quality Control.

Carlo Bagnoli is Professor of Strategy Innovation at the Department of Management, Ca' Foscari University of Venice. Furthermore, he is the scientific director of VeniSIA - Venice Sustainability Innovation Accelerator; founder and scientific director of the Strategy Innovation Master and of the Strategy Innovation Forum. Amongst the various roles that he holds, prof. Bagnoli is a member of the Univeneto Foundation; member of hte management committee and president of the technical and scientific committee of Veneto's Regional Innovation Network named "Smart Destinations in the Land of Venice - 2026". He is the founder, partner, and scientific director of university spin-off Strategy Innovation srl and co-founder of university spin-off Digital Strategy Innovation srl.

Fatma Nur Bayir is an organizational psychologist.

About the Contributors

Marco Borria holds a Business Economics MSc. from Bocconi University and attended specialization courses from the MBA program of the Carlson School of Management, University of Minnesota, in the United States. He was further awarded a Psychology BSc. by Birkbeck College, University of London, and a Psychology PhD. by Brunel University London. During his PhD. he presented his research at nine conferences in Italy, the United Kingdom, and the United States. He is a Chartered Psychologist (CPsychol) with the British Psychological Society (BPS). Marco worked for six years in private equity and leveraged finance for an investment bank, on the buy-side and for a start-up. In addition to that, he worked for eight years in healthcare and pharma in the public sector, in charities and in the private sector. Before teaching at Ca' Foscari University of Venice, he taught at Birkbeck College, University of London, and at Brunel University London. To date he has received 16 national and international awards including research grants, sponsorships, and selections for summer schools. Between 2009 and 2012 he was awarded an Isambard Scholarship by Brunel University London.

Silvana Campos is a Psychologist that received her MD in Social and Work Psychology from the Bahia Federal University (Ufba) in 2016. And now she is doing the PHD on the same program and area. She is currently an analyst at the Municipality of Salvador, having previously been Training Manager at Empresa Baiana de Águas e Saneamento (Embasa). He has experience in research, teaching and consulting Psychology´s field, with an emphasis on recruitment and selection processes, training and development, mapping of technical and behavioral competences, individual development plan, development of teams and managers, performance evaluation, internal coaching.

Dália Costa holds a PhD in Sociology; is assistant professor at the School of Social and Political Sciences of Lisbon University, where teaches since 1996 and coordinates the specialization course in Criminology and Social Reintegration; founder and senior researcher of the Interdisciplinary Center for Gender Studies, cooperating with the Research Centre for Administration and Public Policies. Her research main interests are inequality, including gender inequality; violence and crime; and social policy.

Daniela Costa has a master's in psychology from the University of Minho. She currently attend the PhD in Applied Psychology at the School of Psychology, University of Minho. In recent years, she has dedicated her research to the field of Industrial and Organizational Psychology, addressing topics such as work schedules, especially shift work, and the work-family relationship, among others.

Stephen Deepak is a Faculty at the School of Management, Kristu Jayanti College, Bengaluru. He is a certified Entrepreneurship course educator from IIM – Bangalore and Stanford University ventures program. He has 16 years of teaching experience and teaches several courses in the field of Entrepreneurship, Human Resources Management and Marketing Management.

Cornelia Enger is a Professor of General Business Administration, especially Social Management at the West Saxon University of Zwickau. She received her doctorate at the Martin-Luther-University Halle-Wittenberg, Germany and has a study background in Economics (International Business, MBA) as well as Studies of Pedagogics with focus on Adult Education and Continuing Education (Diploma). Furthermore, she worked as a Certified Business Mediator at the Dresden International University and gained experience as a Scientific Assistant in Teaching and Research at the Chemnitz University of

Technology, Germany. Her specialities and research areas comprise Social Economy/Social Management, Social Policy, Educational Management, the Design and Development of Organizations (also) from a Sociological Perspective and Theory and Methods of Evaluation Research.

Liliana Fernandes has a master's in psychology from the University of Minho.

Maria da Conceição Fonseca is a nutritionist from the Federal University of Pará - UFPA (1993), master's in food and nutrition from the State University of Campinas - UNICAMP (1998) and PhD in Food and Nutrition from the State University of Campinas - UNICAMP (2004). He is currently a professor, associate IV at the Federal University of Bahia - UFBA, at the School of Nutrition - ENUFBA. Experience in the area of nutrition, with emphasis on Food and Nutrition Security and Administration in Food Service, as well as on sustainability applied to Food Service. Coordinator of the Research and Extension group of the UFBA University Restaurant (GPERU - UFBA).

António Frois was European Chess Champion 2014, Internacional Chess Master since 1989 FIDE Trainer since 2006

Alexandra Gomes is an Assistant Professor at Universidade do Algarve, Portugal. PhD in Psychology.

Gabriela Gonçalves works at the CIP - Centro de Investigação em Psicologia.

Sónia Gonçalves completed her PhD in work and organizational psychology in 2011 by ISCTE-IUL. She is an invited assistant professor at ISCSP- Universidade de Lisboa. Sónia is researcher in Centro de Administração e Políticas Públicas (CAPP-ISCSP) and Organizational Behavior and Human Resources Research Group Coordinator. Her research interests focus on how context variables contribute the person health in workplace. She has published 7 chapters and 17 articles in journals. She further organised several scientific international events, and supervised more that 30 MSc dissertations. Sónia also Member of Portuguese Association for People Management and member of the Specialty board of Work, Social, and Organisational Psychology in Ordem dos Psicólogos Portugueses (OPP). In 2016 Sónia P. Gonçalves has been recognized as a specialist in work, social, and organizational psychology, and in occupational healthy psychology (OPP) and in 2017 in Administration and Management by Instituto Politécnico de Tomar.

Sônia Gondim got the Psychology´s degree from the Higher Education Center of Juiz de Fora (1981), the Master's degree in Psychology (Social Psychology) from Gama Filho University (1990) and the PhD in Psychology from the Federal University of Rio de Janeiro (1998). She did the PHD internship from November 2006 to October 2007, having spent 6 months at the Complutense University of Madrid and the remaining months in Cambridge, UK, both with a CNPq scholarship. She did a second post-doctoral internship in Spain in 2013, having been awarded a CAPES Scholarship by the Brazil/Spain International Cooperation Program. She is currently a retired Full Professor at the Institute of Psychology at the Federal University of Bahia and is a visiting professor at the Institute of Psychology at the Federal University of Uberlândia, with postgraduate teaching and research activities.

About the Contributors

Sílvia Luís, PhD in social psychology, is a professor at Universidade Lusófona (Lisbon,Portugal), where she is sub-director of the master in Organizational and Social Psychology. Her research interests focus on how psychosocial variables (e.g.,management support, risk perception) shape the person-environment interaction in different settings. In the organizational context, her research focus on the implications of this interaction for people (e.g.,adaptation to contextual changes, subjective well-being) and for the environment (e.g., public policies, sustainability in organizations).

Maurizio Massaro, PhD, is Associate Professor at Ca' Foscari University of Venice. Before joining academia, he was founder and CEO of multiple consultancy firms. He has also served as a research center Vice President in the field of metal analysis. He has been a visiting Professor at Florida Gulf Coast University and Leicester University. He enjoys several contacts and research partnerships with universities in the USA, continental Europe, UK, Asia and Australia. His research interests include knowledge management, intellectual capital, sustainability in international business, and research methods. His research has been applied in multiple research contexts. Maurizio Massaro is the corresponding author and can be contacted at: maurizio.massaro@unive.it

Carlos Nascimento de Lira is a Nutritionist (2018), Master (2020) and Doctoral Student in Food, Nutrition and Health held by the School of Nutrition of the Federal University of Bahia. He was a member of the Nutrition, Nervous and Immune Systems Group of the Experimental Nutrition Laboratory. He has experience in the field of Collective Feeding, Consulting and Clinical Nutrition. He is currently part of the research groups: Evidence-Based Nutrition (NuBasE) and the Research and Extension Group of the UFBA University Restaurant (GPERU).

Anna-Maria Nitsche holds a PhD on artificial intelligence/machine learning application in supply chain collaboration at the University of Leipzig. Since 2018, she has been working as a research assistant in various projects at the chair of business information systems at the University of Applied Sciences Zwickau. Her main areas of activity are supply chain management, coordination processes, last mile, business informatics, application of innovative technologies, and systemic methods. She is an active member in various organizations such as the Federal Logistics Association Germany (BVL), the Association of German Engineers (VDI) and the British Academy of Management (BAM).

Juliana Paranhos Moreno Batista graduated in Psychology at the Federal University of Bahia (UFBA) in 2015 and pursued a multi-professional residency in Collective Health at IESC/Federal University of Rio de Janeiro (UFRJ) in 2022. She is currently ongoing her Master Degree at the Institute of Scientific and Technological Communication and Information in Health (Icict), one of the technical-scientific units of the Oswaldo Cruz Foundation (Fiocruz). In 2022 she was hired as a sanitarian for the Municipal Health Secretariat of Rio de Janeiro (SMSRio). Her main research topics are health services organisation and management, information for analysis, surveillance, monitoring and evaluation in Public Health; immigration; emotions; emotion regulation; affective management measure.

Syed Perwez is a Professor in OB & HR Division, VIT Business School, VIT University, Vellore, Tamil Nadu, India. Dr. Syed has completed his Graduation in Psychology Honors, P.G in Industrial and Clinical Psychology, MBA in Human Resource Management and Marketing Management, Ph.D. in Psychology, and FDPM in Management (IIM-A). He is designated as Professor in OB & HR area, teaching since more than 12 years to under graduate, post graduate and doctoral management students in VIT Business School, VIT, Vellore, Tamil Nadu, India and Dr. Syed has also 5 years of industry experience in reputed pharmaceutical company like Cipla Ltd, and Nicholas Piramal India ltd as a Middle level Manager.

Miguel Portela holds a PhD in Economics from the University of Amsterdam. He is Associate Professor with Habilitation at Universidade do Minho, Director of the Centre for Research in Economics and Management (NIPE), and Co-Editor of the Portuguese Economic Journal. He is an affiliate of NIPE/UMinho, CIPES and IZA, Bonn. He has an ongoing collaboration with Banco de Portugal and is a member of the Portuguese Council for Productivity. His research interests are labour economics, the economics of education and applied econometrics. He published a set of articles, books and book chapters, emphasising publications in Econometrica, Labour Economics, Scandinavian Journal of Economics, Regional Studies and Studies in Higher Education. He has research collaborations in different countries and leads and integrates research teams whose work has been funded by private and public entities. One highlights his FCT project "It's All About Productivity: contributions to the understanding of the sluggish performance of the Portuguese economy ". He has also written reports to define public policies on the Minimum Wage, Education and Employment in the Portuguese labour market. In addition, he has experience in consulting, both for private and public institutions.

Lígia Portovedo holds a Ph.D. in Organizational Psychology from University of Minho (Portugal) and a degree in Psychology from University of Coimbra. She has been working as HR Manager for the last thirty years in industry, construction, consulting and technology sectors and serves as invited professor at Polytechnic Institute of Viana do Castelo (Portugal). Research Interests direct to psychological variables that impact individual and organizational performance.

Chantal Runte is a research assistant at the chair of business information systems at the University of Applied Sciences Zwickau. After completing a Masters of Science at Uppsala University in June 2021, she has been working in various projects ranging from data-driven solutions in public modernisation, artificial intelligence and ethics to internationalisation strategies as well as knowledge management in higher education.

Özgün Sarımehmet Duman holds BSc in Political Science and Public Administration from METU, MA in Comparative Politics from the University of York (UK) and PhD in Political Science from Ankara University. She completed her post-doctoral research at the University of Sheffield (UK). She conducted research at the London School of Economics and Political Science (LSE) as a Visiting Fellow and at the University of East London as a Senior Research Fellow in European Political Economy. Dr. Sarımehmet Duman's academic research mainly focuses on international political economy, state-market relations, economic crises, Eurozone crisis, labour market relations, social and employment policies, neoliberalism, globalisation and financialisation. She contributed to the field with a number of books and articles in high-impact journals. Her academic productivity and success were acknowledged and rewarded by many institutions including the European Commission and the Research Council of Turkey.

About the Contributors

Christian-Andreas Schumann is Professor of Business Informatics at the West Saxon University of Zwickau. He received his doctorate and habilitation from Chemnitz University of Technology. Currently, he is university representative for international relations, head of the Center for New Forms of Study, director of the Institute for Management and Information, and dean of studies for master's and distance learning programs. He holds leading positions in the Association of German Engineers and is involved in international organizations, for example, the German University Consortium for International Cooperation, the Chinese-German University of Applied Sciences, the Mexican-German University Cooperation, ICDE and SAE International. Additionally, he is chair of the Continental Network of the British, Academy of Management (BAM) and visiting member of the BAM council, a member of the Board of Directors of the Fellows Council of EDEN, a member of the Board of Directors of the Accreditation Agency for Study Programs in Engineering, Informatics, Natural Sciences and Mathematics ASIIN as well as a member of the Delegate Assembly of the Society for Project Management in Germany. His national and international activities include publication activities, conference engagements, such as member of Scientific Committees, Track and Session Chair, Reviewer for Proceedings and Journals, etc. He is co-author of several scientific books and editor in the M&S publishing house. For many years he has been managing large-scale scientific and professional projects in Germany and abroad, as well as working as an international consultant, lecturer, and guest professor, for example, in St. Petersburg and Thessaloniki. His work focuses on digital transformation, open and distance education, information and logistics systems, knowledge management, change management and applied AI.

Khodor Shatila has a Masters' in Business Administration, Sagesse University, Furn El Chebbak Baabda, Lebanon. Researcher in iProcares international research center, Beirut, Lebanon. Research interests: international logistic, transnational supply chains, human resources management, multinational management. Published more than 5 papers in internationally indexed journals, participated in 4 international conference.

Isabel Silva holds a Ph.D. in Work and Organizational Psychology from University of Minho (Portugal). She is a professor at the School of Psychology of University of Minho and an integrated researcher of CICS.NOVA.UMinho. One of her main research interests is the characterization, evaluation and intervention in specific psychosocial factors, such as "shift work", "work-family conflict", "occupational safety" and "violence at work". She has authored and co-authored several publications in the areas mentioned above.

Catia Sousa has a degree in Human Resources Management. Master in Labor Sciences and Labor Relations. PhD in Psychology. Invited Adjunct Professor at the University of Algarve. Member of the Center for Research in Psychology (CIP/UAL).

Başak Uçanok Tan received her B.A. degree in Business Administration from Başkent University. Upon her graduation she was granted the Sunley Management Scholarship and completed MSc in International Management from the University of Northampton, UK. Her master's dissertation focused on the adverse psychological effects of financial crises on layoff survivors. She continued her academic pursuits in Marmara and Istanbul Bilgi University and earned her PhD in Organizational Behavior with her dissertation on the investigation of organizational citizenship behaviors in Turkish SMEs. Her academic research focus concentrates on the dynamics of micro organizational phenomena including work values, organizational citizenship behavior, organizational commitment, alienation, leadership and cooperative behavior. She has served as programme coordinator in Public Relations program in Istanbul Bilgi University from 2010 to 2012 and currently is the director of Human Resource Management Masters programme.

Ana Veloso holds a Ph.D. in Work and Organizational Psychology from University of Minho (Portugal) and a Master degree from the University of Porto. She also has an MBA from University of Porto Business School and a degree in Psychology from University of Coimbra. She is full professor at the School of Psychology, University of Minho. Integrate member of CICS.NOVA.UMinho. Her research interests are focused on Employment Relation (Creativity and Innovation and Work engagement) and Psychology of Human Resources.

Joana Vieira dos Santos is an Assistant Professor at University of Algarve. Degree in Social and Organizational Psychology, Master in Health Psychology, PhD in Psychology (specialisation in Organizational Psychology).

Index

A

adaptation 13, 24, 31, 46, 49, 86, 92, 105, 115, 123, 129, 134, 136-137, 146, 204, 213, 216-217

B

BANI world 19
Better Life Index 5, 11, 18-19
Bion 245-246, 250-251, 254
Blended Value 46, 52, 55, 60
Burnout 62, 77, 89, 114, 117-118, 120-124, 126-127, 129-133, 141, 168, 170, 179-181, 246
Businesses and organisations 1

C

Chess 257-269
Chess Master 261, 263, 266, 269
Conservation of Resources Theory 61, 72, 76, 81, 91-92, 139, 142
COVID 244-245, 250, 256
COVID-19 31, 33, 35, 37-38, 40-41, 53, 112, 135, 147, 150, 202, 216, 218, 221, 226-233, 235, 237-244, 246, 248-249, 253-255, 265
Creativity 154, 156, 159, 185, 248, 250, 258, 263, 265-266, 268-269

D

Digital Ecosystem 40, 47, 51, 58-60
Digital Transformation 44-45, 49, 54, 58
Discrimination 134, 138, 140, 142, 147-148, 161, 166-168, 180, 184, 186, 188-194, 196, 204, 209, 252
Diversity Management 153-164, 182-186, 196

E

Employee Sustainability 1-2, 8, 15, 166
employee wellbeing 132, 155, 182, 244, 253, 255
Employee Well-being 1-4, 15, 18-19, 94, 152, 167-169, 180-181
Equality 46, 48, 127, 150, 155, 158, 162, 166-169, 179-180, 183-184, 186, 189, 220, 238
Equity 3, 166, 169, 175-180
European Stability Mechanism (ESM) 227, 243
Eurozone crisis 226-229, 231-233, 237, 243
exclusion 57, 139-140, 142-143, 146, 150, 158, 190, 194, 201-202, 213, 216, 259, 268

F

Family and Social Life 99-101, 110, 113, 116
Flexibility 99, 112-113, 116, 185, 210, 226-230, 232-233, 238, 240-241, 243
Foulkes 244, 246, 254
Fourth Industrial Revolution 44, 56, 59-60

G

Gender Diversity 166-169, 173-184, 186, 193
Greece 226-229, 232-243
groups 31, 41, 49, 64, 72, 74, 76, 103-104, 106-108, 110-111, 132, 136-137, 139-142, 147, 154-158, 160-161, 164, 167, 169, 185, 189, 199, 201, 203, 209, 213, 216, 223, 240, 244-255

H

Harmonious passion 117-118, 120, 123, 127-128, 131, 133
Health promotion 22, 24, 26, 31, 38
human resource management 2-3, 17-19, 47, 55-56, 58, 62-63, 92-93, 95, 99, 149, 152, 163, 194-196, 221, 223

I

Immigration 136, 146, 150, 198-203, 215-218, 221, 224
Inclusion 8, 14, 33, 52, 106, 140, 150, 153, 155-165, 191-193, 196, 201-202, 215, 218, 257, 259-260, 265, 269
Individuality 156, 183
interview 8-9, 168, 192, 198, 216, 261-262, 265
Irregular Work Schedules 99-103, 106, 110-111, 116

J

Job Insecurity 61-64, 72, 74-76, 78, 81-82, 88-98, 230
Job Satisfaction 42, 63-64, 69, 73, 76, 90, 96, 102-103, 112, 114, 116, 144, 154-155, 163, 168, 179-180, 195, 242

L

Labor Market Transition 40
Labour 114, 146, 158, 160, 184, 226-235, 237-243, 257
Learning 45, 53, 129, 144, 186, 196, 215, 223, 260, 264-265, 269
Levers-Of-Control 244
LGBT 183-184, 187-188, 190, 193, 195-197
Locus of Control 92, 133, 166-167, 169-171, 173-181
longitudinal 87, 95, 132, 145, 198, 203, 216, 218

M

Meaning of Work 198-200, 202, 204, 210, 213-215, 218, 220, 222-225
Meaningfulness of Work 198-202, 204, 213, 215-218, 225
Mediation 62-64, 70, 81, 83, 96, 98, 146, 155, 167, 175-177
Metrics 1, 6, 8-11, 13-15, 20
Moderation 62-64, 70, 81-83, 85-86, 96, 98
MOW 198, 200, 213, 215, 222
Multidimensional approach 20

N

New Forms of Work 40-41, 46, 50-51, 53
Nitsun 244, 246, 251-252, 255
non-standard work schedules 99-102, 105, 112-113
Nonstandard Work Schedules 113-114, 116
Nutrition 22-35, 37-39, 136

O

Obsessive passion 118, 120-121, 123, 127, 129-130, 133
Occupational health and safety 22, 150
Oppression 183, 188, 190, 194
Organizational performance 23, 153, 159, 163, 181
Organizations 1-4, 8, 12-13, 15, 18, 23-24, 43-47, 49-51, 58, 60, 76, 90, 93-95, 99-100, 106, 112, 117, 120, 127-128, 132, 141, 144, 150-151, 153-162, 164-165, 167-168, 180-181, 183-186, 191-196, 217, 223, 250, 255

P

Pandemic 28, 31, 33, 35, 40-41, 53, 57, 112, 135, 218, 226-248, 250, 253, 255-256, 265
People-centered approach 20
Perceived Diversity Climate 153, 156-160
Performance 3-4, 16, 19, 23, 41, 43, 50, 56-58, 61-64, 69-76, 78, 81-83, 86-98, 101, 118-121, 133, 147, 153-155, 157, 159-160, 163-164, 166-168, 173, 175-176, 178-182, 186, 192-193, 196, 240, 244, 249-250, 253-254, 256, 269
Portugal 1, 3, 5, 22, 25, 56, 61, 99-100, 103, 117, 127, 130, 183, 188-191, 193, 195-197, 221, 226-229, 231-243, 257, 260, 262, 265-266
Prejudice 137, 140, 147, 154, 161, 168, 183-184, 189-190, 192-193, 195, 209
PRIMA 225
prisioners 257
Prisoner 258-261, 265-266, 269
Professional Identity 199-200, 204, 209-210, 215-220, 224-225
psychological well-being 90, 112, 117-118, 121-128, 141-142

Q

Quality of life at work 22

R

reahbilitation 257
Recruitment 4, 42, 52, 86, 127, 159-160, 183, 185, 192

S

Social Entrepreneurship 40-41, 43, 51, 54-57, 59-60
Social Exchange Theory 61-62, 72-73, 76, 82, 90
Social Innovation 40, 53, 57

Index

Social Policy 46, 53, 195, 238
Social Transformation 45, 60
Strategy 3, 19, 35, 42-45, 54, 106, 116, 155-156, 160, 167, 182, 189, 195, 202-203, 242, 244, 247, 249, 251, 253-255, 264, 266, 269
Subjective Well Being 134
Sustainability 1-6, 8-9, 13-19, 41-42, 44-47, 49, 52, 55-58, 149, 166-168, 181-182, 228-229, 232, 241, 257
Sustainable citizenship 14, 20
Sustainable Work 40-42, 46-47, 49-50, 52, 55, 60, 168
Syrian Asylum Seekers 134-137, 142-143
Systematic Review 17, 61, 87, 113, 148, 151, 157, 198-199, 201, 217, 225, 239, 241, 253

T

Transgender 184, 187, 194-197
Transphobia 184, 189-192, 195, 197
Triple bottom line 2, 17, 20, 40, 42, 55
Trust 5, 17, 61, 63, 72-78, 81-83, 85, 87-95, 97-98, 155-156, 190, 240, 255, 259-260, 265
Trustworthiness 75-79, 81, 83-86, 88, 90-91, 98
Trustworthiness Dimensions 79, 81, 83-84, 86
Turkey 134-138, 142-143, 145, 147-149, 151, 226, 242

V

VUCA world 19-20

W

Well-Being 1-9, 11-16, 18-19, 41-42, 50, 52-53, 56, 62, 64, 69, 74-75, 81-83, 85-86, 90-91, 94-96, 99, 101-108, 110-118, 120-128, 131, 133-134, 136, 138-139, 141-145, 147, 149, 152, 163, 166-169, 178-181, 190-191, 193-194, 254, 260, 265
Well-being at work 2, 138, 142
Well-being indices 1, 8-9, 11-16
Work 2, 5, 8, 15-16, 18, 22-24, 26, 29, 31, 33, 35, 38, 40-42, 44-53, 55-60, 62-63, 69, 73, 75, 77-78, 81-83, 85-97, 99-108, 110-123, 125-144, 149, 153-159, 161-164, 166-168, 179-183, 190-191, 193-196, 199-202, 204, 209-211, 213-233, 235-241, 243, 245-246, 248-255, 264, 269
Work Compulsively 133
Work excessively 119, 133
Work Identity 199-202, 204, 209-211, 215-218, 225
Work Passion 117-118, 120-127, 130-133
Work Role 60
Work Schedule Management 116
Workaholism 117-133
Work-Family Conflict 101-102, 111, 114-116, 120, 180, 232
Workforce 2, 31-32, 41-42, 44, 50-52, 116, 144, 153-156, 158, 163, 168, 178, 184-186, 193, 195, 223, 230
working time 101, 103, 110-114, 116, 130, 231
workplace ostracism 134, 138, 141-142, 146-147, 149-151

Recommended Reference Books

IGI Global's reference books are available in three unique pricing formats:
Print Only, E-Book Only, or Print + E-Book.

Order direct through IGI Global's Online Bookstore at
www.igi-global.com or through your preferred provider.

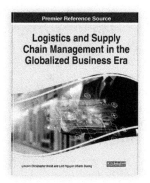

ISBN: 9781799887096
EISBN: 9781799887119
© 2022; 413 pp.
List Price: US$ **250**

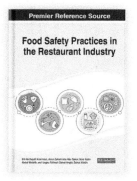

ISBN: 9781799874157
EISBN: 9781799874164
© 2022; 334 pp.
List Price: US$ **240**

ISBN: 9781668440230
EISBN: 9781668440254
© 2022; 320 pp.
List Price: US$ **215**

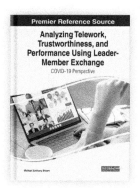

ISBN: 9781799889502
EISBN: 9781799889526
© 2022; 263 pp.
List Price: US$ **240**

ISBN: 9781799885283
EISBN: 9781799885306
© 2022; 587 pp.
List Price: US$ **360**

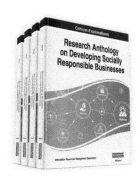

ISBN: 9781668455906
EISBN: 9781668455913
© 2022; 2,235 pp.
List Price: US$ **1,865**

Do you want to stay current on the latest research trends, product announcements, news, and special offers?
Join IGI Global's mailing list to receive customized recommendations, exclusive discounts, and more.
Sign up at: **www.igi-global.com/newsletters.**

Publisher of Timely, Peer-Reviewed Inclusive Research Since 1988

www.igi-global.com   Sign up at www.igi-global.com/newsletters   facebook.com/igiglobal   twitter.com/igiglobal   linkedin.com/igiglobal

Ensure Quality Research is Introduced to the Academic Community

Become an Evaluator for IGI Global Authored Book Projects

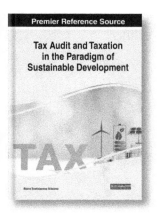

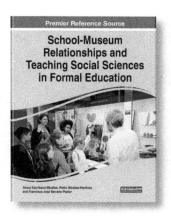
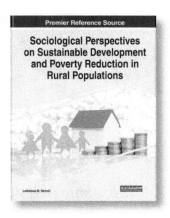

The overall success of an authored book project is dependent on quality and timely manuscript evaluations.

Applications and Inquiries may be sent to:
development@igi-global.com

Applicants must have a doctorate (or equivalent degree) as well as publishing, research, and reviewing experience. Authored Book Evaluators are appointed for one-year terms and are expected to complete at least three evaluations per term. Upon successful completion of this term, evaluators can be considered for an additional term.

If you have a colleague that may be interested in this opportunity, we encourage you to share this information with them.

Easily Identify, Acquire, and Utilize Published
Peer-Reviewed Findings in Support of Your Current Research

IGI Global OnDemand

Purchase Individual IGI Global OnDemand Book Chapters and Journal Articles

For More Information:
www.igi-global.com/e-resources/ondemand/

Browse through 150,000+ Articles and Chapters!

Find specific research related to your current studies and projects that have been contributed by international researchers from prestigious institutions, including:

- Accurate and Advanced Search
- Affordably Acquire Research
- Instantly Access Your Content
- Benefit from the InfoSci Platform Features

"It really provides **an excellent entry into the research literature of the field**. It presents a manageable number of **highly relevant sources** on topics of interest to a wide range of researchers. The sources are **scholarly, but also accessible** to 'practitioners'."

- Ms. Lisa Stimatz, MLS, University of North Carolina at Chapel Hill, USA

Interested in Additional Savings?

Subscribe to
IGI Global OnDemand *Plus*

Learn More

Acquire content from over 128,000+ research-focused book chapters and 33,000+ scholarly journal articles for as low as US$ 5 per article/chapter (original retail price for an article/chapter: US$ 37.50).

7,300+ E-BOOKS.
ADVANCED RESEARCH.
INCLUSIVE & AFFORDABLE.

IGI Global e-Book Collection

- **Flexible Purchasing Options** (Perpetual, Subscription, EBA, etc.)
- Multi-Year Agreements with **No Price Increases** Guaranteed
- **No Additional Charge** for Multi-User Licensing
- No Maintenance, Hosting, or Archiving Fees
- Continually Enhanced & Innovated **Accessibility Compliance Features** (WCAG)

Handbook of Research on Digital Transformation, Industry Use Cases, and the Impact of Disruptive Technologies
ISBN: 9781799877127
EISBN: 9781799877141

Handbook of Research on New Investigations in Artificial Life, AI, and Machine Learning
ISBN: 9781799886860
EISBN: 9781799886877

Handbook of Research on Future of Work and Education
ISBN: 9781799882756
EISBN: 9781799882770

Research Anthology on Physical and Intellectual Disabilities in an Inclusive Society (4 Vols.)
ISBN: 9781668435427
EISBN: 9781668435434

Innovative Economic, Social, and Environmental Practices for Progressing Future Sustainability
ISBN: 9781799895909
EISBN: 9781799895923

Applied Guide for Event Study Research in Supply Chain Management
ISBN: 9781799889694
EISBN: 9781799889717

Mental Health and Wellness in Healthcare Workers
ISBN: 9781799888130
EISBN: 9781799888147

Clean Technologies and Sustainable Development in Civil Engineering
ISBN: 9781799898108
EISBN: 9781799898122

Request More Information, or Recommend the IGI Global e-Book Collection to Your Institution's Librarian

For More Information or to Request a Free Trial, Contact IGI Global's e-Collections Team: eresources@igi-global.com | 1-866-342-6657 ext. 100 | 717-533-8845 ext. 100

Are You Ready to Publish Your Research?

IGI Global — PUBLISHER of TIMELY KNOWLEDGE

IGI Global offers book authorship and editorship opportunities across 11 subject areas, including business, computer science, education, science and engineering, social sciences, and more!

Benefits of Publishing with IGI Global:

- Free one-on-one editorial and promotional support.
- Expedited publishing timelines that can take your book from start to finish in less than one (1) year.
- Choose from a variety of formats, including Edited and Authored References, Handbooks of Research, Encyclopedias, and Research Insights.
- Utilize IGI Global's eEditorial Discovery® submission system in support of conducting the submission and double-blind peer review process.
- IGI Global maintains a strict adherence to ethical practices due in part to our full membership with the Committee on Publication Ethics (COPE).
- Indexing potential in prestigious indices such as Scopus®, Web of Science™, PsycINFO®, and ERIC – Education Resources Information Center.
- Ability to connect your ORCID iD to your IGI Global publications.
- Earn honorariums and royalties on your full book publications as well as complimentary content and exclusive discounts.

Join Your Colleagues from Prestigious Institutions, Including:

- Australian National University
- Massachusetts Institute of Technology
- Johns Hopkins University
- Tsinghua University
- Harvard University
- Columbia University in the City of New York

Learn More at: www.igi-global.com/publish
or Contact IGI Global's Aquisitions Team at: acquisition@igi-global.com